SEMPER FI

SEMPER FI

The Definitive Illustrated History of the U.S. Marines

Col H. Avery Chenoweth, USMCR (Ret.)

with Col Brooke Nihart, USMC (Ret.)

Foreword by James Brady, author of *The Marines of Autumn*

STERLING

New York / London

www.sterlingpublishing.com

Maps created by XNR Productions. Inc.. based on original maps
by H. Avery Chenoweth

Back jacket photograph © Lou Lowery/official USMC photo

Dedication

We proudly dedicate this book to that special brand of
warrior. the United States Marine: to those Marines
of the past who molded the Corps and created its
traditions. to those Marines of the present who carry
the banner forward. and to those Marines who will
comer after us and continue the Corps' inexorable
march toward excellence. fearlessness. invincibility.
and nothing short of victory in battle.

The nineteenth Commandant. Clifton Cates.
succinctly stated the universal truth about the Corps:

"The Marine Corps has no ambition beyond the
performance of its duty to its country. Its sole honor
stems from that recognition which cannot be denied
to a corps of men who have sought for themselves
little more than a life of hardship and the most
hazardous assignments in battle."

Semper Fidelis

FRONT ENDPAPER: Marines of
Company H, 1st Battalion,
pause for a group photograph
during a hike from Olongapo,
the Philippines, in 1901.

CONTENTS

Preface 8

Foreword 12

Tribute to John Glenn 13

Introduction
A Fighting Force Like No Other 14

chapter one
**Don't Tread on Me: The Birth
of the Continental Marines** 32

chapter two
**The Nineteenth Century—
Fortitudine to *Semper Fidelis*** 46

chapter three
Thrust onto the World Stage 98

chapter four
**The Second World War:
1941–1945** 166

chapter five
**Truman's "Police Action" with
the United Nations** 278

chapter six
America's Longest "Hot" War 326

chapter seven
**Tumultuous Decades Climax
with War** 378

chapter eight
The Dawn of a New Millennium 424

chapter nine
Twenty-First Century "Warfighting"

Epilogue   468

Appendix A   469
Marine Corps Rank Insignia
Medals and Decorations
Unit Commendations and Foreign Citations
Marine Corps Battle Streamers
Commandants of the Marine Corps
Sergeants Major of the Marine Corps

Appendix B   476
Military Staff System
Unit Sizes and Commands
Basic U.S. Marine Corps Structure
Structure of Marine Aviation

Appendix C   477
U.S. Marine Corps Innovations in Warfare
Glossary of Marine Lingo
Selected Marine Corps Acronyms

Further Reading   479

Index   484

Preface

First off, this book is written as much for non-Marines as for Marines, all of whom after boot camp know their history pretty well. But the general public, the politicians, the Congress, the other military services, and even the news media don't really grasp the uniqueness and significance of the tripartite structure and mission of the U.S. Marine Corps.

It will be immediately obvious that this book is very biased and chauvinistic. Any Marine or former Marine will understand why.

Personally, the Marine Corps has been the most consistent and influential—although peripheral—part of my own life, while it has been the whole professional life of my co-contributor, Col Brooke Nihart, USMC (Ret.). I was a Marine Reservist, in and out of its uniform, for more than forty-five years. Evaluating my experiences as a Marine, I find that I prize them more than my Princeton fine arts degree and my Masters from the University of Florida, more than my advertising, television, art, and writing awards; I value my "colonelcy" more than any Ph.D. I could have earned—more than any other achievements of my life, including this book and my combat art covering three wars for the Marine Corps (some of this art is featured in my previous book, *Art of War: Eyewitness U.S. Combat Art from the Revolution Through the 20th Century* [Barnes & Noble, 2002]).

Aside from years of continuous Reserve affiliation, I have been in battle in the uniform of a U.S. Marine four times in three wars, and have been with the Marine Corps fighting in the frozen wastes of Korea, the tropical jungles of Vietnam, and the desert sands of Kuwait. But of all things, I take the most pride in having led Marines in combat.

Throughout 1951, as a twenty-two-year-old second lieutenant in Able Company, 1st Battalion, 5th Marines, I led a rifle platoon of eighty-seven Marines, reinforced by mortars, machine guns, artillery, and forward air controllers, into battle against North Korean regulars and Communist Chinese enemies—and prevailed. After that, nothing could ever daunt me.

I have written this "story" of the U.S. Marine Corps for two reasons: as a tribute to an organization that has been so influential in my life and as an introduction for those who want to know more about the role of the military, and who want to gain an understanding of what makes the U.S. Marine Corps unique.

Although my Reserve association was secondary to my nonmilitary career, my half-century of adult life has been more entwined with the United States Marine Corps than with any other aspect of my professional life. Also, having lived that half-century with one foot in the civilian world and the other in the military, I can relate to both—perhaps better than someone who followed only a single path. Thus, what I have written here is a distillation of history and my interpretation of it, informed by my participation in a fair number of the events described. I have tried not to be unduly influenced by what others have written. Instead I have weighed and interpreted things in the light that I have seen them.

Military histories can be stale and prosaic when historians resort to simply rewriting the work of past historians. Even worse, historians sometimes sanitize the facts, glossing over failures and errors in judgment made in the past in order to save reputations or to present things in the most favorable light. The most valuable histories are those that are not afraid to present the events as they occurred, "warts and all." Good examples are T.R. Fehrenbach's magnificent firsthand and freshly written history of the Korean War, *This Kind of War* (Macmillan, 1963), and Army LtCol Melvin Voorhees' *Korean Tales* (Simon & Schuster, 1952). One of the most accurate accounts of the Persian Gulf War is *The Generals' War: The Inside Story of the Conflict in the Gulf*, written by LtGen Bernard E. Trainor, USMC (Ret.), and *New York Times* reporter Michael R. Gordon (Little, Brown, 1995). The brilliant reporting of embedded journalists during the 2003 war in Iraq has factually recorded that conflict. Especially effective examples of such reportage are retired LtCol Oliver L. North's *War Stories: Operation Iraqi Freedom* (Regnery, 2003), based on his front-line coverage of the war as a consultant for the Fox News Network, and retired MajGen Ray Smith and Francis "Bing" West's *The March Up: Taking Baghdad with the 1st Marine Division* (Bantam Doubleday Dell, 2003), both of whom accompanied elements of I MEF during the blitz to Baghdad. And, of course, for fresh, interpretive military history, nothing tops Victor Davis Hanson's *Carnage and Culture: Landmark Battles in the Rise of Western Power* or his *Ripples of Battle: How Wars of the Past Still Determine How We Fight, How We Live, and How We Think* (Doubleday, 2003).

This book, therefore, is not a "history" in the usual sense, because complete, scholarly histories already exist. Instead, this is the "story" of the U.S. Marine Corps, of its uniqueness, and a long list of its innovations in the history of warfare. I have reevaluated some events in Marine Corps history in light of their subsequent historical importance, including the incredible thirty-four days of combat of the 4th Marine Brigade in World War I and its ensuing notoriety. I also discuss the often-overlooked (by others) contributions of the Marine Corps to the history of modern warfare, including such innovations as the amphibious doctrine, dive-bombing, close air support, vertical envelopment, and vertical takeoff and landing. I have also reexamined the importance of Wake Island, the Marine vs. Japanese fighting effectiveness, the

post–World War II atomic-bomb exercises, and the biggest battle of all—the Marine Corps' fight for its very existence in the halls of Congress. Finally, I describe the Corps' unique training, including its martial arts program, plus the critical importance of Marine-Navy task forces and other joint operations in a new century in which new threats are constantly emerging.

In acknowledging those who helped make this work possible, my first expression of deep gratitude goes to my cohort and friend of more than a quarter century, Col Brooke Nihart, USMC, (Ret.). A product of the Platoon Leader Class (PLC) college commissioning program in 1938–39 from Occidental College (as I was a decade later, from Princeton), Col Nihart's first active duty assignment in 1940 was as a second lieutenant commanding a machine-gun and antitank platoon in the 1st Marine Division. Following this he was a gunnery officer on board the aircraft carrier USS *Saratoga*, then commander of the Marine detachment on the USS *Henderson* (AP-1). His last tour during World War II was again with the 1st MarDiv in the Okinawa campaign, as a battalion executive officer.

By the Korean War, Nihart had attained the rank of lieutenant colonel and the command of 2d Battalion, 1st Marine Regiment, 1st Marine Division. Our paths nearly crossed in September 1951 during the last action of the full division at the battle of Kanmubong Ridge, on the east side of the "Punch Bowl." While my unit of the 5th Marines was fighting the NKPA on the left flank, Nihart's was smashing them on the right. After sustaining a particularly vicious night attack, Nihart rallied his men and walked among them—oblivious of the heavy fire all around him—controlling the battle, encouraging his men, and ultimately winning a decisive victory. For his heroic and exemplary professional action, he was awarded the Navy Cross, second only to the Medal of Honor. Following his retirement after thirty years of active duty he was an editor of the *Armed Forces Journal* before

Col H. Avery Chenoweth, USMCR (Ret.)

becoming Deputy Director for Museums at the Marine Corps Historical Center at the Washington Navy Yard, a post he held for nineteen years.

Without Col Nihart's input and expertise in weaponry and his encyclopedic knowledge of Marine Corps history—much of which he has contributed in the form of sidebars—this book would have been incomplete.

I am indebted also to several other distinguished Marine historians, some of whom I have known personally, and to their outstanding works: BGen Edwin H. Simmons, USMC (Ret.), Director Emeritus of the Historical Division, has written the indispensable historical summary of the Corps, *The United States Marines: A History*. The author of numerous books on the Marine Corps and military adviser to Lou Reda Productions of the History Channel, retired Col Joe Alexander's *A Fellowship of Valor: The Battle History of the United States Marines* is a highly readable and exciting page-turner. Retired Marine Reserve colonel and noted author Allan R. Millett's *Semper Fidelis: The History of the United States Marine Corps* is the most detailed and authoritative of them all. Col Millett was the Mason Professor of military history at Ohio State University, and is now

the director of the Eisenhower Center at the University of New Orleans.

In addition to these historians, I have relied on the vast personal knowledge of Marine writers and officers who made some of that history themselves, including my contributing editor, Col Brooke Nihart; former Commandant of the Marine Corps Gen Carl E. Mundy, Jr.; retired MajGen David A. Richwine, Director of Development for the Smithsonian's Air and Space Museum, who as an infantry officer in Vietnam earned the Silver Star before becoming a naval aviator; and BGen Vincente T. "Ben" Blaz, USMC (Ret.), who shared personal information about his boyhood on Guam in World War II. Thanks to BGen Andrew B. Davis, USMCR, Director of Public Affairs, HQMC; and Public Affairs Officer Maj J.A. Johnston and Public Affairs Assistant Bridget White, who provided updated information, as has Davis's successor, BGen Mary Ann Krusa-Dossin, and her staff.

Others who provided insight and suggestions are, from *Leatherneck*, retired Col Walter G. Ford, editor, retired MGySgt Renaldo R. Keene, associate editor, and Jason Monroe, art director; Col John P. Glasgow, editor of the *Marine Corps Gazette*, and retired Maj Rick Spooner, World War II veteran and owner of the legendary Globe and Laurel Restaurant, an unofficial Marine institution located just outside Quantico—probably more famous than the "Tun Tavern" of 1775. The photographs of the Marine memorabilia from his enormous collection are a mark of this book's uniqueness, and his suggestions have been invaluable. Thanks, too, to Jim Phillips, publisher, for his permission to use rare Marine Corps photos from the early part of the twentieth century.

At the Marine Corps Heritage Foundation at Quantico, thanks to LtGen Ron Christmas, president, Mrs. Susan Hodges, VP, Administration and Finance, BGen Gerald L. McKay, COO, retired Col Raymond A. Hord, VP, Development and Marketing, and executive assistants Tina Noonan, Sabrina Linneham, and Christine Goidas. At the

Recruiting Command, appreciation to CG MajGen Walter Gaskin and his advertising and marketing officers, Maj Michael W. Zeliff and Capt David Weidensaul, for their liaison with J. Walter Thompson advertising, which has handled the Marine Corps account since 1946; and special thanks to JWT's Atlanta office director/account supervisor, former Marine and Vietnam veteran 1stLt Jeff White. JWT, which is the fourth-largest advertising firm in the world, placed $52 million of Marine advertising in 2004. (J. Walter Thompson himself was a Civil War Marine who served aboard the USS *Saratoga* before creating the agency in 1878.)

A special thanks, too, to former Marine captain, Korean War veteran, and acclaimed author James Brady for contributing the Foreword, and to world-renowned Marine combat photographer David Douglas Duncan, who so generously allowed the use of his magnificent combat photographs from Korea and Vietnam. And, to retired LtCol Oliver L. North for his invaluable assistance in the Iraq war section.

To those others who ably assisted by providing editorial comments and gathering materials and illustrations: BGen Thomas A. Benes, USMC, president, Marine Corps University, and commanding general, Marine Corps Education Command, including the Historical Division, Marine Corps Base, Quantico; Capt Roger D. Smith, Visual Information Management, Training and Education Command, and MGySgt Ramiro Sanchez of the photo branch at Quantico; Antonio Magnotta, head of the Visual Imaging Repository, and Susan Dillon in the photo archives at the Alfred Gray Center at Quantico; Director of University Archives at the Alfred Gray Research Center in Quantico Kerry Strong, and reference historians Pat Mullen and Mike Miller. At the Historical Division, Marine Corps Historical Center, U.S. Navy Yard, Washington, D.C.: Director of History and Museums Col John Ripley, USMC (Ret.), Retired; Deputy Director of Museums Col Jon T. Hoffman, USMCR; LtCol Ward Scott,

Col Brooke Nihart, USMC (Ret.)

project officer for the Sea Services 50th Anniversary Observance of the Korean War; and Lena Kaljot, photo reference historian. Retired Marine MSgt James A. Fairfax, head of the exhibits section at the Marine Corps Museum, and John T. (Jack) Dyer, retired Marine major and curator, Marine Corps Museum, were both instrumental in arranging for the photographing of important historical artifacts and art, as was the logistical assistance of SSgt J.S. Hernandez. Not least, thanks to retired police officer Gary Paul Johnston for his expertise in weaponry.

At the Quantico Museum: Curator of Material History Kenneth Smith-Christmas, and Assistant Curator Dieter Spenger. At the Weapons Training Battalion: Maj Gregory T. Roper at the Indoor Marksmanship Simulator Trainer; Maj Wesley T. Hayes, public affairs officer, and SSgt Julie Delgado, community relations NCO, G-3, for MCB, Quantico; Col Dave Burgess, USMC (Ret.), director of Professional Development, Marine Corps Association, Quantico, and Jason Pierce, manager, MCA Bookstore, Quantico.

At the Combat Visual Information Center at Quantico: Capt Charles G. Grow, USMC, former photo officer; Sgt Cooper I.

Evans, USMC, for his digital photography of certain weapons; MGySgt James P. Craig at the Weapons Training Battalion, and MGySgt Charles A. Hubbard at the Basic School armory for their help in displaying weaponry for photography. And Col Mark Dudenhefer, Military Awards branch head, Manpower, for guidance and assistance in procuring the medals and battle streamers that we photographed. And to his successor, retired Col Charles Mugno, and his assistant, LtCol Karen Dowling, USMCR, for their help.

At the Marine Corps Aviation Association Dan Meador and former Marine Hank Perry, Marine Corps/Navy liaison officer at Bell Helicopter, Inc., for assistance in acquiring photographs of the MV-22 Osprey; director of the United States Marine Corps Historical Company, retired Marine GySgt Thomas E. Williams, and to Richard W. Claar, specialist in military books and collectibles.

And last but not least, at Barnes & Noble Publishing in New York, my heartfelt thanks to Editorial Director Nathaniel Marunas, Editor Betsy Beier, and Art Director Kevin Ullrich—who, as we say, "went above and beyond the call of duty" with his independent researching and masterful layout of the entire book; to Photography Director Christopher Bain and Assistant Photography Director Lori Epstein, who also put their hearts and souls into collecting visual material. They are not only the most professional and talented people I have ever worked with, but also the most encouraging and understanding as well. They made my previous book on combat art so successful; they have made this one so as well.

And, to those who contributed but somehow have been overlooked—my apologies.

Finally, to my wife, Lise, again for her forbearance (as is the case with writers' wives), and to Brooke Nihart's wife, Mary Helen, for hers.

—Avery Chenoweth
May 2005

Foreword

A daunting task, an impressive feat, putting the United States Marines, their Corps, their history, their spirit, and the many legends all between the hard covers of a single book.

Ask a score of Marines to define themselves and their Corps and you'll get twenty answers. Ask a hundred civilians—or a thousand—and both they and you will end up confused. And here comes Colonels Chenoweth and Nihart to tackle the job—and in words and pictures, to get it right.

As a Marine, and writer about Marines, I once wrote of us and our Corps as a violent priesthood, both sacred and profane, a blend of myth and glorious, often tragic, history. The natural state for United States Marines is in combat; they are uneasy and fretful in times of peace, but leave it to authors Chenoweth and Nihart to give us the Marine in war, in peace, and in just plain ill-temper.

Consider if you will just a few of those who bore the title: Dan Daly, who cursed his men in France and demanded to know if they wanted to live forever. Ted Williams, who flew fighters in two wars and batted .400. Mortarman Lou Diamond, on Guadalcanal a killer with a long white beard, "like Santa Claus." Senator John Chafee, who dropped out of Yale to enter boot camp, fought on the "Canal," went to OCS, fought some more as a lieutenant, and, after Harvard Law School, found himself back in, commanding a rifle company in North Korea. Actor Lee Marvin; *New York Times* publisher "Punch" Sulzberger; Bob Kriendler of the "21" Club; Jimmy Roosevelt, the president's son and a Marine

James Brady served in the 1st Marine Division as a rifle platoon leader, rifle company executive officer, and battalion intelligence officer in 1951–52. He was awarded the Bronze Star for a firefight against the Chinese on Memorial Day of 1952. He writes weekly for *Parade* magazine and for *Advertising Age* and has written fourteen books, including *The Coldest War*, a memoir of Korea, and *Marines of Autumn*, a novel. His most recent novel is *Warning of War*, about the North China Marines of 1941.

Raider; Gene Tunney, the heavyweight champ who beat Dempsey; Jim Lehrer and Don Imus and Mark Shields; Angelo Bertelli of Notre Dame, who won the Heisman and went off to war as a Marine officer; Gene Hackman, who served in North China; David Dinkins, who was mayor of New York.

Such rosters of celebrated Marines go on endlessly, and I haven't even touched on Chesty Puller, "Uncle Joe" Pendleton, or Pappy Boyington. What more can one say about a Corps whose most recent commandant stood six-five and spoke fluent French? And was nominated to command NATO!

When I was a young rifle platoon leader in Dog Company of the 7th Marines in North Korea in 1951 to '52, there was a Korean urchin named Chang who hung about when we came down off the line at Christmas, an engaging, scar-faced rascal of perhaps eleven or twelve. The scars may have derived from an accident, but for the romantic among us, had surely been caused by the sabre of an arrogant Japanese officer in the war. Young Chang, who had seen American films, was sure that John Wayne had been a Marine, perhaps even had been commandant!

"No, Chang, he's an actor, that's all. John Wayne was never a Marine."

The lad could never be convinced. He knew a Marine when he saw one. Hadn't he been among us?

It is Chenoweth and Nihart's achievement that in a single volume they seem able to distinguish between fact and fancy, the historically real and the merely imagined, and to delight, inform, and at times inspire the reader, be he a Marine, or just another mortal.

Well done, sirs.

James Brady
East Hampton, New York

Tribute to John Glenn: Marine, Astronaut, and U.S. Senator

It would be difficult to single out an American who has distinguished himself more in service to his country—and to the Marine Corps—than John H. Glenn, Jr.

In 1992, he was presented with the Congressional Space Medal of Honor for fifty years of outstanding service to his country. That service included twenty-three years in the Marine Corps, ten years as an astronaut at the National Aeronautics and Space Administration (NASA), with which he was the first American to orbit the earth in a space capsule, and three terms as a United States senator from Ohio. That medal, along with innumerable other awards, was added to the five Distinguished Flying Crosses and eighteen Air Medals he earned in combat as a Marine aviator.

A native of the Midwest, Glenn was born in Cambridge, Ohio, in 1921, and graduated from Muskingum College in 1943. He joined the Naval Aviation Cadet Program, earning his wings and commission as a Marine second lieutenant on 31 March 1943. Assigned to the Pacific, he joined VMF-155 of MAG 31, 4th Marine Aircraft Wing (MAW), flying F4U Corsairs in combat during the Marshall Islands campaign of 1944. For fifty-nine combat air missions, he was awarded two Distinguished Flying Crosses (DFCs) and ten Air Medals.

After assignments following the war in China, he was promoted to major and trained in jets in 1952. In February 1953, he joined VMF-311 of 1st MAW at Pohang, South Korea, to fly the F9F Panther jet. Flying this early jet on sixty-three combat missions, he earned a third DFC and six more Air Medals. In an exchange program with the Air Force, Glenn went to the 25th Squadron, 51st Fighter Interceptor Wing, and flew the new supersonic F-86 Sabre jet. In the last three weeks of the war, he downed three Russian-made—and probably Russian-piloted—MiG

Col John H. Glenn, Jr., USMC (Ret.)

fighters over North Korea, earning his fourth DFC and seventh and eighteenth Air Medals. Marine aircraft mechanics had surreptitiously painted on the underside of his Air Force jet, "Join the Marines," and beneath his canopy, "MiG Mad Marine."

After the Korean War, Glenn became a test pilot, and in a record-breaking feat on 16 July 1957, piloting an F-8U1 Crusader jet, "beat the sun" from the West to the East Coast, setting a nonstop transcontinental supersonic flight record of 3 hours, 23 minutes, and 8.1 seconds, earning his fifth DFC.

On 9 April 1959, LtCol Glenn was selected as one of seven astronauts in NASA's first manned space program, "Project Mercury." In 1962, his tiny "Friendship 7" space capsule was propelled into space from an Atlas missile fired from Cape Canaveral, Florida. Fellow astronaut Alan Shepard had already soared into outer space briefly, and a Russian cosmonaut had orbited the earth, but Glenn was the first American to orbit the earth. He did so three times at 17,500 miles per hour at

an altitude of 162 miles. Due to system failures on the pioneering flight, Glenn had to manually control the second and third orbits. Upon reentry into the atmosphere, he deftly maneuvered his craft through the fiery friction created by the atmosphere as parts of his heat shield, instead of absorbing the tremendous heat, began to disintegrate and tear off as he watched helplessly through the windscreen. The American people held their breaths as Glenn's progress was monitored at Mission Control in Houston, Texas, and reported on the broadcast networks.

After four hours and fifty-five minutes of flight, Friendship 7—with its heroic and lucky astronaut—splashed down in the Atlantic Ocean eight hundred miles east of the Kennedy Space Center. A Marine CH-34 Sea Horse helicopter from the USS *Randolph* retrieved him and the capsule from the water.

It would be thirty years from astronaut Glenn's first venture into space to his second on 29 October 1998 at age seventy-seven, when he embarked on a nine-day space voyage aboard the space shuttle *Discovery* with its crew of six.

Ostensibly, Glenn's contribution to the mission would be to further geriatric medical studies in space, although he pulled his weight with everyone else by performing chores aboard the spacecraft. As the shuttle made its customary landing at the Kennedy Space Center at Cape Canaveral, it was a far cry from his earlier splashdown and a fitting tribute to one of the truly great pioneers in space exploration.

Col John H. Glenn, Jr., USMC (Ret.)—astronaut and senator—is perhaps one of the most widely known and admired figures in American history. His life story is inspiring, the markings of a hero, and, certainly, the "Right Stuff." All Marines are proud that he was one of them.

Introduction
A Fighting Force Like No Other

"MARINES—The Few. The Proud." This present recruiting and advertising slogan followed "We Don't Promise You a Rose Garden" during Vietnam and later "A Few Good Men." Such boastful statements would indicate that the Marines think of themselves as a cut above—elite—and that they challenge others to join and be as good as they are...if they can! The standards are high: motivation, physical fitness, intelligence, loyalty, bravery. The bar is not lowered. The simple reason is that as a fighting force, the United States Marine Corps is unique, as are those who comprise it.

No other military force in the world has the configuration or mission of the U.S. Marine Corps. Although some other nations have marines, they usually act as small shipboard units or small landing forces. Since 1914, the Marine Corps has been a unique triple-role organization specialized to fight on land, at sea, and in the air as a self-contained, combined ground and aviation force, coordinating all elements into a formidable war-fighting machine that concentrates on forcible entry from the sea.

Its combat elements—task forces organized into MEFs, MEBs, and MEUs (Marine Expeditionary Forces, Brigades, and Units)—are properly termed Marine Air-Ground Task Forces (MAGTFs). A MAGTF is versatile and flexible enough to react and adapt rapidly to changing situations on the battlefield, a requisite for victory.

A MEF can total between 20,000 and 90,000 Marines, and its mission is to win battles in a major theater of war. A MEB, generally 3,000 to 20,000 Marines strong, responds to crises and smaller-scale contingencies. A MEU is a reinforced battalion-size unit with Special Operation Capabilities (SOC) utilized for first-on-scene rescue missions and to promote peace and stability. A Special Purpose MAGTF (SPMAGTF) is task-organized to accomplish specific missions such as humanitarian assistance, disaster relief, peacetime engagements, or regionally focused exercises. It also contains Fleet Antiterrorism Security Teams (FASTs) and Chemical-Biological Incident Response Forces (CBIRFs), which can respond to higher command for national requirements on a moment's notice.

In Napoleon's time, the word *corps* suggested a large command of two or more divisions with supporting combat and logistic units. Since World War II, a "corps" pertaining to Marines refers to a specialized military body of two or more infantry divisions and air wings comprising a specified unit. Basically, three Marine divisions (MarDivs), each approximately twenty-five thousand troops strong and commanded by a major general, comprise a corps; three corps comprise an "army," commanded by a lieutenant general. The unit between a corps and an army is a "force," which is also commanded by a lieutenant general. Today's U.S. Marine Corps has the capability of fielding three MEFs. Combined, these MEFs, with infantry divisions and air wings, augmented by engineers, artillery, armor, and other support arms, are the actual cutting edge of the U.S. Marine Corps and are called the Operating Forces.

Also unique to the Marine Corps is its mission and structure as a quick-strike force that can be inserted into hostile territory either amphibiously onto a beachhead, by vertical helicopter-borne assaults deeper inland, or both. Termed Operational Maneuver from the Sea (OMFTS)—now updated to Expeditionary Maneuver Warfare (EMW)—such a mission is supported by naval gunfire offshore as well as by bombing and strafing by its own close-air aviation.

This concept works efficiently because of the Corps' basic doctrine: "Every Marine is a rifleman." Even the Marine aviator providing close-air support knows what infantrymen

are experiencing on the ground because before flight training that pilot would have also undergone infantry training and rifle marksmanship at the Basic School in Quantico, Virginia. Neither the Army, the Navy, the Air Force, nor any other domestic or foreign service has such a requirement.

This is the ideal. When Marines find themselves segmented in an otherwise coordinated land-sea-air engagement, they are self-sufficient enough to handle any circumstance. Thus, "The situation is well in hand" has been a truism throughout Marine Corps history.

TRADITION

The Marine Corps has zealously guarded and preserved its traditions. Special occasions, such as the all-inclusive formal Birthday Balls celebrated every 10 November and the formal Mess Nights, preserve the "eliteness" and esprit of the Corps, celebrate its glorious past, and serve as reminders of where Marines came from and why they are the best.

Esprit de Corps

Esprit de corps, the unifying spirit inspiring enthusiasm, devotion, and unswerving regard for the honor of the group, is an intangible attribute, yet one strong enough to motivate fierce loyalty and heroic deeds. In the U.S. Marine Corps, esprit de corps is founded upon and fed by the illustrious tradition that comes from hard-fought battles and victories. It goes from bottom to top and top to bottom

of the entire organization; everyone wearing the Marine uniform possesses it. No matter what the rank, no matter what the job, the same spirit prevails throughout—and for most it lasts a lifetime, remaining with as much vigor after service and into retirement as on active duty. "Once a Marine, always a Marine" is not an empty claim.

An unwavering pride in self, unit, and service to country—the esprit de corps—is instilled from the start, at boot camp for the enlisted Marine and at the Basic School for the officer. It is not indoctrinated; it grows and manifests itself in the individual going through the gauntlet and attaining the tough goal of being accepted as a Marine—on the Marine Corps' terms, not the individual's. From such training, in which honor, courage, and commitment are honed, develops professionalism, leadership, and an unshakable confidence in everything a Marine is called upon to do. One Marine looks at another and knows that that Marine is like himself, is as good as he is, and can be counted on when the chips are down. He knows that whatever enemy he may be

facing, the Marine on his right and the Marine on his left will be there. Marines will fight to the last man, and they will not leave their dead or wounded on the battlefield. Their esprit de corps in battle has been felt by many a foe, to the latter's misfortune.

Even in later life, when a former Marine meets another, he knows instinctively what kind of a person he is dealing with. There is a camaraderie, a perpetual "band of brotherhood," as exemplified by King Henry's exhortation to his men before the Battle of Agincourt in Shakespeare's *Henry V*: "We few, we happy few, we band of brothers. For he today that sheds his blood with me shall be my brother."

Mottoes and Appellations

When the Continental Marines were created during the Second Continental Congress in 1775, various mottoes appeared, including "Don't Tread on Me," which was inscribed on

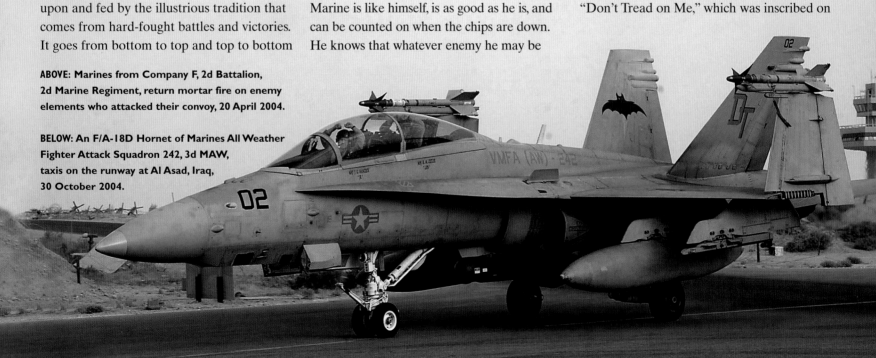

ABOVE: Marines from Company F, 2d Battalion, 2d Marine Regiment, return mortar fire on enemy elements who attacked their convoy, 20 April 2004.

BELOW: An F/A-18D Hornet of Marines All Weather Fighter Attack Squadron 242, 3d MAW, taxis on the runway at Al Asad, Iraq, 30 October 2004.

a drumhead above a coiled rattlesnake. During the Federal period, *Fortitudine*, Latin for "with courage," was inscribed on the brass plates on the Marines' tall shakos. *Per Marem, Per Terram* (often erroneously spelled as *Per Mar, per Terram*), Latin for "by sea, by land," was used during the War with Mexico, as were the mottoes, "By Sea and by Land" and "To the Shores of Tripoli," which was inscribed on the Marine colors.

When, after the Civil War, efficiency experts proposed to do away with the Corps or merge it into the Army, senior Navy officers who had served with Marines at sea or had commanded them in amphibious operations came to the rescue. In a barrage of letters to the White House and Congress, they attested to the professionalism and bravery of their Marines, referring to them as, "Our ever faithful Marines." The description stuck, and *Semper Fidelis*, "always faithful," was adopted by the Corps as the official motto in 1883. It was emblazoned on the riband held in the beak of the eagle on the Marine emblem in 1867. The motto has become universal as both a salutation and a farewell. It has been colloquially shortened to *Semper Fi*.

In addition to mottoes, other monickers came to be associated with the Marines. "Leatherneck" comes from the high leather collar on early-nineteenth-century Marine uniforms, which forced the head to be held high and was supposed to deflect a sword slash to the back of the neck during battle. Marines had been first on the ground in Manila and Cuba in the Spanish-American War, and thereafter earned the description "first to fight."

For a time, during World War I, Marines were referred to as Devil Dogs, a nickname supposedly coined by the Germans, who were impressed by the Marines' ferociousness in battle. However, the Germans never refered to them as such. Thus, the expression *Teufel Hunden*, which is incorrect German (*Teufelshunde*), erroneously came into the lexicon. The "Gung ho" of World War II comes from a Marine colonel's study of Chinese and translates as "work together." It is more often used now as an expression meaning "extremely enthusiastic." The "Old Corps" is an attribution adopted by Marines

to describe those who have considerably more years of service than they do.

"Gyrene" was a slightly pejorative term used by other services when referring to Marines, as was "jar head," which describes the appearance of one's ears standing out after a very short haircut. (The Marines have always favored this kind of cut, not only for its ultimate military appearance but for its practicality in the field and when wearing the steel combat helmet.)

"Force-in-Readiness" epitomized the established role of the Marine Corps when Congress formally defined the Corps' mission during the Korean War in 1952. Based on its readiness and performance during the Persian Gulf War and at the global hot spots thereafter, the Marine Corps has more recently been tapped as America's "911 Force-in-Readiness."

The Marines' Hymn

The traditional Marines' Hymn appeared following the Civil War. Words from an unknown poet were set to the music of nineteenth-century French composer Jacques Offenbach's operetta *Geneviève de Brabant* by Marine Band leader John Philip Sousa. The historical order of Tripoli and the halls of Montezuma were transposed for reasons of euphony; "in the air, on land, and sea" was added circa World War I.

Beginning shortly after World War II, on occasions when the official marches of the various armed services were played, Marines present would stand at attention during the Marines' Hymn. Some civilians assumed that this was the expected tribute to the Marines and began to stand also. After a few years of this practice, members of the other services began to stand when their marches were played. Again, the Marines had led the way.

RIGHT: In 1867 a new—and permanent—Marine Corps emblem was developed by modifying the old eagle and anchor emblem. To signify the expanded role of the Marine Corps, a globe showing the Western Hemisphere was added in front of the anchor. Atop the globe sits an eagle. Thus the "eagle, globe, and anchor" has become the enduring symbol of the United States Marine Corps.

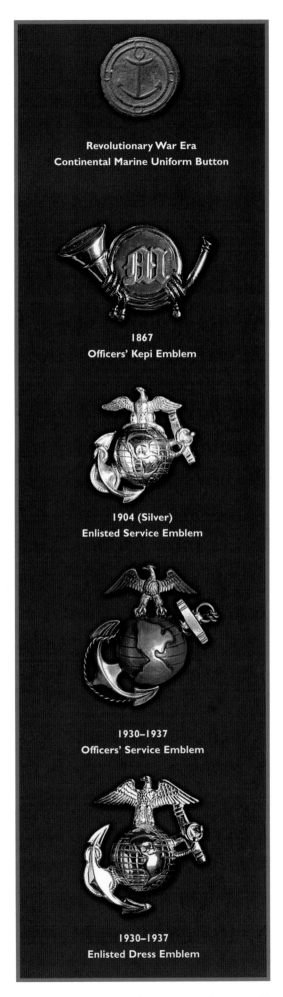

Revolutionary War Era
Continental Marine Uniform Button

1867
Officers' Kepi Emblem

1904 (Silver)
Enlisted Service Emblem

1930–1937
Officers' Service Emblem

1930–1937
Enlisted Dress Emblem

The Marines' Hymm

From the halls of Montezuma
To the shores of Tripoli,
We fight our country's battles
In the air, on land, and sea.

First to fight for right and freedom,
And to keep our honor clean,
We are proud to claim the title
Of United States Marine.

Our flag's unfurled to every breeze
From dawn to setting sun;
We have fought in every clime and place
Where we could take a gun.
In the snow of far off northern lands
And in sunny tropic scenes,
You will find us always on the job—
The United States Marines.

Here's health to you and to our Corps
Which we are proud to serve;
In many a strife we've fought for life
And never lost our nerve.
If the Army and the Navy
Ever look on Heaven's scenes,
They will find the streets are guarded
By United States Marines.

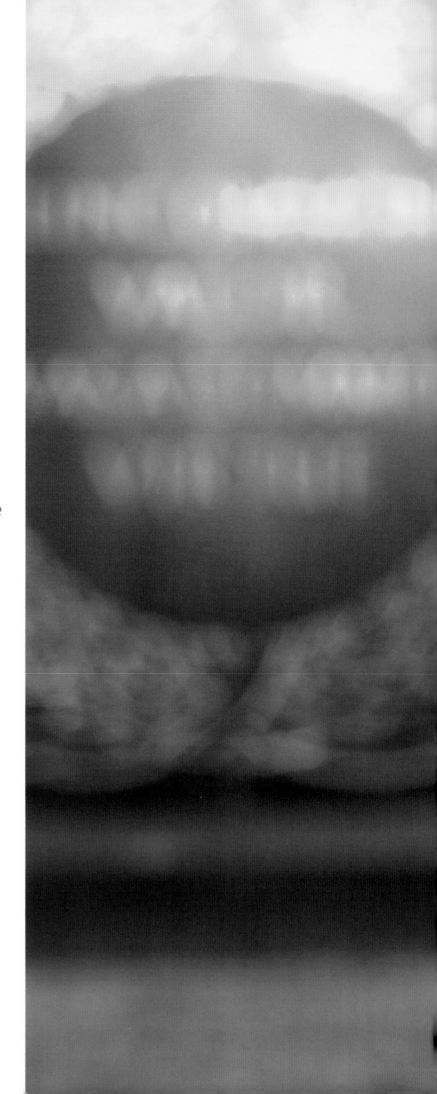

While all branches of the armed forces have the nation's respect, the Marines hold a special place in the hearts of their countrymen. All services have displayed bravery and success on the battlefield, but the Marines have excelled consistently and often spectacularly. Positive publicity has resulted. Both consciously and unconsciously, and often without direction from headquarters, the Marine Corps has built on this reputation in many ways.

Marine Honor Guards, wearing dress blues and executing precise drills, grace many public events, and continue to bolster the Corps' reputation as an elite force.

—BN

The Uniform

The Marine Corps uses the same uniform throughout: green blouse, trousers (skirts), and cover for everyday duty; dress blues for special occasions; Dress Mess for formal; and either brown-side-out or green-side-out camouflage utilities for field and battle. No need for special berets or distinctions, the Marine Corps considers the entire organization elite. Marines always present a sharp image, often the envy of the other services.

Certain details of the uniform are a constant reminder of tradition: the buttons still use the Marine Corps design of 1804, with an eagle atop an anchor under a half circle of thirteen six-pointed stars (later changed to five-pointed stars). The red stripe down the trouser leg of the dress blue uniform was adopted in 1798, but by legend it has come to denote the Marine blood shed at the capture of the halls of Montezuma in the Mexican-American War in 1847. Tradition has it that the quatrefoil on the cover of the Marine officer's barracks cap was added so that Marine sharpshooters in the riggings of vessels in the days of sail could identify Marines below. In fact, it was originally copied from the French officers' uniform in 1859. The Marine officer's sword is based on the Mameluke, sword presented by the brother of the Bey of Alexandria, Egypt, to Marine Lt Presley O'Bannon prior to his famed expedition to capture the fort at Derna from the Barbary pirates in 1804. The fourragère worn over the left shoulder by only the 5th and 6th Marine Regiments represents the Croix de Guerre that the French awarded to those regiments for their victories at Château-Thierry, Belleau Wood, Soissons, Saint-Mihiel, Meuse-Argonne, and Blanc Mont in World War I.

The Marine Band

The Marine Band of professional musicians has been "the president's own" ever since President John Adams so designated it in 1798.

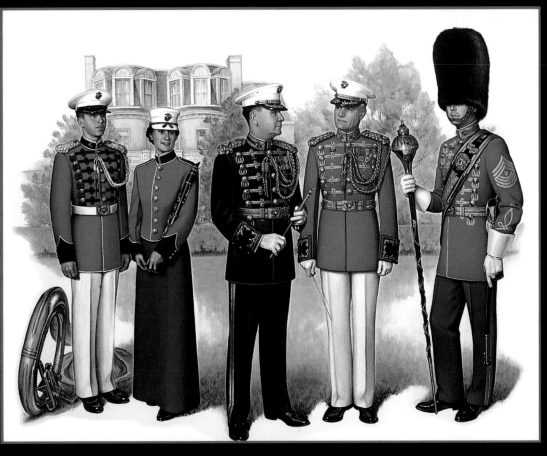

The famed conductor-composer John Philip Sousa was its director throughout the 1880s. Among his many familiar marches, including "Stars and Stripes Forever" and "The Washington Post," Sousa wrote "Semper Fidelis" for the Marine Corps, which was authorized as the service's official march by Congress. Played at all Marine gatherings, it is featured along with the Marines' Hymn at the famed Summer Friday Evening Parades held at Marine Barracks, which has been the site of grand military ceremonies and reviews since its founding in 1801, and at the Tuesday evening Sunset Parades at the Iwo Jima Memorial in Arlington Cemetery overlooking Washington. These ceremonies center on the stirring marches and military precision of the Drum and Bugle Corps and the Silent Drill Team.

OPPOSITE, INSET: Drummer in full dress white uniform, 1942.

LEFT, TOP: Col Donna Neary's uniform print series displaying the noncommissioned and commissioned officers winter Evening Dress uniforms.

LEFT, BOTTOM: Neary's print of the Marine Band summer and winter Full Dress uniforms.

ABOVE: American composer and conductor John Philip Sousa was the leader of the Marine Band from 1880 until 1892.

Presidential Transport

Another long-standing Marine tradition has been providing transport for the commander in chief. *Marine One* is the VH-3D Sea King helicopter assigned to fly the U.S. president on short hops near the nation's capital, and even airlifts passengers to remote locations in the United States and abroad. Marine helicopter squadron HMX-1, headquartered at the Quantico Marine base thirty-five miles south of Washington, is tasked with this prestigious duty. Aircraft are maintained there and at Anacostia Naval Auxiliary Air Station in southeast D.C. The president's helicopter, seen almost daily on television, is painted in a distinctive olive-and-white color scheme.

Battle Streamers

For each major campaign the Marine Corps engages in, a uniquely designed streamer (represented in miniature by a chest ribbon) is added to the top of the staff of the Marine "colors" at Marine headquarters. As of this writing there are fifty battle streamers in all.

ABOVE: *Marine One* takes off from the South Lawn of the White House on 21 September 2001, with President George W. Bush and First Lady Laura Bush on board.

Each campaign streamer includes a bronze star representing each major battle or campaign, or a silver star for each five bronze stars. The Persian Gulf War streamer, for example, has three bronze stars, representing the defense of Saudi Arabia; the liberation and defense of Kuwait; and the Southwest Asia Ceasefire Campaign.

THE EVOLUTION OF THE MARINE MISSION

When the Second Continental Congress raised the two battalions of Continental Marines in 1775 at the beginning of the American Revolution, their original mission was to "serve to advantage by sea." These new American Marines would be knowledgeable of the sea, provide ship and base security, and help man ships' guns, as well as defend against pirates and privateers, prevent mutiny, and provide boarding and raiding parties.

At the start of the twentieth century, the Marines' role was expanded to that of an Advance Base Force (ABF) to defend naval bases on the islands newly acquired from Spain. This marked the beginnings of the later Fleet Marine Force (FMF). During World War I, two regiments of Marines were integrated into the Army 2d Division of the American Expeditionary Force (AEF) and fought conventional infantry warfare in France. The Marine Corps had offered to field an entire division of infantry and artillery supported by squadrons of fighter-bombers, but American commanding general John J. Pershing rejected the offer.

Following the First World War, the Marines always operated with integral aviation, by which they developed the concept of air-ground teams. Marine aviation also originated the concept of dive-bombing, which the German *Luftwaffe* copied, while a broader doctrine of amphibious landing was being devised just prior to its use during the Second World War in the Pacific to defeat Japan. Marines taught their amphibious doctrine to the Army for use in North Africa, Italy, and Normandy. Some Army units using this training were in combined amphibious operations with Marines in the Pacific Island battles.

Stung by the Army's lackluster performance in the opening months of the Korean War—and favorably impressed by the Marine Corps' brilliant record by contrast—both the Senate and the House of the

Eighty-second Congress passed the Douglas-Mansfield Bill in the summer of 1951. President Harry Truman—no admirer of the Marine Corps—reluctantly signed it the following year as Public Law 416. The bill created a permanency for the Marine Corps, with an FMF of three infantry divisions and three air wings, plus a reserve division and wing, with a ceiling of 400,000. It also placed the Commandant of the Marine Corps on an equal level with the chiefs of other services on the Joint Chiefs of Staff in the Department of Defense, and separated the Marine Corps from the Navy, thus amending the National Security Act of 1947. The bill also defined the Corps as a "Force-in-Readiness."

During the Pacific battles of World War II, the Marine Corps had perfected its amphibious Navy-Marine task force doctrine, winning at great cost all the fierce battles it fought. Following the war, as the introduction of atomic weaponry came into play,

Southwest Asia Service Medal

Southwest Asia Service (1990–1995)

BELOW: Marines in Humvees line up in Saudi Arabia in preparation for Desert Storm, 3 January 1991.

Combined Arms: A Marine Corps Tradition

Marines have erroneously been characterized as light infantry. In truth, U.S. Marines have always been familiar with artillery and have usually landed or entered battle with a variety of supporting arms.

From the beginning, they helped man ships' guns. After the Battle of Princeton in the American Revolution, some of Gen George Washington's artillery regiment's enlistments were expired and the soldiers went home, leaving their cannon behind. The Continental Marines with Washington then manned this artillery and accompanied Washington's army into winter quarters.

Navy ships carried some light 4-, 6-, or 12-pound guns on field carriages for landing parties. Upon landing, they might be manned by Marines or by sailors, as at the Battle of Bladensburg in 1814. During the War with Mexico, landing guns accompanied Marines in the conquest of California and in landings along the Gulf of Mexico.

By the time of the Civil War, Navy ordnance specialist John Dahlgren had developed lightweight 6- and 12-pound rifled landing guns on iron carriages. In an expedition on the Carolina coast in 1862, Marine 1stLt William H. Carter wrote home, "I have two rifled howitzers, 6-pounders, and my men know how to use them."

These 6-pounders were used in the 1871 Korean expeditions, but soon thereafter the Navy developed the M1876, a 3-inch breech-loading landing gun, which the Marines used throughout the nineteenth century, including for the seizing of Guantanamo Bay, Cuba, in 1898. During this period, the Marines also used the 10-barreled Gatling gun, firing rifle ammunition, a 1-pound gun, and a Hotchkiss 6-barreled 1-pound cannon—all on landing carriages. Finally, the Marines adopted the Colt-Browning M1895 automatic machine gun, which fired the same 6mm cartridge as their Winchester-Lee 5-shot rifle.

—BN

ABOVE: A French Model 1897 75mm gun used by Marines in the 1920s.

BELOW: Marines at Guantanamo Bay, Cuba, 1898.

the Marine Corps revised its ship-to-shore tactics to include the use of the helicopter in a new vertical-envelopment doctrine. The Marines were the first to introduce the helicopter into combat in the Korean War, and they perfected its deployment in Vietnam.

Since World War II, those serving in the armed forces who can expect to face the enemy one-on-one are Air Force pilots, Navy pilots, roughly 10 percent of the Army's infantry components, and about 75 percent of the entire Marine Corps.

Today, the mission of the Marine Corps is "expeditionary," as it was so designated during the nineteenth century and the Banana Wars of the early twentieth century. Expeditionary missions are accomplished either amphibiously (usually by MEUs, as in Somalia) or strategically deeper into hostile territory, via heliborne assault (by MEBs, as in Afghanistan) or by air/sea lift (by MEFs, as in both the Gulf and Iraq wars).

The twenty-first-century warfighting role of MAGTFs involves a combination of heliborne, vertical ship-to-shore, and other tactics tailored specifically for the plethora of new techniques called for in a fast-moving, high-tech, computer-managed battle scenario.

In the context of recent developments—especially following the terrorist attacks of 11 September 2001—the role of this efficient organization takes on more importance than ever. It is highly mobile and forms the core of joint Navy-Marine battle groups as well as of smaller, self-sustained Amphibious Ready Groups made up of Amphibious Assault Ships (LHAs and LHDs) transporting elements of a Marine Expeditionary Force (MEF), Marine Expeditionary Brigades (MEBs), or Marine Expeditionary Units with Special Operations Capabilities (MEU[SOC]). For larger operations, such as the Gulf War, Air Force air transport (TRANSCOM) as well as commercial airliners are used for strategic lift. Marine supplies, matériel, and ammunition are prepositioned, or sea-based, in the Mediterranean, the Indian Ocean, and the Far East at bases or on attack ships. Modern warfare calls for quick deployment. Marine units are usually the first to arrive, and when they do so, they are ready to fight with all their logistic support, which meets them near the battle site.

One Big Regiment

Most armies' infantry, artillery, and armor units are organized into regiments of five hundred to three thousand men; air forces are in squadrons of a few hundred. Soldiers or airmen enlist in a regiment or squadron and can spend most, if not all, of their careers in that unit. Morale is centered on that unit, its history and traditions, battles won, hardships endured, and past heroism. Although the Marines have had infantry and artillery regiments since the early 1900s and aircraft squadrons since 1917, their organization and training is different.

A Marine does not recruit into a particular regiment, is not trained by a particular regiment, and does not tend to stay in a particular regiment. Instead, he goes to a recruit depot, a "boot camp," either at San Diego, California, or at Parris Island, South Carolina. There, under the stern discipline and guidance of highly skilled drill instructors, he or she is molded into a Marine during a twelve-week period. Among more war-like skills, Marine recruits learn the history and traditions of the entire Marine Corps, not just of a single regiment.

After basic and advanced training, recruits may be posted to a regiment, division, aviation unit, or ship's detachment, but they remain jacks-of-all-trades—and masters of most. Their loyalties are to one big regiment—the Marine Corps. While officers of other services may refer to themselves as a Navy officer, an Army officer, etc., a Marine officer never refers to himself as anything but a Marine.

—BN

As of this writing, the Marine Corps is at an authorized strength of 173,321 Marines or a total force strength of 212,988 augmented by Reservists called up during the War on Terrorism. That gives the Corps its mandated strength of three infantry divisions and three aircraft wings, plus a reserve 4th MarDiv and aircraft wing that are trained but not on active duty. These warfighting elements comprise the Operating Forces, formerly the Fleet Marine Force. Marine bases and stations are referred to as the Supporting Establishment. Two divisions and wings are normally stationed on the West Coast: the 1st MarDiv and 3d Marine Air Wing (MAW) are stationed at Camp Pendleton, California, and the 3d MarDiv and 1st MAW on Okinawa and Hawaii. On the East Coast, the 2d MarDiv is stationed at Camp Lejeune, North Carolina, and the 2d MAW at Cherry Point, North Carolina, and at Marine Corps Air Station in Beaufort, South Carolina.

Until the end of World War II, when the Marine Corps had grown to 458,053 officers and men with six combat divisions and five

BELOW: A CH-53 Sea Stallion helicopter aboard the USS *Nassau*, a Marine Amphibious Assault ship in the Persian Gulf, 7 January 2003.

LEFT: Marine recruits of Lima Company, Series 3117, 3d Battalion, Marine Recruit Depot, San Diego, in the final days of boot camp.

Recruiter's ribbon, established 15 July 1997, awarded retroactive to 28 January 1949.

LEFT, BELOW: The same recruits undergoing the final test, the "Crucible," a three-day exercise that is the culmination of their training. If they pass, they earn the title of U.S. Marine and graduate.

Drill instructor's ribbon, established 15 July 1997, awarded retroactive to 6 October 1952.

aircraft wings, there had not been higher than a three-star lieutenant general rank. Surprising for a force so small, eighty general officers are now authorized. They include the four-star Commandant of the Marine Corps (CMC) and three other four-star general officers: the assistant commandant of the Marine Corps (ACMC), the vice chairman of the Joint Chiefs of Staff, and now the Supreme Allied Commander, Europe (SACEUR/NATO). The

CMC serves as a member of the Joint Chiefs of Staff under the Secretary of Defense. Thirty-second Marine Commandant James Jones was appointed Supreme Allied Commander, Europe for 2003, the first such appointment for a Marine general.

BOOT CAMP: WHERE THE DIFFERENCE BEGINS

Where does all this uniqueness, esprit de corps, and respect for tradition originate? In the past it might have been attributed to attracting a type of aggressive individual who sought adventure and fighting. In the twenty-first century, it is more properly attributed to training. Boot camp training for enlisted individuals takes place at the two recruit depots, at Parris Island, South Carolina, and San Diego, California; officer training takes place at the Basic School at the Marine Corps Base in Quantico, Virginia.

Banners at the boot camps greet recruit and visitor alike: "Where the Difference Begins." That difference refers to what makes the Marine Corps distinguishable from all the

other services. No training of any armed service is comparable to Marine training. A volunteer recruit, having met both the mental and physical requirements, enlists and is sent to a twelve-week boot camp to learn the basics of military discipline, weaponry, marksmanship, and deportment. While there, the recruit sheds extraneous personal impediments in order to find within himself those innate qualities and strengths of character that will enable him to complete the rite of passage and transform himself into a Marine. As the recruit training manual puts it:

"We believe that Marines are forged in a furnace of shared hardship and tough training. This common, intense experience creates bonds of comradeship and standards of conduct so strong that Marines will die for each other. This belief will continue to be the basis upon which we make Marines."

Unique, too, is the fact that in a climate of unity and gender blindness, the Marine Corps refuses to lower its physical standards for males; consequently, men and women do not train together. Although men and women may serve together later, women are prohibited from direct combat roles.

In a concentrated, no-nonsense, twelve-week curriculum, Marine recruits attend

Women Marines

Women in uniform in all the armed forces seem commonplace these days. In today's Marine Corps, almost 6 percent of active-duty Marines are women; 62 percent of non-combat billets and 93 percent of military occupational specialty (MOS) fields are open to women—a far cry from the administrative duties that were opened to Women Marine Reserves in World War I in order to "free a Marine to fight."

Five women have attained flag rank in the Marine Corps, the highest being LtGen Carol A. Mutter, USMC, now retired. Presently serving as director of public affairs, HQMC, is BGen Mary Ann Krusa-Dossin, USMC. The first woman general officer, BGen Margaret A. Brewer, also served in that billet, in 1978.

In August 1918, during World War I, 305 women entered the Marine Corps to relieve men of administrative duties, thus freeing them to join the fighting forces. Although functioning mainly as typists, these "Marinettes," who wore enlisted green uniforms with long skirts, were also instructed in close-order drills and ceremonies and in military discipline. As *Leatherneck* magazine wrote of them after the war: "Everyone is proud of the Marine girls. They carried themselves like real soldiers…and proved they were ready to go anywhere and conduct themselves with honor to the Marine Corps."

Since there was no provision for women in the regular establishment, they were designated Reservists, and some stayed on active duty until World War II, when another influx greatly increased their World War I numbers. The Marine Corps Women's Reserve (MCWR) was established on 13 February 1943. (Eunice

Col Katherine A. Towle

ABOVE: Women Marines pasting up recruiting posters, 21 January 1919.

Lejeune, daughter of former commandant John Lejeune, was present at CMC Alexander Vandegrift's house in 1944 when he announced formally the establishment of the MCWR. She recalled that the portrait of MajGen Archibald Henderson, who had served thirty-nine years as commandant in the nineteenth century, fell from the wall and crashed to the floor.) Women Marines became so plentiful in administrative jobs at HQMC that Commandant Alexander Vandegrift declared that it was thanks to them that the Corps was able to raise the 6th Marine Division in the field for the Okinawa campaign. Of the more than twenty thousand MCWRs on active duty during World War II, 85 percent of the enlisted staff at HQMC were women, and almost two-thirds of the permanent personnel at major posts and stations were MCWRs.

In 1948 President Truman signed the Women's Armed Services Integration Act, and from 1945 through 1952, a cadre of MCWRs remained on active duty as regular members of the armed forces. The Corps established the position of Director of Women Marines and assigned the temporary rank of colonel to Katherine A. Towle, USMC, as director.

By the outbreak of the Korean War, there were more than thirteen WM Reserve platoons composed of 2,787 Marines in the Organized Reserve throughout the country. All were activated for the war. In Vietnam, with thousands of Women Marines on active duty, 28 enlisted women and 8 women officers served in non-combat roles. While many served in non-combat roles in the first Gulf War, in the succeeding war in Afghanistan a female

Serve

WOMEN
MARINES

ABOVE: A 1940s-era recruiting poster.

BGen Margaret A. Brewer

LtGen Carol A. Mutter

BGen Mary Ann Krusa-Dossin

Marine sergeant was killed in a refueler plane crash. In Operation Iraqi Freedom, 1,500 female Marines were deployed to the Persian Gulf region. Many drove trucks that delivered supplies to troops on the fast-moving front lines on the way to Baghdad. Some flew helicopters. Only the ground combat MOSs of infantry, artillery, tanks, and amphibious tractors remain closed to women.

As deputy commandant for Manpower and Reserve Affairs under CMC Charles Krulak between 1996 and 1997, LtGen Carol Mutter eliminated the position of Director of Women Marines. She also directed that the designation "Women" Marine would be dropped, and that, henceforth, every member of the Corps—despite their gender—would be called Marines.

While successful in its present demonstration, the integration of women into the ranks has not been without controversy. From active-duty pregnancies to sexual harassment to ingrained chauvinism in what up through World War II had been an exclusive "white male's club," integration has brought with it a unique set of problems for a Marine Corps that "takes care of its own."

Although they train separately from males, females undergo the same rigorous combat training at boot camp as do their male counterparts. They are taught pugil-stick and hand-to-hand combat, and become proficient in the use of all combat weapons. The adage "Every Marine a rifleman" holds equally true for women Marines. Once again, the Marine Corps leads the way.

—HAC

LEFT: During World War II, Marines with full battle packs march off to war, while members of the Marine Corps Women's Reserve march in to Camp Lejeune, ready to take their places.

military classes on organization, behavior, history, military law (the Unified Code of Military Justice), as well as learning close-order drill, field combat, water survival, marksmanship, and martial arts, all of which involve intense physical training.

This instruction is enhanced by training in Core Values, designed to build self-confidence, character, and a strong moral foundation. Drill instructors take great pains to instill the three components of honor, courage, and commitment from the very first. These attributes, as well as the individual martial arts of judo and tae kwon do, are given top priority, because in combat—which *all* Marines are trained for, no matter what their later specialty—fighting ability and individual and unit integrity are vital.

A recruit is not considered a Marine until he has satisfactorily completed boot training and passes the final test: a fifty-four-hour, sleep- and food-deprived physical and mental ordeal in the field, called the Crucible. Upon completion of the final twenty-four individual and team challenges during this ultimate testing, the recruit has earned the title of Marine. This achievement, and the enormous pride of at last attaining this distinction, is a life-changing experience. Not only does it carry throughout the Marine's career, it marks life beyond the

ABOVE: Wherever Marines are, they train and stay physically fit. Here, within sight of Mt. Fujiyama, in Japan, Marines train in martial arts.

BELOW: In constant training prior to returning to Iraq, members of 3d Battalion, 5th Marines, hone their combat skills at Camp Pendleton. Here, their platoon leader, 2dLt John F. Campbell, signals for ammunition.

Corps. No one can hold his head as high as a Marine who has gone through boot training and the Crucible.

The Corps' Core Values instruction is unique in modern-day military training. The indoctrination of personal and Corps honor, coupled with the courage built up by self-confidence training, results in a commitment that becomes an unshakable loyalty to self, to unit, and to the Corps. These qualities become apparent in the way Marines comport themselves. It is the backbone of the esprit de corps.

That is what the "difference" is all about.

The Martial Arts Program

Another unique element of the Corps' training regimen is the Marine Corps Martial Arts Program (MCMAP), instituted in 2000 for every Marine—male and female—regardless of rank or duty.

Some thirty-eight thousand new recruits are trained every year—98 percent of whom are highly motivated high school graduates. When it comes to training today's recruits, however, the Marines have found them hardly able to defend themselves, much less fight. Consequently, the Marines' new program teaches the martial arts of judo and tae kwon do, plus regular and kickboxing, and awards belts for mastery of each level.

The self-confidence engendered by the personal discipline of both mind and body results in the cultivation of a warrior ethos as well as an overall higher unit combat effectiveness throughout the entire Corps. It reinforces Core Values and high moral principles on an individual level, creating a breed apart. In its mission, termed warfighting, the U.S. Marine Corps is the only service to train every member in the martial arts in order to be individually aggressive and not to hesitate to kill the enemy in close combat.

Facts

Every year, 1,676 commissioned officers are obtained from the Naval Academy, as well as from colleges and university programs, such as Naval Reserve Officer Training Corps (NROTC), Platoon Leaders Class

(PLC), Officer Candidate School (OCS), and selected enlisted and warrant officer programs. Meanwhile, 32,440 enlisted recruits are accepted and trained, while the Reserve feeds enlistments of 6,114, for a total of 38,554 annually. Seventy-five percent of the Marine Corps is under the age of twenty-five. The percentage of female enlisted is 6.13, while that of female officers is 5.2. As with all the other services, an enlisted Marine recruit is paid $964.80 a month; a master sergeant is paid a maximum of $4,060.80 monthly; and a four-star general is paid a maximum of $11,737.20 monthly.

All members can retire after twenty years of service and receive half of their base pay for life, with incremental annual cost-of-living increases. Or, if qualified and needed, service members may stay for thirty or more years on active duty and receive three-quarters or a proportional increase of their base pay at retirement. Mandatory retirement age is sixty-five.

Semper Fidelis

Difficult as it is to imagine topping the achievements of its illustrious 230-year history, the United States Marine Corps of the beginning of the twenty-first century is the paradigm of an efficient, powerful, and formidable fighting force—second to none in the world.

Embodied in its tripartite land, sea, and air components are the professional military skills, the high-tech weapons expertise, and the unassailable traditions and esprit de corps that have consistently made the Marine Corps great, unique, invincible, and, today, America's "911 Force-in-Readiness."

As Congressman and former Marine John Murtha, who championed the adoption of the MV-22 Osprey, so aptly puts it: "Five hundred years from now, Marine officers will still eat last, and sergeants will still run the Corps."

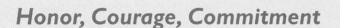

Honor, Courage, Commitment

Core Values of the Corps

While not designed to be any imposition of particular religious or moral tenets, Core Values does attempt to instill the basic universal and positive concepts of honor, courage, and commitment to all Marine recruits. Infractions, such as lying, sexual harassment, cheating, and misdemeanors or felonious crimes, are dealt with swiftly under this personal code of conduct, usually with dismissal of the individual from the Corps. Recruits are taught that:

- *Honor* means integrity, responsibility, and accountability.
- *Courage* means doing the right thing, in the right way, for the right reasons.
- *Commitment* means devotion to the Corps and to fellow Marines.

For some recruits, boot camp is their first exposure to these concepts with such seriousness, and they come to understand that these Core Values ultimately bolster the efficacy of their unit and secure its victory on the battlefield.

—BN

LEFT: Ammunition technician Sgt Ernesto Gonzalez, Jr., MAG 16, 3d MAW, covers a team investigating the crash of a CH-53E Super Stallion near Najaf, Iraq, 21 August 2004.

chapter one

Don't Tread on Me: The Birth of the Continental Marines

"Since 1775 the United States Marines have upheld a fine tradition of service to their country. They are doing so today. I am confident they will continue to do so."

President Franklin D. Roosevelt to CMC, 10 November 1942

By the time of the American Revolution, the thirteen colonies had gained vast maritime experience because they either bordered the Atlantic or had access to large waterways. The shipping of goods, travel by water, and fishing had fostered good boat-handling knowledge. In those times of frequent wars between colonial powers, privateering was a legitimate way of life—and livelihood. This individual piracy against enemy shipping was sanctioned by official government indulgences called letters of marque, which authorized privateers to appropriate captured prizes such as ships and valuable cargo.

Therefore, after the opening battles of the Revolution in April 1775 at Lexington and Concord, the Second Continental Congress' thoughts were toward consolidating independent militia into a Continental Army and raising naval forces to augment it in order to protect the coastal cities and capture incoming enemy arms and supplies.

WHERE DID MARINES COME FROM?

Ask any Marine today and he or she will likely tell you that Marines were created out of thin air early in the American Revolution by proclamation on 10 November 1775. In fact, that order by the Second Continental Congress in Philadelphia officially authorized the raising of two battalions of Marines, the likes of which had been around for a long time. Naval ships had always had a need for seagoing soldiers for protection or assault, and it was known that they should be differently trained than regular soldiers for such a role. Several manuals on marine amphibious operations—primitive as they were in those times—had been published in London prior to the American Revolution. They dealt with basic tactics and the training and deportment of the individual marine. Thus, the role of the marine aboard ship in the days of sail was well established.

American colonials had served as British marines since 1739, when King George III ordered six 1,100-man regiments of marines to be raised to augment naval forces in his seven-year war against Spain and France. Those regiments, three of which were from the American colonies, comprised thirty companies of one hundred men each, with four sergeants, two corporals, two drummers, a captain, two lieutenants, and an ensign (second lieutenant).

In 1741, British admiral Edward Vernon, after whom George Washington's half-brother, Lawrence Washington, named Mount Vernon, and for whom the thirty companies of American-British marines had been raised, set off on a venture to harass the French and Spanish in the Caribbean. He landed his 1,500 British marines and accompanying colonial marines at the outlying forts guarding the Spanish city of

of one Colonel two lieutenant Colonels, two Ma
officers as usual in other regiments, that
consist of an equal number of privates w
other battalions; that particular care be take
no person, be appointed to office or enlisted
Battalions, but such as are good sea men, or
acquainted with maritime affairs as to be
to serve to advantage by sea, when required.
they be inlisted and commissioned to se
or and during the present war between Gre
Britain and the colonies, unless dismiss
y order of Congress: That they be disting
y the marines of the first & second battalion
nerican Marines, and that they be consid
part of the number, which the continental
my before Boston is ordered to consist of.

Resolved

The Tun Tavern Myth

Since the country's sesquicentennial in 1926, Marines have held that colonial Philadelphia's Tun Tavern was the birthplace of their Corps. This is because it was assumed that the first Marines were recruited there. Capt Robert Mullan, whose parents leased the tavern, had raised a company of Marines; therefore, he must have used the family tavern as a recruiting rendezvous, taverns being a favored place for such business. The catch is that the Mullans' lease expired in 1774, and Bob Mullan didn't raise his company until 1776.

Actually, Tun Tavern could be considered the birthplace of the Corps in that John Adams' Naval Committee of the Continental Congress met there in the upstairs room and resolved to form a Navy and to establish the Continental Marines. The rationale was, of course, that you couldn't have an effective Navy without Marines on board to form the nucleus of boarding and landing parties, establish security, prevent mutiny, and assist in manning ships' guns.

The first Continental Marines were probably recruited at another Philadelphia tavern, the Conestogoe Wagon, owned by the mother-in-law of the first Marine officer, Capt Samuel Nicholas.

—BN

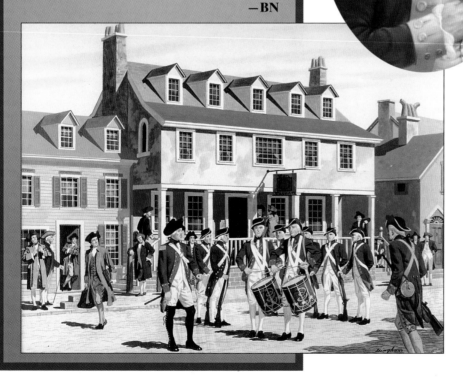

PAGE 33: An excerpt from the Second Continental Congress resolution of 10 November 1775 that authorized the raising of two battalions of Marines to serve with the Continental Navy.

INSET: The author's conceptual portrait of Capt Samuel Nicholas, the first Marine commissioned by action of the Second Continental Congress.

BELOW: An illustration of colonial-era Tun Tavern, the legendary birthplace of the Marines.

Cartagena, Colombia, but they could not take the city, and suffered heavy losses from combat and disease before withdrawing. Before that, in 1664 and 1665, the British and the Dutch, to reinforce their naval forces, had organized marines and trained and armed them to fight aboard and from ships. Spanish marines had served from the early sixteenth century up through the Battle of Lepanto off the coast of Greece, when in 1571 combined European forces defeated the Ottoman incursion into the West.

Even earlier, the Romans had specially trained shipboard infantry called "soldiers of the sea." Centuries before that, the Greeks utilized marines aboard ship, referring to them as heavy-armed sea soldiers. They were instrumental in defeating the encroaching Persians in the Battle of Salamis in 480 B.C. That decisive sea battle stopped the expansion of the Persian empire into the West, and allowed for the blossoming of the golden age of Greek classicism.

The earliest record, however, comes from an Egyptian mural painting, circa 1190 B.C., at Medinet Habu that depicts an offshore naval battle. Supported by infantry both aboard ships and onshore, the Egyptians are shown turning back invaders from the sea. These actions were very primitive; the ships were row-galleys with a single sail enabling them to coast with the prevailing wind. The naval infantry (marines) is shown using bows, arrows, lances, and swords.

MARINES AND THE AMERICAN REVOLUTION

On 19 April 1775, British troops under the command of Maj Pitcairn fired on American militia assembled on Lexington Common, thereby igniting the American Revolution. Soon after, Gen George Washington assembled twelve thousand "minutemen" militia and surrounded Boston. In the meantime, colonials Ethan Allen and Col Benedict Arnold raised a small force to attack the British forts on Lake Champlain to prevent the British from severing the colonies. Washington's little army and several-boat flotilla managed to capture Fort Ticonderoga and Crown Point and raid St. Johns before they were ultimately defeated.

The Second Continental Congress then ordered both Washington's and Arnold's groups to purchase naval vessels and outfit them with seamen and marines. One of Washington's small vessels' payroll records for 5 May 1775 shows marine Lt James Watson as having been paid. The monthly sum would have most likely been $20.

Neither group had satisfactory experiences with marines nor any praise for them afterward. The basic reason—or mistake—was that their marines were chosen and so designated from the army-militia ranks, most of whom had no knowledge of boat handling or seamanship. Even the seamen recruited to man Arnold's and Washington's little fleets were a motley lot, lured by offerings of prize spoils. Unruly and with little interest in the noble aims of the Revolution, the so-called marines were neither skilled nor had proclivity for shipboard duty.

Exasperated by the colonial siege of Boston, on 17 June 2,500 redcoats crossed over into Charlestown and fought the militias at Breed's and Bunker hills. The attacking British sustained heavy casualties; all but a few of the 1,500 colonials withdrew. Later, King George III's troops abandoned the city and retreated temporarily to Halifax, Nova Scotia.

On 5 October, Congress issued a directive to Washington, who was now commander in chief of the militia-merged Continental Army, to procure two vessels on "Continental risque & pay" and to give orders for the "proper encouragement to the Marines and Seamen" expected to serve on his armed ships. Hardly enamored of marines, Washington balked at this and asked to be relieved of the order, as it would take the best soldiers from his small army.

Uniformity

Before the Revolution, Marine recruits had worn civilian clothes or whatever uniforms they could purchase with their own funds. In 1776 the Naval Committee of the Second Continental Congress prescribed new regulations requiring uniforms to be medium-green coats with white-buff facings (lapels, cuffs, and coat lining), buff breeches, and black gaiters. Officers were to wear black cocked (three-cornered) hats with the left brim pinned up with a cockade; enlisted men were to wear round hats with the brim turned up on one side. Also mandated was a leather stock, or high collar, to serve as pseudo-armor against cutlass slashes as well as to keep a man's head erect with military bearing. This rigid collar, which gave the Marines the enduring nickname "Leathernecks," was praised by officers but damned by the men. It was retained until after the Civil War, long after Army troops had discarded theirs.

Some assume that green was chosen because Continental Marines were riflemen. This is in error, as they were armed with smoothbore muskets. The first Continental Marine officer, Capt Samuel Nicholas, was a member of the Gloucester Fox Hunting Club across the Delaware River from Philadelphia, and members in that hunt wore green. Thus green was Nicholas's obvious recommendation to the committee. Later, Marine Lt Robert Mullan's company was noted in a Philadelphia newspaper in 1779 as wearing green coats faced with red. (Mullan apparently did not have the properly designed uniforms at the time.)

—BN

FAR LEFT AND LEFT: Marine artist Col Donna Neary's rendition of a Continental Marine drummer and an officer.

ABOVE: *The First Casualties,* by Marine combat artist Col Charles Waterhouse, USMC (Ret.), depicts the first naval battle of the Revolution. Returning from the little raid on British supplies at New Providence, Bahamas, the American light frigates *Alfred* and *Cabot,* with Continental Marines aboard, encountered HMS *Glasgow* off Block Island, Rhode Island. Marine marksmen in the riggings inflicted the only reported casualties on the British side, while 2dLt John Fitzpatrick became the first casualty of the Continental Marines.

The Continental Marines

The Second Continental Congress then raised appropriate naval forces of thirteen small frigates to fight the growing war, thus creating a Continental Navy. On 10 November 1775 it designated the raising of two battalions of "Continental Marines," which would be specially trained for shipboard duty to provide discipline and security (especially against mutiny), to man guns, and to provide boarding parties and landing forces.

The two battalions were to be the "1st and 2d Battalions of American Marines." They were to be led by one colonel, two lieutenant colonels, and two majors. The battalions were to comprise five hundred men each, divided into ten companies of fifty privates and appropriate officers. The recruiting requirement

was that "no person be appointed to office or inlisted into the Battalions but such as are good seamen, or so acquainted with maritime affairs as to be able to serve to advantage by sea, when required." Monthly pay ranged from $26 for a captain to $6 for a private. The enlistment, while ostensibly for a year, was in effect for the duration of the war. The initial force raised was three hundred Marines, most of whom ended up being recruited for specific ships, rather than in a centralized unit as intended.

To command the fledgling Continental Marine force, Congress commissioned thirty-one-year-old Samuel Nicholas, a well-known Philadelphian, as captain. Nicholas was charged with recruiting other officers and the two battalions. Although Nicholas was able to raise two battalions over time, outfitting the men in proper uniforms and weaponry was not immediately possible. Most served initially in their own civilian clothes, with muskets and carbines solicited from the well-armed local populace. Months later they acquired green cloth locally, and upon seizure of a British arms ship, the Marines appropriated proper weaponry and additional bolts of green cloth for new uniforms.

Those Marine uniforms, in order to differ from the blue and buff of the Continental Army and the blue and white of the Navy, were designated to be green with white facings and britches. Thus, the blue and green of the Americans were easily distinguishable from the despised red coats of the British.

The First Amphibious Operation: 1776

Shortly after creating the small Continental Navy and Marines, the Naval Committee of the Second Continental Congress installed political crony Esek Hopkins as the Navy's commander in chief, and ordered him to use his small fleet to harass British shipping. Aboard Hopkins's flagship, *Alfred*, was Capt Nicholas, the newly appointed head of the Marines.

In January 1776 Hopkins was ordered to clear the British Navy from Chesapeake Bay and the Carolina coast and to attack and destroy British naval combatants in and around Rhode Island. Believing these orders to be too ambitious, he altered them, ostensibly due to foul weather, and sailed to the Bahamas, where he expected to find on the tiny island of New Providence, at Forts Nassau and Montague, naval stores and ammunition that were desperately needed by Washington's army in Boston.

In April, Hopkins put ashore two hundred Marines and fifty sailors to capture the two lightly defended forts. They did so, and the British governor capitulated, but not before sending the highly prized store of gunpowder away surreptitiously before the Americans could seize it.

Thus thwarted, Hopkins and his little raiding party returned to the sea off Rhode Island, where they encountered British warships. After a desultory battle, in which one Marine officer and six enlisted Marines were killed and four were wounded, Hopkins disengaged. A naval inquiry subsequently charged the commodore with disobeying orders and failure to capture

the powder. He was censured and dismissed from service. Nicholas was promoted to major at $32 per month and ordered to raise four more companies of Marines.

The Battles of Trenton and Princeton

The following December, Maj Nicholas was ordered to join his companies of Marines to Gen John Cadwalader's brigade south of Trenton on the Pennsylvania side of the Delaware River, some twenty miles below Washington's army up at McKonkey's Ferry.

LEFT: Revolutionary War dress sword carried by a Continental Marine officer.

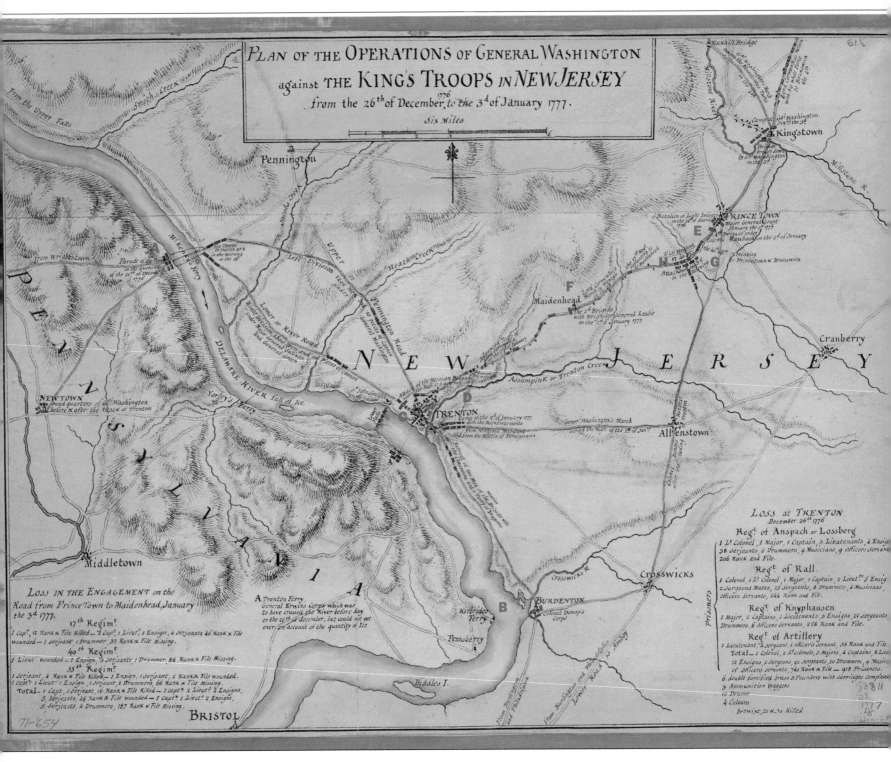

ABOVE: Early British after-action map showing the sites of the battles of Trenton and Princeton (26 December 1776– 3 January 1777), between George Washington's 2,500-man, two-division American army and three mercenary Hessian regiments led by Col Johann Ralls and attached to MajGen Lord Charles Cornwallis's British army. Washington's right flank included Maj Samuel Nicholas's four companies of Continental Marines attached to BGen John Cadwalader's brigade. **(A)** McKonkey's Ferry, where Washington and his men crossed the icy Delaware on the bitter-cold Christmas night, splitting into two columns for his dawn attack on Trenton. **(B)** The position of Cadwalader's brigade, stymied by impassable ice floes. **(C)** Trenton, where the unsuspecting Hessian troops were overcome by Washington's few exhausted soldiers early on the morning of the 26th.

(D) The site where Cadwalader joined his brigade to Washington's for another victory in the small battle of Assunpink Creek. Deceiving the British by leaving his campfires burning throughout the night, Washington slipped away and moved his two divisions up ten miles to **(E)** Princeton, site of the College of New Jersey (now Princeton University), using Nassau Hall as his headquarters. **(F)** Cornwallis's reinforcements streamed in from northern New Jersey and Princeton to meet the approaching Americans; they clashed on the main road from Princeton to Maidenhead, now Lawrenceville. **(G)** The Americans at first were routed—and BGen Hugh Mercer was struck down at the head of his brigade—when Washington, with the help of Cadwalader's brigade, turned the tide to **(H)** an American victory.

BELOW, INSET: This powder horn, used during the Revolutionary War, is the earliest piece of Marine Corps equipment known to exist. It is engraved with an image of a Marine officer and a warship.

RIGHT: A reconnaissance map of the plan of Princeton, created by Gen Cadwalader, shows the area of the Battle of Princeton, which took place on 3 January 1777. The building at center is the Thomas Clarke House, where the gravely wounded BGen Hugh Mercer was carried and later died. Following their defeat, the British retreated north to their winter headquarters via the main north-south route through Princeton. Washington led his victorious troops to Morristown for the remainder of the winter.

BELOW: Marine artist Col Charles Waterhouse's rendition of the high point of the Battle of Princeton. After duping the British at Assunpink Creek outside Trenton, Washington proceeded ten miles up the east road to Princeton, beating back a British rear-guard counterattack. When he reached Nassau Hall (shown in the background), the main building of the College of New Jersey, the bypassed British caught up with his small force and engaged in a pitched battle. With Mercer, his brigade commander, mortally wounded, and sensing a critical moment, Washington valiantly rode his horse, Cincinnatus, into the midst of the wavering Americans and encouraged them with, "It's a fine fox chase, my boys," thus rallying his troops to their third major victory in a hard-fought week. Samuel Nicholas's Marines stood fast with Washington, and because many were experienced naval gunners, they took over his artillery when his own artillerymen's enlistments were up. These first victories of the Revolution turned the tables and gave overall confidence to those fighting for the cause of freedom.

Marine Small Arms: 1775–1855

The individual weapon of the Continental, and later U.S., Marine was a .75-caliber smoothbore flintlock musket called the Brown Bess. Marines used Brown Besses captured from the British as well as copies made by Colonial gunsmiths, who also made shorter, tin-plated, corrosion-resistant versions for shipboard use.

Marines also used a shotgunlike weapon called a blunderbuss, which had a wide, flared muzzle that afforded easier pouring of handfuls of scrap metal down its barrel. Smoothbores were notoriously inaccurate and were effective only at close range; rifled barrels appeared early in the Civil War, but not all Federal Marines were issued them.

Besides firearms, Marines carried edged weapons: swords, knives, eight-foot pikes with steel spear tips, and, on their muskets, 16-inch bayonets. Officers carried a small sword as a badge of office in addition to a brace of flintlock pistols; NCOs carried an infantry hanger, a cutlasslike sword. (Fighting in those days of sail was up close and bloody.) Beginning in 1795, the Springfield Armory turned out copies of the French .69-caliber musket. By the time of the Mexican-American War in 1846, percussion caps had replaced flintlocks, and in 1855 the muskets were rifled. Such rifled .58-caliber guns were effective up to five hundred yards.

—BN

As Washington was capturing the Hessians at Trenton on Christmas Day, Cadwalader could not get his troops across the ice-crusted river to assist. He did, however, cross a week later in time to join his leader for the second decisive victory at Princeton.

Upon learning of the defeat of his Hessians at Trenton, British general Lord Charles Cornwallis had dashed toward the New Jersey town. He was midway between Princeton and Trenton, at Maidenhead (present-day Lawrenceville), when Washington, now augmented with Cadwalader's division and Nicholas's Marines, personally rallied his faltering troops and outfoxed and outflanked the redcoats, soundly whipping them on 3 January. Following that, Cornwallis retired to his winter headquarters at New York, while Washington went to his at Morristown, New Jersey. When Washington's artillery regiment's enlistments expired following the battle at Princeton, Nicholas's Marines stayed and took over artillery for the general.

At Sea with John Paul Jones

Having assumed command of the newly acquired 18-gun frigate *Ranger*, Capt John Paul Jones, with his contingent of twenty-four Marines headed by Capt Matthew Parke, was tasked to take the news of British Gen John Burgoyne's defeat at Saratoga on 17 October 1777 to emissary Benjamin Franklin in Paris.

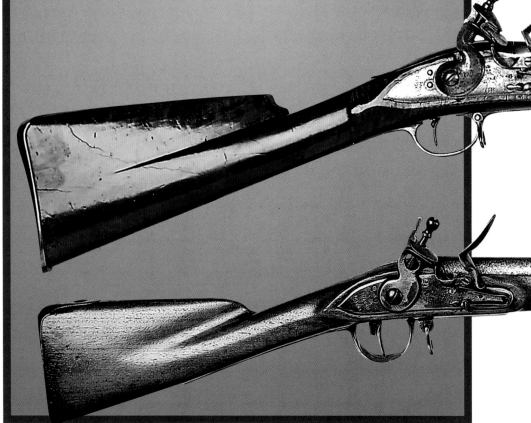

LEFT: British maritime artist Thomas Buttersworth's depiction of the famous naval battle between Capt John Paul Jones' *Bonhomme Richard* and the HMS *Serapis,* which took place off Flamborough Head, England, in the early evening hours of 23 September 1779.

The *Bonhomme Richard* was augmented by French marines and accompanied by the small frigate *Alliance,* with Continental Marines aboard. After the opening broadsides, which inflicted considerable damage on the *Bonhomme Richard,* Jones defied the captain of the HMS *Serapis'* request for surrender by retorting, "I have not yet begun to fight!" Ultimately, a well-dropped grenade exploded the British warship's powder magazine and the enemy vessel surrendered.

TOWER MUSKET (BROWN BESS), 1795

The British "Tower" or "Brown Bess," a .75-caliber muzzle-loading musket much used by the American forces during the Revolution.

CHARLEVILLE MUSKET, 1763

This French .69-caliber musket, known as the Charleville and designed in 1763, was used by Continental Marines. It was later copied and reproduced by the Springfield Armory. It is smooth-bore and muzzle-loading, and fired by flintlock.

RIGHT: Ceramic prototype hand grenade used by Continental Marines and sailors to lob from their own riggings onto the decks of enemy ships locked gunwale-to-gunwale below.

After that, Jones, with Lt Samuel Wallingford and his small party of Marines, began a series of raids against English seacoast towns.

A short time later, Jones acquired a former merchantman in France, converted it, and named it *Bonhomme Richard*, after his good friend Franklin's

Cruising for trouble, Jones found it on the evening of 23 September 1779 off Flamborough Head, England, when his two ships encountered the superior-armed HMS *Serapis*. Initially sustaining the brunt of the attack, with his ship dismasted and riddled by broadsides on the way, Jones' only option was to close in on and board the British frigate. When the British skipper asked for his surrender, Jones famously responded, "I have not yet begun to fight!" Fortuitously, at that moment, one of his seamen lobbed a grenade down the hold of the enemy ship, exploding its powder magazine. Jones' French marines took their toll by firing from the rigging. Thus Capt Jones, his own ship fatally damaged and sinking along with that of his opponent, claimed victory and transferred over to the *Alliance*.

Penobscot Bay: June 1779

Having abandoned Boston in 1775, the British, now based in Halifax, Nova Scotia, decided to build a new naval base in the Massachusetts territory at Penobscot Bay to again threaten Boston.

Upon receiving word of this ominous development, the Massachusetts Bay Colony organized a small fleet of boats and state militiamen, including Marines. Approaching the almost completed British fort at Penobscot, the American commander, Navy commodore Dudley Saltonstall, ordered a Marine reconnaissance party ashore. They secured a small island in front of Fort George for use by artillery under volunteer militiaman LtCol Paul Revere.

The American attack was in three columns, with three hundred Marines on the right. While the other two columns faltered, the Marines charged up a steep incline directly into the awaiting guns of the British. Fourteen Marines were killed, including a Capt John Welsh, and twenty were wounded.

The next day, the Marines again led the attack but were ordered to halt midway by the militia brigadier general, Solomon Lovell. It seems that he and the naval commander had a disagreement over naval gunfire support for the attack: Saltonstall did not want to risk his ships to enemy land batteries. The attack was stalled for a full sixteen days of inactivity—time enough for British fleet reinforcements to arrive and totally destroy the Revolutionary fleet, leaving the Marines, militia, and surviving seamen to find their way back through the uncharted Maine wilderness to Boston.

It had been an incredible blunder, but many found their way back. Saltonstall was court-martialed and summarily cashiered; the Marine commander was subsequently commended and promoted.

Poor Richard's Almanac. While outfitting the ship for war, he manned it with French marines, who—to his dismay—wore red coats similar to those worn by the British. The few American Marines under command of Capt Parke—presumably in proper green—were assigned to the *Bonhomme Richard*'s sister ship, the *Alliance*.

LEFT: Charles Waterhouse's depiction of the single successful assault in an ill-conceived Massachusetts militia operation, under the naval command of Dudley Saltonstall and infantry commander BGen Solomon Lovell, with LtCol Paul Revere as artillery commander. Despite the fact that their commanders had no experience with amphibious operations using Marines, on 28 July 1779 three hundred Continental Marines under Capt John Welsh successfully fought up a 45-degree incline from the shore of the British-held Bagaduce Peninsula in Penobscot Bay, (now) Maine, suffering few casualties and causing the enemy to flee. (This painting, which hung in the Marine Corps legal counsel's office, was destroyed in the 11 September 2001 terrorist attack on the Pentagon.)

RIGHT: Marine artist Col Donna Neary created a series of illustrations depicting the Marine Band and its various uniforms from its early history to the present. This water-color portrays the band fifers and drummers in 1800, accompanying a Marine recruiting party near Independence Hall in Philadelphia.

BELOW: The Marine enlisted uniform of the 1790s, in char-acteristic dark blue with red facings, cuffs, and collar. The instruments dangling from the crossed bayonet belt are a "pick and brush," used for cleaning the touchhole and powder pan of the musket's flintlock. The leather box on the other belt is for holding cartridges, i.e., lead bullets, caps, and black powder wrapped in paper.

FAR RIGHT: An illustration by Marine Col John Magruder, a World War II veteran and for-mer director of the Marine Corps Museum, showing a Marine of the 1800 to 1805 period dressed in dark-blue coat and trousers with red facing and vest. His weapon is the 1763 French Charleville. The black cockade secures the longer brim of his hat to its cylindrical crown.

Final Act

The Continental Marines, who honorably and courageously served throughout the American Revolution on board the *Lexington*, *Reprisal*, *Hornet*, and *Wasp*, as well as smaller craft, committed their last official and important act in September 1781 while Lord Cornwallis was surrendering to Washington at Yorktown. Maj Nicholas, now the senior Marine officer (the designation of commandant would be bestowed on later senior officers), and his last group of Marines escorted from Boston to Philadelphia a treasure trove of French silver crowns loaned from Louis XVI. The loan enabled Continental finance minister Robert Morris to open the Bank of North America.

By the time of the Treaty of Paris in 1783, the Continental Marines had fizzled out of existence; enlistments had ended, and funds had dried up. In all, during the Revolution, there had been 131 officers who held Marine commissions and approximately 2,000 who had enlisted at one time or another over the period. More than 290,000 colonials participated in the American Revolution. Of the 4,435 battle deaths, 49 were Marines.

THE CREATION OF THE UNITED STATES MARINE CORPS

Shortly after the birth of the United States of America in 1789 following the adoption of the Constitution by all thirteen colonies, the new U.S. Congress realized that the country needed proper defenses, especially a Navy to protect its vital sea commerce.

Subsequently, on 27 March 1794, Congress ordered the construction of six new 44- to 50-gun frigates: *Constellation*, *Constitution*, *Congress*, *Chesapeake*, *United States*, and *President* (the last two were added later). Four years later, on 30 April 1798, Congress created the Department of the Navy and within it, in July, the United States Marine Corps.

Within a year, the United States was embroiled in a limited naval shooting war with France, and by 1801 had become involved in a more protracted battle with the Barbary pirates off the shores of Tripoli, one in which the new U.S. Marines were destined to play a never-to-be-forgotten part.

LEFT: World War II Marine combat artist Col Don Dickson's illustration of the conclusion of the first successful amphibious operation of the Continental Marines. Marines captured the lightly defended British fort at New Providence Island in the Bahamas for its supplies and weapons—which the British had managed to send elsewhere before capitulating.

chapter two

The Nineteenth Century—
Fortitudine to *Semper Fidelis*

"From my earliest association with sea life my eyes have been accustomed to see the well-disciplined Marines at their posts on shipboard and at our naval stations, guarding the public property and ensuring discipline on board ship."

RAdm David D. Porter, USN, to CMC, 1863

The nineteenth century started auspiciously for the fledgling U.S. Marine Corps; there was an immediate need for Marines. Revolutionary ally France had commenced an annoying quasi-war with the United States that could have jeopardized the young nation's already shaky start. Furthermore, the unbridled attacks by Barbary pirates in the Mediterranean on new American shipping no longer under British protection presented a dilemma: either pay the heavy bribes to the pirates as other nations did or build a Navy strong enough to protect U.S. ships. The latter was thought to be less costly in the long run.

Riled over the failure of the newly independent United States to side with her against Britain in 1797, France began a campaign of harassment at sea, with French raiders ultimately capturing 316 American vessels. These threats to American shipping not only hastened the completion of the new frigates under construction but also spurred the creation in 1798 of a U.S. Navy to man them and the commissioning of Marines to protect them and fight on board.

The chairman of the House Naval Committee, Samuel Sewall, presented a bill that raised a "Corps" of Marines, consisting of a battalion headed by a major, a complement of officers and NCOs, and five hundred privates and a number of musicians. Marines deployed aboard armed vessels and galleys would be detachments from this Corps.

The bill, after minor amendments, passed, and President John Adams signed into law the "act for establishing and organizing a Marine Corps." He then appointed a Philadelphian, William Ward Burrows, to be Major of the Marine Corps. Burrows also inherited a stock of leftover uniforms that were blue with red facings. These are the basis for the Marines' "dress blues," which have since been modified but are still the distinctive formal uniform today. Decades later the Corps changed back to green for the less formal duty uniform.

A fifty-man Marine detachment was assigned to the new USS *Constitution*, forty-four guns, in May 1799. She and a small sloop, *Sally*, promptly sailed into the waters off Hispaniola (Santo Domingo), where the Marines conducted raids against the French and Spanish.

After the nation's capital was moved in June 1800 from Philadelphia to the north bank of the Potomac River into a newly laid-out Federal City that was to become Washington, in the District of Columbia, Burrows was made Lieutenant Colonel Commandant of Marines.

He had ridden on horseback with the newly elected president, Thomas Jefferson, to choose a site for the new Marine Barracks and the Commandant's House. They chose land between 8th and 9th and G and I Streets in the southeast quadrant, near the Washington

U.S. MARINES WANTED!

YOUNG MEN

Between the ages of 21 and 35 years, enlisting in this corps, are first instructed in their duties as soldiers at the Barrack, Brooklyn, N. Y.; after the acquirement of this knowledge, they are held in readiness to be sent on board U. S. vessels of war, destined for foreign stations.

The following is the amount of Pay, Clothing and Rations that each Soldier receives during the period of his four years' engagement.

AMOUNT OF PAY:

First Sergeants of Barracks and Guards on board vessels of war, - -	$768 00
All other Sergeants, at Barracks and on board vessels of war, - -	624 00
All corporals, - - - - - - - - - - - - - - -	432 00
Privates, - - - - - - - - - - - - - - - - -	336 00

AMOUNT OF CLOTHING:

Uniform Caps.	Pompons.	Stocks.	Uniform Coats.	Epaulets.	Linen Pantaloons.	U. Woollen Pantaloons.	Shirts.	Shoes.	Blankets.	Knapsacks.	Socks.	Fatigue Caps.	Fatigue Jackets.	Fatigue Pantaloons.	Linen Jackets.
1	3	2	2	1	8	4	16	16	2	2	8	2	4	6	5

RATIONS.---IN BARRACKS, ARMY RATIONS ARE ISSUED.

DAILY RATIONS ON BOARD VESSELS OF WAR.

	POUNDS.						OUNCES.							PINTS.			
	Beef.	Pork.	Flour.	Rice.	Raisins or Dried Fruits.	Pickles or Cranberries.	Biscuits.	Sugar.	Teas. (EITHER.)	Coffee. (EITHER.)	Cocoa. (EITHER.)	Butter.	Cheese.	Beans.	Molasses.	Vinegar.	Spirits.
SUNDAY, - - -	1		½		¼		14	2	¼	1	1						¼
MONDAY, - -		1					14	2	¼	1	1			½			¼
TUESDAY, - -	1			½			14	2	¼	1	1	2	2				¼
WEDNESDAY, -		1				¼	14	2	¼	1	1			½			¼
THURSDAY, - -	1		½		¼		14	2	¼	1	1						¼
FRIDAY, - -	1			½			14	2	¼	1	1	2	2		½		¼
SATURDAY, - -		1				¼	14	2	¼	1	1			½		½	¼
WEEKLY QUANTITY,	4	3	1	1	½	½	98	14	1¾	7	7	4	4	1½	½	½	1¾

Any other information respecting the service generally, can be obtained by applying at the RENDEZVOUS,

JOHN GEO. REYNOLDS,
Capt. Com'd'g Recruiting.

LEES & FOULKES' Print, 35 Fulton-st., Brooklyn.

Navy Yard and close enough to reach the Capitol quickly, if necessary. It is still an operating site today.

In France, Napoleon Bonaparte decided to conclude the little war that was never official, thus leaving the fifteen states free to contend with the pirates.

THE BARBARY PIRATES: 1801–1815

For countless centuries the lawless pirates of the potentates along the North African coast of the Mediterranean Sea had harassed merchant shipping. If they were not capturing and ransoming crews, they were pillaging the goods these ships were carrying. Although they had navies strong enough to protect their shipping, Britain, France, and Spain—being fully occupied with the Napoleonic Wars—instead bought off the pirates with annual bribes. The fledgling United States was in no position to do so.

In 1801 the Pasha of Tunis declared war on the new United States of America. President Jefferson, unsure of whether he could legally reciprocate, instead dispatched a squadron including the *Constitution* to the Mediterranean. Aghast that $2 million had already been paid to the pirates and that another $250,000 was being demanded for the release of captive American sailors, Jefferson declared, "Millions for defense, but not one cent for tribute!" For two years the U.S. flotilla cruised and bombarded the pirates' harbors and fortresses. In an untoward mishap, the frigate *Philadelphia* ran aground in Tripoli's harbor and its crew was captured. A Navy raiding party torched the frigate, and the crew was eventually freed.

A thousand miles east at Alexandria, Egypt, a unique expedition formed by U.S. Naval agent Gen William Eaton and led by Marine Lt Presley O'Bannon trudged six hundred miles westward across the desert wastes bordering the sea. Hamet, the exiled brother of the Bey of Tripoli, was persuaded to join this ragtag mission, following along a parallel route. With O'Bannon were his sergeant, six

Uniforms: Marines in the Frigate Navy

When the U.S. Marines were reestablished in July 1798 after fifteen years of broken service following the disbandment of the Continental Marines, they were uniformed in the castoffs of the dissolved legion of Continental Army general Anthony Wayne. Coats and breeches were blue. At that time, blue became the national color of U.S. military uniforms, a tradition that continues to this day. Facings were red, as was a narrow stripe of piping on the breeches' seams. Collars were high "to defend against cold and wet." The braid that reinforced buttonholes was yellow and gold, and the buttons were navy blue. High round hats turned up on one side were prescribed. The colors of this uniform are still used for the Marine Corps' dress blues.

—BN

Marines, and a motley, mutinous bunch of four hundred hangers-on, and camels. Incredibly, they reached their destination, and O'Bannon and his Marines attacked and overtook the fort at Derna, forcing the surrender of the city and the capitulation of the Bey of Tripoli, who controlled Derna. Hamet presented O'Bannon with a Mameluke sword, after which the Marine officer's sword was later patterned. From this event, "to the shores of Tripoli" entered Marine hagiology.

THE SECOND WAR WITH BRITAIN: 1812

The French had not taken the youthful United States seriously, nor had the Barbary pirates. Now it was Britain's turn. With utter disregard of American independence, the British Royal Navy continued to man its ships by impressing able-bodied men of any nationality—mostly English or American—against their wills. At one point early in the new century, there were reportedly more Americans than British in His Majesty's Navy—more than six thousand. Mild-mannered

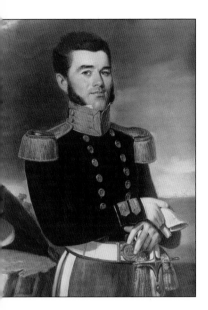

ABOVE: A superb oil portrait by an unidentified artist of U.S. Marine 2dLt Addison Garland in the uniform of 1834. That uniform heralded a return to the green with buff-white facings of the Revolutionary period, although with light-blue trousers. This particular green dye, unfortunately, faded quickly, and eventually the blue uniform was reinstated. Note that the lieutenant's hands are resting on a Mameluke-style sword modeled after the one given to Lt Presley O'Bannon in 1803 by the Bey of Tunis. His chapeau bras sits casually on its side on a tree stump behind him. The artist's treatment of the dramatic sky and sea in the background is reminiscent of portraits of the great French artist Jean-Auguste-Dominique Ingres of the same time period.

Garland rose to major during the Civil War and was sent with a detachment of Marines to secure Mare Island at San Francisco to keep it from falling into Confederate hands. In doing so, he and his troops crossed the Isthmus of Panama through its forbidding swamps and jungles.

RIGHT: A chapeau bras from 1797 to 1802; worn fore-and-aft, rather than broadside.

President James Madison had had enough; he asked Congress to declare war. It did so on 18 June 1812.

The first of a series of sea battles was the *Constitution*'s victory over HMS *Guerrière* off Boston. In the engagement, Marine Lt William S. Bush was killed while boarding the enemy vessel. Other battles up and down the Atlantic coast ensued: the *Constitution* vs. *Java*, *United States* vs. *Macedonian*, *Wasp* vs. *Frolic*, and *Essex* vs. a number of enemy ships. The young American Navy—with Marine detachments on all its new men-of-war—was whipping the tar out of the former "rulers of the waves," which the latter could scarcely believe. Only the USS *Chesapeake* was vanquished, but not before its skipper, James Lawrence, cried the immortal words, "Don't give up the ship!" His crew obeyed.

The fighting spread to the Great Lakes, which British strategists again saw as the back door to the former colonies. Naval battles were fought on Lake Ontario and Lake Erie. Fleets of ships had to be built rapidly by the Americans to meet the threat. Astonishingly, sloops and small schooners could be built onshore within a month, larger frigates in a little more than three months.

While these water battles were thwarting the British from their intended invasion, in the Atlantic Capt David Porter of the *Essex*, with his detachment of Marines under Lt John Marshall Gamble, missed a rendezvous with the *Constitution*. Instead, he ventured around Cape Horn and into the South Pacific and engaged in a year of raids on British whaling, success-fully destroying or capturing a number of enemy ships. To one, HMS *Greenwich*, Porter assigned Gamble as captain. Gamble went on to have his own series of incredible adventures, fighting unfriendly native islanders, being captured by a British ship, gaining his freedom in Hawaii, and eventually voyaging back to Brazil and then to New York.

Capt Porter, in the interim, lost the *Essex* to HMS *Phoebe* and *Cherub* at Valparaiso. He and his remaining crew, including a midshipman named David Glasgow Farragut (who achieved fame later in the Civil War), survived and returned to the United States to fight again.

Land Engagements

Britain, freed from preoccupation with France by the Duke of Wellington's defeat of Napoleon at Waterloo in 1815 and the latter's final exile, now turned her attention to the irritation on her backside: the stinging naval

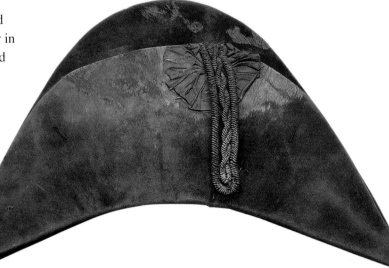

ABOVE: A critical moment in the battle between the USS *Constitution*, "Old Ironsides," and HMS *Guerrière* 750 miles off Boston on 16 August 1812, as reconstructed by illustrator Mort Künstler. Marine Lt William S. Bush, poised in the center on the taffrail and about to board the enemy vessel, turns to ask of his portly skipper, Capt Isaac Hull, "Shall I board her, Sir?" Receiving a nod in the affirmative, Bush jumped aboard the *Guerrière* and was slain by British marine musketry. The boarding was ultimately successful and victory fell to the Americans.

SHORT FLINTLOCK BLUNDERBUSS

A short flintlock blunderbuss with a swivel for mounting on a ship's rail.

defeats inflicted by her erstwhile colony, neighbor to the loyal province of Canada.

Britain's strategy now was to attack American cities. The British began with naval raids at the U.S. Naval Base in the Chesapeake Bay at Hampton Roads, Virginia, where the *Constellation* was anchored. Marine Lt Henry B. Breckinridge and his 50 Marines held off the 2,500 British infantry that landed.

Several months later the British landed four thousand more troops farther north to take the young nation's capital, which was virtually defenseless. The commodore of the U.S. Navy Yard burned his own flotilla of small gunboats and gathered 400 seamen and five guns along with 103 Marines from the nearby barracks, led by Capt Samuel Miller, the Marine Corps adjutant. Their stand was to be made at the bridge across the (now) Anacostia River. The British, however, crossed farther upriver at Bladensburg, east of the capital, on 24 August 1814.

The American Army-Militia commander and the naval commodore were at odds regarding seniority, thereby reducing the effectiveness of the two hastily formed defensive lines. When they were hit, the Army-Militia line disintegrated, and the British began a march down to the Capitol. The Navy-Marine secondary line, of which the British were unaware, caught them by surprise and inflicted many casualties. The British, however, after three costly attacks, overran the Americans, wounding both naval commander Joshua Barney and Marine captain Miller. (The Marine Corps' third commandant, Maj Franklin Wharton, was later admonished for failing to show up for the battle.) British losses totaled 64 dead and 185 wounded. Although Marine casualties were significantly fewer— 8 dead and 14 wounded—this depleted the entire complement of Marines in Washington, D.C.

Unopposed, the British invaders continued on and burned the new Capitol building under construction and then the president's new residence, the White House, causing the Madisons to flee. Dolley, the president's wife, saved what valuables she could. For some unexplained reason, the empty Marine commandant's house and the barracks were not destroyed, although legend has it that the Royal marine officer who had been ordered to burn the Navy Yard refused to burn another marine's quarters.

The British continued to Baltimore. There, by naval blockade, they besieged Fort McHenry, which guarded the harbor. The survival of the fort and its

RIGHT: Having hastily assembled a defensive line to protect the new nation's capital, Marines from the U.S. Navy Yard and Marine Barracks surprised the attacking British at Bladensburg, across the Anacostia River from Maryland, in the District of Columbia. The British had smashed the militia's first line of defense, but were themselves crushed by the Marine line. Nevertheless, the Brits rallied and continued on to burn the newly constructed White House and a good part of Washington, D.C. Col Charles Waterhouse's *The Final Stand at Bladensburg* depicts the Marine line, under Capt Samuel Miller, firing their 12-pound field guns directly at the charging British.

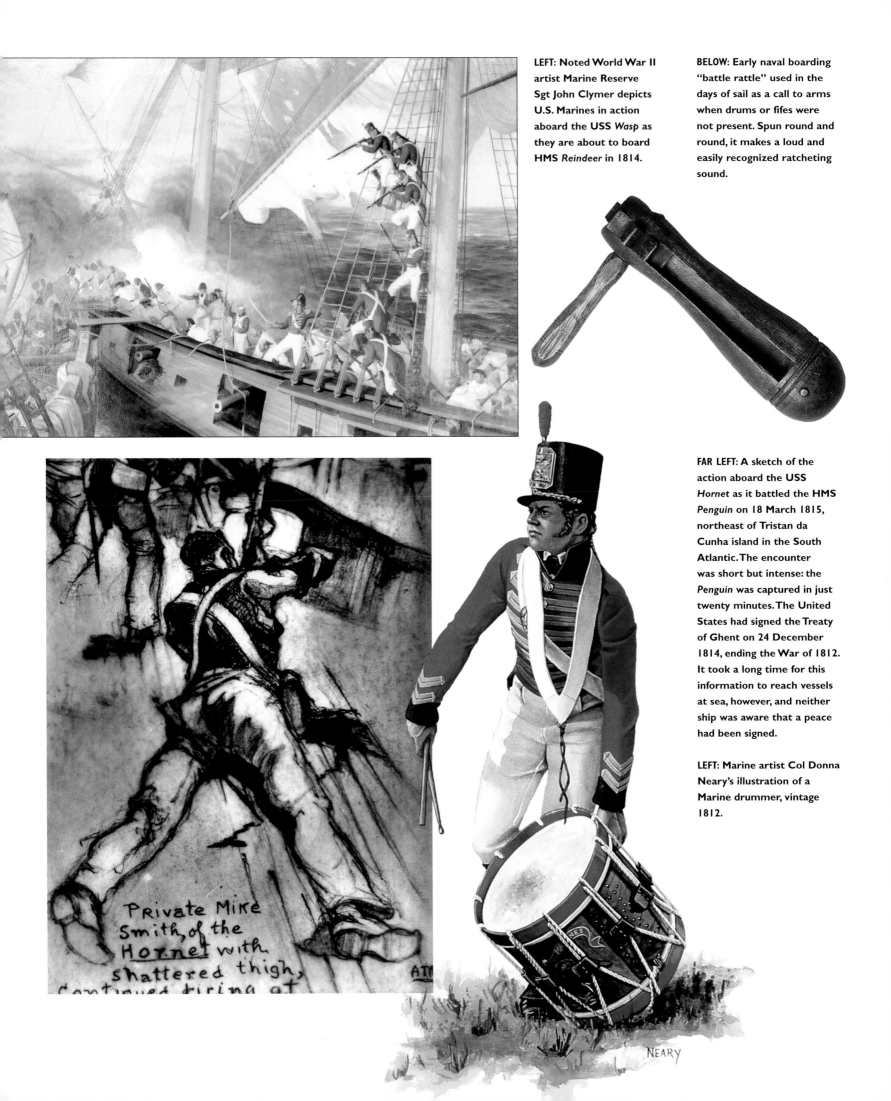

LEFT: Noted World War II artist Marine Reserve Sgt John Clymer depicts U.S. Marines in action aboard the USS *Wasp* as they are about to board HMS *Reindeer* in 1814.

BELOW: Early naval boarding "battle rattle" used in the days of sail as a call to arms when drums or fifes were not present. Spun round and round, it makes a loud and easily recognized ratcheting sound.

FAR LEFT: A sketch of the action aboard the USS *Hornet* as it battled the HMS *Penguin* on 18 March 1815, northeast of Tristan da Cunha island in the South Atlantic. The encounter was short but intense: the *Penguin* was captured in just twenty minutes. The United States had signed the Treaty of Ghent on 24 December 1814, ending the War of 1812. It took a long time for this information to reach vessels at sea, however, and neither ship was aware that a peace had been signed.

LEFT: Marine artist Col Donna Neary's illustration of a Marine drummer, vintage 1812.

Private Mike Smith, of the Hornet with shattered thigh, continued firing at shell-torn fifteen-star-spangled banner was immortalized by an eyewitness, American lawyer and poet Francis Scott Key, who had been a temporary prisoner on a British ship at the time of the incident. Key's poem "The Defense of Fort M'Henry" was set to the tune of "To Anacreon in Heaven," a popular English drinking song of the time. Key's "Star-Spangled Banner" was adopted as the national anthem by the U.S. Congress in 1931.

After their defeat at Baltimore, the British sailed for Jamaica. There, they were joined by Sir Edward Pakenham, the Duke of Wellington's brother-in-law, who along with the British naval commander proposed to attack the American city of New Orleans.

Aftershocks: New Orleans and Further Naval Engagements

Communications in the eighteenth and early nineteenth centuries traveled only as fast as a horse or a sailing ship. News and orders often took months to reach distant destinations, as was the case of the unnecessary Battle of New Orleans, which was fought a month after the Treaty of Ghent had concluded the war in December 1814. Even the USS *Constitution*—by now famed as "Old Ironsides," with a future Marine commandant, Archibald Henderson, aboard—subdued the HMS *Cyane* and *Levant* the following February.

The Battle of New Orleans—acquisition of the city had come by way of Jefferson's 1803 Louisiana Purchase—was the final stamp declaring that the new nation was not to be messed with. Under the command of grizzled frontiersman MajGen Andrew Jackson, forty-five hundred Americans, including Marine Maj Daniel Carmick's three hundred Marines in the center, were strung in a solid defense line of

Why Swords?

In the early days of the Corps, swords were strong and sharp and served as a necessary last-ditch weapon when the single-shot musket or pistol had been fired in a melee. Today the Marine Corps swords are dull-edged and carried by officers and noncommissioned officers (NCOs) in ceremonies as a badge of office.

The uniform regulations of 1804 prescribed "a yellow mounted [brass or gilt] saber with gilt scabbard" but gave no further details. Before Lt Presley O'Bannon in 1804 set out on his expedition to seize Derna in Tripoli, the Bey of Alexandria, Egypt, presented him and seven Navy officers with Mameluke swords. After service in the Mediterranean Squadron, many officers carried these nonregulation swords. They became so popular that they were made regulation items in 1826.

The 1859 regulations changed the officer's sword to the Army pattern M1840 foot officer's sword. In 1875, new regulations returned to the Mameluke sword, with a nickel-plated scabbard instead of the 1826 brass. The M1859 officer's sword was then adopted for NCOs. These swords have continued in use to the present.

—BN

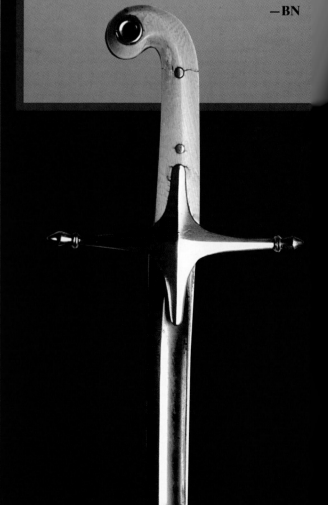

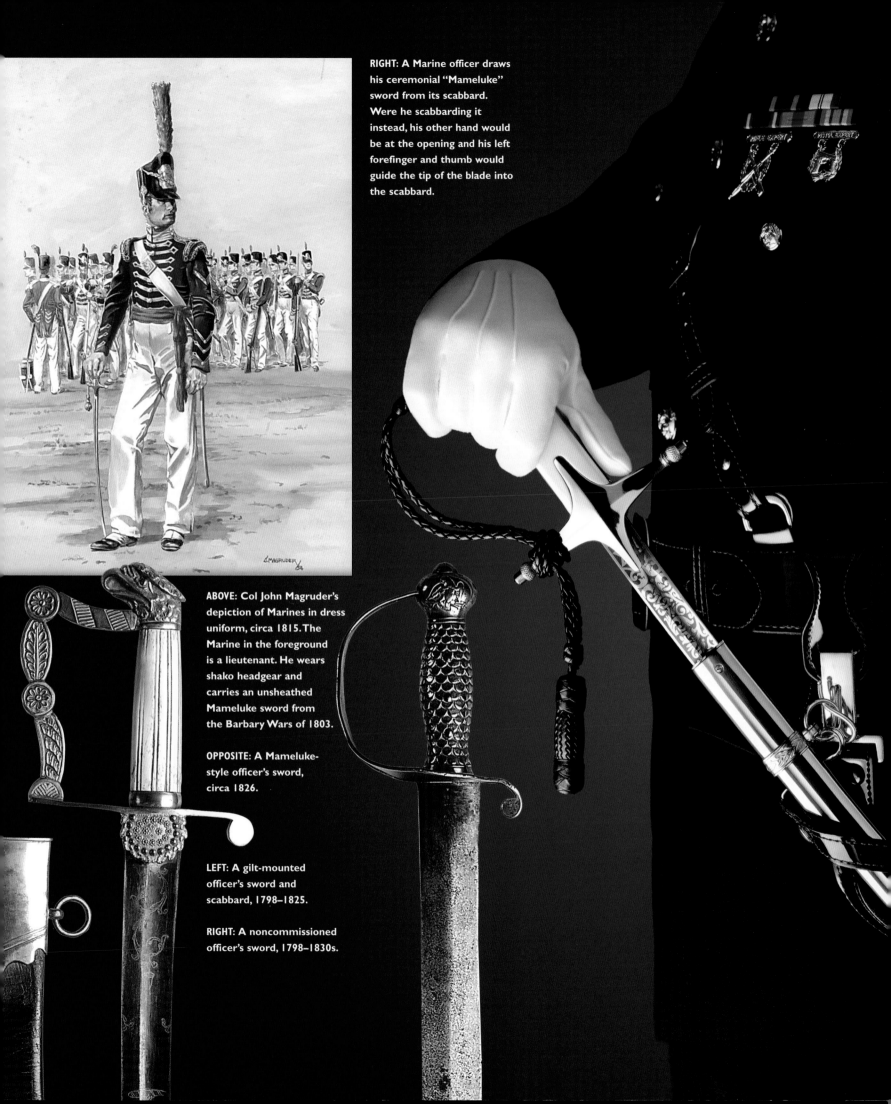

RIGHT: A Marine officer draws his ceremonial "Mameluke" sword from its scabbard. Were he scabbarding it instead, his other hand would be at the opening and his left forefinger and thumb would guide the tip of the blade into the scabbard.

ABOVE: Col John Magruder's depiction of Marines in dress uniform, circa 1815. The Marine in the foreground is a lieutenant. He wears shako headgear and carries an unsheathed Mameluke sword from the Barbary Wars of 1803.

OPPOSITE: A Mameluke-style officer's sword, circa 1826.

LEFT: A gilt-mounted officer's sword and scabbard, 1798–1825.

RIGHT: A noncommissioned officer's sword, 1798–1830s.

RIGHT: Col Donna Neary imagines the Marine Band in 1828 at Great Falls, Maryland, at the ceremonies for the opening of the first section of the Chesapeake and Ohio Canal, visible in the background. Marine Band uniforms for drummers, fifers, and buglers were red, as opposed to the "blues" of the regular-establishment Marines. Red is the color of the facings of the dress uniform in order for officers to better distinguish musicians from the infantry.

LEFT: A Marine private in full-dress uniform, 1819. This tombstone-style hat replaced the earlier cylindrical version. When serving aboard ship, the linen knapsack was painted black. Gaiters over the ankles and tops of the shoes were worn until 1839.

RIGHT AND ABOVE: Early-nineteenth-century drum with drumsticks.

breastworks between the Mississippi River and a cypress swamp.

The 5,300 British troops assaulted straight into the American line. The attack lasted twenty minutes, during which the Brits lost 2,036 killed and wounded, including their commander. The Americans lost eight, and thirteen more were wounded. Gen Jackson allowed the thoroughly defeated and shocked enemy survivors to bury their dead and return to their ships. It was a most decisive, although unnecessary, victory. It did, however, thrust Jackson into the limelight; thirteen years later the frontier Tennessean general became president.

As the nation turned back to peace, the future of the already minuscule Marine Corps was far from secure, despite its exemplary battle record.

RIGHT: LtCol Charles Cureton's watercolor of an orderly sergeant in full-dress uniform, 1827. The "orderly sergeant" was the equivalent of today's first sergeant. Normally, Marines of this rank would carry a noncommissioned officer's sword instead of a musket. Regular sergeants, however, did carry the musket, cartridge box, belt, and bayonet.

BELOW, LEFT: Officer's fatigue cap of the Mexican War period.

ABOVE: A gilt-mounted officer's sword, 1798–1825. The eagle-head pommel stamps it as American. Note design differences compared with the swords appearing on pages 54 and 55.

ABOVE, CENTER: A restrike from the original die in the Marine Museum, Navy Yard, of the eagle and anchor worn on the high shako and cartridge box, from 1820; the emblem was cut from the plate, and worn until 1859.

HANGING BY A THREAD

ABOVE: A portrait of CMC Archibald Henderson by the author based on the portrait of Addison Garland (page 50), a contemporary of Henderson's. Henderson served thirty-nine years as commandant, and died in office at age seventy-five.

RIGHT: Marines guarding a supply wagon are startled by an ambush at Twelve-Mile Swamp near St. Augustine, Florida, in this dramatic painting by Col Charles Waterhouse. The men fire at phantom Seminole Indians and runaway slaves as their horses shy and fall, mortally wounded. Their leader, Capt John Williams, also lost his life in the encounter. The Indian Wars went on for two decades. In the 1830s CMC Henderson lead a battalion of Marines in a fruitless, two-year chase of the recalcitrant Indians, whom the government was trying to force onto land farther west.

The third and fourth commandants of the Marine Corps, respectively, LtCol Franklin Wharton—who despite his failure to take the field at Bladensburg had had a distinguished fourteen-year tenure—and LtCol Anthony Gale, were both court-martialed. The former was acquitted of cowardice and died in office; the latter was found guilty of moral turpitude and cashiered. Fortunately, the 1820 appointment of LtCol Archibald Henderson as their successor redeemed the office. Henderson was the right man for the right time.

Despite the shenanigans at headquarters, Marines were performing a number of expeditionary duties that took them to the far corners of the globe—the Caribbean, the Gulf of Mexico, Key West, West Africa, the Falkland Islands, and Sumatra—all to protect American interests or to free captured U.S. citizens.

It was still, however, a time of peril for the young U.S. Marine Corps, since there was considerable confusion as to whether the Marines were part of the Department of the Navy or the Army.

The 1798 bill that had created the Marine Corps had stipulated that, while at sea, the Corps came under Navy regulations, and while on land under Army rules. Many, including President Jackson, saw no need for the Marines. CMC Henderson, however, had the perspicacity and political skill to influence Congress contrarily behind the scenes. The result of the commandant's covert efforts was the 1834 Act for

M1816 HALL RIFLE

The .69-caliber Model 1816 was produced until 1844 and had the largest production of any U.S. flintlock musket. In addition to 325,000 made by Springfield and more than 350,000 produced by Harpers Ferry, three versions of the Model 1816 were also manufactured by more than a dozen contract arms companies.

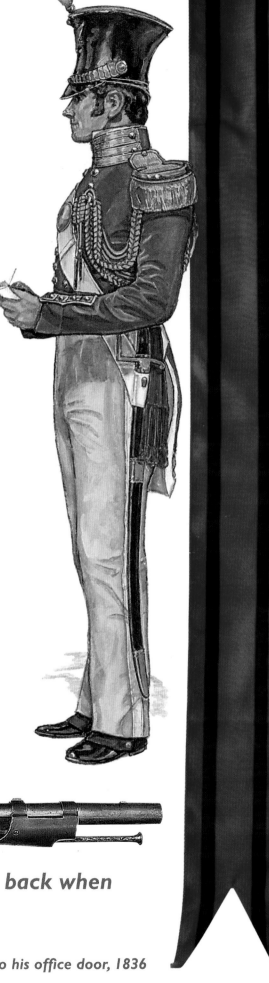

the Better Organization of the Marine Corps. It established that the Corps was a part of the Department of the Navy but not *of* the U.S. Navy. Rather, it was to be a separate, sister service. Furthermore, the president could order Marines to missions he deemed necessary, including reinforcing the Army.

The Marines had finally achieved a reassuring degree of permanence. President Jackson directed the Marines to revert their uniforms back to their original green of the Revolution. Unfortunately, the green dye faded quickly in sunlight, and in 1839 the blue was ultimately reintroduced. The new uniform was a dark-blue coat and light-blue trousers, with a scarlet stripe down the seam for the officers and NCOs.

THE SEMINOLE INDIAN WARS AND BEYOND

When trouble brewed among the Creek and Seminole Indians in Florida and Georgia in the 1830s, the government decided to relocate them to the Arkansas and Oklahoma territories. President Jackson ordered the Marines to assist the Army in trying to oust resisting Indians in Georgia.

In 1836, now-Col Henderson unhesitatingly left his sergeant major in charge of headquarters and went off to lead two battalions of Marines that he had hastily pulled together from various posts. The high point of the government's drawn-out campaign of chasing elusive Indian shadows occurred when Henderson, now commanding a brigade of Marines and soldiers, attacked the cornered Indians at the Hatchee-Lustee River north of Tampa, winning a victory, although only three enemy dead could be counted. Henderson returned to Marine Corps headquarters and was brevetted a brigadier general for his actions.

RIGHT: LtCol Charles Cureton's rendition of the senior noncommissioned officer of the Marine Corps, the sergeant major, in 1835 full-dress uniform. The style is a mixture of both officer and enlisted uniforms. Because the grass-green color faded, the traditional dark blue was reinstated. (Marine "greens" [a forest green] were instituted in the Uniform Regulations of 1912.) The four loops on the slashed cuff represent his rank, while the gold epaulets with gold fringe were authorized for only the top three enlisted grades. The aiguillette (the silk rope strands over the left shoulder to a breast button) indicates assignment to staff duties. The sword is the regulation noncommissioned officer's sword worn from 1827 through 1859.

"Gone to Florida to fight the Indians.... Will be back when the war is over."

LtCol Archibald Henderson, commandant, in a note pinned to his office door, 1836

RIGHT: Col Donna Neary's rendering of a Marine sergeant in the green uniform and black high-crowned leather shako of the 1830s and '40s. Wearing the noncommissioned officer's 1818 sword, this early Marine also carries an M1819 Hall breechloader musket manufactured at the Harpers Ferry, West Virginia, armory, with the bayonet mounted in its lateral position at the muzzle. The sleeve chevron indicates four years of enlisted service.

ABOVE: Enlisted shako with brass eagle plate, circa 1830–1840s. A shako is a tall, cylindrical hat with a plume. The word *shako* is derived from the Hungarian word for "peak" or "point."

M1836 PISTOL

Considered to be the best made and most attractive American martial flintlock pistol, the Model 1836 was also the last of this type. Manufactured by Waters & Johnson, the Model 1836 was a .54-caliber smoothbore and was made until 1844. A total of 41,000 were made, with many later converted to percussion.

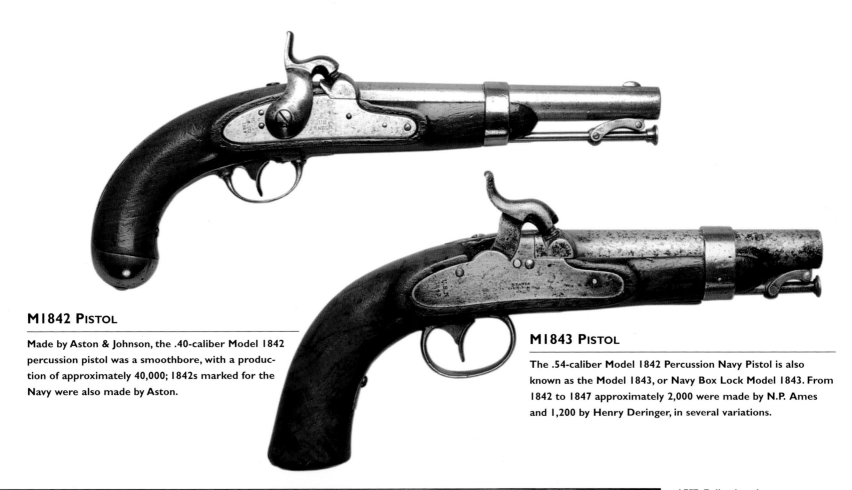

M1842 PISTOL

Made by Aston & Johnson, the .40-caliber Model 1842 percussion pistol was a smoothbore, with a production of approximately 40,000; 1842s marked for the Navy were also made by Aston.

M1843 PISTOL

The .54-caliber Model 1842 Percussion Navy Pistol is also known as the Model 1843, or Navy Box Lock Model 1843. From 1842 to 1847 approximately 2,000 were made by N.P. Ames and 1,200 by Henry Deringer, in several variations.

LEFT: Following the Revolution, the Continental Marines disbanded and their distinctive green uniforms were abandoned. When the new U.S. Marine Corps was created in 1798, it inherited stores of surplus blue uniforms from Gen Anthony Wayne's legion of the U.S. Army. In 1835, President Andrew Jackson ordered the Marines to resume wearing their former "greens." In *Return to Green,* Charles Waterhouse shows Marines swapping their uniforms. The dye used by the manufacturer, however, was fugitive, and the rich green color faded quickly in the sun to a sickly, pale green. Five years later, the Marines reverted to the blue uniforms, which have served as the Marines' "dress blues" to the present.

THE MEXICAN WAR: "FROM THE HALLS OF MONTEZUMA …"

The 1803 Louisiana Purchase from France nearly doubled the size of the United States, adding all the territory of the Mississippi Valley, the Great Plains, and the Rocky Mountains stretching in a great arc toward the Pacific Ocean. Under that arc remained the lightly populated territories of California and south of what is now Colorado, all land claimed by Mexico. Texas was a separate case: it was more densely settled and, after a massacre of settlers by the Mexican army at El Alamo in 1836, had petitioned to join the United States. California was leaning toward becoming a British protectorate. Of course, Mexico would have none of this.

With such territory grabbing in the wind—and with the notion that American expansion westward was the country's "Manifest Destiny"—many schemes to claim land were put into play.

In late October 1845 President James K. Polk decided to send Marine 1stLt Archibald Gillespie on a courier-reconnaissance mission through Mexico and on to California to deliver presidential orders to Army Capt John Frémont, who with guide Kit Carson was on his third western expedition. Perhaps wishing to earn similar Seminole War accolades for his Marines (or perhaps to create a mission to prove a Marine raison d'être), CMC Henderson supported the decision. Such a trek through uncharted, unfriendly Indian areas, following only single trails, was in itself remarkable. The procurement of even basic provisions—food (although game was abundant), adequate weapons, ammunition supplies—was problematic. There were few standards in those days before the mass production of ammunition, and lead had to be melted and poured into bullet molds to replenish supplies. Despite these obstacles, Gillespie prevailed and assessed the

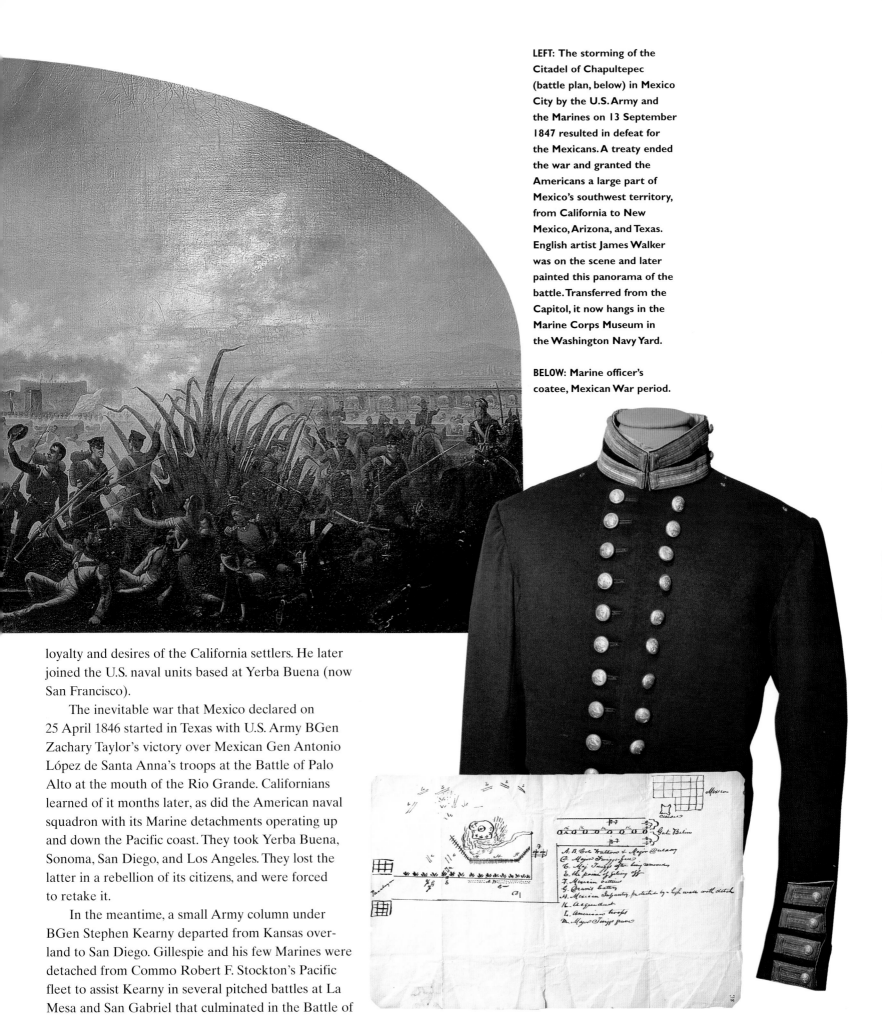

LEFT: The storming of the Citadel of Chapultepec (battle plan, below) in Mexico City by the U.S. Army and the Marines on 13 September 1847 resulted in defeat for the Mexicans. A treaty ended the war and granted the Americans a large part of Mexico's southwest territory, from California to New Mexico, Arizona, and Texas. English artist James Walker was on the scene and later painted this panorama of the battle. Transferred from the Capitol, it now hangs in the Marine Corps Museum in the Washington Navy Yard.

BELOW: Marine officer's coatee, Mexican War period.

loyalty and desires of the California settlers. He later joined the U.S. naval units based at Yerba Buena (now San Francisco).

The inevitable war that Mexico declared on 25 April 1846 started in Texas with U.S. Army BGen Zachary Taylor's victory over Mexican Gen Antonio López de Santa Anna's troops at the Battle of Palo Alto at the mouth of the Rio Grande. Californians learned of it months later, as did the American naval squadron with its Marine detachments operating up and down the Pacific coast. They took Yerba Buena, Sonoma, San Diego, and Los Angeles. They lost the latter in a rebellion of its citizens, and were forced to retake it.

In the meantime, a small Army column under BGen Stephen Kearny departed from Kansas overland to San Diego. Gillespie and his few Marines were detached from Commo Robert F. Stockton's Pacific fleet to assist Kearny in several pitched battles at La Mesa and San Gabriel that culminated in the Battle of

San Pascual (near the present site of the U.S. Marine base at Camp Pendleton). It was a hard-won victory. The Americans suffered nineteen killed and thirty wounded, including Kearny and Gillespie. Nevertheless, they turned northward and finally re-captured the City of Angels.

A second Army assault under Taylor was aimed at the Mexican east coast along the Gulf of Mexico. Taylor's brigade marched south from Texas to Tampico, Mexico, supported offshore by a naval squadron whose Marines had been combined into a two-hundred-man provisional battalion under Marine Capt Alvin Edson.

LEFT: Don Troiani's depiction of a Marine corporal of 1847 in the newly adopted sky-blue kersey (a heavy woolen fabric) fatigue dress and trousers, similar to the Army's. The white cross-chest belts held the cartridge box on the right hip and the bayonet sling on the left. The weapon is still the M1816 Mexico flintlock; the Corps did not adopt percussion-rifled muskets until the mid-1850s. The brass letters *USM* on the cap indicated the U.S. Marine Corps.

Farther down the coast, a larger Army and Marine force under MajGen Winfield Scott landed to secure the major seaport city of Veracruz, which surrendered on 29 March 1847. An amphibious landing force under Navy commodore Matthew C. Perry steamed up the Tabasco River, securing San Juan Bautista.

That done, Scott set off on his vigorous three-hundred-mile uphill march across Mexico to its capital. By now, CMC Henderson had raised a Marine battalion under command of Col Samuel Watson, which was attached to Scott at Veracruz and later to BGen John Quitman's division at Puebla for the assault on Mexico City. Maj Levi Twiggs commanded the Marines when Watson took over the brigade. Unfortunately, Twiggs was one of the first to be killed in the assault on the enemy capital.

Facing thirty thousand Mexicans, Scott's army of eleven thousand, after a month of hard fighting, reached the Citadel of Chapultepec. The high plateau on which it was situated overlooked the causeways across the natural moat surrounding the Mexican capital. On 13 September, after two hours of bombardment, soldiers and Marines stormed the citadel and captured San Cosme Gate, the entrance to the city. The Americans forced their way into the Mexican capital; that night the Mexicans abandoned it. The next morning, the Marines were tasked with clearing the Palacio Nacional, the vaunted "Halls of Montezuma," named for the Aztec chieftain who surrendered to Spanish conquistador Hernán Cortés in 1519, believing the Spanish to be the descendants of the god Quetzalcoatl. The Stars and Stripes were run up after the Mexican colors were cut down.

When the Marine battalion returned to the barracks in Washington, they presented CMC Henderson a flag emblazoned with the words "From Tripoli to the Halls of the Montezumas." Henderson made much of that, perhaps initiating the first of several successful public promotion campaigns for the Corps. From that moment on, Tripoli and the Halls of Montezuma would forever be associated with the Marine Corps.

In the decade following the Mexican-American War, from which the United States acquired the land that became its southwestern states, Henderson's Marines were tasked with numerous global missions with the Navy, in such areas as Panama, China, Liberia, and the Caribbean. The most significant, perhaps, was Maj Jacob Zeilin's Marines accompanying Commo Perry's 1853 expedition to Japan to open diplomatic and trade relations with the West. Zeilin's snappily drilled and uniformed Marines greatly impressed the awed and heretofore isolationist Japanese. Zeilin went on to become commandant in 1864. None then could have foreseen, as the little American flotilla sailed into Tokyo's harbor back in 1853, the vast American sea and air armadas that would enter that same harbor ninety-two years later to accept the surrender of the Japanese Empire after a bitter four-year war against it.

Henderson remained commandant for thirty-nine years, the longest of any in Marine Corps history. His continuity and tenacity in fighting for the Marine Corps in many a struggle against its emasculation or elimination are credited with saving it. He died in office on 6 January 1859 at age seventy-six. The next senior officer, LtCol John Harris, sixty-six years old with forty-five years of service, took over as commandant.

LEFT: A battalion of U.S. Marines figured prominently in the battles on the way to Mexico City, as well as in the capital itself. Marines stormed the Palacio Nacional, which was constructed with materials salvaged from the palace of Montezuma. Noted illustrator Tom Lovell, on active duty as a sergeant at HQMC during World War II, painted this inspiring scene of the hard-bitten Marines entering Mexico City led by Army BGen John A. Quitman.

M1816 SPRINGFIELD RIFLE, MEXICAN-AMERICAN WAR ERA

A Model 1816 .69-caliber musket converted from the original flintlock ignition to percussion.

PRELUDE TO A NATION SPLIT

The practice of slavery in the southern states had been a festering sore since the U.S. Constitution had failed to address the issue in 1789. Morally reprehensible as it was, the slavery system was clung to by the agrarian South as a source of cheap labor for its cotton industry. The inequity of it gnawed at the consciences of many in the North and the South, and hostility over the issue continued to grow. By the 1830s there was a vocal movement in the North calling for slavery to be abolished.

In 1859, a firebrand from Missouri took it upon himself to do just that. With a handful of followers, John Brown seized the lightly guarded Federal arsenal at Harpers Ferry, forty miles northwest of the capital. When news of the raid was telegraphed to Washington, an eighty-six-man Marine detachment under Lt Israel Greene, which was the only regular unit on duty in the capital, immediately traveled by train to the site. Almost simultaneously, the Army dispatched Col Robert E. Lee and LtCol Jeb Stuart to take charge of the situation after first relieving the ineffective local militia on site.

The plan was to demand surrender and, if none was made, to attack. Upon a signal from Stuart, Greene led an assault on the fire engine house occupied by Brown and his supporters, with the Marines battering the door down and charging the defenders. Two Marines behind Greene were shot, but the Marine lieutenant slashed the neck of the bearded abolitionist leader with his sword, and those who were not killed immediately surrendered. It turned out to be the bloody wake-up call for a conflict that would shortly hemorrhage profusely.

RIGHT: Civil War officer's dress chapeau bras. It was worn fore-and-aft, with the gold-braided tassel to the rear, as shown in the illustration above.

BROTHER AGAINST BROTHER: 1861–1865

Before newly elected Abraham Lincoln was inaugurated as the sixteenth president, South Carolina voted to secede from the Union. It would be a tough beginning for the new chief executive. Outgoing President Buchanan immediately sent Marines to secure Fort Washington, across from Mt. Vernon on the Potomac, Baltimore's Fort McHenry, and the Pensacola Navy Yard in Florida.

At the beginning of hostilities, Marine Corps strength was 1,892 officers and men. As was happening in the

OPPOSITE, TOP: An illustration of Marine uniforms of the 1840s by Marine World War II combat artist Maj Donald Dickson. Left to right: private dress, first lieutenant fatigue, commandant dress, fife major dress, major of the staff dress.

LEFT, TOP: Harpers Ferry, West Virginia, site of one of the United States' two principal small-arms factories, was seized by abolitionist John Brown in 1859. Eighty-six Marines from Washington were dispatched to put down the revolt. Brown and his band were holed up in the fire engine house until the Marines stormed the building, shown here in a painting by Don Stivers.

LEFT, BOTTOM: A mid-nineteenth-century photograph of Harpers Ferry and the Federal Armory, located at the junction of West Virginia (foreground), Virginia (right), and Maryland (top), at the confluence of the Shenandoah and Potomac rivers.

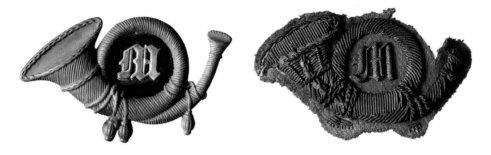

ABOVE, LEFT AND RIGHT: Two variations of the embroidered Marine emblem used on the uniform's kepi cap. The hunting horn signified infantry, the letter *M*, Marines.

BELOW: A navy-blue Civil War–era frock coat, with gold braid. Both Marine officers and enlisted men had two rows of buttons on their coats; in the Army, only officers had two rows. As a result, Marine privates were often saluted by militia and volunteers passing through Washington, a courtesy that they politely acknowledged.

Army and the Navy, the Corps saw the resignation of a number of men who felt they owed their allegiance to the South and to their home states rather than to the Union. Among the officers to resign their commissions and join the new Confederacy were West Pointers Robert E. Lee, Jeb Stuart, and Jefferson Davis, as well as other stalwarts whose names have gone down in history. The Confederacy gained half of the Marine captains and two-thirds of the lieutenants. Lincoln halted the defections upon taking office, summarily dismissing any whose loyalties were not firmly to the Union. The Marines that remained in Washington were mostly senior majors and above, plus new recruits.

Confederate Marines

On 20 May 1861, the newly formed Confederate Congress in Richmond authorized a Marine Corps of ten companies, with a colonel commandant, Lloyd J. Beall. In 1864, as the tide was running out for the Confederacy, Beall reported that the aggregate strength of the Confederate Corps was 539, including 2 captains, 3 lieutenants, and 62 enlisted men who were prisoners of war, with few recruits coming in. Most of the Marines were at Confederate naval stations at Mobile, Savannah, Charleston, Wilmington, and Drewry's Bluff, near Richmond, or on board ironclad steamers in the James River and on the CSS *Tallahassee* and *Chickamauga* at sea. Beall added that all had "displayed the promptness and efficiency of well-disciplined soldiers." Whether they wore distinctive green uniforms is highly doubtful, as few Confederates had official uniforms at all.

Union Marines

Following the defections to the Confederacy, the 13 Marine officers and 336 Marines left at the barracks in Washington were hastily formed into a battalion. They set out in 1861 with Union MajGen Irving McDowell's half-trained Army toward Manassas, Virginia, only thirty miles south of Washington.

The First Battle of Bull Run on 21 July was the first of many disasters to come for the North in the first three years of the war. Named for the little stream that ran through the village of Manassas, the battle turned into a rout of Federal soldiers and the panicked civilians who had come to picnic and watch the "show." Despite their lack of combat experience, the Union Marines, however, made a valiant stand before having to give way when their flanks did so. It was the first—and last—instance of Marines ever turning their backs to an enemy.

ABOVE: Lt F. H. Cameron of the Confederate States Marine Corps.

LEFT: Like their Northern counterparts, the small Confederate Marine Corps saw limited duty during the Civil War. Here, Marines aboard a ship prepare for action, in an illustration by Don Troiani.

BELOW: Button from a Federal Marine's uniform found after the First Battle of Bull Run in 1861.

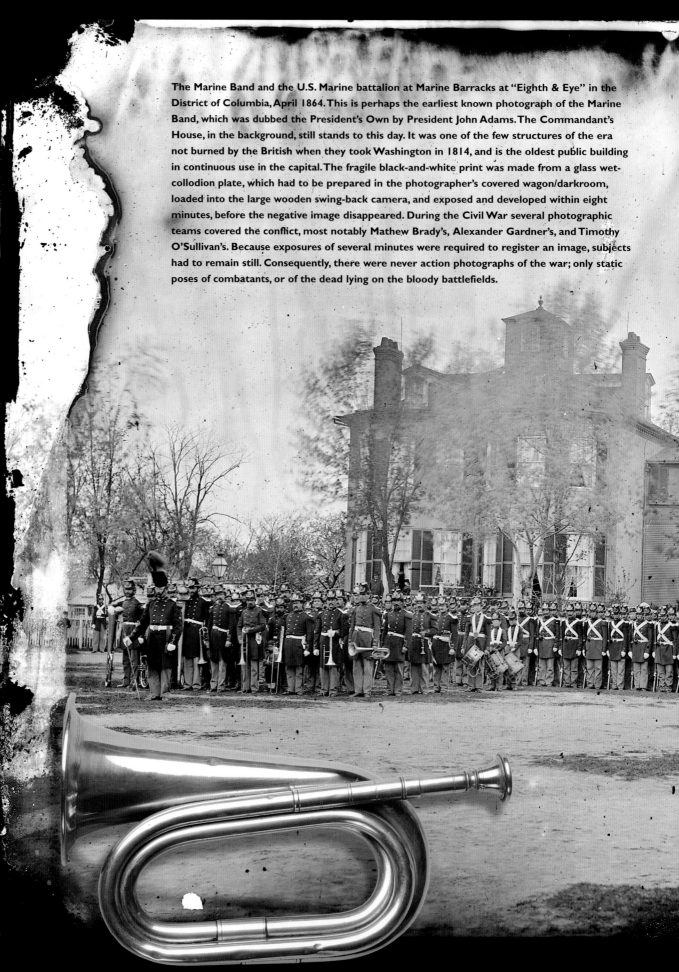

The Marine Band and the U.S. Marine battalion at Marine Barracks at "Eighth & Eye" in the District of Columbia, April 1864. This is perhaps the earliest known photograph of the Marine Band, which was dubbed the President's Own by President John Adams. The Commandant's House, in the background, still stands to this day. It was one of the few structures of the era not burned by the British when they took Washington in 1814, and is the oldest public building in continuous use in the capital. The fragile black-and-white print was made from a glass wet-collodion plate, which had to be prepared in the photographer's covered wagon/darkroom, loaded into the large wooden swing-back camera, and exposed and developed within eight minutes, before the negative image disappeared. During the Civil War several photographic teams covered the conflict, most notably Mathew Brady's, Alexander Gardner's, and Timothy O'Sullivan's. Because exposures of several minutes were required to register an image, subjects had to remain still. Consequently, there were never action photographs of the war; only static poses of combatants, or of the dead lying on the bloody battlefields.

ABOVE: Col John Harris, who became commandant upon the death of Col Archibald Henderson in 1859. Harris served until 1864, when he was succeeded by Col Jacob Zeilin.

BELOW, INSET: The bugle reputedly used by a musician of Company B of the Marine battalion to sound the advance of the Union forces at the First Battle of Bull Run. A hastily organized battalion from Marine Barracks, Washington, accompanied the Army expedition into northern Virginia in July 1861.

In the rebound from Bull Run, Union Marines were used to secure Cape Hatteras and in the naval operation to secure a beachhead at Port Royal Sound, South Carolina, and to capture Hilton Head Island and Beaufort as a Union base. Three hundred Union Marines, under Maj John Reynolds, were on board the river steamer *Governor* in Adm Samuel DuPont's flotilla, which on 3 November 1861 attacked Forts Beauregard and Walker guarding the mouth of deepwater Port Royal Sound.

Unfortunately, *Governor* was caught in a storm and, before she sank, had to transfer the Marines, with only their rifles and ammunition, to the steam frigate *Sabine*. DuPont's successful pounding of the forts in a circling maneuver forced the evacuation of Fort Beauregard covering the northern mouth, but Fort Walker on Hilton Head Island stood firm under its commander, West Pointer BGen Thomas Drayton, now a Confederate. Drayton's brother had stayed in the Union Navy and now commanded the *Pocahontas*, which had been delayed by the storm in joining DuPont's fleet. The delay put the *Pocahontas* in a position offshore to deliver enfilade fire on the Confederate guns, thus preventing the fort from foiling the Union attack.

Under such unexpected bombardment—from his brother, no less—Drayton could not re-aim his guns and had to abandon the fort. Adm DuPont graciously ordered the Marines ashore to capture the unoccupied stronghold. For the rest of the war, Hilton Head Island, Port Royal Sound, and Beaufort remained in Union hands.

LEFT: A Civil War officer's sword.

BELOW: Union Marines aboard an unidentified naval vessel during the Civil War.

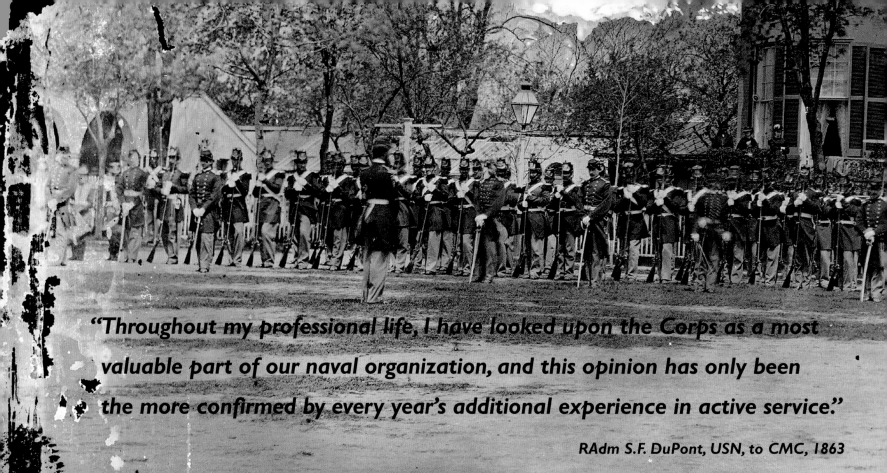

"*Throughout my professional life, I have looked upon the Corps as a most valuable part of our naval organization, and this opinion has only been the more confirmed by every year's additional experience in active service.*"

RAdm S.F. DuPont, USN, to CMC, 1863

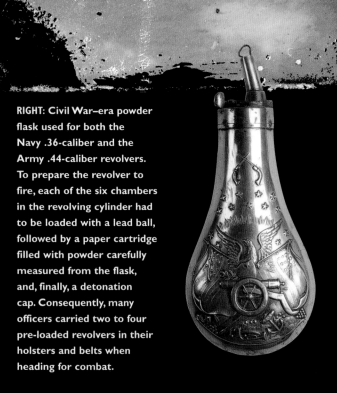

RIGHT: Civil War–era powder flask used for both the Navy .36-caliber and the Army .44-caliber revolvers. To prepare the revolver to fire, each of the six chambers in the revolving cylinder had to be loaded with a lead ball, followed by a paper cartridge filled with powder carefully measured from the flask, and, finally, a detonation cap. Consequently, many officers carried two to four pre-loaded revolvers in their holsters and belts when heading for combat.

M1855 SPRINGFIELD

One of the few pistols made by Springfield Armory, the .58-caliber Model 1855 percussion pistol/carbine has a detachable shoulder stock and uses the Maynard tape self-priming device; only 4,021 were produced. The Model 1855 was designed to be used as a pistol on horseback and as a carbine on foot.

M1851 COLT NAVY REVOLVER

One of the most popular percussion revolvers of the nineteenth century, the 6-shot .36-caliber Colt Model 1851 Navy Revolver was widely issued to the U.S. Navy and the Marine Corps during the Civil War. With a total U.S. production of 215,348, the Colt Navy is found in several variations, including one with a detachable shoulder stock. Approximately 42,000 were produced by Colt's London factory.

OPPOSITE: U.S. Marine Corps officers, circa 1865. From left is Brevet Capt William Wallace, Capt McLane Tilton, and 2dLt George C. Reid.

ABOVE: A group of Union Marines, wearing dress uniforms and carrying Model 1842 muskets, at the Washington Navy Yard in 1864.

OPPOSITE: An illustration by Don Troiani of Union Marines during the attack on Fort Fisher, North Carolina, in the closing days of the Civil War, in what turned out to be an untoward rout of the Union forces. The sergeant in the foreground carries an M1855 rifled musket.

ABOVE AND RIGHT: A Civil War–era dress shako and uniform.

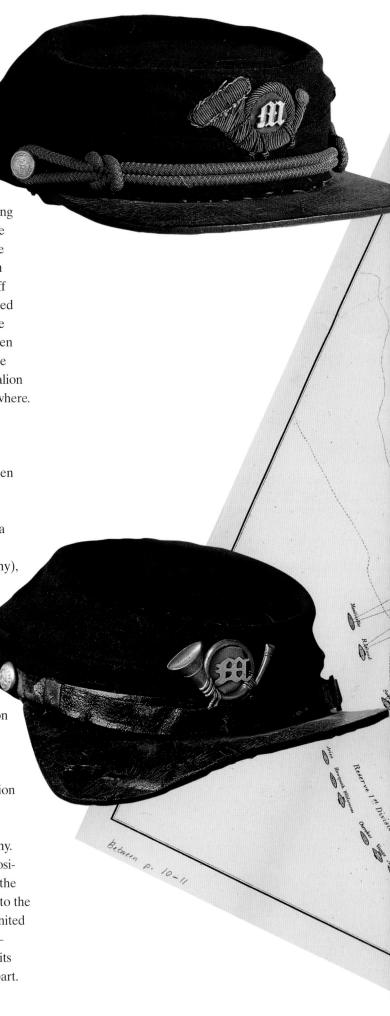

Gen Robert E. Lee had temporarily defended the rail line just west of Beaufort and might have counterattacked and retaken the Union beachhead; however, he was instead ordered to Richmond to take command of the Army of Northern Virginia.

Maj Reynolds' Marines subsequently performed desultory missions, such as capturing the abandoned city of Fort Augustine, before returning to their barracks in Washington.

Top Marine leadership at the time was uninspiring at best. A Marine battalion under Capt John Broome secured the city of New Orleans in April 1862 for the Army to occupy, while the following year, Maj Zeilin was sent with a fresh battalion to join naval forces off Charleston for an attack on Fort Sumter. One hundred and fifty Marines and sailors landed at night onto the rubble-strewn shore of the fort's ruins but were beaten back by rebel fire. Sustaining forty-four casualties, the Marines retired to nearby Folly Island until the battalion was disbanded and the survivors were assigned elsewhere.

The last major engagement involving Union Marines was a similar fiasco at Fort Fisher, at the entrance to Wilmington, North Carolina. An ill-conceived and poorly executed attack led by MajGen Benjamin Butler faltered on the first attempt. Two weeks later a provisional battalion of 8,500 troops, 400 of which were Marines, was hastily formed for a second unsuccessful attack to cover an assault by 1,600 sailors. The divided command (Navy and Army), last-minute "provisional" organizations, inadequate ship-to-shore communications, insufficient naval gunfire preparation, and the fact that the sailors were untrained in infantry tactics, and attacked before the Marines were in position, led to the disaster.

Months later the war was over, but not the fight for the Marine Corps' very existence. The Union Marine Corps had peaked at 4,167 and had lost 148 who were killed in its operations. In 1864 a Congressional resolution was proposed for the Marine Corps to be transferred to the Army. Fortunately, this proposition was tabled. Thus, the Civil War added little to the overall glory of the United States Marine Corps— nor did any accrue to its Confederate counterpart.

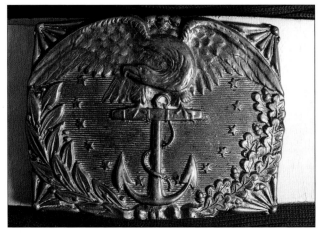

LEFT: Marines in landing boats during the ill-fated attack on Fort Fisher, North Carolina, in a painting by Charles Waterhouse.

LEFT, CENTER: This map of the Union attack on Fort Fisher shows the position of vessels and lines of fire. The second attack on the fort, 13–15 January 1865, was under the command of RAdm David Dixon Porter, son of the famous Capt David D. Porter of the War of 1812. The attack was an unmitigated military disaster, which Porter blamed on the Marines (who had suffered sixty-one killed in action). The fact that the Union forces eventually prevailed glossed over the real story, and perhaps this map contributed to that presentation.

BELOW: A photograph taken after the battle showing the interior defensive guns of Fort Fisher. The barrel of this 10-pounder was shorn off, possibly by an exploding shell of its own.

Weapons for the First Modern War

Shortly before the Civil War, Marines were re-armed with the .58-caliber M1855 rifled musket. It was still a muzzle-loading weapon and could be reloaded as rapidly as the smoothbore, but its hollow-based minié bullet expanded from the explosion of the powder charge and gripped the rifling. The effective range—two hundred to five hundred yards—was several times that of the smoothbore. Later in the war, the M1855 was replaced with the similar M1861 and M1865 Springfield rifled muskets.

Ever in search of increased firepower to compensate for the Corps' small numbers, Marines in the Civil War also used Sharps and Spencer rifles. The Sharps was a single-shot breechloader, using .52-caliber bullets, a paper cartridge, and a percussion cap. The Spencer was a 7-shot, lever-action repeater, using .54-caliber copper cartridges fed by a tubular magazine in the buttstock. Steel parts were tinned to protect against the corrosive effect of salty sea air.

After the Civil War, for economic reasons, the Corps reverted to the M1863 musket. In 1870, Capt McLane Tilton was preparing his company for an expedition to the kingdom of Korea when he was offered the latest Remington breechloaders by that arms company. Before accepting the offer, Tilton checked with HQMC, recommending acceptance and complaining of his old "muzzle fuzzles," as he termed the Springfield muzzleloaders. Headquarters denied his requests, but this was the Corps' last muzzle-loading campaign. The next year, the Navy ordered twenty-two thousand of the .50-caliber Remington rolling-block breechloaders. The Marine Corps used the Remingtons for the rest of the 1870s.

—BN

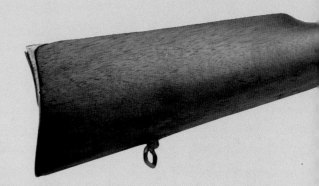

M1862 SPENCER RIFLE

The first lever-action (see inset, opposite) rifle to be patented, the Model 1862 Spencer was chambered for the .52-caliber Spencer cartridge, often referred to as the .56–.50, .56–.52, or .56–.56. It was widely issued during the Civil War as a carbine (shown here), but a longer rifle version was also issued to the Army (approximately 14,500 pieces), and the Navy (only 1,009 pieces).

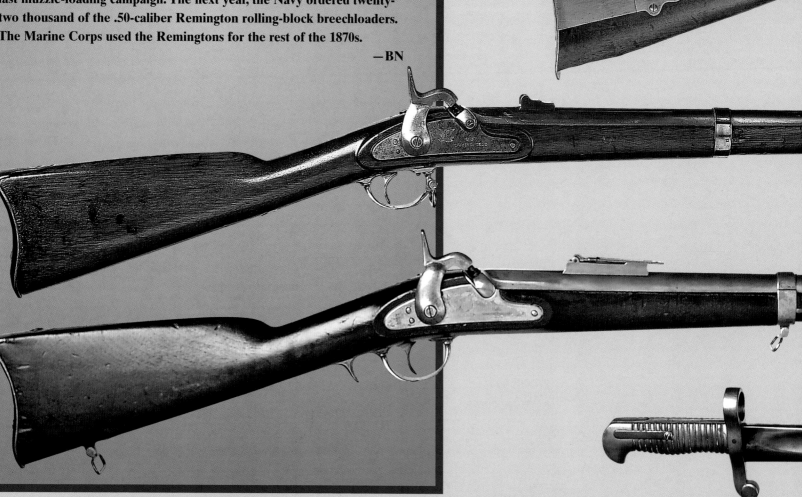

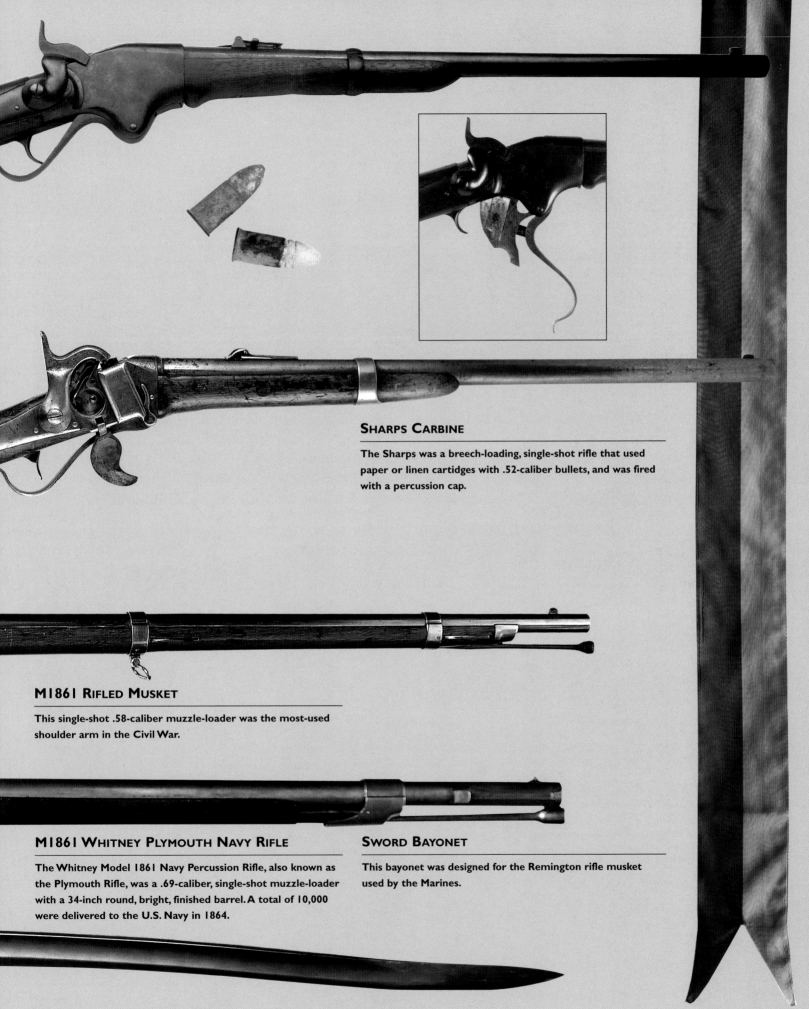

SHARPS CARBINE

The Sharps was a breech-loading, single-shot rifle that used paper or linen cartidges with .52-caliber bullets, and was fired with a percussion cap.

M1861 RIFLED MUSKET

This single-shot .58-caliber muzzle-loader was the most-used shoulder arm in the Civil War.

M1861 WHITNEY PLYMOUTH NAVY RIFLE

The Whitney Model 1861 Navy Percussion Rifle, also known as the Plymouth Rifle, was a .69-caliber, single-shot muzzle-loader with a 34-inch round, bright, finished barrel. A total of 10,000 were delivered to the U.S. Navy in 1864.

SWORD BAYONET

This bayonet was designed for the Remington rifle musket used by the Marines.

NEAR RIGHT: Col Donna Neary's illustration of a Marine drummer of the 1859–1875 period.

FAR RIGHT: A Marine drummer boy. Drums were essential for communicating during bivouac, march, and battle. The distinct, percussive patterns of the drums could be discerned over the din and rumble of battle.

BELOW: Neary's illustration of senior noncommissioned officers, including the drum major, assembled in front of the gate of the cemetery at Gettysburg Battlefield on 19 November 1863. The band stood alongside President Lincoln as he gave his famous address.

ABOVE: Standard military drum used by the Army and Marine Corps during the Civil War. Drums were used to give the cadence count for a march or, like bugles, to signal orders around camp or in battle.

Marine infantry shako device, 1859–1872.

THREE DECADES OF DECADENCE

ABOVE: A U.S. Marine (left) and sailor aboard the USS *Enterprise*, circa 1864.

Marine officer's shako device, 1872–1875. The "eagle, globe, and anchor" emblem was adopted in 1868.

White dress helmet shako plate, 1875–1892.

The thirty years following the war that temporarily divided the Union were both stimulating and stultifying. In the civilian realm, many technical advances came about, including the transcontinental railroad, the harnessing of electricity, ferroconcrete construction, and modernized printing presses.

In the military realm, there was a slow changeover from sail to steam, from wood to iron, and from muzzle-loaders to breechloaders. Besides small wars on the plains to control the remaining recalcitrant Indians, military duty for all services consisted mostly of static garrison duty with snail-paced promotions.

For the Marines, their precarious position was relieved by an 1867 congressional report concluding that "no good reason appears either for abolishing it, the Marine Corps, or transferring it to the Army; on the contrary the Committee recommends that its organization as a separate Corps be preserved and strengthened." As a consequence, Zeilin was promoted

ABOVE: A veteran of the Mexican War, Col Jacob Zeilin was named the seventh Commandant of the Marine Corps on 10 June 1864. After serving for a time as commander of Marine Barracks in Philadelphia and Washington, D.C., in July 1861 Zeilin fought with the Marines at the Battle of Bull Run, where he was wounded. In 1863, now a major, he was given command of the battalion of Marines supporting the naval forces seeking to capture Charleston, South Carolina. Illness cut his command short, however, and he returned to garrison duty, in Portsmouth, New Hampshire. While serving in New Hampshire, he was appointed Commandant of the Marine Corps, and in 1867 was promoted to the rank of brigadier general. Zeilin defended the Corps against its critics after the Civil War, and later approved the design of the Marine emblem, the famed "eagle, globe, and anchor." He retired in 1876 after more than forty-five years as a Marine Corps officer, and died four years later. In the twentieth century, a Navy destroyer and transport were named in his honor.

BELOW: A colonel's epaulet worn by Henry C. Cochrane. The size of the gold fringe increased with rank, making promotions not only slow but expensive.

RIGHT: Marine uniforms of 1875, by artist Donald Dickson. Left to right: private undress, lieutenant colonel full dress, captain mess dress, second lieutenant fatigue, first sergeant full dress, corporal fatigue, drum major full dress, first lieutenant undress.

RIGHT: On 2 May 1867, Col Jacob Zeilin issued an order prescribing a new emblem: a silver hemisphere with gold continents surmounted by a silver eagle with a scarlet cloth border. The order was suddenly revoked on 5 June. This early version of the emblem was eventually superseded by the eagle, globe, and anchor.

to brigadier general and commandant. Thereafter, the Marines embarked on provisional landings to protect American lives, property, and interests in such faraway places as China, Formosa, Japan, Nicaragua, Uruguay, Mexico, Korea, Panama, Hawaii, Egypt, Haiti, Samoa, Argentina, Chile, and Colombia. Reporting on some of these activities, war correspondent Richard Harding Davis coined the phrase "The Marines have landed and have the situation well in hand." The phrase stuck.

It was also during this period that the fabled band impresario John Philip Sousa emerged to take the "President's Own" Marine Band and the stirring marches he composed to national acclaim. Son of a Marine Band member, Sousa had enlisted in the band at age thirteen and became its leader at twenty-five.

Despite the popularity of the Marine Band and the worldwide expeditions, the Corps was in a period of virtual stagnation, mostly due to overage officers still in grade. To revitalize his Corps, ninth Commandant of the Marine Corps Charles Heywood instituted a number of innovations to improve morale and efficiency: fitness reports and promotion examinations, a School of Application for newly commissioned officers, and an infantry tactics textbook based on an earlier Army manual.

In the 1890s some practical changes were made to the Marine field uniform. Influenced by the Army's Indian fighters, a broad-brimmed "campaign," or field, hat with a large Marine emblem on the side was adopted in 1898, as were linen khaki summer field uniforms and canvas leggings. Leggings stayed a part of the uniform into the Korean War sixty years later.

"The Marines were always in the advance, and how well they performed their part, I leave you to judge. To Captain Tilton and his Marines belongs the honor of first landing and last leaving the shore, in leading the advance on the march, in entering the forts, and in acting as skirmishers."

Capt L.A. Kimberly of the USS Colorado reporting to
Commander in Chief, Asiatic Fleet, 1871, on the landing in Korea

ABOVE: Marine 4-inch gun crew aboard the USS Iowa, circa 1900.

RIGHT: Detail of knotted-rope vent from the back of the enlisted dress shako. The vent was located at the top of the rear peak, directly opposite the front pompom.

FAR RIGHT: This modified French shako, originally used in the 1830s, along with the shorter kepi, came back into use following the Civil War.

M1888 SPRINGFIELD TRAPDOOR RIFLE

The Springfield Model 1888 .45–.70-caliber rifle, also known
as the Model 1889, was the last of the single-shot Springfields,
and the last of the ramrod-bayonet "Trapdoor" Springfields,
following experimental models 1880, 1882, and 1884. A total
of 65,000 were made.

BELOW: A Marine skirmish
drill alongside a railroad
track under construction.
The Marine in the fore-
ground, with the canteen,
uses bugle calls to communicate commands. The men
are from the USS *Maine*.

Good Conduct Medal

RIGHT: An 1884 version of the Navy-Marine Medal of Honor, which was awarded to enlisted sailors and Marines only. The first version of the medal, issued on 21 January 1862, was suspended from a fouled anchor. Naval (including Marine) officers were not authorized awards for valor until 1914. The Medal of Honor was created during the Civil War as a citation for distinguished bravery in battle; only seventeen Marines earned it at the time. The medal later became the highest citation for valor in combat. Each of the non-naval services has its own version. It is sometimes referred to erroneously as the "Congressional" Medal of Honor.

Navy-Marine
Medal of Honor, 1884

LEFT: Pvt Harry Lewis MacNeil was an early recipient of the Navy-Marine Medal of Honor. It was awarded to him for braving enemy fire while on board the USS *Brooklyn* during the Battle of Santiago de Cuba, 3 July 1898.

BELOW: Standard-issue Marine water canteen in use from 1875 through 1912. Note that the stenciling style has remained unchanged.

ABOVE: Col Charles G. McCawley was appointed the eighth Commandant of the Marine Corps on 1 November 1876 and served until his retirement on 29 January 1891. A veteran of the Mexican War and the Civil War, CMC McCawley raised the Corps' standards of training, recruitment, and officer selection and instruction. He also assigned John Philip Sousa to serve as leader of the Marine Band.

566.U.S.S.MAINE, MARINES EMBARKING AT HAMPTON ROADS.   DETROIT PHOTOGRAPHIC CO

ABOVE: Marines embark in longboats to board the battle cruiser USS *Maine* for its mission to Havana Harbor, Cuba, to project a U.S. presence during an uprising there against Spain. Twenty-eight of these Marines perished when the *Maine* mysteriously exploded and sank in the harbor on 15 February 1898.

LEFT: Enlisted Marine overcoat with cape, 1875–1912. The chevrons, here indicating the rank of a quartermaster sergeant, were worn on the cuff so the cape would not cover them. The flat bars below the pointed chevrons indicate a "specialty" rank rather than an infantry or arms branch, whose bars were rounded and referred to as rockers.

ABOVE: Marine snare drum— that is, with a taut, coiled wire strung across the bottom head to give it a distinct sound—of the late nineteenth century.

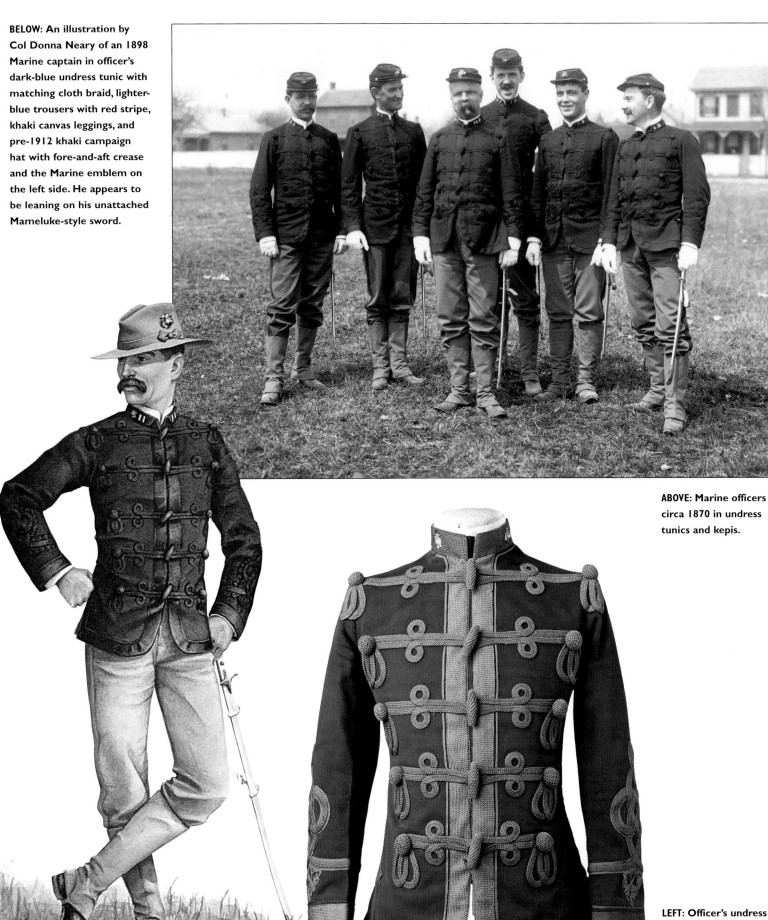

BELOW: An illustration by Col Donna Neary of an 1898 Marine captain in officer's dark-blue undress tunic with matching cloth braid, lighter-blue trousers with red stripe, khaki canvas leggings, and pre-1912 khaki campaign hat with fore-and-aft crease and the Marine emblem on the left side. He appears to be leaning on his unattached Mameluke-style sword.

ABOVE: Marine officers circa 1870 in undress tunics and kepis.

LEFT: Officer's undress tunic, 1871–1900. This example is dark blue with embroidered cloth khaki braid and buttons.

ABOVE: MajGen Charles Heywood was appointed the ninth Commandant of the Marine Corps on 30 January 1891 and served until he retired, after more than forty-five years of distinguished service, on 2 October 1903. During his tenure as commandant, he increased Marine troop strength from 75 officers and 2,100 enlisted to 278 officers and 7,532 enlisted personnel, the greatest strength up to that point. He also set up the officer school system that continues to this day. Heywood was the first Marine to hold the rank of major general.

ABOVE: The shattered hull of the *Maine*, whose explosion on 15 February 1898 ignited the Spanish-American War.

OPPOSITE: A Marine guard aboard the USS *Brooklyn* flagship in Cuba, 3 July 1898.

M1898 Krag-Jorgensen Rifle

Five-shot bolt-action .30-caliber U.S. rifle used during the Spanish-American War and Philippine insurgencies. In the Philippines, the Americans' battle cry was "Civilize 'em with a Krag!"

THE SPANISH-AMERICAN WAR

To quell a potential flash point in a troublesome insurgency on the Caribbean island of Cuba, the battle cruiser USS *Maine* anchored in Havana's harbor. During the night of 15 February 1898, she mysteriously exploded and sank, taking with her 232 sailors and 28 Marines.

Reaction in the United States was fierce. "Remember the *Maine*" swelled into a war cry, fanned by the fiery words of the leading scoop-hungry newspapers, led by William Randolph Hearst's *New York Morning Journal*. Goaded by the jingoistic press and a restless public demanding some sort of retaliation, Congress in April voted for intervention, and President McKinley declared a state of war. (Adm Hyman Rickover, father of the nuclear Navy, speculated in the 1970s that spontaneous

ignition of coal dust in the air had caused the explosion; years after the event, however, a seaman had admitted that the unauthorized smoking of cigarettes was customary next to the powder magazine.)

CMC Heywood immediately ordered a battalion of Marines to be formed. Five days later it was en route by sea to Key West, outfitted with the new Winchester-Lee straight-pull bolt-action .236-caliber rifle using smokeless powder. A Marine artillery battery had also been assembled, and armed with four 3-inch landing guns.

On the other side of the world, in Manila Bay, the Philippines, Commo George Dewey, in command of the American Asiatic Squadron, received his war orders. On 1 May 1898 he opened fire on the Spanish squadron at anchor. Seven enemy ships were damaged severely, as were shore batteries, and 381 Spanish sailors were killed and many others wounded; Dewey's

squadron sustained only several slightly wounded. Marines had manned the ships' secondary gun batteries. Following the victory, a Marine detachment was sent ashore to raise the Stars and Stripes over the Cavite naval station, in the Philippines. Cavite would remain a major U.S. naval facility for almost a century.

Back in Cuba, LtCol Robert Huntington's Marine battalion, which the commandant had ordered raised, was dispatched to seize and secure Guantanamo Bay as an advanced base to support the major assault on the nearby seaport city of Santiago, where the Spanish fleet was bottled up in the harbor. Landing against only sporadic resistance, Huntington's Marines took Guantanamo. The main point of resistance turned out to be at Cuzco Well, which was the water supply for the semiarid city.

On 14 July, two Marine companies and sixty-five Cuban guerrillas advanced to secure the well. Light

naval gunfire support proved ineffective, and some enemy shells began dropping on the Marines. Thinking fast, Sgt John Quick jumped into the open on a small ridge under enemy fire and wigwagged a flag signal to adjust the naval fire onto the five hundred Spanish defenders. The Marines suffered six killed and sixteen wounded. Sgt Quick was awarded the Medal of Honor. Guantanamo has remained a U.S. Navy-Marine Corps base to this day.

In the Philippines, when word of the end of hostilities reached the U.S. Army, which was dug in around the perimeter of the capital, it entered and took the city. Instead of installing the insurgent leader, Emilio Aguinaldo, as the rebel leader had expected, the Army told him to leave. On 4 February 1899 Aguinaldo returned in force and another nasty little war began.

In March, Commo Dewey cabled for a Marine battalion to reinforce Cavite. Two battalions were

BELOW: A Marine skirmish line in battle against the Spanish at Guantanamo, 1898; their sergeant points out the target. The men have stripped to their undershirts to better withstand the tropical climate. This scene was staged for the photographer, who would normally not be in between the opposing sides.

ABOVE: Lt Herbert L. Draper hoists the Stars and Stripes at Camp McCalla, overlooking Guantanamo Bay, Cuba, in June 1898—the first time the American flag had been raised on the island.

BELOW, INSET: Mameluke-Style sword, Spanish-American War era. This particular sword was carried by LtCol Robert Huntington.

dispatched and joined the larger Army operation. It turned out to be a baptism in true jungle warfare, with the Americans fighting ruthless, phantomlike insurgents to whom the jungle was home. A third Marine battalion arrived, as did a reinforced company later that year.

Dewey later remarked that if he had had a regiment of Marines with him after his defeat of the Spanish squadron, the insurgency could have been stopped before it had started.

SUMMARY

Although since its inception the Marine Corps never numbered much above three thousand on average, it managed during the nineteenth century to fly its banner high at home and around the globe, despite the petty political battles behind the scenes. Had it not been for CMC Henderson's persistence and devotion during his long tenure, the story of the Marine Corps might never have been more than a footnote in the history books. Marines, however, performed better than what was expected of military units, from the operations against the Barbary pirates at Tripoli through the War of 1812 and the Mexican-American War, although perhaps with less opportunity to do so during the Civil War. However, they redeemed their Civil War record at the end of the century in the Caribbean, the Philippines, and China, thus setting the stage for their greater role in the twentieth century.

ABOVE: A group of officers of the First Marine Battalion pose in their summer fatigue uniforms with canvas leggings, their felt campaign hats in a variety of positions. Following the Spanish-American War, the fore-and-aft crease was replaced by the four-way "Montana peak," and the emblem was worn at the front and center—which is standard to this day.

RIGHT: Obverse and reverse views of the Dewey Medal, awarded to commemorate the victory of Manila Bay.

LEFT: A rare Marine enlisted summer fatigue campaign coat with gilt buttons, worn during the Spanish-American War.

LEFT: The Marines take a defensive position after seizing Guantanamo Bay for use as a naval base in 1898. The cannon is the M1876 3-inch naval landing gun.

BELOW: LtCol Robert Huntington (front and center) and his First Marine Battalion officers pose at Portsmouth, New Hampshire, before their departure for Cuba in 1898.

BELOW: Huntington's battalion tent camp at Guantanamo Bay. Although the campaign was short, the U.S. Navy and Marines' stay was not; the base continues to be a major naval station to the present day.

ABOVE: The world-renowned composer and bandmaster Col John Philip Sousa, whose triumphal leadership of the Marine Band spanned the 1870s and 1880s. His musical military marches have never lost their popularity. "Semper Fidelis," which he wrote for the Marine Corps, was authorized by Congress as the official march of the USMC. No military band concert is complete without at least one Sousa march.

RIGHT: In 1892 CMC Charles Heywood directed that a new device be designed for the black, Prussian-style, spiked dress helmet, which was adopted following the Franco-Prussian War of 1870. The eagle, globe, and anchor emblem was made of brass for enlisted Marines; the officer's emblem was in silver and gold. Red shoulder knots with silver ornaments (far right) were also prescribed for enlisted Marines. The dress helmet and ornaments were in use until 1904.

ABOVE: The Marine Band of the 1890s, pictured here by Col Donna Neary, debarking a train in Denver for a concert. Sousa initiated nation-wide tours of the Marine Band, which continue to this day. Brass-band music had been popular since before the Civil War, but Sousa raised it to a new, higher standard.

LEFT: A detachment of Marines poses on the porch of the home of the U.S. Consul on the Samoan island of Upolu in April 1899.

BOTTOM LEFT: A Marine drum and bugle corps, circa 1900. This small contingent is dressed in summer khaki with field hats fore-and-aft and emblem to the front.

LEFT: Enlisted dress blue uniform worn from the 1890s through 1912. The blue uniform was the only winter uniform until a forest-green version was adopted in 1912. The web cartridge belt and suspenders were black but often faded to charcoal, as shown here.

ABOVE: Marines in a firefight against members of the Philippine Insurrection that followed the Spanish-American War, 1901.

RIGHT: Leather McKeever cartridge box, showing the canvas loops that held each shell.

M1895 WINCHESTER-LEE NAVY RIFLE

A .236-caliber (6mm) 5-shot, breech-loading rifle. Although used by the Marine Corps for only two years (1898–1899), the Winchester-Lee was the first high-velocity small-caliber military rifle used in the United States. The fragility of the rear sight and an unreliable extractor prevented it from being popular with Marines. It was replaced by the Springfield Krag-Jorgensen .30 caliber in 1900.

INSET: The center-creased campaign hat (later called a field hat by the Marines) was introduced in 1898 and worn until 1912, when it was replaced by the four-dent Montana peak field hat. The high-collar coat of khaki or green continued in use until 1928.

chapter three

Thrust onto the World Stage

"Any officer can get by on his sergeants. To be a sergeant you have to know your stuff. I'd rather be an outstanding sergeant than just another officer."

GySgt Daniel Daly, 1873–1937

From the somewhat forgotten period before World War I stem some of the legendary names of the Marine Corps: Ben Fuller, L.W.T. Waller, John Myers, Smedley Butler, John Quick, Daniel Daly, John A. Lejeune, Harry Lee. Although their names can be seen today on buildings, streets, and monuments throughout the Corps, few can recall the particulars that put them there.

Their heroic exploits took place in China, the Philippines, Samoa, Honduras, Panama, Korea, North Africa, Morocco, Nicaragua, Dominican Republic, Haiti, Beirut, Syria, Abyssinia (now Ethiopia), Russia, and Cuba, and exemplify the diversity of activity for the Marines prior to the world recognition they earned for their actions in the First World War.

A developmental period followed the acquisition of foreign territories (the Philippines, Guam, Puerto Rico, and Hawaii) and bases as a result of the Spanish-American War, and the United States suddenly emerged as a new world power.

Events in the Western Hemisphere and in the Caribbean also reaffirmed the necessity of upholding the Monroe Doctrine to quell unrest in Central American and Caribbean nations as well as to prevent European interference, a role tailor-made for the Marines.

CHINA AND THE AMERICAN LEGATION

In 1900, an indigenous uprising across North China by the "Righteous Fists of Harmony"—called Boxers by the Europeans—set out to expunge all "foreign devils" from Chinese soil. Immediately endangered were the American and other legations in Peking (now Beijing).

In May, two twenty-eight-man ships' detachments of Marines landed near Tientsin (Tianjin), up from the mouth of the Pei Ho River, and moved sixty miles inland to Peking to protect the American legation under siege there. The French, Russians, Germans, Austrians, Italians, and Japanese were also arriving to protect their own legations. The U.S. Marines arrived with a high-wheeled Colt machine gun manned by U.S. sailors. The situation was so tense that Marine Capt John Meyers had to have his Marines clear streets around the legation at bayonet-point.

Boxer and Chinese Imperial troops cut the supply line back to Tientsin, forcing European, Japanese, and American navies to steam offshore with reinforcements. LtCol Ben Waller landed a battalion of Marines and, along with some White Russian sailors, commandeered a locomotive to transport them to Peking. Along the way, they were hit by the Chinese. In the ensuing firefight, the Russians withdrew, leaving the U.S. Marines to fight off the rebels and to collect their casualties. Nearby, at Tientsin, British

ABOVE: LtGen John T. Myers, commander of the American Legation Guard at Peking, China, during the Boxer Rebellion.

PAGE 99: Fanciful post–World War I recruiting poster by John A. Coughlin. Lewis machine guns, like the one pictured here, were all turned over to Marine aviation during the war—they would not have been carried into battle as portrayed. The Lewis machine guns for Marine infantry were replaced by the less-reliable French Chauchat light machine guns.

INSET, RIGHT: Felt field hat with fore-and-aft crease in the crown and the Marine eagle, globe, and anchor emblem on the side, adopted in 1898. At the base of the crown is an encircling silk band tied in a flat bow. A leather chinstrap went around the front of the crown and through a hole in the brim on each side, usually with an adjustable sliding clasp under the chin.

RIGHT: Legation Marines pose on a captured Chinese gun amid the rubble of the Legation defense.

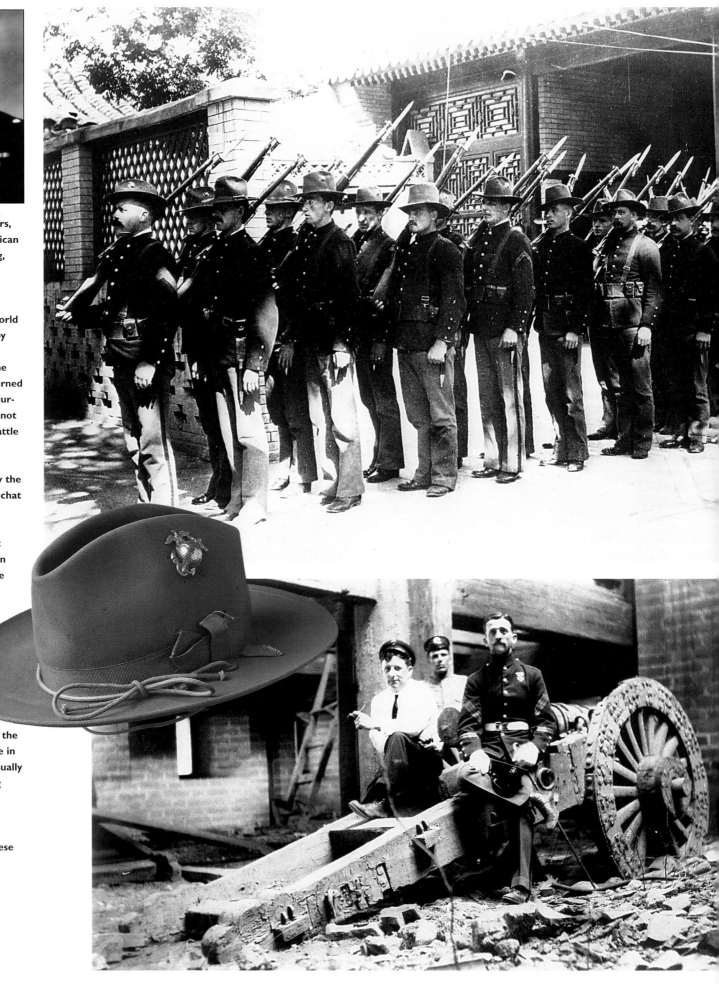

> "To our Marines fell the most difficult and dangerous portion of the defense by reason of our proximity to the great city wall and the main city gate. The Marines acquitted themselves nobly."
>
> *Mr. Edwin N. Conger, U.S. minister,*
>
> *commending the Marines for their part in defense of the Peking legations, 1900*

Royal and American Marines captured an arsenal after heavy skirmishing. When the British commander was wounded, Waller assumed command of the small multinational force.

Heavy fighting continued in Peking. The American legation was built against the high, thick "Tartar Wall" in the southwest corner of the Legation Quarter. British, German, and other legations were in the other quadrants. All sustained heavy attacks as international forces were building up to approximately six thousand, then eventually to more than eighteen thousand.

At one point, Marine Pvt Daniel Daly single-handedly held off attack after attack at his post on the Wall until reinforcements arrived, receiving his first of two Medals of Honor. Fighting in both Peking and Tientsin was fierce. In Tientsin, the city's double rows of ancient walls presented formidable obstacles as American, British, and Japanese Marines fought virtually side by side. Another conglomerate force was finally able to reenter Peking and relieve the hard-hit legations and their defending Marines.

From that major encounter off and on until the beginning of World War II, five hundred American Marines were stationed to protect the U.S. legation in the Chinese capital (thus the beginning of the Marines' additional role as embassy guards). In Shanghai, the larger contingent grew to become the 4th Marine Regiment, which moved to reinforce Gen Douglas MacArthur's American-Filipino army in Manila just days before the Japanese forced the United States into World War II. They, too, were

China Relief Expedition Medal

Medal of Honor, 1914

ABOVE: Henry Lewis Hulbert wears the Medal of Honor awarded to him as a private on 1 April 1899, during the Philippine Insurrection. Hulbert, by then a first lieutenant, was killed at Blanc Mont on 4 October 1918, and was posthumously awarded the Navy Cross and the Croix de Guerre.

BELOW: Marine machine-gun crew manning a belt-fed, .30-caliber Colt machine gun mounted on a tripod, circa 1917.

M1905 COLT .38-CALIBER REVOLVER

A double-action, 6-shot revolver, the M1905 was the first revolver to be manufactured expressly for the Marine Corps. It was used by Marines as the primary sidearm during the Philippine Insurrection and in action in the Caribbean, but performed unsatisfactorily.

M1909 COLT .45-CALIBER REVOLVER

The double-action M1909 was issued as a replacement for the insufficiently powerful .38-caliber M1905 as the primary sidearm of the U.S. military in 1909. It was used until the adoption of the Colt M1911 semiautomatic pistol in 1911.

M1895 COLT MACHINE GUN

A 6mm machine gun manufactured by Colt Arms from a Browning design and converted to .30 caliber as the M1898. Also called the Potato Digger for its downward-moving gas-activated lever. It is belt fed and tripod mounted.

BUCKLEY   UPSHUR   CAMPBELL   GREEN
PATTERSON   WISE CARPENTER   DUNLAP   BRECKINRIDGE   TURRILL   TRACY   WALLACE   EGAN   BERRY   DIETER   SMALL   HALFORD   BERKLEY
BANNON   NEVILLE   MOSES   McKELVEY   WILLIAMS

ABOVE: A unit portrait of the 2d Marine Regiment officers taken during the Spanish-American War.

LEFT: A hard-bitten crew of Marines from D Company, 1st Marine Regiment, in 1901. These men were the first Marines at Subic Bay, Philippines. They have just returned from service with the China Relief Expedition against the Boxer Rebellion of 1900. Seated, left to right: Cpl Jack McDonald, Pvts Wolf, Tingley, Hajek, Hunt. Standing, left to right: Cpl James A. Bevan, Pvts Orsoba, Ormsby, Moon, Laub, Casey, Sgt James Bell.

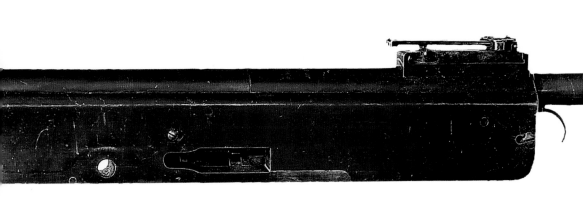

RIGHT: Marine Guard Detachment aboard the USS *Massachusetts,* circa 1890s. Attired in dress blues with white spiked helmets, gloves, and belts, they were the honor guard posted on the quarterdeck for a ceremony, standing at the parade-rest position indicated by the Manual of Arms at that time.

BOTTOM, RIGHT: Marine noncommissioned officers "chowing down" in the Navy petty officers' mess aboard the USS *Massachusetts.*

RIGHT: Enlisted dress helmet, 1892–1904. This is the white summer version of the spiked helmet.

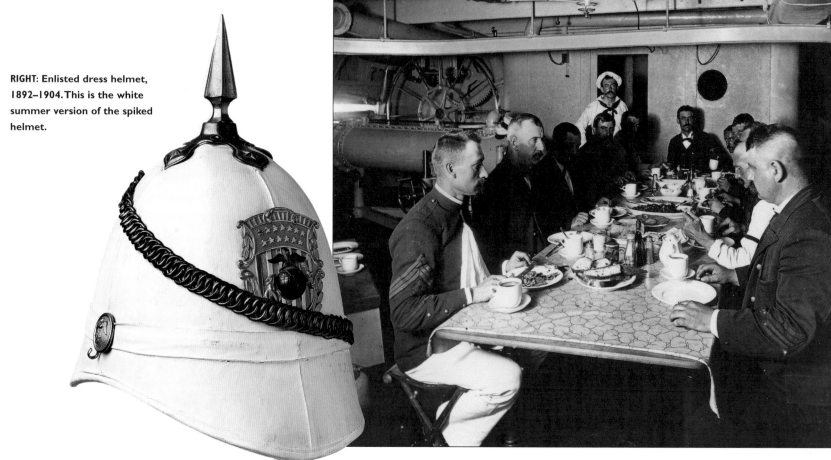

captured with MacArthur's remaining forces (including American Army nurses) by the Japanese on Corregidor and were forced to make the infamous sixty-mile Bataan Death March with other Army and Filipino troops in May 1942.

BEGINNINGS OF THE ADVANCED BASE FORCE

In order to clear up once and for all the status of the Marine Corps vis-à-vis its relation to both the Army and the Navy, on 12 November 1908 President Theodore Roosevelt issued Executive Order 969. It decreed that Marines were to (1) garrison Navy yards in the United States and abroad; (2) be the first line of mobile defense beyond the continental United States; (3) man defenses at advanced bases beyond U.S. shores; (4) garrison the Isthmian Canal Zone in Panama; (5) provide garrisons and expeditionary forces in peacetime; and (6) serve on naval ships. It was also made clear that "small transport ships would be available for the sole purpose and exclusive use of the Marine Corps." Although the Corps had been struggling since 1798 for its continued existence, these orders went a long way toward permanently establishing its missions. President Roosevelt understood Marines. He said in reference to them, "Far

ABOVE: U.S. Marines of ships' detachments on parade in Australia during a stopover on the 1907–1909 around-the-world cruise of the "Great White Fleet." President Theodore Roosevelt persuaded Congress to appropriate only half the funds needed for the venture, but he sent the fleet anyway, and when funds ran out asked Congress to pay for the ships' return trip. It was a tremendous public relations feat for the new American Navy and solidified America's new role as a world power.

LEFT: The Navy 4-inch deck gun in action. The gun was employed for harbor defense for Advanced Base Force (ABF) maneuvers on Culebra Island, Puerto Rico, 1913–1914.

ABOVE, INSET: A Marine
private in dress blues at
the turn of the century.
The photograph was printed
from a glass-plate negative;
the muted colors are a result
of hand-tinting the print.

LEFT: U.S. Marines from
1st Regiment return from
camp at Santa Rita River,
Olongapo, Philippines, 27
January 1910.

better it is to dare mighty things, to win glorious triumphs, even though checkered by failure, than to take rank with those poor spirits who neither enjoy much nor suffer much, because they live in the gray twilight that knows not victory nor defeat."

After much foot-dragging and hassling with the Navy, an Advanced Base Force (ABF) exercise was finally conducted under new CMC William Biddle on Culebra Island, Puerto Rico, in 1914. Despite the lack of necessary heavy equipment such as trucks and surfboats for unloading, Col George Barnett's brigade set up shore, base, and inland perimeter defenses in record time. When the exercise commenced, the umpires began grading Marine efforts very favorably against the attacking naval force, including its assaulting Marines. Thus, the ABF concept—so long in

implementation—spelled success. It not only sealed this most important mission for the Marine Corps, but also loosed the purse strings of Congress for increasing the Corps and ensured the Navy's grudging acceptance of increased ship transport for Marines.

Barnett was elevated immediately to major general and commandant. With Annapolis classmate Col John A. Lejeune as his assistant, Barnett worked closely with Assistant Secretary of the Navy Franklin D. Roosevelt to prepare the Marine Corps along with the Navy for potential hostilities in Europe and the Pacific.

Following the turn of the century, certain internal changes had also been instituted in the Corps. Khaki uniforms were adopted for tropical duty; a khaki flannel shirt replaced the Army blue;

BOTTOM: Whether in peace or war, Marines are always honing their landing skills. Here, in the Philippines in 1911, they practice pulling slip boats onto the beach.

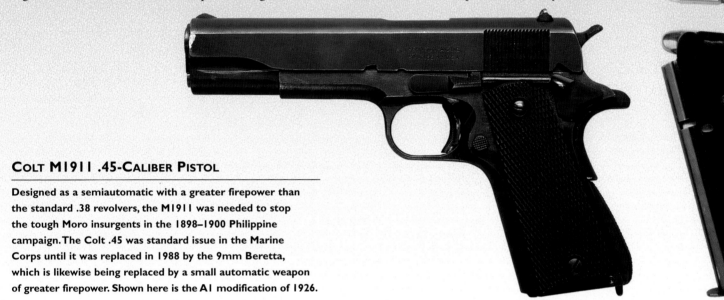

COLT M1911 .45-CALIBER PISTOL

Designed as a semiautomatic with a greater firepower than the standard .38 revolvers, the M1911 was needed to stop the tough Moro insurgents in the 1898–1900 Philippine campaign. The Colt .45 was standard issue in the Marine Corps until it was replaced in 1988 by the 9mm Beretta, which is likewise being replaced by a small automatic weapon of greater firepower. Shown here is the A1 modification of 1926.

U.S.M.C. Expeditionary Force landing stores on beach at Cavacao. P.I.

the emblem on the soft-brim field hat was placed in the front; and a standing-collar khaki blouse was added, as was a bell-crowned visor cap to replace the spiked helmet. A four-dent "Montana peak" hat with stiff brim was adopted in 1912, as was the color forest green for the service uniform. The old, crumbling Marine Barracks at 8th and I Streets were rebuilt in brick in 1912 and stand to this day. The Krag-Jorgensen rifle was replaced by the Springfield M1903, and marksmanship was emphasized. As ABF planning grew after Culebra, additional funds were procured in 1916 for tractor-drawn artillery, trucks, weaponry, and armored cars, as well as improved technical, communication, and aviation units.

EXPEDITIONARY ACTIONS AND "BANANA REPUBLIC WARS"

Through 1917 the Marines conducted a multitude of military excursions. The Panama battalion was dispatched first to Nicaragua, then to Cuba to quell an insurrection, then back to Nicaragua to secure a legitimate election. They then proceeded to Veracruz, Mexico, to prevent German arms from being unloaded to use to unseat the Mexican president. The Marines landed, assisted by companies of sailors, and had "the situation well in hand" (as described in the press) when the Army arrived.

OPPOSITE: A Marine detachment aboard the USS *California*, which landed at Pinto, Nicaragua, in August 1912 to protect American lives and property from insurgent disturbances.

BELOW: A 1912 photograph taken in Panama of Lt Alexander A. Vandegrift (second from left) and three other officers. Vandegrift would rise to major general, commanding the 1st MarDiv on Guadalcanal in the first U.S. counteroffensive of World War II, for which he received the Medal of Honor. He also rose to commandant, serving from 1944 through 1947.

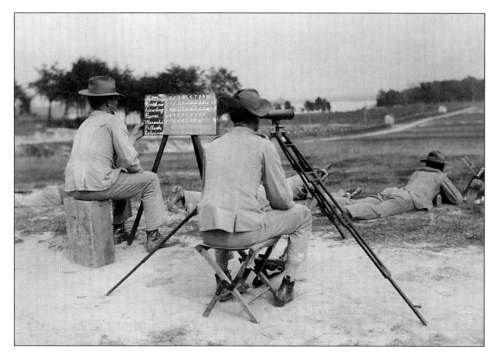

LEFT: Marine firing range, pre-1912. Instructor-spotters tally on a chalkboard the individual scores of Marines firing the .30-caliber Springfield M1903s. At the time, Marine Corps emphasis on marksmanship impressed all the other services. Almost all Marines who went off to the Spanish-American War and World War I wore marksmanship badges.

Marksmanship was emphasized in the early 1900s to the extent that, in 1909, the *Army and Navy Journal* pointed out that the ratio of skilled marksmen in the Corps made the Marines the best shooters in the world. It went on to publish an anonymous poem:

> With a hitch to his trouserloons,
> and a seaman's roll in his gait,
> His handiest tool a Lee straight-pull;
> his home of armor plate.
> Cavalry, guns and foot,
> he one and all combines
> as he charges the foe ashore
> or fights the water mines.
> No gay parade for him,
> his world a watery sheen,
> A rootin', tootin',
> cuttin', shootin',
> Uncle Sam Marine.

RIGHT: Chalk scoreboard used for marksmanship training. The number 5 is either a "possible" (i.e., a bulls-eye) or the number of shots of a 5-round clip that hit the rings of the target. The numbers 1–10 across the top are the "relays," or the number of clips, for each shooter's firing.

LEFT: Recruiting posters by Sidney H. Reisenberg (far left) and noted early-twentieth-century advertising illustrator Joseph C. Leyendecker (near left).

BELOW: Marine artillery battery, with rifles slung across their backs, preparing to "man the drags," that is, move their pieces themselves without the help of draft horses to pull the ropes. An ammunition cart can be seen in the lower right of the photograph.

ABOVE: The "Number One" gun crew of C Company, 2d Regiment, with their 3-inch naval landing gun, at Marine Barracks, Panama, 1913.

RIGHT: A portly Col Joseph H. Pendleton on horseback in 1913 at Guantanamo Bay, Cuba. Pendleton commanded the 2d Regiment of the 2d Provisional Brigade of Marines on temporary duty.

LEFT: Acting Military Governor BGen Harry Lee, USMC (front, extreme right), and his executive and military staffs in the Dominican Republic capital.

BELOW: Marines employed this French 155mm GPF M1918 gun. The gun was used as coastal and field artillery from 1918 through 1942.

Many weak and small Caribbean nations had been defaulting on their debts, and the European countries that had financed them attempted to force restitution. President Teddy Roosevelt's corollary to the Monroe Doctrine thus was put into operation: "The U.S. had the responsibility to force Latin governments to protect foreign lives and pay foreign debts" in order to prevent European powers from establishing a foothold in the hemisphere, as well as to separate parties in a civil war. Venezuela and the Dominican Republic collapsed, as did Haiti.

It was in Haiti where the Marine presence may have been felt most and was sustained for the longest time. In 1914, Marines landed in Port-au-Prince, Haiti's capital, to relieve its treasury of $500,000 and take it for "safe-keeping." When an ensuing election elicited a rebellion, Marines again landed, this time two hundred of them under Capt Smedley Butler and a young Lt Alexander Vandegrift. In clearing the island of rebel "Cacos," they patrolled and engaged in numerous firefights. On 18 November, at the high promontory called Montagne Noir, upon which the fortress Fort Rivière had been built in the eighteenth

RIGHT, TOP: A tugboat nudges a transport loaded with the 1st Marine Brigade shipping out for Veracruz, Mexico, in 1914. Marines took the Mexican city on the Gulf of Mexico and, joined by the Army, continued to stabilize parts of the country and to block moves by the Germans, three years before the United States became engaged in the war in Europe.

RIGHT, BOTTOM: Col L.W.T Waller and his brigade staff at Veracruz in 1915. In the front row, from left, are LtCol Wendell Neville, Col John Lejeune, Waller, LtCol Smedley Butler, and Maj Randolph Berkeley.

BELOW: Panoramic view of the encampment of the 4th Regiment at North Island, California, in 1914. The regiment was commanded by Col Joe Pendleton.

OPPOSITE, LEFT AND RIGHT: Marine recruiting posters, circa 1914 and 1918.

century, Butler won his second Medal of Honor for a particularly fierce skirmish with the Cacos in which the rebel leader was killed.

A Haitian constabulary was established in 1915 and its first commandant of gendarmérie was Butler, who was promoted from Marine lieutenant colonel to Haitian major general. This benevolent "occupation" was to last well into the 1930s. A similar civil insurgency occurred in Spanish-speaking Santo Domingo on the opposite side of the island of Hispaniola from French-speaking Haiti. American Marines fought skirmishes there, restored stability, and stayed for eight years.

In 1911, Marine Corps aviation was born, eight years after the Wright brothers invented and successfully flew their flying machine. The Corps' first aero-

MEDAL OF HONOR

Gunnery Sergeant
DANIEL JOSEPH DALY (Second Award)
Fort Liberte, Haiti
22 October 1915

Serving with the 15th Company of Marines on 22 October 1915, GySgt Daniel Daly was one of the company to leave Fort Liberte, Haiti, for a six-day reconnaissance. After dark on the evening of 24 October, while crossing the river in a deep ravine, the detachment was suddenly fired upon from three sides by about 400 Cacos concealed in bushes about 100 yards from the fort. The Marine detachment fought its way forward to a good position, which it maintained during the night, although subjected to a continuous fire from the Cacos. At daybreak the Marines, in three squads, advanced in three different directions, surprising and scattering the Cacos in all directions. GySgt Daly fought with exceptional gallantry against heavy odds throughout this action.

RIGHT: A 1917 poster created for the Marine Corps by noted American illustrator James Montgomery Flagg. Along with scores of other leading American artists, Flagg contributed his talents to the war effort by painting such posters for all the armed forces.

BELOW: Poster by Sidney H. Reisenberg, 1916.

OPPOSITE, TOP: Unidentified Marine detachment in dress blues in front of a battleship's turret of three 14-inch guns, circa 1920s.

OPPOSITE, BOTTOM: Marine crew of a 5-inch broadside gun on an unidentified battleship. The powder bag is being loaded behind the shell already in the breech. Broadside guns were used for defense against torpedo attacks from destroyers and torpedo boats. Marines, who manned some of the secondary batteries on battleships and cruisers, would compete against Nany gun crews in tests of speed and accuracy. This competition inspired gunner excellence in the Navy.

travel?
adventure?
answer– Join the Marines!
ENLIST TO-DAY FOR 2-3 OR 4 YEARS

RIGHT: Marines firing M1902 3-inch guns in the Dominican Republic.

BELOW: The Marine artillery battery of M1902 3-inch guns in action in the Dominican Republic. This battery was part of a Marine combined arms air-ground team sent to the Dominican Republic to stabilize it against internal strife in 1916.

OPPOSITE, INSET: An armored car mounting a Lewis gun improvised by Marines, circa 1918.

plane was acquired and was flown by 1stLt Alfred A. Cunningham, who had received only an hour and forty-five minutes of instruction. The second aviator, Lt Bernard L. Smith, became the leader of the newly established Aviation Detachment in the ABF.

In 1913, CMC Biddle was instrumental in getting the Navy to allow the naval base at Port Royal, South Carolina, to be turned into the now well-renowned Parris Island Marine Recruit Training Depot. A similar one was set up on Mare Island, San Francisco, later to be transferred to San Diego. The National Defense Act of August 1916 entitled the Marine Corps to commission seven brigadier generals. Never more than four thousand strong throughout the nineteenth century, the Corps' strength grew to almost ten thousand shortly after the turn of the century.

Former president Teddy Roosevelt gratuitously praised the U.S. Marines as one of the three most

efficient military-constabulary forces in the world, along with the French Foreign Legion and the Royal Canadian Mounted Police. The Marines warmly welcomed such unsolicited—but well deserved—compliments.

As the Marine Corps organized itself more tightly and basked in public notoriety, its recruiting efforts emphasized serving from "the Spanish Main to the Orient," as well as being a warrior: "If you want to Fight! Join the Marines" and "First to Fight." The establishment in 1917 of a Marine recruiting publicity bureau in New York City prepared the way for the Corps' big moment, which came with the 1917 entry into the European war.

America's First Armored Vehicle

In 1914, at the beginning of World War I, First Lord of the Admiralty Winston Churchill landed a naval division of bluejackets and Marines on the Belgian coast. Their mission was to guard the British Army's debarkation ports from an extended flank of the German forces. Since the division had no horse cavalry for reconnaissance, motorcars were commandeered for the purpose. The motorcars soon sported mounted machine guns and armored shields, which proved so useful that a fully armored car with a machine gun in a rotating turret was requested. The result was the Rolls-Royce armored vehicle, which served well in Europe until trench warfare immobilized its movement. However, it continued to be useful in the flat, treeless terrain of the Middle East.

As a private venture, in 1915 the Armor Motor Car Company of Detroit developed an armored car that was a near copy of the Rolls. Called the King Armored Car, it was the first armored vehicle fielded by the American military. It combined the chassis of the King Motors luxury sedan with a powerful, for the day, V-8 engine. The revolving turret mounted a machine gun. The first two cars carried the M1895 Colt-Browning or the improved Marlin version. Later cars mounted the Lewis gun, characterized by its large, aluminum cooling shroud.

The Marines, aware of the British experience and ever ready to gain a combat edge by adopting or inventing the latest in weapons, tactics, or organization, sought out an armored car of their own. In 1916 Assistant Secretary of the Navy Franklin D. Roosevelt authorized the purchase of two cars for testing. Tests included road and cross-country mobility and landing over ramps attached to forty-foot Navy motor sailers, which were ships' boats driven by steam or petrol engines instead of oars or sails. When ramps were unavailable, the armor could be detached and the car could be manhandled piece by piece from boat to shore and reassembled.

The tests were considered successful and a total of eight cars were procured and assigned to the 1st Armored Car Squadron of the 1st Marines at Philadelphia, the mobile regiment of the Advanced Base Force and America's first armored unit. The cars were not, however, an unqualified success. Various mechanical problems existed and there was a lack of qualified mechanics for maintenance. The squadron never went to war and was disbanded in 1921. Five of the cars were used in Haiti and Santo Domingo until 1927, when they were returned to Quantico in well-worn condition and finally disposed of in 1934.

—BN

WORLD WAR I

With uncanny foresight, newly appointed commandant MajGen George Barnett had sent Marine officers to France in 1914 and 1915 to observe the fighting. Their reports spurred emphasis back at headquarters on the use of the machine gun, aviation, heavy artillery, trucks, and the techniques of trench warfare. The Marine Corps had four expeditionary regiments in the Caribbean and the Naval Appropriations Act of 1916 had authorized strength at 17,400 enlisted with appropriate officers—a welcome expansion.

Working in Barnett's favor toward doubling that number for the Corps were the pleas from the British and French for at least token American forces to bolster sagging Allied morale. The loss of supplies to submarine sinkings was affecting the British economy drastically, and the French were so weary of the stalemate trench war that whole units of their army were mutinying. The War Department raised one Army division—the 1st Expeditionary Division—and named Army MajGen John J. Pershing commander of the American Expeditionary Force (AEF). Against Army opposition, Barnett was able to get agreement that two Marine regiments would be added to the AEF. "First to Fight" once more, a seasoned though hastily raised 5th Marine Regiment at Philadelphia Navy Yard was the first American unit to sail for France, a month after war was declared.

When the United States was finally provoked to declare war on the Central powers on 6 April 1917 and to join the Allies in the stagnant three-year-old trench war on the European western front, young men flocked to recruiting offices to volunteer. The Marines, with their powerful slogans "Tell It to the Marines!" and "First to Fight," attracted swarms. To accommodate the masses, another training facility had to be created; it was subsequently built on six thousand acres leased around the little Virginia town of Quantico, thirty-five miles south of Washington, D.C. The additional 6th Marine Regiment was raised there in short order.

The Parris Island Marine Recruit Training Depot in South Carolina bulged with trainees. Thousands of volunteers had to be turned away, allowing the Marines to pick the cream of the crop. After the war, even the Army reported that Marines were better trained than their own draftees had been. One difference was that Marine recruit training concentrated two to three weeks on marksmanship, a feature that paid off in France. (Photographs of graduating companies show virtually every Marine wearing an expert rifleman, sharpshooter, or marksman badge.) The training was tough, demanding, and unpleasant in the semitropical heat among the palmettos and sand fleas on the barrier island. One recruit wrote home, "The first day I was at camp I was afraid I was going to die. The next two weeks my sole fear was that I wasn't

ABOVE: MajGen John A. Lejeune, initial commander of the 4th Marine Brigade, consisting of the 5th and 6th Regiments, that was attached to the U.S. Army 2d Infantry Division in France. AEF commander Gen Pershing was reluctant to use Marines and rejected Barnett's offer of a Marine division. After a twelve-month shakedown in country, ostensibly in training with French units, the Marines entered full-scale combat in June 1918, under Army command. A month later, after the battle of Belleau Wood, command of the Army 2d Division was given to Lejeune, who led it to final victory on 11 November 1918. In this photograph, Lejeune is shown wearing the Army 2d Division Indian Head patch on his left shoulder. The Marine Corps dropped patches soon after the war, only to have them reinstated twenty years later for all six of its own divisions in World War II. Lejeune served as commandant from 1920 through 1929.

LEFT: Weapons training at Quantico in 1917 included this exercise in field-stripping and reassembling a Lewis machine gun while blindfolded. The same exercise was assigned with the Springfield M1903 rifle. Such exercises were often lifesavers during night combat.

Sniping: World War I

The Marines began receiving the superbly accurate M1903 Springfield rifle in 1906. The improved long-range accuracy of the rifle made sniping at five hundred to one thousand yards a practicality.

By 1910 the Marine rifle team won second place in the National Matches and by 1911, first place. Naturally, these skills were turned to wartime use.

Springfields mounted with a variety of telescope sights accompanied the 5th and 6th Marines to France. Marine Elton E. Mackin of 67th Company, 2d Battalion, 5th Marines, wrote of a phase of the Belleau Wood battle: "A sniper fired—ours. He had a rifle with a telescopic sight…. Snipers threw long, carefully aimed shots. The leading man went down hard…his comrade jumped for cover…. The snipers kept up the fire."

After Belleau Wood, several Marine battalion commanders were promoted to colonel and detailed to command Army regiments. Col Frederic M. "Dopey" Wise commanded the 60th Infantry for the Argonne Forest offensive. He had encountered German snipers in the treetops at Belleau and anticipated that the same tactic would be used in the Argonne. With this in mind, he organized the best shots of each company as countersnipers to follow one hundred yards behind the attacking front line and watch the treetops. Fifty German snipers were knocked from the trees in a single attack.

—BN

Marine Corps Marksmanship Qualification Badges

| Rifle Expert | Pistol Expert | Rifle Sharpshooter | Pistol Sharpshooter | Rifle Marksman | Pistol Marksman |

SNIPERS' SCHOOL, UNITED STATES MARINES.
QUANTICO, VA. NOV 13TH 1918.
M. MARSDEN CANADIAN ARMY, SENIOR INSTRUCTOR.

M1903 .30-CALIBER SPRINGFIELD RIFLE

The M1903 Springfield was the favored rifle of the Marine Corps for the first half of the twentieth century. This 5-shot, bolt-action clip-fed rifle was very accurate and dependable, and was the infantryman's mainstay from World War I up through the early part of the Guadalcanal campaign in World War II, when it was replaced by the M1 Garand. Marine shooters still use the M1903 in shooting matches. The open-aperture battle-sight was designed by the Marine Corps. Early in World War I, a Kerr web gun-sling was used; this was later replaced by an adjustable leather Brady sling with brass double hooks.

ABOVE: A group photograph, taken a day before World War I ended, of the graduating members of the Scout Snipers' School at Quantico. Capt M.M. Marsden (second row, center, in Scottish cap) of the Canadian Army was the senior instructor. Sniping paid off handsomely during the war, and sniper training went on to become an integral part of tactical warfare in World War II and up through the Iraq War of 2003.

going to die. And after that I knew I'd never die because I'd become so hard that nothing could kill me." Marine Corps recruit training—"boot camp"— has continued in that vein ever since.

The Marine Corps Reserve came into being at this time, as did Reserve Women Marines, who took over administrative chores to release a male Marine for combat duty.

By 14 June 1917, the first contingent of American troops, the 5th Marine Regiment, was sailing for the French port of Saint-Nazaire. There, the regiment served temporarily as military police in the port city until its sister, the 6th Marine Regiment, could subsequently be raised to join it. The two regiments, plus a machine-gun battalion, then became the 4th Marine Brigade. CMC Barnett had successfully championed

doubling the Marine Corps and had even offered a permanent Marine division and aviation force to Gen Pershing, who refused it. Pershing did assign— although reluctantly—the Marine brigade to his rapidly expanding American Expeditionary Force, which would eventually grow to twenty-two infantry divisions of more than a million men. The 4th Marine Brigade was joined to the Army 2d Division, which with its own brigade swelled to twenty-eight thousand men. Depleted by casualties, British and French divisions at the time numbered only approximately ten thousand; therefore, the Marine brigade itself was comparable to an Allied division. With the withdrawal of Russia from the war and the defeat of the Italian armies in northern Italy, the Allies—Britain and France, who were strung across France from the

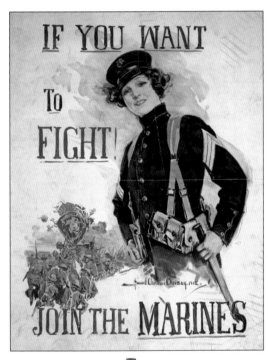

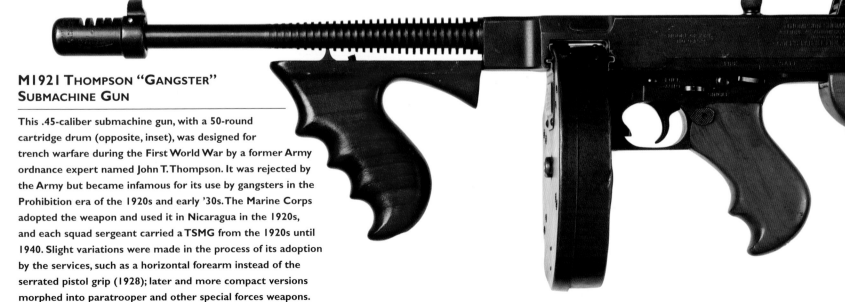

M1921 THOMPSON "GANGSTER" SUBMACHINE GUN

This .45-caliber submachine gun, with a 50-round cartridge drum (opposite, inset), was designed for trench warfare during the First World War by a former Army ordnance expert named John T. Thompson. It was rejected by the Army but became infamous for its use by gangsters in the Prohibition era of the 1920s and early '30s. The Marine Corps adopted the weapon and used it in Nicaragua in the 1920s, and each squad sergeant carried a TSMG from the 1920s until 1940. Slight variations were made in the process of its adoption by the services, such as a horizontal forearm instead of the serrated pistol grip (1928); later and more compact versions morphed into paratrooper and other special forces weapons.

Lust Formation on French soil

LEFT: The first American contingent—the 5th Marine Regiment—arrives at the French seaport of Saint-Nazaire on the Atlantic coast shortly after the United States declared war on Germany in April 1917. Their first duty was to secure supplies and organize before the 6th Regiment joined them to form the 4th Marine Brigade. The Marine brigade joined an Army brigade of the 2d Army Division, forming a 28,000-man heavy division in Pershing's twenty-two-division AEF. Pershing did everything possible to stifle Marine participation in the war, but political influence at HQMC prevailed. The Marine 5th Brigade was formed later, and arrived at Saint-Nazaire a day before the war ended.

LEFT: MajGen Omar Bundy (left), CO of the Army's 2d "Indian Head" Division, and Marine Col Albertus W. Catlin, CO, 6th Regiment, at Sommedieu, France, 30 April 1918. The two men wear "tin hats" and gas masks. Col Catlin is quoted as describing the gas mask in use as being like "fighting with a clothespin on your nose and a bag over your mouth."

To Patch or Not to Patch?

In France during World War I, the American Expeditionary Force (AEF) began the practice of having troops in large formations—divisions and higher—wear identifying patches on the left shoulders of their coats. The 2d Division AEF, which included the 4th Marine Brigade, was one of the first units to adopt the shoulder-sleeve insignia. Their patch pictured the head of an American Indian in a white star. The 5th Marine Brigade, which was in France but was denied a combat role, also adopted a distinctive red shoulder patch, with a globe, an anchor, and a black eagle carrying a red Roman numeral five. After the war the Army continued to wear the patches earned in France, but the Marines ceased the practice, being too small to need such distinctions.

During World War II, the Army, which fielded some ninety divisions and numerous other special units, again used the shoulder-sleeve insignia for easy identification. After Guadalcanal in early 1943, the 1st and 2d Marine Divisions also created shoulder patches. They were worn as a matter of pride and esprit de corps by wounded and transferred Marines returning stateside as being among the first to have seen combat. As the Corps burgeoned to half a million Marines, with six divisions and four aircraft wings, patches for these units were authorized, and soon the Amphibious Corps and Fleet Marine Force, Pacific, special units had their own patches.

While these devices still appear on unofficial signs and publications, the use of patches ceased after the war, never to reappear again. The reason given was that after World War I the Corps was somewhat split between those who had served in the 2d Division, AEF, and those who had not. The post–World War II commandant, Gen A.A. Vandegrift, did not want any such separation or rivalry among Marines. The addition of colored patches to the austere green and khaki uniforms was considered unnecessarily divisive and incompatible with the idea of one unified Corps, loyalty to one big "regiment." The eagle, globe, and anchor on cover and collar, the campaign ribbons, and the marksmanship badges were sufficient adornment for the Marines.

—BN

Headquarters Brigade

6th Machine Gun Battalion

Headquarters Battalion, 5th Marines

1st Battalion, 5th Marines

2d Battalion, 5th Marines

3d Battalion, 5th Marines

Machine Gun Company, 5th Marines

Supply Company, 5th Marines

Headquarters Company, 6th Marines

1st Battalion, 6th Marines

2d Battalion, 6th Marines

3d Battalion, 6th Marines

Machine Gun Company, 6th Marines

Supply Company, 6th Marines

LEFT, TOP: Army Capt George Matthews Harding's *The Capture of Blanc Mont Ridge* illustrates the chaotic nature of trench warfare and close combat. Harding was one of AEF's eight official combat artists and went on to become a Marine major and official combat artist in World War II. Although Harding was an eyewitness to many a battle, and the only one of the eight artists to use a camera as well as sketches to record combat, in this painting he illustrates the action from an impossible point of view. These could be either Army "doughboys" or Marines, since there is some indication of a Marine emblem on one helmet.

Forced by Gen Pershing to wear the same uniform as the Army (when their forest-green ones wore out), the Marines could distinguish one another only by the eagle, globe, and anchor emblems worn on their 1917 British-style steel helmets. Other innovations the Marines Corps made to the uniform, greatly influenced by their comrades in arms, were the over-the-shoulder Sam Browne belt, the "overseas" (fore and aft) cap, and the high collar of the coat rolled down to expose a shirt and field scarf (necktie).

LEFT, BOTTOM: A World War I Marine enlisted coat, made of wool kersey. Here, the coat is shown with M1910 web equipment and a British-type gas mask in the "alert" position.

ABOVE: Col Wendell C. Neville (left), CO, 5th Marine Regiment (future fourteenth CMC, succeeding Lejeune), and MajGen John A. Lejeune, CO, 2d Army Division, and thirteenth CMC. Col Neville took over command of the 4th Marine Brigade from Army BGen James G. Harbord after the first major battle, Belleau Wood. As promotions or reassignments ensued, Lejeune was assigned to command the U.S. Army 2d Division, which he did until the end of the war.

English Channel to Switzerland a short distance north of Paris—faced 191 German divisions on the western front.

As soon as American Army divisions began arriving, Pershing refused to let them be used piecemeal as fillers for Allied units. Nevertheless, he allowed the 1st, 2d, 26th, and 42d Divisions to be temporarily attached to the French for combat training and experience until the remainder of his twenty-two divisions arrived by the summer of 1918.

Newly promoted to lieutenant general, Pershing, ostensibly for logistical reasons, ordered the Marines to wear Army olive-drab uniforms when their own green uniforms wore out. Marines grudgingly obeyed, though they attached the Marine eagle, globe, and anchor insignia onto their helmets above the 2d Division emblem to mark their distinction from the Army. Their basic weapon was the Springfield M1903 .30-caliber rifle with bayonet. Their own automatic weapons, Lewis machine guns, were appropriated for installation for the gunner on the two-seater DeHavilland aircraft, so they were forced to use Chauchat automatic rifles and Hotchkiss machine

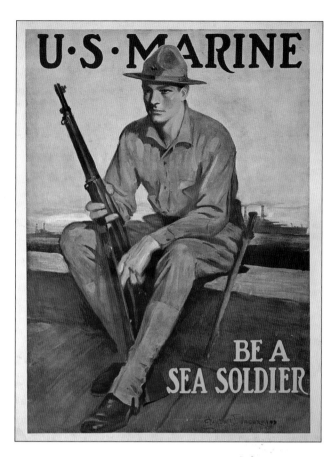

U·S·MARINE

BE A SEA SOLDIER

WORLD WAR I: THE WESTERN FRONT, 1914–1918

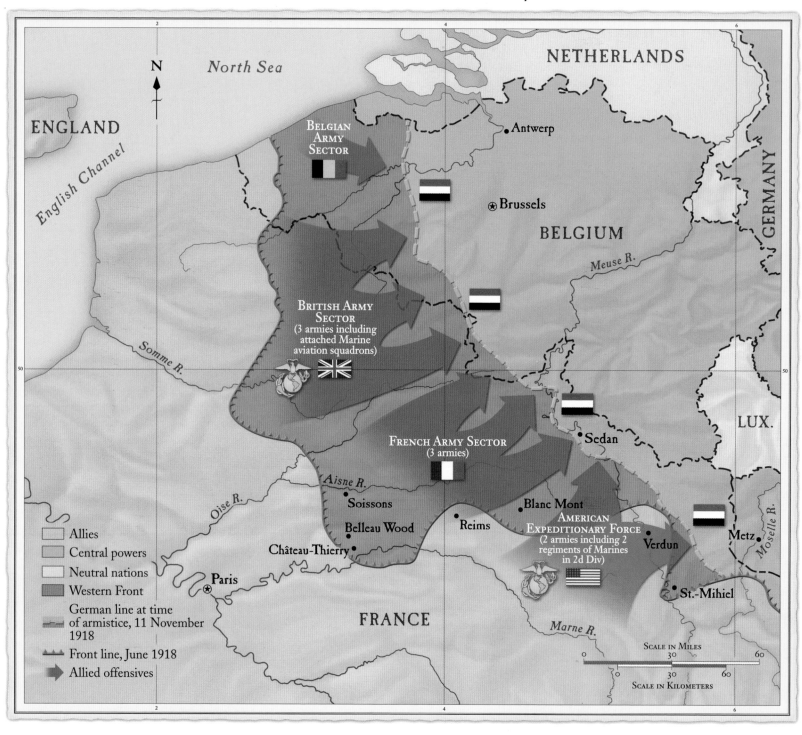

guns provided by the French. They had no trench mortars, no signal flares or Very (flare) pistols, and an inadequate supply of hand grenades; fortunately, they were issued gas masks.

In mid-March 1918, the 4th Marine Brigade, made up of the 5th and 6th Regiments (regiments have been referred to as "Marines" since 1930) of the 2d Army Division, was under the command of BGen Charles A. Doyen. On St. Patrick's Day 1918, the 280 officers and 9,168 enlisted of the brigade dug into positions next to French units near Saint-Mihiel, just southeast of the

previous battle site of Verdun astride the Paris-Metz road, which was a logical German avenue of attack. The Marines received their baptism in fire from the brunt of German probing attacks, including a poison-gas attack that killed forty. Nevertheless, their esprit de corps was high and they performed well. They were relieved on 9 April to join the Army 2d Division northeast of Paris.

When the commanding general of the French division to which they were attached near Château-Thierry learned of a pending German offensive, he

LEFT: An early photograph of the Marine 4th Brigade shortly after their arrival in France in early 1918. They are still in "Marine Green" uniforms and they carry Springfield M1903s and M1913 web equipment, and wear wrap puttees below the knees. The Marine 5th and 6th Regiments did extensive training with both the French and the British—even under fire—before being attached to the Army 2d Division and engaging in battle that June.

BELOW, LEFT: Marine poster from 1917 by C.B. Falls.

BELOW, RIGHT: Battle-hardened Marines pose with a German heavy mortar captured during the Battle of Belleau Wood in June and July 1918. The 2d Army Division, composed of the Marine 4th Brigade and an Army brigade—and later commanded by Marine MajGen John A. Lejeune—captured more enemy machine guns, mortars, and artillery than any other AEF unit.

PREMIERS au FEU MEANS IN FRENCH FIRST to FIGHT IN ENGLISH U.S. MARINES

MEDAL OF HONOR

**Gunnery Sergeant
EARNEST A. JANSON
Château-Thierry, France
6 June 1918**

For conspicuous
gallantry and intrepidity
above and beyond the call of
duty in action with the enemy
near Château-Thierry, France,
6 June 1918. Immediately
after the company to which
GySgt Ernest Janson
belonged had reached its
objective on Hill 142, several hostile counterattacks
were launched against
the line before the new
position had been
consolidated. Janson
was attempting to organize a
position on the north slope of the
hill when he saw twelve of the
enemy, armed with five light machine guns,
crawling toward his group. Giving the alarm,
he rushed the hostile detachment, bayoneted
the two leaders, and forced the others to
flee, abandoning their guns. His quick action,
initiative, and courage drove the enemy from
a position from which they could have swept
the hill with machine-gun fire and forced the
withdrawal of our troops.

LEFT: Navy-Marine Medal
of Honor of 1914. Note that
the thirteen stars of the
ribbon were worn on the
left side, nearest the heart.
GySgt Janson was awarded
both the Army and Navy-
Marine Medals of Honor
for his inspired initiative and
bravery at Belleau Wood. He
wears the Army medal in the
photograph at left.

panicked and suggested to the Marine commander
that the Marines withdraw with the French. Marine
Col Wendell Neville (although it is often attributed to
Capt Lloyd Williams) is reported to have responded
in his booming voice, "Retreat, hell. We just got here!"
That legendary retort reflected the aggressive Marine
attitude that was emulated in later wars.

The attacking Germans got their first taste of
Marine marksmanship on 2 June as their 28th Division
attacked along the Paris-Metz road. To their astonish-
ment, they began taking casualties at eight hundred
yards from the sharpshooting Marines, the new *Teufel
Hunden*, or "Devil Dogs," an apocryphal appellation as
much fabricated by Marines as by the enemy. Four
days later, the barely tested Devil Dogs charged
through a wheat field into a small hunting preserve
named Belleau Wood, laced with German machine
gun, rifle, and artillery fire. Marine casualties mounted
that day to one thousand—more than the Marine
Corps had lost in its entire previous 143-year history—
but they did not halt the advance. At one point, then-
sergeant Dan Daly, of Boxer Rebellion fame, who was
standing in front of his Marines, urged, "Come on you
sons of bitches! Do you want to live forever?" Such
legends were born of that weeklong battle, as was the
term "foxhole" for the shallow protective holes the
men scraped out for some protection from the rain of
enemy artillery shells. At another point, company commander (who later became a commandant) Clifton
Cates captured the bordering town of Bouresches and,
despite mounting casualties, managed to hold it. The
Germans were finally sent reeling back. However, by
18 June the 4th Brigade had been so decimated that it
was no longer battle-worthy and was relieved.

After the brigade had rested and the losses
were replaced, on 25 June, BGen James Harbord,
the Army temporary brigade commander, led the
brigade back into Belleau Wood. On 26 June, he issued
a message: "Belleau Wood now U.S. Marine Corps
entirely." The 4th Marine Brigade had suffered 112
officer and 4,598 enlisted casualties, 1,000 of whom
were killed in action.

On 30 June, the commander of the French 6th
Army decreed that "henceforth in all official papers,
Belleau Wood shall bear the name, 'Bois de la Brigade
de Marine.'"

During the battle Floyd Gibbons, a war correspondent for the Chicago *Tribune*, had been seriously
wounded and evacuated, but in his dispatches back to
his newspaper, his praise of the Marines in action was
so eloquent that it had much to do with the incredible
fame the Marines earned.

Another Notch Chateau Thierry

U.S. Marines

"Why in hell can't the Army do it if the Marines can? They are the same kind of men; why can't they be like Marines?"

Gen John J. "Black Jack" Pershing, 12 February 1918

BELOW: Marines of the 77th Company, 6th Machine Gun Battalion, on 2 June 1918 in the Château-Thierry sector with French soldiers (poilus).

LEFT: M1905 long bayonet used on M1903 Springfield and M1 Garand rifles until 1943.

ABOVE: A view of the village of Château-Thierry and the bridge over the Marne River that was blown up by U.S. troops, thus halting the German advance toward Paris.

RIGHT: Maj Thomas Holcomb's 2d Battalion, 6th Marines, rests following the Battle of Belleau Wood, the first battle of the war for the Marines and one of the bloodiest in Marine Corps history. The 4th Marine Brigade, composed of the 5th and 6th Marine regiments and part of the Army 2d Division, attacked on 6 June; by 18 June it had taken so many casualties— more than half its men—that it had to be relieved to recoup and replace its losses. To honor the bravery and sacrifice of the 4th Brigade, on 30 June the French Army officially changed the name of Belleau Wood to "Bois de la Brigade de Marine," and awarded both Marine regiments the Croix de Guerre with Palm. Holcomb rose to become the seventeenth commandant, serving from 1936 through the beginning of World War II.

VIEW OF CHATEAU THIERRY AND THE FAMOUS BRIDGE WHERE THE MARINE (DEVIL DOGS) STOPPED THE HUN HORDES ON THEIR MARCH ON PARIS.

PHOTOGRAPHED BY W. L. MANN   AUG. 25, 1919

NO. 102-F.   © MANN & LANDRY
325 N. HOWARD ST.
BALTIMORE, MD.

"What shall I say of the gallantry with which these Marines have fought!!! Of the slopes of Hill 142; of the Mares Farm; of the Bois de Belleau and the Village of Bouresches stained with their blood, and not only taken away from the Germans in the full tide of their advance against the French but held by my boys against counter attacks day after day and night after night. I cannot write of their splendid gallantry without tears coming to my eyes."

MajGen James G. Harbord, U.S. Army,
commander of the 4th Marine Brigade and then the 2d Division, AEF

Be Up-to-Date=Be A U. S. Marine

First to Change the Old Campaign Hat for the Modern Helmet

RIGHT, INSET: One of the best combat photographs to come out of the Great War, this dramatic photograph is sometimes said to be of Marines of the 5th Regiment and other times of the Army 1st Division in the Meuse-Argonne. It epitomizes the fierce fighting in World War I. If these were Marines, they would be manning a French M1916 37mm gun during the Battle of Belleau Wood, where their casualties in that monthlong combat exceeded all the casualties the Marine Corps had suffered since its inception in 1775. For their heroic action, which was reported in glowing terms by Chicago *Tribune* reporter Floyd Gibbons, who was also severely wounded, the Marines were awarded the Croix de Guerre, which entitles members of the 5th and 6th Marine Regiments to wear the fourragére over their left shoulder. The French government also changed the name of Belleau Wood to Bois de la Brigade de Marine ("Woods of the Marine Brigade") in their honor. Gibbons's story so highly praised the Marines that it catapulted the two Marine regiments (out of the AEF's sixty-six total) to public acclaim disproportionate (or so thought the Army) to their contribution.

RIGHT: Fighting in Belleau Wood was the heaviest the Marines had ever encountered. The constant shelling by enemy artillery and the crisscrossing, grazing fire of machine guns created a living hell. With very little natural protection, the Marines quickly learned to dig shallow holes in the dirt in which to lie, calling them foxholes, a name still in use today.

LEFT: Marine Pvt John Joseph Kelly of 78th Company, 6th Regiment, 2d Division, was awarded both an Army and a Navy Medal of Honor for his actions in the intense fighting at Blanc Mont, where, dashing one hundred yards in advance of the front line, he attacked an enemy machine-gun nest, killed the gunner and another member of the gun crew, and managed to return through the barrage of fire with eight prisoners. His Army Medal of Honor was pinned on his chest by Gen Pershing. Here, he wears the French Croix de Guerre with Palm, one of a number of foreign decorations he also received.

Fourragères and Waffenstillstandstag

For their gallant action at Belleau Wood, the two Marine regiments, the 5th and 6th, were awarded the Croix de Guerre by the French. To this day, those regiments are entitled to wear a braided rope, or fourragère, over their left shoulder with their service and dress uniforms to commemorate the award.

The Marine 4th Brigade, consisting of the 5th and 6th Regiments, was in combat a total of only thirty-four days, from early June through the capitulation of the Germans on 11 November 1918. The Allies termed the surrender the Armistice; the German word for it is *Waffenstillstandstag*—"Weapons Stand Still Day."

—HAC

RIGHT: A miniature fourragère pin, worn with the Croix de Guerre medal.

RIGHT: Marine aviators of the 1st Marine Aeronautic Company (for antisubmarine patrol) and the 1st Marine Aviation Squadron (flying land-based bombers) relax aboard a transport ship en route to Europe sometime in 1917. The Aeronautic Company was assigned to submarine patrol duty in the Azores off the Portuguese coast; the Aviation Squadron was assigned to northern Europe to augment British aviation. They flew American-built DeHavilland DH-4 biplanes, the only U.S.-manufactured aircraft to see combat in World War I. Marine aviation had no opportunity, however, to engage in the close air support for which it was trained. Note the aviator on the right: under his naval aviator's wings above his left breast pocket is an expert rifle badge. The Marine Corps has always prided itself on training its aviators first to be Marine infantrymen—and still does to this day.

RIGHT: Marine Maj Alfred Cunningham, the fifth Naval aviator and the first Marine aviator, stands before a DeHavilland DH-4 aeroplane. Cunningham was in charge of Marine aviation in Europe during the Great War.

Marine Corps Aviation in World War I

In January 1918, Maj Francis T. Evans sailed to Ponta Delgada in the Azores off the Portuguese coast with the 1st Marine Aeronautic Company, part of the Fixed Regiment of the ABF. It consisted of a squadron of ten American-made Curtiss R-6 and two N-9 seaplanes. There, the Marines flew routine antisubmarine patrols but never sighted an enemy *Unterseeboot*.

Under the first Marine aviator, Maj Alfred Cunningham, the 1st Marine Aviation Force landed near Calais, France, in January 1918 with four cadre squadrons to form the Northern Bombing Group, which was to operate with the British. They brought with them seventy-two unassembled, American-built DeHavilland DH-4 bombers and were assigned initially to Royal Air Force squadrons 217 and 218. Those who went to Squadron 213 flew British-made Sopwith Camel single-seater biplane fighters. In one month of combat, the Marine aviators flew fifty-seven bombing missions in their 340 airplanes, downed twelve German aircraft, suffered four killed in action, and had a pilot and rear-seat gunner receive Medals of Honor. Unfortunately, Marine aviation did not have the opportunity to support Marine ground units in battle as intended.

World War I–era
Navy/Marine Corps Aviator Wings

LEFT: Marine pilot Capt Robert Lytle (right) and his rear gunner, GySgt William Obs, stand beside their DeHavilland DH-4. A similar Marine crew, Lt Ralph Talbot and GySgt Robert G. Robinson, won Medals of Honor for shooting down German planes in a particularly fierce aerial dogfight.

BELOW: Marine DeHavilland DH-4s lined up on an airfield in the British zone near Belgium. Although the airplanes were British-designed, the seventy-two Marine planes were built in the United States and shipped to France disassembled and packed in crates. The two bomber squadrons and a Marine fighter squadron flying British-made Sopwith Camels were in combat for only one month but managed to down twelve enemy aircraft. They were awarded two Medals of Honor, and lost four killed in action.

MEDAL OF HONOR

SECOND LIEUTENANT RALPH TALBOT
Pittham, Belgium
14 October 1918

For exceptionally meritorious service and extraordinary heroism while attached to Squadron C, 1st Marine Aviation Force, in France. 2dLt Talbot participated in numerous air raids into enemy territory. On 8 October 1918, while on such a raid, he was attacked by nine enemy scouts, and in the fight that followed shot down an enemy plane. Also, on 14 October 1918, while on a raid over Pittham, Belgium, 2dLt Talbot and another plane became detached from the formation on account of motor trouble and were attacked by twelve enemy scouts. During the severe fight that followed, his plane shot down one of the enemy scouts. His observer was shot through the elbow and his gun jammed. 2dLt Talbot maneuvered to gain time for his observer to clear the jam with one hand, and then returned to the fight. The observer fought until shot twice, once in the stomach and once in the hip and then collapsed, 2dLt Talbot attacked the nearest enemy scout with his front guns and shot him down. With his observer unconscious and his motor failing, he dived to escape the balance of the enemy and crossed the German trenches at an altitude of fifty feet, landing at the nearest hospital to leave his observer, and then returning to his aerodrome.

RIGHT: Marine combat artist Jim Butcher's *Bombing of Thielt, Belgium* depicts a Marine bombing raid with DeHavillands over a rail yard during the First World War.

Teufel Hunden and the Bulldog Fountain

The ersatz German *Teufel Hunden* entered Marine Corps history as a result of a misspelling on a recruiting poster created by a well-meaning artist in Philadelphia. If Germans ever referred to the Marines as Devil Dogs, it cannot be proven. The term would properly be *Teufelshunde*, but there is no such expression in that language. Noted Marine historian BGen Edwin H. Simmons writes that he is doubtful of the reference, as Marines "began using the term in correspondence while or shortly after being in the quiet trenches near Verdun, before they had done anything to excite the admiration of the Germans. After Belleau Wood, the use became widespread even though the Germans never went further than a begrudging acceptance that with more training and better leadership the Marines would deserve the rating as assault troops." He reports that a German military historian speculates that the most likely reference might have been "they fight like devils from hell."

At the fountain of the Château Belleau, at the edge of the Wood, there is a small statue of a mastiff. As the legend grew, perhaps Marines associated this dog with the saying, thus embellishing it into the ubiquitous bulldog mascot at various bases.

As to appellations, the enemy was less than affectionately referred to as Huns, Boche, and Jerries. American soldiers were referred to as Yanks and Doughboys, while the British were referred to as Brits or Tommys, and the French, as Poilus.

—HAC

RIGHT: This, the most famous Marine recruiting poster to come out of World War I, helped to popularize the nickname *Teufel Hunden*, a moniker that, though misspelled, continues to be a Marine Corps icon. Following the Battle of Belleau Wood in July 1918—where the 5th and 6th Marines earned inordinate praise for their performance—a Philadelphia artist came up with this poster, most likely based on a rumor stating that the astounded Germans thought the Marines fought like "dogs of the devil." The term was probably never used by the Germans, but if it had been, it would have properly been spelled *Teufelshunde*.

OPPOSITE: Noted illustrator Tom Lovell joined the Marine Corps and worked at BGen Denig's Public Affairs office at HQMC during World War II. Here, he depicts Marines attacking Germans in close combat at the Battle of Belleau Wood.

The Last Offensive of the War

The 2d Army Division was attached to the French 4th Army and on 18 July captured a little town called Soissons before boring on to Saint-Mihiel and then going into reserve on 20 July. On 29 July, command of the Army division was turned over to Marine MajGen John A. Lejeune. By this time, the Germans were identifying American Marines as an elite, shock-troop Corps, and were doubly wary.

On 12 September, the 4th Marine Brigade attacked Saint-Mihiel and continued on to Sedan until relieved on 16 September. Ten days later, in Champagne, the French 4th Army, with the two Marine regiments of the U.S. 2d Army Division leading, went "over the top" in the Meuse-Argonne offensive, which turned out to be the final one of the war. In the first three days, the 5th and 6th Marines took their objectives, crashing through two defensive rings of the Hindenberg Line, saving a French unit at Essen Hook, and capturing the long, low mountain range of Blanc Mont and continuing down its slopes to Saint-Etienne on the 6th. In so doing, they sustained their heaviest casualties—2,538—and the French bestowed their coveted Croix de Guerre on the division for the third time. To this day, Marines of the 5th and 6th Regiments wear the green and red braided fourragère signifying this medal over the left shoulder of their service and dress uniforms.

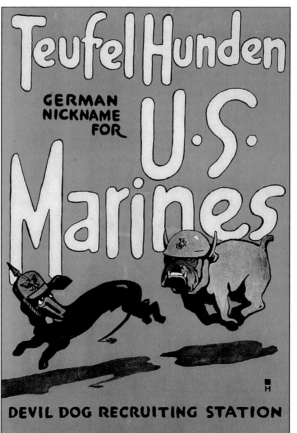

Rested, back up to strength, and back in the American 1st Army's V Corps on 1 November, the 5th and 6th Marine Regiments continued the attack. On the night of 10 November, they crossed the Meuse River to be in position for renewal of the fighting the next day. However, at 11 A.M. that day—the eleventh hour of the eleventh day of the eleventh month—the Germans surrendered, agreeing to an armistice.

Thus the bloody Marine victories of Château-Thierry, Belleau Wood, the Marne, Champagne, Soissons, Saint-Mihiel, Meuse-Argonne, and Blanc Mont entered the annals of Marine Corps lore.

ABOVE: In noted American illustrator F.C. Yohn's *The Last Night of the War*, battle-weary Marines cross the Meuse River on the night of 10–11 November 1918.

RIGHT: A map of the Belleau Wood area indicates machine gun positions, with intersecting lines of fire drawn in red. A young Marine lieutenant, who later became a general, drew the map at the kitchen table in a farmhouse that Marines occupied during the battle. The son of the owner of the farmhouse, now an elderly man but then a child of six, still proudly displays the map to visitors.

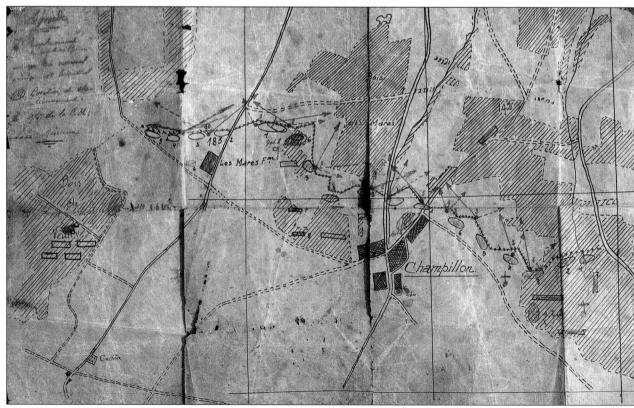

LEFT: Identity card issued to 2dLt Clifton B. Cates by the 2d Division Headquarters, AEF, upon his arrival in France.

"I have only two men out of my company and 20 out of some other company. We need support, but it is almost suicide to try to get it here as we are swept by machine gun fire and a constant barrage is on us. I have no one on my left and only a few on my right. I WILL HOLD."

2dLt Clifton B. Cates (later CMC), 96th Company, 6th Marines, 19 July 1918

LEFT: 2dLt Clifton B. Cates (fourth from left) was the hero of a part of the Battle of Belleau Wood. The little village of Bouresches, an important road junction on the right flank of the 5th Regiment, was taken and held by 2dLt Cates and his platoon. Withstanding vicious counterattacks and high on casualties as well as low on supplies and ammunition, Cates valiantly held his position despite overwhelming odds—virtually saving the day by preventing an enemy envelopment. Cates commanded the 4th MarDiv on Iwo Jima in World War II, and became the nineteenth commandant in 1948.

RIGHT: Capt John W. Thomason, Jr., in an early-1930s photograph. Thomason led a company of the 5th Regiment through the six months of combat in the First World War, and was cited for bravery with the Navy Cross and the Silver Star. An artist and writer, he later wrote and illustrated (see drawing below) the defining book about Marines in the Great War, *Fix Bayonets!*. The stories garnered him a national reputation and brought publicity and further fame to the Marine Corps in general. Col Thomason died early in World War II.

BELOW: Panoramic photograph of the 13th Regiment in Butler Colosseum at Quantico. The regiment trained to become part of the 5th Brigade, which reached France a day before the war ended.

SUMMARY

During the First World War, the Marine Corps grew to 76,000 and sent 32,000 to fight in France, including the 5th Brigade, which arrived in Saint-Nazaire on 11 November. The original 4th Brigade lost 2,459 killed in action and 8,907 wounded. (This averaged 1,200 killed per regiment, which would exceed the average of 750 killed per regiment in the battle of Iwo Jima in 1945. Both had roughly the same days "on the line": the two Marine regiments in France faced intermittent combat for a total of thirty-four days; in World War II, three Marine divisions of eight regiments were in continuous combat on Iwo Jima for thirty-five days, suffering 6,821 killed and 19,217 wounded.) Overall, in its six months in combat in France in World War I, the AEF lost 53,000 killed and more than 250,000 wounded. President Woodrow Wilson stated upon the Marines' homecoming in 1919: "The whole nation has reason to be proud of them."

How could two infantry regiments of fewer than 10,000 out of a total force of 1.3 million accrue such fame and recognition? Certainly the Marines' tight discipline, excellent marksmanship, and unwavering courage in the face of battle were singled out by both French allies and the German enemy, and press coverage played a big part as well. But perhaps the stamp that forever marked the Marines as the "Devil Dogs" of World War I was made by a captain who fought in every battle, John W. Thomason, Jr., of the

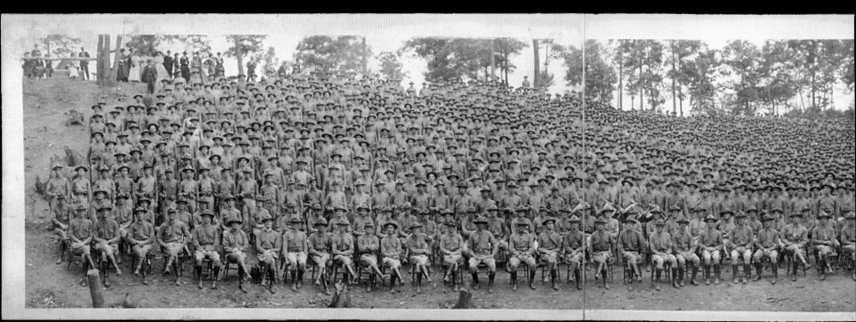

> ## "They were the old breed of American regular, regarding the service as home and war as an occupation."
>
> *Col John W. Thomason, Jr., 1926, referring to the Marines of 1918*

5th Marines. As a company commander, Thomason, besides being cited for bravery and awarded the Navy Cross, was also an artist and a writer. In the mid-1920s his self-illustrated book *Fix Bayonets!* was published by Scribner's, becoming an instant bestseller, and once again elevated the status of Marines in the public's eyes. The *New York Evening Post* raved: "Here is a book. Here is war… and here is the [Marine] as he is, was and always will be in terms of stress and strain and battle…. It runs straight as a cleaning rod. It is keen as a newly ground sword-bayonet. Splendid as the tale itself is, the illustrations all but tell the story themselves."

Overall, unwarlike America had risen to the occasion and its quickly mobilized and trained Army and Marines had distinguished themselves, to the relief and praise of the Allies and the consternation of the enemy. Twenty years later those same nations would go at one another again—sadly, over the same ground.

ABOVE: The "overseas cap," like that worn by MajGen Lejeune in the photo at left, was based on British caps in use during the war. More comfortable and far easier to stow than the rigid-frame barracks cap with visor, the overseas cap gained immediate popularity. The Marine emblem was worn on the left side; officers wore their small insignia of rank on the right.

LEFT: Gen Pershing awarding the Distinguished Service Medal to MajGen Lejeune for his leadership of the 2d U.S. Army Division, which included the 4th Marine Brigade.

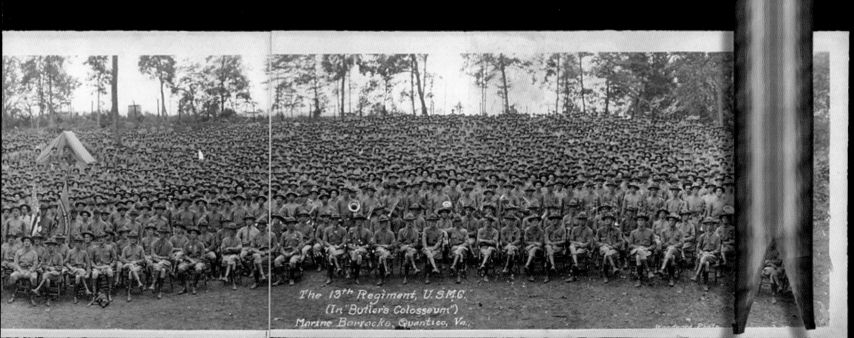

The 13th Regiment, U.S.M.C. (In "Butler's Colosseum") Marine Barracks, Quantico, Va.

BELOW: Marines during
the 1919 engagement with
the rebels of Charlemagne
Peralte in Haiti. The second
man from the right fires a
Lewis light machine gun.

"SEND IN THE MARINES"

In the middle of the Great War, in 1917, Allied Russia underwent a revolution. The resulting civil and governmental chaos caused it to cease hostilities against the Germans on the Eastern Front, thus freeing the Kaiser's armies to augment their lines against the Allies on the Western Front in France.

In the ensuing unrest, the United States sent Marines to Vladivostok in Siberia to forestall Japanese intrusion and to bolster anti-Bolshevik armies there. Meanwhile, in the Caribbean, the newly raised 7th and 9th Marines landed in Cuba that same year to protect strategic sugar cane plantations from German agents and dissident rebels. One battalion of Marines remained at Canaguey, near the Marine base at Guantanamo, until 1922. In 1918, the 9th Marines and its 3d Brigade headquarters group were dispatched with the 8th Marines to the Texas-Mexico border to prevent a suspected German-led Mexican attempt to reclaim the American Southwest. All of this widespread activity occurred while the Marine Corps was organizing the 4th Brigade for battle in France.

Haiti flared up again and the 2d Marines were sent to reinforce efforts to eliminate another Haitian insurrectionist, Charlemagne Peralte. Marine Cpl Herman Hanneken, disguised as a Caco rebel, tracked down and shot the rebel leader and brought his head back to Cap Haitien. Other Cacos soon rose up to take his place and the Marines had their hands full killing or capturing them. In these guerrilla clashes, Marines experimented with aerial dive-bombing. By attaching bomb racks to the wings of DeHavilland DH-4 and Curtiss "Jenny" biplanes, Marines were able to dive at forty-five-degree angles and release the bombs onto targets. In one such action, another Caco leader and two hundred of his followers were killed. In 1920, to avenge a rebel ambush of a Marine patrol and the voodoo ritual of roasting the American lieutenant's heart and liver, Marines found the Caco leader who committed the act and gunned him down. From that moment, a long period of peace ensued under the newly appointed U.S. High Commissioner, Marine BGen John H. Russell.

In Santo Domingo, however, insurrectionists kept arising. Marine patrols under Marine BGen Joe Pendleton's military government had to hunt down and eliminate rebel factions. In all, the full 2d Brigade on the island consisted of the 3d, 4th, and 15th Marines plus a squadron of six DH-4s and the 1st Armored Car Squadron of five King armored cars. The Marines engaged in two hundred firefights in 1918 in Santo Domingo. Under orders from President Wilson, however, the Marines pulled out completely by 1924, having trained a local *guardia* to replace them. Marines had suppressed rising dictatorships there and in Haiti, Cuba, and Nicaragua. They left behind a well-developed police force, improved roads, a hospital, and the foundation for a stable Dominican government.

In the 1920s, MajGen John A. Lejeune, who had led the Marine Brigade and Army 2nd Division in World War I, became commandant. He immediately emphasized Marine Corps readiness and the development of

Marine Corps Brevet Medal

LEFT: A company of Marines in the 1920s prepares for deployment. The Marines wear their campaign hats; their winter service caps lay on top of their "782 gear," or packs, on the ground, and their Springfield '03s are stacked on the right. The packs are actually model 1910 haversacks, and they were one of the most impractical items of equipment ever devised for marching. The pack itself was very heavy and cumbersome to wear. A Marine on the march would be unable to sit down while wearing the complete pack, as shown in the photograph.

M1918 .30-CALIBER BROWNING AUTOMATIC RIFLE (BAR)

The 20-shot gas-operated magazine-fed Browning Automatic Rifle gave tremendous firepower to a Marine squad. In World War II, the BAR would become the mainstay of the four-man Marine fire team. Each of the three squads in a platoon was made up of three such fire teams. Today, the Browning has been replaced by the M249 Squad Automatic Weapon (SAW), which fires a smaller caliber cartridge and has a higher rate of fire.

**1st Sergeant
1922–1944**

**Quartermaster Sergeant,
Supply
1859–1937**

**Drum Major
1935–1937**

LEFT: Marine Corps enlisted chevrons use an inverted "V" so they can be distinguished from the Navy's ratings, which use Vs that point downward. Building from a single V, for private first class, additional stripes denote corporal, then sergeant. Insignia for senior noncommissioned officers include curved "rockers" below the stripes: a single rocker denotes a staff sergeant; two rockers, a gunnery sergeant; and four, a sergeant major. In 1944, a third curved rocker was added for a first or master sergeant. Curved rockers denote combat arms; straight ones are used for specialty ranks. Seam-to-seam chevrons were discontinued in 1912 and were standardized in narrower form. The stripes are either gold, for dress uniforms, or forest green or khaki on a scarlet background, for service uniforms. They were stenciled in black on utilities.

RIGHT, TOP: U.S. Marines leave their experimental armored landing barge and head for shore during maneuvers of the Marine Corps Expeditionary Force (later Fleet Marine Corps) with the United States Fleet at Culebra, Puerto Rico, during the winter of 1923–1924.

RIGHT, BOTTOM: The 5th Marines hit the beach at Culebra during winter maneuvers, 1923–1924. The experience gained from amphibious exercises on Culebra helped win the 1942–1945 landings of the Pacific war.

Uniform Changes

Upon returning from France after the First World War, Marine Corps officers adopted the French-style pegged riding breeches and high-top field boots. The Sam Browne belt, with its strap across the right shoulder to support either a ceremonial sword or a holstered pistol on the left hip, had already become regulation. In 1928, following the British example, the stiff, stand-up collars of the officers' green and khaki uniforms were rolled down to form lapels, and a shirt with necktie (field scarf) was adopted. The dress blues and whites, however, retained the rigid collar. Officers also wore high boots or leather puttees, while the enlisted wore straight khaki or green trousers and, in the field, khaki leggings.

—BN

At right is Col John Magruder's illustration of a Marine officer of the 1920s and 1930s. He wears a campaign hat, a square-ended field scarf, high boots, riding breeches, and a bleached, suspender-supported web "782 gear" belt with first aid pouch, double-magazine holder, and water canteen. His leather holster has a long suspension from the belt to accommodate proper position when its wearer is on horseback. The leather strap through a hole in the bottom of the holster can be wrapped around the upper leg to secure it; here, it is wrapped around the holster to keep it out of the way. The adjustable lanyard hooked to the loop on the butt of the M1911 .45-caliber Colt semi-automatic pistol secured by the holster flap is over the left shoulder and cinched under the right armpit. This lanyard assures that the pistol will not be dropped during action; it also adds a great degree of stability in firing when stretched taut during aiming. If the figure portrayed is a Horse Marine, his right hand is holding a riding crop; however, it could also be a so-called swagger stick, a baton carried by British officers as an elite prop, and which was adopted by the Corps following World War I. The artist here has illustrated the fictional Archie Smallwood, the principal character in a number of popular books by Marine author Verle Ludwig about Marines between the wars, and it epitomizes the small, professional officer cadre that emerged to lead the Corps through the Second World War.

—HAC

ABOVE: A 1920s field hat, more commonly known as a campaign hat. The crown was circled by a matching ribbon with bow at the brim and was pinched in four quarters (a Montana Peak), instead of the previous fore-and-aft crease; the eagle, globe, and anchor emblem was reverted from the side to front and center. Introduced in 1914, the hat went through variations in 1917 and 1922, mostly in regard to the nape strap, which was finally settled upon as leather with an adjustable buckle worn in the front. The officer's version had a scarlet and gold silk cord knotted in the front with the two ends capped by acorn tassels. The campaign hat is still worn by male and female Marine drill instructors at the Marine recruit depots at Parris Island, South Carolina, and San Diego, California, and by members of Marine Corps shooting teams and marksmanship units.

The Air-Ground Team Is Not Light Infantry: 1925–1950

In the 1920s and 1930s, Marines always deployed as a combined arms force and, whenever possible, as an air-ground team. When the 4th Marines were in Shanghai from 1925 to 1941, deployment included heavy infantry weapons, machine guns, mortars, 1-pounder French M1916 37mm anti–machine-gun-nest guns, light Navy landing 3-inch guns, and a motorized unit. The Marine Legation Guard in Peking was similarly organized, with the addition of a horse cavalry unit for reconnaissance. In 1927, when civil war endangered the international settlement in Tientsin, BGen Smedley Butler's Marine brigade arrived in that North China city with artillery, tanks, engineers, and a fighter-bomber aviation squadron—hardly light infantry.

During these years, lesser deployments depended on Marine detachments on Navy battleships and cruisers. The battleships all carried a light 3-inch landing gun that, manned by bluejackets, would support a Marine-sailor landing party. Any serious landings would be supported by Navy or Marine aircraft from carriers.

The Fleet Marine Force (FMF) was formed in the 1930s with a brigade on each coast, at Quantico and at San Diego. The brigades consisted of an infantry regiment supported by an artillery battalion, tank company, antiaircraft battalion, engineer company, signal company, and chemical company with 4.2-inch mortars to fire smoke or gas shells. In 1941, these brigades were expanded into divisions, each with three regiments. It was heavy infantry, indeed, when Marine air units supported.

As the threat of Japan loomed in the Pacific, the defense of U.S. island bases was given priority. The antiaircraft units were expanded into defense battalions, each the equivalent of the ABF fixed regiment of 1914. In addition to the antiaircraft units, the defense battalions included machine guns for beach defense, 5- and 7-inch naval guns or 155mm M1918 GPF heavy field artillery for coastal defense, a tank platoon for counterattack, and aircraft squadrons on Midway, Wake, and Samoa Islands.

World War II in the Pacific validated the Marine Corps' air-ground team in major combat actions. In the Solomon Islands campaign, beginning with Guadalcanal, Marine divisions landed to seize airfields, which were further developed for early arriving Marine aviation units. These units then supported the divisions on land in seizing the island, defending it, and preparing the next island for invasion. This formula was repeated on island targets large enough for airfields: Saipan, Tinian, Guam, Peleliu, Iwo Jima, and Okinawa. For the assault on lesser islands, Navy aircraft from carriers supported the fight.

—BN

BELOW: Enlisted cap from the 3d Marine Brigade's 4th and 6th regiments, worn during the "China incident" of 1927. This cap with red piping (which was adopted in 1904) was worn by Capt Smedley Butler's orderly.

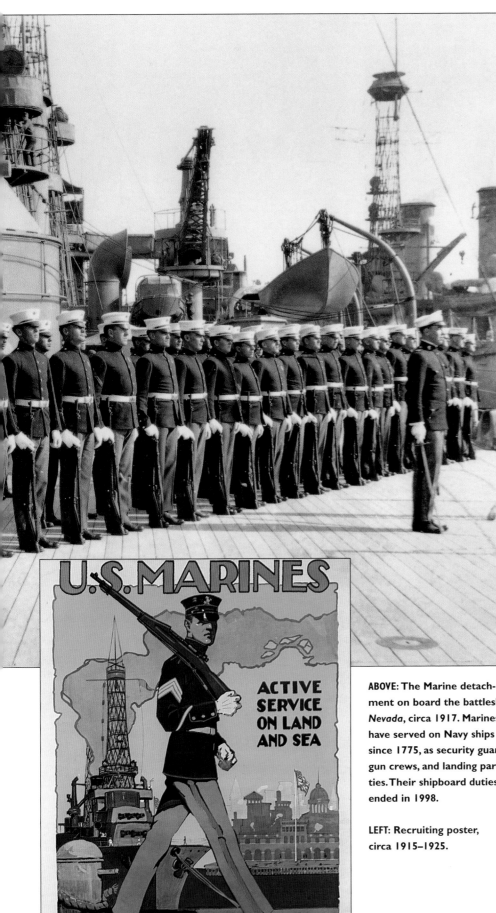

U.S. MARINES

ACTIVE SERVICE ON LAND AND SEA

ENLIST AT

RIGHT: Paymaster sergeant was a specialty rank, as indicated by the straight rockers. The design in the center is of stacked coins (silver dollar, half-dollar, quarter, nickel, dime) with a quill pen angled across them. The slant of the pen point indicated the front; therefore, this chevron would be worn on the right sleeve. The design on the left sleeve would be just the opposite. The gunnery sergeant insignia bears an emblem of an exploding bomb with crossed rifles. During World War II, two lower rockers were added to the insignia, and the rank was made equivalent to a technical sergeant. Gunnery sergeant—referred to individually as gunny—is still a highly revered rank. Along with master gunnery sergeant ("master guns"), the rank denotes weapons expertise, and both ranks are carried over into the commissioned warrant officer rank of "gunner." The assistant mess cook has a C for "cook" as its emblem. Three chevrons designate a field cook; one straight rocker would be added for chief cook, two for mess sergeant. Marine Band musicians wear insignia with a lyre emblem.

ABOVE: The Marine detachment on board the battleship *Nevada*, circa 1917. Marines have served on Navy ships since 1775, as security guards, gun crews, and landing parties. Their shipboard duties ended in 1998.

LEFT: Recruiting poster, circa 1915–1925.

Paymaster Sergeant
1908–1922

Gunnery Sergeant
1898–1937

Assistant Mess Cook

Musician, Marine Band
1935–1937

RIGHT: Capt Gilbert D. Hatfield and his Marine contingent pose following the battle of Ocotal in Nicaragua in July 1927. Hatfield and his forty-one Marines stood off guerrilla leader Augusto César Sandino's daylong attack with assistance from biplanes from VO-1M, which used a new Marine aviation technique of dive-bombing to great effect. One Marine was killed, while more than a hundred Sandinistas were killed or wounded.

RIGHT: 5th Marines about to embark on patrol in the Nicaraguan jungle in 1929. Their broad-brimmed field hats, khakis, and field shoes are augmented by non-standard-issue bandanas, a handy accessory in the intense tropical heat. Light on 782 gear themselves, their heavily laden pack mules carry their provisions, tents, and ammunition.

BELOW: Marines line up for "chow time" at Camp Neville, Maryland, 20 June 1912.

the natural role of the Corps: amphibious operations. He consolidated Marine Corps schools at Quantico on three levels: the Basic Course, the Company Officers' Course, and the Field Officers' Course. He also established the East Coast Expeditionary Force headquartered at the Marine Corps base at Quantico, Virginia, thus replacing the ABF at Philadelphia.

The 1920s and '30s were decades of great innovation for the Corps. An adjutant in the 4th Brigade in France, LtCol Earl Hancock "Pete" Ellis, a superb military strategist, had taken an unusual interest in the Pacific and the potential threat from the Empire of Japan. In 1905, Japan had won its war with Russia and was building up its naval fleet, despite the 1921 Washington Conference for the Limitation of Naval Armaments that limited the battleship ratio of Britain and the United States' five to Japan's three. Ellis wrote a plan for Advanced Base Operations in Micronesia in 1921, expanding on the earlier secret Navy contingency plan "Orange," which would

presage the war that occurred two decades later. The new plan called for the building of a large U.S. naval fleet and Fleet Marine Force to project eventual war in Japanese waters. On 12 May 1923, Ellis undertook a clandestine reconnoitering mission in mufti in the Japanese-ruled Palau island group and mysteriously disappeared.

As the amphibious, close-air support, and aerial dive-bombing doctrines were developing at Quantico, Marines were called upon twice to ride shotgun on U.S. railroads to stop a rash of mail train robberies in the 1920s. They were also called upon for a second campaign in Nicaragua from 1926 through 1933 to try to stabilize that country once more. Again there were skirmishes in the jungles against recalcitrant rebels under Augusto César Sandino. Marine aviators used their old reliable DH-4s and Vought Corsair O2U-1s to good effect, flying evacuation missions under hostile fire while perfecting their dive-bombing and strafing techniques.

ABOVE: LtCol Earl Hancock "Pete" Ellis was commissioned in the Marine Corps following the Spanish-American War. In 1913, while a student at the Naval War College, he participated in drafting a war plan against Japan. As a staff officer for MajGen Lejeune in World War I, he proved to be a brilliant tactician and strategist. In the 1930s, Ellis was sent on a secret mission ostensibly to scout the Japanese-held islands in Micronesia. He was never heard from again. Ellis Hall, at the Command and Staff school of the Marine Corps Education Command at Quantico, is named in his honor. The author painted this portrait of Ellis in 1952.

LEFT: "Horse Marines" of 52A Company, 5th Marines, in formation in front of the bastion where the year before they and their trained native *guardia* were besieged by Sandino and his guerrillas.

U·S·MARINES

SOME QUALIFY AS PILOTS

For further information apply

402 ATLANTIC AVENUE BOSTON, MASS.

In an improved O2U-1 biplane, 1stLt Christian Schilt performed an incredible feat of landing and taking off on the main street of the besieged village of Quilali—under fire. On ten round-trip missions, he brought in 1,400 pounds of supplies and ammunition and evacuated eighteen critically wounded Marines. Over the years, however, Sandino managed to attack and elude such legendary Marines as Herman Hanneken, Merritt Edson, and Lewis "Chesty" Puller.

Back to China: The Mid-1920s

In 1927 in China, the Kuomintang—the self-proclaimed Nationalist Party under Chiang Kai-shek, which had established a new government in the south—marched on Shanghai. Marine detachments from the Asiatic Fleet and the Philippines landed to protect the international settlement once again, and the 4th Marines arrived from San Diego. BGen Smedley Butler was in command of the 3d Brigade, composed of the 4th and 6th Regiments, an artillery battalion with 75mm field guns, tank and engineer platoons, and an air squadron of Boeing FB-1s from Guam. The brigade, less the 4th Marines, occupied Tientsin in North China. The Marine Legation Guard in Peking numbered five hundred and included a troop of so-called Horse Marines. Mounted on Mongolian ponies, these Marines brandished straight-bladed Army sabers in addition to their Springfield '03s and M1911 Colt .45-caliber pistols.

Legation duty, which was exotic yet mostly ceremonial, comfortable, and routine, was highly sought-after. The brigade left Tientsin when the emergency cooled, leaving the 4th Regiment in Shanghai. By this time the Japanese had invaded Manchuria and large parts of China. They had even sunk a U.S. river patrol boat, the USS *Panay*, on the Yangtze River in 1937. The *Panay* was headed for Nanking, and conjecture has it that the Japanese wanted to forestall knowledge of their atrocities there from leaking out. The 6th Marines were sent from San Diego to reinforce the 4th Marines in Shanghai. The winds of a big war were in the air.

In 1937, as the United States was monitoring Japanese moves in Asia, young Marine Capt Evans F. Carlson, who had served in Nicaragua and on two tours in China, and had learned the Mandarin dialect, caught the attention of President Roosevelt. Roosevelt sent Carlson on a clandestine mission in mufti to roam around China and mingle with both the

BELOW: "Horse Marines" of the Mounted Detachment of the Peking Legation at the Imperial Wall in the 1930s.

OPPOSITE, TOP: "China duty" in Shanghai and Peking between the world wars was a coveted assignment. Besides protecting U.S. nationals and property, it involved much "spit 'n' polish" parading and reviewing for visiting dignitaries. This 1937 photo shows a detachment of the 4th Marines in summer service in leggings and 1917-style steel helmets. The officers wear riding breeches and boots and carry the Colt 1911 .45-caliber pistols.

Small Wars Manual

The Marine Corps Schools in the early 1930s distilled and synthesized the Corps' experiences in intervention and pacification operations, mainly in the Caribbean and Central America. These studies resulted in a preliminary *Small Wars Manual* in 1935, with an upgraded, more formal manual issued in 1940. Every type of operation was covered in the manual, from the controlling policies and regulations to such details as organizing a government and civil affairs, humanitarian assistance, logistics, patrols, aviation, riverine operations, and withdrawal from a country.

Shortly after issuance of the 1940 edition, two events occurred: President Roosevelt announced his Good Neighbor Policy toward Latin America; and Mexico, ever sensitive to relations with its powerful neighbor to the north, got wind of the *Small Wars Manual*. Through diplomatic channels, Mexico loudly complained that the manual exacerbated relations with Latin America and was a denial of the Good Neighbor Policy.

The administration, mindful of retaining hemispheric harmony in view of pending war, ordered all copies of the manual to be gathered up and destroyed. The copies were collected from the officers holding them and from unit libraries and shipped to the Marine Corps Supply Depot in Philadelphia. Instead of destroying the copies, a canny supply sergeant of the type that never throws anything away stored them in an obscure corner of the depot. Twenty years later, as guerrilla warfare broke out in Vietnam and the United States sought answers to counter that threat, someone at the CIA, probably a former Marine, remembered the *Small Wars Manual*. Amazingly, a stock of the banned manual was discovered at the supply depot and made available. While it didn't win the war in Vietnam for us, its guidance was far better than relearning the lessons. Today, the manual has been republished privately.

—BN

BELOW: LtCol Harvey L. Miller wears the typical cotton khaki field uniform used in the late 1930s and into World War II: web pistol belt with suspenders, a binocular case strap across the right shoulder, and a chain anchored in the right chest pocket flap to a compass in the left pocket. The jaunty angle of the steel helmet and the way the chinstrap is worn indicates that he is in formation rather than in a field exercise. The insignia on his collar are the larger, shoulder type.

ABOVE: This 1933 photograph of Pfc Curtis W. Knight of the mounted legation guard in Peking epitomizes the spirit of China duty from the Boxer Rebellion through the 1930s. Pfc Knight is wearing his winter dress blues with riding breeches and leather puttees, and a white belt. His gloved hands rest on a World War I U.S. Army cavalry saber and he strikes a haughty pose for the camera.

BELOW: A view inside the Grumman "Ironworks" facility in Bethpage, Long Island, shows the production line in the background; in the foreground are two Marine F3F-2 "Flying Barrels." The Marine planes—the precursor of the famous F4F Wildcat—are marked with the insignia of Marine Fighting Squadron 1, VMF-1: note the eagle, globe, and anchor on the fuselage, below the cockpit canopy, and the red circle in the white star on the wing insignia. Armament consisted of one .30-caliber and one .50-caliber Browning machine gun, synchronized and cowl-mounted, and racks for two 116-pound bombs. The aircraft's hand-cranked retractable landing gear and enclosed cockpit gave it increased aerodynamics. The fuselage was a sealed construction that allowed it to float in water.

Nationalist and Communist armies. Carlson soon became enamored of the Communists' egalitarianism and programs of social reform. He recommended to the president social reforms for U.S. forces and, resigning from the Marine Corps, went about preaching pro-Chinese intervention. He later rejoined the Corps after Pearl Harbor and would end up commanding a Raider battalion on Guadalcanal. The only Communist-egalitarian reform he successfully instilled was the war cry "Gung ho!," which means "work together." This has stuck with the Marines ever since.

The Japanese had occupied Peking as early as 1927 and by 1931 had moved into Shanghai; Marines remained to protect the international settlements in each. Having conquered Manchuria and renamed it Manchukuo, the Japanese clashed on 8 August 1937 with Chinese troops, and the Sino-Japanese war was on. The 4th Marines went into action to man their perimeters and to protect the settlements. The 6th Regiment soon joined them, but the Marine positions became so perilous that the 6th Marines were ordered out in 1938, leaving the 4th surrounded by Japanese. By 1940, all other nationalities had withdrawn their legations' troops. At the end of November 1941, however, the

Headquarters Peking

Headquarters Tientsin

Company A

Company B

Company C

Company D

4th Marines, too, had to move out and reinforce Gen Douglas MacArthur's conglomerate American-Filipino army in Manila. The 4th did so and ended up in the infamous Bataan Death March when MacArthur's forces surrendered to the Japanese the following May. On 8 December the Marines of the 4th remaining in Peking were immediately interned as POWs.

Amphibious Doctrine Development

In 1933, now-CMC John Russell persuaded the Secretary of the Navy to designate the former ABF-Expeditionary Force as the FMF and as an integral part of the U.S. fleet. Reinforced brigades were to be stationed at Quantico and San Diego.

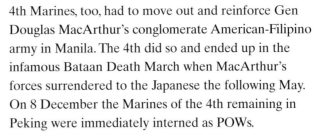

OPPOSITE, TOP: BGen Smedley Butler (left) and MajGen John A. Lejeune in winter dress blues shortly after World War I.

TOP RIGHT: China Marines of the 4th Regiment, in winter uniforms and gear with steel helmets with Marine emblems, pose in a sandbagged 37mm gun position overlooking Soo Chow Creek, Shanghai, during the 1937 troubles.

RIGHT: A "Mongolian piss-cutter," the unique headgear of the "Old Asiatic Station" Marines of the U.S. Legation Guard in Peking and Tientsin, China, during the first half of the twentieth century. Made of either lamb's wool or, reputedly, cat's fur, it was a necessary item in northern China and in Icelandic service. The diamond device has six distinctive designs that indicate the companies of the regiment on duty in China, up to the Second World War. This one is the device for the only officer of D Company, the detachment popularly referred to as the Horse Marines.

The "thinkers" at Quantico were collecting the results of their studies into codified doctrine, such as the Tentative Manual for Landing Operations. The Navy followed suit with their manual FTP-167 in 1938, and the Army brought out FM-100 in 1941, an edition almost verbatim to the Marine manual. All were based on Marine Corps studies and developments.

As these studies were being refined, equipment was also. A Florida Everglades amphibious tractor called the *Alligator* was adopted in 1940 and became the prototype LVT (Landing Vehicle, Tracked) of the Pacific war.

The Depression Years: 1930s

The Marine Corps continued to attract officers and enlisted men to its ranks after its heralded exploits during the war in France and the following action-filled decades in the Caribbean and the Orient. An adventurous life was undoubtedly appealing; combining that with the $125 a month earned by junior officers made it irresistible to some, as employment was generally hard to come by—even for college graduates—during the Great Depression. Many college men, unable to finish school because of financial problems, enlisted and became officers or senior NCOs prior to the coming war. Many also jumped at the opportunity to join as war clouds loomed in 1940 and '41.

For several decades the Corps had been looking to the Naval Academy at Annapolis for its young officers; however, when not enough could be garnered from the Navy school, the Corps opened the door to honor graduates of college Army and Navy ROTC programs and to land-grant and other state and private universities. The Platoon Leaders Class (PLC) was inaugurated in 1935, whereby a college male could sign up and be trained in two six-week summer sessions and receive his Reserve second lieutenant's commission upon graduation. A number of distinguished commandants came both from the Naval Academy and from military and civilian colleges during the period: Randolph Pate, David Shoup, Wallace Greene, Robert Cushman, and Leonard Chapman. Noted generals did also: Victor Krulak, Lewis Walt, Keith McCutcheon, Raymond Davis, Donn Robertson, William Jones, and Marion Carl.

Marines in the Movies

Capt John Thomason's book *Fix Bayonets!* popularized the image of the tough Marine and inspired portrayals of Marines in magazine stories. In the mid 1920s, playwright Laurence Stallings, a former Marine major wounded at Belleau Wood, also brought the tenacious fighting Marine to the silver screen, with such films as *The Big Parade* and *What Price Glory.* As Marine historian BGen E.H. Simmons describes it: "The public image of the United States Marine (usually played by Victor McLaglen or Wallace Beery) was taking shape: lean, sunburned, in faded khaki and rakish field hat, rattling through some jungled banana republic on board a narrow-gauge railroad, an '03 rifle in one hand and a bottle in the other, or in olive drab with a tin helmet and heavy marching order. Shouldering arms and starting down a shell-rutted road for the Western Front… turning to grin and wave good-bye to Mademoiselle, the innkeeper's gallant if naughty daughter."

Since 1925 the Marine Corps has offered varying degrees of consultation, personnel, and equipment to motion picture companies. Most of the resulting films fostered a positive image of the Corps; however, during Vietnam, some films were controversial and the Marines' public image was tarnished. This author, as a nine-year-old in 1937, was inspired by the movie *The Singing Marine,* which featured crooner Dick Powell. While the film was not totally sanctioned by the Corps, it included songs with unforgettable lyrics: Over the sea

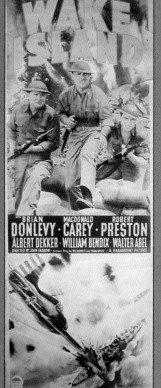

let's go, men! / We're shovin' right off, / We're shovin' right off again; / … It may be Shanghai, / Farewell and good bye; / Sally and Sue, don't be blue; / We'll just be gone for years and years and then, / We're shovin' right off for home again!

In the 1940s during and following World War II, actors John Wayne, Brian Donlevy, James Cagney, Dan Daly, Sterling Hayden, and even Marine hero Maj Peter Ortiz portrayed Marines on the silver screen. Before the climactic battle scene, these movie Marines would invariably end up in a bar brawl with a bunch of swabbies until the MPs arrived threatening to bust them to lower ranks as a consequence. These same upstarts would then inevitably go off and almost single-handedly win the battle against the Japanese.

—HAC

LEFT, BOTTOM: 20th Century Fox's 1943 film *Guadalcanal Diary* was based on novelist Richard Tregaskis' account of the August 1942 first counterattack against the Axis powers onto the Japanese-held Solomon Island of Guadalcanal in the South Pacific. It was an unusually accurate and non-melodramatic depiction of that battle.

LEFT, TOP: The film *Wake Island*, which came out in 1942 when U.S. morale was low due to Japanese victories in the Pacific, did much to elevate American spirits and to put the Marine Corps back in the forefront of the American public's mind.

LEFT AND INSET: The most unforgettable Marine World War II movie—and possibly the most frequently rerun on television—is the *Sands of Iwo Jima*. John Wayne's performance as the paradigm of platoon sergeants, Marine SSgt Stryker, has become iconic. Oddly, the majority of the battle scenes feature real Marine SSgt Norman Hatch's film footage shot on Tarawa. The film has Stryker and his Marines fighting their way up Mt. Surubachi (see below)—SSgt Stryker is ultimately killed in the process. The photograph below is a production still taken during the filming on the Hollywood set.

A GREAT HUMAN STORY
....MAKES A MIGHTY
MOTION PICTURE

THE MARINES' GREATEST HOUR

SANDS OF IWO JIMA

starring
JOHN WAYNE

co-starring
JOHN AGAR · ADELE MARA · FORREST TUCKER

with
WALLY CASSELL · JAMES BROWN · RICHARD WEBB · ARTHUR FRANZ
JULIE BISHOP · JAMES HOLDEN · PETER COE · RICHARD JAECKEL

A REPUBLIC PICTURE

chapter four

The Second World War: 1941–1945

"If the Battle of Waterloo was won on the playing fields of Eton, the Japanese bases in the Pacific were captured on the beaches of the Caribbean [Culebra and Vieques]."

LtGen Holland M. Smith, 1949

After its brief, hard-fought moment in the spotlight in France during the "war to end all wars," the Marine Corps took center stage in the Pacific battles of the second worldwide conflagration of the twentieth century.

From its 1798 inception up to World War II, the U.S. Marine Corps had engaged in more than 180 combat operations around the world. With the exception of the American Revolution, the War of 1812, and the Civil War, America's wars and military engagements up to 1941 had been fought on foreign soil against foreigners. The Mexican-American War was distant enough and affected so few Americans as to be an abstraction, while the proximity of Cuba elicited all sorts of jingoistic exhortations for war. In World War I, the nation was incensed enough to rise to the occasion, even swallowing the inordinate number of casualties that were ultimately suffered.

The American involvement in World War II stemmed from something entirely different— something America had never before experienced: a surprise attack on its own soil. The reaction to this shocking event was electrifying and galvanizing. The nation of 130 million Americans unified as never before, raised an unprecedented armed force, and fought the war all over the globe until Nazi, Fascist, and Imperial aggression was decisively and unconditionally defeated. The Allied effort was perceived as a righteous cause: Good against Evil.

Two of the opening episodes of the conflict— Pearl Harbor and Wake Island—demonstrated American fiber and showed the enemy what it would be up against. Having been caught off guard by the surprise attack, sailors at the naval base at Pearl Harbor, adjacent to Honolulu and other Army, Army Air Corps, and Marine installations on Oahu in the Hawaiian Islands, dished back what they could; heroically, civilians did, too. On tiny Wake Island, in the central Pacific, the small Marine ground defense unit and aviation squadron protecting the Navy and its civilian construction crew gave the attacking Japanese a battle they had not bargained for.

WAR IN EUROPE AND ASIA

Although numerous invasions, civil wars, and other up-risings—such as Soviet pogroms, the Japanese invasion of China, Italy's invasion of Ethiopia and Albania, the Spanish Civil War, the German Anschluss of Austria, and the annexation of the Rhineland and Sudetenland—presaged World War II, it was Nazi German Chancellor Adolf Hitler's blitzkrieg ("lightning war") attack across the Polish border on 1 September 1939 that brought almost all major nations into the most horrendous war the world had ever experienced.

As former Allies Britain and France braced shoulder-to-shoulder once more, President Roosevelt

ALWAYS ON THE ALERT

AT SEA ON LAND IN THE AIR

U·S·MARINES

ABOVE: The second most senior Marine officer on board the *Arizona* when it was hit was Maj Alan Shapley (shown above in the rank of lieutenant general). On 6 December Shapley received orders transferring him to the 2d MarDiv, but he remained aboard an extra day to play in a baseball game against the team from the USS *Enterprise*. When the battlewagon was hit on 7 December, many were blown into the water. In the confusion that followed, Shapely helped many men make their way to the safety of a pipeline attached to Ford Island. One of those men was a fellow Marine, Cpl Earl Nightingale. When Nightingale's strength began to give out as he swam for the pipeline, he told Shapley to save himself. But Shapley refused to leave him, and pulled Nightingale to safety. Shapley survived the attack and was awarded a Silver Star for "meritorious conduct at the peril of his own life."

PAGE 167: An early World War II Marine recruiting poster depicting a Marine manning a Browning M2 water-cooled .50-caliber machine gun.

proclaimed a "limited national emergency" and began expanding the U.S. armed forces. The Marine Corps jumped from 18,000 to 25,000, then was augmented by the call-up of its Organized Reserve of 5,240. The following year Congress inaugurated the universal military draft for all eligible males.

In December 1940, CMC MajGen Thomas Holcomb designated the East Coast 1st Marine Brigade as the 1st Marine Division (1st MarDiv). He did likewise on the West Coast with the 2d Marine Brigade at San Diego, which became the 2d Marine Division (2d MarDiv). (Four more divisions would be raised in the coming war.) Facilities for both were expanded: adding Camp Lejeune in North Carolina and Camps Pendleton, Elliott, and Gillespie in southern California, with nearby aircraft wings at Cherry Point and El Toro, respectively. A provisional brigade of the 6th Marines landed in Iceland in July 1941 to free British troops for their Home Defense, a deal FDR and Prime Minister Winston Churchill worked out along with lend-lease and the exchange of fifty U.S. WWI destroyers for access to British bases in the Western Hemisphere in the short period of U.S. neutrality.

Eight months later, the brigade was relieved by a unit of the U.S. Army and joined other Marine units that were concentrating on amphibious warfare in the Pacific theater. American military planners had been aware of a possible Japanese threat in the Pacific since World War I. Marine defense battalions had already been stationed in the Hawaiian Islands, as well as on Guam, Samoa, Wake Island, Midway, Johnston, and Palmyra Atoll. In response to Japanese expansion into China in the 1920s and 1930s and refusal of the U.S. demand to withdraw from the Dutch East Indies, FDR froze assets and embargoed oil and scrap-metal exports to Japan in 1941. By December of that year, tensions were already running high.

PEARL HARBOR: A DAY OF INFAMY

From the dastardly Japanese surprise attack on 7 December 1941 well into the summer of the following year, the advancing Japanese army and naval forces overwhelmed and captured the meager American and Allied forces in the western Pacific.

In a ninety-minute assault over Oahu, two waves of almost two hundred Japanese aircraft, each from task forces aboard six aircraft carriers 250 miles north

of the island, attacked every American military installation. Marines aboard naval ships and those of the defense battalions responded quickly by firing whatever weapons they could muster, most of which had been locked away along with the ammunition that peaceful early Sunday morning. At Ewa Mooring Mast Field, Marine Aircraft Group 21, consisting of fighter, scout-bomber, and utility squadrons, was caught with all its aircraft neatly lined up—making them easy to defend against saboteurs but inviting targets for the strafing Zeros. Because Japanese pilots used Ewa as a final target to expend all ordnance, no Marine aircraft were able to get airborne. In all, 265 American warplanes were destroyed. Seventeen Army Air Corps Curtiss P-40s managed to get aloft and accounted for eleven of the twenty-nine

OPPOSITE, INSET: The USS *Arizona* taking a direct bomb hit in its below-deck magazine from attacking Japanese planes at Pearl Harbor, 7 December 1941. Of the 109 Marines that were killed during the attack on Pearl Harbor, 71 of them were from the USS *Arizona*, the majority of which were killed when the ship's forward magazine exploded. An additional 69 Marines were wounded on various ships, harbor installations, and airfields.

BACKGROUND: The *Arizona* four days later, settled on the bottom of Pearl Harbor with 1,100 of its crew entombed in its hull. The above-water superstructure was later removed, while the hull remained as a submerged sarcophagus. After the war, a memorial was built above the hull, allowing visitors to peer down into the remains.

RIGHT: Panoramic view of the aerial dive-bombing and torpedo attack on the almost defenseless berthed capital ships of the U.S. Pacific Fleet shortly after 8 AM on what should have been a quiet Sunday morning. The small black specks clustered above the anchored ships indicate that the attackers were met with some return Navy and Marine defensive antiaircraft fire.

RIGHT, CENTER: The bugle used by Marine Pvt Roy F.W. Rieck at Marine Barracks to sound general quarters when the aerial attack began. The bugle is the old regulation USMC bugle in the key of G.

BELOW: Skin fabric from a Marine SB2U-3 scout-bomber that was heavily damaged during the attack on the airfield at Ewa.

enemy torpedo planes, dive-bombers, and fighters that were shot down. All eight U.S. battleships anchored dockside at Battleship Row were bombed or torpedoed out of commission. Three were sunk, the *Oklahoma* capsized, and the *Arizona* settled to the bottom. Ten of the other ninety-six ships in the harbor were severely damaged. Fortunately, all three U.S. aircraft carriers were at sea. American losses totaled 2,403 killed and 1,178 wounded; 108 Marines from ships' detachments were killed, another 4 were killed from aerial attack, and 64 were wounded. Marine gunners, both at the Ewa air station and on the cruiser *Helena*, downed a total of four Japanese aircraft.

(Ironically, the aerial attack was copied exactly from a 1932 U.S. Navy simulated demonstration exercise to which Japanese naval observers had been invited.)

The U.S. carrier *Enterprise*, on its way back from delivering twelve new Wildcat fighter planes of a Marine squadron to Wake Island, heard of the attack on its radio: "This is no drill." Sadly, nine of its own planes that had flown off to land back at Pearl Harbor after the attack were mistakenly shot down by U.S. Navy gunners, who thought they were returning Japanese planes.

Concurrent with the attacks on Pearl Harbor on 7 and 8 December 1941 (it was the next day across the international date line in the western Pacific), the Japanese launched assaults and captured Burma, Malaya, Singapore, Java, and Hong Kong and invaded the Philippines. One hundred and forty Marines in Peking, forty-seven in Tientsin, and seventeen in Chinwangtao were immediately interned. In preparation for a major attack on the U.S. island of Midway in mid-1942, the Japanese attacked and occupied the American-held islands of Attu and Kiska in the Aleutian chain off Alaska.

BELOW: An hour and a half after the surprise attack, stunned Marines at Marine Barracks at Pearl Harbor muster on the parade grounds. Billowing smoke from the devastation rises from nearby Battleship Row. By this point, Marine weapons and ammunition lockers have been opened, and an organized defense is being inaugurated.

Advanced Base Force to Defense Battalions

Following the Spanish-American War, the Advanced Base Force (ABF) concept was developed to guard overseas U.S. holdings acquired from Spain against Japanese expansionism in the Pacific and against German designs on territory in Latin America and the Caribbean.

The final organization of the ABF of 1914 consisted of one fixed regiment and one mobile regiment. The former included coast defense guns, beach defense machine guns and field artillery, harbor mines and searchlights, and reconnaissance aircraft. The mobile regiment consisted of infantry that would counterattack a successful enemy landing. In 1914 units were landed at Veracruz, Mexico, and during World War I elements of the ABF provided a harbor defense and a seaplane antisubmarine patrol in the Azores while the main ABF was poised for deployment to the Adriatic Sea. The ABF was disbanded in 1919.

In the 1930s the Orange Plan for a possible war in the Pacific with Japan called for the defense of Midway and Wake islands west of Hawaii, and the atolls of Johnston and Palmyra to the southwest. In 1937 battalion-size detachments for the defense of these islands were discussed. By 1938 the Orange Plan included a 456-man Marine force at Midway, armed with 5-inch guns, 3-inch antiaircraft (AA) guns, searchlights, and machine guns. Wake had a similarly armed garrison of 445 Marines, while Johnston and Palmyra had only 135 Marines each, with just antiaircraft guns, searchlights, and machine guns.

By 1940 the Orange Plan was superseded by the Rainbow Plan for a joint Anglo-American war against Germany, Italy, and Japan in both hemispheres. The proposed base defenses were not yet implemented, but in 1939 the Marine Corps Schools at Quantico organized the ten-month Base Defense Course. The fiscal mood of Congress at the time was such that it was more willing to allocate funds

for defensive rather than offensive units. CMC Thomas Holcomb seized the opportunity to increase the strength of the Corps by requesting money for base defense.

The first 900-man defense battalion (DefBn) was organized by expanding the 3-inch AA battery, which included searchlights, sound detectors, and .50-caliber AA machine guns. Five-inch Navy battleship broadside guns were manned by former seagoing Marines experienced in their use, and heavy .30-caliber machine guns and gunners for beach defense were added.

By 1941 the 3-inch AA guns began to be replaced by the new 90mm guns, and some of the 5-inch guns by M1918 GPF 155mm guns or the new M1A1 155mm "Long Toms." The sound-detecting microphones, unreliable in the constant ocean winds of the Pacific Islands, began to be replaced by the early SCR-268 and then the improved SCR-270 RADARs. The average defense battalion grew to 1,372

ABOVE: The Marine 3-inch antiaircraft gun emplacement No. 3 of Battery F, 3d Defense Battalion, on Bougainville suffered two direct bomb hits on the same day in November 1943. The Japanese "Daisy Cutter" bombs that knocked this gun out of commission exploded a few feet above the ground. All six Marines of the gun crew were killed.

Marines by mid-war. Each manned eight 155mm guns, twelve 90mm AA guns, sixteen 40mm light AA guns, and twenty-eight 20mm and thirty-five .50-caliber AA machine guns, plus, in some battalions, eight M3 light tanks.

Battalions began deploying well before the Japanese attack on Pearl Harbor: the 7th DefBn to Samoa in March of 1941, the 5th to Iceland in June, the 6th to Midway, the 1st to Wake, Johnston, and Palmyra. In early 1942 the 2d reinforced Samoa, the 8th was deployed to the Wallis Islands, the 4th to Espírito Santo, the 3d to Guadalcanal with the 1st MarDiv, and the 5th from Iceland to Tulagi in the Solomons in September 1942. In all, 19 defense battalions were raised, totaling 26,685 Marines and Navy medical personnel.

By April 1944, with the Japanese fleet and airpower all but destroyed, the battalions reorganized. The 155mm coast defense groups became heavy field artillery battalions for general support at corps level. The 90mm AA groups became antiaircraft battalions and continued in that role. Remaining Marines became replacements according to individual specialties.

The success and value of the defense battalion early in World War II validated the ABF concept, which originated in the early twentieth century and came to fruition in its midyears. The gallant defense of Wake by elements of the 1st Defense Battalion cost Japan dearly and inspired America after the humiliation of Pearl Harbor. The defense of Midway by the 6th and Guadalcanal by the 3d brought further honors to the Corps, as did the effective antiaircraft fire throughout the Solomons while Japanese airpower was still a factor.

—BN

51st Defense Battalion Insignia

52d Defense Battalion Insignia

ABOVE: Marines on Guadalcanal man a 90mm antiaircraft gun. Used constantly to fire at Japanese planes during the air raids that occurred many times a day, the gun could also be effectively employed as high-velocity ground artillery, when necessary.

LEFT: Marines of 9th Defense Battalion man a .50-caliber water-cooled Browning M2 antiaircraft gun during the invasion of Rendova in the Solomon Islands on 30 June 1943. This gun took down the first Japanese plane to attack the American invasion force. This photograph was taken just minutes before an air raid alarm sounded to indicate yet another in a series of relentless enemy air raids.

ABOVE: Members of the ill-fated 1st Marine Defense Battalion pose for a group photograph in mid-1941, prior to shipping out for duty on Wake Island. They would be American heroes all by the end of the year. Forty-three of the 453 lost their lives; all the others were imprisoned by the Japanese.

OPPOSITE: A letter from Capt Henry Talmage Elrod to his wife and carried off Wake Island by Maj Walter L.J. Bayler, the last man to leave the island. Elrod was killed in action three days after this letter was written.

WAKE ISLAND: "SEND US MORE JAPS"

Reeling from the sucker punches of the simultaneous sneak attacks on Pearl Harbor, Guam, Manila, and, later in January, on Midway Island, the United States momentarily stunned an overconfident aggressor with a reflexive uppercut from its tight little fist on Wake Island. The Marine garrison there had been under siege for two full weeks before the inevitable invasion, and the apocryphal reply to the question of what they needed was "Send us more Japs." The quip was a filler portion of normal radio message traffic, but the words were picked up by the American press and lifted the country's wounded pride sky-high. The phrase joined the ranks of other rally cries, such as "Don't give up the ship" and "Don't fire until you see the whites of their eyes." The Marines were quick to claim it as their own.

The last thing Wake Island needed during the final weeks of December 1941 was more Japanese—the island was being bombarded by Japanese aircraft day and night, and after repelling one invasion attempt, the meager Marine and Navy defense forces were bracing for the final blow. Still, newspaper and "Extra" headlines blazoned: MARINES STILL HOLD WAKE; MARINES AT WAKE SINK TWO JAP SHIPS; WAKE ISLAND RESISTS ATTACK; JAPANESE SHIPS FLEE FROM BATTLE. These and other such banners riveted Marine heroics forever in the minds of the public.

What the Japanese anticipated as an easy seizure of this isolated U.S. naval facility 2,300 miles due west of Pearl Harbor instead ended up being an unexpected and bloody battle. Fragments of the fight were fed through military radio traffic to Pearl Harbor, then to the press. Overall communications in 1941, however, were very primitive by today's standards. Submarine telegraphic cable had connected the United States to England since 1858 and to Japan since 1903. The first round-the-world cable and wireless company had put a station on Midway Island in 1903, but not on Wake. Furthermore, transatlantic telephone cable had been laid to Europe in 1927, but none had spanned the Pacific. A thousand miles of underwater cable stretched from Pearl Harbor to Midway in 1941, but again none to Wake. Military long- and short-range radio was effective between surface and air units, but, being of amplitude modulation, it wasn't always clear or reliable. Under ideal atmospheric conditions, shortwave radio transmissions can reach about halfway around the Earth but are subject to much interference. Radar was new and Wake had none. Official radio message traffic was limited to succinct and sparse communications, with no superfluous details.

Just days before the island fell, communications expert Maj Walter L.J. Bayler was ordered to depart in the only PBY seaplane that managed, under a low ceiling, to fly and land in the inner lagoon. Bayler was needed on Midway; his debriefing and most likely his full description of the battle to that point fed the insatiable press. The full story of the heroic stand of 453 Marines, 69 sailors, and the 1,200-man civilian construction crew was not pieced together until after the war, however, when, after almost four years of brutal captivity, Navy Cdr Winfield S. Cunningham and Marine CO Maj James P. Devereux wrote their own versions.

MEDAL OF HONOR

CAPTAIN HENRY TALMAGE ELROD
Wake Island
8–23 December 1941

For conspicuous gallantry and intrepidity at the risk of his life above and beyond the call of duty while attached to Marine Fighting Squadron 211, during action against enemy Japanese land, surface, and aerial units at Wake Island, 8 to 23 December 1941. Engaging vastly superior forces of enemy bombers and warships on 9 and 12 December, Capt Elrod shot down two of a flight of twenty-two hostile planes and, executing repeated bombing and strafing runs at extremely low altitude and close range, succeeded in inflicting deadly damage upon a large Japanese vessel, thereby sinking the first major warship to be destroyed by small-caliber bombs delivered from a fighter-type aircraft. When his plane was disabled by hostile fire and no other ships were operative, Capt Elrod assumed command of one flank of the line set up in defiance of the enemy landing and, conducting a brilliant defense, enabled his men to hold their positions and repulse intense hostile fusillades to provide covering fire for unarmed ammunition carriers. Capturing an automatic weapon during one enemy rush in force, he gave his own firearm to one of his men and fought on vigorously against the Japanese. Responsible in a large measure for the strength of his sector's gallant resistance, on 23 December, Capt Elrod led his men with bold aggressiveness until he fell, mortally wounded. His superb skill as a pilot, daring leadership, and unswerving devotion to duty distinguished him among the defenders of Wake Island, and his valiant conduct reflects the highest credit upon himself and the U.S. Naval Service.

AIR MAIL

UNITED STATES NAVY

Saturday, 20 December, 1941

My Dearest Darling Sweetheart

I never suspected this afternoon when I wrote my other short note that I would be sitting down writing another tonight. But here we are. I just got in a few minutes ago and have just learned that Walt Bayler is returning and he has kindly consented to deliver this personally, so I am very thankful for the moment.

Of course there isn't a lot of news that I can write about. And you probably know more real news than I do anyhow. I am missing you terribly and am undergoing a few new experiences but also is everyone else. We have had considerable rain today and it is still cloudy. The wind has been very low however. The weather on the whole is nothing to complain about but I would like to see a good old fashioned typhoon sweep this entire area.

I imagine there is an awful lot of whitewashing going on now in high places. It certainly will be a criminal shame if they succeed in covering over everything.

I am writing this in something of a hurry and under somewhat difficult circumstances. I'll think of a million things that I should have said after I have gone to bed tonight. But I want to say that I love you and you alone always and . . . . or so. Give my love to

ABOVE: A depiction by aviation illustrator John D. Shaw of the airstrip on Wake during the heroic defense by VMF-211. The Grumman F4F-3 Wildcat was the Marines' and Navy's first-line fighter, having recently replaced the less effective bi-wing Brewster Buffalos. Although not as maneuverable or as fast as the Japanese Zero, the Wildcat was better armed and protected, and proved to be very effective against enemy bombers.

BELOW: First lieutenant bars and eagle, globe, and anchor collar/cap emblem worn by Woodrow M. Kessler while CO of Battery B, 1st Defense Battalion, during the siege of Wake Island. The 5-inch guns of the defense battalion took a heavy toll on Japanese aircraft and ships.

ABOVE: The twelve original Wildcats were cannibalized when damaged to keep the remaining ones flying. When the last plane became inoperable, squadron leader Maj Paul S. Putnam had his pilots join Maj Devereux's infantry Marines in their defensive trenches on the beaches for the expected final assault.

What little was known at the time about the heroism at Wake gave America something to cheer about in those grim days. It also gave the enemy second thoughts about how easy a victory would be over the "sleeping giant" it had so rudely awakened, as Japanese Adm Isoroku Yamamoto had phrased it after he launched the attack on Pearl Harbor.

For some months before the Pearl Harbor attack, feverish construction to improve Wake's airstrip and shallow atoll harbor had been under way. The island was also a stopover for the Pan American Airways China Clipper civilian "flying boats," and there was a small hotel where passengers could spend the night. Four days before the Japanese attack, twelve new Grumman F4F Wildcat fighter planes of VMF-211 under Maj Paul Putnam had been flown in from the carrier *Enterprise*. Marine Maj James P. Devereux commanded the 1st Defense Battalion on the ground, outfitted with old World War I–style tin-pot helmets. The Marines and the Navy construction supervisors were under the command of Navy Cdr Winfield S. Cunningham, holder of two Navy Crosses. There was also a five-man Army Air Corps communications detachment. Under a cautionary alert, work proceeded at a rapid pace and Devereux solidified his beach defenses. The tiny land areas that rimmed the atoll's lagoon comprised no more than two and a half square miles, mostly of fine, white coral sand that glinted in the bright tropical sunlight. Not only was there little maneuver room, but supplies, ammunition, and aviation fuel had to be stocked close by—too close for comfort.

While receiving garbled radio reports of the attack on Pearl Harbor, Wake suffered its first devastating aerial attack by thirty-six Japanese bombers flown 720 miles from Roi, located to the south on the Kwajalein Atoll in the Marshall Islands. In a matter of minutes the island was ablaze. Eighty-four defenders were killed and seven of the eight Wildcats not in the air were reduced to burning hulks. The 3-inch antiaircraft and 5-inch sea-

coast gun batteries in their sandbagged emplacements survived. When on 11 December the Japanese attempted a follow-up landing from four assault transports with one thousand assault troops protected by six destroyers and three heavy cruisers, Maj Devereux had a deadly welcome for them. Sustaining a fierce bombardment from the covering destroyers, the Marine commander patiently waited until the enemy ships were well within the can't-miss range of 4,500 yards before giving the order for his six shore batteries to open fire.

The subsequent salvos surprised the Japanese, hitting two enemy destroyers, a troop transport, and a covering cruiser. The destroyers were sunk, and six other ships were damaged. The stunned attacking task force quickly withdrew, and the Japanese postponed their landing while they licked their wounds and added reinforcements of two more cruisers and support from two aircraft carriers for the next attempt. As the task force was retreating, Marine pilots sank another destroyer and a submarine. A couple of hours later during a bombing raid, Marines shot down three bombers while the antiaircraft crews on the ground bagged three

INSET: Insignia (designed after the battle) of VMF-211, the Marine fighter squadron that landed on Wake Island just days before the Japanese attacked, and which fought valiantly until all of their aircraft were damaged beyond repair. Pilot Capt Henry Elrod, who had sunk one of the Japanese destroyers, was posthumously awarded the Medal of Honor for leading an infantry attack against the invading Japanese, the first Marine aviator to be so honored.

BELOW: Illustrator Marc Stewart's painting *Cat and Mouse Over Wake*. Despite the ever-dwindling supply of aircraft, VMF-211's Wildcats were nevertheless always able to give a hot welcome to Japanese bombers. All told, the squadron shot down twenty-one bombers and sank a destroyer and a submarine. It only encountered Zero fighters in the second invasion attempt, when the enemy task force was reinforced with two carriers.

ABOVE: Marine Maj James P. Devereux, commander of the 1st Marine Defense Battalion on Wake, staged a remarkable defense of the tiny atoll, repulsing the first and severely compromising the second Japanese amphibious landing before being ordered to surrender by the senior Navy commander. He and his four hundred surviving Marines, along with some eight hundred civilian workers and Navy personnel, were imprisoned in Japan for the remainder of the war. Devereux was awarded the Navy Cross (his medal is shown at right).

ABOVE RIGHT: Aerial view of the southern tip of Wake atoll after a Japanese attack. The limited space on the tiny landmasses forced supplies and fuel to be stored in close, thus increasing their vulnerability to aerial attack.

Devereux's Command Post

more. It is estimated that the Japanese lost more than 850 men in the aborted assault; 4 Marines were wounded and none were killed in that first action. For the Americans, the eleventh of December had been a long but gratifying day.

For a brief time there was a spark of hope when news of a relief force was received; the aircraft carrier *Saratoga* (with contributor Brooke Nihart, then a young lieutenant and gunnery officer, on board) was reportedly sailing toward Wake Island from Pearl Harbor with Marine fighter and dive-bomber squadrons on board. However, with word of the intense Japanese bombing and the attempted landing, the carrier turned back in order to avoid losing what few U.S. Navy ships remained operable after Pearl Harbor.

Wake continued to be pounded, and its quickly diminishing fighter squadron was patched again and again, until its last Wildcat was no longer airworthy. The remaining five aircraft managed to fight for most of the two-week period, but when there were no more planes to fly, the five surviving pilots attached themselves to Devereux as infantrymen. One of them, Capt Henry Elrod, who had sunk one of the destroyers, led a charge against the enemy landing forces and was posthumously awarded the Medal of Honor, the first Marine aviator to be so honored in World War II.

On 23 December at 0400 the final invasion began. Japanese special naval landing forces debarked at several spots on the beach perimeter, and fierce bayonet

Navy Cross

and hand-to-hand fighting ensued in the darkness. The civilian workers had by this time begun to pitch in and attend to the wounded, carry supplies and ammunition, and pass shells to the antiaircraft and coastal gun crews.

The battle was heroic but futile. In the late morning, after issuing the message "Enemy on island. Issue in doubt," the Navy commander ordered all forces to surrender—a tough decision for some of the Marines, who continued to fight on their own for a while. Maj Devereux had no choice: attaching a white T-shirt to a stick, he walked in front of his lines to stop the firing and met with his enemy counterpart.

The surrendering Marines knew the Japanese had the reputation of not taking prisoners—of killing them instead. Nevertheless, they hoped to be treated properly as prisoners of war. Like the captured Marines in China, on Guam, and in Bataan, they were to be disappointed. The humane treatment of POWs mandated under the Geneva Convention was ignored by the Japanese. They beat, starved, enslaved, and beheaded many Marines on their way to and while in miserable prison camps in China and Japan. Eight Marines, three sailors, and one hundred civilians who had been on Wake died in captivity. Battle deaths totaled forty-three Marines, three sailors, and thirty-four civilians. The 1st Marine Defense Battalion had shot down twenty-one aircraft and damaged fifty-seven others. It, along with VMF-211, had sunk five enemy ships and damaged eight others. The 410 Marines—many of them wounded—killed almost 2,000 Japanese invaders during the two landing attacks on the island. In effect, it was a major loss of face for the Japanese, who had thought themselves invincible. One of the Japanese task force commanders wrote afterward: "Considering the power accumulated for the invasion of Wake Island and the meager forces of the defenders, it was the most humiliating defeat the Japanese navy had ever suffered." That Imperial Japanese Navy would suffer many more defeats at the hands of the U.S. Navy and Marines in the coming months.

Wake Island was one of the most courageous and stirring fights in Marine Corps history—indeed, in the nation's history. What it demonstrated more than anything else was the indomitable fighting spirit of Marines—not only of seasoned Marine officers and senior NCOs, which is to be expected, but also of the inexperienced young Marines unbaptized by fire. Although they were perhaps naive about war, when the time came to fight, they proved to be hardy products of the generation toughened and honed by the Great Depression. All were willing to fight and die, virtually to the last man, and they swallowed hard at having to surrender. Most had responded, "Marines don't surrender!" All knew, though, that the U.S. Navy commander had no choice but to order it.

The story of the atrocities the Japanese committed against the captured Americans from Wake was not widely known at the time. When it became public, the commander of the Japanese garrison who surrendered to the Marines on 4 September 1945 was convicted of war crimes and executed for massacring one hundred civilians on the island. Besides allowing the inhumane treatment of the captive Marines, he had had five of them beheaded. (Other grisly Japanese atrocities contrary to the Geneva Convention were eventually disclosed in Hong Kong, Singapore, and other places overrun by the conquering Japanese. In retaliation for the Doolittle Raid on Tokyo the following April, the Japanese slaughtered 250,000 innocent Chinese civilians and beheaded several of the captured U.S. airmen in Tokyo.)

The last man to have left Wake Island, Bayler, now a colonel, was given the honor of being the first to return. President Roosevelt, in his 6 January 1942 State of the Union message, praised the Marines' stand at Wake Island and said that because of it, "their fellow citizens have been inspired to render their own full share of service and sacrifice." During a later press conference, when newsmen contrasted the Marines' performance at Wake against the debacles at Hong Kong, Singapore, and Clark Field in the Philippines, CMC MajGen Holcomb responded, "What the hell did you expect, anyway?"

Marine Expeditionary Medal

ABOVE: The only time the Marine Expeditionary Medal was awarded in World War II was for service in the Wake Island battle. It is the second service medal in USMC history. For specific expeditionary operations, a gold bar and letter is worn with the medal, signifying that action. Here, the _W_ on the ribbon denotes Wake Island.

LEFT: A sketch by Albin Henning depicting the final action on Wake Island.

BELOW: Marines embarking for Midway. The presence of the Vought bi-wing single-float seaplane on the deck of the docked ship suggests that it is either a heavy cruiser or a battleship.

RIGHT: Marine-manned 20mm antiaircraft guns at the port bow gallery, or Sector 2, on board the carrier *Yorktown* on its way to the decisive battle of Midway in early June 1942. These gun crews numbered three: the gunner, the loader, and the trunnion operator. The rate of fire was 450 rounds per minute. The *Yorktown* had been severely damaged only a month before in the Battle of the Coral Sea; incredibly, Navy and civilian crews at Pearl Harbor got enough repairs done to allow her to join the *Enterprise* and *Hornet* in time for the momentous naval battle.

BATAAN AND CORREGIDOR IN THE PHILIPPINES

On 6 May 1942, Marines of the 4th Regiment defending "the Rock" (Corregidor Island), which guarded the mouth of Manila Bay, were forced to surrender with the remainder of Gen MacArthur's American-Filipino army. MacArthur had escaped with his family in a fast patrol torpedo boat, leaving LtGen Jonathan Wainwright—with the remnants of his whipped army of 17,000 Americans, 120,000 Filipinos, and the Marines—to endure the brutal 65-mile Bataan Death March to a Japanese prison camp farther up the peninsula. Thousands died along the way. (After the war, MacArthur awarded all the survivors a unit citation—except the Marines. That deliberate oversight sealed a long-standing disdain by Marines for the famous general. It was somewhat mollified by the successful Marine amphibious landing at Inchon in Korea nine years later, which MacArthur had called upon Marines to do.) Again, the American press led their stories with the Marines: U.S. Marines Fight With MacArthur; Marines Aid Bataan Defense. Clearly, the U.S. Marine Corps was considered America's front line against Japan.

In April, the daring Doolittle Raid on Tokyo by sixteen B-25 Mitchell twin-engine Army Air Corps bombers flown off the aircraft carrier *Hornet* bolstered sagging U.S. morale. In May, the first direct naval confrontation between the Imperial Japanese Navy and the U.S. Navy took place in the Coral Sea, just northeast of Australia. Although it ended in a draw, it stopped the Japanese advance and the threat to Australia. The U.S. aircraft carrier *Lexington* was sunk, however, and the *Yorktown* was heavily damaged. This battle—and the very decisive one that followed—demonstrated that naval warfare had changed: the aircraft carrier had replaced the battleship as the backbone of the fleet. Navy aircraft had done the damage. The United States lost seventy-seven, the Japanese, ninety-seven and a small carrier.

RIGHT: A Vought SB2U Vindicator takes off on a mission on Midway. The three Marine squadrons (integrated with Navy land-based air components) of MAG 22 on Midway were made up of obsolete Brewster Buffalos and Vindicators. During the decisive naval battle of 3 to 6 June 1942, all Marine aircraft proved ineffective or were destroyed.

RIGHT, INSET: A USMC field message from Maj James S. O'Halloran, CO, Battery E, 3-inch Antiaircraft Group, 3d Defense Battalion, reporting at 1600 hours on 4 June 1942: "Three enemy planes seen shot down from this position—one by fire of this battery. Fourth plane seen trailing heavy smoke toward south, losing altitude fast. 262 rounds H.E. expended, no casualties. Everything now in readiness for further assaults."

BELOW: Marines receive the flag-draped coffins of their buddies who died in the defense of Midway Island.

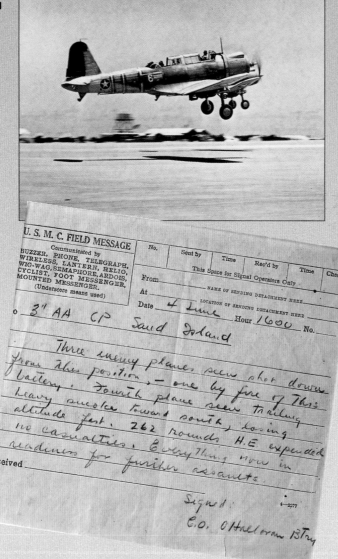

A month later, American and Japanese naval forces clashed again, this time north of the end of the Hawaiian Island chain at Midway Island, 1,300 miles from Pearl Harbor. Having broken the secret Japanese naval code, the U.S. fleet, with its three remaining carriers, was lying in wait for the Japanese naval task force, which had four carriers. A three-day battle ensued, spreading hundreds of miles over the sea.

On Midway, the Marine 6th Defense Battalion and MAG-22 were subjected to fierce aerial attacks. Although they were augmented by seven superior Wildcat fighters and nineteen SBD Dauntless dive-bombers (delivered from the *Lexington* in December), Marines were still flying obsolete Brewster Buffalo fighter planes and Vought SBU-2 dive-bombers. Nevertheless, they fought valiantly.

Marine fighters and dive-bombers intercepted an attacking force of 108 Japanese aircraft, losing 15 of their own fighters. Marine dive-bombers, along with Navy torpedo squadrons from the *Enterprise* and *Yorktown*, attacked the enemy carriers *Akagi*, *Kaga*, and *Soryu*, losing eight of their nineteen planes (the Navy lost three complete TBD torpedo squadrons). At the end of the first day, only two Marine fighter planes and eleven dive-bombers were airworthy. Navy dive-bomber squadrons fortuitously spotted the three Japanese flattops as they were rearming and refueling planes on their flight decks. They dived out of the clouds (using dive-bombing techniques Marines had developed) to rain a torrent of bombs that caused chain reactions of explosions and gasoline infernos that sent three of the four enemy carriers to the bottom. The next day, the remaining carrier, *Hiryu*, met the same fate, and the first clear-cut American victory of the war was sealed—a blow from which the Imperial Japanese Navy never recovered. It had lost its major aircraft carriers and most of its best pilots in the 320 aircraft that were shot down—a portent of things to come.

Mr. Higgins's Landing Craft

As the Marines Corps developed doctrine for amphibious operations in the mid-1930s—including the organization of the Fleet Marine Forces in 1935 and the 1934 publication of the *Tentative Landing Operation Manual*—solving the problems of ship-to-shore movement became paramount. Using ships' boats, which were designed to travel from moored ships to dockside, proved unsatisfactory. They tended to broach in even moderate surf, and troops had to debark by clambering over the side into often chest-deep water.

The search for a suitable boat was on. Many were tried—fishing boats, Coast Guard surf boats, Boston whalers—and all were unsatisfactory. Finally, New Orleans boat builder Andrew J. Higgins submitted his 30-foot Eureka, a special shallow-draft boat he had designed for the use of trappers and oil drillers along the lower Mississippi and Gulf Coast. It had a tunnel stern, which protected the propeller and extended almost to the bow. The "spoonbill" bow enabled the craft to run well up onto a beach for an almost dry troop landing, and when the engine was reversed, the propeller pushed a stream of water under the bow that easily lifted the beached boat clear of the shore.

Higgins's boats were warmly embraced by the Marine Corps. By 1941, the small Amphibious Forces, Atlantic and Pacific, with a few old cargo/passenger steamers converted to APAs (Auxiliary Personnel Amphibious), were outfitted with up to twenty-four 36-foot Higgins LCPs (Landing Craft, Personnel) and suitable davits and cranes to quickly launch them. These LCPs still had shortcomings. Troops had to clamber over the side into knee- to waist-deep water. Also, vehicles could not be landed from the LCPs.

These problems were soon corrected. An LCPR (Landing Craft, Personnel [Ramped]), with a narrow bow ramp that allowed a single file of Marines to debark into ankle-deep water or even onto a dry beach, was fielded before the end of 1941. An LCV (Landing Craft Vehicle), which had a wide bow ramp and could land a Jeep (1/4-ton truck) with trailer or 37mm antitank gun or 75mm pack howitzer, appeared that summer as well. There were so many LCPs in the system that the transports that landed the 1st MarDiv on Guadalcanal still carried them.

Meanwhile, Andrew Higgins had designed and built a 50-foot LCM-3 (Landing Craft, Mechanized) to land heavy trucks and light tanks. A 56-foot LCM-6 that could land a 30-ton M4 Sherman medium tank soon followed. By 1943, the LCPs, LCPRs, and LCVs were replaced by the LCVP (Landing Craft Vehicle, Personnel), which became the standard troop-landing craft through the Korean War and beyond. Based on the LCV, the LCVP had a ramp and armor-plated side that offered protection against small-arms fire. In contrast to the LCV, the LCVP had a protected coxswain's position, where the "cox" stood erect on the stern.

The LCVP, in the opinion of LtGen Holland M. Smith, commanding general of Fleet Marine Force Pacific, "did more to win the war in the Pacific than any other single piece of equipment."

—BN

BELOW: Marines scramble down cargo nets over the side of a transport ship into an LCV for the invasion of Bougainville in 1943.

WORLD WAR II: NAVY-MARINE AND ARMY BATTLES
December 1941–September 1945

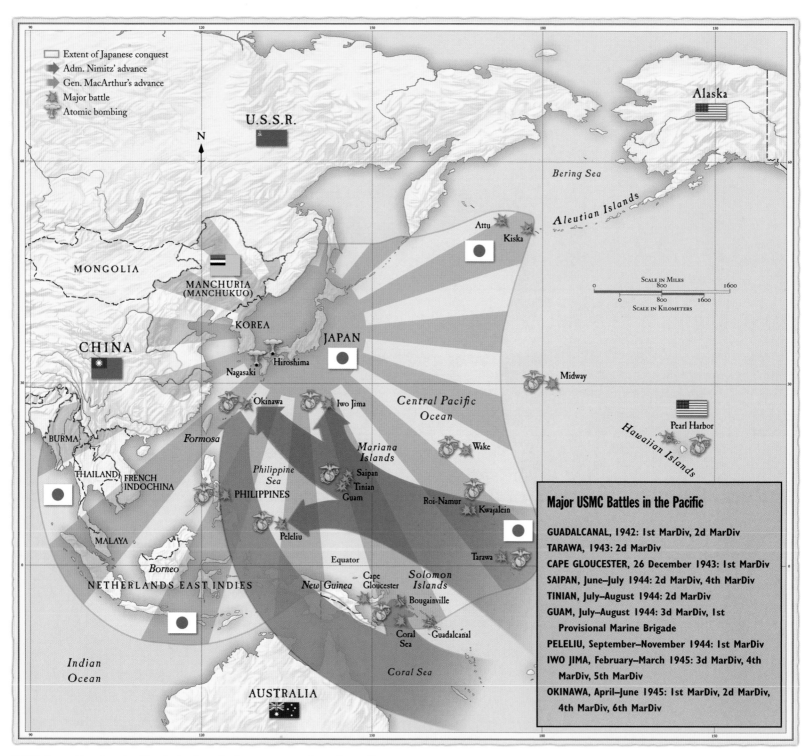

Major USMC Battles in the Pacific

GUADALCANAL, 1942: 1st MarDiv, 2d MarDiv

TARAWA, 1943: 2d MarDiv

CAPE GLOUCESTER, 26 December 1943: 1st MarDiv

SAIPAN, June–July 1944: 2d MarDiv, 4th MarDiv

TINIAN, July–August 1944: 2d MarDiv

GUAM, July–August 1944: 3d MarDiv, 1st
    Provisional Marine Brigade

PELELIU, September–November 1944: 1st MarDiv

IWO JIMA, February–March 1945: 3d MarDiv, 4th
    MarDiv, 5th MarDiv

OKINAWA, April–June 1945: 1st MarDiv, 2d MarDiv,
    4th MarDiv, 6th MarDiv

ABOVE: Army Gen Douglas MacArthur's main thrust came up from Australia over the larger landmasses of the Solomons, New Guinea, and the Philippines. It consisted of Army infantry divisions supported by some Marine units and transported by Navy surface ships. Adm Chester Nimitz's primary central Pacific thrust was by Marine amphibious assaults (supported by some Army units) on Japanese island strongholds to obtain airfields and bases nearer to Japan. Both MacArthur and Nimitz bypassed numerous other Japanese strongholds, and after three years of intense land, sea, and air battles, their forces converged in a final battle on Okinawa. This Japanese home island would then become a jumping-off base for the planned invasion of Japan itself.

ABOVE: Marine aviator Capt Marion Carl, who eventually racked up 18.5 Japanese kills in the air, later went on to fly combat missions in Vietnam as a brigadier general in the air wing, and rose to the rank of lieutenant general.

LEFT: Roy Grinnell's painting of one of the Marine Wildcats scoring a kill during a routine flight of Japanese dive-bombers over Henderson Field on Guadalcanal. Note that the red ball that once appeared in the center of the white-star insignia on American aircraft (see page 177) has been eliminated, lest there be any confusion in distinguishing American from Japanese planes. Such air battles occurred daily above the embattled Marines on the ground.

LEFT, INSET: This Japanese hand-cranked siren was captured by Marines at the uncompleted airstrip on Guadalcanal. It was immediately put to use at the "Pagoda," or operations shed, to warn of approaching enemy aircraft at the newly named Henderson Field, completed by Marine engineers and Navy Seabees under continuous enemy aerial and naval bombardment.

TULAGI-GUADALCANAL: FIRST GROUND COUNTEROFFENSIVE OF WORLD WAR II

A Japanese airfield had been discovered under construction on the large island of Guadalcanal in the Solomon Islands within bombing range of Australia. In order to prevent its completion, the quickly assembled 1st Marine Division and elements of 2d MarDiv landed on the beach on 8 August 1942 and began the first Allied ground counteroffensive of World War II.

The 1st Marine Parachute Battalion (on foot) and the 2d Marines, having first taken the adjacent small island of Tulagi in a sharp engagement, made way for the 1st and 5th Marine Regiments to land unopposed on the north shore of the larger island. At first the Marines faced only the Japanese construction crews and captured the airstrip, naming it Henderson Field after Marine pilot/hero Maj Lofton R. Henderson, who had been killed at Midway while attacking the carrier *Akagi*. The Japanese, however, were not long in reinforcing the defenders with crack infantry troops shuttled in nightly by destroyer and assault transport.

The battle grew fiercer by the day. The Marines' tight perimeter encircling the airfield sustained vicious nightly attacks. Both the beachhead and the airfield, with its growing force of Marine F4F Wildcat fighters and SBD Dauntless dive-bombers, as well as Army Air Corps P-38 Lightnings and Bell P-39 Airacobras, were subjected to relentless daily aerial bombings and nightly bombardments from the Japanese battleships' 14-inch naval guns—sometimes a thousand bombs a day and a thousand rounds a night. The protecting and supporting U.S. naval ships themselves were in constant battle in the neighboring waters as the land, sea, and air battles raged on for six bloody months.

For the Marines of the 1st Division, it was hellish, disease-ridden jungle warfare in searing tropical heat and monsoon deluges. These new conditions would be

Sniping: World War II

Sniping, as a specialized skill, was not emphasized between the wars. Marksmanship, however, was stressed for all Marines. If a long-range shot was necessary, the best shots in the outfit would be called up for the task.

The United States' entry into World War II changed this informal practice. A scout-sniper platoon was added to the table of organization of the Marine rifle regiment. Special equipment was produced and sniper schools were created on both coasts. Maj George Van Orden, commanding officer of the rifle range at Quantico, added a Unertl 8-power telescope to National Match grade M1903 rifles to create the standard Marine sniping rifle that was used in both World War II and Korea. M1903A4 and M1C rifles with various scopes were also used.

Sniper schools were organized at Jacques Farm, near San Diego, under distinguished shot Reserve Capt Walter R. Walsh and at Quantico under the eagle eye of Maj Van Orden. Graduates of these schools joined Marine rifle regimental scout-sniper platoons.

—BN

ABOVE: Volunteer Marine glider-pilot trainees listen to an instructor at Page Field on Parris Island in early 1942. Even before the glider invasion of Crete by the Nazis in May 1941, the Marine Corps had inaugurated a glider program, which resulted in the formation of Glider Group 71. The program never took off, however, as design and production of troop-carrying gliders never materialized for the Marine group. Furthermore, as proven on Guadalcanal, the terrain of the South Pacific was not well suited for glider landings. The Army proceeded with its program but used gliders only once in combat, in 1944 at Normandy, which offered more favorable, flat terrain.

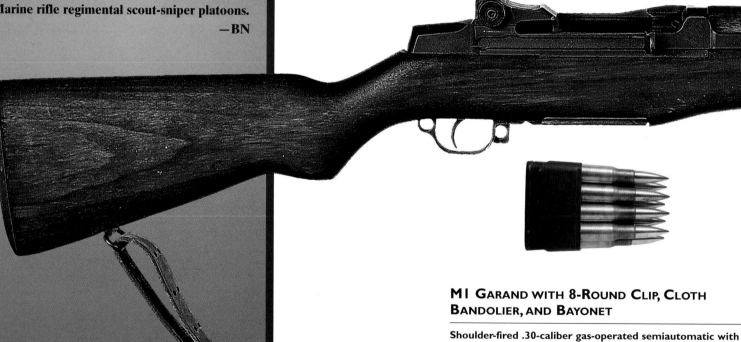

M1 GARAND WITH 8-ROUND CLIP, CLOTH BANDOLIER, AND BAYONET

Shoulder-fired .30-caliber gas-operated semiautomatic with an 8-round clip, the M1 Garand became the standard-issue infantry weapon in World War II and Korea. The M1 proved just as accurate as the revered M1903 and had a faster rate of fire. The ease with which it could be field-stripped for cleaning also added to its popularity; the cloth bandolier could hold six additional clips and was easy to carry.

faced by a newly equipped Marine. The updated uniforms and combat gear were far different from the look of World War I, which characterized those courageous defenders of Wake. The American warrior of the modern war wore a newly designed cloche helmet with liner and the jungle utility uniform. Until improvements could be made, the weapons were the same used in the war twenty years earlier: the 1903 Springfield rifle, the Browning Automatic Rifle (BAR), and the .30-caliber air-cooled Browning M1919A4 light and the M1917 heavy water-cooled machine guns. It was only after the reinforcing Army 164th Regiment, equipped with the new M1 Garand 8-shot-clip semiautomatic rifle, demonstrated its more rapid firepower that the 1st Marine Division gave up their beloved '03s and adopted the Garands.

By December 1942, the 1st Marine Division was exhausted. Battle casualties, malnutrition, and malaria had brought it below 50 percent effective, despite reinforcements by elements of the 2d Marine Division and two Army regiments. The 1st Marine Division was relieved on 9 December by the Army Americal Division, which would finish the mopping up of the evacuating Japanese, and retired to Australia for well-deserved rest, recuperation, and the rebuilding of the division.

The 1st Marine Division had performed superbly and had turned the tide against the Japanese. The Japanese had not expected Americans to fight so tenaciously—even after Wake—but they soon learned to respect the American Marines, who proceeded to defeat them in battle after battle, forcing them to fight defensive ground actions, while steadily advancing toward the Japanese homeland.

ABOVE: Marines of a tank crew scramble back to their M3 light tank with its 37mm main gun and light .30-caliber machine gun on top of the turret. The tanks were most useful in the flat terrain near and on the beaches.

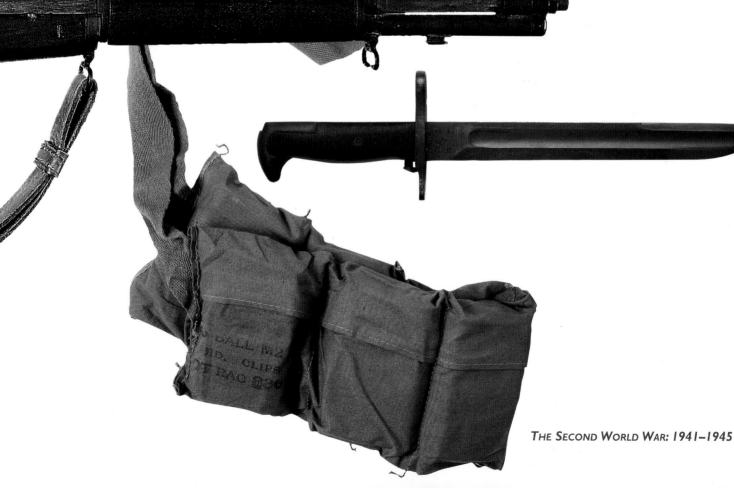

MEDAL OF HONOR

SERGEANT CLYDE THOMASON
Makin Island Raid
17 August 1942

For conspicuous heroism and intrepidity above and beyond the call of duty during the Marine Raider Expedition against the Japanese-held island of Makin, 17–18 August 1942. Leading the advance element of the assault echelon, Sgt Thomason disposed his men with keen judgment and discrimination and, by his exemplary leadership and great personal valor, exhorted them to like fearless efforts. On one occasion, he dauntlessly walked up to a house which concealed an enemy Japanese sniper, forced in the door, and shot the man before he could resist. Later in the action, while leading an assault on an enemy position, he gallantly gave his life in the service of his country. His courage and loyal devotion to duty in the face of grave peril were in keeping with the finest traditions of the U.S. Naval Service.

RIGHT: On Bougainville, Marine dog-handler Pfc Finley holds the leash of a true Marine Devil Dog: "Jack," a three-year-old Belgian shepherd. Jack was hit by a Japanese sniper's bullet while carrying a message from one unit to another. Nevertheless, the dog completed his mission, and was commended by the commandant for "outstanding performance against the enemy."

BELOW: On 26 August 1942, Marines from the 2d Raider Battalion, on the deck of their transport submarine, return to Pearl Harbor after the ill-fated raid on Makin Island led by LtCol Evans F. Carlson. Some still wear the khaki uniforms that had been dyed black for the raid, while others are in borrowed sailors' jumpers and bell-bottoms.

LEFT: Three of the dozens of legendary names that came out of Guadalcanal (left to right): MajGen A.A. Vandegrift, CG, 1st MarDiv; Col Gerald Thomas, G-3, who nine years later would lead 1st MarDiv in Korea; and Col Merritt Edson, who gained additional fame by leading his "Edson's Raiders" in small incursions against the Japanese. Vandegrift was awarded the Medal of Honor for his heroic action in battle on "the Canal," as was Edson, for defense of the ridge named for his heroism.

BELOW: Marines cross the Matanikau River in one of two major battles in the same area. Both the Marines and the Japanese faced difficulties with resupply, casualty evacuation, and reinforcement. Finally, after six months of intense fighting, the Marines prevailed, and those Japanese who survived gave up the battle and were evacuated.

M3 SUBMACHINE GUN

The .45-caliber M3 submachine gun, equipped with a 30-round magazine. Known as the Grease Gun, it is light, compact, made from stamped metal, has a retractable buttstock, and was versatile in airborne and special operations during World War II.

"Take your time. Stay away from the easy going. Never go the same way twice."

GySgt Charles C. Arndt,
on patrolling on Guadalcanal, 1942

Marine Innovations: Knives

Knives have always accompanied military men, from the daggers of the Bronze Age and the Greek skopus to the Roman legionary's iron dagger and the medieval knight's left-handed poniard, and, more recently, the Confederate soldier's Bowie knife.

Lt Presley Neville O'Bannon carried a naval dirk (now on display at the Marine Corps Museum), while World War I–era Marines used a trench knife with a brass knuckle hilt.

From the 1930s into the 1940s, Philadelphia Marine Reserve Officer Anthony Drexel Biddle taught new Marine lieutenants at Quantico's Basic School knife and bayonet fighting as well as hand-to-hand combat. Three of his students—Lieutenants Yeaton, Moore, and Taxis—were ordered to the 4th Marines in Shanghai, and later distinguished themselves in World War II. They continued their study of Close Quarter Combat (CQC) with Capt William Fairbairn and Sgt Eric Sykes, the famed British officers of the Shanghai Municipal Police of the International Settlement. The three Marines, in cooperation with Fairbairn, developed a fighting knife called a Stiletto.

Fairbairn and Sykes left Shanghai for England in 1940 and, after Dunkirk, trained commandos in Scotland in CQC. There they developed a slightly modified Shanghai knife that became known as the Fairbairn-Sykes knife. British commandos carried the knife throughout World War II, as did the four Marine Raider battalions.

Encounters between Marines and Japanese soldiers in the jungles of

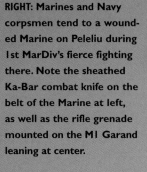

RIGHT: Marines and Navy corpsmen tend to a wounded Marine on Peleliu during 1st MarDiv's fierce fighting there. Note the sheathed Ka-Bar combat knife on the belt of the Marine at left, as well as the rifle grenade mounted on the M1 Garand leaning at center.

Stiletto Knife with Sheath

Ka-Bar

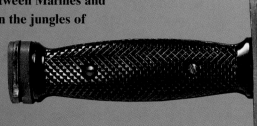

M7 Carbine Bayonet

Guadalcanal led to a demand for American-style hunting knives, which had a shortened Bowie-type blade ideal for both cutting though jungle and engaging the enemy at close quarters at night. Sporting goods stores at home were quickly emptied of such knives, as they were sent overseas or purchased to equip men on their way. The Marine Corps soon decided it required an official knife. Gen Clifford H. Shuey, then a captain and head of the engineer division of HQMC, was given the task of designing and procuring a knife. Shuey developed specifications, and the Ka-Bar knife company was engaged to make a sturdy, modified Bowie-type hunting knife with an 8-inch blade. To meet the demand, a number of other knife makers made the "K-Bar," as it came to be known. It continues to be standard equipment in the Corps to this day.

In the 1950s, retired brigadier general and ordnance specialist George Van Orden developed a shortened version of the Ka-Bar with saw teeth on the back edge of the blade. The serrated edge was designed to cut through a Plexiglass aircraft canopy or the aluminum sheet of the fuselage of a crashed aircraft. It was adopted by the U.S. Navy as an escape-and-evasion knife. The Marine Corps also developed a folding pocketknife with a stainless steel handle and multiple blades. It is marked "USMC" and is issued only on deployment.

It has been said that the Marines are always on the cutting edge of warrior craft. As of this writing, the Marine Corps is receiving a new bayonet that will replace both the Ka-Bar fighting/utility knife and the puny M7 bayonet. Its 8-inch blade includes a serrated edge just forward of the grip, which is capable of sawing through body armor and other material, and the hard-plastic scabbard includes a whetstone for sharpening the blade. The drop point is reminiscent of the famed Randall knives of thirty years ago.

—BN

LEFT: A Marine recruiting poster that erroneously depicts a Marine Raider team landing under air cover by Curtiss P-40 Kittyhawks, which were not used by the Marine Corps and which are marked with non-American rudder stripes.

BELOW: Marine Navajo "code-talkers" pose on Bougainville. Native Americans were often called upon to transmit messages by phone and radio in their native languages. Despite their code-breaking skills, the Japanese, who cracked the codes used by the Army and its Air Corps, were never able to decipher the Marine Corps' code—the Navajo language.

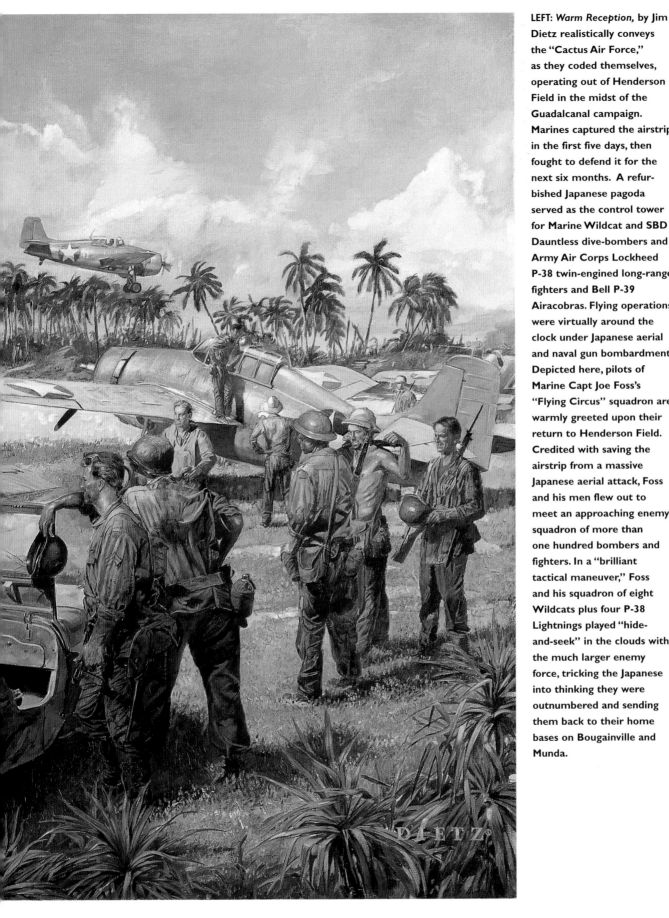

LEFT: *Warm Reception,* by Jim Dietz realistically conveys the "Cactus Air Force," as they coded themselves, operating out of Henderson Field in the midst of the Guadalcanal campaign. Marines captured the airstrip in the first five days, then fought to defend it for the next six months. A refurbished Japanese pagoda served as the control tower for Marine Wildcat and SBD Dauntless dive-bombers and Army Air Corps Lockheed P-38 twin-engined long-range fighters and Bell P-39 Airacobras. Flying operations were virtually around the clock under Japanese aerial and naval gun bombardment. Depicted here, pilots of Marine Capt Joe Foss's "Flying Circus" squadron are warmly greeted upon their return to Henderson Field. Credited with saving the airstrip from a massive Japanese aerial attack, Foss and his men flew out to meet an approaching enemy squadron of more than one hundred bombers and fighters. In a "brilliant tactical maneuver," Foss and his squadron of eight Wildcats plus four P-38 Lightnings played "hide-and-seek" in the clouds with the much larger enemy force, tricking the Japanese into thinking they were outnumbered and sending them back to their home bases on Bougainville and Munda.

ABOVE: Equaling Capt Eddie Rickenbacker's record of twenty-six kills in World War I, former South Dakota farm boy and Marine F4F Wildcat fighter pilot Joseph J. Foss knocked twenty-six Japanese bombers and fighters out of the sky over Guadalcanal in forty-four days in 1942 to 1943. The Marine flying ace led two four-plane groups of VMF-121, dubbed Foss's Flying Circus. He was also credited with sixteen probables. Foss was shot down several times, but was rescued and hospitalized with wounds and malaria. For his amazing feat, he was awarded the Medal of Honor; he also earned the Distinguished Flying Cross, the Silver Star, and the Purple Heart. After the war and a stint in the Air National Guard in Korea, he retired as a brigadier general, served two terms as governor of South Dakota, was president of the National Rifle Association, and was the first commissioner of the American Football League. He also hosted the popular television show *The American Sportsman* on ABC. Foss was laid to rest in Arlington National Cemetery on 22 January 2003.

Let's give him
Enough and On Time

BELOW: Battle-hardened Marines pause briefly to pose for a combat photographer. Note that the two on the right are not wearing steel helmets over their helmet liners. They are probably on the perimeter of Edson's ridge on Guadalcanal, where bloody hand-to-hand fighting occurred constantly from August through September 1942, in that first U.S. ground counteroffensive. Their beloved bolt-action Springfield 1903 rifles would soon be replaced by the new semiautomatic M1 Garands, introduced by the Army 164th Regiment, on their left flank.

ABOVE: A poster by noted illustrator Norman Rockwell pays tribute to both Marines and soldiers with its depiction of a machine-gunner in a tattered uniform manning a heavy water-cooled .30-caliber gun.

BELOW: Extremely rare today, the unofficial George Medal was made for a few members of the 1st Marine Division after they reached Australia following the Guadalcanal campaign. The medal depicts the hand of a sailor dropping a hot potato into the hands of a Marine; the suspension ribbon was cut from a set of herringbone utilities, and the motto in Latin translates roughly as "Let George Do It." It marks the occasion when U.S. Navy ships withdrew from Guadalcanal on D+3, leaving the 1st MarDiv open to Japanese naval bombardment and aerial attacks.

The Fire Team

Being small, and often deploying small units such as ships' detachments into hostile areas, the Marine Corps always sought to get more combat power from fewer Marines. Thus, during the so-called Banana Wars of the 1920s and 1930s, the Marines improved on the standard eight-man squad of the Army and Marine Corps of the period.

The squad included a BAR (Browning Automatic Rifle) man and an assistant BAR man. In addition to the Browning, Marines added a second automatic weapon, the Thompson submachine gun (TSMG), a.k.a. the Tommy gun, which was carried by the corporal squad leader. The squad could thus be divided into two four-man fire teams, and the team with the BAR could provide covering fire while the team with the TSMG maneuvered and assaulted the objective.

During World War II, with these experiences in mind, the Corps again increased the squad, to thirteen men under a sergeant squad leader, with three four-man fire teams under corporals; each team had a BAR. This high-firepower squad proved to be so successful that during the Korean War the Army copied the idea, but with two BAR-armed fire teams per squad. Today, the Corps uses squads with two or three fire teams, each with a M249 5.56mm light machine gun.

—BN

LEFT: A scene typical of the South Pacific jungle warfare engaged in by Marines. Here, a heavy water-cooled M1917A .30-caliber machine-gun crew fires from as protective a position as they can muster among the trees and foliage, fighting not only an unseen enemy but also a host of insects, varmints, and snakes in the suffocating tropical heat.

For conspicuous gallantry and intrepidity at the risk of his life above and beyond the call of duty as leader of a section of six fighter planes in Marine Fighting Squadron 112, during aerial operations against enemy Japanese forces off Kolombangara Island in the Solomons group, 31 January 1943. Taking off with his section as escort for a strike force of dive-bombers and torpedo planes ordered to attack Japanese surface vessels, 1stLt DeBlanc led his flight directly to the target area where, at 14,000 feet, our strike force encountered a large number of Japanese Zeros protecting the enemy's surface craft. In company with the other fighters, 1stLt DeBlanc instantly engaged the hostile planes and aggressively countered their repeated attempts to drive off our bombers, persevering in his efforts to protect the diving planes and waging fierce combat until, picking up a call for assistance from the dive-bombers, under attack by enemy float planes at 1,000 feet, he broke off his engagement with the Zeros, plunged into the formation of float planes, and disrupted the savage attack, enabling our dive-bombers and torpedo planes to complete their runs on the Japanese surface disposition and withdraw without further incident. Although his escort mission was fulfilled upon the safe retirement of the bombers, 1stLt DeBlanc courageously remained on the scene despite a rapidly diminishing fuel supply and, boldly challenging the enemy's superior number of float planes, fought a valiant battle against terrific odds, seizing the tactical advantage and striking repeatedly to destroy three of the hostile aircraft and to disperse the remainder. Prepared to maneuver his damaged plane back to base, he had climbed aloft and set his course when he discovered two Zeros closing in behind. Undaunted, he opened fire and blasted both Zeros from the sky in a short, bitterly fought action which resulted in such hopeless damage to his own plane that he was forced to bail out at a perilously low altitude atop the trees on enemy-held Kolombangara. A gallant officer, a superb airman, and an indomitable fighter, 1stLt DeBlanc had rendered decisive assistance during a critical stage of operations, and his unwavering fortitude in the face of overwhelming opposition reflects the highest credit upon himself and adds new luster to the traditions of the U.S. Naval Service.

Meanwhile, Marine and Navy pilots were knocking Japanese airplanes out of the skies in staggering numbers. The surface Navy had it particularly tough, however, losing as many of its own ships as it sank of the enemy's.

The strategy after Guadalcanal was for Adm Chester Nimitz's Navy and Marines to blast northward up the Solomon Islands and then the central Pacific, while Gen Douglas MacArthur and his Army to the west secured the larger landmasses of New Guinea, New Britain, and the Philippines, both pincers to converge for the final onslaught on Japan itself.

UP THE SLOT

For the next year, Marine divisions and Raider battalions, supported by Marine Air and naval gunfire, fought their bloody way up the so-called Slot, the central waterway between the Solomon Islands, down which Japanese replacements had come nightly and below which the floor of the sea was so littered with sunken Japanese and American ships that it was referred to as Iron Bottom.

Marine and Navy air, sea, and land task forces battled island by island—New Georgia, Choiseul, and Vella Lavella—reinforced by the Army 43d Infantry Division, with the 3d Marine Division taking Bougainville and the 1st MarDiv, back from rest in Australia, taking Cape Gloucester on New Britain. The two Marine divisions were attached to MacArthur's Southwestern Pacific Theater forces along with his Army divisions, to which the Marines taught amphibious-landing techniques. The Marines made amphibious landing after landing, perfecting their ship-to-shore movement and naval gunfire and close air support to a sharply honed edge.

The strategy for the Marine-Navy thrust was to seize airfields closer and closer to Japan. While combined Marine divisions and air wings were fighting through the Solomon Islands, it was deemed strategically necessary to control the Gilbert Islands two thousand miles to the east in the central Pacific by taking its dominant atoll, Tarawa.

RIGHT: MajGen Archer A. Vandegrift, CG, and LtGen Thomas Holcomb, CMC, (seated in foreground at right) in a high-level 1st MarDiv conference on Guadalcanal in November 1942.

LEFT, CENTER: The islands where Marines fought in the South Pacific were hardly tropical paradises. Despite their coconut plantations and sandy beaches, they were plagued with disease, insects, and venomous reptiles and other crawling creatures. Here, a patrol flushes out an enemy bunker in a coconut grove. It is early in the Guadalcanal campaign, as evidenced by their M1903 rifles and the one rifleman wearing leggings. The leggings were abandoned after a month or so; in the intense heat and monsoon torrents the uniforms were virtually rotting off the men's backs, while malaria had taken a toll greater than the bullets of the Japanese. Wearing the helmet chinstraps unbuckled lent a certain swagger to the uniform but was actually quite uncomfortable—when moving fast, the helmet bobbled, requiring one hand to steady it. It was better to keep the chinstraps securely buckled in a firefight. (They were ordered to be unbuckled only when descending cargo nets and loading into landing boats.) Shortly after witnessing the effectiveness of the reinforcing Army 164th Regiment's M1 Garands, Marines gave up their cherished 1903s. Note the Marine who has his Colt .45 M1911 at the ready.

RIGHT: The unique Marine tropical sea-green herringbone-twill utility uniform was beloved by the Old Corps of World War II and Korea. It was durable, had practical pockets, and its loose fit afforded a degree of ventilation in hot climates. The cartridge belt with individual pockets for M1 8-round clips was often augmented by a cloth magazine bandolier, worn over the shoulders as seen in the photograph above. A first-aid pouch was also attached, as was a bayonet scabbard and water canteen.

American Campaign Medal

M1941 JOHNSON RIFLE

Invented by Marine Reserve Capt Melvin Johnson, the M1941 is a recoil-operated .30-.06-caliber semiautomatic rifle with a rotary 10-round magazine and a prong bayonet. In World War II, it was produced in limited quantities for the Dutch government for use in the Dutch East Indies. When these islands fell to the Japanese, the Marine Corps procured some of the Dutch rifles to arm Marine parachutists and Raiders. The M1941 fell out of use by the end of the war and was replaced by the M1 Garand.

Marine Inventions: The Johnson Rifle

Marines have always been weapons-oriented. World War I infantry used bolt-action 5- or 10-shot rifles. At least one semiautomatic, or self-loading, rifle was tried, but it was too heavy and unreliable. After the Great War, several major countries experimented, unsuccessfully, with lighter models. By the late 1930s John Garand, civilian armorer for the Army, had developed a workable semiauto rifle, and it was put into limited production for service testing. Marine Reserve Capt Melvin Johnson, as a private venture, invented a rifle and accompanying light machine gun based on the same mechanism as Garand's rifle. In 1940 the two weapons were tested competitively. Because the Johnson was not in production and suffered from initial quality problems, the Garand—designated U.S. Rifle M1—was selected.

The M1 armed American forces during World War II and Korea and proved very successful. Johnson and his associates put his rifle into production and it was adopted by the Dutch East Indies forces. Because it could be dismantled into two short pieces for attachment to a parachutist, the rifle and light machine gun were adopted by Marine parachute battalions. The joint U.S.-Canadian 1st Special Service Force also used them in Italy and France, as did the French Expeditionary Corps in North Africa. Later, the Israelis, too, used Johnsons that had been meant for the Dutch.

—BN

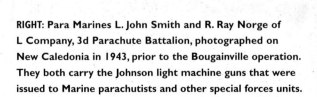

RIGHT: Para Marines L. John Smith and R. Ray Norge of L Company, 3d Parachute Battalion, photographed on New Caledonia in 1943, prior to the Bougainville operation. They both carry the Johnson light machine guns that were issued to Marine parachutists and other special forces units.

1st Marine Amphibious Corps
Headquarters

1st Marine Amphibious Corps
Parachute Marines

1st Marine Amphibious Corps
Raider Battalion

CENTER, INSET: A rare color photograph of a Marine 75mm pack howitzer in action at Torokina Field, Bougainville, 15 December 1943. The gun crew has draped a tattered Japanese flag over the camouflage netting.

BELOW: In January 1943, native guides lead a combat patrol of the 2d Marines up the Tenaru River, which had seen heavy fighting six months earlier. By this time, 2d MarDiv and the Army Americal Division had relieved 1st MarDiv, which had gone to Australia for rest and recuperation.

The Marines Transform Warfare

Warfare is not transformed by new technology alone. Old modes of warfare, doctrines, and tactics are transformed by leaders who conceive of new ways to exploit available technologies. Germany's use of tanks to exploit breakthroughs is one example of this. Another is the Marine Corps' development of amphibious landings, a concept that was brought to fruition by the innovation of landing craft and landing vehicles.

The next transformation of warfare was the development of an integrated sea-land-air operational mode in the South Pacific by the Marines and the Navy. The sequence of events was as follows:

The Japanese were building an airfield on Guadalcanal, the southernmost island of the Solomons chain. The Japanese field would support a further jump five hundred miles southward to the island of Espíritu Santo, then to New Caledonia, and, ultimately, to Australia and New Zealand.

The United States preempted Japan by occupying New Caledonia and establishing an airfield on Espíritu Santo. Then the 1st Marine Division, under naval air and gunfire support, landed on Guadalcanal while the airfield was under construction. The airfield was quickly completed and named Henderson Field. It became the base for Marine Air operations, and eventually for Navy aircraft from the sunken and damaged carriers *Hornet* and *Enterprise*.

After the bitter defense of Henderson Field, the next step for the Americans was to seize a Japanese field on Munda, in the central Solomons, although at severe cost to the landing force. The field on Munda then supported a jump to Bougainville, the northernmost Solomon island. There, to avoid a Japanese defense of the existing airfield, the 3d Marine Division landed in an undefended area where a field could be built. The 1st Marine Division's landing at Cape Gloucester on the island of New Britain was accomplished in the same manner. From airfields on these two islands the large Japanese base at Rabaul to the north was neutralized. New Zealand troops carried aboard U.S. Navy amphibious force ships seized Green Island, and Marine Air was based there to neutralize Kavieng, on New Ireland, to the north of New Britain and Rabaul.

These later operations were in MacArthur's Southwestern Pacific Command Area, and he monitored the successful technique appreciatively. Using the same operational scheme, he overcame his initial stalemate in New Guinea in a series of jumps along the New Guinea coast, bypassing Japanese defenses and constructing airfields to support the next two-hundred-mile jump. MacArthur continued to employ this Marine Corps–Navy warfighting technique all the way to his return to the Philippines. Then, six years later, he used it again when he sent the 1st Marine Division, covered by Marine Air and naval gunfire, to land at Inchon and unhinge the North Korean deep invasion of South Korea.

The sea-land-air transformation continues today with the enhancement of helicopters and expeditionary airfield equipment. In 2003, Marines in helicopters from carriers in the Indian Ocean landed to establish a base at a friendly field in Pakistan. From there they jumped several hundred miles into landlocked Afghanistan to seize an airfield. Marine and other U.S. and allied forces then entered by air transport to conduct operations throughout the country.

The Marine air-ground teams backed by Navy ships and aircraft have again entered the annals of an enduring warfare transformation.

—BN

TARAWA

Tarawa was a narrow strip in a necklace of several small islands of sand surrounding a lagoon that was the sunken crater of a long-extinct volcano. Betio—3 miles long and 800 yards wide—was the principal landmass. Its capture would be a snap, or so thought the Navy task force commander, RAdm Kelly Turner. Both Turner and his superior, VAdm Raymond Spruance, decided to limit prelanding bombardments and refused a request by landing force CO Marine MajGen Holland M. "Howlin' Mad" Smith to seize the adjacent islets for artillery positions.

Having reluctantly agreed to only three days of heavy aerial and naval gunfire by the Navy to soften up the 2,619 Japanese defenders, Marine commanders on 20 November 1943 sent the 2d Division of Smith's V Amphibious Corps to ride the 6 miles from their transports in LVTs (Landing Vehicles, Tracked—"amtracs" carrying twenty to twenty-four troops) into the atoll's lagoon to assault the main island of Betio. There, the 6th, 8th, and 2d Marines plunged ashore and ran into unexpected—and lethal—opposition.

As the 8th and 2d Marines (the latter commanded by Col David M. Shoup, who would not only be wounded and awarded the Medal of Honor but would become the twenty-second commandant), and later the 6th Marines, came ashore from inside the lagoon, they met devastating small-arms, mortar, and artillery fire from supposedly destroyed enemy positions. The first wave of amtracs made it through, sustaining heavy casualties, and the assaulting Marines secured the 500-yard-long pier. But the succeeding waves of smaller LCVPs (deeper-draft Landing Craft Vehicles, Personnel, carrying thirty-six troops, or a platoon) could not cross the coral reef that lay several hundred yards from the beach, forcing Marines to jump into the waist-deep surf and wade the distance through withering automatic-weapons fire. Five hundred Marines did not make it out of the water.

Once the Marines had reached the beach, there was little room to maneuver among the coconut-palm-log barriers and debris and concrete pillboxes of the tenacious enemy, which in its customary Bushido tradition had chosen to die to the last man. Die they did, except for seventeen wounded who survived. The Marines lost 984 KIA; another 2,072 were wounded.

V Amphibious Corps
(Lieutenant General Command)

MEDAL OF HONOR

COLONEL DAVID MONROE SHOUP
Betio Island, Tarawa Atoll
20–22 November 1943

For conspicuous gallantry and intrepidity at the risk of his life above and beyond the call of duty as commanding officer of all Marine Corps troops in action against enemy Japanese forces on Betio Island, Tarawa Atoll, Gilbert Islands, from 20 to 22 November 1943. Although severely shocked by an exploding enemy shell soon after landing at the pier and suffering from a serious, painful leg wound which had become infected, Col Shoup fearlessly exposed himself to the terrific and relentless artillery, machine-gun, and rifle fire from hostile shore emplacements. Rallying his hesitant troops by his own inspiring heroism, he gallantly led them across the fringing reefs to charge the heavily fortified island and reinforce our hard-pressed, thinly held lines. Upon arrival on shore, he assumed command of all landed troops and, working without rest under constant, withering enemy fire during the next two days, conducted smashing attacks against unbelievably strong and fanatically defended Japanese positions despite innumerable obstacles and heavy casualties. By his brilliant leadership, daring tactics, and selfless devotion to duty, Col Shoup was largely responsible for the final decisive defeat of the enemy, and his indomitable fighting spirit reflects great credit upon the U.S. Naval Service.

RIGHT: A member of "Denig's Demons" combat art team at HQMC, noted illustrator Tom Lovell painted this startlingly realistic portrayal of the Tarawa amphibious landing based on Marine combat cinematographer SSgt Norman T. Hatch's eye-witness description. Lovell depicts here the fourth wave of 2d MarDiv in its shallow-draft LCVP. Unlike the previous waves of LVTs, the LCVPs could not clear the reef that was several hundred yards off the beachhead. To reach the beach, Marines had to jump into the chest-deep surf and wade through a hailstorm of enemy gunfire. Five hundred didn't make it.

RIGHT: The bunched-up landing forces here use a low coconut-palm-log seawall for protection as they wait for the signal to continue the attack off the beachhead. Despite its ferocity, the three-day prelanding naval and aerial bombardment of Betio had not sufficiently softened enemy resistance on the beaches. As a result, the crouching Marines had no choice but to charge forward into the murderous fire as subsequent waves landed behind them. In a day of vicious fighting, they traversed the 800-yard island and began killing the remainder of the 2,600 defenders.

LEFT: New camouflaged utilities were introduced at Tarawa. Shown here are the shirt, cartridge belt, and inflatable life belt. A hand grenade and a jungle first-aid pouch are hooked onto the cartridge belt.

The four-day battle was the roughest the Marines had encountered so far, and important lessons would be gained from it. The Navy had much to learn from it as well: there had been bad naval air and fire-support coordination. And Navy interference with preplanning had led to the Navy amphibious force CO having to relinquish command to the Marine landing force CO once ashore. It became obvious, too, that the Marine commander needed to have his own command ship. The Army regiment's sluggish performance on nearby Makin Island was studied as well in light of the Marines' speedy but deadly assault against heavier resistance.

In succeeding amphibious landings on heavily fortified beachheads, aerial and naval gunfire preparatory bombardments would be more prolonged, more intense, and at closer, more effective ranges. Additionally, landing craft would be significantly improved. The Marine mission henceforth would be to assault Japanese-held island strongholds across the central Pacific in order to secure airfields closer and closer to the enemy homeland.

By 1944 the Marine Corps had increased to five 25,000-man infantry divisions with supporting artillery and tanks and four air wings. The Corps would leapfrog from one horrendous island battle to another,

LEFT: A civilian artist for Abbott Laboratories, fifty-two-year-old Kerr Eby went in with the fourth wave at Tarawa and sketched this firsthand impression of the bloody carnage in the shallow water off the beach. Eby had also done combat sketches while serving as an Army engineer in World War I.

BELOW, LEFT AND RIGHT: This sequence of photos taken by combat photographer Cpl Obie Newcomb shows the living among the dead on the Tarawa beachhead. SSgt Norman T. Hatch, cinematographer for the 2d MarDiv, also shot motion pictures of the battle.

PAGES 208–209: Marines of the 2d and 8th regiments hunker down among the chunks of concrete, pieces of coral, and coconut-palm logs that made up the seawall on Betio. The photograph at far right was taken by Obie Newcomb while under fire from Japanese defenders.

BELOW: Commanders of the assault forces on Tarawa confer during the battle. Seated is Col Evans Carlson, CO, 8th Marines; standing in the foreground with hands on hips is Col Merritt Edson, CO, 6th Marines; and standing at center, holding the map case, is Col David Shoup, CO, 2d Marines, who led the initial attack on Tarawa.

OPPOSITE, INSET: Marine combat cinematographer SSgt Norman Hatch gives water to a kitten he found under a destroyed Japanese tank.

first clearing the Gilbert Islands (Tarawa), the Marshalls (Kwajalein, Roi-Namur, and Eniwetok), the Marianas (Saipan, Tinian, and Guam), the Palau Island group (Peleliu), and the Bonin Islands (Iwo Jima) just 660 miles due south of Tokyo before converging with the Army in the invasion of Okinawa. Each bloody battle provided an airfield not only for supporting amphibious operations but also for longer-range interdiction. Saipan-Tinian was perhaps the most critical, for from there the new B-29 Superfortresses were able to fly to and bomb Japan itself. Marine blood flowed copiously for the tiny island of Iwo Jima to become an emergency landing field for combat-crippled B-29s returning from bombing missions over the enemy homeland and a base for Army Air Corps P-51 Mustang escort fighters.

World War II—Asiatic-Pacific Campaign (1941–1945)

BELOW: A sweeping view of the congestion and litter on the beach at Betio, where the Marines of 2d MarDiv overwhelmed the dug-in Japanese defenders. There was little room to fight on the tiny island, and combat was often close-in and hand-to-hand. Front-line air strikes were largely impracticable in such close quarters, but flamethrowers and tanks provided valuable support.

RIGHT: "Boondockers" worn by Col David M. Shoup when he was regimental commander of the 2d Marines, 2d MarDiv, on Tarawa in November 1943. Shoup was awarded the Medal of Honor for his part in the action, and later became CMC. The comfortable, almost indestructible high-quarter field shoes were beloved by Marines.

"Casualties many; percentage of dead not known; combat efficiency: we are winning."

Radio message from Col David M. Shoup (later CMC) on Tarawa to MajGen Julian C. Smith, 21 November 1943

The Corps Led the Way in Combat Cinematography

The Marine-Navy assault on Tarawa in November 1943 was the first successful amphibious attack against a heavily fortified beachhead in modern warfare. Fortunately, Marine combat photographers captured the historic—and bloody—seventy-six-hour battle for posterity.

Marine SSgt Norman T. Hatch, trained by the March of Time newsreel staff before the war, was senior cinematographer for 2d MarDiv. With him was his assistant, Pvt William F. Kelliher, and still photographer Cpl Obie Newcomb. Hatch shot 35mm black-and-white motion pictures in 100-foot reels with his spring-wound Bell & Howell Eyemo, which had a swivel mount for a wide-angle, normal, or telephoto lens;

Newcomb used the standard 4 x 5 Speed Graphic still camera. Hatch and SSgt John Ercole had trained several younger cinematographers using Kodak and Bell & Howell 16mm color cameras, which they had culled from every camera store in Los Angeles prior to going overseas.

The result was some of the greatest combat footage ever filmed. The film

BELOW: SSgt Norman Hatch (circled) shooting 1stLt Alexander Bonnyman's daring attack against a bombproof Japanese emplacement on Betio, Tarawa. His assistant, Pvt William F. Kelliher, stands right beside him. Bonnyman was awarded a posthumous Medal of Honor for his action. Footage of the assault shot by Hatch and others was turned into an Oscar-winning documentary the following year.

quickly reached Los Angeles for processing and editing at Warner Brothers and was released by Universal motion picture studios into theaters nationwide. Titled *With the Marines on Tarawa*, it won the 1944 Academy Award for Most Outstanding Documentary Short Subject, and the footage has since been used in countless movies, notably in the 1949 film *The Sands of Iwo Jima*. For Tarawa, SSgt Hatch was awarded the Navy Commendation Medal.

Promoted to warrant officer, Hatch became the photo officer for 5th MarDiv in the Iwo Jima operation. Sgt Bill Genaust, one of his combat cinematographers, shot the flag-raising sequence in 16mm color (see page 244) before he was

killed in action. After the battle, WO Hatch, working with photo officers Lt Herb Schlosberg and Capt Karl Soule of 3d and 4th MarDivs at Warner Brothers, edited a theatrical release of the battle, which was nominated for an Academy Award in 1946. For his action on Iwo, WO Hatch was awarded a Bronze Star.

During World War II, many noted Hollywood film producers and directors joined the services: Frank Capra was a major in the Army at the Pictorial Center in Astoria, Queens, and John Ford was a captain in the Navy. Following the war, Hatch co-produced a film for then LtCol Victor H. "Brute" Krulak titled *Bombs Over Tokyo*, which Krulak circulated in the corridors of Congress and at the White House as ammunition against the very real threat of the elimination of the Marine Corps. Krulak advised Hatch and Lt Carlos P. Steele, the G-3 photo officer, that the heads of Unification, House, and Senate Armed Services committees stated that the film was instrumental in ensuring a Marine Corps in the 1947 National Security Act. Public Law 416, signed in 1952 after the Corps' brilliant combat record at Pusan, Inchon, Seoul, and the Chosin Reservoir in Korea, had further cemented the Marine Corps' survivability.

Reverting to the Marine Corps Reserve at war's end and rising to major, Hatch was a motion picture cameraman and film and television producer before becoming senior audio-visual adviser to the Secretary of Defense and a consultant to the White House Press Office and to the House and Senate photo and TV galleries in the National Capital.

During the Korean War, the bitter Chosin Reservoir withdrawal in December of 1950 was recorded on 35mm black-and-white film by Marine MSgt Heber D. Maxwell. How Maxwell protected both his camera and film under such harsh, frigid conditions is incredible. His footage was

MEDAL OF HONOR

FIRST LIEUTENANT ALEXANDER BONNYMAN, JR.
Betio Island, Tarawa Atoll
20–22 November 1943

Acting on his own initiative when assault troops were pinned down at the far end of Betio Pier by the overwhelming fire of Japanese shore batteries, 1stLt Bonnyman repeatedly defied the blasting fury of the enemy bombardment to organize and lead the besieged men over the long, open pier to the beach and then, voluntarily obtaining flamethrowers and demolitions, organized his pioneer shore party into assault demolitionists and directed the blowing up of several hostile installations before the close of D-Day. Determined to effect an opening in the enemy's strongly organized defense line the following day, he voluntarily crawled approximately 40 yards forward of our lines and placed demolitions in the entrance of a large Japanese emplacement as the initial move in his planned attack against the heavily garrisoned, bombproof installation which was stubbornly resisting despite the destruction early in the action of a large number of Japanese who had been inflicting heavy casualties on our forces and holding up our advance. Withdrawing only to replenish his ammunition, he led his men in a renewed assault, fearlessly exposing himself to the merciless slash of hostile fire as he stormed the formidable bastion, directed the placement of demolition charges in both entrances, and seized the top of the bombproof position, flushing out more than 100 of the enemy who were instantly cut down, and effecting the annihilation of approximately 150 troops inside the emplacement. Assailed by additional Japanese after he had gained his objective, he made a heroic stand on the edge of the structure, defending his strategic position with indomitable determination in the face of the desperate charge and killing three of the enemy before he fell, mortally wounded. By his dauntless fighting spirit, unrelenting aggressiveness and forceful leadership throughout three days of unremitting, violent battle, 1stLt Bonnyman had inspired his men to heroic effort, enabling them to beat off the counterattack and break the back of hostile resistance in that sector for an immediate gain of 400 yards with no further casualties to our forces in this zone. He gallantly gave his life for his country.

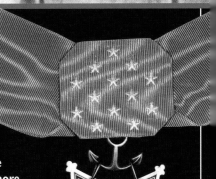

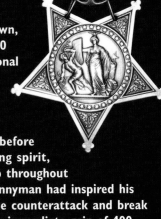

shown in newsreels in theaters all over the country shortly afterward. David Douglas Duncan was there as well, taking still shots for *Life* magazine.

In the early 1960s, Marine Reserve Col William Hendricks, a VP heading animation and shorts at Warner Brothers Studios and CO of the Reserve West Coast Public Affairs Unit, produced a color theatrical release titled *Force in Readiness*, which won an Academy Award in the documentary category in 1962.

These pioneering Marine cinematographers deserve recognition, as they were in a league unto themselves. No other military service has achieved such recognition since then.

—HAC

ABOVE: The 2d Marine Division Photo Section, under the direction of Capt Louis Hayward, poses for a group photo on Tarawa in November 1943. Bottom row, left to right: SSgt Carlos P. Steele, Pfc Jack Ely, Pfc Fermin Dixon, SSgt John F. Ercole, Cpl Obie Newcomb, Sgt Ernest J. Diet. Center row, left to right: Pfc Christopher Demo, Sgt Forest Owens, Cpl James Orton, Cpl Raymond A. Matjasic. Back row, left to right: SSgt Roy Oland, Capt Louis Hayward, WO John F. Leopold, SSgt Norman T. Hatch. Not shown in this photo is Pvt William F. Kelliher.

RIGHT: Dashing young cameraman SSgt Norman Hatch, with a well-deserved Navy Commendation and an Expert Rifleman Badge, went on to cover Iwo Jima as a Warrant Officer, receiving a Bronze Star. The straight bar instead of a curved rocker under his three sergeant stripes indicated specialty ranks at the time, in this case combat photographer.

LEFT: Marines in close combat with Japanese defenders in the Marshall Islands. Note the bayonet mounted on the M1 of the Marine on the left.

BELOW: Marines take a breather, "the smoking lamp is lit," and they "chow down" on Roi-Namur on 18 February 1944. These men secured the two small islands in the Kwajalein Atoll relatively quickly.

PACIFIC ISLAND–HOPPING

Kwajalein–Roi-Namur

Following a long breather after Tarawa, Adm Nimitz's island-hopping plan to secure airfields in the central Pacific closer and closer to the Japanese homeland called next for the seizure of Kwajalein Atoll in the Marshall Islands group 700 miles north-northwest of the Gilbert Islands. The main island in this largest of the world's atolls was assigned to an Army regiment, while the 23d and 24th Marine Regiments were given the task of capturing two linked islands at the north rim of the atoll: Roi-Namur, home to the large airfield used by the Japanese to attack Wake Island two and a half years earlier.

From 31 January to 2 February 1944, the new 4th Marine Division, under MajGen Harry Schmidt, landed in amtracs launched from new LSTs (Landing Ship Tanks) after the 25th Marines had taken five adjacent islands from which to set up artillery positions for the 14th Marines to support the landing on Roi and Namur. This direct-fire support, plus battleship and other naval gunfire closing to within eight hundred yards of the beach, corrected the earlier mistakes at

**Fleet Marine Force Pacific
Artillery Battalion
1944**

**Fleet Marine Force Pacific
Supply & Service
1944**

**Fleet Marine Force Pacific
Amphibious Tractor Battalion
1944**

**Fleet Marine Force Pacific
Headquarters
1944**

Tarawa. As a result, casualties were much lighter at Roi-Namur.

The 23d Marines raced across the airstrip on Roi and secured it. The 24th Marines had a tougher time on adjacent Namur and had to use tanks and half-tracks before smashing all Japanese resistance. In all, 3,563 Japanese defenders were killed, while 313 Marines were killed in action and 502 were wounded. The Army seized Kwajalein itself.

Eniwetok

From Roi the next target was Eniwetok, a 400-mile leap northwestward at the extremity of the Marshalls, again to gain an airfield and anchorage closer to Japan.

On 17 February 1944, V Phib Corps Reserve, a brigade consisting of the 22d Marines and the 106th Infantry of the Army, landed on the atoll. The Marines took Engebi, the northernmost island, in a single day of hard fighting. The 3d Battalion then joined the Army regiment to secure Eniwetok after two more days of fighting. Marines suffered 254 killed and 555 wounded; the enemy lost 3,400 killed and 66 taken prisoner.

RIGHT: Having just come ashore, a Marine .50-caliber machine gun crew sets up under fire on an enemy beachhead.

Strategy

Marine Air Group 31 and MAG-13 had been quickly flown in and became operational on Roi and Kwajalein, and with MAG-22 echeloned from Midway to Eniwetok, they began pummeling four other major Japanese bases in the Marshalls that had been purposely bypassed. The ten fighter and four bomber squadrons accounted for three-quarters of the casualties of 2,564 inflicted on these enemy bases. It is estimated that 3,500 of the original 13,701 enemy isolated eventually died from disease and starvation.

By 1944, the U.S. Navy had amassed vast armadas of powerful task forces centered on new, fast, *Essex*-class aircraft carriers, with light carriers (CVL) and escort carriers (CVE) for close-air and antisubmarine protection. With now five powerful Marine divisions and four air wings, it was a formidable force. That was proven in the summer of 1944 with the incursion 1,300 miles northwestward into the Mariana Islands, which contained the large neighboring string of islands of Saipan, Tinian, and Guam. The latter, a U.S. territory inherited from Spain following the Spanish-American War, had been lost in the first days of the war.

Tarawa—Problems Met; Kwajalein—Problems Solved

While Marines continued fighting jungle warfare in the Solomons and Cape Gloucester during 1943, the 2d Marine Division faced a different challenge in November of that year at Tarawa Atoll, in the central Pacific Gilbert Island group: the direct attack of a heavily fortified beach. The unanticipated problems encountered at Tarawa were solved for the next operation, Kwajalein Atoll, two months later.

The first problem was that of intelligence. While aerial photographs plotted enemy defenses accurately, hydrographic information was limited to the logbook entry of an 1840 visit by a whaling ship. The whaler noted that there was enough depth of water over the coral reef for ships' boats to pass through. However, a coral reef is a living organism, and this one had grown at least one foot in the intervening one hundred years since the whaler's visit, and landing craft could no longer pass over it. During the assault on Betio, the first waves of Marines crossed to the beach in LVT amphibious tractors, but there were too few LVTs to accommodate subsequent waves. They instead came across in Higgins boats, which got hung up on the barrier reef, forcing the men to wade ashore for several hundred yards in waist- to neck-deep water amidst unrelenting Japanese fire. Casualties were heavy.

Naval gunfire from 5-inch to 14-inch guns was delivered from a safe distance at sea; in effect, area fire. But the loose coral sand absorbed the explosions, and a direct hit on a defensive position was pure luck. Close air support by Navy Air was poorly controlled and delivered.

There were other lessons to be learned, and they were, but these were the most important ones. For the 4th Marine Division landing on the Roi-Namur islands of Kwajalein Atoll on 31 January 1944, more LVTs were available

ABOVE: The coconut-palm-log, coral, and concrete seawall on the three-mile-long, six-hundred-yard-wide island of Betio prevented most amtracs from reaching the battle further inland. It did, however, serve as a temporary shelter for those coming ashore, enabling them to regroup and mount successive attacks. In four days the battle for Betio was over, but the lessons learned during the assault would continue to play a role in later battles.

due to increased production, and the landing was made from inside the lagoon, where the reef was less of a barrier. Fire support, too, was greatly improved. Naval fire, including that of battleships, confined the beach to as little as eight hundred yards using "pointer" (aimed) fire on concrete blockhouses and bunkers.

During December and January, Navy carrier aircraft practiced close air support of advancing troops to ensure accuracy and responsiveness. Equally important, artillery of the 14th Marines was landed prior to D-Day on islets adjacent to Roi-Namur. When aerial and naval gunfire bombardment was lifted just before the landing, the artillery opened up with close-in fire under front-line troop control.

The two islands were secured in two days of fighting, with casualties less than one-quarter of those at Tarawa. This was another demonstration of the Marines' quick adaptation to circumstances in solving problems presented by evolving warfare.

—BN

**Fleet Marine Force Pacific
Bomb Disposal Company
1944**

**Fleet Marine Force Pacific
Dog Platoon
1944**

**Fleet Marine Force Pacific
Separate Engineer Battalion
1944**

**Fleet Marine Force Pacific
Antiaircraft (AA) Battalion
1944**

The Marianas: Saipan, Guam, and Tinian

On 15 June 1944, Adm Spruance's Fifth Fleet escorted Marine LtGen Holland M. "Howlin' Mad" Smith's Expeditionary Troops and his Northern Troops and Landing Force (NTLF), which included the 2d and 4th Marine Divisions, for a tough landing on Saipan, the northernmost of the large islands of the chain, 1,500 air-miles due east of Manila. On Saipan—14 miles long, 6 miles wide, mountainous, and ringed by a coral reef barrier—was the main headquarters for the Japanese Central Pacific Fleet Command. It was garrisoned with 29,662 sailors and soldiers.

The object of taking the Saipan-Tinian-Guam group was twofold: to secure advanced airfields for longer-ranged bombers to strike Japan and to draw the Imperial Japanese Navy out of hiding for a final showdown.

The amphibious landing on Saipan on 16 June, by the 2d MarDiv on the left, the 4th MarDiv in the center, and the Army 165th Infantry of the Reserve Army 27th Division on the right, met stiff resistance. The 2d MarDiv alone sustained two thousand casualties on the first day. After fierce fighting, the units took their objectives and lined up abreast for the final sweep to clear the northern part of the island. The 2d MarDiv was still on the left, the entire 27th Army Division was now in the center, and the 4th MarDiv was on the right. When the Marine divisions advanced against heavy resistance and the Army division did not, Howlin' Mad Smith summarily relieved the Army CO, MajGen Ralph Smith, of his command. That action would have deep repercussions for Marine-Army relations for years to come.

As Saipan was being cleared of enemy stragglers, work on the runways got under way. B-29 Super-fortresses, the new, improved, and longer-range versions of the old B-17s, would soon arrive to make daily and nightly bombing runs over Japan.

The fighting was over on 10 July. Of the 16,525 American casualties, 10,570 Marines were wounded

OPPOSITE: Marines use a satchel charge to dislodge enemy fighters from a dug-in position on Saipan. They wait for survivors to emerge to mow them down with gun-fire—or a flamethrower, if necessary.

LEFT: A Marine 37mm gun crew fires from point-blank range at entrenched Japanese on Saipan. Their gun shield appears to be a wooden road sign, yanked up and placed over the gun to afford some protection. Note that it is riddled with bullet holes.

BELOW: Marines toss hand grenades during close-in fighting on Saipan. With a range of about the distance from home plate to second base, the grenade would explode ten seconds after pulling the pin.

The Art of Interrogation

The roots of the Marine interrogator date to well before World War I, but the godfather of the modern interrogator was Sherwood F. Moran, USMCR, whose work with Japanese POWs in World War II— when anyone in the Corps with an applicable second language was assigned interrogation duties and known as an Intelligence Marine—has become legendary.

Moran's reputation in part stems from the extraordinary success he enjoyed, but also because of his technique, which was based on treating prisoners with dignity, speaking their language fluently, and being conversant with their history and culture. Moran, who had lived in Japan for decades as a missionary, also tended to the wounded and sick, fed the malnourished, and in general encouraged prisoners to consider themselves "safe" once they had been captured. In fact, he preferred the term "interviewer" to interrogator, and considered it essential to think of the prisoner not as an enemy, but as a new acquaintance. In his famous report dated 17 July, 1943, he likened the process to making love: that is, that prisoners were to be "wooed" and that every interrogator needed to develop his own special touch.

There have been various critiques of Moran's methods offered over the years by fans of a more "hard-boiled" approach (to borrow Moran's own description of his detractors), who suggest that the Japanese who allowed themselves to be captured alive were already "soft." The strength of his approach was confirmed not only by results, however, but by the parallel success of his charismatic counterpart in German intelligence, Luftwaffe interrogator Hans Joachim Scharff, who used comparable methods to extract valuable information out of his prisoners (mainly Allied airmen).

INSET: Intelligence Marine Pvt Kenneth N. Portteus and a couple of Japanese prisoners share a light moment on Okinawa during an interrogation. Few Japanese soldiers surrendered, but those who did were treated humanely by their captors.

ABOVE: Aviation illustrator Nicolas Trudgian's *Gunfight Over Rabaul* shows gull-winged F4U Corsairs of VMF-214—the "Black Sheep" squadron—attacking the Japanese naval base at Rabaul, on the northeastern tip of New Britain Island. The flamboyant squadron racked up a total of 126 victories and 34 probables by war's end.

RIGHT: 1stLt Paul A. Mullen, shown here on 25 June 1943, scored 1.5 victories while flying with VMF-122 and an additional 5 victories with VMF-214. He was awarded the Distinguished Flying Cross.

World War II Air Medal (awarded for every ten combat missions)

OPPOSITE, BOTTOM: Marine pilots of VMF-214, Maj Gregory "Pappy" Boyington's famous "Black Sheep" squadron, in the central Solomons in January 1944. Boyington (holding papers) came to Marine aviation via Gen Clair Chennault's famous all-volunteer American "Flying Tigers," who fought in China. Bringing a total of six kills with him, Boyington downed nineteen more as leader of the Black Sheep, elevating him to second place in victory totals in World War II, behind Joe Foss.

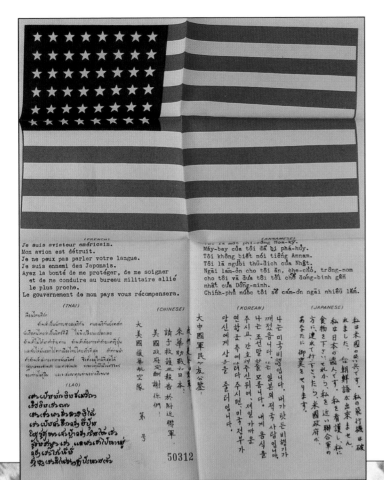

LEFT: The Navy-Marine aviators' "Safe Conduct" or POW pass was carried at all times for use in the event of being shot down or captured over enemy territory. Made of silk, the panel measures 9 1/2 inches by 12 inches and was often sewn into the lining of the pilot's flight jacket. This particular pass was used by former Navy radioman Robert Plouffe.

RIGHT: The naval aviator's life vest—referred to affectionately as the Mae West because of its buxom silhouette when inflated—saved many a downed flier at sea. It could be quickly inflated by yanking the two lower tabs, which released a burst of carbon dioxide; it could also be inflated by mouth via a tube near the wearer's head.

and 2,365 were killed in action. All but 1,000 of the 30,000 defenders were killed. Following the loss of Saipan and the naval defeat in the Philippine Sea, Japanese premier Hideki Tojo resigned. (Adm Yamamoto had been killed earlier, after Japanese codes had been broken and Marine Air intelligence officers in the Solomon Islands had plotted the enemy officer's flight plan so that Army Air Corps P-38 Lightnings could intercept his aircraft and shoot it down.)

The consequence of the attack on the three Marianas islands was as intended: the Japanese fleet appeared and one of the most horrendous sea-air battles of the war ensued. On 19 June, Adm Marc Mitscher's Navy Task Force 58 engaged the Imperial Japanese Navy in the Battle of the Philippine Sea some several hundred miles to the west, sinking the last two Japanese aircraft carriers and losing one hundred of its own planes in the process. However, Mitscher's Navy and Marine aircraft downed 346

Japanese planes in that single day's raging battle. It was thenceforth dubbed the Great Marianas Turkey Shoot.

After Saipan was secured, MajGen Roy Geiger, the former aviation commander on Guadalcanal and now III Amphibious Corps commander, sent his 3d MarDiv and the 1st Provisional Brigade of the 22d and 29th Marines and the Army 77th Division, held in reserve, onto Guam on 21 July. The three regiments of the 3d MarDiv went in abreast, with armored amphibians mounted with 37mm and 75mm guns.

After progressing through a hard-fought day, the Marine units linked up and braced for the inevitable nighttime counterattack—which came in the form of a suicidal banzai attack through a mangrove swamp. The enemy penetrated between two units and reached a rear field hospital, where wounded, bandaged Marines in their Skivvies grabbed weapons and beat them back.

By 4 August, MAG-21 began operations out of the captured airfield at Orote and was quickly built up to twelve squadrons. By 10 August, it was all over. More than 1,350 Marines had been killed and 6,964 wounded; Japanese losses were more than 17,000 killed and 485 taken prisoner. For years after the war, enemy stragglers who had tried to hole up in the far reaches of the island would give themselves up, half-crazed from starvation.

Just two miles across from the southern shore of Saipan lay a smaller island, Tinian. Relatively flat, it was cultivated for sugarcane and was home to several airfields. Tinian was an ideal locale for the eight-thousand-foot runway envisioned for the new B-29s.

After a breather, 4th and 2d MarDivs came over from Saipan and landed on 24 July. All of their artillery had been left grouped on Saipan across the waterway and was called in to fire in front of the two divisions now attacking on Tinian. Air support also came from Marine aircraft on the new fields on Saipan as well as aircraft carriers offshore. On 1 August, the island was secured. The Japanese lost 6,050 killed and 255 taken prisoner; however, 13,262 civilians were saved from the fate others had chosen on Saipan and Guam: suicide by jumping off the steep cliffs. The Marines lost 290 killed and 1,515 wounded; 24 remained missing in action.

BGen Vincente "Ben" Blaz, USMC (Ret.)

Little could thirteen-year-old Guamanian Ben Blaz have foreseen on 8 December 1941 how his life would be affected when the Japanese invaded and captured his Pacific island home, Guam, a "possession" ceded to the United States at the end of the Spanish-American War.

Big for his age, Blaz was herded with other native Chamorros into a labor battalion. Forced to use only hand tools to dig and burlap sacks to drag the dirt, they built a landing strip for Japanese aviation as Guam was quickly turned into a Japanese high command center. The labor was grueling, and the Japanese decapitated uncooperative civilians and raped and murdered others during their brutal thirty-one-month occupation.

In July 1944, a U.S. naval preinvasion bombardment signaled an impending landing by U.S. Marines. The Japanese quickly rounded up most of the Guamanians—including Blaz, his eight siblings, and his parents—and threw them into barbed-wire concentration camps in the jungle, without food or shelter. While scavenging food for their families one night, Blaz and two friends, who were brothers, managed to escape. The boys drifted down a river to return to their homes in the hope of finding food to bring back to their hungry families.

On their return, one of the brothers, who had lagged behind, took a wrong turn and ran right into a Japanese patrol and was captured (he was later found tied to a tree—decapitated). Blaz and the other brother continued toward the concentration camp and, fortunately, stumbled into a patrol of the 9th Marines. Speaking very little English, they were mistaken for Japanese and interned as POWs until a former Guamanian teacher vouched for them and the Marines freed them. Unable to locate his family after the camp was

liberated, the young Guamanian stayed with the Marines, who were by then mopping up the island. He even accompanied a few patrols but was kept in the rear of the column for safety.

As things returned to normal, Blaz went back to high school, graduated in 1947, and won a scholarship to the University of Notre Dame in the United States, where, upon graduating in 1951, he was commissioned a second lieutenant in the U.S. Marines. During an outstanding professional career in the United States Marine Corps, he served three overseas tours with the 9th Marines, who had been his rescuers. On his first tour, as a first lieutenant, he served as regimental legal officer; on his second tour, as a major, he was the 9th Marines' operations officer in Vietnam; and on his last tour—which he considers his finest—Blaz, then a colonel, served as commanding officer of the regiment that had liberated him a quarter century before.

Capping his Marine Corps career, the former teenage prisoner of the Japanese was promoted to brigadier general in 1977 and assigned director of information at Marine Corps headquarters. Following that, he served as deputy chief of staff of Reserve affairs.

Retiring in 1980 with twenty-nine years of service, he returned to his island home, taught at the University of Guam, and was elected to the U.S. Congress as a delegate from Guam, serving four terms from 1984 through 1993.

In his memoir, Gen Blaz reflected on his life-changing experiences in World War II:

"While this difficult period deprived those of my generation most of our tender teen years, it taught us more about life, family, and ourselves than I, for one, had ever learned before or since.… The Chamorro spirit was not an abstraction; rather, it was demonstrably real during those years and I have drawn inspiration and sustenance from that reality my entire life."

"Challenged by the threatening experience of war and pressed to our limits, we learned things about human nature and ourselves that we might not have been able to grasp in peaceful, less demanding times."

—HAC

THE NEXT MOVES

At this point, two military strategies conflicted: MacArthur's forces had secured the larger land-masses up the southern Pacific and were poised to invade the Philippines. In preparation, the general wanted his right flank protected by the elimination of any air threat from Peleliu in the Palau Island group a thousand miles to the east of Mindanao, the large southernmost island of the Philippine Island group.

Adm Nimitz's Navy and Army Air Forces, how-ever, saw the Bonin archipelago—with its dominant island, Iwo Jima, only two and a half flying hours due south of Tokyo—as an essential base for shorter-range fighters to be able to escort the B-29s and thus cut the inevitable losses. In addition, Iwo Jima would be an emergency landing field for damaged Superfortresses on their return leg from the incessant bombing runs that had begun over the enemy homeland. The seizure of Peleliu, however, was ordered a priority. By the middle of 1944, Marines in the Pacific numbered approximately 200,000 with supporting weapons and logistical units. The 5 Marine air wings totaled 28 Marine Air Groups with 126 squadrons manned by 10,457 pilots.

Peleliu

The assault on Peleliu got under way on 15 September 1944. Even Marine planners thought it would be a short, four-day affair. The 1st MarDiv, reinforced to 28,484 strong (1st, 5th, and 7th Marines and sup-porting arms), landed under fire and found itself in the iron jaws of well-dug-in Japanese defenses. The enemy waited until the Marines were bunched up on the beaches before opening up fierce mortar and artillery barrages, knocking out twenty-six LVTs. A tank-infantry counterattack between the 1st and 5th Marines was stopped, but slowed the Marines'

ABOVE: Marines take cover behind a half-track during their slow, torturous advance on Peleliu. Evidently, the action was too hot to man the exposed .50-caliber and .30-caliber machine guns, which appear loaded to fire.

RIGHT: A Marine was never without his dog tags, the two small metal tags stamped with his name, serial number, and blood type. (Today, the tags have a DNA ID.) If wounded, he could be easily identified and treated. If he were killed, one of the tags would go to casualty collection; the other would stay with the body to ensure a proper burial. The water canteen and cup were other essentials that a Marine always had at hand. These items belonged to John S. Roche of the 11th Marines, 1st MarDiv, whose boot camp photo is shown at right. Roche was wounded on Peleliu when a Japanese shell exploded near him and sent shrapnel flying into his leg. A piece also hit his canteen, as evidenced by the small dent.

advance to their objectives. The next day, the Marines took the airfield with staggering casualties while Chesty Puller's 1st Marines were bloodying themselves against "Bloody Nose" Ridge. Five days later, Chesty's regiment, which suffered 56 percent casualties, was replaced by the 321st Army Regimental Combat Team of the 81st Infantry Division.

Marine Air began moving in as soon as the airfield was cleared. On 24 September, Corsairs from VMF-114 arrived, as did those of VMF-122 a week later. The new inverted-gull-winged F4U Corsairs, uniquely rigged with rockets and napalm, delivered their ordnance on the enemy a thousand yards from takeoff without even time to retract their landing gear.

Peleliu turned out to be even more devastating than Tarawa. By 12 October the battle was, thankfully, over. The struggle had lasted twenty-nine days and had taken 1,241 Marine lives, leaving 5,500 wounded. The defending Japanese lost 10,695 dead and 301 taken prisoner.

Ironically, the operation might not have been necessary at all. Even before the battle was over, MacArthur upped his timetable and invaded the Philippines. He bypassed Mindanao and instead landed hundreds of miles farther north, on the middle island of Leyte. Naturally, he wanted to redeem his earlier defeat at Bataan— and to demonstrate his pledge to return. However, it took three Navy task forces with Marine aviation to land and cover MacArthur's Army forces at Leyte and, later, on the north island of Luzon.

Any enemy threat from Peleliu was moot at that point.

Marines played a major role in MacArthur's return to the Philippines. Artillery from V Phib Corps was loaned to the Army, and by December 1944 five Marine squadrons, including night fighters, were in support of the Army 77th Division landings on Leyte, Mindanao, and Luzon, supporting the 1st Cavalry Division's drive on Manila. They supported numerous other smaller Army landings as well. The crusty Marines circulated signage to needle MacArthur: "BY GRACE OF GOD AND A FEW MARINES, MACARTHUR'S BACK IN THE PHILIPPINES."

Silver Star

ABOVE: Marine Pfc George R. Weiland of 3d Battalion, 7th Marines, 1st MarDiv, was killed at Peleliu as his unit advanced under furious attack by the entrenched Japanese forces on 4 October 1944. The young Marine was awarded a post-humous Silver Star for his unwavering gallantry.

LEFT: A Marine bulldozer tank crew fires at dug-in enemy positions on a steep ridge on Peleliu. The terrain on Peleliu was rougher than any the Marines had encountered so far. Almost insurmountable jagged cliffs rose steeply from rocky beaches, affording the enemy innumerable caves, nooks, and crannies in which to hide. Marines suffered a high rate of casualties in fer-reting them out. Air-dropped napalm and flamethrower tank-fire were necessary.

Another Side of the Marine Corps

Combat Correspondents

At the beginning of World War II, Marine BGen Robert L. Denig was called out of retirement by CMC LtGen Thomas Holcomb to lead the Department of Public Relations (later termed Public Information, DIVINFO, and now Public Affairs) at HQMC. He was the right man at the right moment. Denig envisioned a department that would generate authentic on-the-scene war stories written by Marine combat correspondents and accompanied by eyewitness combat art by Marine artists. These reports would serve not only as a means to record history, but also as a way to keep the public informed and to raise the morale of the families back home. To assemble his group of artists and writers, Denig looked both inside and outside the Corps.

From the flood of volunteers in those frantic months after Pearl Harbor, Denig wisely sought only practicing, professional newspapermen. He had 1stSgt Joe Shipman, resplendent in his dress blues, march into the newsrooms of the major Washington newspapers and guarantee sergeant stripes to anyone with five years' journalistic experience who joined the Marines and passed boot camp. This, he

BELOW: A foursome of "Denig's Demons" on New Britain in 1943 (left to right): combat photographer Sgt Al Monteverdi; combat correspondents SSgt Sam Stavisky and SSgt Jeremiah O'Leary; and Sgt Bob Brenner, combat photographer.

promised, would be followed by combat duty. It was just the experience for which many young reporters were then eager. Once interviewed and approved, they were enlisted by Denig—regardless of age or physical limitations—and sent to Parris Island for rigorous infantry indoctrination. They were then given their sergeant stripes and sent off to the Pacific battle zones. Newspaper photographers were also recruited, ostensibly to form writer-photographer teams, a concept that was not fully worked out until the end of the war.

Dubbed Denig's Demons, the *Washington Star*'s Jeremiah O'Leary, the *Washington Post*'s Sam Stavisky and Al Lewis, the *Washington Times*' Art Mielke, the *Chattanooga Times*' Paul Long, the

Philadelphia Bulletin's John Black, and the *Buffalo Courier Express*' Joe Alli were the first to reach the battle zones in the Solomons during and following the Guadalcanal campaign's final days, in the fall of 1942 to 1943.

The first reporter to become one of Denig's Demons was Jeremiah A.P. "Jerry" O'Leary, a twenty-three-year-old who had started at the *Star* as a copy boy in 1937. Reaching the Solomon Islands combat zone in early 1943, he covered the 1st MarDiv's amphibious landings at Cape Gloucester on New Britain, and the 3d MarDiv's recapture of Guam in the Marianas. From there he accompanied the 1st MarDiv in the horrendous landing at Peleliu. On New Britain, he teamed up briefly with Sam Stavisky and combat photographers Al Monteverdi and Bob Brenner, the latter killed in action. During his tour, O'Leary was awarded four battle stars, the Bronze Star for valor, and a Purple Heart for wounds.

A native of Chelsea, Massachusetts, twenty-seven-year-old Sam Stavisky joined the *Post* in 1938 and had worked his way up to assistant city editor when war broke out. The son of Ukrainian Jewish immigrants, the patriotic Stavisky tried to join the Army the day after he heard the news of Pearl Harbor, but the Army—and later the Navy—rejected him because of his diminutive stature and poor eyesight. When he got wind of BGen Denig's quest for professional news reporters, he presented himself and practically demanded to be allowed to join the Marines. Denig saw immediately that Stavisky was the right kind of writer for the Corps and enlisted him.

Stavisky proved his worth. He covered the final battles on Guadalcanal, then moved on to Pavuvu, the Russell Islands, New Georgia, New Britain, and, accompanying the 1st Marine Tank Battalion, Hollandia on Dutch New Guinea. Most of this time was spent in the thick of the fighting. He also rode as a rear gunner in an SBD Dauntless raid, on the top-of-the-mast Marine machine-gunners' platform on a battleship, on a PT Mosquito-boat raid, and even in an Army Air Corps B-24 Liberator, which was attacked by Japanese Zeros on a bombing run over Hollandia on New Guinea. Stavisky and combat photographer Brenner accompanied Col Chesty Puller's famous Itni River patrol of the western part of New Britain Island, during which they engaged in heavy firefights with die-hard Japanese troops and suffered the hardships of the elements, insects, and disease along with other combat Marines.

In the memoir he wrote a half century later, *Marine Combat Correspondent* (Ballantine, 1999), Stavisky offers a vivid account of Denig's Demons in battle. As he describes it, "We packed an 8.5-lb. Swedish [Hermes] typewriter along with the rifle and battle gear. [We] fought first, wrote later." Keeping the invaluable typewriter in operating condition and the paper dry in the monsoon rains was as great a concern as the dangers and deprivations of battle. Nor could he avoid contracting malaria, bouts of which plagued him for years.

After his three-year hitch, which included a war-bond tour stateside, TSgt Sam Stavisky returned to the *Washington Post*, first covering the returning veterans, then writing editorials. He also contributed articles to *The Saturday Evening Post*, *Collier's*, *Look*, *Nation's Business*, *American Legion*, *Harper's*, and other magazines. In 1954 he left the *Post* and created a successful PR-lobbying firm.

Jerry O'Leary, too, was mustered out after the war as a technical sergeant and returned to the *Washington Star*. The others returned to their respective papers as well. O'Leary, however, took a commission in the Marine Corps Reserve, only to be called up five years later for the Korean War, which he covered from 1951 through 1952 as a public information officer. Following Korea he returned to the *Star* until it ceased publication in 1981, when he became spokesman for the national security director in the Reagan White House. Joining the *Washington Times*, he was forthwith assigned as White House correspondent. He was ultimately elected president of the White House Correspondents, was promoted to colonel in the Marine Reserves, and wrote a column, "O'Leary's Washington," for the *Times*. Jerry O'Leary died on 19 December 1993 at the age of seventy-three.

Combat Photographers

Although Denig's original concept was for combat photographers to accompany correspondents as writer/photographer teams, this did not really gel at first. Photography in the Marine Corps has bounced from small organizational units to G-3 Operations to DIVINFO. Today it belongs to the Visual Imaging section, along with, of course, *Leatherneck* magazine, which has always employed its own staff of photographers. In World War II, Marine photographers used the cumbersome but sturdy 4 x 5 format, sheet-film Speed Graphic and the 2 x 2, film-spool Rolleiflex cameras. Cinematographers used the 16mm Bell & Howell "Eyemo" with a triple-rotating lens. Most film was shot in black and white.

Two of the greatest Marine photographers were on Iwo Jima: Lou Lowery of *Leatherneck*, who snapped the less well-known photo of the first flag-raising (Joe Rosenthal took the more famous flag-raising photo later that same day), and Sgt Bill Genaust, a cinematographer under SSgt Hatch who caught the raising on 16mm motion picture film. Later, in Vietnam, photographer Tom Bartlett of *Leatherneck*, shooting 35mm color, would also make a name for himself. Of course, as for individual talent, none can top former World War II Marine David Douglas Duncan, whose photographic coverage of the Korean and Vietnam wars as a civilian is unmatched.

Combat Artists

Technically a part of Denig's Demons in the Public Relations Office, the Combat

ABOVE: Marine combat still photographers Cpl Obie Newcomb (left) and Cpl Raymond Matjasic pose beside the wreckage of Japanese aircraft on Tarawa. Newcomb, holding a standard Speed Graphic camera, was a former New York City freelance photographer; Matjasic, a former staff photographer for the Cleveland *Plain Dealer*. They took still shots while SSgt Norman T. Hatch, 2d Division photo chief, and Sgt John Ercole covered the action using 35mm black-and-white motion pictures.

RIGHT: An unidentified combat correspondent in the midst of battle, oblivious to the dead Japanese soldier in the foreground.

ABOVE: A civilian war correspondent beloved by Marines, sailors, and soldiers in all war theaters, Ernie Pyle is shown here aboard a troop transport on its way to Okinawa in early 1945. Oblivious to danger, Pyle lived and went into battle with the troops. Sadly, on 18 April, while accompanying an Army patrol on the tiny isle of Ie Shima off Okinawa, he was cut down by enemy machine-gun fire. The entire nation mourned.

Clymer, Tom Lovell, Tom Dunn, and Howard Terpning, as well as a famous cartoonist, Reserve Maj Alex Raymond, creator of the popular newspaper comic strips *Flash Gordon, Jungle Jim,* and *Rip Kirby.* These illustrators created inspirational depictions of major moments in Marine Corps history that became widely known throughout the Corps in reproductions and lured many a recruit.

Vic Donohue, Hugh Laidman, and Elmer Wexler were the first artists to go into combat on Guadalcanal, and they produced a number of sketches of that long, arduous battle. Laidman received a battlefield commission and contracted debilitating malaria, but he nevertheless managed to execute dozens of sketches of the battles and supporting activities.

Also on Guadalcanal was a Reserve captain, Donald L. Dickson, a former advertising art director who was assigned to the Public Information section of the 1st MarDiv. He had created the popular newspaper comic strip *Sgt. Stoney Craig.* Dickson's sketches of the modern Marine wearing the newly designed cloche helmet with liner (different from the World War I–style helmet worn at the beginning of the war) and the updated twill combat utilities—some carrying the beloved old Springfield 1903 .30-caliber rifle, others, the new M1 Garand—were to become the image of the Marine in World War II. Dickson later became the editor of *Leatherneck* magazine.

Sixty-three artists in the ranks covered Marine combat during the war. BGen Denig put a young captain, Raymond Henri, who had a passing knowledge of art, in charge of the program. He was another man for his time. Henri assembled the art from the battlefronts, mounted exhibits for the public in locales throughout the country and in major museums, disseminated information and news releases, and was responsible for the beginning of the great Marine Corps Combat Art collection.

Both the correspondents and the artists experienced fierce combat and were

Artist Program instituted for Marines to produce war art no doubt benefited from the input of the first and foremost Marine combat artist, Col John W. Thomason, who was still on active duty despite his declining health. He assisted Denig in bringing aboard nationally noted fine artists and commercial illustrators, such as John

LEFT: Eighteen-year-old Pfc Harry Jackson's combat painting of the action on Tarawa.

BOTTOM LEFT: Combat artist Harry Jackson on Tarawa. Landing with one of the first waves, Jackson had to run one hundred yards down a pier under intense enemy fire. Hit twice, he not only survived the battle but also managed to make a number of sketches. He was again wounded on Saipan. Following the war, Jackson rose to national and international prominence as an avant-garde artist and sculptor.

BELOW: One of Capt Donald L. Dickson's battle-field sketches made on Guadalcanal captured the universal image of the modern Marine "grunt." Formerly a civilian comic strip artist, Dickson served as the Public Information officer with 1st MarDiv and as adjutant with the 5th Marines.

trained as infantrymen to fight when called upon. One important distinction emerged between the combat correspondents and the combat artists: the former documented what they wrote by getting the accurate names of participants in their stories, their correct ages, and their hometowns, as well as the battles they were engaged in. Perhaps because the artists did their work on the run and from a distance—or later from memory—they usually failed to identify their subjects, the locations or battles (perhaps due also to censorship), or the dates and/or units they were depicting. The correspondents were professional news reporters for whom these details were essential; the artists, however, were given no directives on what to do or how to document their art. Later efforts to identify or caption their artwork posed many problems.

straggler

Marine Corps Magazines

While Denig's Demons were under the publicity wing of HQMC (three decades later to be transferred to the History and Museums Division), there were two other major internal publications (aside from base newspapers) that called for writers, photographers, and graphic artists. These were the *Marine Corps Gazette* (the professional monthly) and *Leatherneck* (the popular monthly), both under the aegis of the Marine Corps Association. They were strictly Marine-oriented, as opposed to the Army's and Defense Department's *Yank* and *Stars and Stripes,* which covered all the services.

During World War II, two Marine cartoonists emerged at *Leatherneck* who gained great followings and lasting reputations: Fred Rhoades for his humorous cartoon strips *Sad Sack* and *Gizmo and Eightball,* and Fred Lasswell for his *Snuffy Smith.* Later, in the Korean War, TSgt Norval Packwood's *Leatherhead in Korea* and a stream of other cartoons were popular, as were the zany cartoons of Sgt George Booth, who after service rose to national prominence at *New Yorker* magazine.

Denig's Demons grew to more than 250 combat correspondents and combat photographers and 60 combat artists by the end of the war. The correspondents covered every aspect and detail of Marine air, sea, and land operations, as well as writing stories about supporting Army, Navy, and Coast Guard personnel. And out of the organization—which was unique to the Marine Corps—came the Marine Combat Correspondents Association (MCCA), which continues to this day, with both active duty and former Marines as members. A later organization, the Marine Corps Reserve Public Affairs Unit 1-1 in New York City also continues its annual, voluntary, weeklong seminar for the regular establishment in specialized media and publicity training on a national level.

—HAC

ABOVE: On assignment for Abbott Laboratories, civilian combat artist Kerr Eby executed a masterful eyewitness series of charcoal-pencil sketches of the battle for Tarawa's Betio Island, including this drawing of the aftermath. The casualties, debris, and carnage depicted offer mute testimony to the brutality of the battle. The sketch also highlights the futility of the battle, in which so many lives were lost for a tiny hill of sand that would ultimately be abandoned once its strategic significance ceased to exist. Many Japanese-held islands were simply bypassed, rather than attacked, in the Pacific Fleet's push toward Japan, saving countless lives.

IWO JIMA: THE BLOODIEST BATTLE OF WORLD WAR II

While the U.S. Army and the Marines were recapturing the Philippines, on 19 February 1945 Marine MajGen Harry Schmidt's V Amphibious Corps, consisting of the 3d, 4th, and the new 5th Marine Divisions, landed on a barren, pork chop–shaped volcanic rock 5 miles long and 2 1/2 miles wide protruding from the rough waters of the northern Pacific and cooled by strong, salty breezes 660 miles due south of Tokyo.

Iwo Jima (translated as Sulfur Island) has a distinctive silhouette, with its near-extinct volcano, Mount Suribachi, rising 555 feet at the island's southern tip. The Marine assault forces would land on the southeastern shore under this militarily dominant terrain feature, from which the enemy had a commanding view not only of the landing beaches but also of the whole island and the conduct of battle.

Having learned from past actions, the Marines bombarded the target incessantly for seventy-four consecutive days with heavy naval gunfire and aerial bombing and strafing. It was subsequently discovered that all of these efforts failed to inflict much harm or damage on the deeply entrenched enemy, who had dug more than six hundred bunkers, pillboxes, caves, and gun emplacements deeply into the compacted volcanic ash. Interlocking tunnels connected these spots with heavily protected weapons sites and fields of fire to cover virtually every square meter of the island.

The terrain itself, often chilled by sudden rains in the temperate climate, would be like none the Marines had ever encountered. Instead of landing on a tropical sandy beach with warm, lapping, turquoise water, V Amphibious Corps plowed through a rough surf onto a steep shore of dark, hot, shifting ash that gave way under vehicle tracks and the Marines' "boondockers" (field shoes) topped by calf-high canvas leggings. Every step was an ordeal and it was virtually futile to dig even a shallow foxhole—the granular grit kept filling the hole back up. Both vehicular and foot progress was almost impossible, causing a gigantic backup of men, material, and vehicles on the steep incline of the

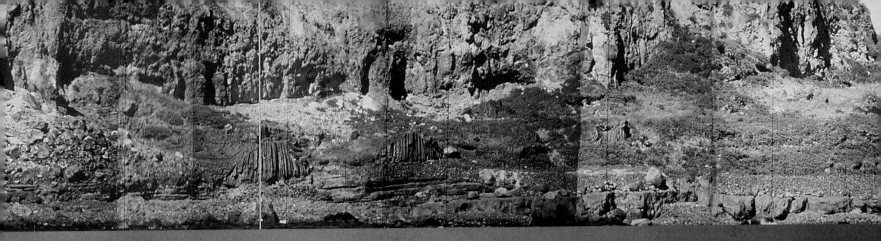

LEFT: On the first day, some thirty thousand Marines, hunkered down against enemy fire, were landed in waves in LCVPs.

BELOW: As Marines hit the beach and dispersed to attack, the Japanese opened up with withering, intersecting lines of fire in preplotted targeted areas that covered virtually the entire landing beach. The casualties were horrific. Mount Suribachi, where Marines would later raise the flag that has come to symbolize American victory in war, looms in the distance.

RIGHT, INSET: In "the sleep of death," a Marine who did not make it past the shifting volcanic ash of the beach on Iwo. Around the clock, for thirty-six consecutive days and nights, a Marine was either killed or wounded every two minutes.

RIGHT, BACKGROUND: Incoming Japanese fire on the beachhead was incessant until the southern half of the island was secured. There was nothing tropical about Iwo Jima; it was chilly and digging a foxhole in the loose ash was nearly impossible. As Navy landing craft brought troops and supplies in, they took casualties back out to the hospital ship.

BELOW: The hulks of damaged landing craft and other debris litter the beach midway through the battle. After the enemy fire on the beach was eliminated, the beachhead operation became logistically efficient.

"beach"—exactly what the enemy had anticipated before opening a relentless fire from their preplotted guns. Burning, bullet-ridden, sinking, floundering, and swamped landing craft—coxswained by valiant Coast Guardsmen and sailors—littered, bobbed, and piled up at the shoreline as supporting rolling barrages and close air strikes chopped up the surface just yards over the shore rise. By first day's nightfall, the first two assault divisions, 4th and 5th MarDivs, had landed 30,000 men on a beachhead 3,000 yards long and 700 to 1,500 yards deep, taking 2,300 casualties. Tons of supplies, guns, and weapons were piled in a confined area choked with wreckage and body fragments, the result of the continuous and murderous enemy barrage.

The first day was an indescribable nightmare. As a survivor later wrote, it was incredible that anyone on that beach could escape the explosions and metal that filled the air like buzzing bees. Yet the worst lay ahead.

Defiantly, wave after wave of the 4th and 5th Marine Divisions barged ashore. MajGen Keller Rockey's untried 5th Division was on the left; Cates' seasoned 4th Division was on the right. Col Harry Liversedge's 28th Marines of the 5th Division fought fiercely all day long; by the second day ashore, they had gained only two hundred yards. Led by their Sherman tanks, they slowly cut across the island at the base of the volcano and sustained heavy casualties. On the fourth day, incredibly, they scaled the heights and secured Suribachi. The first patrol to reach the top tied a small boat flag one Marine had been given to a pole, but it was too small to be seen from afar. A couple of hours later, a larger flag from an LST was brought up and attached to a piece of water cistern pipe found in the vicinity. As a Marine 16mm combat motion picture cameraman cranked away and civilian Associated Press photographer Joe Rosenthal stood ready with his 4 x 5 Speed Graphic still camera, five Marines

ABOVE: MajGen Keller E. Rockey, CG of the untried 5th MarDiv on Iwo. Rockey's units crossed the island, isolating Suribachi and swiftly taking it. His division then wheeled right and positioned itself on the left flank of the 4th and 3d Divisions. All three rolled up the tiny island in horrific combat until victorious.

LEFT, INSET: Navy corpsmen and Marines help the wounded get to medical treatment stations and to evacuation sites.

BELOW: Camouflaged "brown-side out" helmet recovered from the battle.

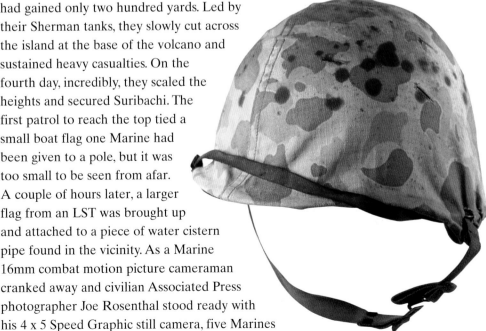

GySgt "Manila John" Basilone

GySgt "Manila John" Basilone was a New Jersey Marine who had been awarded the Medal of Honor on Guadalcanal for single-handedly gunning down wave after wave of attacking Japanese—at times holding his water-cooled .30-caliber heavy machine gun in his arms. After a stateside war bonds tour, he commanded a machine-gun platoon in the 1st Battalion, 27th Marines. Landing on the right extremity of the Iwo Jima beachhead near the so-called boat basin, he rallied his men, shouting, "Come on, you guys. We've got to get these guns off the beach!" With that, he slogged his way up the shifting incline, reached the top, and was blown to bits with four others by a mortar blast. He was posthumously awarded the Navy Cross, the only enlisted Marine in World War II to be awarded a Navy Cross and Purple Heart in addition to a Medal of Honor. Following Guadalcanal in 1942, Basilone had "Death Before Dishonor" tattooed on his left arm.

—HAC

"In the Army, shock troops are a small minority supported by a vast group of artisans, laborers, clerks, and organizers. In the Marines, there are practically nothing but shock troops."

Combat correspondent John Lardner
in a 6 March 1945 report

joined by a Navy corpsman raised the larger flag that could be seen all over the island and by ships offshore. As the pole went upward, Rosenthal clicked his shutter and unwittingly enshrined an unforgettable wartime moment. Considered the greatest battle photograph of all time, his shot came to signify victory as well as the undying valor of the U.S. Marine Corps.

Below, on the hot surface of the island, the 5th and 4th Divisions had cut all the way across to the opposite shore in vicious fighting and had secured the nearer airfield. As the two Marine divisions wheeled abreast and headed upward to the larger, rocky, rising northern part of the island, they were joined by two regiments of the newly landed 3d Division, under MajGen Graves Erskine, who kept his 3d Regiment afloat in reserve. (In truth, Erskine did not want to commit all of his seasoned troops, harboring the regiment for the soon-to-come invasion of Japan.) With no room for flanking maneuvers, the three divisions of 71,245 Marines continued a grueling frontal assault against an unseen enemy who fought for every inch, meting out devastating defensive fire from hidden positions in caves, bunkers, and subterranean dugouts. Hand-carried flamethrowers and special tanks equipped with flamethrowers instead of guns worked closely with demolition teams to eradicate these obstacles, sending up seething pillars of smoke and debris. The rock formations the Marines encountered were more like quarries, and hot sulfur springs belched from cauldronlike terraces. Volcanic ash from explosions along with the fire from flamethrowers, napalm, and demolished pillboxes and caves choked the air. Wreckage, metal, the debris of war, and body parts were strewn everywhere, entangled

BELOW: The typical terrain across which three Marine divisions fought for five solid weeks on Iwo. Here, Marines have moved up to a destroyed Japanese pillbox. The Japanese defenders had honeycombed the island with connecting tunnels, gun emplacements, interlocking fire, and hidden caves. To oust the enemy, the Marines had to fight for every square meter.

ABOVE: MajGen Harry Schmidt, CG, V Amphibious Corps (VAC), was overall landing force commander on Iwo Jima, commanding the largest force of U.S. Marines ever committed to battle up to that time. VAC consisted of the 3d, 4th, and newly formed 5th divisions—a total of 80,000 Marines, including supporting units.

RIGHT, TOP: As members of E—"Easy"—Company prepare to ascend Mount Suribachi, LtCol Chandler Johnson, CO of 2d Battalion, 28th Marines, calls in the order to suspend naval bombardment of the area. Before the patrol left, Johnson handed E Company CO 1stLt Harold G. Schrier a small flag from the attack transport Missoula (APA-211), telling him to raise it if he made it to the top.

RIGHT, BOTTOM: Knowing that they might not make it back, photographer Lou Lowery took this picture of Easy Company ascending the exposed north face of Mount Suribachi carrying the small 4 1/2-foot American flag.

> "We're not accustomed to occupying defensive positions. It's destructive to morale."
>
> LtGen Holland M. "Howlin' Mad" Smith at Iwo Jima, 1945

LEFT AND BELOW: On Iwo, there was a three-hour period between the raising of the first, smaller flag and the raising of the second, during which the position was defended against sniper attack and flamethrowers were used to blast out enemy caves and dugouts. The enemy defenders, lethargic from oxygen depletion as a result of the napalm-fueled flamethrowers, put up only sporadic resistance.

ABOVE: LtGen Holland M. "Howlin' Mad" Smith, CG, Fleet Marine Forces, Pacific (FMFPAC). His role in the Iwo Jima operation was loosely defined and did not override VAC commander MajGen Schmidt's, although "Howlin' Mad" gained as much publicity. After Okinawa, Smith was succeeded as CG, FMFPAC, by LtGen Roy S. Geiger, CG of III Amphibious Corps during that battle.

ABOVE: Marines of Easy Company tie the small flag, which patrol leader 1stLt Harold G. Schrier had brought from the *Missoula*, to a piece of cistern water pipe found at the summit.

RIGHT: Sgt Lou Lowery's photograph of the first flag-raising. Left to right are Pfc Louis C. Charlo; Sgt Henry O. Hansen (without helmet); platoon Sgt Ernest I. "Boots" Thomas (seated); 1stLt Schrier (behind Thomas); Pfc James R. Michels (foreground, holding carbine); and Cpl Charles W. Lindberg (standing). After the flag was raised on 23 February 1945, Marines were still alert to enemy retaliatory attacks. Unfortunately, the flag was too small to be seen from afar. Consequently, 5th MarDiv CG MajGen Keller E. Rockey ordered it replaced by a larger one; chief photo officer, WO Norman T. Hatch, ordered cameraman Sgt William H. "Bill" Genaust and still photographer Pfc Robert R. Campbell to hightail it up to the top and catch the raising of the second flag. Along the way, they encountered AP photographer Joe Rosenthal. The three cameramen arrived shortly before the five Marines and a Navy corpsman hoisted the larger flag, which had been scrounged from LST-779 on the beach.

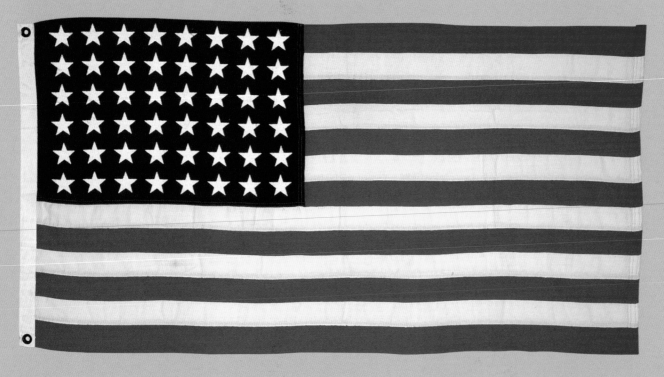

LEFT: The first American flag raised on Mount Suribachi, Iwo Jima. This, the smaller of the two flags, is now displayed with the second flag in the National Museum of the Marine Corps Quantico.

OPPOSITE, BOTTOM: The six men who raised the second flag atop Mount Suribachi. Their portraits are shown in the order in which they appear in Rosenthal's famous photograph.

"The raising of that flag on Suribachi means a Marine Corps for the next 500 years."

Secretary of the Navy James Forrestal to LtGen Holland M. Smith, 23 February 1945

BACKGROUND: Almost caught off guard as the second, larger flag was readied to be raised, AP photographer Joe Rosenthal, perched precariously on a pile of rocks, quickly pulled his film slide, took aim with hyper-focal distance set at fifty feet, and barely caught the middle of the event with his trusty but cumbersome 4 x 5 Speed Graphic camera. He did not realize what he had shot—the image was small in his viewfinder. He then posed several photos with Marines gathered beneath the waving flag, which could be seen from practically everywhere on the island and from ships offshore. His film was developed on Guam and an alert photo editor took a closer look at the small image in the center of the film. He cropped the print to create the famous photograph and sent copies to the Associated Press and HQMC. Before the fighting ended, Norm Hatch—still wearing combat gear—was flown to HQMC for a conference with CMC Vandegrift and the heads of AP and Time/Life to negotiate rights to the photograph. Hatch bluffed both civilian entities by intimating that the Corps had its own shot of the action, whereupon the Marine Corps was given all rights to use the photograph at no cost in perpetuity.

Cpl
Ira H. Hayes

Cpl
Rene A. Gagnon

Pfc
Franklin R. Sousley
(Killed in Action)

Sgt
Michael Strank
(Killed in Action)

Pharmacist's Mate
Second Class
John H. Bradley
(Navy Cross Recipient)

Cpl
Harlon H. Block
(Killed in Action)

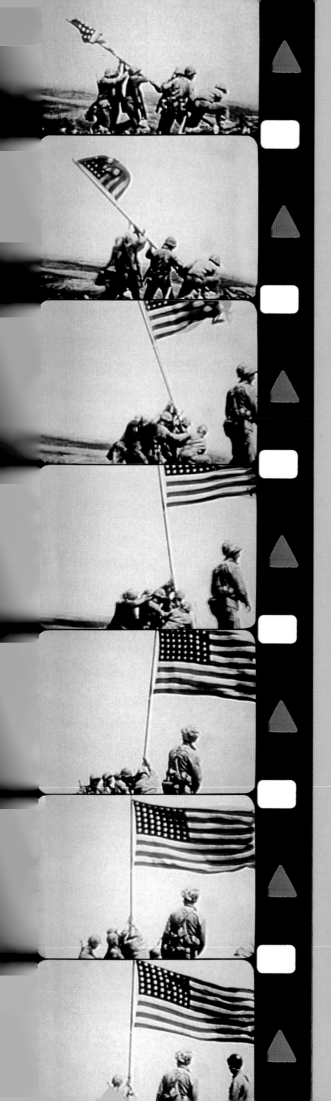

LEFT: Motion picture footage shot by cinematographer Sgt Bill Genaust, who stood slightly to the right of Rosenthal during the filming. Genaust was killed nine days later.

RIGHT: AP photographer Joe Rosenthal gained international fame for shooting the most famous battle picture in history, which became an icon for victory and won Rosenthal the Pulitzer Prize. Yet he had no idea he had taken such a great picture until he saw what was done with it by an astute photo editor.

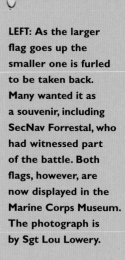

LEFT: As the larger flag goes up the smaller one is furled to be taken back. Many wanted it as a souvenir, including SecNav Forrestal, who had witnessed part of the battle. Both flags, however, are now displayed in the Marine Corps Museum. The photograph is by Sgt Lou Lowery.

BELOW: Rosenthal's photograph of the larger flag and the group responsible for raising it. Shortly afterward, in a press conference back on Guam, Rosenthal was asked if he had posed the shot of the flag-raising. Not having seen the great shot as yet, and thinking they were referring to this one, which he had obviously posed, he innocently replied, "Yes," thus sowing confusion about the famous photograph.

ABOVE: The second American flag raised on Mount Suribachi was an 8 x 4 1/2-foot flag rescued from a salvage depot at Pearl Harbor and stored in a locker on LST-211. It was given to 2dLt Albert T. Tuttle, who quickly brought it to the summit to replace the smaller one.

FAR LEFT: The torturous, alien battlefield of Iwo Jima resembled a scene from Dante's *Inferno*—or the no-man's-land of World War I, minus the trenches. From the plain below Suribachi the island sloped north, with rugged outcroppings giving way to sheer 100-foot cliffs, over which many Japanese defenders chose to jump to their deaths rather than surrender. Iwo still stands as the fiercest battle in Marine Corps history.

LEFT, TOP: A dug-in 105mm howitzer position on the right flank of the 3d MarDiv. Between it and Mount Suribachi, visible in the background, the 4th and 5th Divisions had severed the island, and would soon advance abreast to subdue the more formidable northern half. Even before that was secure, Marine engineers and Navy Seabees were constructing under fire the first airstrip for damaged Army Air Force B-29 Superfortresses to make emergency landings on their way back from bombing runs over the Japanese homeland.

LEFT, BOTTOM: Negro Marines on Iwo Jima pose holding their carbines and M1s shortly after the island was secured on 26 March 1945. Although not integrated with white Marines until President Truman issued an executive order in 1947, African-American Marines served in separate stevedore and shore-defense battalions under white officers. Front row, left to right: Pfc H. Ross, Jr., Cpl F. Tanner, and Cpl Ernest J. Scott. Back row, left to right: Pfc V. Kleitt, Pvt John W. Lee, and Cpl P. Shepherd.

ABOVE: Harry Liversedge as a brigadier general. Liversedge commanded the 28th Marine Regiment, 5th MarDiv, on Iwo Jima. It was one of the 28th's units that captured Mount Suribachi on the fourth day of fighting and raised the two flags atop it.

RIGHT: A Navy corpsman, carrying a canvas stretcher over his shoulder, and Marines make their way through the twisted hulks of wrecked Japanese Mitsubishi G4M3 "Betty" bombers and Naka-jima Ki-43 "Oscar" fighters at one of the Japanese airfields on Iwo. Such debris was quickly removed by Marine engineers and Navy Seabees, and the airfields were rendered operational even before the fighting was over.

OPPOSITE, INSET: The web belt carried on Iwo Jima by Marine Joseph C. Lanzalotto, who served in Easy Company, 2d Battalion, 28th Marines. Attached to the belt is a first aid pouch, a double .45-caliber magazine holder, and a holster with a .45-caliber pistol and Ka-bar knife. Lanzalotto is pictured on page 245; he is the Marine standing directly in front of the flagpole in Rosenthal's posed group photo atop Mount Suribachi.

with crisscrossing strands of chopped-up communications wire.

Marine casualties were appalling: nineteen of the original battalion commanders were casualties. As officers and senior NCOs became casualties, leadership of what was left of companies and platoons fell to sergeants and corporals—young men hardly twenty years old—who rose to the occasion heroically. The front was everywhere on Iwo Jima. Collecting and evacuating the wounded was difficult enough; the dead were simply covered temporarily with ponchos or shelter halves and left for later. A cemetery would eventually be plotted and the dead would be buried. Following the war, the interred would be removed to a cemetery on Hawaii.

One particularly difficult objective, Hill 382 (the number refers to its height in feet above sea level), became known as the Meatgrinder because it changed hands so often and created so much carnage. The battle raged for five solid weeks until the last resistance ended—punctuated by a final, futile banzai charge consisting mostly of the remaining enemy officers against a tent camp of newly arrived Army Air Corps pilots. Some two hundred Americans were killed in desperate hand-to-hand fighting. Before the shooting had ended in the northern sector, crippled B-29s had begun returning from their missions over the Japanese homeland.

On 26 March, Iwo Jima was declared secure and the battle over. The three Marine divisions entirely wiped out 21,000 Japanese defenders. In so doing, 5,931 Marines died and 17,372 were wounded. Twenty-five Marines were awarded Medals of Honor, most posthumously. More than 500 unarmed and noncombatant Navy corpsmen and doctors were also casualties. In the environs, Navy and Marine aviators, sailors, and Coast Guardsmen sustained another 2,500 or so casualties. In fact, it was the only battle in which the enemy inflicted more total casualties— but not killed in action—on attacking Marines. Press coverage of the battle—including Rosenthal's inspiring photograph—had been thorough and honest, but some criticism arose stateside decrying the inordinate loss of life. Iwo Jima had, indeed, been costly, but in succeeding months more than 25,000 Army Air Forces airmen used the island for emergency landings as intended, and the fighter escorts based there saved untold numbers of B-29s from being shot down.

The thirty-five days on Iwo Jima were the bloodiest of World War II and ever in the history of the U.S. Marine Corps. No greater tribute could have been

given to the Marines than those immortal words spoken by Commander in Chief of the Pacific Adm Chester Nimitz: "Uncommon valor was a common virtue."

Leyte Gulf

Although desperate enemy pilots had deliberately flown their aircraft into U.S. Navy ships before, it was during the greatest of naval battles, that of Leyte Gulf in the Philippine campaign in October 1944, that they resorted to bomb-loaded aircraft as weapons to destroy ships. They called themselves kamikazes ("divine wind"), for to sacrifice their lives for the emperor was a divine calling.

As a result of heavy losses to kamikazes at Leyte and the still ongoing Iwo Jima campaign, Marine fighter squadrons had been put aboard the attack carriers *Essex, Wasp, Bunker Hill,* and *Bennington,* as well as a number of CVE escort carriers, to supplement subsequent Navy task force raids in January and February 1945 against Indochinese ports and airfields and Japan's home islands. Marine pilots had been

quickly carrier-qualified to master the tricky takeoff and trickier tail-hook landings that were often referred to as controlled crashes on the moving and pitching flight decks. In March, the carrier *Franklin,*

Wear the "*FIGHTIN'EST*" wings in the service

FLY WITH THE MARINES

APPLY, OR WRITE, TO NEAREST RECRUITING STATION

LEFT: Marine Maj Alex Raymond, famous for his cartoon strips *Flash Gordon*, *Rip Kirby*, and *Jungle Jim*, copied a photograph for this ink-and-watercolor painting of Marine pilots being debriefed after a mission. Note the red, white, and blue arm-patch insignia indicating that the pilot had served in China with the "Flying Tigers."

OPPOSITE, INSET: A recruiting poster for Marine pilots pays homage to the fierce air battles of the Pacific war.

BELOW: The carrier escort USS *Franklin* after being hit just sixty-five miles off the coast of Japan in the midst of a Navy task force on 19 March 1945. A lone twin-engine Japanese "Betty" bomber on a weather mission had dived into lower clouds to avoid Navy fighters and emerged right over the *Franklin*—unfortunately, just as its loaded Marine aircraft were about to take off. The two dropped bombs caused the entire flight deck to go up in flames; all Marine aircraft loaded on her flight deck were lost, as were 832 crew members.

Marine Flying Aces

The more than 10,000 Marine pilots in the Pacific war shot down or destroyed a total of 2,344 enemy planes. In the process, 125 of the pilots achieved the status of ace, for which each had to bag 5 enemy aircraft in aerial combat. Many became multiple aces: Maj Gregory "Pappy" Boyington, who had previously flown for the American volunteer Flying Tigers squadron in China (where he had claimed to bag 6, but was officially credited with 3.5), led his famous Black Sheep squadron in their Corsairs up the Solomon Islands and added 19 more. Maj Joe Foss, flying the old F4F Wildcat off Guadalcanal, shot down the first 3 of his 26 on his first mission. Capt Marion Carl ended up with 18.5 kills (the half shared with another pilot) in his Corsair. Maj George Axtell at Okinawa bagged his 5 in a single half hour. Eleven pilots received Medals of Honor, four posthumously. Most of the squadrons received Presidential, Navy, and Distinguished (Army) Unit Citations. A total of 551 pilots were killed in combat; 1,000 more died in noncombat operational crashes.

—HAC

ABOVE: Marine crewmen aboard the USS *Hancock* admire the victory symbols painted on the flight deck bulkhead. The bomb images denote, of course, bombing missions, the rising-sun Japanese flags indicate the number of enemy aircraft downed by Marine and Navy shipboard pilots, and the red-dot flags account for enemy planes downed by the ship's antiaircraft batteries.

1stLt Robert M. Hanson
VMF-214, 215
25 Victories
Medal of Honor Recipient

Maj Gregory Boyington
VMF-214
22.5 Victories
Medal of Honor Recipient

Maj Archie G. Donahue
VMF-112, 451
14 Victories
Navy Cross Recipient

Capt Kenneth D. Frazier
VMF-223
12.5 Victories
Navy Cross Recipient

LtCol Harold W. Bauer
VMF-212
11 Victories
Medal of Honor Recipient

1stLt Franklin C. Thomas, Jr.
VMF-112
9 Victories
Navy Cross Recipient

Capt Donald N. Aldrich
VMF-215
20 Victories
Navy Cross Recipient

1stLt James E. Swett
VMF-221
15.5 Victories
Medal of Honor Recipient

1stLt Harold E. Segal
VMF-221
12 Victories
Distinguished Flying Cross
Recipient

2dLt Eugene A. Trowbridge
VMF-223
12 Victories
Navy Cross Recipient

2dLt Frederick R. Payne
VMF-212, 223
7.5 Victories
Navy Cross Recipient

1stLt John F. Bolt, Jr.
VMF-214
6 Victories
Navy Cross Recipient

Navy Unit Citation

MEDAL OF HONOR

FIRST LIEUTENANT KENNETH AMBROSE WALSH
Solomon Islands Area
15 August and 30 August 1943

For extraordinary heroism and intrepidity above and beyond the call of duty as a pilot in Marine Fighting Squadron 124 in aerial combat against enemy Japanese forces in the Solomon Islands area. Determined to thwart the enemy's attempt to bomb Allied ground forces and shipping at Vella Lavella on 15 August 1943, 1stLt Walsh repeatedly dived his plane into an enemy formation outnumbering his own division six to one and, although his plane was hit numerous times, shot down two Japanese dive-bombers and one fighter. After developing engine trouble on 30 August during a vital escort mission, 1stLt Walsh landed his mechanically disabled plane at Munda, quickly replaced it with another, and proceeded to rejoin his flight over Kahili. Separated from his escort group when he encountered approximately fifty Japanese Zeros, he unhesitatingly attacked, striking with relentless fury in his lone battle against a powerful force. He destroyed four hostile fighters before cannon shellfire forced him to make a dead-stick landing off Vella Lavella where he was later picked up. His valiant leadership and his daring skill as a flier served as a source of confidence and inspiration to his fellow pilots and reflect the highest credit upon the U.S. Naval Service.

WORLD WAR II ERA
NAVY/MARINE CORPS WINGS

Navy/Marine Corps Aviator

Navy/Marine Corps Observer

Navy/Marine Corps Flight Nurse

Navy/Marine Corps Flight Surgeon

Navy/Marine Corps Air Crew

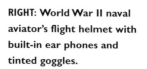

RIGHT: World War II naval aviator's flight helmet with built-in ear phones and tinted goggles.

BELOW: Pilots of Marine Fighter Squadrons 124 and 213 pose on one of their F4U Corsairs on the flight deck of their carrier, the USS *Essex* (CV-9), in the Pacific in March 1945. The two squadrons produced a total of eleven aces. The three-bladed prop indicates an earlier model Corsair; at the end of the war the more powerful F4U-4Bs had four-bladed props.

ABOVE: One of the most astounding careers in the Marine Corps was that of Roy S. Geiger. Commissioned in 1909, he served at sea and in China and the Philippines. Joining the Naval Aeronautic Station at Pensacola, Florida, he earned his wings as a naval aviator in 1917, just in time for World War I. In France in 1918, he flew with the RAF and commanded the first Marine Aviation Force. After air service in the Banana Wars between the First and Second World Wars, Geiger commanded 1st MAW on Guadalcanal. In the war in the Pacific, he rose to command III Amphibious Corps, and during the joint Navy-Marine-Army operation on Okinawa, Geiger was named deputy commander of the Tenth Army. When Army LtGen Simon Bolivar Buckner, the commander of the Tenth Army, was killed in action, LtGen Geiger took over, becoming the first Marine ever to command a U.S. army. At the Japanese sur-render ceremonies, Geiger was the senior Marine representative, as Commander Fleet Marine Forces, Pacific.

newly arrived just sixty-five miles off the coast of Japan with its decks loaded with Marine aircraft, succumbed to aerial attack. All aircraft were destroyed, 832 crew members were killed, and she was rendered inoperable—yet would nevertheless be able to limp twelve thousand miles back to the Brooklyn Navy Yard for repair. The heroism displayed in the attack by both sailors and Marines aboard resulted in two Medals of Honor, nineteen Navy Crosses, and twenty-two Silver Stars.

OKINAWA

In the spring of 1945, with the entire Pacific won back from the conquering Japanese after three years of hard fighting, U.S. forces were now on the doorstep of the Japanese homeland. The next move was to capture Okinawa, on the Ryukyu Archipelago chain 360 air miles south-southwest of the southernmost home island. The 60-mile-long and 2- to 18-mile-wide island had a civilian population of 130,000. Its seizure would afford a near air base and staging area for the ultimate invasion of the main islands of Japan.

It was the logical place for both the southwestern pincer of MacArthur and the central Pacific one of Nimitz to converge for the ultimate invasion of Japan itself. That invasion was scheduled—come hell or high water—for November. It would involve the six Marine and twenty-two Army divisions, which would be augmented by many transferred from the European Theater, in several huge, simultaneous amphibious assaults. It would also be larger, more difficult, and vastly more bloody than even D-Day at Normandy or Iwo Jima. Two million American casualties were predicted.

First, though, a large base of operations close enough to the Japanese home islands had to be secured and established. Okinawa, although perfect, was formidable. A thousand miles north of Luzon in the Philippines, the island presented incredible logistical, as well as naval and air, support problems. Furthermore, there was still an undetermined threat from the Imperial Japanese Navy's ships that were unaccounted for—possibly aircraft carriers, lesser ships, and especially the super battleship *Yamato* with new 18.1-inch guns. In lieu of absent long-range naval air or gunfire, the Imperial Japanese Navy's ultimate weapons, introduced in the preceding battle of Leyte

Gulf, were the suicidal kamikaze attacks. The Japanese lashed a single large bomb to an unarmed aircraft with minimal fuel. After making his final vows to the emperor, a kamikaze pilot would take off from Japan and fly his aircraft into the largest surface ship he could spot in the vast armada of 1,200 U.S. ships in the waters off Okinawa. The kamikazes were formed into 350-plane waves called *kikusui* ("floating chrysanthemums") to attack the U.S. fleet en masse. Although they did not sink any capital ships or carriers, kamikazes did hit and sink many smaller ones, causing much damage and taking many lives on all that they did hit. Such attacks numbered in the thousands.

The Battle

Two Marine divisions, the 1st and the new 6th, with the 2d as a floating decoy, composed the III Amphibious Corps under MajGen Roy Geiger. They were designated the Northern Landing Force of the U.S. Tenth Army, which was commanded by Army LtGen Simon Bolivar Buckner, the son of a famous Confederate general. The Southern Landing Force was composed of the XXIV Army Corps, under MajGen John Hodge, and was made up of the 7th, 77th, and 96th Divisions, with the 27th Division as floating reserve. The 2d MarDiv would be attached to this corps for its initial feint during the main landing. In all, the Tenth Army totaled 182,112, of which 81,165 were Marines.

Marine MajGen Francis Mulcahy was overall tactical air commander of the operation. Cruising offshore were eighteen CVEs with four Marine squadrons, in addition to other, Navy, squadrons.

Defending Japanese Gen Mitsuru Ushijima's strategy was to allow the American forces to land and mass in front of the first of his three lines of defense across the southern part of the island in front of the capital, Naha. Then he would launch an all-out counterattack to wipe out the invaders. Fortunately for the Americans, even after seven days of preliminary bombardment and with a diversionary decoy nonlanding of the 2d MarDiv off the southern coast, the bulk of the Tenth Army landed on 1 April 1945 on the southwest side of the island with little opposition or casualties. It turned out to be mostly a logistical ship-to-shore off-loading, under cover of naval gunfire and Marine and Navy Air. The 1st and 6th MarDivs put 16,000 ashore in the first hour, including their Sherman tanks and 155mm "Long Toms" heavy artillery.

The objectives were the northern, sparsely populated, wooded, mountainous parts of the island positioned on the left flank of the two Marine divisions

LEFT: In the fierce fighting near the Okinawan capital, Naha, a 6th MarDiv tank receives counter-battery fire from the strong Japanese defenses.

BELOW: Epitomizing a Marine charging into battle, this often reproduced photo is of assistant BAR man Pfc Paul E. Isom, 5th Marines, at the battle of Shuri Castle.

Valorous Unit Award (Army)

and the southern half, including Naha, which was flatter, afforded more maneuver room, and accounted for most of the inhabitants. There were also an estimated 100,000 Japanese defenders who manned the three major defense barriers that spanned east and west in front of the capital. The commander's CP was on the second defense barrier, the Shuri Line, in a significant architectural feature, Shuri Castle.

The 6th MarDiv, built up from MajGen Shepherd's 1st Provisional Brigade with the addition of the 29th Marines, quickly conquered Yontan airfield and the northern part of the island. The 6th MarDiv encountered stiff opposition at Nago and Mount Yaetake, where the 29th Marines suffered two hundred killed and eight hundred wounded. They then joined 1st MarDiv, under MajGen Pedro del Valle, which had cut the island in two on the third day and was on line on the right flank west of the Army divisions. Four abreast, the American divisions then engaged in warfare similar to that which had occurred in Europe before the Germans' surrender on 5 May 1945.

By 12 April the advance of the Army 7th and 96th Divisions against the first defensive barrier had lost momentum. The 29th Marines were sent in as reinforcements for eight more days of heavy fighting against the east-west ridgelines, Shuri Castle, and Naha. It took the two Marine divisions a solid month to breach the Shuri Line. Marines used one particular tactic that saved many of their tanks from suicidal sapper attacks: a squad of three fire teams escorted each tank. They found, too, that the new M7 self-propelled 105mm guns of regimental weapons companies were better in blasting out caves and bunkers than conventional artillery or napalm air strikes.

On 19 April, while the Army was still bogged down, Marine Gen Geiger proposed an end-run amphibious landing by the 2d MarDiv already afloat. Tenth Army CG Buckner, who did not appreciate the amphibious specialty of Marines, decided against it, insisting instead on continuing a stubborn, wasteful, shoulder-to-shoulder frontal assault. By 27 April, 1st MarDiv once again had to relieve the Army 27th Division on the line.

OPPOSITE, BOTTOM: Marines storming the so-called Little Siegfried Line of the Japanese defense at Naha, the capital of Okinawa, use a satchel charge to blow up a cave where the enemy was holed up.

BELOW: When the 1 April 1945 invasion of Okinawa by the U.S. Tenth Army (which included the 1st and 6th Divisions of III Marine Amphibious Corps plus the 2d Marine Division, in reserve as a floating decoy) began to get bogged down in fighting the strong Japanese defensive lines, the Army commander, LtGen Simon Bolivar Buckner, refused to consider using the Marines for amphibious assaults behind enemy lines, thus prolonging the carnage. Here, Marines sweep through a field of grain searching for enemy defenders.

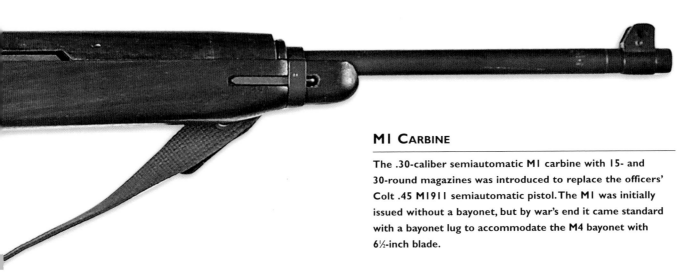

M1 CARBINE

The .30-caliber semiautomatic M1 carbine with 15- and 30-round magazines was introduced to replace the officers' Colt .45 M1911 semiautomatic pistol. The M1 was initially issued without a bayonet, but by war's end it came standard with a bayonet lug to accommodate the M4 bayonet with 6½-inch blade.

Early Control of Tactical Aviation

By the midpoint of the war in the Pacific, the island objectives were larger and the United States had gained air superiority. This meant that many more friendly aircraft were in play, and developing a system more sophisticated than an airfield control tower became essential.

On the basis of experience in the Solomons and Marianas with multidivision multiair group operations employing close air support, air defense, inderdiction, and air transport missions, air control centers were created. Known as Landing Force Air Support Control Units (LFAS-CU), they were first employed under then Col Keith McCutcheon to control Marine Air in support of MacArthur's forces in the Philippines. Use by V Phib Corps on Iwo Jima and by the Tenth Army on Okinawa followed.

By the Korean War, such a control unit was termed the Direct Air Support Center and controlled Marine Air for 1st MarDiv and, at Inchon-Seoul and the Chosin operations, for X Corps.

At the division level, for Marine Corps landings, close air support, and naval gunfire support, control and beach communications were integral in the Marine division. Marine and Navy officers and communicators were used. As more Army divisions were trained in amphibious warfare by the Navy-Marine Corps Amphibious Training Command and programmed for the Pacific, these communications were provided by a newly created Joint Amphibious Signal Company (JASCO). The company was joint in that it included Army Air Force air liaison officers (ALOs) and forward air control (FAC) parties, Navy naval gunfire liaison officers (NGLOs) and shore fire control parties (SFCPs), Army shore party communications, and Navy beachmaster communications.

—BN

ABOVE, INSET: LtGen Vernon Megee was the commander of all Marine Landing Force Air Support Control Units at Okinawa.

ABOVE: A Marine F4U Corsair in a rocket-strafing run during the battle for Okinawa. Note the smoke of the combat raging on the ground below.

RIGHT: Early in the invasion of Okinawa, the 1st MarDiv secured the northern half of the large island, then joined the newly formed 6th MarDiv and two Army divisions in the assault southward toward the capital. On the way, Marines wiped out stubborn Japanese resistance with flamethrowers and close-in fighting.

The expected big Japanese counterattack came on the night of 4 May. The 6th MarDiv was immediately moved in on the right of 1st MarDiv, providing a complete two-corps front of two Marine and two Army divisions. Marines, utilizing their naval support, called for illuminating and preregistered gunfire, and their own artillery and mortar barrages shot the attackers to pieces. The 1st Marines, with their flank on the west coast, intercepted and thwarted an enemy amphibious envelopment attempt, killing seven hundred in the water before they could set foot ashore. As the major enemy attack faltered at one point, 1st MarDiv counterattacked and carried the day. Although further combat was futile for the Japanese, they resisted for seven more bloody weeks.

The 1st MarDiv hammered through the tough Awacha Pocket and was joined by the 6th MarDiv. Then, the semi-monsoon "plum rains" deluged the battlefield, turning everything into quagmire. Despite the inhospitable conditions, the Marines trudged forward, fighting hard for their objectives. The 6th MarDiv attacked the western anchor of the Shuri Line and Sugar Loaf Hill, which was taken in fierce fighting by the 22d Marines. Joined by the 29th Marines, they breached the Shuri defensive line and reached the outskirts of Naha. That fighting almost debilitated both regiments. Other vicious little battles for Half Moon and Horseshoe ridges took great and courageous effort on the part of attacking Marines. The 7th Marines lost seven hundred men taking Dakeshi Ridge and five hundred more in the first five days at Wana Draw, where the 1st Tank Battalion had to be called in. In a single day, the tanks fired 5,000 75mm cannon shells and 173,000 .30-caliber machine-gun rounds, and flamethrowing tanks expended six hundred gallons of napalm. Opposition was sometimes so stiff that the 1st MarDiv gained only an average of fifty-five yards a day for more than eighteen days. The Japanese mastered reverse-slope defense. After reaching the hard-fought crest of a hill,

ABOVE: Marines of the 22d Regiment in an intense firefight north of the outskirts of the Okinawan capital, Naha, 4 May 1945.

LEFT: A tank spurts fire at an enemy position on a hillside. Flamethrowing tanks became indispensable in the tough, close-in fighting on Okinawa.

the exhausted Marines would suddenly find themselves engaged in hand-to-hand fighting with the enemies who had merely popped back over from the other side of the ridge from their prepositioned defensive points. And every night, Marines could expect infiltrators to seek out their foxholes and either lob

Unsung Heroes

The Navy corpsmen, doctors, and chaplains who served with the Marines as part of their duties deserve special mention. Unarmed and heedless of their own safety, they were there with the Marines in every battle. Corpsmen (the equivalent of the Army's medics) attended the injured on the battlefield, and many were wounded or killed in the process. It was perhaps the toughest duty in the Navy. Navy surgeons were not far behind, and they, too, became casualties. They often worked in makeshift field hospitals or even in covered areas just behind the battle. On Iwo Jima a Navy corpsman had helped raise the flag on Suribachi, and two earned the Medal of Honor. Navy chaplains were also on the spot in battle, comforting the wounded and administering to the dying. Many of them were wounded and many received decorations for valor in combat. Navy nurses on board the hospital ships were heroines as well; their medical assistance, succor, and compassion either helped many a Marine through his ordeal or comforted him in his final moments.

—HAC

Navy Corpsman
Petty Officer First Class
(World War II–era insignia)

Navy Corpsman
Petty Officer First Class
(Modern insignia)

ABOVE, RIGHT: A wounded Marine is helped off the battlefield by a Navy corpsman.

RIGHT: A Navy corpsman attends to a wounded Marine near where he was hit during the battle, using his M1 as a makeshift blood-plasma drip. Under such conditions, corpsmen could also apply bandages to stop bleeding, inject morphine to ease pain, and sprinkle sulfa powder on wounds to allay infection. It would probably be several hours before this Marine arrived at a major field medical facility or hospital ship. Since the advent of the helicopter, those hours have been reduced to minutes.

OPPOSITE, ABOVE: After a jolting stretcher-lift—possibly a rough ride in a jeep—and a short journey over choppy seas in an LCVP, a wounded Marine is lifted aboard a transport ship with medical facilities.

OPPOSITE, BELOW: A Navy emergency field hospital near the battlefield. Some critical cases could be treated here before further evacuation to a hospital ship.

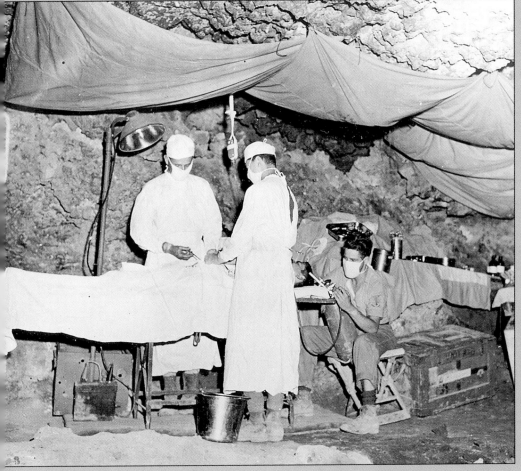

CORPORAL RICHARD EARL BUSH
Mount Yaetake, Okinawa
16 April 1945

For conspicuous gallantry and intrepidity at the risk of his life above and beyond the call of duty as a squad leader serving with the 1st Battalion, 4th Marines, 6th Marine Division, in action against enemy Japanese forces, during the final assault against Mount Yaetake on Okinawa, Ryukyu Islands, 16 April 1945. Rallying his men forward with indomitable determination, Cpl Bush boldly defied the slashing fury of concentrated Japanese artillery fire pouring down from the gun-studded mountain fortress to lead his squad up the face of the rocky precipice, sweep over the ridge, and drive the defending troops from their deeply entrenched position. With his unit, the first to break through to the inner defense of Mount Yaetake, he fought relentlessly in the forefront of the action until seriously wounded and evacuated with others under protecting rocks. Although prostrate under medical treatment when a Japanese hand grenade landed in the midst of the group, Cpl Bush, alert and courageous in extremity as in battle, unhesitatingly pulled the deadly missile to himself and absorbed the shattering violence of the exploding charge in his body, thereby saving his fellow Marines from severe injury or death despite the certain peril to his own life. By his valiant leadership and aggressive tactics in the face of savage opposition, Cpl Bush contributed materially to the success of the sustained drive toward the conquest of this fiercely defended outpost of the Japanese Empire. His constant concern for the welfare of his men, his resolute spirit of self-sacrifice, and his unwavering devotion to duty throughout the bitter conflict enhance and sustain the highest traditions of the U.S. Naval Service.

ABOVE: MajGen Pedro A. del Valle, CG, 1st MarDiv on Okinawa. Born on Puerto Rico and a class of 1915 graduate from the Naval Academy, del Valle served aboard ships in WW I and in the Banana Wars that followed. At Guadalcanal he commanded the 11th Marine Artillery Regiment and—for a short time in 1943—all Marine forces on the island. In 1944 he led III Corps artillery in action on Guam and in 1945 became the commanding general of 1st MarDiv. An aggressive leader, del Valle had his division cut in front of a stalled Army division to capture Shuri Castle.

grenades into them or stealthily cut the throats of any Marines caught sleeping.

To the left, 1st MarDiv's 1st and 5th Marines were converging on Shuri Castle itself, the enemy CP. On 29 May, crossing over the boundaries of a stalled Army unit, they secured it after bitter fighting. Gen del Valle was severely chastised for having authorized the move, but the objective was taken by the Marines where the Army had not. Perhaps, too, the criticism came because the Marine company commander had flippantly raised the Confederate Stars and Bars over the castle—which was shortly replaced by the Stars and Stripes.

Marine Air was giving the enemy a rough time as well. In an odd reversal of the traditional Navy and Marine aviation roles, Marine Corsairs were tangling with the Japanese over the East China Sea, while Navy Hellcats ended up providing close air support of the two divisions' front lines. MAG-33 scored 214 confirmed kills. Marine Maj George Axtell, of the VMF-323 "Death Rattlers," downed five Japanese raiders in thirty minutes of whirlwind aerial dogfighting. Navy aircraft also sank the *Yamato*, which had no air cover, and fifteen other enemy ships.

The III Phib Corps had gotten four VMO (observation) spotter-plane squadrons ashore quickly, and within ten days of the initial landing, two hundred Marine aircraft were shore-based. By June, twenty-two squadrons, composed of Corsairs, the new F6F Hellcats, and TBF Avenger torpedo planes, were operating ashore with ten at sea off the CVEs *Block Island* and *Gilbert Islands*. The attack carrier *Bunker Hill* was crippled by kamikazes, leaving only two VMF squadrons on the *Bennington*, which in five months of continuous operations since January shot down 82 enemy aircraft, destroyed 149 more on the ground, and dropped 100 tons of bombs, losing 48 aircraft and 18 pilots. Marine carrier-based Corsairs and F6F night-fighters proved highly effective against kamikazes.

The next objective was the Oruku Peninsula across from Naha that jutted out in front of the 6th MarDiv. Gen Buckner reluctantly gave Gen Shepherd permission for a shore-to-shore landing—that is, an embarkation in landing craft from his own shore, going in LCVPs around the flank of the enemy line, and making an amphibious landing behind it, in order to compress the Japanese naval defenders into one last pocket for annihilation. The landing took the Japanese completely by surprise. The 22d Marines attacked frontally and the pocket was wiped out in a week of hard combat.

Marine generals all the way up to CMC Alexander Vandegrift—as well as Navy admirals— urged the Army commander to utilize the Marine amphibious capabilities at hand and make an amphibious landing behind enemy lines on the southern tip of the island. Lacking any real comprehension of how to capitalize on this unique maneuvering arm, Gen Buckner acted slowly and with unnecessary caution, which did not sit well with the Marines, who were used to fighting hard and advancing rapidly to keep the enemy off balance. The Army's less aggressive strategy was to use overwhelming fire support to subdue an enemy before walking in and taking over. This conflict in strategy accounted for many unnecessary casualties and continuing friction between the Army and the Marines.

In most of the fighting in the Pacific, the Americans fought by day and the Japanese by night. Thus, against the particularly nasty objective of Kunishi Ridge, Col Ed Snedeker had his 7th Marines attack at 0330. Ninety minutes later, they caught the Japanese completely off guard at breakfast and secured the ridge. The Japanese could not conceive of being attacked at night by Americans. The 7th, however, had to be resupplied by the 1st Tank Battalion, which also had to take out the wounded. This was done in an extraordinary manner: a tank would drive over the supine body of a wounded Marine, who would lie very still; once the tank was positioned over him, the bottom hatch would be opened and the Marine would be lifted into the tank and driven back through a hailstorm of bullets to safety and medical attention. Also, the light two-seater Piper L-5 "Bird Dogs" of the VMO-6 squadron replaced the rear seat with a stretcher and could escort the more seriously wounded to the newly set-up hospital at Kadena in a matter of minutes, as opposed to the bone-jolting, six-hour vehicle ride over rough roads. In eleven days, 641 critically wounded Marines were evacuated in this manner.

While Buckner was watching the 8th Marines of the 2d MarDiv come in to reinforce the chewed-up 1st MarDiv, he was struck fatally by a coral fragment from a nearby enemy shell explosion. Marine LtGen Roy Geiger, the next senior officer, immediately took over the Tenth Army—to the utter consternation of the Army high command. He was the first and only Marine officer—and aviator, to boot—to ever command a field army, if only for a short time. Meanwhile, 1st MarDiv finished off Kunishi Ridge, the last major stronghold, in four more days of hard fighting.

LEFT: Trying to keep themselves and their equipment dry during the "plum rains" of late spring, Marines of 1st Battalion, 4th Marines, take advantage of a lull in the intense fighting on the reverse slope of part of Sugar Loaf Hill.

BELOW: A Marine BAR-man leads a patrol through the ruins of the Okinawan capital, Naha, alert to the dangers of lurking snipers.

RIGHT: A Marine colonel buries his son, killed in battle. Kneeling is Col Frank Fenton, CO, 17th Marines, 1st MarDiv. Draped with the Stars and Stripes, the body of his son Mike will be buried near the field of battle where he paid the supreme price. Another of Col Fenton's sons, Capt Ike Fenton, fought in the Pusan Perimeter in Korea five years later. (See page 284.)

BELOW: Marines and Navy corpsmen dash across open space under enemy fire to assist casualties from a previous attack, one of which lies in the foreground amid the battle litter of weapons and 782 gear.

LEFT: Weary Marines of an 81mm mortar platoon carry tubes of ammo lashed to packboards up to the front-line positions. Fighters on Okinawa had to contend not only with exhaustion and constant enemy fire, but also with stifling heat, torrential rain, and glue-thick mud. It was some of the roughest going of World War II.

BELOW: With bazooka rocket support, a Marine squad assaults the almost impregnable defensive line north of Naha.

Change of Command

Army LtGen Simon Bolivar Buckner's first combat command was on Okinawa as Tenth Army commander (Army XXIV Corps and Marine III Amphibious Corps [1st, 6th, and 2d MarDivs and 2d MAW]). With no appreciation of the amphibious flanking capabilities of his Marine forces, Buckner stubbornly attacked with two Army and two Marine divisions abreast, in a grueling, yard-by-yard battle.

On 18 June 1945, after the bloody fighting had dragged on for two and a half months, Gen Buckner made a broad-daylight visit to the temporary command post of the 8th Marines, on the crest of the east shoulder of Ibaru-Mezado Ridge. Buckner and his entourage arrived in a six-jeep convoy, with all vehicles displaying the long radio antennae that denoted a command group, attracting the attention of the enemy below the ridge. Buckner proceeded to climb to the top of the ridge for a look-see. The 8th Marines CO, Col Clarence Wallace, urged Buckner to don his helmet—which he reluctantly did—and cautioned him not to venture down the forward slope to observe Marines on the line below engaging the enemy. But the Tenth Army CG brushed off Wallace's admonition with foolish bravado. Seconds later a Japanese artillery shell hit nearby, sending up a jagged chunk of coral rock that crushed Buckner's chest: a wound that would prove to be fatal.

Fortunately, Buckner's deputy commander was Marine MajGen Roy S. Geiger, pioneer aviator and wing commander of the Marine "Cactus Air Force" on Guadalcanal and the Amphibious Corps commander in the Bougainville, Guam, and Peleliu landings. Geiger was immediately promoted to three stars and took command of Tenth Army for the next ten days of fighting—the only Marine and aviator ever to command so large a force, and a U.S. Army one at that. Geiger, as commanding general of FMFPAC, was also the senior Marine officer at the signing of the Japanese surrender in Tokyo Harbor the following September.

Capt Ishihara, the Japanese artillery officer who had personally sighted and fired the shell that killed Buckner, thought his round had missed the man standing on the ridge, and that he had failed his emperor. Long after the war, Marine Maj Richard T. Spooner, who as a private first class witnessed the death of the general, located the former Japanese officer in Japan—and even found the gun that had fired the fatal shot on display in a museum.

—HAC

All organized resistance ended on Okinawa on 21 June, and LtGen Geiger held a flag-raising ceremony in front of Tenth Army headquarters. At the same time, on the southern extremity of the island, the Japanese commanding general and his chief of staff donned their dress uniforms and committed ritual suicide. Their graves were found later.

The battle for Okinawa had been the largest amphibious operation of the Pacific war, although its initial landing had not been a hard-fought one. Unfortunately, 107,539 Okinawan civilians had been killed along with the Japanese combatants, and prisoners of war totaled more than 7,000. Marine and Navy pilots and ships' antiaircraft fire shot down 3,041 enemy aircraft, and more than 4,700 kamikazes destroyed themselves. The Navy, Marine, and Army Air Forces lost 763 aircraft. The U.S. Navy took the heaviest losses: 36 ships sunk, 368 damaged. Navy dead amounted to 4,907, with 5,100 wounded; 3,244 Marines died and 11,677 were wounded. Army casualties totaled more than 25,000. Ten Marines earned the Medal of Honor, as did three Navy corpsmen. Eleven of those were posthumous. The Secretary of the Navy awarded the Presidential Unit Citation to both Marine divisions, the 2d Marine Air Wing, and VMO-6.

ABOVE: Marine Sgt Richard T. Spooner, in a photo taken after World War II. Spooner served on Saipan, where he was wounded, and in the Okinawa campaign. During the latter, Cpl Spooner was near Tenth Army commander LtGen Simon B. Buckner when Buckner was struck and killed by a coral fragment set loose by a Japanese artillery round. Spooner was later commissioned and rose to the rank of major. After retirement, he founded—and still runs—the famous Globe and Laurel restaurant, located outside the gate at Quantico. Much of the early Marines memorabilia that appears in this book is from Maj Spooner's extensive collection.

ABOVE: The 8th Marines of 2d MarDiv (the only unit of that division engaged) move across captured Kadena Airfield as a Piper L-3 "Bird Dog" from VMO-6 banks to come in for a landing.

LEFT: Early in the Okinawa invasion, Marine and Navy aircraft destroyed all Japanese land-based aircraft. Shown here is Yontan Airfield, with a Marine F4U Corsair landing in the distance. After Seabees and Marine engineers bulldozed the wreckage away, the airfield quickly became operational.

OPPOSITE: Ignoring the warnings of 8th Marines CO Col Clarence R. Wallace (center) and his regimental S-3 operations officer, Maj William C. Chamberlain, LtGen Buckner stepped down the forward slope of Ibaru-Mezado Ridge to watch the action below. He was struck and killed just seconds after this photo was taken. Marine MajGen Roy S. Geiger, Marine pioneer aviator, veteran of the Banana Wars, wing commander at Guadalcanal, and amphibious force commander at Bougainville, Guam, and Peleliu, assumed command of the field army upon Buckner's untimely death in the final days of the fighting.

Marines in the European and North African Theaters

ABOVE: Dashing young Marine officer Peter J. Ortiz, shown here as a captain, served in both North Africa and France as a member of the Office of Strategic Services (OSS). Ortiz was awarded numerous high military decorations by the Marine Corps and by the French and British governments.

Aside from those Marines serving aboard U.S. Navy ships, a number of Marine officers and NCOs were assigned other duties in Europe, including many who performed undercover work. The Marine embassy detachment in London grew to 120 and performed special duties for the Navy. Other Marines served (some clandestinely) in Albania, Algeria, Austria, Belgium, Bulgaria, Corsica, Germany, Greece, Italy, Romania, and Yugoslavia. At the American Legation in Tangier, Morocco, were LtCol William A. Eddy, 2dLt Franklin Holcomb, the CMC's son, and petroleum specialist Otto Weber, a Reserve lieutenant.

Peter J. Ortiz

Destined to become the most famous was Maj Peter J. Ortiz, a native-born American raised in France who spoke five languages. He had served in the French Foreign Legion and had been wounded and captured by the Germans in 1940. Having escaped, he reached the United States and was ultimately commissioned in the U.S. Marine Corps.

Assigned to the Office of Strategic Services (OSS, precursor to the CIA) in London, he parachuted with an Allied team into Nazi-occupied France to lead Free-French "Maquis" Resistance fighters. He assisted downed Allied fliers, ambushed Germans, and prepared the Forces Françaises de l'Intérieur (FFI) for the coming Allied invasions. Such clandestine teams always wore their service uniforms in combat situations, sometimes under civilian clothes; Ortiz proudly wore his Marine service greens with barracks hat, sans wire frame.

In one story told about Ortiz, he was in a nightclub in Lyon, dressed as a civilian, when he overheard a group of German officers berating the United States, President Franklin Roosevelt, and the United States Marine Corps, which they had likely never encountered. Incensed, Ortiz quickly left the restaurant, went back to his room, put on his Marine uniform—with rows of ribbons—donned a trench coat, and returned to the club. Striding over to the table full of Germans, he flung open his trench coat to reveal a U.S. Marine standing before them and at the same time whipped out his pistol and aimed it at the startled Wehrmacht officers.

Holding them at gunpoint, Ortiz ordered them in their own language to lift their glasses to toast first the United States then President Roosevelt. Ordering another round of drinks, he then offered a special toast to the United States Marine

Corps and ordered the Germans to join in. When they had obediently drained their glasses, the Marine officer abruptly turned and disappeared into the night.

Later, unintentionally confronting a German motorized column, Ortiz and the two Marine NCOs with him, sergeants John Bodnar and Jack Risler, held off the enemy battalion until Ortiz realized that the Germans would take reprisals on the French citizens and execute scores of them if he and the sergeants continued to resist. He stood up and marched his team out in smart military fashion and surrendered, reminding their startled captors that, as Marines, they were uniformed enemies and were required to give only name, rank, and serial number. Unable to escape from the German POW camp to which they were taken near Bremen, they were liberated fourteen months later, when British troops secured that area at the end of the war.

Ortiz became one of the most highly decorated Marines of World War II. In addition to his several previous French Foreign Legion decorations, from the U.S. Navy Department he received two Navy Crosses, the Legion of Merit with combat "V," and two Purple Hearts for wounds. From the British, he was made an Officer of the Most Excellent Order of the British Empire, and from the French, he received five Croix de Guerre (two palms, a gold and a silver star), the Croix de Combattant, the Ouissam Alaouite, the Médaille Coloniale, and the Chevalier de la Légion d'Honneur. In gratitude, the village of Centron in the Haute-Savoie region renamed its town center Place Peter Ortiz.

After the war, two Hollywood motion pictures were made about his life and he played minor roles in others. After his retirement in 1955 he was promoted to colonel. He died at age seventy-five in May 1988 and was interred at Arlington Cemetery.

—HAC

THE ABRUPT END

Cleanup following the battle was done quickly in order to clear the way for the amassing of men, matériel, weapons, aircraft, and ships for the next phase: the invasion of Japan, dubbed Operations Olympic and Coronet. Okinawa would be the jumping-off place. Operation Olympic, scheduled for 1 November 1945, entailed the assault of Japan's southern home island, Kyushu, by the 3d, 4th, and 5th Marine Divisions and ten Army divisions. The following March, in Operation Coronet, the 1st and 6th MarDivs along with nine Army divisions would land on the Tokyo plain on Honshu. The Joint Chiefs' plan for a ground assault won over the Air Corps' plan for heavy aerial bombardment as an alternative. Of the twenty-four American attacking divisions, the JCS fully expected to lose entirely the first three waves on the beaches and for estimated casualties in the first few days to exceed 100,000.

Meanwhile, on 21 June, an incredible detonation deep in the New Mexico desert marked the unleashing of a new weapon that would change the war—and the world. Two more of the explosive devices were quickly assembled and transported "Top Secret" on the cruiser USS *Indianapolis* (which was sunk by a submarine on its return trip) to the island of Tinian. There, the first was readied and loaded into the bomb bay of a gleaming, aluminum-skinned B-29 of the 509th Bomb Group of the USAAF. The plane was nicknamed *Enola Gay*, after the mother of its pilot, LtCol Paul Tibbets, Jr. (Tibbets was unaware that his promotion to colonel had come through that very day.)

The *Enola Gay*, escorted by another Superfortress, lifted off on its unique mission at 0245 on the morning of 6 August 1945. It flew at an altitude of thirty thousand feet for five hours to reach its unusual target, the virtually unscathed Japanese military logistics base and harbor city of Hiroshima, and drop its deadly cargo, a 20-kiloton atomic bomb dubbed Little Boy. At 0815, the bomb exploded two thousand feet above the city. As the pilots turned to head home, both B-29s shuddered momentarily from the shock of the blast, and Tibbets and the crews saw behind them a gigantic mushroom-shaped cloud rising to the stratosphere. Even they had not known exactly what the device was. It obliterated forty-six square miles of the Japanese city in one enormous, blinding, pinkish-white flash of atomic radiation. Some 40,000 people on the ground died almost instantly. (By contrast, previous firebombing raids on Tokyo and other major Japanese

ABOVE: Maj George C. Axtell, Jr., twenty-three-year-old commanding officer of the "Death Rattlers," the famed 2d Marine Air Wing fighter squadron credited with downing 124 Japanese planes over Okinawa. On 22 April 1945, Axtell intercepted two enemy aerial attacking forces of great numerical superiority and "by a fearless, daring, and skillful attack, thwarted the enemy attack against the U.S. naval forces, shipping, aircraft, and installations." The Marine major was credited with five kills, three probables, and three damaged. He was awarded the Navy Cross for his actions.

cities had claimed as many as 90,000 lives in each of several night attacks. Japan had been bombed more heavily than Europe.)

The extent of the devastation staggered the Japanese—and the world—when President Harry S. Truman, who had succeeded the late President Roosevelt, announced it. It was hoped that this event would end the war. Due to an internal struggle among Japanese leaders, however, an immediate surrender was not forthcoming. To convince the Japanese of America's resolve and to demonstrate that the United States possessed additional bombs, another type of atomic bomb, euphemistically named Fat Boy, was dropped on 9 August, obliterating the Japanese city of Nagasaki, killing 23,753. With that, the Japanese accepted "loss of face" and surrendered unconditionally on 15 August 1945.

Thus, the dreaded invasion would not be necessary after all—possibly saving hundreds of thousands of lives on both sides. The bloody four years of war (ten years in Asia) brought on by the Japanese Empire was now terminated in the sacrificial destruction of two of its major cities—as well as the utter defeat of its armed forces in the Pacific by the United States and its Allies.

Reevaluated in hindsight, the dropping of the two atomic bombs, while arguably saving hundreds of thousands of both American and Japanese lives, also instigated an arms race between the two emerging world superpowers, the United States and the Soviet Union, to develop ever more powerful weapons of mass destruction. Thus the bombings would usher in almost half a century of cold war on the heels of the six-year global hot one they had

ended. The bombings at Hiroshima and Nagasaki also warned the world of the catastrophic effects of atomic warfare—unless it was controlled and possibly outlawed.

By the time a moratorium on nuclear weapons was agreed upon, their destructive power had escalated from the 20-kiloton bomb dropped at Hiroshima to a 100-megaton weapon tested by the Soviets in 1962. Had either the Germans (who were very close to developing) or the Japanese been able to develop the A-bomb first, the world would quite possibly be a very different place today. It is likely that neither enemy would have hesitated to use the bomb indiscriminately.

THE JAPANESE SURRENDER

On 2 September 1945, ninety-two years after Commo Matthew C. Perry had sailed his little steam-and-sail flotilla to the isolated, still-medieval world of Japan, portions of the U.S. Navy—the greatest fleet the world had ever seen—under five-star Fleet Admiral Chester W. Nimitz sailed into Tokyo Harbor for the formal surrender of the Japanese Empire to the United States and its Allies.

As hundreds of Navy and Marine aircraft flew overhead in "V for victory" formations to impress the vanquished Japanese, the articles of surrender were signed by representatives of the Allies and Japan aboard the battleship USS *Missouri* (which President Truman had requested as a tribute to his home state). Signing for the victors was five-star General of the Army Douglas MacArthur, who had also been designated Supreme Allied Commander, Far East, and who would stay on in Tokyo to lead the occupation and guide the defeated nation toward democracy. Among the top admirals and generals witnessing the momentous event was a lone Marine officer, LtGen

Roy Geiger, now Commanding General, Fleet Marine Force, Pacific. He and the Marines had come a long way from Wake Island and Guadalcanal to this hard-fought moment of triumph.

At the time of surrender, the Japanese still had 3 million men in one hundred infantry and armored divisions in Japan and 1 million troops overseas in Asia. Although the Imperial Japanese Navy no longer existed thanks to the U.S. Navy, the Japanese still had four thousand kamikazes in reserve for the anticipated American landings. Civilians, too, were prepared to fight to the death, if only with bamboo spears. The invasion of Japan would most likely have been the biggest bloodletting in history.

The Marine III and V Amphibious Corps had been preparing for the invasion that was canceled when the Japanese capitulated. Instead, Marine and Army units entered Japan as occupation troops. The 4th Marines took over the Yokosuka Naval Base on Honshu. The Marine 2d and 5th Divisions took over Sasebo and, for several months, the annihilated city of Nagasaki on the lesser island, Kyushu. Thus, some Marines were exposed to the then-unknown lingering effects of atomic radiation. By April 1946 all Marine units had been removed and the area turned over to the U.S. Army.

The imprisoned survivors of the 4th Marines captured at Corregidor, as well as the Wake Island defenders, were quickly found and freed. These 4th Marines were honored in ceremonies in Japan with the presentation of their new regimental "colors"

The Myth of the Invincible Japanese Warrior

World War II Victory Medal

At the outset of World War II, the impression in Western circles was that the Japanese soldier was virtually invincible—fierce, ruthless, and willing to fight to the death. As the Pacific campaign progressed and the tides turned in favor of the American forces after Midway, the myth of the invincibility of the Japanese soldier persisted despite the fact that the Imperial forces were losing the war. In light of the success of the U.S. efforts in the war, particularly as exemplified by the Marines, this myth is due for some reevaluation.

At Midway, the U.S. Navy and Marines devastated the Imperial Japanese carrier and surface fleet and killed many of its best pilots, a crippling blow from which the Japanese would never fully recover. Once the "sleeping giant" of the West had been awakened, by contrast, there was no lulling it back to sleep. Indeed, the U.S. Navy was astonishingly quick to rebuild in the wake of the attack on Pearl Harbor, and in general the swift and efficient U.S. production of matériel throughout the war put the Japanese (and ultimately all the Axis powers) at a growing disadvantage. In light of this, the fact that the Japanese continued to fight with increasingly less (and increasingly inferior) equipment certainly contributed to their aura of toughness.

The Guadalcanal campaign and the associated offshore naval engagements were brutal slugfests that eventually drove the Japanese from the island. But again, the tenacity of the Japanese soldier was a highlight of reports of the action on the ground: the soldiers fought to the death rather than submit to capture, yielding surprisingly few POWs for the Americans. To be sure, the Marines were given credit for the hard-won victory, but still the myth of the steely Japanese endured.

In the Solomon Islands campaign, the enemy had had strong naval, air, and logistic support, unlike in the central Pacific campaign, where each of the Japanese fortified beachheads (Tarawa, Roi-Namur, Saipan, Tinian, Guam, Peleliu, and Iwo) was isolated. Okinawa had even built up reserves and enjoyed a short—though impossible to defend—supply line to the homeland. In all these cases, though, the Japanese lost, too. Certainly, the overwhelming firepower of the Americans accounted for much of the difference: by the Iwo campaign, for

instance, the Navy had one hundred combat carriers, the Marine Corps had six divisions and five air wings, and the Army Air Corps deployed fleets of long-range bombers. But that wasn't the only difference.

It seems crucial to distinguish between the operation of the Imperial Japanese forces as a whole and the comportment of the individual soldiers. For as the Pacific campaign progressed and the Japanese forces were clearly losing the war, the specter of the Japanese soldier nevertheless continued to inspire fear. The nagging question remains: why?

The well-equipped and trained Japanese army defeated poorly equipped and inadequately trained Chinese irregulars (peasant militia, really). And the Japanese army swarmed down through undefended Burma and Indonesia, ultimately crushing a half-hearted defense by the British. These were victories, certainly, but why did the soldiers of the German Wehrmacht—who had defeated the French, British, and Polish armies, and nearly overcame the Russian army, too—not enjoy the same fearsome reputation?

The answer seems to be cultural, and it had direct consequences in the field. The Japanese soldier of World War II was the product of a monolithic, hierarchical, and militaristic culture based on the Bushido code, which valued honor above life and stressed sacrifice in the name of the emperor. The U.S. Marine of World War II, by contrast, was raised in a democratic society that stressed working together as a community to accomplish goals, and then trained to become a professional killer. When the Japanese soldier and the U.S. Marine fought, these two cultural ideologies clashed, too—and the democratic ideology (backed as it was by the military-industrial complex of a huge nation with vast natural resources) prevailed.

In addition to personal bravery—which both Japanese and American soldiers displayed on occasions too numerous to mention—both had the will to win. And when it came down to mortal, one-on-one combat, the American Marines turned out to be just as ferocious as the enemy (not surprisingly, in the passion of such life-or-death moments, the instinct for survival rose to the fore). So what else could have made the difference?

The average American Marine of World War II was a kid between seventeen and twenty-one years

old, raised during the Great Depression, with perhaps a couple years of public high school, who had been transformed almost overnight into a warrior. These young men were then expected to fight in the terrifying, alien jungles of Guadalcanal and Bougainville, face murderous fire slogging through the shallow waters of Betio, scale cliffs and mountains on Saipan, Guam, and Peleliu, and fight in desperate circumstances on Iwo and Okinawa. And, yes, like the Japanese soldier, the Marine was expected to, and often did, fight to the death—but for different reasons.

The Marine fought for Corps, for Country, for God—in that order. If anything, the U.S. forces prevailed in the Pacific Theater in part because the American Marine was primarily motivated by a democratic esprit de corps rather than mindless self-sacrifice in the name of an abstract code of honor or a godlike emperor. In the end, what put the Japanese soldier at a disadvantage when facing a Marine was precisely the same suicidal quality that gave the reputation of the Japanese soldier its mythic quality. The Japanese laid down their lives for their emperor, but the Marines laid down their lives for each other.

—HAC

1st Marine Division
Guadalcanal, Cape Gloucester,
Peleliu, Okinawa, North China
Returned to U.S. 1946

2d Marine Division
Guadalcanal, Tarawa, Saipan,
Tinian, Okinawa, Japan
Returned to U.S. 1946

3d Marine Division
Bougainville, Guam, Iwo Jima
Disbanded December 1945

by the later-formed 1st and 3d Battalions from Guam. The original colors had been destroyed on Corregidor in May 1942 to prevent their falling into enemy hands—an ignominious acquiescence of defeat for any military organization. All Japanese units that had faced Marines lost their colors in defeat.

DEMOBILIZATION

Following V-E Day in Europe and V-J Day in Japan in 1945, America's 16 million men and women in uniform could not return to civilian life fast enough. Nine million were released the first year, flooding the job market or attending college on the new GI Bill as a bonus for their sacrifices. The Marine Corps was no exception, but first there were some loose ends to tie up.

Just three days before the Japanese surrendered, the Soviet Union had declared war on Japan and had invaded Japanese-held Manchukuo. Three years later the Soviets would obstruct free access to Berlin and, in the words of Prime Minister Winston Churchill, drop an "iron curtain" across Europe. Erstwhile Ally, dictator Joseph Stalin, suddenly appeared to be a new aggressor.

Following the surrender, the 1st and 3d Battalions of the 4th Marines had gone ashore and secured the Yokosuka naval base in Tokyo Bay. Fortunately, the Japanese honored the terms of surrender and there were no untoward incidents as American forces landed. Even enemies still in uniform did not obstruct the occupiers; they simply bowed courteously as the American forces went about taking over their country.

While attending to occupation duties in Japan and partial demobilization in the Pacific and the United States, the Marines were tasked with a mission that would take them back to their old stomping ground, China. They were to oversee the surrender of the remaining 630,000 Japanese soldiers still in China and to separate the Chinese warring factions of Gen Chiang Kai-shek's free and Mao Tse-tung's Communist armies. But behind the mission was also the desire to thwart any further advancement of the Soviet Union in that part of the world, to prevent that country from accomplishing the subjugation of conquered countries as it was beginning to do in Europe.

The 1st Marine Division went back to occupy Tientsin and the American Legation compound in Peiping (formerly known as Peking, then later renamed Beijing when the Communists took over), and four Marine Aircraft Groups were also sent in. Before its disbandment in 1946, the 6th MarDiv, less the 4th Marines, was sent farther south to Tsingtao near Mao's forces. Both there and at Peking, in a general environment of anarchy, the Marines accepted the surrender of 100,000 Japanese but allowed them to keep their weapons. (Who knew but that the Americans and Japanese might be fighting side by side again one day as they had done in the same area in 1900 during the Boxer Rebellion?) During this chaotic time, Marines guarded the railroads and railroad bridges in that area of China. They were ambushed dozens of times by Mao Communists and sustained ten killed and thirty-four wounded. All Marines were brought out of China by 1949.

The Marines, as did the Army, occupied Japan following the war, and in 1950 they would be called upon again to fight in the Far East. In 1945, Congress authorized the peacetime strength of the Marine

Corps at 107,000, much larger than before the war but a quarter of its wartime strength. The 1st and 2d Divisions would remain at strength and constitute FMF Pacific and FMF Atlantic. The 1st MarDiv would remain at Camp Pendleton, California; the 2d MarDiv and the cadre of the Reserve 4th would be at Camp Lejeune, North Carolina, with corresponding aircraft wings at El Toro and Cherry Point.

RECAP OF MARINES IN WORLD WAR II

From the single 4th Brigade, consisting of 9,000 men, which fought so valiantly for six months in the First World War, the Marine Corps had grown to six combat divisions (compared with the Army's ninety-three activated divisions), five air wings (four in the Pacific), and four carrier groups in the Second World War for a total of 485,053 Marines. More than 450,000 served in the Pacific Theater, where 19,215 were killed, more than 72,000 wounded, and 2,220 taken prisoner, 518 of whom died in captivity. Eighty-one received the Medal of Honor "for conspicuous gallantry and intrepidity… in combat above and beyond the call of duty," forty-eight of them posthumously. Marines also served on capital ships around the globe, with the American Office of Strategic Services (OSS), and with the British in Europe and the Middle East. Others served with partisans in Yugoslavia and with guerrillas in the Philippines and China.

Women had also joined the Marine Corps Reserve, as they had in World War I. Nineteen thousand women served as stenographers, motor mechanics, cryptographers, and parachute riggers, freeing men for combat. They were referred to this time not as Marinettes but as Women Marines (WMs). In a time of national segregation, it was difficult for African Americans to join the Corps; however, enough did enlist to form several defense and service battalions. Many fought on Iwo Jima and at other hostile landings. Immediately following the war, the Marine Corps was the first military service to desegregate, as President Truman had ordered.

BACKGROUND: The U.S. Marine Corps War Memorial, created by Navy veteran and sculptor Felix de Weldon, overlooks the U.S. Capitol from its lofty site at the edge of Arlington Cemetery. Based on Joe Rosenthal's famous photograph of the Iwo Jima flag-raising, the monument commemorates the sacrifices of all Marines who have fought and died for their country.

4th Marine Division
Saipan, Tinian, Iwo Jima
Disbanded November 1945

5th Marine Division
Iwo Jima
Disbanded January 1946

6th Marine Division
Okinawa, Tsingtao
Disbanded April 1946

chapter five
Truman's "Police Action" with the United Nations

"Request immediate assignment Marine Regimental Combat Team and supporting Air Group for duty this command...."

Gen Douglas MacArthur, on 2 July 1950, calling for Marines to help in Korea

At 0400 hours on Sunday, 25 June 1950, seven infantry and armored divisions of the communist North Korean People's Army (NKPA), with 150 Russian-made T-34 tanks, launched simultaneous attacks down six major avenues of approach across the 38th Parallel demarcation line into South Korea.

The eight light infantry divisions of the defending Republic of Korea (ROK) Army, with no armor and little artillery, were mostly asleep—at least the 40 percent who were not absent on weekend passes. Their senior officers were just winding up their customary Saturday night revels, making the rounds to the parties that were usually hosted by foreign embassies or by the Korean Military Advisory Group (KMAG), a U.S. organization under State Department, rather than Army, authority. U.S. Army occupation troops had been pulled out of Korea two years before, and U.S. Secretary of State Dean Acheson had publicly stated that South Korea was not in the U.S. security orbit.

As the partygoers were tumbling into bed, no doubt vaguely dreading the inevitable hangovers they would wake up with, telephone reports of artillery and tank attacks began to come in to various ROK headquarters and to KMAG. No one took them seriously or realized the consequences of these attacks. Despite the recent increase in serious North Korean guerrilla activity, most thought it was a feint, the usual

jockeying for position of the Soviet and Chinese Communist–controlled people of the North. The 38th Parallel was only an arbitrary demarcation, a last-minute footnote to the Japanese surrender drawn up by State-War-Navy officers to keep the Soviets at bay following their last-minute entry into the war after occupying parts of Manchuria and Korea. To the civilians, Korea was all one country; the artificial separation into North and South was the result of the puppet regime installed by the Communists.

Korea had just been liberated from forty years of brutal domination by Japan, which exploited the populace and sought to assimilate it culturally. When the Japanese left upon surrendering to Allied forces at the end of World War II, with them went the colonial ruling structure, leaving behind a chaotic and ravaged country—especially in the agrarian south. Two-story buildings were a rarity among the mud-and-thatched-roof hovels, and few roads in the rugged, mountainous country had been paved.

Though tasked with training the ROK Army, KMAG also had to ensure that the South Korean military was not strong enough to attack the North. As a result, KMAG's work with the ROK Army was mere window dressing; weapons, vehicles, and armor were inadequate and in short supply, and training was lackadaisical. Nor did there seem to be any urgency for improvement. No one could conceive of a war erupting in such a place.

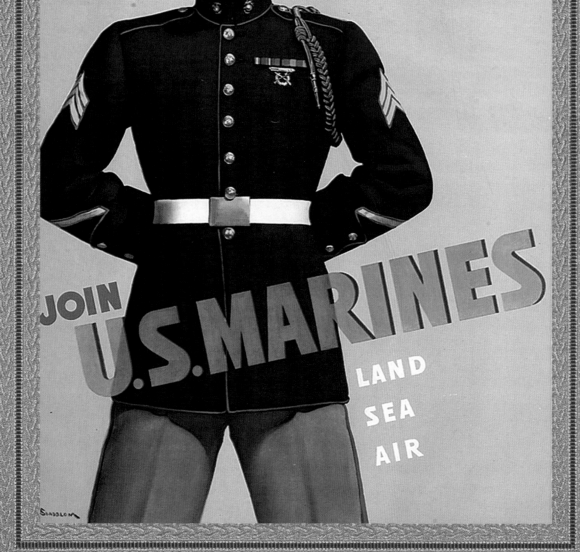

PAGE 283: A Marines recruiting poster by Haddon Sundblom, circa 1950.

PAGES 284–285: Photographer David Douglas Duncan, who served with the Marines in World War II, was a freelance photographer on assignment for *Life* magazine when he captured these remarkable images of the 2d Battalion, 5th Marines, fighting North Korean regulars on the Naktong River line in the last-bastion Pusan Perimeter.

When the North Korean army overran South Korea, capturing its capital, Seoul, smashing all South Korean opposition, and eliminating the 24th and 25th U.S. Infantry Divisions in June and July of 1950, it drove remnants of the South Korean army and what was left of the U.S. Eighth Army into a tight perimeter at the tip of the peninsula.

Hastily assembled from the 5th Marine Regiment, the 1st Marine Provisional Brigade was brought in as a "Fire Brigade" to stop enemy penetrations and back up faltering U.S. units.

(Continued on opposite page)

PRESIDENT TRUMAN'S RESPONSE

Awakened with the news of the unmistakable invasion of South Korea, President Truman demonstrated his oft-repeated motto, "The buck stops here." Without hesitation, the feisty chief executive made a decision that almost equaled his earlier one to drop the two atomic bombs to end World War II. As his advisers were steering toward a meeting of the United Nations (UN) Security Council, Truman ordered Gen George E. Stratemeyer's weak Far East Air Force to immediately destroy North Korean airfields and aircraft and to protect allied shipping in and out of South Korea.

UN Secretary-General Trygve Lie quickly convened the Security Council. At that time, the permanent members—those with veto powers—were the United States, Britain, France, and the Soviet Union; China had not yet become a member of the United Nations. In what was either a gross miscalculation or a deliberate test of the West's determination, Soviet Deputy Foreign Minister Andrei Gromyko—who usually cast the customary nullifying vote against the West—was absent. Consequently, the free nations quickly agreed to assist South Korea militarily, thus initiating the first military action of the newly created United Nations and giving the United States carte blanche to take whatever actions it deemed necessary.

Truman told the press that he was undertaking a "police action." It was a daring move on the president's part, for the U.S. military was in no shape to go to war. Neither were any of its World War II allies.

STATUS OF THE U.S. MILITARY IN 1950

Secretary of Defense Louis Johnson—and the Joint Chiefs of Staff (JCS)—had to eat crow. Under Johnson's watch, the once formidable American armed forces had deteriorated drastically.

In effect, the U.S. Army was a disgrace, the newly created U.S. Air Force was just getting organized, and the Navy was mothballing its once victorious fleets. The green occupation troops were spread all over Japan; most were raw replacements with no training—few of them had ever fired a weapon. The United States was so far from anything approaching a war footing that it almost exceeded its total lack of preparedness prior to both world wars. From a high of one hundred divisions in World War II, there were only ten infantry and four armored divisions left, and they were at only 60 percent of their former strength, under-equipped and ill-trained. In this atmosphere, the Marine Corps had valiantly tried to maintain enough

resources for a single full-strength division that could respond to any contingency.

Washington's attention, through the newly created North Atlantic Treaty Organization (NATO), was securely fixed on Europe to defend against what had by then become a clear Soviet threat. It was assumed that the great Gen Douglas MacArthur had the situation in the Far East under control, so that region was largely neglected by Washington, and only four divisions were in the Pacific. What was to

(Continued from previous page) After virtually saving the allied lines again and again, the Marines turned the tide at the Naktong. The Marine Provisional Brigade fought for the whole month of August before it was pulled out to form the spearhead of the mid-September amphibious landing at Inchon. These scenes show the closeness and ferocity of the fighting.

M9A1 2.36-INCH ROCKET LAUNCHER

This improved version of the 1942 2.36-inch M9 rocket launcher—a carryover from World War II—was still incapable of penetrating the slanted, heavy armor of the Russian-made T-34 tanks used by the North Koreans in 1950. It was somewhat effective against pillboxes and personnel, but not as effective as the M20 3.5 rocket and launcher used by the Marines.

ABOVE: A Marine 3.5-inch rocket launcher crew trains somewhere behind the lines. The Marines were fortunate to have these 3.5s; the Army had only 2.36s, which would just bounce off enemy tanks.

RIGHT: The typical southern terrain of rolling hills and rice paddies cut by unpaved roads in the Pusan Perimeter offered little protective cover, but did afford room for classic military formations. It also gave Marine gunners great fields of fire against enemy tanks, as the burning Russian-made T-34 here attests.

OPPOSITE: After hard fighting in the unbearable heat of the Korean summer, a Marine light-machine-gun crew comes off the line for a break. Note the helmet covers and leggings. As the battles wore on the leggings and the covers wore out and were discarded.

Initiative and Quick Response—Meeting the North Korean Tank Threat

In the early days of the Korean War, NKPA Soviet-supplied T-34 tanks were virtually unstoppable. The 2.36-inch rocket launcher, which had been used in World War II, proved to have insufficient range and penetrating power to stop the T-34s, and the new 3.5-inch antitank rocket launchers were initially unavailable. The Marine Corps responded to the threat by purchasing quantities of the new Belgian ENERGA antitank rifle grenade. The ENERGA could be fired from existing launchers attached to the muzzles of the Marines' M1 rifles. A planeload of the grenades was flown to the Marine brigade in the Pusan Perimeter.

—BN

be found, however, was that no one—not even MacArthur—had given the slightest thought to a threat from that quarter.

What was almost worse than the physical neglect of the armed forces was the deterioration of discipline and morale, thanks mostly to the effects of the "Doolittle Commission," named after MajGen James E. Doolittle of Tokyo raid fame. Based on interviews conducted in 1945 with forty-two disgruntled GIs, the commission had determined that the entire armed forces should be "civilianized," with rank structure and discipline de-emphasized—a formula for failure. The Marines quietly ignored this.

When it finally dawned on some of the seasoned U.S. military in Japan that T-34 tanks (which had been used in the Battle of Stalingrad in World War II) were opening the way for the invading North Koreans, they discovered that their own resources—in the entire Far East—consisted entirely of three M26 Pershing tanks with 90mm cannons and ninety M24 light tanks with 75mm guns, which were as ineffective as the paltry 2.36-inch antitank rockets that they would soon learn simply bounced off the T-34s. Worse yet, all ninety-three tanks had to be totally rebuilt before they would be battle-ready.

ABOVE: The stark stare of battle exhaustion marks the face of Capt Ike Fenton, commander, "Baker" (in the phonetic code of that time) Company, 1st Battalion, 5th Marines, in this photograph by David Douglas Duncan. Fenton's Marines had been in intense battle for three days and would endure two more before the defeated enemy pulled back—fortunately, for Fenton's Marines were out of ammo, rations, and water.

Ike Fenton came from a Marine family; his father was a brigadier general on Okinawa, where Ike's brother was killed. (See page 266.)

As if it weren't bad enough, it turned out that there was insufficient ammunition for the tanks, for the artillery, and even for the 75mm recoilless rifles that could stop a tank. Incredibly, there were not even any extra steel-cored fan belts, and each M26 required ten of these, eight of which had to be replaced after every seven hours of operation.

However, there were a few old Air Force P-51 Mustangs and Navy F6F Hellcats and Corsairs that were able to knock the prop-driven Russian-made YAK-3s out of the skies. MacArthur, now advised that he was in charge of the war, started beefing up MajGen Walton Walker's Eighth Army, assembling the 24th and 25th Divisions in Japan and the 1st and 2d Cavalry from the States. At the end of the first week, however, an advance echelon of the 24th was sent into battle piecemeal, without proper reconnaissance, G-2 Intelligence

OPPOSITE, TOP AND BOTTOM, AND LEFT: A sequence of combat action caught on camera by David Douglas Duncan. Having received fire from a hidden enemy machine gun, a Marine squad dashes over a dike to the edge of a rice paddy. They run low and fast to avoid the enemy fire. At far left, top and bottom, an ammo carrier stumbles at the sight of a headless enemy corpse; at left, the corporal fire team leader sloshes ahead of his BAR man. As Duncan described it, "The bullets hummed off-key tunes just overhead." He also poetically described the oppressive heat: "The air was suffocating and the sun reached down through the brain of anyone who moved in the open. It grabbed the stomach and tried to yank it inside out." (This and other quotations are from Duncan's *This Is War.*)

The Corps' Biggest Battle

Even with the war over, the second half of the 1940s was by no means tranquil. The United States would have much work to do to get itself—and the rest of world—back to normal. At home, U.S. leaders would have to demobilize the largest armed force in history, revert from a wartime to a peacetime economy, and readjust the returning GIs into society and absorb them into the job market. Abroad, they would have to occupy Germany and rebuild Europe, occupy and democratize Japan, and try to forge a peaceful world through the newly created United Nations, all while dealing with the new threat of Soviet Communism, which now dominated half the planet and threatened to continue expanding its influence.

The situation facing the victorious U.S. armed forces was complicated to say the least. While there was public pressure to "bring the boys home," there were also arguments about how best to reorganize to confront the Soviet Union. President Truman, backed by top Army leaders George C. Marshall, Dwight D. Eisenhower, Omar Bradley, Lawton Collins, Carl Spaatz, Hap Arnold, and others, pressed for a "unification" plan that would combine all branches of the armed services into a single force, presumably run by the Army. Now that nuclear weapons were a reality, these officers felt that ground wars—especially amphibious landings—were a thing of the past. Spaatz and Arnold, however, pushed for an Air Force separate from the Army, claiming that the necessary change in strategy would give the Air Force the leading role of long-range bombing in any future war. Not surprisingly, the unification concept, expressed in the so-called Collins Plan, alarmed the Navy. The Marine Corps, however, was not even invited to voice an opinion.

Thus the stage was set for the biggest battle the Marine Corps ever waged, a showdown for its very survival. It would be a two-front fight: the first pitted against the Army, the Air Force, and the president; the second, against budget cuts in Congress, directed by the president, that would debilitate the Corps and, in effect, phase it out of existence. The threats were nothing new in the history of the Marine Corps, but they were far more serious this time, and would take seven years to resolve.

From 1947 through 1949 there was a virtual standoff between anti-Marine forces (Truman, the Army, the new Air Force, some in the Navy, and congressional budget-cutters) and a Marine Corps that had been forcibly decimated from its top strength of 485,000 Marines to just 50,000. The Marine Corps was not represented among the Joint Chiefs of Staff, nor was it recognized as a separate service, although by law it should have been. Secretary of the Navy James Forrestal assumed the Navy spoke for the Marine Corps, even though he himself had been aboard ship and witnessed the battle of Iwo Jima.

The Army, though, continued to be the main instigator for doing away with the Marines. Throughout the Marine Corps'

170-year history, the Army (more so than the Navy, which was naturally more closely associated with the Corps) had constantly nipped at the Marines' heels and had sought to influence presidents and congresses to eliminate it. The mere existence of the Marines rankled the Army, which feared that the Corps was duplicating its own role by constituting a second land army. It wasn't until President Teddy Roosevelt's executive order of 1908, which defined the unique role of the Marines as distinct from that of the other armed forces, that the Corps considered their advanced-base expeditionary role to be firmly established, and their readiness, adaptability, and fighting professionalism to be officially recognized. Fueling the Army's animosity was the inordinate amount of press and public admiration given to a single brigade of Marines (in an Army of eighty-four brigades) during World War I. After that conflict, the Marine Corps continued to excel in its unique role, quelling brush fires in China and the Caribbean while developing its own amphibious doctrine—neither of which the Army was doing.

It was the "big war" that brought about the showdown between the Army and the Marines. Army officials were stung by the praise and attention won by the Marines for their brilliant performance in the Pacific over one less so by an Army not highly trained in amphibious or jungle warfare. The resentment was exacerbated by the "Smith versus Smith" incident during the battle of Saipan, in which Army National Guard 27th Division MajGen Ralph Smith was relieved of his command by Marine LtGen "Howlin' Mad" Smith, and on Okinawa by Marine LtGen Roy Geiger, who briefly took over command of the Tenth Army in the last battle of the war. Coupled with the Army's own air arm now demanding separation into its own branch, while the Navy and the Marines were keeping theirs, the battle lines were drawn following V-J Day.

Truman stated in December 1945 that he wanted all U.S. armed forces to be unified into a single service under the War Department, with a civilian secretary and a single military commander to control the roles and missions of all the other services. Of course, that single service would be the Army. General of the Army Eisenhower would be the chief, and the other services would be subordinate to the Army chain of command. The Marine Corps would ostensibly be reduced to light infantry regiments in the Army or the Navy, with no air components.

Fortunately, the Senate Military Affairs Committee's adoption of the Collins Plan for the unification of the services was tabled long enough for the Senate Naval Affairs Committee to air the Navy-Marine criticisms of the plan. On 6 May 1946 CMC Vandegrift testified to Congress and gave the reasons for the Marine Corps' opposition. A select group of combat veterans—generals Gerald Thomas and Merritt Edson and colonels Merrill Twining, Victor Krulak, Robert Hogaboom, James Kerr, and Robert Heinl, as well as some lieutenant colonels, the most influential with Congress being James Hittle—worked diligently, preparing and coaching the arguments. They were dubbed the Chowder Society, after the popular comic strip of the day, *The Little Men's Chowder and Marching Society*. Vandegrift testified first to the extraordinary role of Marines in the war, while pointing out the obvious prejudice in the proposed Collins Plan. Contrary to Army Gen Bradley's fatuous statement that there would never be amphibious operations in future wars, Vandegrift reiterated the need for amphibiously trained forces such as the Marines, emphasizing that regardless of present conditions, the Marines would always be needed as a "Force-in-Readiness." Pointing out the Corps' standards of bravery, success, and economy not found in the Army, to quote Marine historian Allan Millett, he stated unequivocally that "the Marines are ready," but *only* if they remain with the fleet and retain their air-ground capability

> "Eliminate the Marine Corps and you will no longer have a measuring rod to apply to the Army.... I sometimes suspect that is why some Army men want to eliminate the Marine Corps, because they will not then be subject to the test of competition."
>
> Senator Paul Douglas to a sub-committee of the Committee on Armed Services, 13 April 1951

in the Fleet Marine Force (FMF). He stressed to Congress that the Corps had the right to have its fate decided by the body that created it, not by executive fiat. He further stated:

> Sentiment is not a valid consideration in determining questions of national security. We have pride in ourselves and in our past, but we do not rest our case on any presumed gratitude owed us from the nation. The bended knee is not a tradition of our Corps … if the Marine must go [he has] earned the right to depart with dignity and honor, not by subjugation to the status of uselessness and servility planned for him by the War Department.

Vandegrift's speech, reported nationwide, elicited favorable support for the Corps and stopped the wheels of unification. Still, the battle went on, differing only in the degree of skulduggery employed. Agitation for the Marine point of view began to grow and further hearings followed. The result was that through the machinations of the Chowder Society, and public condemnations of the president's and the Army's tactics, the tide began to turn. Marine Gen Howlin' Mad Smith retired in a huff to write a scathing pro-Marine article for *The Saturday Evening Post*. Other voices, too, were raised, while new CMC Clifton Cates, pleased, looked the other way as the battle climaxed.

Mired in the controversy, Congress soon became aware of the anti-Marine hostility behind the plan for unification—especially Eisenhower's, as he revealed in confidential papers. Congress accepted the Marine and Navy argument that service roles and missions should be included in the final version of the National Security Act of 1947. The Marine Corps Reserve Officers Association, the Veterans of Foreign Wars, the National Guard Association, the National Rifle Association, and even RAdm Ellis Zacharias, the Navy's intelligence genius, all testified on behalf of the Corps. The ultimate result was legislative protection of the Marine Corps and naval aviation, which had also been in jeopardy.

An Army ploy to have legislation written to its specifications—after reassuring the Navy and the Marines to the contrary—backfired when the Chowder Society sold their cause to Congressman Clare Hoffman, who managed the House hearings so that they turned out to be very pro-Marine. The press had a field day, exposing to the public the rampant anti-Marine hostility in Washington and accusing the unification proponents of plotting to dominate defense spending to the detriment of the other services. Consequently, a new House bill, H.R.2319, was written, assigning proper responsibilities to the Marine Corps.

Gen Alexander Archer Vandegrift

Gen Clifton Bledsoe Cates

MajGen Merritt Austin Edson

Gen Gerald C. Thomas

At the same time, the Navy Reorganization Act of 1947 threatened the integrity of the Marine Corps as a separate branch from the Navy. There were still many brush fires remaining.

The second phase of the continuing battle against the Collins Plan came in 1948. An amendment to the earlier National Security Act created the Department of Defense to replace the War Department and had created a chairman for the Joint Chiefs of Staff. Louis Johnson, who had succeeded James Forrestal, the first Secretary of Defense, was a political crony of Truman's and an avowed Marine-Navy hater. General of the Army Omar Bradley (no lover of Marines either) became the new chairman of the Joint Chiefs of Staff. The two men continued to tilt unabashedly against the Navy and the Marines.

When Congress, at the insistence of the new Air Force, cut more Navy funding in favor of the Air Force's new ten-engine B-36 bombers, the Navy objected strenuously and the "revolt of the admirals" occurred, which the Marine Corps reciprocally and heartily supported. All of this resulted in a case for more congressional protection for the Corps. Championing the Marine and Navy cause, members of Congress such as Chairman of the House Armed Services Committee Carl Vinson plus influential former Marines Donald Jackson, Paul

Douglas, Mike Mansfield, and George Smathers, forced the matter to be tabled. Subsequent legislation would incorporate all the necessary protections the Marine generals had been fighting for, and it would be finalized in 1952, when the performance of the Marine Corps in battle once again demonstrated its unmatched proficiency, leadership, and bravery.

As late as the fall of 1949, Cates was still fighting for the Commandant of the Marine Corps to become a member of the Joint Chiefs of Staff. A new act incorporated in House Bill 4214, Sect. 206(c) (drafted by the Chowder Society) would reaffirm the Corps' traditional duties and finally give the Marine Corps primary responsibility for developing its own warfare doctrine and equipment. The bill also asserted its wartime right to expand. This would conclusively and indisputably make the Marine Corps a separate service within the Navy Department while maintaining the combined Navy-Marine concept of the necessity to project sea power, despite what the Army and the newly created Air Force were advocating to the contrary.

CMC Cates would finally win the battle for the Corps' survival, but the next challenge—one that could also prove to be fatal—would be budgetary.

As if all this politicking were not enough, the Marine Corps' demobilization from six to ostensibly two skeletonized

divisions and wings caused much disruption in the officer corps, which wished to remain on active duty. Senior officers were urged to retire (an offer sweetened by "tombstone" promotions to the next higher rank if an officer had distinguished himself in combat) or else be reverted to the next lower rank if retained. Aviators were hardest hit; if they wanted to stay on active duty, many had to revert to infantry billets. Few new aviators were trained between 1946 and 1950, although Reserve recruiting, especially for the PLC (college Platoon Leaders Class), remained healthy. And new training programs were introduced in aviation, vehicle maintenance, ordnance, and supply to attract skilled enlisted. A small number of women Reservists were kept on active duty as a cadre and were integrated into the Regular establishment. Racial integration had been ordered in all the armed services by presidential executive order in 1948, although the Marine Corps had been de facto integrated two years earlier.

Vandegrift, Cates, and the headquarters staffs had been wrestling with these reductions-in-force at the same time that they were fighting behind the scenes in Congress for the very survival of the Corps. Yet even in the anti-Marine atmosphere of the Truman administration, there had been a faint conciliatory reference to a Marine role in time of war, which would include its seizing and holding Iceland, the Azores, and

Gen Merrill B. Twining

Gen Robert Edward Hogaboom

BGen James Donald Hittle

LtGen Victor H. Krulak

especially protecting the oil refineries in the Persian Gulf. While the Marines would be assigned these important but peripheral tasks, the Army and Air Force would run the show and concentrate on confronting the Soviet threat in Europe, thus keeping the Marines and its aviation from encroaching on the Army's and Air Force's jealously guarded larger roles. No repeats of World War I! The Defense Department overlooked Asia, however, unable to foresee the consequences of a Communist takeover in China, where Marines were involved in protecting U.S. interests. When Truman and the Army chiefs failed to push the unification of the services through Congress, they hoped at least to accomplish the reduction of the Marine Corps to a virtual constabulary role.

As if in retaliation for the ignominy of having lost the battle against the Marines and the Navy, Secretary of Defense Johnson immediately ordered sharp cuts in the FMF budget for fiscal year 1949–50, forcing the Corps to pare down to eight light, reduced-strength infantry battalions and twelve air squadrons. Johnson even went so far as to ban all 10 November Marine Corps birthday celebrations because they rivaled the ambassadors' Fourth of July receptions in American embassies, an arbitrary act that put him in league with MacArthur as a Marine adversary.

The Saving Grace of the Corps

Always ahead of the game, as they had been in the Advanced Base Force concept and the amphibious doctrine that proved itself so splendidly in World War II, Marine planners at Quantico devised a defense against the claims of the Army and Air Force that atomic bombs had made amphibious landings obsolete and unworkable. LtGen Roy Geiger had witnessed the Bikini atoll atom bomb test in 1946. He urged CMC Vandegrift, in light of nuclear weapons, to rethink World War II–type amphibious operations, with their emphasis on mass and concentration of forces.

Thus began one of the most extraordinary achievements in the annals of military doctrinal development. Assistant CMC Lemuel F. Shepherd headed a board of innovative thinkers—mostly combat-hardened generals—and quickly came up with the recommendation that Marine ship-to-shore movement had to be rethought if it was to go against an enemy with nuclear weapons. Plowing through the water in slow, vulnerable amphibious landing craft was no longer viable. Getting the troops ashore and reaching the enemy quickly—and dropping behind his lines—would preclude the use of atomic weapons for the enemy's fear of destroying his own troops. Movement, therefore, must be accomplished by air—by means of a vertical-takeoff-and-landing helicopter. Thus vertical envelopment would

become the Marine Corps' next major contribution to military concepts. Unfortunately, the development of a practical helicopter was still in its infancy.

Incredibly, in the space of three years, Marine planners worked in a crash program with two aircraft designers—helicopter pioneers Igor Sikorsky and Frank Piaseki along with Bell Aircraft Corporation—to create a practical true rotary-wing helicopter. The new aircraft was to be capable of lifting up to 5,000 pounds to an altitude of 15,000 feet, and fly 200–300 miles at 100 knots.

The first helicopter squadron was activated at Quantico and designated HMX-1. It would be on-the-job development and training. In early June 1950, HMX demonstrated a Piaseki HRP-1 twin tandem-rotor "Flying Banana" to President Truman—who was unimpressed. That was two weeks before the North Koreans invaded South Korea.

That Flying Banana would evolve into the Boeing Vertol CH-46 Sea Knight, which is still in service. In two year's time, Sikorsky's main-and-tail-rotor HO3S would evolve into the HRS utility helicopter that could lift six Marines or 1,420 pounds of cargo and would prove itself in the coming unexpected war—a conflict that would virtually exonerate the Marine Corps' fight for existence and more than prove its worth.

Once again, the Marine Corps was leading the pack.

—HAC

RIGHT: Marines dash for cover behind one of their M26 Pershing tanks. In the perimeter action and later at Inchon and Seoul, there was plenty of work for armored tanks, and their 90mm cannons knocked out T-34s at will.

BELOW: Marines of a 155mm howitzer battery in the Pusan Perimeter relax at their posts during a break in the action.

assessment, maps, weaponry, or support. LtCol Charles B. Smith's four-hundred-man task force was consequently chopped to pieces. Trying desperately to stem the tide of the overwhelming NKPA offensive and the utter collapse of the ROK defenses, more U.S. units were sent piece by piece to the slaughter in the arrogant but naive belief that the mere presence of American forces would halt the Communists. Both the 24th and 25th Divisions were virtually wiped out; the commanding general of the 24th Division was captured after he lost his entire division in battle. Only by ramming replacements into new cadres did the brass maintain the illusion that they had not lost their colors.

As the U.S. military floundered, CMC Clifton Cates saw what was needed—a Marine division. Personally promising the Joint Chiefs that the 1st MarDiv would be ready to fight in thirty days, he then conveyed that message to MacArthur, who in turn ordered all Marine commands to feed the 1st MarDiv at Camp Pendleton while alerting organized Reserve units around the country that Truman was about to authorize their call to active duty. Individual Reservists would be next. The Marine Corps was going to war again and was mobilizing fast.

Thus it was at this critical point that MacArthur's much-touted genius rose to the fore. He knew that the only way to defeat the enemy was by inflicting a flanking attack where it was least expected—amphibiously, in the rear of his front-line columns. Knowing also that none of Walker's Eighth Army, which after a month of retreating was pinned down in a small perimeter at the southern tip of the peninsula, could do it, MacArthur once more called for the Marines.

1ST MARDIV PREPARES FOR COMBAT: THE "FIRE BRIGADE"

While building up 1st MarDiv and shipping it to Korean waters, commanding general Oliver P. Smith ordered a 1st Provisional Brigade of the understrength 5th Marines, reinforced by artillery and tanks and commanded by BGen Edward Craig, to reinforce Walker at the Pusan Perimeter. Dubbed the Fire Brigade, this was a highly trained unit made up of tough veteran Marines. Quickly moving from one hot

ABOVE: MajGen Oliver P. Smith, CG, 1st MarDiv, a reserved intellectual as well as a tough combat commander, served in the Banana Wars and in World War II. Taking over 1st MarDiv in June 1950, he led it through the Inchon-Seoul and Chosin Reservoir battles. Resisting superior Army commands to string out his division unprotected deep into North Korea, he maintained unit integrity, outfought ten Chinese divisions surrounding his own, and led his unit in a fighting withdrawal for seventy miles in thirteen days in subzero conditions. Smith's 1st MarDiv was the only U.S. unit to survive the Chinese attack intact.

ABOVE: Marine BGen Edward A. Craig, deputy commander of 1st MarDiv and CO of 1st Marine Provisional Brigade, which was quickly organized and inserted into the Pusan Perimeter to save the remnants of the U.S. Eighth Army. In a month of heavy fighting, plugging enemy breakthroughs, it earned the title of "Fire Brigade," before rejoining the division and spearheading the amphibious landing at Inchon on 15 September 1950.

RIGHT, TOP: A Navy crewman signaling a Marine Skyraider pilot to rev up prior to the take-off signal from the flight deck of the USS *Midway* on station in the Sea of Japan.

RIGHT, BOTTOM: A combat shot of troops on the line by a Marine photographer.

OPPOSITE: David Douglas Duncan caught one of Ike Fenton's casualties as he was being taken back to an aid station by South Korean laborers ("cargedores," who were probably volunteers; later they would be paid as Korean Service Corps to assist U.S. troops in logistics). The wounded Marine is being lifted on a makeshift stretcher made of a poncho/ shelter half wrapped around bunches of captured enemy rifles. One such seriously wounded sergeant, upon being evacuated, weakly implored Fenton, "Don't let them fall back, Captain, don't let them fall back no matter what they throw at you."

BELOW: The first objective in the Pusan Perimeter for the 1st Marine Provisional Brigade —the "Fire Brigade"—was to extinguish enemy opposition at Yangsan on the northeast side of Pusan. Succeeding objectives came fast and frequently. The Marine brigade was used to plug breaks in the weak lines defended by U.S. and South Korean remnants that had retreated before the North Korean onslaught. In vicious combat for all of August 1950, the brigade was moved out to join the rest of 1st MarDiv for the planned amphibious landing on 15 September at Inchon, near the capital of Seoul, far behind the enemy line at Pusan.

spot to another to plug breaches in the Army and ROK lines, the Marines, in their camouflage-covered helmets and khaki-colored leggings (which resulted in their being branded Yellow Legs by the enemy), stopped the enemy with the help of tightly coordinated air support from strafing, bombing, and napalming F4U gull-winged Corsairs from CVE escort carriers. This Marine Provisional Brigade virtually saved the Pusan Perimeter. After four weeks, they were pulled out of hard and constant fighting to join the amphibious landing of the entire division at Inchon, the port city of the capital, Seoul. This would be MacArthur's brilliant masterstroke to end the war.

Even though the operation had been a poorly kept secret, and had been derided by military and civilian higher-ups back at the Pentagon, on 15 September 1950 the combat-ready Marine division, with the Army 7th Division as backup, landed in classic amphibious fashion and quickly took Inchon before fighting its way against stiff resistance farther inland to Seoul. The amphibious operation broke the back of the NKPA attack, to the chagrin of Gen Omar Bradley and the Joint Chiefs, causing the invaders to streak back to the North across the 38th Parallel in disorderly retreat, with Walker's formerly pinned-down U.S. Eighth Army in pursuit.

INCHON-SEOUL

The main reason an amphibious landing was scoffed at by higher-ups—and possibly by the enemy as well— was that the harbor at Inchon was one of the most inaccessible in the world, with tides rushing in and out some thirty feet twice a day. Sandbars shifted treacherously and clogged entrance channels, especially around the outlying islands that would have to be taken first. One such island was Wolmi-do, which guarded the main channel. The high tide lasted only briefly, so it would have to be taken quickly, then defended from shore fire for seven hours until the tide rose again and the main assault waves could come in. Few thought it possible—except, fortunately, MacArthur and the Marines. The Navy was more than a bit skeptical.

Against all odds, LtCol Bob Taplett's 3d Battalion, 5th Marines, skimmed over the shallow waters, landed on the steep shore of Wolmi-do, and secured the island, eliminating its small garrison of NKPA troops. Then all awaited the flood of the next tide, when the other assault battalions of the 1st, 5th, and 7th Marines landed on the shore of Inchon and scaled the seawall under intense fire. MacArthur, his staff, and the Marine commanders all watched what would be the last full-scale amphibious landing on a beachhead under fire in military history.

"I have just returned from visiting the Marines at the front, and there is not a finer fighting organization in the world."
Gen Douglas MacArthur, on the outskirts of Seoul, 21 September 1950

Chinese "potato masher"   Chinese percussion grenade   Chinese smoke/chemical grenade   Japanese fragment grenade   U.S. M1 fragment grenade

RIGHT: Arduous going for the 5th Marines in rugged hills along the Naktong River in the Pusan Perimeter in the stifling heat of August. Carrying limited equipment, including two canteens of water, a couple of days' rations, ammo, and light packs with entrenching tool and canvas shelter half—with no helmet cover but wearing leggings—they got more than their share of action. In fact, the Marine Fire Brigade, led by BGen Edward A. Craig and with awe-inspiring close air support, astonished the Army and became the anathema of the North Korean invaders.

ABOVE: A section of the 75mm recoilless rifle platoon of Antitank Platoon, 5th Marines (AT-5), during action in the Pusan Perimeter. Pfc Gordon W. Leahy, of Cincinnati, loads for gunner Cpl Jerome D. Tuttle, of Delhi, New York, as Sgt Rolland L. Snyder, to their left, spots.

LEFT: An M26 Pershing from the other platoon of the antitank company prepares to fire from the military crest of a low hill. The 75mm recoilless rifles, together with the 90mm cannon and .50-caliber top-mounted machine gun of the Sherman, destroyed all the enemy T-34 tanks they encountered.

True to form, the Marine assault regiments smashed through Inchon, dispatching tank counterattacks, capturing Kimpo airfield, and fighting on to the capital twenty-five miles inland. There, they had to cross the Han River without the benefit of bridges, which had all been destroyed, and fight street by street to capture the city. The Marines accomplished all their objectives within a week of solid fighting. As they did, the enemy lines down to the south at Pusan collapsed, and they and the defenders around the capital were pushed back up toward the 38th Parallel. The tried-and-true Marine Corps demonstrated to the world what it did best—fight the tough battles it was always ready for.

ABOVE: The seawall at Inchon, where the treacherous tides ebbed and flowed some thirty feet twice a day. These LSTs carried Marines from the 5th, 1st, and 7th regiments in the last major amphibious landing in the history of warfare, on 15 September 1950.

OPPOSITE: This is one of a series of combat photographs taken during the Marine amphibious landing at Inchon—the landing that the JCS and especially Gen Omar Bradley scoffed could never be done again. Going up the ladder and over the seawall is 1stLt Baldomero Lopez, commander of 3d Platoon, Able Company, 5th Marines. He and his platoon had fought all through the Pusan Perimeter. Leading his men through hostile fire across the open wharf, Lopez, an Annapolis graduate, was hit twice as he was about to throw a grenade, dropped it and purposely fell on it, sacrificing his life to save those of his men. (The next officer to lead the 3d Platoon after it came through the Chosin Reservoir battle was the author of this book.)

MACARTHUR'S MONUMENTAL FOLLY

At this point, MacArthur made two disastrous mistakes: 1) he ordered Eighth Army to pursue the enemy all the way to the Yalu River, the border with China, ignoring signs that the Chinese were preparing to enter the war, and 2) he ordered the Army X Corps, commanded by Army MajGen Ned Almond, which had just made the Inchon landing, to operate out of MacArthur's own headquarters in Tokyo instead of from Walker's Eighth Army HQ, robbing the overall ground commander of an essential maneuver element. This was worse for the Marine division. It was still assigned to X Corps, which now was ordered to re-embark for the east coast of North Korea.

Gen Almond's ability and tactics at the time were suspect, and he did not hide the fact that he wanted to reach the Yalu before his West Point classmate Walker did. The Marines found themselves caught in the middle. MacArthur assured President Truman that there was nothing to worry about, for the Chinese would not dare enter the war, an assertion belied by the fact that Chinese prisoners were being captured by all forward units.

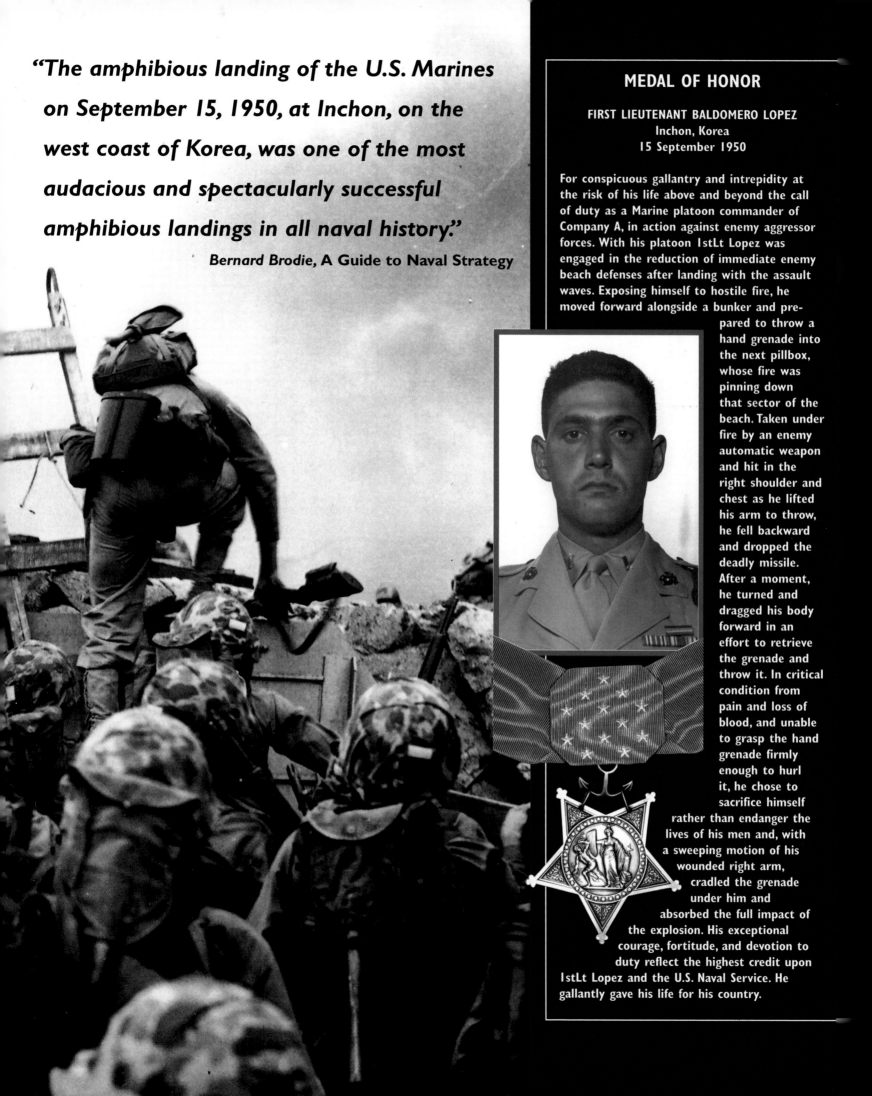

"The amphibious landing of the U.S. Marines on September 15, 1950, at Inchon, on the west coast of Korea, was one of the most audacious and spectacularly successful amphibious landings in all naval history."

Bernard Brodie, A Guide to Naval Strategy

MEDAL OF HONOR

FIRST LIEUTENANT BALDOMERO LOPEZ
Inchon, Korea
15 September 1950

For conspicuous gallantry and intrepidity at the risk of his life above and beyond the call of duty as a Marine platoon commander of Company A, in action against enemy aggressor forces. With his platoon 1stLt Lopez was engaged in the reduction of immediate enemy beach defenses after landing with the assault waves. Exposing himself to hostile fire, he moved forward alongside a bunker and prepared to throw a hand grenade into the next pillbox, whose fire was pinning down that sector of the beach. Taken under fire by an enemy automatic weapon and hit in the right shoulder and chest as he lifted his arm to throw, he fell backward and dropped the deadly missile. After a moment, he turned and dragged his body forward in an effort to retrieve the grenade and throw it. In critical condition from pain and loss of blood, and unable to grasp the hand grenade firmly enough to hurl it, he chose to sacrifice himself rather than endanger the lives of his men and, with a sweeping motion of his wounded right arm, cradled the grenade under him and absorbed the full impact of the explosion. His exceptional courage, fortitude, and devotion to duty reflect the highest credit upon 1stLt Lopez and the U.S. Naval Service. He gallantly gave his life for his country.

Marine division commander MajGen O.P. Smith was ordered to take 1st MarDiv to the Yalu—fifty miles from their landing point on the coast of the China Sea—via a narrow mountain road west of North Korea's Chosin Reservoir. Smith, however, balked at the idea of sending his regiments on such wild, sense-less missions into the trackless interior, as the Army 7th Infantry Division and the ROK I Corps farther east of X Corps were doing. Despite having his 1st, 5th, and 7th Marines dangerously strung out the length of the road paralleling the reservoir some thirty-five miles from Koto-ri to Yudam-ni, Smith was determined to maintain unit integrity above all else. While the division was engaging the NKPA along the way, it began taking more and more Chinese prisoners. Still, both Almond and MacArthur persisted in their stubborn denial of any Chinese Communist (ChiCom) entry until 25 November, when the Chinese opened a massive counteroffensive against the U.S. Eighth Army and ROK units to the west above the North Korean

capital, Pyongyang, and X Corps to the east. The unforeseen attack coincided with the onset of the region's fierce winter conditions, with temperatures dropping far below zero at night and snow covering the landscape. Since the JCS, on MacArthur's promise, believed the "boys would be home for Christmas," they had failed to give priority to the shipment of winter clothing. Most of the Eighth Army shivered in their light field jackets, their hands bare because they had no gloves. Back in the United States, there was a frantic effort to rush winter parkas, supplies, ammunition, and weapons to the beleaguered U.S. forces now built up to five battered Army divisions and an intact Marine division, which, fortunately, had its winter gear.

December 1950 was perhaps the darkest hour in U.S. military history. When the Chinese entered the war, the entire UN line of five Army and eight ROK divisions collapsed, with the exception of the Marine division. More distressing, the collapse was a "bug out," a disorderly retreat with the appearance of a

ABOVE: The fighting on the way to Seoul was fierce. The remaining North Koreans threw everything they had left at the Marines, including tanks.

stirred-up nest of insects. ROK units dropped their weapons, fled to the hills, and headed home; U.S. Army units also broke and ran, throwing down their weapons, helmets, and any other impediments to flight. All order was lost; vehicles and artillery were abandoned, the latter left complete with operating manuals. The dead and wounded were left behind as well. It was a shameful time for the American military, as the entire UN line retreated back below the 38th Parallel, abandoning Seoul and Inchon in the process.

THE 1ST MARDIV AT THE CHOSIN RESERVOIR

The story of the 1st MarDiv, however, was different. With its supply train reaching fifty miles from the seaport of Hungnam up a narrow unpaved road that rose into the mountains, 1st MarDiv passed through Koto-ri just to the west of the southern end of the gigantic Chosin Reservoir. Col Lewis "Chesty" Puller's 1st

Marines operated this division anchor and supply point. About midway up the reservoir, where the road became a narrow cut into the side of a range of bleak mountains, was Hagaru-ri, a small hamlet in which the 7th Marines, under Col Homer Litzenberg, were positioned. This village included a primitive airstrip that was immediately improved for Marine aviation operations.

A dozen or so miles to the west of the northern tip of the reservoir were the 5th Marines, under LtCol Ray Murray, veteran of the Pusan Perimeter, and a battalion of the 7th Marines. The little cluster of huts was identified as Yudam-ni; beyond it lay nothing but higher mountains and desolate, untracked wastes. With only old, inaccurate Japanese maps to rely on, Gen Smith and his Marines were ordered by the Army X Corps to go deeper into this wilderness.

Smith, however, smelled trouble. It was not a good military move. Not only were the 5th and 7th now taking uniformed Communist Chinese Forces (CCF) prisoners, but the prisoners could identify their units of the 9th Army Group, made up of ten People's Liberation Army (PLA) divisions. Marine G-2 Intelligence informed Almond and MacArthur of the presence of Chinese troops, but got no response. There were two other predictable responses, however: from the weather, which turned bitterly cold and delivered fresh snowfall, and from the PLA, which attacked the Marines at Yudam-ni with devastating force. The PLA also attacked the main body of the 7th and the 1st back down the line, severing many points in the road, which was the Main Supply Route (MSR) between units. Hagaru-ri, where the new 2,900-foot airstrip was now operational, weather permitting, for resupply and medical evacuation, was hit the hardest.

What ensued was to be the 1st MarDiv's fight of their lives, and one of the most extraordinary feats in military history.

"RETREAT, HELL!"

Hit with the full might of ten attacking ChiCom divisions (some 100,000 men against the Marines' 20,000), the Marine regiments, with only the 5th and 7th in physical contact, pulled in their perimeters, and fought the enemy that surrounded them. While the Marines' winter equipment—parkas, boots, wool caps, gloves, and the like—had just been air-dropped to them, the Chinese, though laden with Soviet-made rifles, machine

ABOVE: MajGen Raymond L. Murray (then a lieutenant colonel) commanded the 5th Marines in Korea in the battles at the Pusan Perimeter, Inchon, and Seoul, and in the 1st MarDiv's legendary break-out from the Chosin Reservoir. In World War II, as CO of the 2d Battalion, 6th Marines, at Tarawa, Guadalcanal, and Saipan, Murray had been awarded the Navy Cross and two Silver Stars. He was cited again for extraordinary heroism in Korea, and was awarded a second Navy Cross, as well as a third and fourth Silver Star. Murray retired from active duty in 1968.

OPPOSITE: House-to-house, street-by-street, close-in fighting was waged to capture Seoul from the North Koreans. Here an NCO fires his bayonet-mounted M1 carbine at an enemy, as two of his squad join him. This was the first taste of urban fighting since the Okinawa campaign five years earlier.

MEDAL OF HONOR

STAFF SERGEANT ARCHIE VAN WINKLE
Vicinity of Sudong, Korea
2 November 1950

For conspicuous gallantry and intrepidity at the risk of his life above and beyond the call of duty while serving as a platoon sergeant in Company B, in action against enemy aggressor forces. Immediately rallying the men in his area after a fanatical and numerically superior enemy force penetrated the center of the line under cover of darkness and pinned down the platoon with a devastating barrage of deadly automatic weapons and grenade fire, SSgt Archie Van Winkle boldly spearheaded a determined attack through withering fire against hostile frontal positions and, though he and all the others who charged with him were wounded, succeeded in enabling his platoon to gain the fire superiority and the opportunity to reorganize. Realizing that the left-flank squad was isolated from the rest of the unit, he rushed through forty yards of fierce enemy fire to reunite his troops despite an elbow wound that rendered one of his arms totally useless. Severely wounded a second time when a direct hit in the chest from a hostile hand grenade caused serious and painful wounds, he staunchly refused evacuation and continued to shout orders and words of encouragement to his depleted and battered platoon. Finally carried from his position unconscious from shock and from loss of blood, SSgt Van Winkle served to inspire all who observed him to heroic efforts in successfully repulsing the enemy attack. His superb leadership, valiant fighting spirit, and unfaltering devotion to duty in the face of heavy odds reflect the highest credit upon himself and the U.S. Naval Service.

RIGHT, TOP: When three Chinese armies attacked at Yudam-ni at the northernmost penetration by the 1st MarDiv, Marines of the 5th Regiment fought on their front and then their rear, maintaining unit integrity in a grueling two-week battle back to their debarkation point. Weather permitting, Marine Corsairs strafed and napalmed the enemy that surrounded the Marines. (Photographs on these pages are by Marine combat photographer Sgt F.C. Kerr.)

RIGHT, BOTTOM: With meager supplies and ammunition— and picking up Army stragglers in subzero ice and snow—the Marine column, augmented with the 7th and 1st Marines, fought its way from the Chosin Reservoir seventy miles back to the Sea of Japan. Exhausted, they nevertheless dealt the Chinese a devastating blow, and brought all of their wounded, as well as the dead they could not bury at Hagaru-ri, back with them.

FAR RIGHT: Typical of the fighting in frigid weather, the parka-clad Marines were continually called upon to leave the trudging column to mount counterattacks or to clear the enemy from the surrounding high ground. The ice, snow, and freezing temperatures often caused weapons to malfunction. Personal hygiene was impossible, and during the two-week period many subsisted on only crackers and candy bars from their limited rations and relied on snow for thirst.

"Don't you forget that you're the 1st Marines!

Not all the Communists in hell can overrun you!"

Col Lewis B. "Chesty" Puller, rallying his regiment

in the attack from the Chosin Reservoir, 1950

MEDAL OF HONOR

CAPTAIN WILLIAM E. BARBER
Chosin Reservoir Area, Korea
28 November–2 December 1950

For conspicuous gallantry and intrepidity at the risk of his life above and beyond the call of duty as commanding officer of Company F, in action against enemy aggressor forces. Assigned to defend a three-mile mountain pass along the division's main supply line and commanding the only route of approach in the march from Yudam-ni to Hagaru-ri, Capt Barber took position with his battle-weary troops and, before nightfall, had dug in and set up a defense along the frozen, snow-covered hillside. When a force of estimated regimental strength savagely attacked during the night, inflicting heavy casualties and finally surrounding his position following a bitterly fought seven-hour conflict, Capt Barber, after repulsing the enemy, gave assurance that he could hold if supplied by airdrops and requested permission to stand fast when orders were received by radio to fight his way back to a relieving force after two reinforcing units had been driven back under fierce resistance in their attempts to reach the isolated troops. Aware that leaving the position would sever contact with the 8,000 Marines trapped at Yudam-ni and jeopardize their chances of joining the 3,000 more awaiting their arrival in Hagaru-ri for the continued drive to the sea, he chose to risk loss of his command rather than sacrifice more men if the enemy seized control and forced a renewed battle to regain the position, or abandon his many wounded who were unable to walk. Although severely wounded in the leg in the early morning of the 29th, Capt Barber continued to maintain personal control, often moving up and down the lines on a stretcher to direct the defense and consistently encouraging and inspiring his men to supreme efforts despite the staggering opposition. Waging desperate battle, throughout five days and six nights of repeated onslaughts launched by the fanatical aggressors, he and his heroic command accounted for approximately 1,000 enemy dead in this epic stand in bitter subzero weather, and when the company was relieved only 82 of his original 220 men were able to walk away from the position so valiantly defended against insuperable odds. His profound faith and courage, great personal valor, and unwavering fortitude were decisive factors in the successful withdrawal of the division from the deathtrap in the Chosin Reservoir sector and reflect the highest credit upon Capt Barber, his intrepid officers and men, and the U.S. Naval Service.

guns, and submachine "burp" guns, were only lightly clad in padded cotton clothing and canvas sneaker-type shoes. They managed to climb up the ridgelines on each side of the mountainous road on which the Marines had to travel and harass the U.S. force during the two-week ordeal.

Realizing now that they were facing three CCF armies of ten divisions, and cognizant that the entire UN line was collapsing under the weight of the new war at this juncture, the 1st MarDiv tightened its three 360-degree perimeters and began to fight its way out by attacking in the opposite direction. Gen Smith was able to fly into Hagaru-ri and establish his divisional headquarters there. On 29 November, the 1st Marines put together a relief column of some nine hundred men (including a stray Army company) and twenty-nine tanks at Koto-ri. Under the leadership of LtCol Douglas Drysdale of the British 41 Royal Marine Commando, it hacked its way through several ambushes and roadblocks set up by the ubiquitous enemy. Drysdale and the front echelon made it to Hagaru-ri, but his remaining column was cut into four segments, and all of the troops were killed or captured. When a journalist asked Gen Smith if the Marines were retreating, he replied, "Retreat, hell! We're just attacking in another direction."

And that they did. The Marines fought the entire way back for seventy miles through snow and ice and in subzero temperatures, bringing their dead and wounded with them. They draped their dead over the hoods of vehicles or lined them up in truck beds to absorb incoming rifle fire from the enemy. Overcast weather prohibited close air support or evacuation of wounded by air most of the time. It was a fighting withdrawal, often with exhausted Marine squad patrols fighting their way up hills to clear them of harassing fire so the trudging column could continue. U.S. soldiers and ROK stragglers—unarmed, wounded, half-frozen, and half-starved—managed to join the relative security of the moving Marine column. Some were fortunate enough to survive; thousands lost were never accounted for. Soldiers succumbed to the fierce cold and enemy ambushes; truckloads of Army wounded were set afire by the CCF soldiers who found them on the ice of the reservoir.

The nasty weather, with its snow and ice, whipping winds, and temperatures that dropped to thirty degrees below zero at night, was devastating. Even with hooded parkas, double gloves, wool sweaters under their utilities, and rubber shoepacs, they could not stave off the elements, which began to take a heavier toll than the enemy was taking. Frostbite was endemic. The unlined shoepacs proved worthless; even with two or three pairs

LEFT, TOP: Former Marine photo officer David Douglas Duncan, on civilian assignment for *Life* magazine, accompanied the Marines from Pusan, through Inchon-Seoul and the Chosin Reservoir battle. This shot shows the stark reality of survival against overwhelming odds. The Marines did not abandon their dead, wounded, or equipment. Duncan had to keep his camera under his coats next to his body, and whenever he felt the mechanism thawing out enough, he would quickly take a series of shots before the shutter froze up again.

LEFT, BOTTOM: Sgt F.C. Kerr's memorable photo of exhausted Marines taking a brief break in the subzero weather in the North Korean mountains, ignoring the lightly falling new snow that would just add to their misery.

RIGHT: Midway through its fighting "in another direction," the Marine column "crapped out" below Koto-ri. Despite the ordeal—like none other in military history—these Marines managed a smile for Sgt F.C. Kerr. The tougher it got, the higher the morale. Not one Marine doubted they would make it. Most of the ten Chinese (CCF) divisions surrounding 1st MarDiv did not; they were left decimated and un-battle worthy. The Communist Chinese commander was duly executed.

of wool socks and a fabric insole they absorbed sweat and froze. Changing socks—if there were any to change—under the conditions of moving and fighting while somehow trying to stay warm was impossible.

What few C-rations there were could not be heated under the circumstances; when opened, they were found to be simply blocks of ice—if the cans could be opened at all. The little key-twist can openers could not be handled with gloves, and if the gloves were removed—even for a minute—the already cold hand would freeze to the metal. Men would throw the cans into whatever fires could be built and retrieve them with gloved hands, in hopes the contents would be thawed enough to eat. Most Marines simply lived on the candy bars and crackers that came with the rations. Water was simply the snow around them. Their bodily functions slowed, imposing further burdens on the exhausted Marines. Elimination slowed to almost non-function—except for those who developed systemic dysentery; when the need did occur, it was impossible to remove clothing to urinate or defecate. Most just let go in their clothing and stumbled along as it eventually froze. There was neither thought nor possibility of proper sanitation or personal hygiene. Most soldiers went more than a month without taking their clothes off, much less bathing.

On the ridgelines, the CCF soldiers could easily be seen silhouetted against the sky—through binoculars the arrogant Chinese general could be seen strutting in polished, tan, high-top riding boots. Sporadically, they would open fire, especially at some point on the road where the further bunching up of Marines would offer easy targets. The Marines eventually came to ignore the bullets that constantly buzzed past their ears and became stoic about being hit. They also fought back every step of the way, smashing the enemy with fire from rifles, machine guns, recoilless rifles, and 90mm tank cannons. Occasionally, even 105mm howitzers would be able to fire in battery. Small patrols were constantly sent up the hills to flush out troublesome enemy pockets. That the Marines could do this under such conditions is nothing short of miraculous—not to mention courageous.

The 1st Battalion, 7th Marines, under LtCol Ray Davis, set out cross-country to come from behind against heavy odds (Davis was awarded the Medal of Honor for this action), and relieve a company still holding the critical Toktong Pass between Yudam-ni and Hagaru-ri. LtCol Bob Taplett's 3d Battalion, 5th Marines, leading the column out of Yudam-ni, pushed fourteen miles to Hagaru-ri in seventy hours of hard marching and fighting. There, the 5th and

"Retreat, hell! We're just attacking in another direction."
MajGen Oliver P. Smith, on fighting from the Chosin Reservoir to the sea, 1950

MEDAL OF HONOR

CAPTAIN CARL L. SITTER
Hagaru-ri, Korea
29–30 November 1950

For conspicuous gallantry and intrepidity at the risk of his life above and beyond the call of duty as commanding officer of Company G, in action against enemy aggressor forces. Ordered to break through enemy-infested territory to reinforce his battalion on the morning of 29 November, Capt Sitter continuously exposed himself to enemy fire as he led his company forward and, despite 25 percent casualties suffered in the furious action, succeeded in driving through to his objective. Assuming the responsibility of attempting to seize and occupy a strategic area occupied by a hostile force of regiment strength deeply entrenched on a snow-covered hill commanding the entire valley southeast of Hagaru-ri, as well as the line of march of friendly troops withdrawing to the south, he reorganized his depleted units the following morning and boldly led them up the steep, frozen hillside under blistering fire, encouraging and redeploying his troops as casualties occurred and directing forward platoons as they continued the drive to the top of the ridge. During the night, when a vastly outnumbering enemy launched a sudden, vicious counterattack, setting the hill ablaze with mortar, machine-gun, and automatic-weapons fire and taking a heavy toll in troops, Capt Sitter visited each foxhole and gun position, coolly deploying and integrating reinforcing units consisting of service personnel unfamiliar with infantry tactics into a coordinated combat team, and instilling in every man the will and determination to hold his position at all costs. With the enemy penetrating his lines in repeated counterattacks that often required hand-to-hand combat, and on one occasion infiltrating to the command post with hand grenades, he fought gallantly with his men in repulsing and killing the fanatic attackers in each encounter. Painfully wounded in the face, arms, and chest by bursting grenades, he staunchly refused to be evacuated and continued to fight on until a successful defense of the area was assured, with a loss to the enemy of more than 50 percent dead, wounded, and captured. His valiant leadership, superb tactics, and great personal valor throughout thirty-six hours of bitter combat reflect the highest credit upon Capt Sitter and the U.S. Naval Service.

MEDAL OF HONOR

LIEUTENANT COLONEL RAYMOND G. DAVIS
Hagaru-ri, Korea
1–4 December 1950

For conspicuous gallantry and intrepidity at the risk of his life above and beyond the call of duty as commanding officer of the 1st Battalion, in action against enemy aggressor forces. Although keenly aware that the operation involved breaking through a surrounding enemy and advancing eight miles along primitive, icy trails in the bitter cold with every passage disputed by a savage and determined foe, LtCol Davis boldly led his battalion into the attack in a daring attempt to relieve a beleaguered rifle company and to seize, hold, and defend a vital mountain pass controlling the only route available for two Marine regiments in danger of being cut off by numerically superior hostile forces during their re-deployment to the port of Hungnam. When the battalion immediately encountered strong opposition from entrenched enemy forces commanding high ground in the path of the advance, he promptly spearheaded his unit in a fierce attack up the steep, ice-covered slopes in the face of withering fire and, personally leading the assault groups in a hand-to-hand encounter, drove the hostile troops from their positions, rested his men, and reconnoitered the area under enemy fire to determine the best route for continuing the mission. Always in the thick of the fighting, LtCol Davis led his battalion over three successive ridges in the deep snow in continuous attacks against the enemy and, constantly inspiring and encouraging his men throughout the night, brought his unit to a point within 1,500 yards of the surrounded rifle company by daybreak. Although knocked to the ground when a shell fragment struck his helmet and two bullets pierced his clothing, he arose and fought his way forward at the head of his men until he reached the isolated Marines. On the following morning, he bravely led his battalion in securing the vital mountain pass from a strongly entrenched and numerically superior hostile force, carrying all his wounded with him, including twenty-two litter cases and numerous ambulatory patients. Despite repeated savage and heavy assaults by the enemy, he stubbornly held the vital terrain until the two regiments of the division had deployed through the pass and, on the morning of 4 December, led his battalion into Hagaru-ri intact. By his superb leadership, outstanding courage, and brilliant tactical ability, LtCol Davis was directly instrumental in saving the beleaguered rifle company from complete annihilation and enabled the two Marine regiments to escape possible destruction. His valiant devotion to duty and unyielding fighting spirit in the face of almost insurmountable odds enhance and sustain the highest traditions of the U.S. Naval Service.

7th Marines, division headquarters staff, and accumulated stragglers were led out by the 41 Royal Marine Commando, back the eleven miles to Koto-ri, to consolidate with the 1st Marines. Smith informed Almond, who had suggested leaving everything behind, that the Marines would leave no vehicles, no equipment, and no dead or wounded behind them. Whatever was unserviceable was dumped over the side of the road into the deep ravines. After their dog tags were collected and their names recorded, the dead were buried at Hagaru-ri in deeply bulldozed pits. As many wounded as possible were evacuated by air when the weather permitted. Some who had been taken out wounded only days before were flown back in as replacements. As the hardships increased, so did morale. Each Marine knew that he would make it—his pride in himself and his unit would not allow for any alternative.

ANOTHER INCREDIBLE FEAT

Below Koto-ri, the Chinese had destroyed a crucial bridge at Funchilin Pass, over which the retrograde Marine column had to pass. It could not bypass the destroyed bridge by climbing down into the chasm and up the other side; the structure had to be repaired. Incredibly, sectional steel bridge spans were flown to the spot in Marine "flying boxcars," twin-boom R4Q/C-82 cargo planes. Miraculously, the weather cleared for a short time, and the bridge spans were dropped from low altitude onto the cleared roadway in front of the lead unit. One span tumbled down the embankment, but the others were quickly assembled and set in place by Marine engineers, allowing the column to make the arduous trek back with all vehicles, equipment, and men.

The enemy fire had begun to taper off. With the realization of their heavy losses—eight out of ten enemy divisions totally destroyed by the Marines—the Chinese withdrew, having suffered more than twenty-five thousand casualties. The Chinese commanding general was subsequently executed for his battlefield failure—no doubt with his boots on.

The Marines returned to their waiting ships at Hungnam filthy and exhausted, but with heads held high, their colors intact. What equipment was not salvageable was destroyed, and what was still serviceable was loaded aboard with them.

In addition to many other awards for valor and Purple Hearts for wounds, fourteen Medals of Honor were bestowed, seven posthumously. Not to be overlooked were the brave Navy corpsmen attached to Marine battalions; they suffered with the rest as they went about ministering to the wounded as best they could with depleted medical supplies and the inability to dress wounds properly in the intense cold.

On 15 December, the 1st Marine Division disembarked at Masan, on the southern tip of the peninsula, for much needed rest and rehabilitation. Of the 4,400 battle casualties, 730 were killed; uncountable others suffered from frostbite and pneumonia. Regardless, the Marine Corps had shown both ally and foe just what Marines were made of. The Chosin Reservoir battle was one of the most remarkable feats in military history. Survivors still refer to themselves as the "Chosin Few."

As some military units are recognized as having "served their time in hell," the 1st Marine Division certainly did—albeit in a frozen one.

1951: SEESAW AT THE 38TH

With the UN forces having been pushed below the 38th Parallel after the loss of Seoul and Inchon, the Marine division rested and regrouped to go back into battle. In the five months from August through the end of 1950, Marine regulars and Reservists called up in organized units had engaged in heavy fighting. In 1951 they would be augmented by individual Reservists called up by the thousands and put through accelerated basic training and boot camp. The individual Reservists outnumbered the regulars at one point. Many were World War II veterans; others had joined to train on a monthly weekend basis. It was a period of strong patriotism. Newly commissioned second lieutenants from the platoon leaders class, fresh out of college, were put into

BELOW, BOTTOM: Combat-loaded Marines move through a village on the central Korean front in the spring of 1951.

BELOW: M14 Antitank grenade with mount for M1 Garand. Used in World War II, Korea, and the early part of Vietnam.

> *"Our tactical air arm should spend a few months with the Marines. I don't know what causes the difference, but it is there. The Marine pilots give us the impression that they are breaking their hearts to help us out."*
>
> *An Army captain in Korea, quoted in* Combat Forces Journal

RIGHT: Marine pilots wore this type of World War II leather naval aviator helmet with built-in ear phones and goggles when flying Corsairs and other propeller-type aircraft during the early part of the Korean War.

BELOW: Returning from a close air support mission, a Marine F4U Corsair from VMF-312 comes in for a tail-hook-down landing on the USS *Bairoko* (CVE-115) off South Korea.

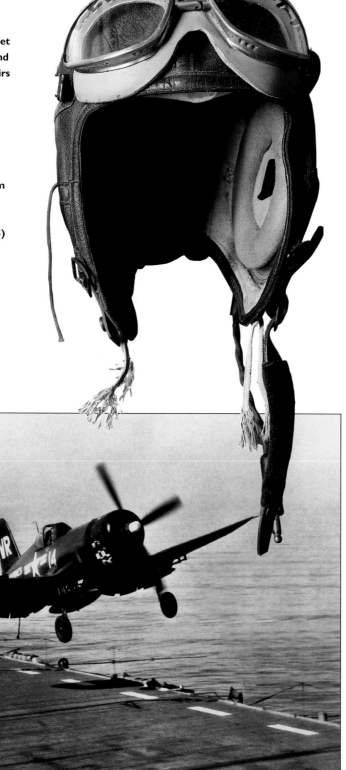

replacement drafts and sent by air and ship to reinforce 1st MarDiv.

After a short respite in the "Bean Patch" at Masan, in January the restless veteran Chosin Marines displaced forward a short distance to Pohang to receive replacements. Instead of the usual in-camp training, the division had a unique opportunity to engage against guerrillas of the NKPA 9th Division, which had been cut off two hundred miles behind the UN lines and was operating in the vicinity. In long, motorized, and ground platoon and company patrols, the division kept its sharp edge, while giving the replacements necessary on-the-job training.

The Truman Gaffe

That January, while the Marines were hunting down guerrillas and the U.S. Army was trying to retake Seoul, President Truman could not have been a happy man. Not only had MacArthur betrayed him, but he was also facing the results of the disastrous reduction-in-force policy of Secretary of Defense Johnson (and the complicit JCS), which had brought about the most humiliating defeat in U.S. military history. Stung by public criticism—and with the outstanding combat record of the Marines at Pusan, Inchon, and the Chosin smack in his face—Truman offered a hot-headed response to a congressman's inquiry as to when the Marine commandant would receive JCS status: "For your information, the Marine Corps is the Navy's police force, and as long as I am president that is what it will remain. They have a propaganda machine that is almost equal to Stalin's…. The Chief of Naval Operations is the Chief of Staff of the Navy of which the Marines are a part…." A huge public outcry ensued; the president offered apologies but did not recant. Thus the Marines added Truman to their list of least favorite leaders, which already included MacArthur. They even chalked "Horrible Harry's Police Force" on their trucks and tanks.

The time had come, obviously, to clarify the Marine Corps' status—especially after it had demonstrated in Korea that it could do what others seemingly could not. Senator Paul Douglas, a former Marine captain, and Congressman Mike Mansfield jointly sponsored a bill that would forever define the missions of the Corps. The bill established the Corps' peacetime strength at three divisions/wings, made it indisputably a service separate from the Navy (yet in the Navy Department), and—the coup de grâce—gave the Marine commandant equal membership with the Joint Chiefs of Staff on Marine affairs. Truman reluctantly

LEFT: The "Black Sheep" of VMF-214 World War II fame fought again in Korea. The squadron's F4U-4B Corsair fighter-bombers of 1st MAW operated out of an airfield near 1st MarDiv's rear.

BELOW, INSET: Marine top ace Maj John Glenn, while on temporary duty with the Air Force, flew his F80 Sabre jet and downed three North Korean Russian-piloted MiGs. His aircraft was appropriately named "MiG-Mad Marine."

LEFT: A Marine aircraft ground crew combat-loads a Corsair with rockets and napalm for another close air mission. For a time in 1951, the USAF won control over all allied aviation over Korea, thus crippling the Marine specialty of close air-ground support. After much wrangling, the Marine command was able to regain control of its own aviation.

RIGHT: The hard-plastic gold naval aviator flight helmet of both Marine and Navy pilots accompanied the introduction of jet aircraft, for which more protection was needed in the higher-tech and supersonic fighters. The plastic facemask is not shown.

ABOVE: Maj John F. Bolt, a Marine ace from World War II, became the first Marine "Jet Ace" in Korea when, temporarily attached to the U.S. Air Force 25th squadron, 51st Fighter Interceptor Wing, flying F86 Sabre jets, he downed six Russian-made (and no doubt Russian-piloted) MiG-15s.

RIGHT: This more advanced helmet, shown with oxygen mask but not facemask, was worn by Marine Col Neil MacIntyre in his F9F Panther jet.

signed the Douglas-Mansfield Bill, which became Public Law 416 in 1952. Gen Lemuel Shepherd became commandant.

Yo-Yo at the Parallel

As some veterans of the six months of heavy fighting were rotated home, commands changed. Gen Matthew Ridgway took over the Eighth Army after Walker died in a motor vehicle accident, and MajGen Gerald Thomas, who, nine years earlier, as chief of staff, had steered the battle for Guadalcanal, assumed command of 1st MarDiv. (When Truman fired MacArthur the following April, Ridgway took his place. His successor at Eighth Army was Army LtGen James Van Fleet.)

The forward element of the fourth replacement draft arrived by air at Pohang on 11 January 1951; the rest came by ship two weeks later. This heralded the greatest influx of individual Reservists, who had been called up in September 1950, and who in 1951 would constitute the bulk of 1st MarDiv. At one point, forty of the forty-two officers of the 5th Marines were Reservists.

By this time, the allied forces in Korea were composed of units representing twenty-one member countries of the United Nations. The allied counter-offensive, "Killer," began on 21 February. The Marines, now in central Korea in IX Corps, jumped off from Wonju and headed for Hoengsong. The overall counter-offensive recaptured Seoul and again sent the NKPA and CCF reeling north across the 38th Parallel. The second phase, "Ripper," commenced on 7 March and took the allies past Seoul and across the parallel in a line extending northeastward.

This run of success came abruptly to a halt on 21 April, when, with bugles blowing, hordes of the enemy attacked the entire UN line. The Marines took the brunt of the Chinese attack west and east of the little town of Hwachon on the Pukhan-gang (river). ROK units on their left and right flanks gave way, forcing the Marines to withdraw some thirty miles before the UN lines began to hold.

In May, the yo-yo took the Marines into the low ring of mountains east of Hwachon that had been dubbed the Punch Bowl. The slugfest continued through the summer, when a temporary break occurred with the initiation of peace talks in Paris. When no peace was forthcoming, Van Fleet ordered another advance along the entire front.

Helos and Jets

Vertical-lift flying machines had been experimented with as early as 1910. In 1923 the Pitcairn company successfully flew its "autogyro," a new type of flying machine with three overhead rotor blades that allowed it to take off and land vertically, and a front propeller for forward motion that allowed it to fly normally, albeit slowly. The Marines experimented with three autogyros in Nicaragua in the late 1920s, but the aircraft's lack of payload capacity precluded its wartime operability. Awed Nicaraguans called the strange-looking OP-1s Turkey Hens.

By 1943 the Germans had an operational rotary-wing helicopter that was used for reconnaissance and rescue missions. After World War II, the British and French developed successful models that could carry up to ten passengers, but they were not commercially viable. In 1948 the U.S. Navy and Air Force adopted the Sikorsky H-5, a main-and-tail-rotor craft that proved useful for sea search and rescue. The Army was also looking into its limited use.

Jet propulsion had been experimented with before the war, but the Germans were the first to use it tactically, to propel their V-1s, flying bombs that terrorized England. Then, in the last air battles over Europe, the Germans stunned Allied aviators with their twin-jet Me-262 fighters, which could streak past the Allies at supersonic speeds.

After the war, the Air Force and Navy were rapidly developing jet aircraft. So, too, was the Marine Corps, despite its budget battles. In 1948 the Marines acquired McDonnell-Douglas FH-1 Phantom and Grumman F9F-2 Panther jet aircraft.

—HAC

BELOW, INSET: A Marine F9F Panther twin jet with almost enough mission decals to obscure its fuselage. This straight-wing Panther was superseded by a swept-wing version, termed an F9F Cougar.

BELOW: A strafing-napalm run by Panther jets in later action over the centralized Korean front in 1951.

ABOVE: Marine ace BGen Robert E. Galer, then a major, led VMF-224 in the Guadalcanal campaign, shooting down eleven enemy planes in twenty-nine days; he was awarded the Medal of Honor in recognition for his heroism in aerial combat during this campaign. Galer had been commissioned in 1936 and received his wings in 1937. He was at Ewa, Oahu, during the Japanese attack on Pearl Harbor. After the Guadalcanal action, Galer participated in three D-Day landings in the Pacific: at Iwo Jima, as ground leader of a close air support team, in the Philippines, and then at Okinawa.

In 1952, Galer, now a colonel, was the assistant chief of staff, G-4, for 1st MAW in Korea, and went on to be named commanding officer of MAG 12, 1st MAW. On 5 August 1952, he was shot down behind enemy lines and rescued by helicopter, and Galer finished his career at HQMC and was promoted to one star rank upon his retirement in 1957.

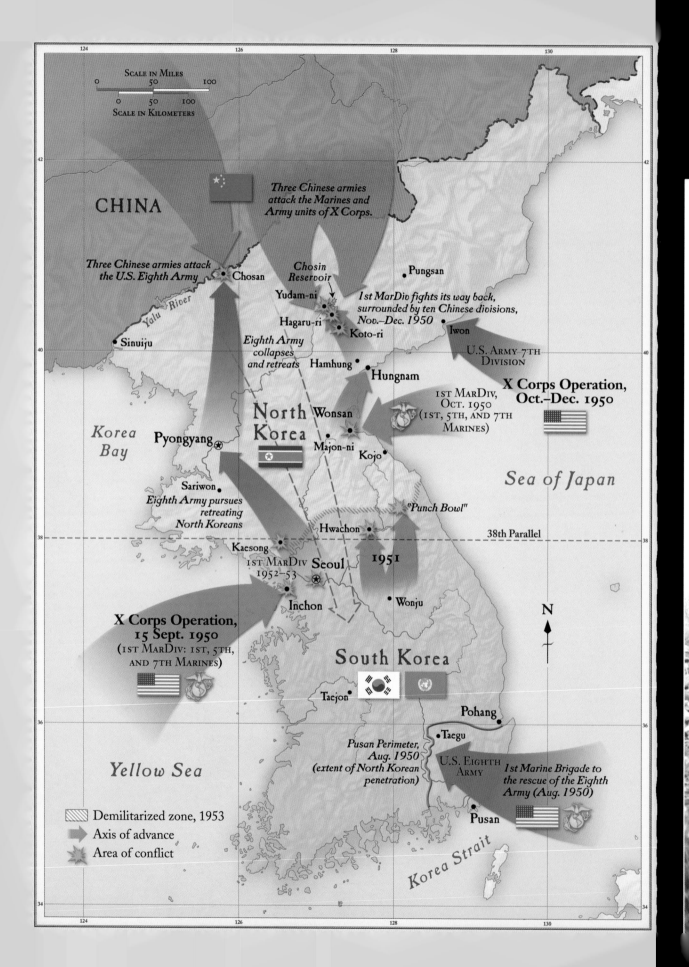

SCALE IN MILES
0   50   100

SCALE IN KILOMETERS
0   50   100

CHINA

Three Chinese armies
attack the Marines and
Army units of X Corps.

Three Chinese armies attack
the U.S. Eighth Army

Chosan

Chosin
Reservoir

Pungsan

Yudam-ni

*1st MarDiv fights its way back,
surrounded by ten Chinese divisions,
Nov.–Dec. 1950*

Hagaru-ri

Koto-ri

Iwon

Sinuiju

Eighth Army
collapses
and retreats

Hamhung

Yalu River

U.S. ARMY 7TH
DIVISION

Hungnam

North
Korea

Wonsan

1ST MARDIV,
OCT. 1950
(1ST, 5TH, AND 7TH
MARINES)

X Corps Operation,
Oct.–Dec. 1950

Korea
Bay

Pyongyang

Majon-ni

Kojo

Sea of Japan

Sariwon

Eighth Army pursues
retreating
North Koreans

"Punch Bowl"

38th Parallel

Hwachon

Kaesong

1ST MARDIV
1952–53

Seoul

1951

Inchon

Wonju

N

X Corps Operation,
15 Sept. 1950
(1ST MARDIV: 1ST, 5TH,
AND 7TH MARINES)

South Korea

Taejon

Pohang

Taegu

Pusan Perimeter,
Aug. 1950
(extent of North Korean
penetration)

U.S. EIGHTH
ARMY

1st Marine Brigade to
the rescue of the Eighth
Army (Aug. 1950)

Yellow Sea

Pusan

Demilitarized zone, 1953
Axis of advance
Area of conflict

Korea Strait

**BELOW: Marines of 3d
Battalion, 7th Marines, move
forward to new positions
above the 38th Parallel into
North Korea, to the west of
the Hwachon Reservoir, in
April 1951. On 23 April, the
entire line, including the 7th,
5th, and 1st Marines, bore the
brunt of a major Chinese
attack, forcing a complete
withdrawal of the UN lines
back some thirty miles.**

LEFT: In a gun emplacement on the front lines, Marines Pfc Ronald F. Johnson and Sgt Jerry M. Debusk of 1st MarDiv load their M2 60mm mortar.

RIGHT: Designed for the Army, this winter pile-lined, ear-flapped headgear was issued to all U.S. forces in Korea, including the Marine Corps. Marines wore it under their camouflage-covered helmets.

MARINE CLOSE AIR SUPPORT

A unique Marine specialty is coordinated close air support from its indigenious air wings. The combat effectiveness of this tactic had been indisputably demonstrated at the Pusan Perimeter, Inchon, Seoul, and, when weather permitted, at the Chosin Reservoir.

In 1951 that concept was shattered when the U.S. Air Force sought to control all air operations over Korea from Tokyo. Marine Forward Air Controllers (FACs) on the ground would normally communicate directly to the pilots and steer them to targets. Now, front-line FACs had to obtain clearance from the Air Force, which determined what aircraft was available in the vicinity—whether USAF, Navy, or Marine—and ordered the flight to the target. Not only did the resulting delays threaten combat effectiveness, but non-Marine pilots were not skilled in low-level strikes. The Air Force's new F-80 Shooting Star jets were not designed for this kind of close support; their higher speeds precluded their following a looping pattern. Instead, they would overshoot and devolve into figure eight patterns that, after a few runs, had them firing back into the direction of the Marine lines. Sparks flew among Marine commanding generals, X Corps, and 5th Air Force headquarters until control of Marine Air was finally returned to the Marines, where it belonged.

Marine Corsairs continued as the faithful workhorses of close air support. In all, 436 Marine aircraft were lost to ground fire and operational accidents during the war. Although they acquired F9F Panther jets in 1952 and 1953, the Marines stuck to their close air missions, leaving the new air-to-air battles to the Air Force and Navy jets while they headed far to the north to tangle with Soviet-built MiG jets flown mostly by pilots from the USSR on behalf of North Korea.

TOP: The ubiquitous two-seat, bubble-front Bell 47G helicopter was in constant use for observation, transportation of VIPs, artillery spotting, and (using its two outside-mounted stretchers) for MedEvac.

RIGHT: The workhorse Sikorsky HRS-I helicopter, with a crew of two and a load of combat-equipped Marines. Designed in 1949, the HRS-I was first introduced into combat by Marine HMR-161 in September 1951, in the Punch Bowl area, for the lifting of troops of the 2d Battalion, 1st Marines, commanded by LtCol Brooke Nihart (co-author of this book). They also lifted resupplies and evacuated casualties.

FIRST USE OF HELICOPTERS IN WARFARE

The Marines' crash program to develop the concept of "vertical envelopment" was brought to fruition in the early fall of 1951. From the beginning of the war, two-seat Bell 47G helicopters, with their Plexiglas bubble-fronts, had been used to take commanders over battle areas, to conduct observation, and, with a stretcher lashed on to each side, to assist with medical evacuation from the battlefield to hospitals.

ABOVE: Gen Keith B. McCutcheon, as a colonel, commanded Marine Helicopter Transport Squadron 161 (HMR-161) in Korea.

LEFT: In the first use of helicopters in warfare, Marine HMR-161, in Sikorsky HRS-1 helos, transported troops, ammunition, and supplies back and forth on the Main Line of Resistance (MLR) in the Punch Bowl area of North Korea in the fall of 1951.

BOTTOM, FAR LEFT: A Forward Air Control team talking down a resupply helicopter.

BOTTOM, LEFT: Cpl C. Papake, assistant gunner, carries a tripod for the .30-caliber water-cooled heavy machine gun in the arms of J.J. Raferty, on a ridge top on the central front. Marines always controlled the "high ground," which earned them an additional appellation of "Ridge Runners."

Marines Develop Body Armor

The armor worn to protect soldiers against high-velocity rifle and machine-gun bullets was much too heavy to be worn by infantry, who must be able to move and shoot. But, as World War II statistics revealed, many more casualties are caused by artillery and mortar-shell fragments than by small arms.

To address this problem, in 1943 an Army-Navy committee began testing lightweight plastics for use in body armor. One prototype was composed of Doron, a rigid slab of fiberglass ⅛-inch thick, bonded with thermosetting plastic. For areas needing flexibility, a 12-ply basket-weave nylon was utilized. These products were found to stop .45-caliber submachine-gun bullets as well as hand grenade and shell fragments. They were successfully field-tested by the Marine Corps in the final stages of the Okinawa campaign in 1945.

Between 1947 and 1951 LtCmdr Fred L. Lewis Jr., director of the Body Armor project at the Naval Medical Research Laboratory, developed an armored vest at the request of the Marine Corps. It weighed an acceptable 8.5 pounds and combined Doron plates with heavy nylon cloth. The vest was designated M1951. In early 1952 the front-line units of the 1st Marine Division in Korea were equipped with 2,500 of these vests, and an order for 25,000 followed. Incidences of wounds to the torso quickly dropped, although the less life-threatening leg wounds continued.

In the years following the Korean War, the Marines made frequent improvements to their body armor, adding groin protection and collars to protect the neck. More resistant and flexible materials were also developed. Ceramic add-on plates, which could stop rifle bullets, were provided for helicopter crews and other immobile exposed Marines.

—BN

ABOVE: The first serviceable armored vest was introduced in the Korean War in 1952. Styled M1951, this vest shows a bullet hole that did not penetrate and thus saved the life of Cpl R. Cameron (pictured at top). This new body armor was improved with Kevlar plating during the Vietnam and later wars and has since been referred to as a flak vest.

Marine transport helicopter squadron HMR-161, flying the now operational Sikorsky HRS-1s, was the first to achieve actual vertical movement of Marines and supplies into battle positions under fire. Not only did the HRS-1s quickly and effortlessly lift supplies and ammunition to fighting positions on the tops of ridgelines, but they also brought whole Marine infantry battalions, rocket batteries, and reconnaissance companies to front-line positions. Helicopters quickly became indispensable, and the Marines' innovation set the stage for the next war, in which the helicopter would reign supreme. Again, the Marine Corps had developed, tested, and proven a new tactical doctrine.

THE LAST BATTLES OF THE KOREAN WAR

In early September 1951, 1st MarDiv launched its last major coordinated full-strength attack against the enemy, on the Yoke and Kanmubong ridges, located on the eastern ridges of the Punch Bowl. There would not be another full divisional operation for forty years. After a week of hard fighting and heavy casualties, and still only halfway to their final objectives, all units were ordered to stop. Gen Van Fleet had decided, under political pressure, to advance no farther, so as not to impede the peace talks. The Marines withdrew to previous positions and waited until March 1952, at which time the 1st MarDiv took up static positions north of Seoul, just behind Panmunjom, where the talks were now being held. There they dug into World War I–type trenches and bunkers and conducted harassing and

"The safest place in Korea was right behind a platoon of Marines. Lord, how they could fight. The Reds told us they were afraid to tangle with the Marines and avoided them when they could be located."

MajGen Frank E. Lowe,

presidential observer reporting on the war

BELOW: The second section of the 75mm recoilless rifle platoon of the Antitank Company, 5th Marines, in action on the central front. After two or three rounds were off, sending up clouds of dirt and dust behind the gun that revealed their position, enemy mortar fire would rain down and the gun section would hastily deplace. (The author commanded this platoon during the latter half of 1951.)

MEDAL OF HONOR

CORPORAL DAVID B. CHAMPAGNE
Vicinity of Sudong, Korea
2 May 1952

For conspicuous gallantry and intrepidity at the risk of his life above and beyond the call of duty while serving as a fire team leader of Company A, in action against enemy aggressor forces. Advancing with his platoon in the initial assault of the company against a strongly fortified and heavily defended hill position, Cpl Champagne skillfully led his fire team through a veritable hail of intense enemy machine-gun, small-arms, and grenade fire, overrunning trenches and a series of almost impregnable bunker positions before reaching the crest of the hill and placing his men in defensive positions. Suffering a painful leg wound while assisting in repelling the ensuing hostile counterattack, which was launched under cover of a murderous hail of mortar and artillery fire, he steadfastly refused evacuation and fearlessly continued to control his fire team. When the enemy counterattack increased in intensity, and a hostile grenade landed in the midst of the fire team, Cpl Champagne unhesitatingly seized the deadly missile and hurled it in the direction of the approaching enemy. As the grenade left his hand, it exploded, blowing off his hand and throwing him out of the trench. Mortally wounded by enemy mortar fire while in this exposed position, Cpl Champagne, by his valiant leadership, fortitude, and gallant spirit of self-sacrifice in the face of almost certain death, undoubtedly saved the lives of several of his fellow Marines. His heroic actions served to inspire all who observed him and reflect the highest credit upon himself and the U.S. Naval Service. He gallantly gave his life for his country.

reconnaissance raids along what was now a well-defined, neutral Demilitarized one (DMZ)—but the North Koreans and Chinese had no intention of respecting it. Much blood was shed on both sides in countless exchanges of artillery barrages and meaningless patrol clashes. Finally, in the late summer of 1953, a real cease-fire took effect, and shortly thereafter, the Marine division was withdrawn.

SUMMARY

The United Nations' war in Korea had been a noble experiment. Unlike World War II, in which attacked countries allied in self-defense and turned the aggressors back, the Korean War saw twenty-one countries band together to save an attacked nation from subjugation. It turned out to be a new kind of "limited war," the harbinger of many to come. It has been critiqued as the first war the United States has ever lost; however, in hindsight, it is clear that South Korea was successfully saved from being overtaken by a hostile power. It can also be seen as a victory if one considers South Korea's freedom to progress from an undeveloped, pre-modern nation to a prosperous country with first-world status—in contrast to the starving North, which still clings to its unworkable communist ideals. It also demonstrated the West's determination to block communist expansion, even if it took the shedding of first blood to do so.

The cost was high: 33,686 Americans killed and more than 100,000 wounded in three years of fighting. Of those numbers, the Marine Corps lost 4,262 killed and 21,781 wounded. American prisoners of war totaled 7,190, of which only 227 were Marines; more than 8,000 American soldiers and airmen are still listed as missing. Many more thousands of South Korean soldiers and civilians were slain, and the casualties inflicted on the North—and on their Chinese allies—

Korean Service Medal

**United Nations Service Medal
(Korean Service)**

OPPOSITE, INSET: 1stLt James Brady, who later became a famous publisher and author, earned a Bronze Star in Korea, in World War I–type trench warfare that lasted a year and a half. The Marines' cordon was to protect the peace talk site at Panmunjom and the capital, Seoul; the Chinese placed their toughest units opposite them and harassed the Marines with surprise attacks and bayonet charges. The Marines sent out their own patrols and clobbered the enemy at every opportunity. From 1952 to mid-1953, when the truce was signed, was anything but quiet. The Marines suffered more casualties during this period than in the previous year and a half.

OPPOSITE: The typical state of Marine dug-in positions— shown here under an artillery bombardment—was harrowing. While the first year and a half had been a period of being constantly on the move, the latter phase of the war was entirely static, with only probing patrols of both sides moving. Bullet-and-shrapnel-deflecting "flak jackets" were issued at this time (a first in warfare) and saved countless lives.

LEFT, INSET: Marine Commandant Gen Lemuel Shepherd takes a look through a periscope in a fortified bunker at enemy activity in front of 1st MarDiv in 1952.

RIGHT: A Marine 81mm heavy mortar crew take a special 1952 Thanksgiving chow break in their bunker on the MLR. The "mess gear" shown below was used for at least one hot meal a day. All of the utensils compacted into the two halves; the metal tray was only available at a few mess tents. Upon entering the chow line, each Marine dipped his mess gear into a deep barrel of water kept boiling by an inserted heater with a high chimney pipe; when finished eating, each Marine then went to the end of the chow line and dipped his mess gear into a similar tub of soapy water, swished things around, then rinsed in a final tub of boiling water. This was a luxury compared with being in the field on patrols or in battle, where hygiene was a big problem.

ABOVE: Korean War–era mess kit. The knife, fork, and spoon were packed inside the folding aluminum top and bottom. The canteen cup fit under the canteen in its canvas cover. The compartment tray was provided only by larger unit "messes" in bivouac.

are calculated to have been more than 2 million. Since the end of hostilities on 27 July 1953, the United States has had to keep more than 37,000 Army troops stationed along the DMZ to assure compliance with the now half-century-old truce.

REHEARSING FOR ATOMIC WARFARE

While the battles still raged in Korea, preparations for a new kind of warfare were fermenting behind the scenes back at the Pentagon. To study the effects of nuclear weapons on the battlefield, the JCS, in conjunction with the Atomic Energy Commission, ordered a series of atomic tests involving ground troops to be conducted at the Yucca Flat test site in southern Nevada, north of Las Vegas. Designated the Desert Rock series, a number of almost weekly tests began in April 1952. Following an Army test, the Marines were assigned to Desert Rock IV, and also participated in two later atmospheric atomic tests at the Nevada site.

Marine advance echelons observed the Army test while perched on a rocky outcropping ten miles across the desert from ground zero. This explosion was also the first ever televised live. At the time, television was relatively primitive, black and white, and not yet connected across the continent by coaxial cable, so station KTLA installed a series of relays for the signal to reach Los Angeles.

The Marine test called for a brigade of Marines to stay in long, 3-foot-deep trenches 2,000 yards from ground zero. No protective gear or dark goggles were provided. On signal, the Marines were to crouch face-down in the trenches and close their eyes. Overhead, at an altitude of 30,000 feet, a B-29 would drop a Hiroshima-type, 20-kiloton A-bomb, which would burst at 2,000 feet above the desert floor.

As it did so, there was a ghastly white flash that seemed to turn things chalky white or inky black. The searing heat and harmful radiation dissipated quickly, and seconds later the Marines were given the order to rise, enabling them to see the blast effect kicking up desert sand and debris as it raced toward them. Above the ground was a churning, donut-shaped fireball that measured 1,500 feet in diameter and sounded like a hundred freight trains. As the cloud cooled, it sucked up desert debris, creating in a few minutes the characteristic "mushroom" appearance.

While the Marines gazed in awe, the giant still-churning cloud and its column continued to grow and rise to the stratosphere, with a clearly visible ice cap forming on top of it. After an hour, the cloud would become a long, wide trail across the sky to the northeast. The Marines, led by monitors reading Geiger counters to measure acceptable radiation levels, walked onto ground zero. The heavy equipment, tanks, artillery, and vehicles used as simulated targets had been driven halfway into the ground by the extraordinary force.

Further tests followed, and much was learned about absorption tolerances for the radiation emitted from an airburst. No Marine received doses of more than eight roentgens—comparable to a dental X-ray.

During the next ten years, however, the United States and the Soviet Union raced each other to develop weapons of greater and greater destructive power. By the time aboveground testing of nuclear weapons was halted in 1961, the Soviets had exploded a 100-megaton bomb. The dawn of the 1960s saw the two world superpowers locked in a cold war that increasingly threatened to flare up into actual conflict.

The characteristic mushroom cloud of an atomic bomb, this one dropped in front of Marines during an atmospheric atomic test in April 1952 at the atomic testing grounds at Yucca Flat, Nevada. A 20-kiloton bomb, like that dropped on Hiroshima seven years earlier, was air-dropped by an Air Force B-29 and exploded 2,000 feet off the ground. The Provisional Marine Brigade was hunkered down in shallow trenches. When the initial heat and radiation expired in a flash, the blast wave could be seen traveling across the 4,000 yards of desert as the 1,500-foot diameter fireball churned, roaring like a hundred freight trains overhead, until the desert debris was sucked up to form the cloud seen here.

chapter six

America's Longest "Hot" War

"First there was the Old Corps, then there was the New Corps. And now there's this goddamned thing."

Quote from a veteran gunnery sergeant in Allan Millett's Semper Fidelis

For the Marines, the twelve years between the end of the Korean War—with the cease-fire in place along the DMZ, where more than one U.S. Army division would remain for the next half-century—and the next major shooting war was a period of activity and innovation.

During this period, the Force-in-Readiness role of the Marine Corps, finally established by law in 1952, was put to the test a number of times. In 1954, Communist insurgents defeated the French at their outpost at Dien Bien Phu, in Indochina. The Geneva Peace Accords, which sealed that defeat and called for the withdrawal of the French from their Indochinese colonies, created a Communist North and a free South Vietnam, separated at the 17th Parallel, as well as two neighboring countries bordering on the west, Laos and Cambodia. Marines were called upon to assist in the evacuation of the more than 300,000 civilians who chose to flee the new, ruthless regime of Ho Chi Minh in the North to resettle in the South. In 1955, Marines conducted an evacuation from mainland China to Taiwan of 24,000 Nationalist soldiers who had been driven out by Mao Tse-tung's Red Army.

Communist activity was increasing all over the globe. Although the Soviet Union's Nikita Khrushchev (Stalin's successor) and China's Mao Tse-tung were far from bosom buddies, the Communists now controlled half the world. Fearing a domino effect of one country after another falling under Communist rule, the West was on nervous alert. While keeping a wary eye on the Soviets and insisting on the maintenance of beefed-up NATO forces in Europe, several U.S. administrations used the Marine Corps as a quick response force for minor shows of force. When the British and French seized the Suez Canal from Egypt in 1956, 3d Battalion, 2d Marines, afloat with the Sixth Fleet in the Mediterranean, covered the evacuation of civilians from Alexandria. Also, in view of the unrest in the Middle East and along the North African coast, the Marine garrison at Port Lyautey, Morocco, was reinforced.

In 1958, the first of several U.S. incursions into Lebanon took place. Two Marine Battalion Landing Teams (BLTs) from the Sixth Fleet surged across a tranquil beach filled with gawking sunbathers just south of Beirut International Airport. After much political inveigling by the U.S. ambassador and leaders of the fighting Christian, Druze, and Muslim factions, Marines took up positions at the American Embassy as well as at important bridges, docks, and road junctions. A British brigade arrived from Cyprus to assist, and the U.S. Army 24th Airborne Brigade came from Germany to further expand the force. The Marines remained for three uneventful months before returning either to the Sixth Fleet or to Camp Lejeune in North Carolina.

That same year, a Marine Special Landing Force and MAG-11 were ordered to Taiwan, where the defeated Nationalist Chinese had fled, to show a U.S. presence to the Chinese, who were threatening to

THE MARINE CORPS
BUILDS MEN

ABOVE: The first so-designated Sergeant Major of the Marine Corps was Wilbur Bestwick, who assumed the newly established post on 23 May 1957. Bestwick saw duty in both World War II and Korea. He died in 1972.

PAGE 327 AND RIGHT: Vietnam-era Marine recruiting posters.

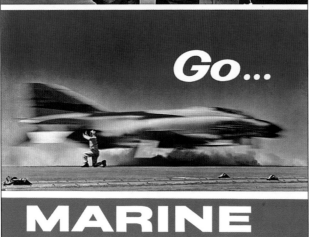

invade. Two years later, a Communist civil war erupted in neighboring Laos. A Marine helicopter squadron was sent into Thailand across from the Laotian border as a show of force and to render assistance if needed, and, in 1962, 3d Marine Amphibious Unit (MAU) conducted a large exercise there. This was the start of the fifteen-year Marine involvement in Southeast Asia.

Meanwhile, back in the Western Hemisphere, the cold war heated up to the boiling point—and the United States called up Air Force Reserves—when the Soviet Union constructed a concrete wall across Germany in 1961 to physically seal off the Communist world from the West. Unrest, such as that in Hungary and Czechoslovakia, was quickly squelched by the Soviet iron fist backed by tanks and soldiers. The United States monitored Soviet nuclear testing, discovering that Soviet premier Nikita Khrushchev was sending as many as twenty thousand troops, forty bombers, and forty nuclear-tipped Intermediate-range Ballistic Missiles (IBMs) to its ally Cuba.

In 1962, U.S. satellite surveillance, then in its infancy, along with U-2 reconnaissance planes returned photographic evidence of the Soviet missile buildup in Cuba. These weapons—which could reach such American cities as New Orleans, Atlanta, and even Washington, D.C.—posed a direct threat to the security

of the United States and, indeed, to the entire free world. A global crisis ensued.

In a televised address on 22 October 1962, President John F. Kennedy denounced Khrushchev's actions and ordered a naval "quarantine" blockade of Soviet shipping around dictator Fidel Castro's Cuba. He also vowed to strike back—not at Cuba, but at the Soviet Union—if any missiles were launched. In exchange for the dismantling of the Cuban missile bases, the United States agreed to withdraw the missiles it had positioned in Turkey, which were aimed at the Soviet Union. During the crisis, the entire 2d MarDiv was afloat in the Caribbean, joined by 5th Marine Amphibious Brigade (MAB) from 1st MarDiv, which had sailed via the Panama Canal. The Guantanamo garrison was reinforced with three battalions from 2d MarDiv and one from 1st MarDiv. The 2d MAW at Cherry Point, North Carolina, sent squadrons to Puerto Rico and to Florida to augment U.S. forces building up for an invasion of Cuba if the Soviets failed to back down. Khrushchev finally relented, and World War III was very narrowly averted.

LOOSE ENDS

Following the Korean War, a number of internal struggles had a marked impact on the Marine Corps. In 1958, the Corps faced a reevaluation of its primary mission by President Eisenhower—the Corps' old archnemesis. Again, the Corps, this time under CMC Randolph Pate, held its own and emerged unscathed. In 1960, after John F. Kennedy became president, and with feisty CMC David Shoup at the helm, the Corps' "flexible response" role was strengthened even more, although Shoup resisted Kennedy's desire to add a counterinsurgency mission. Short of a nuclear confrontation, however, Shoup believed that a counterinsurgency mission was better left to the Army because it would have interfered with the Corps' amphibious nature, mobility, versatility, and Force-in-Readiness role.

Despite the perpetual budget crunch, the Corps managed to accomplish a number of significant improvements and innovations. Helicopters became dependable and relatively plentiful; both Atlantic and Pacific FMFs had been restructured so that they could transport helicopters. Heavier tank, artillery, and engineer elements were moved from division to force troop level. A number of escort carriers were converted to Landing Platform Helicopters (LPHs) exclusively for the Marine Corps. Portable aluminum matting, termed Short Airfield for Tactical Support (SATS), was developed for tactical airstrips on land. The trusty old M1 Garand rifle was replaced by the new automatic M14, configured for the new standardized NATO 7.62mm cartridge, and a newly designed M60 machine gun replaced the venerable old BAR. In 1964, the Corps conducted forty-five landing exercises worldwide, often in conjunction with the armed forces of friendly countries.

In 1965, a Communist-insurgency civil war became a threat in the Dominican Republic. The Marines had previously occupied the country from 1916 to 1924, and now another American intervention was deemed necessary. In late April, 6th MEU was ordered in just west of the city of Santo Domingo to evacuate three thousand U.S. citizens. A makeshift helipad was cleared in the parking lot of the Hotel Embajador for the Marine choppers. When the local police could no longer control the situation, two platoons of Marines—then a full Battalion Landing Team—were sent in to help restore order. BLT 3/6 came ashore under sporadic sniper fire throughout the city, as did two brigades of the Army 82d Airborne Division. Soon, the entire Marine 4th Brigade—led by BGen John H. Bouker but under overall Army command—had landed. In total, eight thousand Marines were put ashore before the operation was turned over to an Inter-American Peace Force composed of soldiers from Brazil, Paraguay, Honduras, Nicaragua, and Costa Rica. The U.S. Marines withdrew after suffering thirty-nine casualties—nine killed and thirty wounded—in random firefights.

ABOVE: Commandant of the Marine Corps, Gen David M. Shoup. A Medal of Honor recipient for his actions at Tarawa, Shoup stood up for the Corps while under pressure from President John F. Kennedy on numerous occasions. He served as CMC from 1960 to 1963, during the increasing involvement in South Vietnam by first the Kennedy and then the Lyndon Johnson administration.

LEFT: Large, troop-carrying helicopters—developed by the Marines—in the early 1960s. Dubbed Flying Bananas for their obvious shape, they were ridiculed by President Truman; following rapid improvement they were reintroduced after 1965 in upgraded form as the CH-46 Sea Knight. The Marine workhorse, however, remained the smaller UH-34 Sea Horse, which carried seven combat-equipped troops, except when it was too hot for the chopper to lift that heavy a load. The smaller, ubiquitous UH-1, the "Huey," darted all over the countryside on observation, command, MedEvac, and even gunship missions; 1st MAW eventually had some 350 UH-34s.

LEFT, INSET: Although the M1 steel helmet afforded great protection from ricochets and deflected fragments, it could not withstand a direct rifle hit. This helmet was worn in the Dominican Republic operation by Pfc Michael Feher, who was killed in action on 3 May 1963.

Marines and the POW Code of Conduct

By the summer of 1955, American prisoners of war in Korea had been returned by the Chinese and North Koreans. Debriefing of POWs revealed that many, even a few Marines, had succumbed to the cruelty and brainwashing techniques of their captors. What to do to avoid such conduct in the future?

I was a young officer serving in HQMC at this time when I was summoned to report to the commandant. Apprehensively, I stood before Gen Lemuel C. Shepherd in his second floor corner office in the Navy Annex, which overlooked the Pentagon. Shepherd told me that the Secretary of Defense had convened an advisory committee on prisoners of war in an endeavor to study the failure of some of our POWs to resist their captors and to seek a solution to avoid such occurrences in the future. Retired general and flag officers were to constitute the committee, and Marine MajGen Meritt A. "Red Mike" Edson would represent the Marine Corps. "You," he said, "will represent the Corps on the committee staff." The commandant then issued his brief guidance. He explained that Air Force and Navy aviation wanted to protect their pilots by allowing them to

tell their captors anything they wanted to hear to avoid mistreatment. We Marines, he emphasized, couldn't allow such laxness. We were to stick by the Geneva Convention and give the enemy only name, rank, and serial number, period. "Your job and General Edson's is to see that we hold the line," he said. With an "Aye aye, sir" I departed for the Pentagon, and an interesting summer.

The committee heard the testimony of former prisoners from World War II and Korea and the views of senior military officers, religious leaders, educators, psychologists, heads of veterans' organizations, lawyers, and politicians. Deliberations of the committee members followed, with staff members sitting in. The task of drafting a report with the recommended POW code of conduct fell to me. I conceived of the code as a catechism in the first person: "I am, I will," etc. A draft was submitted and then returned with further instructions. A second draft was accepted and turned over to professional wordsmiths for fine-tuning.

The code that emerged from this process has been learned by all servicemen and has stood the test of the Vietnam and Gulf wars.

RIGHT: When the UN Coalition and Communists exchanged prisoners at the cease-fire in July 1953, 77,000 North Koreans and Chinese were returned while 9,130 South Koreans and 3,597 American POWs were repatriated—minus 21 who defected. Still missing are 5,178 Americans. News of the behavior of U.S. Army POWs caused a national scandal. Too many had succumbed not only to physical brutality at the hands of the Communists, but to a new psychological, ideological indoctrination technique referred to as "brainwashing." This not only caused a general breakdown of morale, but also led to large-scale collaboration with the enemy. The few Marine POWs, however, were lauded by the DoD and Senate investigating committees for their discipline and courage, and their high rate of survival. Five even received meritorious awards for exemplary conduct in captivity. The result of this new kind of mental torture by an enemy that did not abide by the rules of the Geneva Convention was a new Code of Conduct for U.S. Prisoners of War.

I am an American fighting man. I serve in the forces which guard my country and our way of life. I am prepared to give my life in their defense.

I will never surrender of my own free will. If in command, I will never surrender my men while they still have the means to resist.

If I am captured, I will continue to resist by all means available. I will make every effort to escape and aid others to escape. I will accept neither parole nor special favors from the enemy.

If I become a prisoner of war, I will keep faith with my fellow prisoners. I will give no information or take part in any action which might be harmful to my comrades. If I am senior, I will take command. If not, I will obey the lawful orders of those appointed over me and will back them up in every way.

When questioned, should I become a prisoner of war, I am bound to give only name, rank, service number, and date of birth. I will evade answering further questions to the utmost of my ability. I will make no oral or written statements disloyal to my country and its allies or harmful to their cause.

I will never forget that I am an American fighting man, responsible for my actions, and dedicated to the principles which make my country free. I will trust in my God and in the United States of America.

These statements are further expanded and explained in the full code of conduct.

—BN

MEDAL OF HONOR

CAPTAIN DONALD GILBERT COOK
Republic of Vietnam
31 December 1964–8 December 1967

For conspicuous gallantry and intrepidity at the risk of his life above and beyond the call of duty while interned as a prisoner of war by the Vietcong in the Republic of Vietnam during the period 31 December 1964 to 8 December 1967. Despite the fact that by so doing he would bring about harsher treatment for himself, Col (then a captain) Cook established himself as the senior prisoner, even though in actuality he was not. Repeatedly assuming more than his share of responsibility for their health, Col Cook willingly and unselfishly put the interests of his comrades before that of his own well-being and, eventually, his life. Giving needier men his medicine and drug allowance while constantly nursing them, he risked infection from contagious diseases while in a rapidly deteriorating state of health. This unselfish and exemplary conduct, coupled with his refusal to stray even the slightest from the code of conduct, earned him the deepest respect from not only his fellow prisoners, but his captors as well. Rather than negotiate for his own release or better treatment, he steadfastly frustrated attempts by the Vietcong to break his indomitable spirit, and passed this same resolve on to the men whose well-being he so closely associated with his own. Knowing his refusals would prevent his release prior to the end of the war, and also knowing his chances for prolonged survival would be small in the event of continued refusal, he chose nevertheless to adhere to a code of conduct far above that which could be expected. His personal valor and exceptional spirit of loyalty in the face of almost certain death reflected the highest credit upon Col Cook, the Marine Corps, and the United States Naval Service.

RIGHT: In the early days just
after their arrival in Vietnam,
before the "stuff hit the fan,"
a bunched-up column of
Marines casually crosses a
stream near Da Nang. No
doubt their first firefight
jolted them out of such
complacency; the sunglasses
would go, and the silver officers' insignia would be worn
under the collars of their new
lightweight jungle utilities, so
as not to single leaders out as
targets to the enemy. Some
would find out the hard way,
too, that pipe, cigar, and
cigarette smoke could tip
off the VC to their presence
from a good distance away.
In addition, their trusty M14
rifles would be replaced by
M16s two years later.

BELOW: Much of the early
mission in 1965 involved
support of the South
Vietnamese Army (ARVN),
as this Marine UH-34 Sea
Horse crew is doing here.

THE VIETNAM WAR: 1965–1975

The ten-year war in Vietnam, part of the former
French colony of Indochina in Southeast Asia, is difficult to summarize. What began as a unilateral effort
by the United States to help save a sovereign country
from Communist aggression and domination—similar
to the U.S.-UN enterprise in Korea but without UN
sanction or participation this time—ended in an
inconclusive stalemate. The U.S. involvement in the
conflict would eventually become bogged down in
civilian-governmental mismanagement, military mistakes, relentless criticism by the press, and the
American public's growing opposition to the war,
which turned society virtually upside down.

Under the leadership of President John F.
Kennedy, who had been intrigued by the concept
of counter-guerrilla warfare since the rediscovery of
the Marine *Small Wars Manual* (written before World
War II), Army and Marine advisers were sent to assist
the South Vietnamese by as early as 1960. President
Lyndon B. Johnson, who inherited the entanglement
after JFK's assassination in November 1963, escalated
the American presence in Vietnam soon after taking
office. After an alleged attack on U.S. Navy ships
operating in international waters by North
Vietnamese gunboats in August 1964, Johnson asked
Congress to pass the dubious Tonkin Gulf Resolution,

MEDAL OF HONOR

SERGEANT ROBERT E. O'MALLEY
Republic of Vietnam
18 August 1965

For conspicuous gallantry and intrepidity in action against the Communist (Vietcong) forces at the risk of his life above and beyond the call of duty. While leading his squad in the assault against a strongly entrenched enemy force, his unit came under intense small-arms fire. With complete disregard for his personal safety, Sgt O'Malley raced across an open rice paddy to a trench line where the enemy forces were located. Jumping into the trench, he attacked the Vietcong with his rifle and grenades, single-handedly killing eight of the enemy. He then led his squad in the assistance of an adjacent Marine unit that was suffering heavy casualties. Continuing to press forward, he reloaded his weapon and fired with telling effect into the enemy emplacement. He personally assisted in the evacuation of several wounded Marines, and again regrouping the remnants of his squad, he returned to the point of the heaviest fighting. Ordered to an evacuation point by an officer, Sgt O'Malley gathered his besieged and badly wounded squad, and boldly led them under fire to a helicopter for withdrawal. Although wounded three times in this encounter, and facing imminent death from a fanatic and determined enemy, he steadfastly refused evacuation and continued to cover his squad's boarding of the helicopters while, from an exposed position, he delivered fire against the enemy until his wounded men were evacuated. Only then, with his last mission accomplished, did he permit himself to be removed from the battlefield. By his valor, leadership, and courageous efforts in behalf of his comrades, he served as an inspiration to all who observed him, and reflected the highest credit upon the Marine Corps and the U.S. Naval Service.

ABOVE: Sgt Robert O'Malley was the first Marine to receive the Medal of Honor in the Vietnam War. There would be fifty-seven others awarded to Marines, most posthumously, before their withdrawal in 1971. A group of Marines was flown out to Austin, Texas, in 1966 for ceremonies and the personal awarding of the medal by President Lyndon Johnson. Top dignitaries of the government, including SecDef Robert McNamara, were also present. This photograph of the ceremony was taken by the author.

through dense undergrowth in the A Shau Valley. They are a bit bunched up by the necessity of not losing sight of the Marine in front, and it was rough going through the rocky terrain and often tall elephant grass that not only hid the enemy but also an occasional tiger.

OPPOSITE, BOTTOM LEFT: The author, a Korean veteran on leave from his New York advertising agency, voluntarily served on active duty as a Reserve lieutenant colonel in 1967, on a combat artist assignment for DIVINFO, HQMC.

OPPOSITE, BOTTOM RIGHT: A reconnoitering mission by division staff near the coast above Da Nang. Upon disembarking the UH-34 choppers, they were met with a short mortar attack. Included in the group was veteran war correspondent Jim Lucas. When radioed for, three UH-34s swooped in low under cover of the distant dunes and retrieved the group.

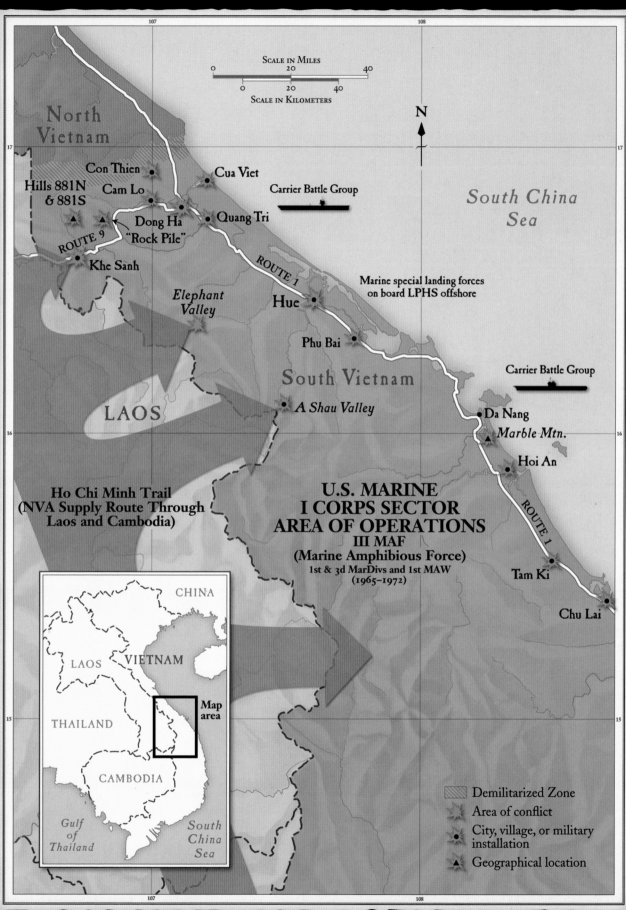

North Vietnam

Hills 881N & 881S

Con Thien

Cam Lo

Cua Viet

Quang Tri

Dong Ha "Rock Pile"

ROUTE 9

Khe Sanh

Elephant Valley

ROUTE 1

Hue

Phu Bai

LAOS

South Vietnam

A Shau Valley

Ho Chi Minh Trail (NVA Supply Route Through Laos and Cambodia)

U.S. MARINE
I CORPS SECTOR
AREA OF OPERATIONS
III MAF
(Marine Amphibious Force)
1st & 3d MarDivs and 1st MAW
(1965–1972)

Carrier Battle Group

South China Sea

Marine special landing forces on board LPHS offshore

Carrier Battle Group

Da Nang

Marble Mtn.

Hoi An

Tam Ki

ROUTE 1

Chu Lai

SCALE IN MILES
0   20   40

SCALE IN KILOMETERS
0   20   40

N

CHINA

LAOS

VIETNAM

THAILAND

Map area

CAMBODIA

Gulf of Thailand

South China Sea

Demilitarized Zone

Area of conflict

City, village, or military installation

Geographical location

ABOVE: Two unidentified Marines man an outpost near Da Nang in 1966. The gunner in the foreground is firing the new M60 7.62mm machine gun that replaced the BAR as the automatic weapon of the Marine "fire team." Another fire team member feeds the ammo belt into the gun. It was not unusual for all members of a rifle platoon to carry extra belts of ammunition over their shoulders—sometimes even the officers. Marine firepower consumed a lot of ammo. A Marine in the background aims his M14.

which gave him the "war powers" needed to escalate American involvement. Johnson's go-it-alone policy ultimately led to the commitment of more than a half-million U.S. troops in South Vietnam by 1967.

The president and his Secretary of Defense, Robert McNamara, were ostensibly concerned that the loss of the Vietnamese republic to the Communists would lead to the similar fall of other small countries in the region, and even around the world. To prevent this from happening, Johnson and McNamara, whose team of corporate "whiz kids" from Ford Motor Company had no combat

experience, decided to micromanage the war from the basement War Room of the White House.

In trying to plan every aspect of the war, McNamara and Johnson, who had served in the Navy in World War II but had never seen combat, engineered a disaster. Civilian policy was allowed to overrule the advice of military commanders on military matters, strategy, and tactics, and the war was handicapped by imposed rules of engagement. Underestimating the power of television, the government also allowed journalists to wander freely throughout the war zones in Vietnam.

BELOW: Marines and Navy corpsmen were quick to befriend and assist South Vietnamese civilians. They helped support orphanages (later populated by American-fathered children), and even collected funds to build a small children's hospital at Hoa Khanh, just north of Da Nang. Marine squads in the Combined Action Program actually lived in Vietnamese villages to protect them from the VC and to provide security during their rice harvests.

M60 MACHINE GUN

The M60 7.62mm belt-fed machine gun with bipod replaced the venerable Browning automatic rifle (BAR) and the .30-caliber light and heavy machine guns of WWII and Korea. The M60 has since been replaced by the M240 machine gun and the M249 squad automatic weapon (SAW).

Combined Action Program

Although they went largely unreported by the press, the Marines inaugurated a number of humanitarian efforts to assist the Vietnamese people, such as the support of local orphanages (many populated by children fathered by Marines and GIs), MedCAP (Medical Civic Action Patrols) divisions that provided medical treatment to many civilians, and the construction of a children's hospital at Hoa Khanh funded entirely by personal donations from Marines.

The Combined Action Program (CAP) was first begun by volunteers from the 3d Battalion, 4th Marines, at Phu Bai, north of Da Nang; the CAP effort later grew to regimental size. The program formed a number of Combined Action Companies (CACs), from which a Marine squad would work closely with the indigenous Popular Forces and actually live in a particular village in order to protect it from marauding Vietcong. Where there were no Marines, the VC would prey upon villages, mostly at night, stealing food supplies, killing men—especially village leaders—women, and children, and taking any military weapons they could find.

As the Combined Action Program began to show some signs of success, LtGen Lew Walt, CG, III MAF, and LtGen Victor Krulak, CG, FMFPAC, became convinced that "pacification" and building local friendships would more effectively win the hearts and the support of the people than would ephemeral pitched battles. The Marines' "ambassadors in green" concept evolved into two valuable aspects: "County Fairs," which had Marines cordon off a village to search for VC efforts, and "Golden Fleece," in which Marines would guard farmers harvesting rice in the paddies. Though these Marine efforts both north and south of Da Nang were very successful, they went unreported. The press was interested only in firefights and body counts.

In the end, sadly, the CAP often resulted in civilians the Marines were trying to save becoming targets of the VC.

—HAC

The result was a veritable feeding frenzy of reporting that turned out the most sensationalized war coverage Americans had ever seen. A constant stream of gruesome battle scenes and images of body bags carrying home slain Americans (an average of two hundred a week) was served up to the American public every evening on their televisions. Any beneficial or humane aspects of the U.S. effort were not reported. Considering the combination of these images with an increasingly radicalized antiwar movement, which encouraged such acts of civil disobedience as the burning of draft cards and American flags and rioting against authorities, it is no wonder the war effort failed. Never in its history had the United States changed its mind and disengaged in the midst of a war, as President Nixon ordered the military to do in 1972. The consequence of this act was the ultimate conquest of South Vietnam three years later by the Communist North—and a waste of American blood and treasure.

Despite all the negativity back home, the Marine Corps fought valiantly. Limited to a geographical area in the northernmost sector of South Vietnam below the Demilitarized Zone (DMZ), their battles—like the Army's—became ephemeral, repetitious search-and-destroy missions, with no retention of real estate—only tallies of enemy body counts. And unlike in previous wars, there was no front line, no Main Line of Resistance (MLR). There were only strongpoints and fire-support bases, which had to be defended

LEFT: The shock of the deadly gunfire and the condition of his fatally wounded comrades shows on Cpl James Farley's face. The corporal's chopper, Yankee Papa 13, was also hit by enemy ground fire on its way back to Da Nang. This photo by UPI photographer Larry Burrows appeared on the cover of the 16 August 1965 issue of *Life* magazine.

LIEUTENANT HARVEY C. BARNUM
Republic of Vietnam
18 December 1965

For conspicuous gallantry and intrepidity at the risk of his life above and beyond the call of duty. When a rifle company was suddenly pinned down by a hail of extremely accurate enemy fire and was quickly separated from the remainder of the battalion by more than five hundred meters of open and fire-swept ground, and while casualties mounted rapidly, Lt Harvey Barnum quickly made a hazardous reconnaissance of the area, seeking targets for his artillery. Finding the rifle company commander mortally wounded and the radio operator killed, Barnum, with complete disregard for his safety, gave aid to the dying commander, then removed the radio from the dead operator and strapped it to himself. He immediately assumed command of the rifle company, and moving at once into the midst of the heavy fire, rallying and giving encouragement to all units, reorganized them to replace the loss of key personnel and led their attack on the enemy positions from which deadly fire continued to come. His sound and swift decisions and his obvious calm served to stabilize the badly decimated unit, and his gallant example as he stood exposed repeatedly to point out targets served as an inspiration to all. Provided with two armed helicopters, he moved fearlessly through enemy fire to control the air attack against the firmly entrenched enemy while skillfully directing one platoon in a successful counterattack on the key enemy positions. Having thus cleared a small area, he requested and directed the landing of two transport helicopters for the evacuation of the dead and wounded. He then assisted in the mopping up and final seizure of the battalion's objective. His gallant initiative and heroic conduct reflected great credit upon himself and were in keeping with the highest traditions of the Marine Corps and the U.S. Naval Service.

OPPOSITE, TOP: Transporting the Special Landing Force of the Seventh Fleet standing off the coast of the I Corps sector, the LPH *Okinawa*'s UH-34 Sea Horses heloed many Marine incursions to sweep coastal parts of the DMZ clear of enemy troops.

OPPOSITE, BOTTOM: Combat-loaded Marines on patrol near Da Nang assist one another in crossing rice-paddy dikes (hopefully with their M14 safeties on). The rice paddies were fetid with human fertilizer—typical in Southeast Asia—and often the VC would lace them with *punji* sticks, or sharpened bamboo spikes, to inflict hideous wounds and infections upon unwary Marines.

in 360-degree perimeters called Tactical Areas of Responsibility (TAOR). From them, patrols either set out on foot or were dropped by helicopter near intended targets for sharp, sporadic, and inconclusive battles against phantom Vietcong (VC) guerrillas in the jungles and the piedmont.

The enemy, mostly peasant farmers, resorted to all sorts of primitive and barbaric traps, including *punji* (needle-sharp dung-dipped bamboo spikes) in covered pits and around helicopter landing zones; swinging Malayan whips (*punjis* on heavy, rope-sprung tree trunks that would crash down when a wire was tripped); Bouncing-Betty mines (Russian-made mines that when stepped on sprang three feet above the surface and exploded in a shower of thousands of bits of shrapnel); bear traps; and other lethal and unorthodox devices. And unlike in World War II and even Korea, U.S. forces did not face large enemy units, heavy artillery, armor, naval gunfire, or air combat. The war was essentially a ten-year series of small-unit firefights in the jungles. Only occasionally would larger, regular units of the North Vietnamese Army (NVA) be confronted, and they never fought in a conventional manner.

Enter the Marines

Before 1965, both Kennedy and Johnson had sent upwards of twenty thousand military advisers into South Vietnam, and the Marines had a helo squadron in Operation Shufly actively supporting the Army of the Republic of Vietnam (ARVN) in the Mekong Delta below Saigon. When North Vietnam attacked the major airfield outside Saigon, destroying many U.S. aircraft, President Johnson ordered the first American ground troops, a Marine Expeditionary Brigade (MEB), to land in-country. The 9th MEB, cruising offshore for two months, finally landed on 8 March 1965 at Da Nang in the northern I Corps sector. Led by BGen Frederick Karch, BLT (Battalion Landing Team) 3/9 crossed Red Beach on the coast, while BLT 1/3 was brought by Marine C-130 transports to the South Vietnamese air base to the northwest of the city.

The landings were unopposed and warmly welcomed by the inhabitants. A perimeter of strongpoints was immediately established around the city, and preparations were made for the III Marine Amphibious Force (MAF) headquarters to be set up on the peninsula at the mouth of the harbor. Across the Tourane River, a former French brothel was taken over and turned into the Combat Information Bureau (CIB), run by DIVINFO (Division of Information) from HQMC; the small cubicles were turned into accommodations specifically for visiting press and VIPs. The CIB had the distinction of being the only air-conditioned bar-restaurant in the area and was also frequented by higher-ranking Marines.

Following the securing of the area in 1965 by the 9th MEB, the III Marine Amphibious Force, consisting of 3d MarDiv and 1st MAW units, moved into the I Corps sector, the northernmost four provinces below the DMZ that stretched across the country and separated North from South. The 3d MAB soon secured the city of Chu Lai, south of Da Nang. Eventually, 85,000 Marines would compose III MAF. The MAF, and later 1st MarDiv, was headquartered one hundred miles south of the DMZ in Da Nang, where the major airfield was situated. Other ground units were located between the DMZ and Da Nang in the major provincial towns of Con Thien, Dong Ha, Quang Tri, and Phu Bai. Westward along the unpaved Route 9, just below the DMZ, were Marine combat camps at Cam Lo, the "Rock Pile," Camp Carroll, Ca Lu, and Khe Sanh. South of Da Nang were the strongholds of An Hoa, Hoi An, and Chu Lai. Elements of the Army American Division also operated in I Corps; overall command in Vietnam belonged to the Army Military Assistance Command, Vietnam (MACV), at Saigon. Marine fixed-wing aviation was based mainly at Da Nang and Chu Lai, while the primary helicopter field was at Marble Mountain, just south of Da Nang. The helicopters used during most of the war were the Sikorsky UH-34 Sea Horse utility choppers with a capacity of seven combat-laden Marines, and the smaller, ubiquitous Bell UH-1 Hueys. The CH-46 tandem twin-rotor Sea Knights came in later, as did the new AH-1G Cobra gunships, and in the early 1970s, the CH-53 Sea Stallions.

On 7 May 1965, the 3d MAB landed seventy miles south of Da Nang at Chu Lai, which would become an important 4,000-foot SATS fixed-wing and helicopter field. By 11 May, all three Marine headquarters were in Da Nang: III MAF, 3d MarDiv, and 1st MAW. LtGen Lewis Walt commanded the MAF, MajGen William Collins led the division, and BGen Keith McCutcheon commanded the wing. Marine A-4 Skyhawks from the Philippines were flown in on 1 June; F-4 Phantoms followed later.

By late summer, four regiments (3d, 4th, and 9th of 3d MarDiv, and 7th of 1st MarDiv) were "in-country," as were four MAGs (11th and 12th with A-4s, and 16th and 36th with UH-34 helicopters). In August, the 1st Vietcong regiment threatened the base at Chu Lai. On 18 August, the 7th Marines conducted Operation Starlite, a three-pronged attack by river crossing, helicopter insertion, and a small amphibious assault that resulted in driving the VC away, leaving a thousand of them dead.

M14 7.62MM RIFLE

The M14, an improved version of the M1 Garand, fired the standardized NATO 7.62mm cartridge with a 20-round magazine, and was designed primarily for shoulder use as a semiautomatic rifle, though it could also be mounted on a bipod and used as a fully automatic rifle. It was used in the early part of the Vietnam War and was the Corps' standard-issue rifle until it was replaced by order of SecDef McNamara with the new Stoner-designed M16 in April 1967.

ABOVE: When President Johnson ordered Marines to be landed in Vietnam on 1 January 1965 as the first commitment of U.S. ground units, the 9th MEB standing offshore did so, not as an amphibious assault but as an administrative landing. Here, Marines arrive in Da Nang to the welcoming cries and flower garlands of the populace.

LEFT: Other units landed at later dates to augment the 9th MEB. Typically, these were unopposed administrative landings, as shown here, combat loaded but with no magazines or ammo in their rifles.

Expeditionary Airfields

The need for a short, transportable hard-surfaced airfield for naval carrier-type aircraft became apparent by as early as 1942. Early experiments using a wooden plank surface and primitive arresting gear and catapults were unsuccessful, and the idea was shelved for higher priority matters during World War II. In the Pacific, Marines improved and used captured Japanese airfields. New 5,000-foot airstrips, made either of decomposed coral or surfaced with PSP (Pierced Steel Planks) and sufficient for piston-powered aircraft, could also be built quickly by Marine Corps engineers or by Naval Construction battalions.

In the 1950s, the development of jet fighters and attack aircraft that required much longer airstrips caused the short airfield equipped with aircraft carrier–like arresting gear and catapults to be reconsidered. The idea was pitched in 1953, and in 1956 the CMC set forth the requirements for a Short Airfield for Tactical Support (SATS). Development of the matting for runway and taxi strips began the following year, and research was started on a portable launch-and-recovery system, with elements being tested at Quantico's airfield in the early 1960s. The result was an all-weather airfield, complete with a portable control tower that was almost entirely air-portable and completely reusable. It looked and operated like the deck of an aircraft carrier: upon touchdown, the plane's tail hook engaged the arresting gear. A short catapult launch had the plane airborne in seconds. The new field was ready in time for the Vietnam War, and one was installed at Chu Lai.

The SATS landing strip is 72 feet wide and 2,210 feet long and is surfaced with interlocking aluminum mats measuring 2 feet wide by 12 feet long and weighing 144 pounds each. A three-hundred-man Naval Construction detachment or Marine Corps engineers working two six-hour shifts can lay 400 feet a day. The catapult uses two J79 turbojet engines, and the M21 arresting gear cables, which are attached to a turbine wheel in a fluid-filled tub, bring fighters as heavy as the F-4 Phantom or F-14 Tomcat to a soft stop in as little as 600 feet.

Pilots use a TACAN (Tactical Air Navigation System) navigation beacon to locate the field, while controllers of a MCATCU (Marine Corps Air Tactical Control Unit) pick up the plane on ground-control-approach radar and talk it down. The edge of the field is lined with orange lights; if the pilot sees the center light as an orange ball he knows he is on the correct landing angle to hook onto the arresting gear. A TAFDS (Tactical Airfield Fuel Dispensing System), consisting of collapsible fabric and rubber bags, connecting plumbing, filters, and dispensing nozzles, accommodates the heavy fuel consumption of jet aircraft. The system can be filled from flexible pipelines from offshore tankers or by tanker trucks from the nearest port.

The tactical situation may govern the extent of field development, which is flexible. Normally, a SATS is constructed in three phases. Phase I sets up the minimum 2,200-foot runway and one parallel taxiway and hot-pad areas for twelve tactical aircraft and minimum support and maintenance capabilities. Phase II includes amassing material and equipment to accommodate two squadrons. Phase III, attained after twenty-six days, sets up a runway of 7,000 feet and three squadrons. At Chu Lai work began on 8 May, and the first plane landed twenty-three days later. The total load of material and equipment needed to install a SATS is only a small fraction of what would be needed for construction materials alone for a conventional field.

The SATS—another Marine innovation that has transformed warfare—gives the Marine Expeditionary Force the valuable capability of having an early air base in an objective area that has no existing fields. From there, timely close air support and air defense can be provided without the delay of flying from distant bases.

—BN

LEFT: A Marine A-4 Skyhawk is loaded for a bombing run behind protective revetments on the SATS landing strip at Chu Lai. The belly tank gave the small, twin-engine jet fighter/bomber extended range.

Marble Mountain and Chu Lai

The main Marine helicopter squadrons were located near Marble Mountain—the unique, domelike rock outcropping on the coast just below Da Nang, near China Beach. In late October 1965, VC sappers (demolitions specialists) hit the area, destroying twenty-four helos, damaging twenty-three others, and killing forty-one; at the same time, they attacked the airfield at Chu Lai, where they destroyed two A-4s and damaged six others. In December, battalions from the 7th and the 3d Marines had to rescue the ARVN 5th Regiment from a severe firefight north of Chu Lai, in an operation dubbed Harvest Moon.

Operation Double Eagle

In late January 1966, Task Force Delta combined with the Army 1st Cavalry Division to rescue the district headquarters at Que Son to the west of Chu Lai, which had been under attack by the North Vietnamese Army (NVA) 325A Division. There was heavy fighting between the Americans and the 36th NVA and 1st VC regiments.

ABOVE: A Marine A-1 Skyraider drops phosphorous bombs from low altitude on the tiny village of Ban De, where VC were hiding.

LEFT: A Marine examines a U.S. M1 carbine of WWII and Korean War vintage. The enemy VC were provided with whatever weapons the Communists could muster— mostly the Russian-made Kalashnikov AK-47s.

RIGHT: *Life* photographer Larry Burrows covered the battles on Hills 484 and 400, where he took the memorable photos on this page. Here, under fire during a fight for Hill 484 near Dong Ha in 1966, Marines extract a wounded buddy for MedEvac. In the background is noted French photographer Catherine LeRoy, later seriously wounded, but who after recovery went back into the field with both Marines and Army troops. American TV reporter Dickie Chapelle was not so fortunate; accompanying a Marine patrol, she stepped on a land mine and was killed. Her death instituted the Marine policy forbidding female photographers or journalists on combat operations.

BELOW: Marines wounded in the fight for Hills 484 and 400 await evacuation by helicopter.

In March, the remainder of the 1st MarDiv, consisting mostly of the 5th Marine Regiment, landed in the two southern provinces of I Corps, under command of MajGen Jeff Fields. That spring, an internecine struggle erupted within the South Vietnamese military. A senior general in the I Corps sector was relieved of his command and ordered out of the country, causing the revolt of those loyal to him, many of whom were Buddhists. The distracting uprising had to be quelled by the South Vietnamese, and it interfered for a time with the cohesion of the allied effort in the sector.

The DMZ

In the spring of 1966, elements of the 324B NVA Division crossed over into the DMZ, triggering the Marine response termed Operation Hastings, launched in July. That operation dragged on and merged into another that lasted into May of the following year and was dubbed Operation Prairie.

ABOVE: On a 9th Marines battalion patrol during Operation Union II southwest of Da Nang in April 1967, a radioman cautiously checks a South Vietnamese "hootch" for hidden VC. Although the first several days of the patrol were uneventful, it concluded in a terrific firefight when VC emerged from hidden "spider holes" and other ambush sites to engage Marines.

The battleground for both was the DMZ and Route 9, which ran roughly parallel to and south of the zone, stretching from the South China Sea to the Cambodian border. The 3d MarDiv was moved forward and its advance CP (Command Post) was placed at Dong Ha, where Route 9 and the north-south Route 1 crossed. As numerous battles ensued, 1st MarDiv was moved up to Da Nang, leaving the southern part of I Corps mostly in Army hands.

In March 1967, the villages of Gio Linh, Con Thien, an outpost called the Rock Pile, Cam Lo, and Khe Sanh along the DMZ came under sustained attack by North Vietnamese forces. From 27 April through 3 May, 3d Marines fought severe battles against two NVA regiments on Hills 881 North and 881 South, which dominated the approaches to the firebase just above Khe Sanh, until relieved by the 26th Marines arriving from the reactivated 5th MarDiv at Camp Pendleton, California. Worse, the new—but untested—M16 semiautomatic rifles that McNamara insisted replace the Marine M14s proved problematic in these battles, at the cost of numerous Marine casualties.

In April, the Army's 25th Division was placed under III MAF control, and the 5th Marines engaged in Operation Union I and II to the southwest of Da Nang.

MEDAL OF HONOR

PRIVATE FIRST CLASS JAMES ANDERSON, JR.
Republic of Vietnam
28 February 1967

For conspicuous gallantry and intrepidity at the risk of his life above and beyond the call of duty. Company F was advancing in dense jungle northwest of Cam Lo in an effort to extract a heavily besieged reconnaissance patrol. Pfc James Anderson's platoon was the lead element and had advanced only about two hundred meters when it was brought under extremely intense enemy small-arms and automatic-weapons fire. The platoon reacted swiftly, getting on line as best they could in the thick terrain, and began returning fire. Pfc Anderson found himself tightly bunched together with the other members of his platoon only twenty meters from the enemy positions. As the firefight continued several of the men were wounded in the deadly enemy assault. Suddenly, an enemy grenade landed in the midst of the Marines and rolled alongside Pfc Anderson's head. Unhesitatingly and with complete disregard for his personal safety, he reached out, grasped the grenade, pulled it to his chest, and curled around it as it went off. Although several Marines received shrapnel wounds from the grenade, his body absorbed the major force of the explosion. In this singularly heroic act, Pfc Anderson saved his comrades from serious injury and possible death. His personal heroism, extraordinary valor, and inspirational supreme self-sacrifice reflected great credit upon himself and the Marine Corps and upheld the highest traditions of the U.S. Naval Service. He gallantly gave his life for his country.

The New M16 Rifle and Other Improvements

In the spring of 1967, SecDef McNamara and MACV (Military Assistance Command, Vietnam) insisted that III MAF adopt the new M16 5.56mm semiautomatic rifle the Army was using in order to standardize the supply chain. Its performance in the battles for Hills 881 North and South brought many complaints, mostly about malfunctions caused by chamber imperfections, the inability to properly clean the weapon during combat, and its tendency to jam in heavy rain and muddy conditions. The matter was looked into immediately and the rifles were retrofitted. The M79 40mm grenade launcher, with an operator, was added to each squad. Protective flak jackets were standard issue, and a new lightweight, quick-drying uniform with a bush jacket and pants, styled after that used by U.S. paratroopers during World War II, was adopted, along with a new jungle boot that had a mesh top on a rubber sole, resulting in quicker drying in the humid tropical environment.

—BN

ABOVE RIGHT: Following their first mission, UH-34s return to the flight deck of the LPH *Okinawa* off South Vietnam in the China Sea with its sister LPH *Princeton*, after inserting a BLT of the Special Landing Force into the DMZ during Operation Beaucharger in April 1967. The lead chopper, with the battalion CO and the Navy intelligence staff, inadvertently landed on an enemy machine-gun nest; they took severe casualties and numerous hits but made it back nevertheless.

ARMALITE (COLT) M16

Designed by a former Marine corporal, Eugene Stoner, this new 5.56mm M16 semiautomatic, 20-round-magazine rifle was adopted by all armed services in early 1967 by order of SecDef McNamara. Although it had a high muzzle velocity (3,250 feet per second), its initial jamming and cleaning defects caused many a Marine casualty when first used in the battles of Hill 881, North and South, above Khe Sanh. The remedies resulted in the M16A and, up to the present time, the M16A2. The straight barrel-stock design allows for less recoil and greater accuracy. Its simple construction, with plastic stock, pistol grip, and barrel cover, and easy disassembly make it the best combat rifle in the world, especially in close combat—better than the enemy's ubiquitous stamped-metal Russian Kalashnikov AK-47s that the Marines faced in Vietnam.

LEFT: In the midst of the intense fighting on the strategically important Hill 881, in April 1967, Navy corpsman Vernon R. Wike (left) treats a mortally wounded Marine while another Marine assists. Corpsmen braved the dangers just as the combatants did. Note that the corpsmen wear their helmet chinstraps secured tightly. Unlike the devil-may-care Marines portrayed by John Wayne in the movies, real Marines never leave their chinstraps flapping while in battle.

BELOW: The eleven-day battles for Hill 861 and Hills 881 North and 881 South, overlooking the new firebase at Khe Sanh on the western end of Route 9 paralleling the DMZ near the Laotian border, were particularly vexing. Some of the Marines had been issued the new untested and unfamiliar M16 prototype rifles, many of which malfunctioned, causing additional casualties. The fighting was close and relentless. This platoon commander has his Colt .45 M1911 semiautomatic pistol ready for the enemy looming just over the military crest of the ridge. His radioman is in contact with company or battalion headquarters, quite possibly requesting mortar, artillery, or close air support. Notice that an unexploded enemy fragment grenade lies menacingly in the foreground, unnoticed in the heat of battle.

> *"There's two ways to get off Hill 881—*
>
> *flown off or blown off."*
>
> *Sgt Joseph Michael Jones*

OPPOSITE: Except for the helmet styles and ponchos, this could be a scene from World War I: trench/bunker warfare just below the DMZ at Con Thien—worse, during the monsoon season. In this photograph by David Douglas Duncan, Marines of Mike Company, 3d Battalion, 9th Marines, stoically man this forward outpost, which was the only high ground for miles. Called the "Hill of Angels" in Vietnamese, this was an important observation post and a trip wire for infiltrating the NVA. Consequently, it was under constant bombardment from enemy heavy artillery, mortar, and rocket fire. On the rows and rows of defensive barbed wire surrounding the perimeter dead enemy bodies hung for days following their constant and random night attacks.

RIGHT: Marines of Lima Company, 3d Battalion, 4th Marines, in a wooded area south of Con Thien fire M79 grenades at enemy snipers.

LEFT, TOP: In another photo by Duncan, a break in the harsh fall weather allows these cooped-up Marines to emerge from their underground lairs and watch an air strike on forward enemy positions in the supposedly unoccupied DMZ. Empty ammo boxes are strewn about, and the Marine on the right wields a combat shotgun, very effective when the enemy closed in during night attacks—just as it was in the trench warfare of 1918. Marine heavy artillery was set up back near Dong Ha to support all Marine ground units in the area.

M79 GRENADE LAUNCHER

Grenade launcher, M79, 40mm single-shot breech-loaded weapon. Introduced in the Vietnam War for close-in fighting, it was more lethal than a sawed-off shotgun. Bridging the gap from a hand-thrown grenade, the M79 launched a spherical explosive with 300 fragments up to 300 meters at 75 meters per second. Its rifled bore rotated the shot at 3,700 rpm, in turn arming it.

Stingray Patrols in Vietnam

Once a firm base had been established in the Da Nang area of South Vietnam in 1965, the Marines began to advance inland to secure territory from the Vietcong (VC) and the North Vietnamese Army (NVA). The area featured jungle, mountains, scattered clearings, and villages. The VC and NVA were an elusive enemy and it was difficult to bring them into action on favorable terms. They easily detected Marine movements by platoon, company, and battalion and simply moved out of the way or set ambushes in the close country. Marines again demonstrated their ability to quickly adapt to a changed terrain and tactical situation with the initiation of the Stingray Patrol program in 1966.

Stingray Patrols usually consisted of five or six highly trained, lightly armed Marines from Force Reconnaissance Companies or Division Reconnaissance Battalions. Equipped with a radio, they were inserted into enemy territory by helicopter. They then moved to high ground or other positions where they could observe a wide area of trails, stream crossings, or other locations where the enemy might pass. They would not engage with their weapons, but would instead call in artillery fire or air strikes on the enemy.

From 1967 to 1971 more than eight thousand Stingray Patrols were run; only one was lost and not one was captured. The 8,317 patrols had 15,680 sightings of 138,252 enemies. They called in 6,463 artillery-fire missions and 1,328 air strikes, resulting in 9,566 confirmed kills, 85 captured, and more than 300 weapons secured. In terms of enemy killed versus American losses, the Stingray Patrols showed a four or five to one advantage over infantry units. Making use of highly trained men, modern radio communications, and overwhelming artillery and air firepower, Marine reconnaissance in Vietnam developed one aspect of future warfare: in the Gulf War of 1991, sniper teams and Stingray-type patrols were inserted into the vast, flat deserts of Kuwait and Iraq with results similar to those achieved in Vietnam.

—BN

LEFT: Sanctuary. Exhausted, slightly wounded members of 1st Battalion, 9th Marines, irreverently rest on the altar of a small Vietnamese Catholic church a few miles below the DMZ. Although damaged slightly by the surrounding battle, the structure did offer a temporary safe haven, despite the fact that the Communist enemy had no compunction about destroying such places of Christian worship in the country.

RIGHT, TOP: Marine CH-53 Sea Stallions, like the one shown in this David Douglas Duncan photograph, were introduced at the end of 1967. Capable of lifting eight thousand pounds, these heavy-duty helicopters brought in replacement troops and tons of rations, equipment, and ammunition—sometimes slung in cargo nets beneath. They loaded out with casualties.

RIGHT, BOTTOM: Duncan's photograph captures the vacant, dog-tired, "thousand-yard stare" that comes with experiencing constant combat. This young Marine will endure more bombardment and personal privation before it is his turn to be rotated—if he is still alive by then.

On 18 May, the Special Landing Force from the LPH *Okinawa* was inserted into the DMZ near the mouth of the Ben Hai River, sustaining moderate casualties, while three Marine battalions worked with ARVN units to clear the Gio Linh and Ben Hai areas of enemy infiltrators just to the west of the landing force.

In June, LtGen Robert Cushman relieved LtGen Lew Walt as CG, III MAF. Walt returned to the United States to become assistant commandant of the Marine Corps. In September, hard fighting broke out again along the DMZ at Khe Sanh and Con Thien. Operations were also conducted in the A Shau Valley, farther to the south and west. On 14 November, 3d MarDiv commander MajGen Bruno Hochmuth was killed in a helicopter crash, and command went to MajGen Rathvon Tompkins. The 1st MarDiv was commanded by MajGen Donn Robertson.

Khe Sanh

In November of 1967, intelligence reports indicated that several NVA divisions were assembling above the western end of the DMZ. The 26th Marines and a battalion from the 9th Marines, supported by an ARVN Ranger battalion at the combat camp at Khe Sanh, a hamlet in the northwestern corner of South Vietnam twelve miles south of the DMZ, were alerted. The camp was situated in a U-shaped valley rimmed by two- to three-thousand-foot rolling mountains. The firebase camp was also positioned to interdict the Ho Chi Minh trail, located just over the border in Laos and Cambodia and from which the North constantly

MEDAL OF HONOR

CORPORAL WILLIAM THOMAS PERKINS, JR.
Republic of Vietnam
12 October 1967

For conspicuous gallantry and intrepidity at the risk of his life above and beyond the call of duty while serving as a combat photographer attached to Company C. During Operation Medina, a major reconnaissance operation in force southwest of Quang Tri, Company C made heavy combat contact with a numerically superior North Vietnamese Army force estimated at from two to three companies. The focal point of the intense fighting was a helicopter landing zone that was also serving as the Command Post of Company C. In the course of a strong hostile attack, an enemy grenade landed in the immediate area occupied by Cpl William Perkins and three other Marines. Realizing the inherent danger, he shouted the warning "incoming grenade" to his fellow Marines, and in a valiant act of heroism, hurled himself upon the grenade, absorbing the impact of the explosion with his body, thereby saving the lives of his comrades at the cost of his life. Through his exceptional courage and inspiring valor in the face of certain death, Cpl Perkins reflected great credit upon himself and the Marine Corps and upheld the highest traditions of the U.S. Naval Service. He gallantly gave his life for his country.

BELOW, LEFT: A battle-damaged combat film camera. The ubiquitous, spring-wound, Bell & Howell "Eyemo" 16mm film camera, with swivel turret-mount for wide-angle, normal, and telephoto lenses, was the workhorse for combat cameramen in World War II, Korea, and into early Vietnam. This particular camera was damaged by the same grenade that killed its operator, Marine Cpl William T. Perkins, in Operation Medina in Vietnam in 1967.

RIGHT: Cpl William T. Perkins (left, background) taking pictures with his Bell & Howell camera.

RIGHT: A heavy-lift cargo helicopter—basically a skeletonized CH-53, called a Flying Grasshopper or Jolly Green Giant—airlifts ammunition and supplies to an artillery position at Khe Sanh. These giant lifters were occasionally called on to extract downed Hueys and UH-34s. They could also airlift artillery pieces.

BELOW: The beloved rough-side-out boondockers of WWII and Korea had been replaced by black versions (as were all services' shoes, visors, belts, etc.). But Vietnam's tropical jungles and monsoons called for something more practical. Thus a rubber-soled, leather-instep boot with a breathable, quick-drying mesh-fabric upper was adopted by all U.S. combatants. The boots shown here were worn by William J. Farrister, H&S Company, 106th Platoon, 2d Battalion, 26th Marines, at Khe Sanh, 18 January through 20 April 1968.

sent secret deliveries of troops and weapons to the VC in the South.

Khe Sanh had all the negative attributes of the ill-fated 1954 French outpost at Dien Bien Phu, several hundred miles to the north. Nevertheless, the Marines had manned it, reinforced its perimeter, and bulldozed a 2,000-foot airstrip. And, unlike the vulnerable French, who had not had outposts on the higher ground, nor heavy artillery and air support, the Marines had installed pickets all around, had laid warning and explosive barbed-wire protective rings, and had air-dropped metal motion-detecting devices to monitor the enemy's every move. The NVA 325th and 304th divisions composed of 15,000 troops were now identified. (An NVA division was approximately 7,000 men compared with the Marine division of 25,000.) Although the enemy had only limited armor and no air support, they did possess heavy artillery.

The siege began on 21 January 1968; it would be the second battle of Khe Sanh—and the last.

The J2 intelligence group at General of the Army William C. Westmoreland's MCAV headquarters in Saigon, as well as the CIA there, had been collecting intelligence that portended a large-scale buildup across the western end of the DMZ for just such an enemy attack. The activity at Khe Sanh was interpreted, therefore, to be the prelude to the long-expected, all-out attempt to overwhelm the Marine, Army, and ARVN forces in I Corps. Others, including the CIA, cautioned that it might be only a feint for something bigger. Westmoreland, a virtual yes-man for SecDef McNamara (who, along with the president, had increased his level of micromanaging the war to the point of installing a three-dimensional scale model of Khe Sanh, accurate down to its maze of trenches, in the White House War Room), ignored the possibility of a feint, and his J2 experts failed to properly interpret their intelligence information, especially that from the competing agency, the CIA.

Since Tet, the festival of the lunar new year and Vietnam's most important holiday, was to be observed throughout South Vietnam from 27 January through 3 February, a temporary cease-fire was announced for the South Vietnamese army, and more than half of their forces went home to celebrate. The winter-spring monsoons were now bringing especially hazardous conditions to Khe Sanh. Persistent fog and mists meant low visibility, which hampered air operations, especially helicopter resupply.

President Johnson, more fearful than ever of the consequences of losing Khe Sanh, especially during an election year, demanded that his Joint Chiefs of Staff personally guarantee that the Marine firebase would not fall.

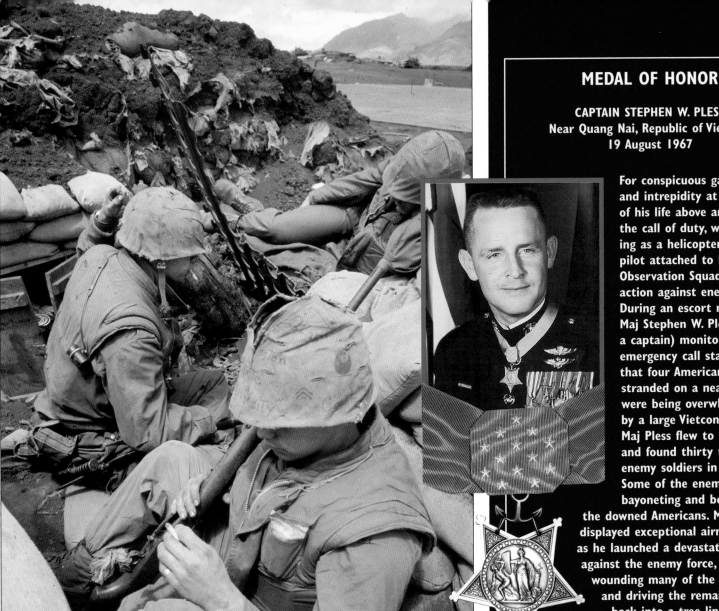

ABOVE: Marines along a perimeter of the Khe Sanh combat base grab a moment of fresh air during a lull in the constant enemy shelling in March 1968. The Marine in the foreground holds a sniper rifle.

As the battle raged at Khe Sanh through January, more intelligence, intercepted message traffic, and prisoner interrogations predicted yet more activity elsewhere, but was not disseminated to proper commands down the line. Incredibly, MACV remained somewhat oblivious to the coming threat, although some units suspected trouble—as did the Marines— and initiated alerts on their own.

The Tet Offensive

In what was almost a repeat performance of the previous war, with KMAG officers partying on the eve of the invasion of South Korea in 1950, on 26 January two hundred MACV-J2 U.S. colonels were at the officers'

MEDAL OF HONOR

CAPTAIN STEPHEN W. PLESS
Near Quang Nai, Republic of Vietnam
19 August 1967

For conspicuous gallantry and intrepidity at the risk of his life above and beyond the call of duty, while serving as a helicopter gunship pilot attached to Marine Observation Squadron 6 in action against enemy forces. During an escort mission, Maj Stephen W. Pless (then a captain) monitored an emergency call stating that four American soldiers stranded on a nearby beach were being overwhelmed by a large Vietcong force. Maj Pless flew to the scene and found thirty to fifty enemy soldiers in the open. Some of the enemy were bayoneting and beating the downed Americans. Maj Pless displayed exceptional airmanship as he launched a devastating attack against the enemy force, killing or wounding many of the enemy and driving the remainder back into a tree line. His rocket and machine-gun attacks were made at such low levels that the aircraft flew through debris created by explosions from its rockets. Seeing one of the wounded soldiers gesture for assistance, he maneuvered his helicopter into a position between the wounded men and the enemy, providing a shield that permitted his crew to retrieve the wounded. During the rescue the enemy directed intense fire at the helicopter and rushed the aircraft again and again, closing to within a few feet before being beaten back. When the wounded men were aboard, Maj Pless maneuvered the helicopter out to sea. Before it became safely airborne, the overloaded aircraft settled four times into the water. Displaying superb airmanship, he finally got the helicopter aloft. Maj Pless's extraordinary heroism coupled with his outstanding flying skill prevented the annihilation of the tiny force. His courageous actions reflect great credit upon himself and uphold the highest traditions of the Marine Corps and the U.S. Naval Service.

club of the BOQ (Bachelor Officers Quarter) in Saigon, most likely enjoying their customary happy hour, just hours before all hell broke loose throughout South Vietnam in what was later called the Tet Offensive.

The next morning, the senior intelligence colonel found himself on the roof of the senior officers' quarters firing a .50-caliber machine gun at attackers who seemed to come from everywhere. He still had no idea that a countrywide battle had erupted. Gen Westmoreland, who was also unaware of the scale of the attacks, had to be rescued from his quarters by Military Police as firefights raged all around him. Vietcong had even broken into the American Embassy, only to be killed immediately by Marine guards. Throughout the South, 5 provincial capitals and 105 villages were attacked simultaneously by some 80,000 NVA regulars and VC. The enemy was unable to penetrate Da Nang, which was protected by the Marines. The Communists' strategy was to hit hard everywhere during the religious holiday, when least expected, and urge the populace to rise up against their American and ARVN oppressors and join the Communists in taking over the country. Indeed, Khe Sanh had been only a feint.

The general uprising, however, did not occur, and within a few days—a week in some cases—the NVA and VC were killed or driven off. They failed to capture and hold a single town, village, or capital, and they sustained 33,000 killed, 40,000 wounded, and 6,000 taken prisoner. The ARVN lost 2,800 killed, the United States, 1,100. Only in the ancient capital of Hue, between Da Nang and the DMZ, was there a prolonged fight.

One Shot, One Kill: Sniping in Vietnam

After World War II, sniping skills languished. Regiments no longer included scout-sniper platoons. In the Korean War, sniping was an ad hoc matter that depended on the initiative of individual commanders. Typically, an M1903 with Unertl scope, or one of the other sniping rifles of the previous war, would be put into the hands of the best shots, who were then told to snipe. The higher skills of long-range shooting and the fieldcraft essential to acquiring a good sniper hide were all but lost, except in the memories of a few. One of these few was Maj E.J. Land, of the Marksmanship Training Unit at Quantico, who, along with other enthusiastic Marine shooters, sparked a revival of interest in sniping.

Super-accurate rifles were developed, culminating with the M40, which was based on the Remington 700 rifle. In 1960, a formal sniping school was established. Shooting skills were honed by top Marine rifle competitors; tactics and skills in camouflage, fieldcraft, stalking, and gathering intelligence about the enemy were taught; and a sniping training manual was published. These skills were transferred to the Fleet Marine Force with a table of organization (T/O) and a table of equipment (T/E), plus a military occupational specialty number (MOS) for snipers.

The payoff came in the Vietnam War. The changes wrought at Quantico were in place. Shots were often at a range of one thousand yards or more. One of the more successful Marine snipers, GySgt Carlos Hathcock, was credited with ninety-three confirmed kills.

—BN

RIGHT: A Marine sniper in Hue uses a sandbag to take aim at a long-range target. Enemy soldiers were completely astonished when they or one of their comrades would suddenly crumple to ground, hit by a sniper bullet fired from a mile away.

.30-CALIBER SNIPER RIFLE

The .30-caliber bolt-action single-shot sniper rifle with telescopic sight had an effective range of more than a thousand yards and was used effectively throughout the Vietnam War.

Hue

In the Marines' I Corps sector, the beautiful, ancient imperial capital city of Hue, halfway between Da Nang and the DMZ, had been more or less neutral; there were no ARVN units or Marines there, only a small MACV contingent. Nevertheless, a regiment of NVA regulars—wearing civilian clothes that they later discarded to reveal their uniforms—infiltrated and took over the defenseless, historic city. The MACV advisory group called for help, and two battalions from the 1st Marines and an ARVN unit nearby were rushed in to rescue the encircled group south of the Perfume River, across from the city, and then clear out the enemy. After heavy fighting, the Marines secured the bridge into the city but were momentarily stopped by a strong NVA force occupying the heavily fortified Old Citadel Wall. The 2d Battalion, 5th Marines, was called in to reinforce the drive into the city, and by the time the street-by-street, house-by-house battle was over, the three Marine and thirteen ARVN battalions (with two Army brigades in blocking positions on the north side of the city) had defeated between eight and eleven heavily entrenched NVA battalions. The monthlong fight was one of the fiercest of the war.

Before the battle of Hue was over, an ARVN Special Forces camp near Khe Sanh was overrun by NVA Russian-built PT-76 amphibious tanks—the first and last such use of these vehicles. Meanwhile, under constant siege, Khe Sanh had to be continuously resupplied by Marine and Air Force C-123 and C-130 aircraft (four were destroyed by enemy fire) and cargo helicopters. Gen Westmoreland stated afterward, in an

OPPOSITE, CENTER: A three-Marine sniper team working the hills around Khe Sanh. LCpl Albert Miranda sights in as LCpl David Burdwell spots, while Lt Alec Bodenwiser checks. Miranda, resting the .30-caliber rifle on his left hand and forearm, indicates that the target is relatively close—only a few hundred yards or so. For longer ranges, up to two thousand yards, a sandbag or rock formation would be used to further steady the rifle.

RIGHT: A wounded Marine is attended to by a Navy corpsman during the fighting in Hue. The Marine will be evacuated by chopper to appropriate medical facilities, and will perhaps return to fight another day.

RIGHT: After eighteen days of intense close-in fighting in Hue, Marines and the ARVN had captured most of the city. Here, a Marine fires from the rubble of the crest of the citadel wall.

LEFT: The bitterest and longest aggressive battle of the war: the battle for the neutral, ancient capital city of Hue. It was the culmination of the Communists' unsuccessful Tet Offensive, January–February 1968. Three Marine and seven ARVN battalions retook Hue after four weeks of grueling street-to-street, house-to-house fighting against NVA regulars. As they retreated, the vengeful enemy massacred five thousand innocent South Vietnamese civilians, leaving four thousand of their own dead behind. UPI combat photographer Kyoichi Sawada fearlessly covered the battle, capturing remarkable moments like this.

effort to be conciliatory, that the resupply effort—designated Operation Pegasus—had been the "premier air logistical feat of the war." He might have added, "and an ill-advised, strategically and tactically impossible battle to win conclusively—at unnecessary loss of life." The battle ended on 30 March. More than 100,000 tons of bombs had been dropped on the surrounding enemy; 205 Marines had been killed, 800 wounded; the North Vietnamese lost an estimated 10,000 killed.

Although the Tet Offensive initially took the Marines by surprise, they responded quickly and effectively, knocking back the attacks and killing 6,000 enemy soldiers. The Marines lost 142 killed. For the North Vietnamese, the offensive was militarily disastrous—the VC was virtually wiped out—but they nonetheless claimed a tremendous propaganda coup. The international press blazoned headlines across their news reports that were mostly critical of the United States and the Johnson administration (which had suggested that the war was all but won) and portrayed Tet as a victory for the North, all but ignoring the fact that the retreating North Vietnamese forces had planted mines throughout the devastated city and brutally massacred 5,000 civilians. The misreporting of the Tet Offensive contributed much to the American public's increased opposition to the war.

Defeat Snatched from the Jaws of Victory

During the battle of Tet, not only had the U.S. military been caught off guard, but the media had been as well. Pinned down by the rifle fire themselves, television reporters were able to film only glimpses of the fighting. This out-of-context footage often focused on images of destruction and of dead bodies that were not clearly identified as those of the enemy. In Hue, reporters filmed scenes of Marines firing and taking casualties—all of which reached the TV sets of the American public on the evening news and gave the impression that the Tet attacks had been a major defeat and setback for the U.S. The president and McNamara were shocked and took it that way as well.

Unintentionally or not, the news reporters covering Vietnam, many of whom were not knowledgeable about military matters and were sympathetic to the antiwar voices being raised back home, often told a slanted story, or editorialized rather than reported the news objectively. To the fighting men there, journalists appeared to be unduly sympathetic to the enemy's cause. (Certainly the troops were aware of the favorable attention that journalists gave to the trips to

OPPOSITE: The casualties at Hue mounted steadily, and 142 U.S. Marines were killed in action. Here, Navy corpsmen give a wounded Marine first aid amid the rubble and debris of battle before he is evacuated to appropriate medical facilities, probably aboard one of the two venerable hospital ships standing offshore, the *Repose* or the *Sanctuary*.

LEFT, TOP: The Swedish hospital ship *Helgoland* docked in the Tourane River in Da Nang. The neutral country's contribution was to help South Vietnamese civilians, but Sweden did not turn away wounded Vietcong or enemy NVA. Few foreign countries favored U.S. policy in the Vietnam War, and many openly aided the North Vietnamese.

LEFT, BOTTOM: Marines of Golf Company, 2d Battalion, 9th Marines, cross a small river northwest of Hue on a pontoon raft. The vehicle is a half-ton M274 mechanical "mule." Some innovations like this were tested in Vietnam, including a tracked vehicle called an Ontos, with four 106mm recoilless rifles mounted on top.

ABOVE AND OPPOSITE: David Douglas Duncan captured this harrowing sequence of four photos of a C-130 cargo plane taking a direct hit during a mortar attack. A ground crewman is also hit; other crewmen exit the aircraft as it starts to burn. In most cases these sorts of airlifts resulted in the planes being on the ground for only a moment or so before taking off again, to avoid just such an occurrence. The enemy mortar hit was a "lucky" shot. (Note: all photos on this page and opposite are by David Douglas Duncan.)

RIGHT: A wounded Marine crewman from another C-130 that was hit later is placed on a stretcher for evacuation.

North Vietnam by the likes of former U.S. attorney general Ramsey Clark and movie actress Jane Fonda—not to mention the "Peace" groups that visited U.S. POWs in Hanoi and dutifully played back the propaganda they were fed.) The press and TV never alluded to the bodies of five thousand slaughtered innocents left behind in Hue by the whipped, retreating NVA. And many stories that disparaged U.S. efforts were manufactured or were flat-out misleading.

Even Ho Chi Minh himself was stunned that an out-and-out victory by the Americans was transformed into a total, psychological defeat. Hanoi's strategy for the Tet Offensive was to orchestrate a public opinion nightmare for the Americans as much as it was to pull off a military victory, and it had succeeded beyond expectations. Tet also played a part in unseating President Johnson, who decided not to run for reelection. Westmoreland was bumped upstairs to

LEFT: Another C-130 four-engine prop cargo plane disintegrates in a consuming fireball. Loaded with aviation fuel, it was hit by machine-gun fire as it came in for its touch-and-go landing, careening in flames down the runway and killing a crewman and five passengers. Cargo aircraft that had to land on "hot" runways did so by diving steeply and pulling out to a virtual stall for a short landing, then hesitating just long enough to unload and reload casualties before taking off quickly at the steepest angle possible to avoid enemy gunfire. They often made a jet-assisted takeoff (JATO), in which rockets under the wings gave an initial boost, almost heaving the giant bird back into the air.

become chairman of the Joint Chiefs of Staff, where he would be under the thumb of McNamara, who would soon resign in humiliation. Westy was replaced by his deputy, Gen Creighton Abrams, who faced a thankless task to disengage from an unwinnable war.

In essence, the Tet Offensive, although it was a U.S.–South Vietnam victory, was inadvertently the turning point of the war. The incoming Nixon administration despaired and threw in the towel, and within two years all U.S. forces would be out of South Vietnam and the country would be left to fend for itself.

The Spring Counteroffensive

Operation Pegasus was followed by operations west of Da Nang on the Laotian border into the A Shau Valley by 9th Marines and elements of Army 1st Cavalry and 101st Airborne divisions. An NVA

divisional attack on Dong Ha was labeled a "mini-Tet" and was just as indecisive. In May, MajGen Raymond Davis, a Medal of Honor recipient for action at the Chosin Reservoir in Korea, took over 3d MarDiv. Operation Task Force Hotel was mounted to reinforce Khe Sanh and to defeat decisively the 304th NVA division, which had been surrounding the base. By 19 June, the NVA had retreated. In August, the NVA conducted a third offensive across the DMZ, on Go Noi Island and all the way down to Da Nang. All of the enemy attacks were thwarted.

On 14 April 1968, III MAF commander LtGen Robert Cushman ordered Khe Sanh to be abandoned after deciding it was no longer militarily viable. The besieged firebase had suffered untold casualties from as many as a thousand rounds of enemy artillery a day, and had withstood constant massed frontal attacks and infiltrations—not to overlook the thirty thousand aircraft sorties required to protect and resupply it. By 23 June it was bulldozed over, and hardly a trace of the city remained. The Marines wrote off Khe Sanh as a victorious standoff; the North Vietnamese propagandized it throughout the world as a victory against the "Imperialists." Thus the U.S. victories at Tet and Khe Sanh were twisted into U.S. defeats.

With the coming of the autumn monsoons, operations were somewhat curtailed. The Marines developed a concept called Stingray, in which six-man patrols were dropped into remote areas to surreptitiously direct artillery and air strikes; this totally bewildered the enemy. In November, the "Accelerated Pacification Plan" was inaugurated at "Dodge City," a beleaguered outpost west of Da Nang. A strong cordon was tightened around the area, which boxed in 1,300 NVA and 100 VC, killing 1,210 of them.

Operation Dewey Canyon

At the beginning of 1969, the war was once again repeating itself as Marines returned to the site of Operation Starlite for another sweep by one of the SLFs (Special Landing Forces) offshore. At the end

MEDAL OF HONOR

LANCE CORPORAL KENNETH L. WORLEY
Bo Ban, Quang Nam Province
Republic of Vietnam
12 August 1968

For conspicuous gallantry and intrepidity at the risk of his life above and beyond the call of duty, while serving as a machine gunner with Company L, 3d Battalion, 7th Marines, First Marine Division in action against enemy forces in the Republic of Vietnam. After establishing a night ambush position in a house in the Bo Ban Hamlet of Quang Nam Province, security was set up and the remainder of the patrol members retired until their respective watch. During the early morning hours of 12 August 1968, the Marines were abruptly awakened by the platoon leader's warning that grenades had landed in the house. Fully realizing the inevitable result of his actions, LCpl Kenneth Worley, in a valiant act of heroism, instantly threw himself upon the grenade nearest him and his comrades, absorbing with his own body the full and tremendous force of the explosion. Through his extraordinary initiative and inspiring valor in the face of almost certain death, he saved his comrades from serious injury and possible loss of life, although five of his fellow Marines incurred minor wounds as the other grenades exploded. LCpl Worley's gallant actions upheld the highest traditions of the Marine Corps and the United States Naval Service. He gallantly gave his life for his country.

of January, Operation Dewey Canyon, the most successful of the regimental-size operations of the war, took place. In April, fresh NVA units were again spotted at Cam Lo, up on Route 9, also necessitating clearing operations.

The Unprecedented Pullout

President Lyndon Johnson, recognizing that he had been politically destroyed by the war, had declined to run for reelection in 1968. In 1969, newly elected president Richard Nixon, after initiating a devastating B-52 bombing campaign against Hanoi and a semi-successful incursion (not an "invasion," as reported by the press) into Cambodia to sever the clandestine Ho Chi Minh supply trail, began to fulfill his election promise to end the war in Vietnam, by simply pulling out. Accordingly, in June the 9th Marines were withdrawn to Okinawa, along with elements of the 1st MAW. By midsummer, things had quieted down to the extent that it was possible to travel by Jeep, and without escort, on the newly paved Route 9 from Dong Ha all the way west to the Rockpile. One Montagnard village along Route 9 had even returned to normal, with schoolchildren attending classes in their cute, freshly laundered blue-and-white frocks and short pants.

In July, the immortal words of astronaut Neil Armstrong after landing on the moon were heard by everyone in South Vietnam—who all seemed to have transistor pocket radios they had purchased in the Post Exchanges (PXs). (There was no satellite television transmission at the time.)

In September, there was a second incremental withdrawal. By October, the 3d MarDiv was entirely out of South Vietnam, and all Marine helicopter operations were consolidated at Marble Mountain. It is incredibly complicated to remove combat units during an active war, but the Marine units were extracted without incident. U.S. Army units replaced the Marines until they, too, were withdrawn, leaving the South Vietnamese Army and South Vietnamese marines to fend for themselves. The withdrawals were results of the new peace talks taking place in Paris. Between January and April 1970, 12,600 more Marines were withdrawn. The 26th Marines went back to

OPPOSITE: There was a long quiet spell along the DMZ and Route 9 in the middle of 1969. Nevertheless, Marine 105mm howitzer artillery support for 3d MarDiv units was at the ready at the Dong Ha fire-support base, here being resupplied by a CH-46 Sea Knight with its load slung in an external cargo net.

LEFT, TOP: A distraught commander in chief. President Lyndon Johnson listens to one of the weekly audio tapes sent from the battle zone by his son-in-law, Marine Capt Charles S. Robb. Critics blamed the so-called Vietnam debacle on Johnson's and SecDef McNamara's personal and political intrusions in micro-managing the war from the White House. After the Tet Offensive, Johnson admitted defeat by not running for a second term.

LEFT, BOTTOM: Marine combat artist Maj Mike Leahy accompanied India Company, 3d Battalion, 7th Marines, on Operation Mameluke Thrust. His on-the-spot sketch shows a Marine F-4 Phantom delivering an air strike forward of the company's position. The company commander, Capt Charles S. Robb, son-in-law of then-President Lyndon Johnson, directs the strike. Robb later went on to become Democratic governor and then U.S. senator from Virginia.

Air Naval Gunfire Liaison Company (ANGLICO)

The ANGLICO is a unique Marine Corps organization designed to exploit the firepower of a Navy-Marine team in support of a U.S. Army or allied division. The two active ANGLICOs were activated in 1949 and 1951. A third ANGLICO is in the Reserve establishment.

ANGLICO provides a liaison team for division and brigade teams. Brigade teams furnish Supporting Arms Liaison Teams (SALTs) for maneuver battalions. SALTs in turn have two Firepower Control Teams (FCTs). FCTs include an Air Liaison Officer and communicators, Forward Air Controllers (FACs), a Naval Gunfire Liaison Officer and communicators, and Shore Fore Control Parties (SFCPs).

The first ANGLICO teams saw action in Korea and Vietnam as well as in joint exercises. The second ANGLICO saw action in Lebanon in 1958 and 1982, NATO exercises in Europe and in the Mediterranean, and was active in Grenada, the Dominican Republic, and the Gulf War of 1991.

As a result of the Defense Department's Quadrennial Review, the two ANGLICOs were deactivated in 1998 and 1999. As of this writing, however, these two valuable units are in the process of being reactivated due to the possibility of further conflict in the Middle East.

—BN

BELOW: After surviving enemy sniper fire for three hours as he strung explosives under the bridge at Dong Ha, Capt John L. Ripley still came under sporadic mortar fire. This incredible photograph by a South Vietnamese photographer catches a tense moment as a round explodes at Ripley's heels as he dashes for cover.

Camp Pendleton and were deactivated. Only one helicopter and three fixed-wing squadrons remained. The III MAF turned over its sector to the U.S. Army XXIV Corps and departed.

Minor operations, mostly in support of ARVN units, occupied the remaining 7th Marines, until they left in September. By October, only 18,600 Marines remained in the country. Their duties consisted mostly of assisting in the evacuation of civilians in the wake of the devastation of typhoon Kate.

In January 1971, Marine Tactical Air supported an ARVN incursion into Laos, and on 15 February, the 5th Marines stood down and left the country. On 14 April, the commanding general of III MAF removed his colors and headquarters to Okinawa. All Marine ground and air operations in South Vietnam ceased on 7 May, and all Marines, except five hundred embassy guards, air and naval gunfire support officers, and advisers, were out of the country by 26 June 1971.

With the South Vietnamese left to defend themselves, in 1972 the NVA opened their "Easter Offensive," with four armored divisions leading sixteen infantry divisions across the DMZ and invading the South, while the 9th MAB stood offshore just in case. At Dong Ha, the NVA's mechanized units had to cross the only bridge over the Cua Viet River. In one of the remaining U.S. advisory groups there happened to be a Marine captain, John Ripley, who was also a demolitions expert. Seeing that the ARVN was not capable of destroying the bridge and delaying the enemy advance, Ripley, without hesitation, took it upon himself to strap on explosives.

Incredibly, he advanced hand over hand under the bridge girders and worked his way from one giant piling to another, hanging by one hand and placing the charges with the other, while crimping the detonators with his teeth. All the while, both friendly and hostile eyes watched in amazement, and enemy snipers intermittently tried to stop him. After three hours he had placed enough explosives, and worked his way back under the steel structure to the south shore, attached the fuses to the detonator, and plunged the lever. The bridge blew sky high, and the two hundred attacking enemy tanks and thirty thousand troops were stranded on the opposite bank for the several days it took to erect a temporary bridge. For his heroic action, Ripley was awarded the Navy Cross. (In retirement, he became the director of the Marine Corps History and Museums Division.)

Some elements of fixed-wing F-4 Phantom, A-4 Skyhawk, and A-6 Intruder squadrons were left at Da Nang to support ARVN incursions into Laos, Cambodia, and, occasionally, North Vietnam.

The Ignominious End

The Paris Peace Accords, which were signed in 1973 by North Vietnam, South Vietnam, the Vietcong, and the United States, formally ended the Vietnam War and allowed for the release of 649 prisoners, 26 of whom were Marines. Forty-seven Marines still remain missing in action.

In 1975, the North Vietnamese flagrantly ignored the treaty when their twenty rebuilt divisions, including mechanized, smashed down from I Corps, scattering the disintegrating thirteen South Vietnamese divisions; the U.S. Congress refused to authorize logistical support to the retreating ARVN or the bombing of the invading NVA as they barreled all the way down to Saigon. The whole country fell to the Communists in a matter of months.

With the 9th MAB standing offshore, a five-man Marine advance party was sent in to Tan Son Nhut airfield, where they helped evacuate the 6,000 Americans—mostly civilians—who remained. A platoon also landed at the airport on 26 April to assist the Marine embassy guards in the evacuation. Two were killed by sniper fire. Three days later, BLT 2/4, with 865 Marines in two helicopter squadrons, also landed to assist the 171 Marines at the U.S. Embassy. Marine CH-53s began carrying 395 Americans and 4,475 Vietnamese out to awaiting ships.

As the NVA were storming the city, at the American Embassy, which was mobbed by frantic refugees, CH-46s had to land on the roof of the building while the heavier CH-53s landed in the parking lot. From there, 978 more Americans and 1,120

ABOVE: John L. Ripley is one of the true heroes of the Vietnam War. As a Marine adviser to the South Vietnamese in 1973, after all U.S. forces had left the country, Ripley single-handedly halted—albeit temporarily—the North Vietnamese final invasion of the South at Dong Ha just below the DMZ. Swinging hand over hand along the girders of the only bridge over the Cua Viet River, he laboriously laid explosives and then blew the bridge up, thus delaying some two hundred enemy tanks and thousands of invading NVA troops. He was awarded the Navy Cross for his actions. A retired colonel, Ripley is now head of the Marine Corps History and Museums Division.

LEFT: A high-altitude reconnaissance photo shows the bridge at Dong Ha just moments after Ripley plunged the detonator to bring it down, thus halting the advance of North Vietnamese forces. The railroad bridge on the left had already been severed by an earlier aerial bombing.

SONG MIEU GIANG RIVER

DROPPED SPAN

DROPPED SPAN

Combat Action Ribbon

ABOVE: Established in 1969 by SecNav John Chafee (a former Marine and Korean War veteran), the Combat Action Ribbon is equivalent to the Army's Combat Infantryman Badge. Retroactive to 7 December 1941, it is awarded to all Marine and Navy personnel from the rank of colonel or captain (0-6) who have actively participated in ground or sea combat under enemy fire with satisfactory performance.

RIGHT: During the final battle, as the NVA was capturing Saigon in April 1975, Marines from BLT 2/4 disembark from giant CH-53 choppers on the U.S. Embassy parking lot to provide security as refugees embark to be airlifted to LPHs offshore.

FAR RIGHT: Marines assist refugee South Vietnamese families as they arrive by chopper on the flight deck of the LPH *Blue Ridge* on 29 April 1975. The UH-1 Huey in the background, which had airlifted the refugees, broke its landing skids and was later unceremoniously dumped overboard to make room for more refugees, who were ultimately taken to Okinawa for further immigration to the U.S. and other receptive countries.

Vietnamese and foreign nationals were evacuated. The image of the last helicopter lifting off the embassy roof at 0735 on 29 April—leaving behind many pleading, crying souls for whom there was no more room—will be forever etched in the American psyche. Fortunately, there were no U.S. combat casualties during the evacuation.

Later that day, the Communists of the North took over Saigon. Shortly afterward, North Vietnamese leadership changed its name to Ho Chi Minh City.

The Marines in the Vietnam Era

The involvement of the Marine Corps in Vietnam was hindered by many impediments. The 1st and 3d MarDivs, the 26th Regiment, which had been reactivated from the 5th Division, and the 1st Marine Air Wing, made up of six aircraft groups of twenty-six tactical squadrons (186 CH-34 and UH-1 Huey utility helicopters, and 242 fixed-wing F-4 Phantoms, A-6 Intruders, F-8 Crusaders, and A-4 Skyhawks at five major fields), were ultimately sent into the northern I Corps sector below the DMZ. The 2d MarDiv retained its core position back in the States in FMF Atlantic, although individual troops were rotated back and forth to the divisions in combat. Unlike in Korea, neither the Reserve 4th MarDiv nor its organized Reserve

components nor any individual Reservists were ordered to active duty. Many did volunteer, however.

The universal draft of eligible males provided the bulk of replacement manpower, mostly for the Army, but, during several periods, also for the Marines. The Air Force and the Navy—like the Marine Corps—tried to maintain their all-volunteer status in the face of a generation of increasingly antiwar youth. Midway through the war, the Army and the Marines were forced to accept 18 percent of their recruits from those scoring in the subaverage Mental Group IV on the Armed Forces Qualification Test (the lowest category of recruit legally allowed to serve), and even those with criminal records, who by law could not be investigated. For a time, the Marine Corps suffered severely as a result of being forced to lower its standards.

The perennial friction between the administration/Army/Air Force and the Marine Corps raised its ugly head again in 1967 when the Army criticized Marine Corps helicopter usage. The Navy saw no need for Marine fixed-wing aircraft, while the Air Force took its case to President Johnson to control all aviation, including Marine.

Nineteen sixty-eight was a year marked by drug abuse and racial unrest both stateside and in Vietnam. Drug use became rampant (mostly in the Army), especially in Vietnam, where the enemy provided it cheaply on the streets to hooked GIs. During Robert Cushman's tenure as Commandant of the Marine Corps (1972–1975), at Camp Lejeune and other bases and in Vietnam, military discipline suffered. Black Marines attacked white Marines, causing great upheavals in morale and in senior and lower officer retention. There were incidents of open defiance of orders and the appearance of a disturbing new phenomenon: the assassination of officers, called fragging. Discontented, undisciplined members of the lower ranks—in either drug- or race-related undertones—would drop a live hand grenade into an officer's tent at night, killing or injuring the victim. It took drastic steps by the succeeding commandant, Louis Wilson, to curb the situation; he did so mostly by limiting the acceptance of recruits to only those who had completed high school and by allowing administrative discharges in lieu of courts-martial.

The war in Vietnam turned out to be far different from previous U.S. wars in many ways. Of the 500,000 American troops in Vietnam, only about 100,000 were in combat infantry battalions; the rest provided rear-echelon support. Even when not "on the lines"—that is, on defensive perimeters in dug-in positions—the troops lived in long, tin-roofed barracks, or "hootches," constructed of plywood, wired for electricity, and featuring long, screened windows for the tropical climate; these were quite different from the almost windowless

> "I still need Marines who can shoot and salute.
> But I need Marines who can fix jet engines
> and man sophisticated radar sets, as well."
>
> *Gen Robert E. Cushman, Jr., CMC, 1974*

ABOVE: Gen Robert E. Cushman, Jr., twenty-fifth commandant, 1972–1975, was graduated from the Naval Academy and commissioned in 1935. Assigned to sea duty, he was aboard the USS *Philadelphia* at Pearl Harbor, subsequently participating in the battles of Bougainville, Guam, and Iwo Jima. In the Vietnam War, LtGen Cushman commanded II MAF from 1967 through the pullout of III MAF in June 1971. Following this command, Cushman was assigned to the CIA, then to HQMC; he served as CMC during a period of internal turmoil in the ranks of the Corps.

RIGHT: "The wall" at the Vietnam Veterans Memorial on the Mall in Washington, D.C., includes the names of the more than thirteen thousand Marines who died in the war. Dedicated on 13 November 1982, the memorial is, unfortunately, an epitaph to defeat.

Quonset huts of past wars. Thus a squad in rear duty lived in "squad bays," slept on cots, had electric lighting, and could purchase refrigerators, radios, hi-fis, all the beer they could drink, and all the snacks they could eat from any of the five PXs set up in Da Nang. Whereas PX facilities in past wars had been spartan, those in Vietnam were almost on a par with today's Wal-Marts. Almost anything could be bought, from cameras to condoms, both of which produced a brisk business.

from the north and east. The 34th MAU and the headquarters of 4th MAB waited offshore as the landing force of the Sixth Fleet as a precaution.

In July of the following year, the 34th MAU was called upon to evacuate U.S. citizens and foreign nationals from the island of Cyprus as Turkish paratroops invaded and seized the disputed northern half of the island from the Greeks. Mobs attacked the U.S. Embassy in Nicosia, the capital, overcoming Marine guards and killing the U.S. ambassador, Rodger Davies.

In the Meantime ...

In November 1973, the two-week Yom Kippur War broke out when Egyptian forces attacked Israel across the Suez Canal while Syria and Jordan attacked

Recapitulation

No war is easy, and anyone who has ever seen combat will tell you that it is hell. All battles and firefights are ugly, violent, lethal, fearful, and unforgettable;

however—not to diminish in any way anyone's participation in Vietnam—there simply were no battles of great significance or ferocity that could compare with Marine battles in Korea or in the first and second world wars. None of the battles in Vietnam were decisive to the point that they changed the course of events; they were indecisive repeats of repeats. That alone contributed to the malaise the war created. Worse, when those who fought such tough battles returned to the United States, they did so not to national acclaim, not as heroes, but to national indifference, even scorn.

The total force-level high for III MAF in South Vietnam had been 85,755. By 1973, 12,929 Marines had been killed in combat and 88,542 had been wounded—almost as many as in World War II. Eighty percent of those wounded returned to combat duty. Total Marine Corps strength had grown to 317,400 during a period of combat that spanned almost seven years. In that period, from 1965 to 1971, 794,000 Marines served; only 669,000 had served in World War II. Fifty-seven Medals of Honor were awarded to Marines for action during the course of the Vietnam War.

The war in Vietnam was ultimately a fiasco, largely because misguided civilian politics interfered with any hope for clear-cut military objectives. What could have been a victory of sorts instead turned into a humiliating defeat for the United States. After expending so much American blood and treasure over so long a time, it was a terrible tragedy to witness the beautiful country the United States had tried to save succumb to the enemy—although to those opposed to the U.S. actions it was a relief.

Inscribed on the Vietnam Veterans Memorial in Washington, D.C., are 58,000 names of Americans who died during this long conflict. These names are not a tribute to victory, but a testament to a senseless defeat.

ANTICLIMAX

A month after the United States' ignominious abandonment of and evacuation from South Vietnam, the communist Khmer Rouge of neighboring Cambodia seized the American container ship *Mayaguez* off their coast while that vessel was en route to Thailand. With Navy and Marine units no longer on the scene, the U.S. Air Force commander in Thailand, by order of President Gerald Ford, ordered fifteen Air Force helicopters and a Marine battalion from Okinawa

to attempt a rescue of the captured civilian crew. When the Marines boarded the ship two days later, they found it abandoned; it was presumed that the crew had been taken to nearby Koh Tang Island.

The events that followed were an unmitigated disaster. The Air Force commanders—ignorant of Navy-Marine assault tactics—ordered Air Force helicopters onto the island without prior aerial surveillance, intelligence gathering, or air strikes. Untrained in vertical-assault operations, the Air Force choppers, carrying Marines, met with fierce ground fire, and two of them went down in flames—with their human cargo still aboard. After unloading the Marines, another helicopter crashed into the sea. The two hundred Marines found themselves stranded in the midst of hostile territory without naval support, close air support, or means of resupply. Unskilled in close air support, Air Force fighters proved ineffective, as did a single, covering Air Force AC-130 gunship.

Some Marine reinforcements finally arrived much later and helped hold a landing zone for extraction under fire. Forty-one Marines were wounded and eleven were killed; three others were inadvertently left behind, subject to the brutal vengeance of the Khmer Rouge, when Air Force choppers refused to return to rescue them for fear of exposure to ground fire. Two seamen and two airmen also died. Worse, it was later discovered that the hurried operation that cost so many lives had been unnecessary, since the merchant marine crew of the *Mayaguez* had already been taken to another island and were in the process of being freed when the Marines initiated their attack on Koh Tang.

It was a humiliating finale to the larger humiliation of the defeat in Vietnam, and it presaged future ill-conceived ad hoc "joint" operations that would also fail, although well-trained Navy-Marine teams would most likely have conducted the operation successfully.

Vietnam Service Medal

Republic of Vietnam Campaign Medal

Vietnam Gallantry Cross with Palm

"Some people spend an entire lifetime wondering if they made a difference in the world. But the Marines don't have that problem."

President Ronald Reagan, 1985

The wound to the nation caused by the war in Vietnam continued to fester, and the rest of the 1970s and the 1980s offered little redemption. Mercifully, the draft had ended in 1973, and in the face of the bitter aftertaste of Vietnam and a youthful culture turned increasingly antiwar, antimilitary, and antiauthority, the armed services resorted to an all-volunteer status. Furthermore, during these two decades, the Marine Corps still had to fight against hostile administrations and congressional critics, despite previous laws guaranteeing its existence and its numerous successes as the nation's premier Force-in-Readiness.

EXPEDITIONARY OPERATIONS

Meanwhile, the Marine Corps was active around the globe. In 1975, Marine Amphibious Units (MAUs) participated in joint NATO exercises in Norway. By 1980, a totally new concept in logistics had been developed and put into operation by the Marine Corps: the prepositioning of supplies in parts of the world where armed conflicts were likely to occur. On the small island of Diego Garcia in the Indian Ocean, for example, supplies, equipment, and ammunition for a Marine Expeditionary Brigade (MEB) were stockpiled on Maritime Prepositioned Ships (MPS) for future emergency use. Later in the decade, the Corps was involved in putting down Communist insurgencies and combating illegal drug trafficking in Central America and the Caribbean, especially in El Salvador.

In November 1979, the U.S. Embassy in Tehran, Iran, was seized by anti-American militants and sixty-five Americans were taken hostage, including the eighteen-man Marine security guard. The stumbling efforts of the Carter administration to negotiate their release proved ineffective, and they were held in captivity for more than a year. In April 1980, an attempt to rescue these hostages through a joint effort of Navy, Army, Air Force, and Marine special ops, designated Operation Eagle Claw (JTF 1-79), ended in utter disaster. On 25 April, eight Navy RH-53D long-range mine-sweeping helicopters (without engine sand filters) piloted by Marine aviators took off from the nuclear carrier *Nimitz* in the Arabian Sea to land an Army Delta Force and Marine Special Ops force on the outskirts of the Iranian capital, a journey of four hundred miles each way. Three were forced to turn back when they experienced engine trouble, jeopardizing the mission.

At the halfway refueling point over the Iranian desert, called Desert One, one of the Navy helicopters collided with an Air Force C-130 refueler. Both of the aircraft crashed, killing three Marines and five airmen. Left with fewer than the minimum number of helicopters required, the mission was abruptly aborted. The hostages were ultimately released on the day of President Ronald Reagan's inauguration, 20 January 1981.

We don't promise you a rose garden

THE MARINES ARE LOOKING
FOR A FEW GOOD MEN.

RIGHT: A Marine AAV positioned in a well-fortified bunker in the Christian sector of Beirut.

BELOW: At the request of the president of Lebanon, U.S. president Ronald Reagan sent Marines to Lebanon to train the Lebanese Christian militia. This action alienated the opposing Muslim and Druze political factions, leading to resistance against the presence of the Marines, and, ultimately, to the destruction of the Marine barracks in 1983.

ABOVE: Gen Louis H. Wilson, a Medal of Honor recipient for service during the battle for Guam, served as the twenty-sixth commandant from 1 July 1975 to 30 June 1979. In a time of national social unrest, Wilson's innovations put straight the turmoil in the ranks that lingered following the Vietnam War.

PAGE 379: This recruiting poster, which features drill instructor Sgt Charles A. Taliano "welcoming" a new recruit, ran from late 1971 to mid-1984.

BELOW: An officer's cover from the 1980s. In the mid-1960s, SecDef Robert McNamara ordered all U.S. military services to conform to black uniform accessories: black shoes, black cap visors and straps, black Sam Browne belts, and black gloves. The Marine Corps thus lost the distinctive, rich cordovan leather that had graced the uniform since the beginning of the twentieth century. Gold leaves (often referred to as "scrambled eggs") on the visors of general officer ranks had been customary since the beginning of the century; it was only in the 1980s, however, that they were approved for field grades (from major to colonel) with the service uniform.

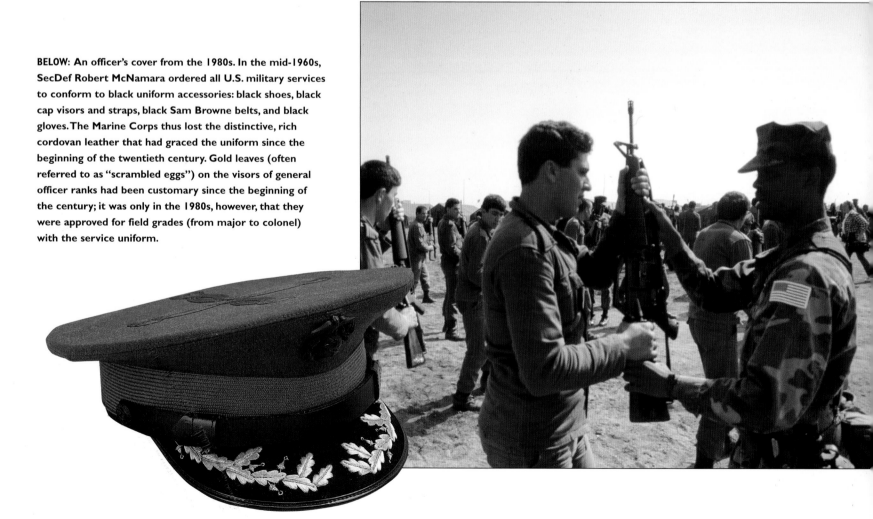

TURMOIL IN THE RANKS

During the 1970s and early 1980s, the Marine Corps and the other services suffered unrest in the ranks— a symptom of the times. The Corps, however, was hit harder than the other branches because the under-qualified recruits it was forced to accept from the draft during Vietnam represented a wider gap from its historically high standards. Until the troublemakers, misfits, and drug users could be eliminated and replaced with better recruits, the Corps was plagued by demoralizing turmoil. In the all-volunteer climate introduced after the Vietnam-era draft ended, the other services tried to attract recruits by dangling enticing benefits and perquisites while minimizing toughness and hazards. The Marine Corps, by contrast, stuck to its tougher, higher standards. Its very successful Vietnam-era advertising campaign, created by the J. Walter Thompson advertising agency in New York, used the slogan "We Don't Promise You a Rose Garden," which was inspired by a popular song of the time. A more challenging slogan was adopted later: "We're Looking for a Few Good Men." The campaigns were successful in attracting a higher caliber of recruit, and the Corps' personnel problems slowly abated.

For a brief period, the Marine Corps had the worst rates of imprisonment, absences without leave, and courts-martial of any of the armed forces. Drug and alcohol abuse within its ranks was second only to that of the Navy's personnel. The tall and imposing CMC Louis H. Wilson, Jr.—a Medal of Honor recipient for Guam—was responsible for bringing the Marine Corps out of its doldrums. Wilson combated the drug problem head-on by divesting the Corps of the troublemakers and misfits and seeking more high school graduates as recruits. One positive factor was the increase in female recruits from three thousand to more than nine thousand by the early 1980s. Women Marines tended to have fewer disciplinary problems and were a leveling factor in male behavior. By trimming the Corps and bringing it back up to former standards, Wilson restored its professionalism.

CMC Wilson also had been legislative assistant to former commandants and knew his way around Capitol Hill. Staunch Marine Corps advocates, such as Senator John Stennis, chairman of the Senate Armed

Chesty Puller: Legend of the Corps

A feisty, formidable fighter, Lewis B. "Chesty" Puller, Jr., spent thirty-seven years from the 1920s through the 1960s fighting Haitian and Nicaraguan guerrillas, Japanese, North Koreans, and Chinese. On the way, he accumulated five Navy Crosses (the award next highest to the Medal of Honor), Silver and Bronze Stars for valor, the Army Distinguished Service Cross, three Air Medals, Purple Hearts for wounds, and a slew of campaign ribbons, making him the most decorated Marine in history. After a rough start during the downsizing of the Corps following World War I, Puller's aggressiveness, harsh discipline, and popularity with the troops he led—plus an undisguised disdain for rear-echelon staff work—earned him his reputation and career advancement. A lieutenant colonel at the beginning of World War II, the tough, small-framed, barrel-chested Puller led the 1st Battalion, 1st Marines, at Guadalcanal. Two years later, he was a colonel and regimental commander in the assault on Peleliu in the toughest of its fighting.

Although he feared his career might be over with the drastic cutbacks in the armed forces in 1946—especially in the Marine Corps—he was picked for infantry commands, and later led the 1st Marines into Korea in 1950 at Inchon, on to Seoul, and into the frozen Chosin Reservoir in North Korea. His exploits, fame, and military decorations continued to amass, and he was written about extensively, becoming a living legend.

Promoted to brigadier and then major general, his postwar assignments were equally successful and heralded. But his health began to deteriorate in his late fifties and a mild stroke forced him to retire, despite his vociferous objections and legal challenges.

His son, Lewis B. Puller III, on whom he doted, was commissioned a second lieutenant and served in Vietnam in 1968. Tragically, he was severely wounded by a land mine, losing both legs and parts of both hands. The shock of seeing his son's condition no doubt hastened Chesty's demise. He succumbed on 11 October 1971 at the age of seventy-three.

Lewis III wrote a book about his life as the son of a famous Marine hero entitled *Favored Son*. The agony of his wound-handicapped life proved too much, however. The favored son took his own life in 2000.

—HAC

"You don't hurt 'em if you don't hit 'em."

LtGen Lewis B. "Chesty" Puller, 1962

Forces Committee, and other senators and congressmen, wrote a clause into the Defense Authorization Bill of 1978 that firmly placed the CMC as a full member of the JCS—a position that the CMC had theretofore held only for affairs specifically involving the Marine Corps.

THE LEBANON DEBACLE

Between 1982 and 1984, Marines again landed in Beirut, Lebanon, this time in the midst of an Israeli invasion to oust the retreating Palestinian Liberation Organization (PLO) under Yasser Arafat. In late

August 1982, the Marines, serving as part of a multinational peacekeeping force, guarded the docks to ensure the safe evacuation of Arafat and his PLO irregulars to Libya.

The following April, terrorists car-bombed the U.S. Embassy in Beirut, killing sixty-three people, including one of the Marine embassy guards. A month later, the 24th MAU landed to augment the 22d MAU. In August, the Christian president-elect of Lebanon, Bashir Gemayel, who had originally invited the Marines in, was assassinated, leading to the Israeli takeover of West Beirut. Further complicating a nasty situation, Lebanese-Christian militias entered two Palestinian refugee camps in Israeli-controlled areas, where they massacred hundreds of civilians. The slain president's brother, Amin, became president in his place and asked the Marines to train his Christian faction army; the Reagan administration agreed. This turned out to be a costly mistake that alienated the heretofore balanced Druze and Muslim factions. The result was that the Marines were looked upon as stooges of the Lebanese government, and attacks against Marines in the streets of Beirut—stonings and grenade bombardments—became common. The era of goodwill toward the United States had ended.

That end was punctuated at dawn on 23 October 1983, when a Mercedes truck loaded with six tons of TNT sped past startled Lebanese and U.S. Marine guards (who were not allowed to carry loaded weapons) at the Marine compound and exploded as it crashed through the glass front doors of the temporary barracks. The explosion blew away the vertical posts holding up the four concrete-slab floors, which crumpled down in a crashing heap of debris and

LEFT: The commander of BLT 1 of the 8th Marines, LtCol Larry Gerlach, addresses his troops in front of a civilian building contracted for use as their barracks, on 9 October 1983. Little did anyone realize that only fourteen days later a suicide bomber would crash into the building at that very spot, detonating tons of explosives that would totally destroy the structure and kill 220 Marines and 21 other service members. Gerlach himself was injured in the attack, after which more than 80 survivors were pulled from the wreckage.

BELOW: The explosion and subsequent cloud of debris rising from the collapse of the four-story building that fateful morning was caught by a Marine photographer from several miles away.

ABOVE: Col Timothy Geraghty, commander of the 8th Marines, of which the ill-fated 1st Battalion suffered the brunt of the terrorist attack. Unfortunately, the rules of engagement for the operation disallowed the Marines guarding the building from arming their weapons, or they could have possibly been able to stop the racing vehicle carrying the explosives.

ABOVE: An official Marine Corps photo of the aftermath shows Marines searching the rubble for survivors and the dead immediately following the tragedy. As this was taking place, intermittent enemy sniper fire pinged around them.

ABOVE: The twenty-eighth commandant, Paul X. Kelley (1 July 1983–30 June 1987), had the unfortunate Beirut barracks incident occur on his watch—a blight that could tarnish an otherwise brilliant career.

RIGHT: The 22d MAU—minus its 1st Battalion, 8th Marines, wiped out in the barracks attack—was ordered out of Lebanon in February 1984, thus ending their extended "peacekeeping" mission in the once-prosperous but now war-torn country. Here, 2d Battalion, 8th Marines, embarks on landing craft to reboard their LHA, standing offshore in the Mediterranean.

RIGHT: An on-the-spot pen-and-ink sketch of Marines in Lebanon in 1983 by Marine combat artist Maj Jack Dyer, USMCR. A combat artist in the previous Vietnam War, Dyer became curator of the Marine Corps Museum at the Navy Yard, a post he has held for a quarter of a century.

human remains. Eighty Marines and many other survivors were pulled out of the wreckage—under intermittent sniper fire—but the attack still claimed 220 Marine lives (the equivalent of an entire Marine infantry company). This ghastly attack resulted not only in numerous deaths, but also in the ending of the career of the commanding officer, Col Timothy J. Geraghty. Repercussions were felt all the way up the chain of command to the commandant, Gen Paul X. Kelley, whose chance of becoming the first Marine to be chairman of the Joint Chiefs of Staff went up in smoke. Within a month, all Marines had been pulled out of Beirut.

As a living memorial to those who died in the Beirut barracks attack, trees were planted near the entrance to the main gate at Camp Lejeune, each with a plaque bearing the name of one of the fallen.

OPERATION URGENT FURY

A few days after the Lebanon fiasco, a joint task force operation, Urgent Fury, gave the Marine Corps the opportunity to remove some of the sting of Beirut. The tiny independent island nation of Grenada, in the Windward Islands chain in the Caribbean Sea, had been in political turmoil for some time and had been virtually taken over by Cuban Communists.

On 25 October 1983, the 82d Airborne, 75th Rangers, Navy SEALs, Army Special Ops teams, and the 22d Marine Amphibious Unit invaded the island. The effort was plagued with interservice operational confusion and totally inadequate intelligence gathering. In six days of desultory landings and movements—including the Marine rescue of a SEAL team and the Marines' capture of four-fifths of the island—five thousand U.S. forces finally overcame Grenada's ragtag People's Revolutionary Army, most of which gladly surrendered, along with its Cuban military advisers and militiamen. Thirty-six Cubans, thirty-three U.S. soldiers, and three Marine helicopter pilots were killed, but the country was liberated, the American citizens were evacuated, and a reasonably stable representative government was installed. For the Marines, it had been a successful live-fire exercise with few casualties.

CMC ALFRED M. GRAY'S "WARFIGHTING"

Gruff Gen Alfred M. Gray took the helm as Marine commandant in July 1987 and immediately put his personal stamp on the Corps. "Amphibious" was changed to "Expeditionary," so Marine Amphibious Units became Marine Expeditionary Units, and the Development and Education Command at Marine Corps Schools, Quantico, became the Marine Corps Combat Development Command. The revised command had five components: 1) the Marine Air-Ground Task Force, whose new mission was termed Warfighting, 2) Training and Education, 3) Intelligence, 4) "Wargaming" and Assessment, and 5) Information Technology. The commandant's desire was to establish the Warfighting Center as a brain trust for the areas of operational concepts, studies, doctrine, and plans. He also streamlined the acquisition of weapons, vehicles, and equipment by creating a Marine Corps Research, Development, and Acquisition Command at Quantico.

The Marine Corps would now roll up the sleeves of its camouflage-green utilities and concentrate on its mission in the field. Gray even carried his no-frills

LEFT: Although in reality only a live-fire exercise against a motley group of semi-trained Cubans garrisoned there, the U.S. invasion of the tiny Caribbean island of Grenada to oust Cuban Communists was a rapid success, providing a distraction, at least, a week after the barracks tragedy. Here, Marines patrol a street in the capital, St. George's.

BELOW: Reviewing the Marine guard contingent at the U.S. Naval Academy is academy graduate Col John Ripley. Ripley, the hero of the bridge battle at Dong Ha, Vietnam, in 1972, returned to teach at the academy before retiring. For his action in single-handedly destroying the bridge during the North Vietnamese "Easter Offensive" he was awarded the Navy Cross.

Sea Duty

From the Continental Marines of 1775 until 1998, detachments of Marines have served on board U.S. Navy warships. In the eighteenth and nineteenth centuries, Marine detachments used small arms and ships' guns to fight enemy ships, boarded enemy ships, and formed landing parties for assaults ashore. When a larger force of Marines was called for—as it was for the Seminole, Mexican, Civil, and Spanish-American wars—ship detachments and Navy Yard guards were merged into provisional battalions. In the twentieth century, sea duty became less important. It was still useful, however, in its traditional shipboard role and to retain a close identity with the Navy as part of the Navy-Marine Corps Team.

During World War II, more than ten thousand Marines served aboard thirty-eight fleet aircraft carriers, twenty-five battleships, and seventy-four cruisers. They manned the ships' 5-inch, 40mm, and 20mm antiaircraft guns, served as orderlies for admirals and ships' captains, and provided security aboard ship and in port. Carrier and battleship detachments numbered up to one hundred Marines, while cruisers carried up to fifty. Although landing parties were not used in the Pacific, Marines from cruisers were landed to accept the surrender of Vichy French and German garrisons in the Mediterranean. In addition, Marine Transport Quartermaster teams served on APAs (amphibious transports) and AKAs (amphibious cargo ships) to ensure the proper loading of equipment and supplies for landings. Such teams are still in use as Combat Cargo Officers.

In the 1970s, ships' landing parties were no longer organized. By the 1990s, few of the ships that required Marines were left. Battleships and cruisers were now smaller and packed with guided missiles, leaving little room for Marines. Nevertheless, eleven aircraft carriers remained, each with a small detachment of one officer and twenty-five enlisted Marines to provide security for the nuclear weapons on board. On 1 January 1998, the last detachments were ordered to disband and non-deployed detachments stood down on 31 January. Upon return to the States of the USS *George Washington* (CVN-73), its detachment was disestablished on 1 May. The eleven officers and 275 enlisted men in these detachments created a second Fleet Anti-terrorism Security Team (FAST) company. Marines from the two FAST companies are rotationally deployed and placed under the control of Naval Forces Europe, Pacific Fleet, and Naval Forces Central Command. One of their missions is shipboard security.

—BN

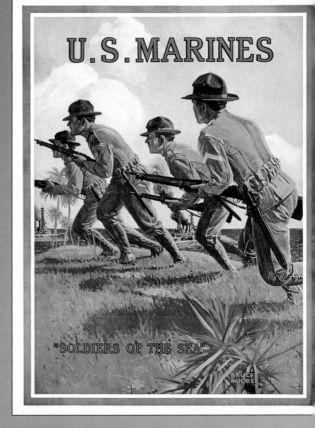

ABOVE: An early-twentieth-century recruiting poster depicts a Marine landing party in Cuba or the Philippines.

LEFT: A postcard showing a Marine detachment aboard an unidentified ship circa 1900. It is likely that they were photographed during the around-the-world cruise of the Great White Fleet. They appear to be equipped with Kraig-Jorgensen rifles.

U. S. Sailors Life "Marines Drill"

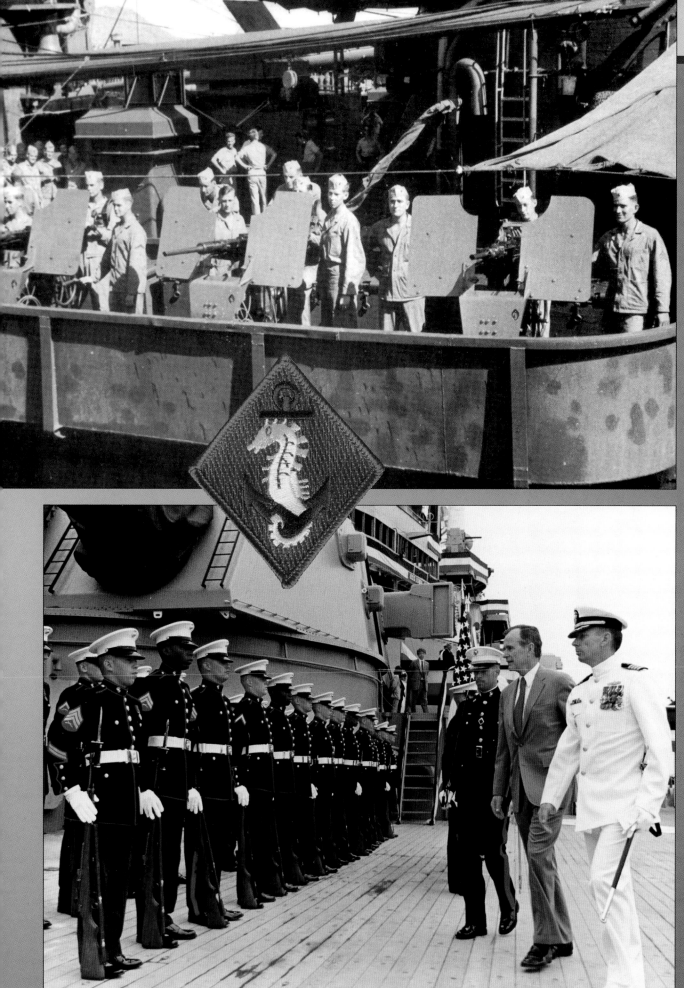

Navy Sea Service Deployment Ribbon

LEFT: Marine 20mm antiaircraft gun crews on board the USS *New Mexico* (BB-40), during World War II, in the Pacific.

INSET: The Sea Duty patch (ca. 1946) worn by Marines of shipboard detachments.

LEFT: Vice President George H.W. Bush inspects the Marine detachment at the recommissioning of the USS *Iowa* on 28 April 1984. The vice president is flanked by the Marine commander on his right and the ship's skipper, Capt Gerald Gneckow, USN, on his left. Bush himself was a naval aviator in World War II, and was shot down by hostile fire during the Iwo Jima campaign while flying a TBF Avenger torpedo bomber over Chiji Jima, just north of Iwo. He was rescued from the water by a U.S. submarine.

ABOVE: The "Field Commandant," Gen Alfred M. Gray. As twenty-ninth CMC (1987–1991), Gray took the Corps back to basics as a field expeditionary force. A no-nonsense, to-the-point Marine, he eschewed the dressier uniforms, preferring field attire—even when addressing congressional committees on Capitol Hill.

RIGHT: A Marine self-propelled 155mm howitzer configured for desert fighting.

style into the halls of Congress, where he testified on Marine matters dressed not in a Service "A" uniform with ribbons, but in neat, starched camouflage utilities. He personified a field—not a parade—Marine, leading a "Field" Expeditionary Corps.

Gray also established the Marine Corps University at Quantico, the core of which would be the existing schools: Amphibious Warfare, Command and Staff, Staff NCO Academy, Communications Officers' School, and the Basic School for junior officers. A $12 million research center named after him was built at Quantico in 1993 to house the university.

CMC Gray had turned the Corps around and taken it out of the post-Vietnam stand-down of the 1970s and 1980s.

All the while, MEUs were active in the Persian Gulf in numerous patrol actions in a continuing "tanker war" instigated by the Iraqis, who were irritated by their stalemate against their archenemy, Iran.

OPERATION JUST CAUSE

In December 1989, an operation was conducted in Panama to oust corrupt dictator Manuel Noriega. As in Grenada six years earlier, this effort combined different branches of the U.S. military. U.S. Army troops and Marine Expeditionary Units were flown in to augment the Army garrisons stationed in Panama. Although often erroneously referred to as an invasion, it was nothing of the kind: U.S. forces had been permanently stationed to guard the Panama Canal

since the United States completed the excavation and construction of that waterway in 1915. An "invasion" implies the seizing of territory from another country where the attackers' presence had never been felt before—as had been the case in Grenada.

After a short siege, Noriega was finally flushed out, and imprisoned in the United States on drug-trafficking charges. Marines guarded a petroleum tank farm, and other American units took over Panamanian traffic control and secured bridges and roadways while restoring law and order and reinstating a duly elected president. Few civilians were hurt and 1,200 hostile Panamanians surrendered and were disarmed.

UPDATED WEAPONRY AND EQUIPMENT

A long list of new weapons was adopted during the 1980s. The trusty old Colt .45-caliber Model 1911 semiautomatic pistol was replaced by the Italian-made 15-clip 9mm Beretta. The M16A semiautomatic rifle was upgraded to the M16A2; the M249 Squad Automatic Weapon (SAW) took over the role of the old BAR; and the M240 replaced the M60 machine gun. For a short time, the three four-man fire-team squads were reduced to two five-man fire teams around the SAW,

ABOVE: An M-240 40mm grenade launcher mounted atop an AAV added tremendous short-range firepower to the vehicle's 25mm cannon.

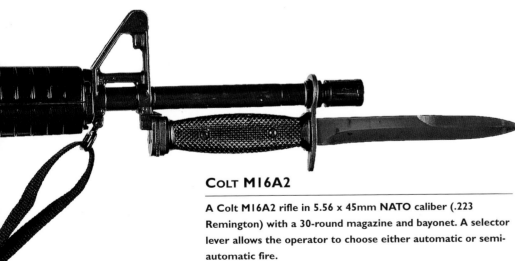

COLT M16A2

A Colt M16A2 rifle in 5.56 x 45mm NATO caliber (.223 Remington) with a 30-round magazine and bayonet. A selector lever allows the operator to choose either automatic or semi-automatic fire.

9MM BERETTA SEMIAUTOMATIC PISTOL

Replacing the venerable Colt M1911 semiautomatic pistol in the early 1980s, this 9mm Italian-made pistol offered certain advantages over the three-quarter-century-old .45-caliber Colt. Its trigger guard was designed for a two-handed grip, and its 15-shot magazine, with one round in the chamber, offered a bit more firepower. During the first Gulf War, however, only fifteen rounds of ammunition were distributed to the staff officers who carried it. (The author convinced the armory in Al Jubail to give him an extra magazine, so he went into Kuwait with thirty rounds!)

thus reducing the number of Marines in a platoon
from forty-eight to thirty-six, and an additional battalion was added to
each regiment,
thus configuring
a quadrangular
rather than trian-
gular formation. The Dragon Anti-tank (AT) missile
system was introduced, as was the AT-4 anti-armor
rocket, the M2 .50-caliber heavy machine gun, the M19
40mm machine gun, and new 60 and 81mm mortars.

The little workhorse of the previous three wars,
the Jeep ¼-ton vehicle was replaced by the larger,
automatic-transmission High Mobility
Multipurpose Wheeled Vehicle (HMMWV,
or Humvee). Light Armored Vehicles
(LAVs) were also tried out for the
first time in the Panama operation, and they proved highly
proficient and adaptable.
A newly designed helmet,
somewhat similar in appearance to that
used by the Germans in the two world wars, was
adopted, as was an improved flak jacket. Both were
made of Kevlar, which is lighter and more impervious
to bullets and shrapnel than the metal used in the
Marines' previous helmet.

Vehicle-mounted, Tube-launched, Optically-
tracked, Wire-guided (TOW) missiles came into the
inventory, as did light 155mm howitzers, replacing
the trusty 105s. In 1985, the Marine Corps adopted
the M1A1 as its main battle tank, with its 120mm

smoothbore gun replacing the aging M60s; the new tanks, however, were slower in delivery than the fast, 8-wheeled LAVs, with their 25mm rapid-fire automatic cannon. The LAVs added rapid mobility to ground units and would prove their worth in the 1991 Gulf War.

A unique sea-surface vessel was also developed to augment the conventional landing craft nested in the rear hulls of the LHAs. Called the Landing Craft Air Cushion (LCAC), this raftlike pontoon platform, with externally mounted aircraft-type, pusher-type propellers, skimmed over the water at a little more than forty knots and could transport 60-ton payloads of troops, supplies, tanks, or other vehicles from ship to shore.

A minor milestone in development that affected all troops was the change in the individual combat ration, the Meal, Ready-to-Eat (MRE). Packaged in hermetically sealed foil packets that fit easily into pockets, MREs could be eaten cold or hot and were fortified with vitamins, proteins, and energy boosters. They were so rich that one meal would often suffice for an entire day. The evolution from the canned "Bully Beef" of the Spanish-American War through the "monkey meat" (corned beef) and "goldfish" (canned salmon) with hardtack biscuits of World War I, the K- and C-rations of World War II and Korea, and Vietnam's modified C-rations to the MREs was a major step forward. Nevertheless, the improved chow was given the jocular appellation "Meals Rejected by Everyone" by the troops.

M2 BROWNING .50-CALIBER MACHINE GUN

In continuous use since World War I, the Browning .50-caliber machine gun is now standard in the U.S. military as the M2. Affectionately known as the "Ma Deuce," the M2 is short-recoil operated and fires from a disintegrating-link belt at the rate of 450 to 550 rounds per minute, with an effective range of one mile. (Note: The gun shown is the Belgian FN version, slightly different from the U.S. issue.)

ABOVE, TOP: A Marine artillery gunner trains an M109 towed howitzer on a target.

ABOVE: The gun crew of an M109 howitzer rams a round into the breech.

Marines Confront Russians Over North Atlantic

Little-known episodes of the cold war were the confrontation of Russian aerial reconnaissance patrols with Marine combat air patrols over the North Atlantic and the Sea of Japan.

In the autumn of 1979, Marine fighter/attack squadron VMFA-115, flying F-4J Phantoms with smokeless engines and upgraded weapons systems, rotated three weeks' duty with an Air Force squadron at Keflavik, Iceland. With their own Marine KC-130 aerial refuelers accompanying them, the Marine air patrols were able to extend their range by three hundred nautical miles. Since this was farther than the Air Force patrols they were accustomed to, the Russians became mistakenly concerned that the U.S. Navy had an aircraft carrier operating in the North Atlantic. The Marine squadron had several close encounters with four-engine Russian Bear patrol-bombers.

—HAC

TOP: During the height of the cold war, Marine aviation provided combat air and reconnaissance patrols, tracking Russian long-range patrol planes on both sides of the world. Flying an F-4 Phantom with VMFA-531 out of Atsugi, Japan, in 1965 Capt Robert Hanke, USMC, approached to within ten feet of the wingtip of a Russian Badger—close enough for the pilots to exchange hand greetings. Hanke served as a regular and Reserve Marine Corps officer for more than twenty-two years before retiring as a colonel in 1984.

RIGHT: 1stLt Tom Benes, USMC, in a deployment in 1979 of VMFA-115 from Iceland in Exercise Blue Ice, overtakes a Russian counter-rotating propeller-driven, long-range Bear patrol-bomber over the North Atlantic. The Marine squadron's presence confused the Russians into thinking there was a U.S. aircraft carrier operating in the area. Benes rose to command a squadron in the Gulf War and to the rank of major general.

MARINE AVIATION

Marine Corps aviation during the 1970s and 1980s was marked by considerable progress. Although the CH-46 Sea Knight was still the operational workhorse for vertical envelopment, a new, larger CH-53 Sea Stallion and CH-53E Super Stallion were introduced for longer, heavier-lift missions. Future planning for the fast-approaching twenty-first century called for even faster heavier-lift-capable choppers with longer range for vertical envelopment. Thus, a rocky path of research and development lay in store for the concept of a tilt-rotor aircraft, the V-22 Osprey, which would eventually replace the CH-46s and 53s.

The V/STOL AV-8A Harrier started as a small, experimental fighter aircraft that perched vertically on its tail in order to take off straight upward. In its final, perfected incarnation, its two lateral jet-engine exhaust ducts swiveled to thrust downward in order to push the Harrier up into a horizontal position, then swiveled horizontally to assume conventional forward flight. The Harrier could even slow its forward flight in midair, stop, hover, rotate 360 degrees while hovering, and descend vertically. It was ideal for operating off ships' decks or from small clearings during infantry operations. By 1990, there were eight Harrier squadrons on LHAs in Expeditionary MAGTFs.

As for high-performance and close air support, McDonnell-Douglas FA-18 Hornets replaced the A-4 Skyhawks and F-4 Phantoms. The reliable A-6 Intruders, however, continued to be used as longer-range bombers and, in their EA-6B configuration, as electronic warfare mainstays.

Marine Fighter Attack Squadron (All Weather)-242

Marine Fighter Training Squadron-401

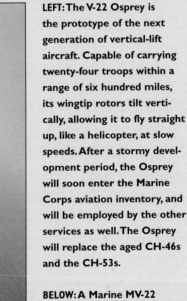

LEFT: The V-22 Osprey is the prototype of the next generation of vertical-lift aircraft. Capable of carrying twenty-four troops within a range of six hundred miles, its wingtip rotors tilt vertically, allowing it to fly straight up, like a helicopter, at slow speeds. After a stormy development period, the Osprey will soon enter the Marine Corps aviation inventory, and will be employed by the other services as well. The Osprey will replace the aged CH-46s and the CH-53s.

BELOW: A Marine MV-22 Osprey with tilt-rotors in the takeoff position revs up on the runway as a Marine F/A-18 Hornet taxis after landing at MCAS (Marine Corps Air Station) Miramar in California.

Marine Fighter Attack Squadron-115

END OF THE COLD WAR

The cold war between the West and Communism—specifically between the two superpowers, the Soviet Union and the United States—fizzled out in 1989 under Soviet premier Mikhail Gorbachev. The detested Berlin Wall came tumbling down, the Soviet Union disintegrated, and Communism in the former Soviet bloc slowly gave way to a shaky form of capitalism. Former Soviet satellites became independent nations to adjust to a fast-changing world. Only hard-line Cuba, North Korea, and China stuck to the unworkable, despotic Communist system.

The removal of the threat of international Communism did not, however, put an end to the necessity of military alertness on the part of the free world. Nuclear weapons and other military hardware formerly under Soviet control were now in less secure hands, and "rogue" nations began to arise, setting the stage for a new kind of trouble. When the whistle blew in August 1990, the Marines were ready.

THE PERSIAN GULF WAR: 1990–1991

The last thing anyone could have imagined at the beginning of August 1990 was that the world would have another major war on its hands, much less in

southwest Asia. But a major war did begin when Iraq's Saddam Hussein, in a lightning stroke, invaded and conquered Kuwait, his tiny, peaceful neighbor situated near where the Tigris and Euphrates rivers join to form the Shatt al-Arab River and empty into the northern end of the Persian Gulf. Defenseless, oil-rich Kuwait watched helplessly as Iraq's vaunted Republican Guard armored divisions swept all the way through itsmassive oil fields and down its coastal highway to the southern border with Saudi Arabia.

The world was thrown into near panic. The Kuwaiti oil fields were already captured; and if those of Saudi Arabia were taken as well, more than half the world's oil supply would be either lost or under the control of elements unfriendly to the West—the biggest consumer of Persian Gulf oil. Furthermore, the members of the ruling Saudi royal family were at risk of being deposed should the country fall, and there was no secondary level of bureaucracy to carry the country forward.

Saudi Arabia, a theocratic monarchy dominated by Muslims of the fundamentalist Wahhabi sect, had only in the previous three decades transformed itself from a medieval, desert kingdom peopled by nomads into a superficially modern country, with a major north-south divided superhighway system laid down over its sandy wastes. The danger was immediately apparent to Western nations dependent on Middle East oil, as well as to the beleaguered Israelis, who feared a wider confrontation with the hostile Arab world that surrounded them.

Unhesitatingly, President George H.W. Bush reacted by forming a coalition of Western and friendly Arab countries, while badgering Congress for war powers that would enable him to act. Rather than waiting for everything to come together, Bush acted, ordering U.S. forces to Saudi Arabia to defend it. He was fortunate to be surrounded by a strong team of advisers, especially SecDef Dick Cheney. The chairman of the Joint Chiefs of Staff was Army Gen Colin Powell. Command of CENTCOM, the military headquarters at McDill Field in Tampa, Florida, that controlled U.S. military activities in the Middle East and southwest Asia, had only recently passed from Marine Gen George Christ to Army Gen Norman Schwarzkopf. Powell urged sanctions against Saddam Hussein, rather than military action, but Bush and Cheney overruled him. Thus a military buildup, dubbed Operation Desert Shield, got under way quickly, while the coalition of affected nations was still coming together.

**Marine Attack Training
Squadron-203**

LEFT: A Marine pilot of
VMFA-121 flies his F/A-18D
Hornet.

BELOW: Marine pilot Maj Fred
Schenk sits silhouetted in the
cockpit of his Marine AV-8B
Harrier in the Persian Gulf,
awaiting the signal for his
non-catapult takeoff down
the flight deck of its "mother"
LHA, *Nassau*, which was the
flagship for the 4th MEB.

ABOVE: The venerable Marine
EA-6B Prowler, a four-place,
greatly modified version
of the earlier A-6 Intruder
of the Vietnam era. During
the Gulf War, most Prowlers
were based at Sheik Isa Air
Base on the island of Bahrain
off the Saudi coast.

ABOVE: The unit patch of
the 3d Marine Aircraft Wing,
Aviation Combat Element
(Forward), more commonly
known as the 3d MAW
ACE(F).

The Marine Corps was immediately alerted to prepare one—possibly two—Marine Expeditionary Forces for deployment as soon as possible to southwest Asia. MEBs and MEUs already afloat steamed toward the Persian Gulf. The Corps mobilized at a rapid pace; by 7 August Reservists were also being called up.

To bolster a shaky Saudi Arabia, presumably a staunch ally of the United States, a show of force was necessary. Air Force fighters immediately flew to the airport of the capital, Riyadh, as did elements of the 82d Army Airborne Division. Their presence reassured the Saudis and played well on television back in the United States. The press, however, missed the big story. While the TV cameras were rolling at the Riyadh airport, the Marine prepositioning ships from Diego Garcia and the 7th MEB were arriving at the Saudi port city of Al Jubail and its airport. Thus a full Marine Expeditionary Brigade with all its supplies was landing, ready to fight and hold back the Iraqis, if necessary. Meanwhile, the battalion of the 82d had landed with only a two-day supply of food and ammunition, and would have had to be supported by the Marines if fighting had occurred.

Despite the critical nature of the situation, the Saudis wrestled internally with a wrenching decision: whether to allow Western infidels to profane their holy soil. (That soil was no different from that of neighboring Kuwait, Iraq, the United Arab Emirates, Oman, or Yemen, except that arbitrary lines drawn on a map by the British in 1919 after the Ottoman Turks were driven out had demarcated Saudi Arabia as "holy." The actual holy sites of Mecca and Medina were on the opposite side of the country, far from any conflict.)

When the reluctant decision was made by the Saudis to allow U.S. troops to land in their country, it came with conditions. The Americans were not to stray from their military compounds or venture into any towns, nor were they permitted to fly the American flag; female military personnel were not allowed to wear skirts, had to keep their sleeves rolled down, and had to stay virtually out of sight; Christian chaplains could not wear visible crosses; and no alcohol could enter the country (the one Jewish Navy chaplain brought Manischewitz wine for his services anyway). The U.S. troops were forced to accede to these stipulations.

Maritime Prepositioning Force

Marine Expeditionary Units (MEUs), afloat on three to five ships of a Navy amphibious-ready force, are the "first responders" to any overseas crisis requiring the attention of American troops. The MEU is a combined-arms force built around an infantry battalion, with reinforcing artillery, tanks, engineers, logistic units, and aircraft. When a larger unit is required—a brigade-size MEB or a division air-wing-size MEF—it can take as long as a week to assemble ships, then load and steam from East or West Coast ports, and another week or two to steam the two thousand to eight thousand miles to the beachhead seized by the MEU.

In the mid-1980s, the Marine Corps found a solution to cut this time to less than a week: the Maritime Prepositioning Force. Thirteen large ships were procured or built by the Navy's Military Sealift Command. They are organized into three squadrons, with four ships stationed in the Mediterranean, five on Diego Garcia in the Indian Ocean, and four on Guam and Saipan in the Pacific. The squadrons are under the command of Navy officers, while the ships themselves are commanded and manned by Merchant Marine crews.

Each squadron carries enough heavy weapons, equipment, fuel, food, ammunition, etc., to sustain a seventeen thousand–man MEB for thirty days. The Marines of the MEB, along with their personal gear and weapons and infantry-crew-served weapons, would be flown by Air Force or Civilian Air Fleet (CAF) transports to an airfield seized by the MEU, at which point the Marine Prepositioning Force (MPF) squadron would set sail to meet it. The ships would then be unloaded at dockside in a port or over a beach with lighters carried on board. The MPF can unload and equip an MEB in just three days.

This loading list of a squadron illustrates the magnitude of the operation:

- 5.2 million gallons of fuel
- 30 M1A1 tanks
- 2,174 50,000-pound cargo containers
- 24 Light Armored Vehicles (LAVs)
- 14 50,000-pound container handlers
- 105 Amphibious Assault Vehicles (AAVs)
- 8 25-ton cranes
- 76 TOW missile launchers
- 16 7.5-ton cranes
- 30 155mm howitzers
- 47 floodlight sets
- 6 motorized road graders
- 123 electric generators
- 4 wheeled scraper tractors
- 1 field hospital (200 beds)
- 50 tractors
- 104 3,000-gallon collapsible fuel tanks
- 282 5-ton trucks
- 203 cargo trailers
- 7 Tactical Airfield Fuel Dispensing Systems (TAFDSs)
- 89 powered trailers
- 22 wrecker trucks
- 107 forklift trucks
- 45 dump trucks
- 41 Reverse Osmosis Water Purification Units (ROWPUs)
- 530 Cargo troop carriers (HMMWVs)

The MPF had its first test in Operation Desert Shield, the first phase of the Persian Gulf War, 1990–91. The operation was seamless; the MEU afloat in the Persian Gulf landed and defended the airfield provided by Saudi Arabia. All three MPF squadrons arrived just as the two-division I MEF arrived by air. At the conclusion of the war, the MPF back-loaded the equipment and supplies and returned to their home ports, where the loads were topped off with new gear and the equipment was refurbished for the next mission by civilian and Marine maintenance gangs.

The MPF was so successful that one senior Marine officer joked, "Now everybody [meaning the Army and Air Force] wants one."

—BN

ABOVE: One of the Maritime prepositioned ships unloading at dockside at Al Jubail, Saudi Arabia. Marine Corps planning paid off handsomely when these fully preloaded ships, stationed at Diego Garcia in the Indian Ocean, responded immediately, and within days unloaded supplies for an entire MEB as ground and air troops were arriving during Operation Desert Shield.

The Formidable Enemy

Analysts billed the Iraqi Army as the fourth strongest in the world. In addition to its three specially trained Republican Guard divisions there were forty-four others, including a dozen or so armored, with Russian-made T-55 and T-72 tanks.

All of these forces were soon concentrated in Kuwait, except for the better-trained and better-equipped elite Republican Guards, which remained as a buffer on the northern Kuwaiti border with Iraq. The vast desert wastes west of Kuwait were devoid of Iraqis; the terrain was virtually uninhabited and unmapped, and little was known of its topography. It was considered impenetrable.

Despite the Iraqis' lackluster performance in the preceding war with neighboring Iran, Hussein's weaponry was considered formidable. He had used poison gas in that war, and afterward had massacred an entire town of Kurdish rebels in his own country. There were fears that he had stockpiled large quantities of lethal gas, as well as biological weapons, and would not hesitate to use them. He was known also to have an arsenal of intermediate-range Soviet-made surface-to-surface SCUD missiles, which he could launch at Saudi Arabia and perhaps Israel; he later attacked both countries with such missiles. The strength of his air force of MiG fighters was not known. His armored brigades had an estimated four thousand Russian-made tanks—a match, perhaps, for the Marine M60s and maybe even the as-yet-untested new M1A1 Abrams. He was rumored also to have an artillery piece with a range of one hundred miles. President Bush and the coalition had no illusions as to what they were up against.

Operation Desert Shield

The first phase of the Western-Arab coalition operation, the buildup, was termed Desert Shield. While Congress was debating and President Bush was arm-twisting NATO and friendly Arab countries, U.S. forces were being marshaled and shipped as rapidly as possible to Saudi Arabia. Marine air components of 3d MAW flew into Bahrain, an island country just off the coast of Saudi Arabia in the Persian Gulf. The bulk of the Marine I MEF either landed by ship or was flown in by commercial airliners or in Air Force C-141s to the airfield at Al Jubail. During the height of the U.S. buildup, troops were arriving at the rate of more than 2,000 a day. U.S. forces ultimately reached 500,000 troops.

The 7th MEB had been first to land and was shortly merged into I MEF as it built up to two divisions, the 1st and 2d MarDivs, with the attachment of the British 1st Armoured Division, which was named after the famed "Desert Rats" who fought in North Africa in World War II. Offshore, 4th and 5th MEBs were in PhibRons (Amphibious Squadrons) 2 and 3, cruising on station in the Gulf. They would provide an ever-present threat of an amphibious landing near Kuwait City that would pin down six Iraqi divisions.

OPPOSITE: Newly arrived Marines in formation during the Desert Shield build-up phase of the pending Gulf War. Most would have received desert-warfare training at the Marine Corps Air Ground Combat Center (MCAGCC) at Twentynine Palms, California, prior to arriving in Saudi Arabia.

LEFT, TOP: A Marine in self-made netting camouflage assumes a firing position with his M249 SAW behind a natural berm as two LAV-25s provide backup for him and his squad. The fast-moving Light Attack Vehicles mount a lethal 25mm cannon.

LEFT, BOTTOM: Marines during a training exercise prior to the four-day ground phase of the war. During the actual attack, these Marines would be in MOPP-2, wearing basic gas-protective suits, against the possible threat of chemical weapons.

The "Camps"

The compounds where the rear echelons were billeted were formerly imported-workers' camps. They consisted of long, flat wooden buildings laid out on the sand like city blocks, with mess halls that were kept open twenty-four hours a day. The Marine combat battalions positioned in the desert, however, lived in the customary tent camps, and most of their messes dished out only a single hot meal a day to supplement the daily MREs.

Personal weapons, of course, were carried at all times. Only the sentries on duty possessed live ammunition, however; to check that each weapon was unloaded, it had to be aimed into a special sandbox and the trigger pulled before it would be allowed into any compound. Telephone booths were situated on the corners of each block. Pity the poor enlisted Marine who did not stop to think before using his credit card to phone his sweetheart or wife back home; many monthly telephone bills exceeded a corporal's base pay.

—HAC

Operation Desert Storm: Plan of Battle

The original plan of battle for Desert Storm was for both Marine divisions to provide the attack north along the Kuwaiti coast, where they could receive naval gunfire and amphibious assault support. That plan was compromised, however, by a source within the coalition. Thus, as the coalition consolidated and the U.S. Army's eight (plus two British and one French) divisions began massing, the main attack mission of the two Marine divisions was shifted farther west to central Kuwait, primarily as a diversion or holding force. These troops would confront the main force of eighteen Iraqi divisions behind a double minefield barrier that stretched the width of southern Kuwait. Replacing the Marines on the coastal approach would be Saudi National Guard, Kuwaiti, Qatari, and Moroccan units, and on the Marines' left flank, Egyptians, Syrians, and other Saudi elements.

While the Marines held the attention of the Iraqis, Gen Schwarzkopf's obvious left hook by two Army corps a hundred miles farther to the west would provide flanking envelopment to cut off the remnants of the retreating Iraqi forces. As these plans developed and all allied units adjusted westward, the British 1st Armoured Division asked to be removed from I MEF. To make up for this loss of armor, especially since most Marine tank battalions were still using M60s, I MEF commander LtGen Walter Boomer requested the Army Tiger Brigade of Abrams M1A1 tanks to spearhead the attack of the 2d MarDiv, which also had an Organized Reserve tank company of M1A1s of its own that would distinguish itself in the coming battle.

Operation Desert Storm: The Aerial Phase, 16 January 1991

Despite the continued protestations of the U.S. Army that it was not ready, most of the coalition air units for the attack phase of Desert Storm were in place when President Bush ordered the commencement of air operations on 16 January 1991. Navy aircraft were on board aircraft carriers in the Gulf, the Arabian Sea, and the Mediterranean; Air Force fighter-bombers were located at various airfields in Saudi Arabia; and long-range heavy B-52 bombers flew from Diego Garcia and from continental U.S. bases. Marine F/A-18 Hornets, A-6 Intruders, and some AV-8B Harriers were based at Sheik Isa Airbase near Al Jubail and in Bahrain; others were operational from carriers, and there were more Harriers on LHAs in 4th and 5th MEBs afloat in the Persian Gulf.

Before dawn on 16 January, low-flying Army helicopters initiated the air-war phase by destroying Iraqi forward radar stations and surface-to-air missile (SAM) sites, thus enabling high-performance aircraft to attack airfields and military targets throughout Iraq. All of the Iraqi air assets that were not destroyed in those initial attacks flew to comparative safety at former enemy Iranian airfields. The Americans, with British and French air components, achieved air supremacy from the outset.

The threat of hidden SAM missiles was never totally eradicated; therefore, F/A-18s and Harriers had to stay above twelve thousand feet when they made their bombing and strafing runs. With proper aerial protection, Air Force A-10 Warthogs and accompanying Army Apache and Marine Cobra helicopter gunships attacked at low altitudes. Small radio-controlled drones, unmanned aerial vehicles (UAVs), also performed a new phase of low-altitude aerial reconnaissance over enemy troop concentrations. The faster Marine OV-10 Bronco observation aircraft also flew low-altitude missions. Enormously destructive 15,000-pound "Daisy Cutter" bombs were rolled out of the backs of C-130 propeller-type four-engine cargo planes, and the C-130 configured as a gunship was also employed.

The thirty-two-day aerial campaign was highly successful in destroying enemy armor and troop concentrations—especially when using the newer laser-guided weaponry—and in maintaining pressure in preparation for the subsequent ground phase. But the main benefit of the air war was that it destroyed all lateral communication between Iraqi units; none, it was found out later, knew where its adjacent or supporting units were. A total fog of war had been imposed on the enemy, so that when the ground attack began, the Iraqi divisions were at a complete loss as to the situation on the battlefield. Furthermore, they couldn't even cry for help from supporting units.

Meanwhile …

While 92,000 Marines were assembling in and around Saudi Arabia for the assault into Kuwait, other Marines afloat still had their typical Force-in-Readiness roles to perform. In late August, as Desert Shield was coming together, the 26th MEU had arrived off Monrovia, Liberia, on the African coast to relieve the 22d MEU, which had been evacuating Americans and neutrals from the scene of that minor civil war.

In January 1991, just before the start of the Desert Storm air phase, Marines afloat in the Seventh Fleet in the Indian Ocean had been flown by helicopter into Mogadishu, the capital of Somalia on the eastern African coast, to evacuate the American legation and others from another minor civil war. They would return to Somalia the following year in a humanitarian mission to feed the starving populace.

Preparation for the Ground Phase

While the air campaign was in full swing, the Iraqis initiated probing and diversionary attacks at the Saudi border, one of which penetrated several miles. On 29 January, at Al Khafji on the coast, ten miles south of the Kuwaiti border, two Iraqi armored columns attacked a I MEF reconnaissance outpost backed up by Task Force Shepherd. A stiff battle ensued, including close air support from Marine F/A-18 Hornets and Air Force A-10 Warthogs. Two Marine recon platoons were trapped in the small town and were rescued by combined Saudi and Qatari units.

Simultaneously, thirty Iraqi tanks attacked Outpost 4, a former Saudi police station, at Umm Hajul at the "elbow" in 2d MarDiv's zone. A sharp battle ensued, with Marine ground and air units and A-10 Warthogs. Unfortunately, as had happened at Al Khafji, another Marine LAV was hit by friendly fire, causing additional casualties. All thirty Iraqi tanks were destroyed.

ABOVE: The "Trip Trey" Shamrocks of MCAS Beaufort, South Carolina, flew their F/A-18 Hornets to Sheik Isa airfield on Bahrain for Desert Storm. Commanded by LtCol Tom Benes, the pilots racked up an impressive, accident-free record, yet the squadron was decommissioned following its return after the war.

ABOVE: The All-Weather, A-6E Intruder squadron VMA(AW)-533 also flew to and operated out of Sheik Isa during the Gulf War. They have since transitioned to F/A-18s and are stationed at MCAS Beaufort, South Carolina.

ABOVE: A view forward of the short flight deck of the LHA *Nassau*, command ship of 4th MEB operating off the Kuwaiti coast during Desert Shield and Storm. The complement of AV-8B Harriers was augmented with utility Hueys and AH-1W Cobra gunships.

RIGHT: A Harrier executing a vertical landing on the flight deck of the *Nassau* after a mission. Although the Harrier takes off toward the bow in a conventional manner, when it returns it comes abeam the mother ship's port side, hovers, then is talked down by the Air Boss as it moves sideways and then settles onto the deck. It is then moved by deck crews to a lashed-down parking position, sometimes hanging over the side, as shown here.

I MEF Liberates Kuwait

The arbitrary western boundary on the map of Kuwait angles sharply southward until it abruptly changes direction, heading due east, then south, then due east again; the upper angle suggests an armpit, the lower, an elbow. On the Saudi side, a twelve-foot-high earthen berm extends for the length of the border. Between the armpit and the elbow, 1st MarDiv's sector was on the right, 2d MarDiv's on the left. The 5th MEB (in "green-side-out" camouflage, not having been issued desert cammies) was brought ashore as an MEF reserve below the Kuwaiti-Saudi border. As the two divisions shifted to jumping-off positions westward, the 5th MEB aimed across the border amplified loudspeakers that played recordings of tracked vehicles and other noises, traversing back and forth from the elbow to the sea, thus fooling the Iraqis into believing that the Marine divisions were massing in their original positions.

Directly ahead of both MarDivs, some seven miles inside Kuwait, the Iraqis had installed two deep lines of minefield barriers. Both divisions would have to penetrate these formidable obstacles before confronting the forty-four Iraqi divisions behind them. The solution was to mount bulldozer blades on lead M60s tanks along with an innovative device that threw a section of chain-link fencing over the tank it was attached to, which then smacked the ground in front of it. Thus the mines were detonated, clearing a pathway wide enough for a single column of vehicles. The ominous tops of the scattered, unexploded, still-lethal mines could be seen on both sides of the pathway as wind gusts swept them clear of sand.

The twin breaches were accomplished quickly and effectively, taking both the defending Iraqis and Gen Schwarzkopf's headquarters totally by surprise—so much so that the jump-off of the two left-flank Army corps had to be advanced, lest the Marines get too far ahead and into Kuwait City ahead of the Army, instead of being a holding force as Schwarzkopf had planned. The VII Army Corps took three days to make its slow end run over the desert, only to arrive and engage the retreating forces in southern Iraq in short, wrap-up firefights on the final day. The airlifted XVIII Army Corps on the extreme western left flank also arrived on the third day, to intercept what was left of the retreating Iraqi Republican Guard divisions near the Euphrates River on the road back to Baghdad. Arab coalition forces postured in the allied lineup but generally were reluctant to fight fellow Arabs. The Marine divisions, however, despite being only a "holding force," advanced in constant combat for the entire four days, and liberated Kuwait.

The 100-Hour Ground War: 24–28 February 1991

G-Day, the commencement of the ground-attack phase, was 24 February, a cold, wet, rainy Monday. The desert sand had turned into gritty mud. At 0400 the two Marine divisions—with the troops in Mission Oriented Protective Posture-2 (MOPP-2), with gas-protective suits on but not special boots, gloves, or gas masks—jumped off and blasted their way into Kuwait with 194 M60 and 74 M1A1 tanks, 301 LAVs, and 216 artillery pieces; 532 tracked amphibious assault vehicles were used to carry supplies behind them over the sandy wastes. Leading the attack for 1st MarDiv were two mechanized task forces: Shepherd, made up of two Light Armored Infantry Battalions, and Ripper (RCT-7). The latter was composed of 1st Battalion, 7th Marines; 1st Battalion, 5th Marines; 3d Battalion, 9th Marines; and 1st Tank Battalion. Following on foot were Grizzly (RCT-4), with its 2d and 3d battalions, 7th Marines, and recon platoons, and Papa Bear (RCT-1), consisting of battalions from 1st and 9th Marines, plus combat engineers and other specialty units. Taro (RCT-3) was made up of units from 3d Marines and was motorized. Leading 2d MarDiv was the attached Army "Tiger Brigade" of M1A1 Abrams.

As the mine barriers were breached on the morning of the first day, the Marines were met with sporadic artillery and fire from T-72 tanks that were half-buried behind sand bunkers, reducing their ability to maneuver and making them sitting ducks for

BELOW: A Marine M1A1 70-ton Main Battle Tank with its 120mm smoothbore cannon. I MEF had only 194 of these to augment their older M60A1/A3s. For the invasion, the U.S. Army "Tiger" Brigade, with its 118 M1A1 Abrams, was attached to 2d MarDiv, serving as its mechanized spearhead.

advancing Marine tanks and close air supporting aircraft, mostly Cobra helicopter gunships.

The Marine task forces barreled through the mine barriers and faced an unanticipated phenomenon: the mass surrender of thousands upon thousands of Iraqi troops. These soldiers had thrown their weapons away, some had no shoes, and all were exhausted, undernourished, and weary of the air bombardments they had managed to live through. All seemed happier to surrender to the Americans rather than follow Saddam's order to fight them. They were so docile that only a few handfuls of Marines were necessary to keep guard over them until they were corralled into compounds, counted, and interrogated.

Led by their fast-moving mechanized task forces, the advancing Marine divisions took out everything in front of them with their TOW missiles and other weapons, and reached their objectives ahead of their timetables. They pummeled the retreating Iraqis—or those that chose to stand and fight—for two days, until a severe sandstorm obliterated everything. By that time, both divisions were in the center of Kuwait, between the two major oil fields, some wells of which were burning. In the early morning of the third day, the Iraqis began torching the remaining oil-well heads in all of Kuwait's oil fields. The 1st MarDiv also repulsed a counterattack at the south end of the Burqan oil field. Even LtGen Boomer's CP group got caught in a brief but fierce firefight. At the same time, Marine artillery opened up a prescheduled "time-on-target" artillery barrage, firing every piece in the two Marine zones. The combination of the exploding wells and the noise of the artillery was an indescribable nightmare. The sky turned blood-red and became so bright that one could

read by it. The surreal inferno and cacophony continued well into the next morning—but the sun never rose that day. The thick, black pall that rose from the blazing oil wells turned day into night; dawn could be determined only by consulting a watch. The eerie darkness was punctuated by the reverberating thunder of artillery and bombs. By noon the cloud had become so impenetrable—much darker than a starless night—that even the headlights of vehicles failed to pierce the gloom. Despite this impediment, the task forces continued to advance, crushing all resistance ahead of them.

As 2d MarDiv moved through the Al Jabar airfield and on to its objective on the west side of Kuwait City, it knocked out everything in its way.

Before the dawn of the second day, the Organized Reserve Bravo Company of the 4th Tank Battalion, 4th Marine (Reserve) Division, which was the only Marine unit to have the new M1A1 main battle tanks and which had been called up for active duty and attached to 2d MarDiv, had spotted through their thermal-imaging scopes a column of thirty-five Iraqi T-55 and T-72 tanks angling across their front. Reserve captain and commanding officer Chip Parkison, a wine salesman from Seattle, Washington, was preparing his fourteen tanks for the coming day's operation when the report of advancing enemy tanks reached him. His tanks were stationary and the enemy's guns were aimed straight ahead, so they had not detected the Marines. Holding their breath as they waited for their tanks to warm up and then cool down, which they had to do before they could operate, the Marines in the lead tank were just able to fire off a round at the lead enemy T-72, from the tank's smoothbore 120mm high-velocity 4,000-yard-range cannon, as it was turning its gun toward them. The other thirteen tanks joined in, firing round after round—just like on the firing range. The M1A1 battle tank indisputably proved its superiority against the vaunted Russian T-72s. So did the Marine tank operators.

The Marine Reservists destroyed twenty enemy tanks in the first ninety seconds; the impromptu battle lasted only seven minutes. When the smoke cleared, the weekend warriors from Yakima, Washington, could see that their fourteen M1A1 tanks had destroyed thirty T-72s and four T-55s. In the four-day war, Bravo Company went on to destroy a total of fifty-nine tanks, thirty-two armored personnel carriers, twenty-six non-armored vehicles, and one artillery gun. They took no casualties in their remarkable hundred hours of combat before returning to their civilian lives and their weekend Reserve training. That training had not only paid off handsomely, but also had proved beyond a doubt its value to the Marine Corps.

Task Force Ripper, under Col Carlton W. Fulford, Jr., led 1st MarDiv straight into Kuwait City under the engulfing blackness of the burning oil cloud, smashing its way through enemy armor and delaying actions. At the outskirts of the capital, the cloud formed a sharp edge where it ended, and a bright, sunny sky could be seen beyond. On the way to their objective, the Kuwait International Airport, Ripper blasted its way through and totally destroyed a hundred enemy tanks, armored personnel carriers, and other military vehicles, all without taking a single casualty. The 1st MarDiv van followed on its heels and set up on the tarmac and in the terminal buildings at the captured airfield, under the

BELOW: The command group of Task Force Ripper confers at Observation Post 4 on the Kuwaiti border on 23 February 1991, the day before the ground offensive. The nearest figure is Marine Col Carlton W. Fulford, TF CO; his staff behind consists of (from left) Col Chris Cortez, CO, 1/5, and Col James N. Mattis, CO, 1/7. Kneeling over the map are LtCol Rick Zilmer, S3, 7th Marines, and LtCol Drew Bennett, S3, 1/7. All of these officers rose to flag rank following the war; Fulford to four-star and SACEUR commander; Mattis to CG, 1st MarDiv, in the Afghanistan and Iraq wars. The author's camouflaged Jeep Cherokee can be seen in the background.

Staff Vehicles

The new Humvees, which had replaced the venerable Jeeps, presented some drawbacks. Although the Humvee's automatic transmission made the vehicle more serviceable in sand than the shift-gear Jeep, it was a gas-guzzler. Officers and senior NCOs, who in the past had nearly unrestricted use of the smaller Jeeps in such field situations, could not simply requisition a Humvee to run errands, and their units and living camps were spread out all over the northeastern coast of Saudi Arabia. To fill the gap, the Japanese provided hundreds of Honda, Toyota, Nissan, and other sedans for such use. These efficient vehicles were prized and widely used as staff cars. Few of them had four-wheel-drive capability, however, so most were useless off-road.

The week before the ground phase of the war began, in mid-February, four-wheel-drive Jeep Cherokees just off the factory assembly lines began to be shipped to Al Jubail, where they were loaded onto 18-wheel rigs. Many officers and NCO drivers traded their Japanese cars for these new vehicles, taking them straight to the motor pool to be spray-painted a sand color. The motorized columns of both Marine divisions went into battle with these Cherokees plowing along in four-wheel drive in the deep ruts of the larger vehicles. MEF CG Walter Boomer's Command Group had many Cherokees and four-wheel-drive Toyota pickup trucks in addition to its LAVs.

—HAC

RIGHT: The VII and XVIII Army Corps, consisting of eight American, British, and French divisions, attacked on the far-left flank and reached lower Iraq for short battles on the final day.

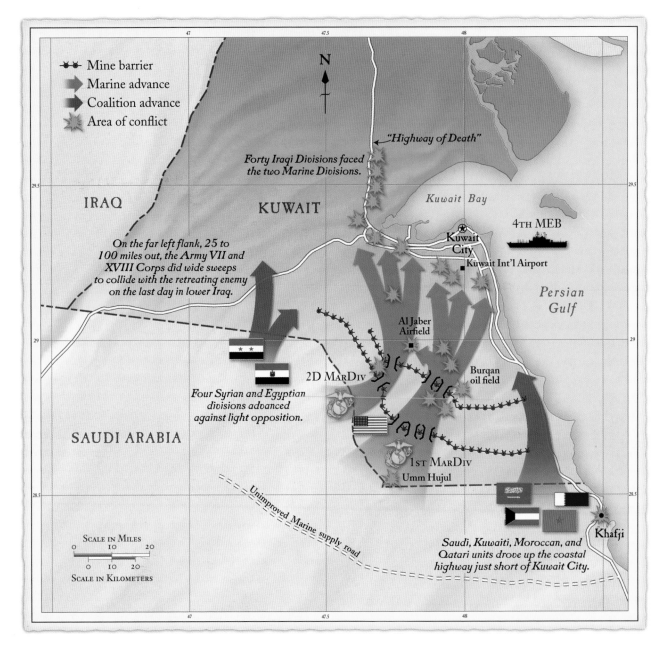

Mine barrier
Marine advance
Coalition advance
Area of conflict

"Highway of Death"

Forty Iraqi Divisions faced the two Marine Divisions.

IRAQ

KUWAIT

Kuwait Bay

4TH MEB

Kuwait City

Kuwait Int'l Airport

On the far left flank, 25 to 100 miles out, the Army VII and XVIII Corps did wide sweeps to collide with the retreating enemy on the last day in lower Iraq.

Persian Gulf

Al Jaber Airfield

2D MARDIV

Burqan oil field

Four Syrian and Egyptian divisions advanced against light opposition.

SAUDI ARABIA

1ST MARDIV
Umm Hujul

Unimproved Marine supply road

SCALE IN MILES
0   10   20

SCALE IN KILOMETERS
0   10   20

Saudi, Kuwaiti, Moroccan, and Qatari units drove up the coastal highway just short of Kuwait City.

Khafji

Kuwaiti Liberation of Kuwait Medal

continuing red glow of the adjacent oil fires. There it held up while 2d MarDiv did the same thing on the other side of the city. Marine and Navy Air then wreaked havoc and total destruction on the roadway leading north out of Kuwait City as they caught the fleeing Iraqis in their tanks and vehicles in devastating bombing and strafing attacks on what became known as the Highway of Death.

I MEF commander LtGen Boomer took his CP group into the deserted city to reconnoiter and meet with whatever Kuwaiti officials had remained. Word came later that night that President Bush had ordered a cease-fire for 0800 the following morning, 28 February. The lightning war was over in only one hundred hours.

The author of this book, on duty as a combat artist for the Historical Division, HQMC, detached the following day from 1st MarDiv and drove his Jeep Cherokee into the deserted capital to find the American Embassy, passing burned buildings and abandoned Iraqi tanks strewn with loot—mostly women's lingerie and children's toys stolen from smashed stores and shops. At the American Embassy, the author met a Marine force recon team, Piglet-2-1, that had dashed to the embassy in the middle of the war, secured it, checked for booby traps, and raised the American flag, then waited for the rest of I MEF to reach them. The leader, 1stLt Brian Knowles, was awarded a Bronze Star personally by LtGen Boomer. Later in the day, after the cease-fire had gone

RIGHT: Force (I MEF) Recon team, Piglet-2-1, as assembled at 0730 on 28 February 1991 at the abandoned American embassy in Kuwait City. They had secretly entered the city two days earlier, had entered the embassy, checked it for booby traps, raised the American flag, then simply awaited the advancing Marine units. The action of the recon team was not met with gratitude by General Schwarzkopf at CENTCOM headquarters; he had wanted the liberation of the American embassy to be a U.S. Army show. Consequently, he ordered an Army helicopter to fly over the embassy at 1300 that day and rope down an Army team for a photo op for the assembled television cameras and reporters.

ABOVE: Walter E. Boomer, assistant Commandant of the Marine Corps. During the Gulf War, LtGen Boomer was commanding general of the First Marine Expeditionary Force (I MEF), which consisted basically of 1st and 2d MarDivs, 3d MAW, 4th and 5th MEBs, and assorted support units.

into effect, the press, which had gathered there by that time, was advised by Gen Schwarzkopf's headquarters that an Army Special Forces team would arrive by helicopter at 1300 and would rappel down to "liberate the embassy." They did so, making a fine photo op for the TV cameras—and an amusing incident for the Marine recon team that had actually secured it two days before.

LEFT: Left to right are MajGen William M. Keys, CG, 2d MarDiv; MajGen James M. Myatt, CG, 1st MarDiv; and LtGen Walter E. Boomer, CG, I MEF.

The Final Tally

With the victory in the Persian Gulf war, the American military finally left the specter of Vietnam behind and regained the admiration and respect of the American people. The Marine Corps had performed brilliantly. Their method of breaching the mine barriers entered the textbooks, while their prepositioning of supplies so impressed the Army that it looked into doing the same. Once more, the Navy-Marine team and MAGTF-combined ground-close-air-support concept reaffirmed the Corps' status as the nation's premier Force-in-Readiness.

Desert Storm was the largest combat operation in Marine Corps history. More than 92,000 Marines were either ashore or afloat during the war, and twenty-four infantry battalions and forty Marine air squadrons had engaged in battle. Only 6 of 194 Marine fixed-wing aircraft were lost, and only 3 out of 178 helicopters. Marines destroyed 1,040 enemy tanks, 608 armored personnel carriers, and 432 artillery pieces. More than

23,000 prisoners of war were captured. Twenty-four Marines died in combat and ninety-two were wounded. The two-man crew of an OV-10 Bronco that had crashed was captured and later released.

Following the war, the elements of victorious I MEF stood down from Kuwait and Saudi Arabia and re-embarked for their home or expeditionary stations. Reservists were released from active duty to return to civilian life, and some regular units, like F/A-18 Hornet squadron VMA-333, "Trip Tray," at MCAS, Beaufort, South Carolina, were deactivated. Nevertheless, perpetually "on call," the Marine Corps immediately responded to crises as far flung as those in Bangladesh, Somalia (again), Haiti, Bosnia, and Kosovo.

Saudi Arabian Liberation of Kuwait Medal

THE THIRTIETH COMMANDANT: CARL MUNDY

When Alfred M. Gray stepped down as CMC, the baton was passed to a more genial—but still firm—leader, Gen Carl E. Mundy, Jr. Gray's was a hard act to follow: only a 180-degree change of personality would make a transition successful. Mundy sought to re-instill some traditional values in the Marines while retaining the sharp edge Gray had honed. He best expressed his intentions in a field manual (FMFM 1-10) titled *Leading Marines*, of which he expounded in such chapters as "Our Ethos," "Every Marine a Rifleman," "Soldiers of the Sea," "Setting the Example," "Unit Spirit," "Being Ready," and "Fighting Power and Winning." He was—and is—a consummate communicator. Very importantly, he was also able to ele-vate the Marine Corps to the level of full operational part-ner in unified commands, now termed Jointness. Working closely with his Navy counterpart, Mundy steered the Corps' sea partners toward reshaping a new, post–cold war national strategy of Navy-Marine team cooperation in power projection and littoral orientation, and away from the former deep-water-confrontation concept used against the Soviet Union. This would become the doctrine "From the Sea: A New Direction for the Naval Services." Gen Mundy was also successful in keeping the base-strength level of the Corps at 174,000 active-duty Marines.

CONTINUING EXPEDITIONARY MISSIONS

The brief war in the Persian Gulf had concluded in victory for the thirty-nation coalition, but the loose ends that had been left dangling quickly became snags. Having accom-plished the UN mandate to eject Iraqi forces from Kuwait, President George H.W. Bush had not pressed the coalition on to Baghdad to overthrow dictator Saddam Hussein. Gen Norman Schwarzkopf, too, had made an unwise concession to the defeat-ed Iraqis at the cease-fire talks in allow-ing them the continued use of their remaining helicopters; the first thing they did was use them to attack the Shiite Muslims in southern Iraq and Kurdish tribes in the north.

Kurdish tribes held a large northern portion of the country and

had resisted Hussein for some time. Their situation soon became critical, however. Immediately following the war, Hussein drove the fiercely independent and rebellious Iraqi Kurds from their homes and villages and into the hills. Hundreds were dying daily from malnutrition, disease, and exposure. To give them humanitarian assis-tance, Combined Task Force Provide Comfort was formed with U.S. Army and Marine elements. The 24th Marine Expeditionary Unit (Special Operations Capable), with its helicopter squadron HMM-264's twenty-three CH-46 choppers, delivered a million pounds of relief supplies to the tent camp set up for Kurds near the Turkish border by Army engineers and Navy Seabees. French, British, and Dutch units joined in the effort as well. Provide Comfort lasted from April through May 1991.

U.S. Central Command had ordered the Iraqis out of the Kurdish area and had imposed two wide no-fly zones across northern and southern Iraq to forestall any further attacks by Saddam on the Shiites or Kurds.

DEVASTATION IN BANGLADESH

Also in April of that year, the small, impoverished Muslim country of Bangladesh, situated between India and Burma, was hit by a devastating typhoon that brought raging winds of almost 150 miles per hour. An estimated 100,000 people were killed by a twenty-foot tidal wave and subse-quent flooding; bridges were downed, transportation was stopped, and food and potable drinking water were in desperately short supply. Immediate humanitarian relief was needed.

Help came in the form of Operation Sea Angel. The Joint Task Force commander was Marine LtGen Henry C. Stackpole III, CG of III MEF on Okinawa. With attached Army and Navy relief units and the 250-man water-purification Contingency Marine Air-Ground Task Force 2-91 (CMAGTF 2-91), using watercraft and helicopters including Landing Craft Air Cushions (LCACs), an LCU (Landing Craft, Utility), and Amphibious Assault Vehicles (AAVs), MedCAP teams from the 5th Marine Expeditionary Battalion offshore lifted in food and supplies. In all, the Air Force moved 2,430 tons; the Army, 886 tons; and Navy and Marine air, 700 tons. Navy and Marine surface units delivered 1,487 tons of food and 266,000 gallons of water.

ABOVE: LtGen Henry C. Stackpole, USMC, a Princeton graduate, led Operation Sea Angel as commander of the Contingency Joint Task Force (CJTF) formed to provide humanitarian assistance to the people of Bangladesh following the devastating typhoon of the spring of 1991. He later assumed command of Marine Forces Pacific in 1992, and retired in 1994 after more than thirty years in the Corps.

LEFT: Marines distribute grain to civilians in Somalia as part of Joint Task Force Provide Relief.

RETURN TO SOMALIA

In September 1992, chaos again erupted in Somalia when local warlords began to vie with one another for power at the expense of the impoverished populace. Armed with rusty AK-47s, ragtag, pseudo-militia bands prowled their warlords' claims, driving any kind of old vehicle they could get running. These thugs confiscated the food that had been donated by international relief agencies, wreaking havoc and intensifying the famine that was already rampant in that destitute country perched on the Horn of Africa. Joint Task Force Provide Relief was formed to fly in the thousands of tons of food needed. United Nations Pakistani Frontier Forces were landed as the 11th MEU stood by offshore.

Control of Central Command, headquartered at McDill Air Force Base in Tampa, Florida, reverted from Army Gen Norman Schwarzkopf to Marine Gen Joseph Hoar, who alerted I MEF for deployment. Its commanding general, LtGen Robert Johnston, would be Cdr JTF Somalia. The 1st MarDiv and the Army 10th Mountain Division, composing the joint task force, would secure the areas of Mogadishu, Kismayo, Baidoa, Bale Dogle, and Bardera, but would remain neutral in regard to the local warlords. Close offshore, the 15th MEU(SOC) was ready to prepare the way for a UN peacekeeping force and to deliver food to alleviate the famine.

The 15th MEU ultimately landed from AAVs on the beach at Mogadishu under the glaring lights of the TV camera crews that had gotten wind of the operation and were on the shore to welcome them. A French Foreign Legion parachute battalion joined in as the U.S. Embassy was reoccupied by Marines under intermittent sniper fire.

Marine and U.S. Army units, along with those of other countries (France, Belgium, Kuwait, Saudi Arabia, Morocco, Egypt, Botswana, Zimbabwe, Turkey, Nigeria, Pakistan, and the United Arab Emirates), continued to supervise the distribution of humanitarian supplies, while engaging in non-decisive, harassing firefights. By May 1993, the Marines' part of the mission had been successfully completed, and they departed.

In October 1993, President Bill Clinton sent the Army back into Somalia to engage in an ill-advised operation to chase down one of the local warlords; it ended badly with the loss of several Black Hawk helicopters, eighteen dead soldiers, and seventy-five wounded. The 13th and 22d MEUs were hastily dispatched to assist, but were withdrawn in March 1994.

LVTs to AAAVs

The Marine Corps' penchant for persistence in seeking a technological solution to a tactical problem is best exemplified by its exploitation of a civilian vehicle: the amphibious tractor, better known as the LVT (Landing Vehicle, Tracked), or amtrac. As it was refined over the course of sixty years—and four major wars—the LVT morphed into the AAAV, or Advanced Assault Amphibious Vehicle, and the new EAV (Expeditionary Amphibious Vehicle).

Japan manifested its expansionist intentions in the Pacific through its reaction to the U.S. seizure of the Philippines and its victory over Russia in the Far East during 1904 to 1905. Earl H. "Pete" Ellis, a forward-thinking Marine at the Navy War College in 1911 to 1913, wrote several studies of advanced-base operations against Japanese expansion into Pacific islands. Following World War I, Japan was given control of German-held islands in the Pacific, which would later provide bases for Japan's attacks on Guam, Hawaii,

ABOVE: Having yet to secure the beachhead at Peleliu in 1944, these 1st MarDiv Marines hunker down behind the protection of an LVT-A2 during the fierce fighting on the tiny island. LVT-A2s weighed 32,800 pounds and were armed with an M6 37mm gun, as well as three .30-caliber light machine guns. They could transport a Marine squad of twelve.

Australia, and New Zealand. In 1921, Ellis produced "Advanced Based Operations in Micronesia," which in 1922 became "Operations Plan 712" and later the "Orange Plan" for war against Japan.

One of the essential needs perceived for these operations was a means for crossing the coral reefs that enclosed the Pacific islands. In 1922, the CMC got wind of a floating tracked vehicle designed by automotive engineer Walter Christie. One model had the additional attraction of mounting a 75mm gun. With Christie's cooperation, tests were made in the Potomac and then

at Culebra, near Puerto Rico. While Christie's vehicle was just the thing for climbing across protective reefs, it proved unseaworthy in open-ocean ship-to-shore movement, and had difficulty plunging through the surf at the beach. But the idea's attraction became embedded in Marines' minds.

The distractions of Nicaragua, Haiti, and China in the 1920s and '30s, combined with the funding cutbacks of the Great Depression, prevented further exploration of the amphibious vehicle idea. But in 1938, with Japan's threat looming ever larger, the Corps discovered the remarkable tracked amphibious vehicle invented by engineer Donald Roebling, who intended his boat-tractor for use in post-hurricane rescue in the swamps of the Gulf Coast. The Navy had neither the interest nor the money for such foolishness, but the Marines saw it as a solution to the nagging problems of moving across reefs and advancing inland rapidly. By 1940, the Marines had successfully tested the Roebling vehicle and won over the Navy. By mid-1941 it was in production at Dunedin, Florida, as the LVT-1. Powered by an automotive engine, it could attain speeds of six miles per hour in the water and twelve miles per hour on land. The first LVT-1s were used in the Guadalcanal landing in August 1942 and again at Tarawa in November 1943, although in insufficient numbers to land any but the assault wave.

Improved models quickly followed: the LVT-2 in late 1942, and in 1943 the LVT-A2, an armored version mounting a light tank turret with a 37mm gun. Also fielded in 1943 were the LVT-3, powered by two Cadillac V-8 engines and with a rear ramp for discharging men and vehicles, and the LVT-4, powered by a radial aircraft engine. The LVT-A4 mounted a turret with a short 75mm howitzer and was employed in the first wave for last-minute beach-defense suppression. The LVTs became so useful

LEFT: Marines climb down cargo nets from an APA transport ship into Landing Craft, Infantry (LCI) for the invasion of Kwajalein in the South Pacific in World War II.

BELOW: Left front view of an LVT-A4 with a late-model cab.

PAGES 414–415: An AAV plows through heavy seas all buttoned up during a training exercise. Newer AAAVs (Advanced Amphibious Assault Vehicles) will travel at 20 knots on water and 45 mph on land.

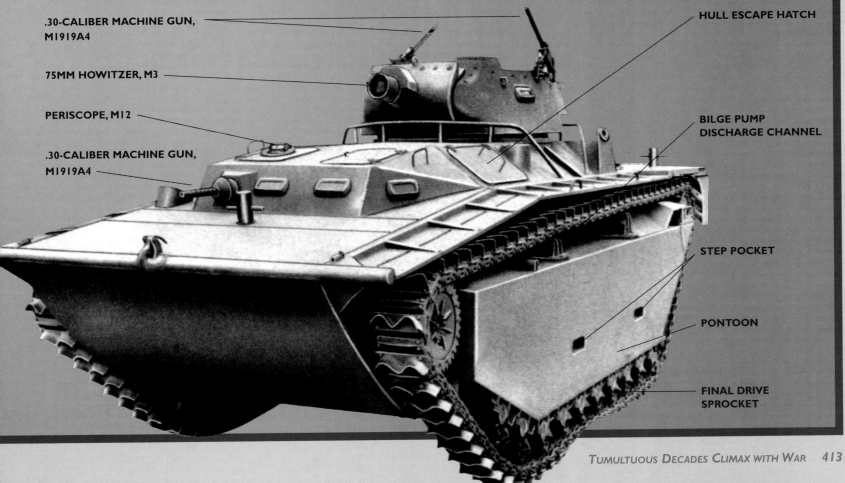

.30-CALIBER MACHINE GUN, M1919A4

75MM HOWITZER, M3

PERISCOPE, M12

.30-CALIBER MACHINE GUN, M1919A4

HULL ESCAPE HATCH

BILGE PUMP DISCHARGE CHANNEL

STEP POCKET

PONTOON

FINAL DRIVE SPROCKET

for landings and advances inland that the U.S. Army and British Army used the later models. The LVT-3s and A4s were used in the Korean War as well.

The LVTP-5, a much larger amphibious vehicle developed in the 1950s, was used in the Vietnam War. Powered by a V-12 tank engine, it had a 30-mph land speed, but its water speed was little more than that of earlier LVTs. The LVTP-7 was developed in the 1960s and, with modifications and improvements, is still in use today. Powered by a diesel engine and propelled in the water by a combination of tracks and ducted propellers, its water speed is 8.4 mph, while its land speed is 45 mph. It was employed successfully in the 1991 Gulf War (Desert Storm) as an armored infantry carrier in the advance across the desert and through Iraqi defenses into Kuwait.

By the time of the Gulf War, the LVTP-7 was thirty years old, and a replacement was needed. Meanwhile, the P-7 underwent improvements and modifications to extend its service life, becoming the AAVP-7. During the 1990s, a new amphibious vehicle was conceived, and by 1999 a prototype was tested. The Advanced Amphibious Assault Vehicle (AAAV) will be fielded between 2007 and 2017, with a total of 1,013 planned. With a planing hull and powered by an 850 hp turbo-charged V-12 diesel engine, the AAAV can do 25 mph on water and 45 mph on land. Armored and mounting a 30mm automatic cannon, it will carry eighteen Marines. Instead of being launched from a mile or two offshore as LVTs were in the past, the AAAV can be launched from over the horizon in a surprise attack. Waves of AAAVs will cross the beach at full speed and attack inland in a seamless maneuver. No more slow ship-to-shore movement in full sight of the defense after a long naval bombardment. After seventy years of development, the ultimate (for now) amphibious assault vehicle has arrived.

—BN

TOP: Marines of AAV platoon, A Company, Combat Assault Battalion, 7th Marine Regiment, participate in a Landing Force Cooperation Afloat Readiness and Training (LF CARAT) exercise in Southeast Asia in 2002. CARAT is an annual exercise designed to promote cooperation between U.S. armed forces and those of allied nations in Southeast Asia.

BOTTOM: An LCAC (Landing Craft Air Cushioned) from 15th MEU stocked with humanitarian relief supplies lands on a debris-strewn beach on the Indonesian island of Sumatra in January 2005 as part of Operation Unified Assistance, a nine-day humanitarian operation. Sailors of LHD-6 USS *Bonhomme Richard* and Marines of 15th MEU delivered more than a million pounds of supplies to survivors of the devastating tsunami of December 2004.

ABOVE: Marines of 3d MEB inside an AAV during Operation Crocodile, a 2003 joint exercise with Australian armed forces.

LEFT: Along with the MV-22 Osprey tilt-rotor aircraft and the LCAC, the Marine Corps' new AAAV completes the "Amphibious Triad" that gives the Corps superior expeditionary warfare capability. The AAAV is more than three times faster on the water than the AAV and has twice the armor protection and greater firepower. It is equally effective on land, with as much mobility as an M1A1 tank, and provides Nuclear, Biological, and Chemical (NBC) protection for both crew and embarked personnel.

HAITI REDUX

In July 1994, as the Caribbean island of Haiti (which had played an earlier role in Marine history) found itself in political upheaval and civil chaos, Operation Uphold/Support Democracy was launched by the Clinton administration to restore Jean-Bertrand Aristide to the presidency. Special-Purpose Marine Air-Ground Task Force (SPMAGTF) Carib, a "special" Battalion Landing Team, was organized by the Marine Corps and sent to Haiti to secure the northern area of Cape Haitien, the old battleground of the 1930s, while the Army secured the capital, Port-au-Prince.

As a high-ranking American peace delegation went ashore at the capital, the SPMAGTF landed peacefully and tried to enlist the cooperation of the locals to restore law and order. A small firefight was the only overt incident to mar the Marine landing, until Haitian soldiers and policemen began reverting to rebel guerrilla tactics—whereupon ten locals were killed in a firefight with Marines. A clean-up operation was turned over to Army units, and the Marines backloaded to the LHAs waiting offshore.

CMC CHUCK KRULAK

Gen Charles C. Krulak is the scion of another famous Marine general, Victor Krulak, who had been a member of the Chowder Society and had been instrumental in the early Marine participation in the Korean War. Former director of Recruiting Command, the younger Krulak

LEFT, INSET: Marine waist gunners, sergeants Todd Abbott and Andrew McInally, man their .50-caliber machine guns as their CH-53D heavy helicopter—carrying the first contingent of Marines from the 26th MEU(SOC)—lands at Skopje, Macedonia, in June 1999. Marines played a major role in NATO peacekeeping efforts in the Balkan country.

BELOW: On 10 June 1999, LCACs transport the first wave of 1,200 Marines of 26th MEU from LHD-3 *Kearsarge* to Litohoro in northern Greece to support NATO security forces in Kosovo.

had raised recruiting standards and lengthened training, adding the "Crucible" as a final, defining challenge at the Marine Recruit Depot at Parris Island. His focus was on "Making Marines and Winning Battles." As such, he introduced the "Three Block War" concept, which assumed that future conflicts would most likely be short-lived and take place in urban environments, and could simultaneously involve humanitarian assistance, peacekeeping, and mid-intensity conflict—all taking place within twenty-four hours and spread across no more than three city blocks. He also instituted the twin touchstones of Valor and Values in training and career motivation. A decorated combat officer in the Vietnam War, Charles Krulak also served as CG for the 2d Force Service and Supply Group (FSSG) in the Gulf War. He had done a remarkable job in preparing logistics for the two Marine divisions as they attacked into Kuwait, setting up a supply and medical base at Kibrit, Saudi Arabia just south of the border to funnel thousands of tons of materials and ammunition to the assault troops. A virtually miraculous feat was his discovery at Kibrit of a major and long-forgotten source of well water capable of supplying the sixty thousand Marines in the assault. Krulak's FSSG, along with the 1st FSSG at Al Jubail, was

a textbook demonstration of an efficient logistic operation. Just before being tapped to become commandant, he had served as CG, FMF Lant, then CG, Marine Corps Combat Development Command, at Quantico.

THE BALKAN TINDERBOX

The Balkans, the territory on the east coast of the Adriatic Sea across from Italy, has rarely known stability. The assassination of Archduke Ferdinand in Sarajevo in 1914 ignited World War I; Marshal Tito's amalgamation of diverse ethnic entities into the independent Communist nation of Yugoslavia following World War II held together only until his death. In the last two decades of the twentieth century, Yugoslavia began to fall apart, with each ethnic group claiming old hegemonies: Croatia broke away, then Bosnia-Herzegovina, followed by Kosovo. Neighboring Montenegro, Albania, and Macedonia tried not to get involved, despite the slaughter of Albanian Muslims by the Serbs under

ABOVE: The thirty-first commandant, Gen Charles C. Krulak (1995–1999). Krulak's father, LtGen Victor "Brute" Krulak, was a major figure in World War II, Korea, and Vietnam.

BELOW: An LCAC unloads Marines of 26th MEU on the beach of Litohoro, Greece, in June 1999.

The Bunny Rabbit and the Super Stallions

One particular incident of Marine daring stood out during the fighting in the Balkans: the Marine rescue of a downed Air Force pilot in hostile territory while under fire.

An F-16C Fighting Falcon piloted by Capt Scott O'Grady was hit by a surface-to-air missile (SAM) on 2 June 1995. At first, it was not known whether O'Grady had survived; five days later, however, a weak radio signal from him on the ground indicated that he not only had survived, but had somehow managed to elude the surrounding enemy.

Two hours after that signal was received, a Marine Tactical Recovery of Aircraft and Personnel (TRAP) team aboard the LHD-3 USS *Kearsarge* in the Adriatic Sea mustered two rescue teams aboard two CH-53E Super Stallions. These helicopters were covered by AH-1W Super Cobra helicopter gunships and Harriers, while forty Hornets and EA-6B Prowlers from Aviano, Italy, and the USS *Roosevelt* circled overhead on combat air patrol.

Col Martin Berndt, commanding officer of the 24th MEU, accompanied the mission commander, LtCol Chris Gunther, in his Super Stallion, *Dash-1*. Leaving the LHD at dawn, the rescue team flew eighty-seven miles into northern Bosnia to the area where the downed pilot had been detected. Dropping through a thick fog, they managed to spot O'Grady, and landed precariously among trees and rocks. The twenty-man TRAP team hit the ground, grabbed the dazed and weak pilot, whisked him into the chopper, and headed back to the *Kearsarge*. It was not easy going—they had to fly low, performing evasive maneuvers to dodge SAMs and AAA (Anti-Aircraft Artillery) fire. Both aircraft sustained hits, but the damage fortunately proved minor.

Once he was safely back in the United States, Capt O'Grady—denying that he was any kind of hero and saying he felt more like a scared little bunny rabbit—credited the Marines who saved him with being the real heroes, risking everything to go in and get him. The TRAP team had been trained for just such an operation and had pulled it off with perfect precision—and the Air Force pilot, who had gone through the tough Air Force Survival School in California, had showed his mettle as well.

—HAC

President Slobodan Milosevic, who still held forth in Serbia and its capital, Belgrade.

The fifty-five-year-old North Atlantic Treaty Organization (NATO) dragged its feet militarily on initiating Operation Allied Force in a region that fell outside of its sphere of influence. With no cohesive goal in the troublesome Balkans, NATO exhibited more eagerness to negotiate rather than force the matter. With the urging of the United Nations, however, the alliance initiated surgical air strikes in Bosnia-Herzegovina in 1994. U.S. Marine and Air Force fighter/bomber squadrons were deployed to Aviano, Italy, as were other NATO forces, while British and U.S. Navy task forces assembled in the Adriatic Sea, off the coast of the Balkans. It was an awkward situation: the West wanted to avoid a large-scale war and not wreak collateral damage beyond specific targets. Allied aerial bombings continued as the Serbs, Croats, and Muslims fought it out on the ground, despite the presence of United Nations peacekeeping troops in various areas. The once-beautiful city of Sarajevo, site of the 1984 Winter Olympics, was almost completely destroyed as NATO and the United Nations stood by impotently.

On the Ground in Kosovo

When Milosevic's ethnic cleansing—the genocide of Muslim Albanians—increased in ferocity, NATO's first effort to bring him under control was an aerial-bombing strategy, which leaders felt would force the dictator to capitulate. After three months of the surgical bombing of military and industrial targets, he still had not changed his ways, so NATO had no choice but to begin Operation Joint Guardian and send in ground forces to try to separate the warring parties.

A U.S. Navy-Marine Amphibious Ready Group (LHD-3 *Kearsarge*, LPD-15 *Ponce*, and LSD-44 *Gunston Hall*) steamed into the Aegean Sea to northern Greece, and on 10 June 1999, the 26th MEU(SOC) landed its BLT 3/8, a force of 1,200 Marines and 168 tactical vehicles. The BLT motored in convoy across Macedonia and into Kosovo, amid the cheers and hurrahs of the locals lining the roads.

Passing evacuating Serb army units as they entered their objective, the district of Gnjilane, the Marine column carefully wove through marked minefields to take over positions from a French brigade. On 15 June, the Marines confronted the Kosovo Liberation Army (KLA) and prevented a victory march it had planned, which not only would have broken the fragile Dayton Peace Accords, but also would have provoked the Serbs and further challenged NATO. Later, the Marines stopped the KLA, arrested their commanders and disarmed them, all without resistance. They also took over and disarmed the Kosovo Ministry of Interior Police. The U.S. forces continued to be subject to sporadic sniper fire from Kosovars and Serbs while the perimeter was being set up and Marine patrols were securing the town. In the days that followed, Marine patrols were extended to the countryside to confiscate arms and deter violence at ethnic flash points.

Humanitarian and MedCAP helicopter flights were conducted, and Marines and Navy corpsmen took over the hospital and the city fire department. Sporadic firefights were quickly quelled, and the Marines imposed a curfew. In one instance, a sniper killed a person on a street. Witnesses identified where he was hiding, and a Marine platoon stormed the building, captured the sniper, put him under arrest for murder, and turned him over to civilian authorities.

Normal life returned to Gnjilane as Albanian Kosovar refugees returned from Macedonia behind the retreating Serbs. Soon both sides were looking to the Marines for protection, and the displaced Albanians again cheered the Marines, who had allowed them to return to their homes.

On 10 July, BLT 3/8 turned its positions over to U.S. Army units and redeployed.

OPPOSITE: At Camp Hope, Albania, Marines of 26th MEU board CH-53E Sea Stallions that will take them back to the *Kearsarge*, operating in the Adriatic Sea, 4 June 1999. The Marines were relieved by U.S. Air Force security personnel.

ABOVE: A Harrier pilot performs a final flight check before a mission.

LEFT: Marines in an AAV keep on high alert as they ride through an ethnic Albanian village in Yugoslavia in June 1999.

RIGHT: Marines of BLT 2/8, attached to 24th MEU(SOC), participate in an urban warfare training exercise on the Albanian island of Sazan in July 2000. Such training is designed to give Marines the edge in urbanized combat environments.

BELOW: An AAV of 13th MEU(SOC) lands on the black volcanic sand of Green Beach on Iwo Jima, the site of the bloodiest battle of World War II, on 26 January 2001. While there, the Marines dedicated a plaque as a memorial to their brothers who fought with "uncommon valor" on that hallowed ground.

SUMMARY

The twentieth century was an incredible era in the history of the United States and that of the entire globe. Massive social, political, and economic changes occurred around the world, as well as conflicts that took the lives of an estimated 200 million people. The United States entered the century as a neophyte on the global scene, but emerged at the end as the single most powerful country the world had ever seen. Gone were the major challengers to democracy, but left in their wake were emerging so-called third world countries that demanded voices and places in the global community. Their places were basically in the semi-workable United Nations, the organization of 170 countries that ostensibly presented a level of fairness to all parties.

New threats to life itself, however, appeared in the form of nuclear power, biological and chemical warfare, and the use of space as a new arena for warfare. Space had been conquered in the span of a person's lifetime; it was only sixty-six years from humankind's first flight in 1903, in an air machine that took a man 5 feet off the ground for 120 feet, to the 25,000 mph trip to the moon in 1969. The conquest of space also made possible remarkable scientific and technological innovations in satellite communications and surveillance, including, ultimately, a palm-size global-positioning transponder capable of pinpointing any holder's location on earth.

In the 1990s, the Internet—a connecting network of major computer servers worldwide—afforded instant communication anywhere on earth, as did the handheld cellular telephone, which could place calls via satellite and which became as ubiquitous as personal computers. The crude, flickering, black-and-white moving pictures available around 1900 gave way to color television by mid-century, which brought real-time reporting into everyone's living room.

The century was not spared war; two major, worldwide hot conflicts were followed by several decades of a cold one, bracketed by numerous minor ones in every part of the globe. With them came the introduction of newer and more lethal weapons of war, both for one-on-one use and for mass destruction.

The nineteenth-century Marine Corps, which never had many more than three thousand men, grew to its maximum size of almost a half-million in the twentieth century. Unmatched battle glory in the mid-century world wars ensured that this unique organization kept its sharp edge, against a plethora of enemies, throughout the remaining half-century. The Marines Corps also fulfilled its role as the nation's Force-in-Readiness—and military standard-setter—in the Western Hemisphere and around the world, while introducing innovations that increased the efficiency of the Corps and those of other military organizations that adopted its innovations.

M1014 COMBAT SHOTGUN

Adopted by the USMC for close-range security and other operations, the H&K Benelli 12-gauge shotgun is semiautomatic in operation and uses a special retractable buttstock and separate pistol grip. It is also equipped with adjustable sights, an M1913 "Picatinny" receiver rail for mounting an optical sight, and an extended 6-round magazine tube.

M16A2 WITH M203 40MM GRENADE LAUNCHER

The M16A2, shown here mounted with an M203 grenade launcher, is a lightweight air-cooled, gas-operated, magazine-fed rifle that can be fired from either the shoulder or the hip. A selector lever allows the operator to switch between semi-automatic and automatic fire; in automatic mode, a burst-control device limits the number of rounds to three per trigger pull, which saves ammunition and increases accuracy. The lightweight, compact M203 has a maximum effective range of 400 meters. It replaced the Vietnam War–era M79 grenade launcher.

HECKLER & KOCH MP5 9MM SUBMACHINE GUN

Used for close-quarter battle (CQB) by special units, the H&K MP5 fires the 9 x 19mm NATO cartridge from a 30-round magazine and can be equipped with a collapsible buttstock and a special SureFire Tactical Light, as seen here. It fires at the rate of 750 rounds per minute.

chapter eight

The Dawn of a New Millennium

"No better friend, no worse enemy than a U.S. Marine."

MajGen James N. Mattis, USMC
CG, 1st MarDiv

Computers, those incredible digital devices that were developed to a practical degree in the fourth quarter of the preceding century, were ubiquitous by the beginning of the twenty-first century, just as common in U.S. households as the television set. By that time the military was completely dependent on them as well—they were used at every level, from the coordination of infantry to the targeting of high-tech weapons in the air and space arenas.

The Marine Corps continued to hone its role, especially in combined amphibious exercises (Phibex) with member countries of the North Atlantic Treaty Organization. In 2000, NATO conducted a Phibex with the newly independent Croatia, which had broken from Yugoslavia. One hundred and fifty miles northwest of Montenegro, on Croatia's west coast along the Adriatic Sea, Company G, Battalion Landing Team 2/2, of the 26th Marine Expeditionary Unit (Special Operations Capable), and MEU Support Service Group 26, from LHA-5 *Peleliu*, joined Croatian units in military exercises in that Balkan country.

On 1 July 1999, the Marine Corps reins passed from thirty-first CMC Chuck Krulak to Gen James L. Jones. Jones was truly a Marine for the twenty-first century. The son of a World War II Marine officer, he was raised in France, and graduated from the Georgetown University School of Foreign Service in 1966 before being commissioned a second lieutenant.

Climbing quickly up the ladder of command, he won combat decorations in Vietnam, led all types of units, served as Marine liaison to the U.S. Senate, and graduated from the National War College. He commanded main components of Joint Task Force operations in Iraq, Turkey, Bosnia-Herzegovina, and Macedonia. Before being selected as commandant, he served as military assistant to the Secretary of Defense in the Clinton administration.

One of Gen Jones's first challenges as commandant concerned the experimental MV-22 Osprey, the tilt-rotor transport in development by Bell/Boeing to replace the aging CH-46s and 53s. Several Ospreys had crashed over the previous decade of development—events not unexpected in view of the aircraft's experimental nature. Similar accident rates have been experienced during the development of almost all high-performance aircraft, especially the V/STOL Harrier. However, critics in Congress, backed by opponents from the other services, blindly threatened to curtail funding for the program. The situation was made worse by an internal scandal in Marine Corps aviation that arose when it was discovered that a squadron commander, pressured by higher-ups, had ordered maintenance records to be falsified. The officers were relieved of their commands and reprimanded. The Osprey program slowly regained momentum, and the aircraft is scheduled to enter the Marine Corps inventory around 2007, and those of the other three services soon thereafter.

Marines

TERROR STRIKES AT HOME

In the fall of 2001, terrorism came to American soil; 11 September 2001 has since superseded 7 December 1941 in the American psyche. The horrendous terrorist attacks of that morning were viewed live by most of America (and much of the world), who sat horrified in front of their television sets. The sight of commercial airliners flying straight into the Twin Towers of the World Trade Center in New York's Lower Manhattan was a mesmerizing nightmare that was punctuated shortly afterward with scenes of a similar attack at the Pentagon, a portion of which was destroyed by another airliner crash, and with news of a fourth airliner, believed to have been headed for the White House or the Capitol, which crashed with all aboard in a Pennsylvania field.

Those terrifying acts, executed within a two-hour period, shocked not only the nation, but the world, and set the United States and its allies on a course toward a war different from any that had ever been fought before. President George W. Bush, son of the Gulf War president, immediately declared a war on terrorism.

The U.S. armed forces quickly went on full alert. All commercial and private air traffic was halted, and military air units flew combat patrols over major cities while surface units intercepted coastal shipping. The people of the United States coalesced visibly in the same manner in which they had following the attack on Pearl Harbor. American flags were flown everywhere, the military received newfound respect, and President Bush saw his approval ratings soar. The nation waited for an offensive response to deliver some degree of retaliation against those responsible for the terrorist plot, Osama bin Laden and his al-Qaeda organization, which had allied itself with the de facto government of Afghanistan, the Muslim fundamentalist Taliban. President Bush proclaimed that this would be a totally different war from any the U.S. had ever fought, and that it would be a dirty and protracted effort. Although Congress did not "declare war," since the al-Qaeda terrorists did not represent a particular country, it did give the president powers to engage in "hostilities" to protect the United States from foreign enemies.

Marine Expeditionary Units from all over the globe converged in the Indian Ocean and the Arabian Sea

south of Pakistan and Iran, as other U.S. forces prepared to load out of the United States. One month after the attacks of 11 September, the Marine Corps organized an "Anti-Terrorism Brigade" from the 4th Marine Expeditionary Brigade by bringing together the previously organized Chemical-Biological Incident Response Force (CBRIF), an infantry battalion of the 8th Marines, and two Fleet Anti-Terrorist Security Teams (FAST). Designated to function under the Marine Corps Atlantic headquarters at Norfolk, Virginia, this brigade would work closely with the newly established Homeland Security Department. Homeland defense was termed Operation Noble Eagle; the operation outside of the continental limits of the United States was termed Operation Enduring Freedom.

Operation Enduring Freedom (OEF)

Forty-four days after the terrorist attacks, the United States launched aerial strikes in Afghanistan against the Taliban and al-Qaeda, hitting the caves that the military suspected hid bin Laden. Small, clandestine CIA and Army Delta Special Forces units were brought in by helicopter to liaise with the friendly Northern Alliance, a loose coalition of Afghani forces supported by the United States, and to guide the air strikes and aerial bombardments. Air strikes were conducted by Navy and Marine F/A-18 Hornets from carriers, by Marine Harriers from LHAs operating five hundred miles away in the Arabian Sea, and by the full inventory of Air Force combat aircraft. B-52 and Stealth bombers flew combat missions from their bases in the United States and on the island of Diego Garcia, in the Indian Ocean.

The first Marine air strikes were conducted on 18 October 2001 by VMFA-251, the "Thunderbolts," from the Marine Corps Air Station in Beaufort, South Carolina. Flying their Hornets from the nuclear carrier USS *Theodore Roosevelt* (CVN-71), Marine pilots flew an average of one seven-hour mission every other day, which included several air-to-air refuelings to reach their targets in northern Afghanistan. V/STOL Harriers from the 15th MEU(SOC) on the LHA-5 *Peleliu* dropped their 500-pound bombs on targets during night attacks using night-vision technology.

The 15th MEU(SOC), on the USS *Peleliu* and *Shreveport* (LPD-12), along with *Dubuque* (LPD-8) and *Comstock* (LSD-45), was on station in the Arabian Sea below Pakistan in PhibRon 8, where it was joined by the 26th MEU(SOC) recently out of Camp Lejeune in PhibRon 7, on board the USS *Bataan* (LHD-5) and the *Whidbey Island* (LSD-41). Both PhibRons composed Naval Task Force 58—commanded for the

first time in history by a Marine, BGen James N. Mattis—which centered around the nuclear carriers *Theodore Roosevelt, Enterprise* (CVN-65), *Carl Vinson* (CVN-70), and *Kitty Hawk* (CV-63). The Marines making up the two MEBs numbered nine thousand, as many as had served in the 4th Brigade in France in World War I. In the early phase, U.S. Army Rangers were inserted into Afghanistan by helicopter from aircraft carriers in the Arabian Sea.

The deployment of these forces to secure an airstrip below the city of Kandahar was the first commitment of large numbers of U.S. ground units, and the longest-distance amphibious and air deployment in Marine Corps history. The Marines penetrated into the interior of a country four hundred miles from their sea base. During the insertion, the CH-53E Super Stallion heavy helicopters landed first and refueled in allied Pakistan, then continued on and were air-refueled by Marine KC-130 Hercules tankers over southern Afghanistan before landing unopposed at their objective. Within an hour and a half, while the perimeters and other necessary areas were being set up, Marines readied the abandoned desert airstrip to receive fixed-wing and transport aircraft. The flag that had been flown at the site of the destroyed World Trade Center was sent to them to fly over this forward base in the country from which the attack had originated. SecDef Donald Rumsfeld described their mission as to "establish, hold, and patrol" their forward operations base.

By 27 November, more than a thousand Marines had secured the airstrip, established a 360-degree Tactical Area of Responsibility compound, checked for minefields, and sent out motorized and helicopter combat patrols in the vicinity to ferret out lingering Taliban and al-Qaeda forces. As they were debarking, Navy F-14 fighter-bomber pilots spotted and destroyed a fifteen-vehicle enemy motorized column headed their way. Marines in AH-1 Cobra helicopter gunships, using their night-vision equipment, finished off the job. Marine aircraft began using the airstrip, and target-designator teams pinpointed objectives for air strikes.

The Marines held the base for more than three months, engaging the enemy in sporadic firefights without suffering any combat casualties. Additionally, they received Taliban and al-Qaeda "detainees" (a new term for POWs), who were

Marine Aerial Refueler Transport Squadron 252 (VMGR-252)

BELOW: Two Marine CH-53E Super Stallions refueling at low level from a Marine KC-130 *Hercules* tanker over the LHD-1, USS *Wasp*, in the Atlantic in 2002. The heavy-lift CH-53E can be distinguished from the earlier model by its distinctive slanted tail fin and a seventh rotor blade. On deck are other CH-53Es from VMS-261, CH-46s, and AH-1W Cobra gunships. All are aviation combat elements in support of the 22d MEU(SOC) stationed on board. The *Wasp* later became the nucleus for ESG-2.

subsequently flown to an impoundment at the American naval base at Guantanamo, Cuba. Several accidents accounted for some injuries, and seven Marines of the crew of a KC-130 refueler died when it crashed into a mountain at night. In early February, the Marines turned the base over to the Army for long-term occupation, having served their role as "first in" to seize the objective.

They then redeployed at sea, in their expeditionary modes, to await the next call to action.

MARINE CORPS LEADERSHIP

Every four years, the president, upon recommendation of the Secretary of Defense, chooses a new Commandant of the Marine Corps from the top generals in the Corps. The choice is not made in a vacuum or by

lot. The senior generals constantly confer on strategy and the direction of the Marine Corps, so that whoever is chosen from the group knows the overall plan for the Corps and will continue the direction that has been decided upon, with room for each new commandant to apply his personal stamp. The personal contribution of CMC James Jones, Jr., came in the form of the "Capstone Concept" of Expeditionary Maneuver Warfare (EMW).

Expeditionary Maneuver Warfare caps a hierarchy composed, in descending order, of Integrating Concepts, Operational Concepts, Functional Concepts, and Core Concepts. As stipulated by CMC Jones, this basic structure addresses how to confront "the fundamental nature of war—a violent struggle between hostile, independent, irreconcilable wills characterized by chaos, friction, and uncertainty— [which] will remain unchanged as it transcends advancements in technology…. Sea-basing enables

LEFT: A dangerous cordon-and-search mission in Oruzgan province, Afghanistan. Two marines from BLT 1/6, the ground-combat element of the 22d MEU(SOC), weapons at the ready, search a building during Operation Cadillac Ranch in June 2004.

ABOVE: The thirty-second Commandant of the Marine Corps, Gen James L. Jones, Jr. Following his term as CMC, Jones was appointed by President George W. Bush to the post of Supreme Allied Commander, Europe (SACEUR).

forces to move directly from ship to objectives deep inland and represents a significant advance from traditional, phased amphibious operations...." Jones goes on to state:

> True expeditionary forces are those that not only can displace and go to far-flung places and operate, but [can] operate over a sustained period of time, without necessarily being reinforced the next day, or two or three days later.... [They are] sustainable...almost one-third of the logistics available to U.S. ground combat units is in the structure of the Marine Corps. We do not have to go to our Reserves to be expeditionary.
>
> Our armed forces need a certain portion that are expeditionary and a certain portion that are deployable follow-on forces right behind them. These follow-on forces will always be tethered to the flow of logistics that will support them.... The Marine Corps goes nowhere without the U.S. Navy. In the joint expeditionary world, the primacy of logistics and supportability must be considered.... We don't want to have to depend on a very short period of time where you can't do anything unless you have logistics. For about six percent of the defense budget, we provide about twenty percent of the expeditionary combat power, twenty

percent of the infantry battalions, twenty percent of the fighter and attack squadrons, seventeen percent of the attack helicopters, and about one-third of the logistics that is in the active-duty inventory for U.S. ground forces. On any given day, about thirty thousand Marines are forward-based or forward-deployed.

ABOVE: Machine gunner LCpl Michael Hahn of Lima Company, 3d Battalion, 2d Marines, on patrol in Iraq in April 2005. He mans an M240 machine gun.

4th Marine Expeditionary Brigade (Anti-Terrorism)

The Marine Corps has ever been ready to create new organizations to meet new conditions or challenges. In the nineteenth century, the small Corps was cobbled together from Navy Yard guards or ships' detachments battalions for expeditionary duty. From the Seminole Wars of the 1830s to Huntington's Battalion of 1898, the Marines made do when called upon for larger efforts than a ship's landing party could undertake.

With a larger force in the twentieth century, the Marine Corps developed special units, such as the Defense, Raider, and Parachute battalions of World War II, that meshed seamlessly with the core combat units of battalions, MEUs, and aircraft squadrons and groups.

In response to the terrorist attacks of 11 September 2001, a realignment of certain Marine forces was called for. Elements of the Marine Security Guard Battalion, the Security Force Battalion, and the Chemical-Biological Incident Response Force were pulled together under a reactivated 4th Marine Expeditionary Brigade (Anti-Terrorism). The new task force was "stood up" at Camp Lejeune on 29 October 2001 by the commandant, Gen James L. Jones.

The 4th MEB (AT) is designed to provide the National Command Authority and unified commanders with specialized, rapidly deployable anti-terrorism forces to detect, deter, and defend against terrorist threats, and to conduct initial incident responses worldwide in the event of a terrorist attack.

—BN

Global War on Terrorism (GWOT) Service Medal

Global War on Terrorism (GWOT) Expeditionary Medal

CONTINUING UNREST IN SOUTHWEST ASIA

Following the defeat of the Taliban in 2002 by U.S. and Afghani forces and the installation of a new, indigenous government in Afghanistan, the world's attention turned again to Iraq, this time because of allegations that dictator Saddam Hussein continued to possess weapons of mass destruction in defiance of the United Nations' mandate to get rid of them. Some also suspected Hussein of being in collusion with the al-Qaeda terrorist organization.

Although Iraq had straight-line borders arbitrarily drawn on the Mideast map by the British in World War I, the country was actually composed of three more-or-less ethnic divisions: the north, the center, and the south. The northern region is part of an area dominated by ethnic Kurds that spreads into Turkey and Iran (and over which the United States has imposed a "no-fly" zone for the Iraqis); the center, location of the capital, Baghdad, is predominantly Sunni Muslim (Sunnis are the self-proclaimed legal successors of Muhammad); the south, under the southern U.S.-imposed no-fly zone, is populated primarily by Shiite Muslims (descendants of the anointed followers of Muhammad). Centuries-old ethnic-tribal tensions ensured that "ne'er the trey shall meet."

Increasingly convinced that Saddam had weapons of mass destruction, and that he posed an immediate threat to the United States, in 2003 President Bush brought the matter to the United Nations, via Secretary of State Colin Powell, with a challenge to respond to the threat. The result was UN resolution 1441, which all member nations agreed upon, and which laid out extreme consequences for Saddam if he failed to cooperate with UN weapons inspectors. Saddam, however, subtly refused to fully cooperate, giving false and incomplete information and threatening any Iraqi who cooperated.

After six months of frustration and mounting opposition to his promise to remove Saddam if he did not comply, President Bush, allied with British prime minister Tony Blair, formed a coalition that included Spain and Poland to oust Saddam's regime unilaterally—and preemptively, if necessary. Former allies France and Germany—as well as Russia—vehemently opposed any preemptive attack on Iraq. China, never one to side with the United States, also objected. Therefore, it was impossible to procure sanction from the UN Security Council for military action.

Finally, giving both the United Nations and Iraq an ultimatum, Bush and his coalition of now some forty nations (with only the United States, Great Britain, and Australia contributing combat forces) were poised to launch a preemptive invasion of Iraq.

OPERATION IRAQI FREEDOM

During the six-month period in which the UN weapons inspectors in Iraq had been trying to make a case that war was not necessary, Army general Tommy Franks, commander of U.S. Central Command (CENTCOM), began moving his command and control and tactical units into place in the Persian Gulf. Franks then moved CENTCOM itself "forward" to Doha, the capital of the small, friendly, peninsular nation of Qatar. (SecDef Donald Rumsfeld and his chairman of the Joint Chiefs of Staff, Air Force general Richard Myers, oversaw the operation from the Pentagon.) Air units were stationed in Qatar and in neighboring Bahrain.

LEFT: Heavy equipment is off-loaded from a Maritime Prepositioning Force ship at a dock in Kuwait on 17 January 2003, during the buildup for the invasion of Iraq. This particular equipment load includes tanks, howitzers, and enough food and ammunition to supply seventeen thousand Marines for thirty days of combat. All supplies went to the Camp Pendleton–based I MEF, which was assembling just south of the Iraq border.

BELOW: During continual training exercises in Kuwait just ten miles south of the Iraq border, Delta Company, 1st Tank Battalion, is caught in a desert "Tooz" sandstorm while on a firing range, a month before the beginning of Operation Iraqi Freedom.

Marine Tactical Electronic
Warfare Squadron 2
(VMAQ-2)

RIGHT: A Marine pilot performs a preflight check of
his AV-8B Harrier on board
an LHA, prior to a mission
over Iraq.

FAR RIGHT: A Marine deck
crewman stands at the
ready to perform his role
in the smooth coordination
of both mission takeoff and
recovery phases.

BOTTOM RIGHT: Marine
Medium Helicopter Squadron
266 (HMM-266) CO LtCol
Joel Powers watches two
of his CH-46 Sea Knights
lift off on a mission from
Kandahar Air Field (KAF),
Afghanistan, near the end
of their four-month tour,
in late July 2004. KAF had
been the first objective in
the war, captured by U.S.
Marines two years earlier.

OPPOSITE, TOP: Capt Llonie
Cobb, a pilot in VMAQ-2,
climbs into his EA-6B
Prowler for a mission. The
venerable EA-6Bs have been
in service for decades and are
constantly upgraded. Their
performance is unequalled.

OPPOSITE: Marine Maj Robert
"Horse" Rauenhorst snags
the tail hook of his F/A-18
Hornet on the arresting cable
on the deck of the carrier
USS *Harry S. Truman* (CVN-
75), decelerating his aircraft
from 150 knots to zero in
some fifty feet. The *Truman*
was operating a Marine
squadron as well as its own
Navy squadrons in the
Persian Gulf during OIF.

Marine Helicopter Training
Squadron 301
(HMT-301)

**Marine Fighter Squadron 214
(VMF-214)**

**Marine Light Attack
Helicopter Squadron 775
(HMLA-775)**

"When I give you the word, together we will cross the Line of Departure, close with those forces that choose to fight, and destroy them. Our fight is not with the Iraqi people, nor is it with members of the Iraqi army who choose to surrender. While we will move swiftly and aggressively against those who resist, we will treat all others with decency, demonstrating chivalry and soldierly compassion for people who have endured a lifetime under Saddam's oppression.... You are a part of the world's most feared and trusted fighting force. Engage your brain before you engage your weapon. Share your courage with each other as we enter Iraq. Keep faith in your comrades to your left and right and in the Marine Air cover overhead.

For the mission's sake, for our country's sake, and the sake of the men who carried the Division's colors in past battles—'who fought for life and never lost their nerve'—carry out your mission and keep your honor clean. Demonstrate to the world there is 'no better friend, no worse enemy' than a U.S. Marine."

—MajGen James N. Mattis, USMC
CG, 1st MarDiv, prior to the invasion of Iraq

Six Navy aircraft-carrier battle groups assembled in the Gulf and the Arabian Sea, as prepositioned Marine Corps supply ships moved out from Diego Garcia toward Kuwait, and the 3d Army Infantry Division (ID) began displacing out of Ft. Stewart, Georgia.

Unlike in the first Gulf War, Arab participation in the coalition was absent. Saudi Arabia, no longer the United States' principal Arab ally, refused the U.S. request to build up forces or use bases on their soil to attack neighboring Iraq. Worse, anti-American sentiment was spreading throughout the entire Arab world. Incredibly, even in Qatar, where the American presence was welcomed, a newly formed Arab television network, Al-Jazeera, telecast a nonstop stream of anti-American programming, as did the Abu Dhabi network, from the United Arab Emirates.

Turkey, located on Iraq's northern border and a staunch U.S. ally throughout the cold war, balked, too, and ultimately refused to allow the U.S. Army's 4th Mechanized Division to transit its territory and attack Iraq from the north. This upset the U.S. timetable and jeopardized the overall operation to a great extent. The British contributed their 7th Armoured Brigade, the "Desert Rats," and their 40 Royal Commando Regiment, which operated in the south to secure the vital seaports of Um Qasr and Faw, on the Shatt al Arab waterway, and the major Shiite city of Basrah.

In the early morning hours of 20 March 2003, two days after a deadline had expired for Saddam to exile himself from Iraq, two USAF F-117A Stealth bombers streaked undetected over Baghdad, each dropping two 2,000-pound JDAM (Joint Direct Attack Munitions) bombs in succession. Each bomb penetrated deeper than the one that preceded it, down to a depth of some four floors underground—totally destroying Saddam Hussein's main palace on the bank of the Tigris River. It was earlier reported that the dictator, his two sons, and other high-ranking officials had been seen entering the palace. This shocking explosion rocked the Iraqi capital, stunned its residents, and signaled the beginning of Operation Iraqi Freedom. Neither Saddam nor his sons, Uday or Qusay, died in the attack. Regardless, intercepted telephonic traffic indicated that the regime had been rendered headless.

Later the following day, after nightfall, U.S. Marine, Army, and British ground forces, using night-vision equipment, crossed over from Kuwait and invaded Iraq. They were supported by U.S. Air Force, Navy, Marine, Army, and British air components, which were also using night-vision equipment.

LEFT: The lethal business end of a Marine AH-1W Cobra helicopter gunship. The wing pods mount laser-guided bombs and rockets, and below the front gunner (the pilot sits behind him in a separate cockpit) is a swivel three-barrel machine gun.

BELOW: Marines would never bunch up like this in combat; the perspective here has been distorted by a telephoto lens, making them look closer together. They are actually strung out about a hundred yards, with a good distance between each. These Marines are part of Task Force Tarawa, engaging stubborn resistance from Saddam Hussein's vaunted Republican Guard divisions during fighting in and around the southern Iraqi city of Nasiriyah, before blitzing forward and capturing Baghdad.

Camouflage and Copycats

In the days of close combat with smooth-bore muskets, each country had its own uniform color, so that on the battlefield its soldiers could be distinguished from their opponents. The Russian czar's army wore green, Frederick the Great's Prussians wore blue, France and Austria, white, and Britain, red. The United States chose blue as the national uniform color.

The custom changed during the American Civil War with the development of long-range rifles, machine guns, and rapid-fire artillery. Soldiers needed to be hidden rather than seen, and the traditional national colors gave way to duller shades. Probably one of the best colors for a battle uniform was the Confederate gray of the Civil War, since it blended in with the smoke of battle and the morning mists. In Britain's nineteenth-century colonial wars in India's Punjab region and the Northwest Frontier, the white robes of the quickly raised native units were dipped in mud and became "khaki," the Hindi word for mud.

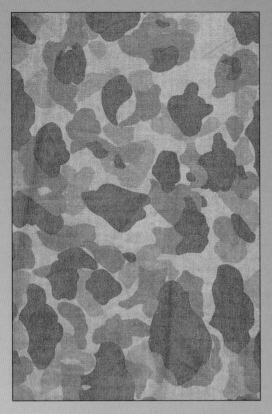

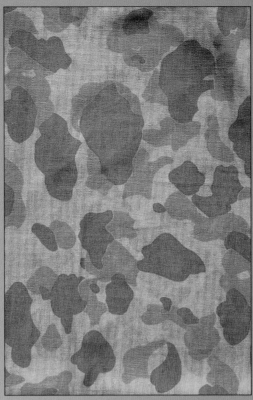

World War II Pattern
"Green Side Out"

World War II Pattern
"Brown Side Out"

Vietnam "Tiger Stripe" Pattern

Before World War I, Britain's army adopted wool khaki uniforms, Germany's donned *feldgrau*, or field gray, and in 1908 the U.S. Army began wearing olive drab. The Marine Corps followed suit with forest green in 1912. France went to war in 1914 in dark-blue coats and red pants, but soon changed to what they called horizon blue, a pale blue with the same effect as Confederate gray. These drab shades were widely used during World War II, except in the tropics of the Pacific war.

Before World War II, the U.S. Army and Marine fatigues for working-party duties were inexpensive blue-denim coveralls. Shortly before the war, the Marines changed to cotton herringbone-twill, sage-green jackets and trousers for work and field, called utilities. The Army followed suit with a darker-green cotton uniform. Early in the Pacific war, the Marine Corps developed a two-sided camouflage-pattern cloth—brown on one side, green on the other. Depending on the terrain and season—sandy atolls, deserts, or green

jungle—the order was "brown side out" or "green side out." This cloth was made into helmet covers for all hands and became the hallmark of the Marines in World War II and Korea. The two-sided cloth was also made into suits to be worn by regimental scout sniper platoons, raiders, parachute troops, and reconnaissance units. These special hard-to-get uniforms were popular with other Marines, who would beg, borrow, or steal them whenever they could.

Under the Department of Defense unification policies of the 1960s, Marines had to give up their beloved cotton utilities (as well as their cordovan for black leather) and went to Vietnam wearing the Army-style dark-green bush jackets and patch-pocket pants made of a heavier, synthetic material. The Army also produced a "woodland"-pattern green helmet cover, which both services used.

The Army of the Republic of South Vietnam (ARVN) wore a snappy "tiger stripe" camouflage uniform, which American advisers for the ARVN also

Woodland Pattern

Desert "Chocolate Chip" Pattern

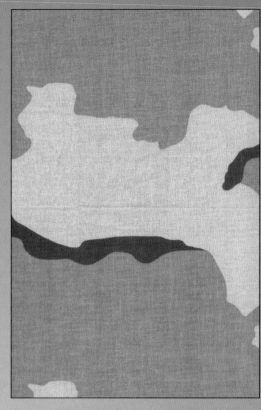

Three-Color Desert Pattern

RIGHT: As sometimes happens, supplies of certain brown- or green-side-out cammies are exhausted. Here, a Marine from Task Force Tarawa, during the battle for Nasiriyah, has a desert helmet cover and a green-camouflage gas suit, probably worn over his desert cammies. The flak jackets at first also were a mixture of desert and green. In the previous Gulf War, elements of the 4th MEB that came ashore to back up the lower border of Kuwait, while 1st and 2d MarDivs advanced, also wore green camouflage.

wore. These suits were popular with American troops, and the U.S. Army soon produced combat uniforms with its own woodland-pattern green cloth. For uniformity, the Marines wore these as well.

After the withdrawal from Vietnam, the Army returned to its dark-green combat uniform. The Defense Logistics Agency announced that it had a surplus of several hundred thousand suits of the woodland-pattern camouflage to dispose of at no charge. Marine Corps commandant Gen Louis Wilson said, "We'll take them," and Marines began to wear camouflage to distinguish themselves from the Army. Soon everyone was copying the Marines and wearing camouflage. The Naval Construction battalions (Seabees), Air Force police, and then the Army all started wearing camouflage. Meanwhile, armies around the world soon adopted camouflage, assuming it was the mark of an elite military, with countries developing their own distinct patterns.

MARPAT Digital Forest Pattern

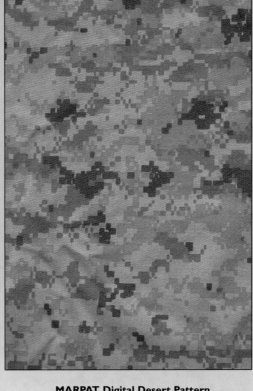

MARPAT Digital Desert Pattern

In response to the cheapening of their woodland-pattern camouflage as the badge of elite combat units, and to enter the twenty-first century in style, the Marine Corps developed its own distinct pattern of camouflage with a pixilated design to confuse digital imaging—a pattern that, one hopes, will remain unique to the Marines. The irony is that the Marine sage-green utilities of World War II and Korea, the Confederate gray of the Civil War, and the French horizon blue of World War I, all of which blend well into their surroundings, are still the best camouflage of all.

Just prior to the Gulf War, the Corps and the Army designed a camouflage pattern of tan, brown, and black—best described as chocolate chip—to be used in a desert environment. It was later modified by eliminating the contrasting darker areas for an overall light-sand look. In 2000 the Marine Corps redesigned the utility/battle uniform once again, to a light monotone with the characteristics of light deflection, digital-camera confusion, and nonregistration by night-vision devices.

—BN

ABOVE: Opinions differ as to who first designed the digital cammies, shown above. The Canadian Army (CADPAT) claims it did, and the U.S. Marine Corps (MARPAT) collaborated with them to adapt it. An independent designer, Guy Cramer, posted a similar design on his website in 1998 as PIXELPAT. It also appears that Finland has adopted a variation for its army, as China has for its marines. Not to be left behind again, the U.S. Army is adopting the pixilated design as well. Marines lead the way; the others follow.

LEFT: Marines patrol the area around Daly Airfield in Iraq, in April 2003. They wear desert cammies with green, woodland-pattern flak jackets.

ABOVE: Early in Operation Iraqi Freedom, Marines from Charlie Company, 1/7, observe enemy Russian-made T-55 tanks near the oil refinery at Az Zubayr, Iraq. Marines captured their oil-field objectives without suffering any damage and facing only light resistance.

BELOW: Pfc David R. Bailey of Gold Company, 2d Battalion, 6th Marines, on security patrol near Iraq's Daly Airfield in April 2003. His helmet is in the new MARPAT digital desert pattern.

"Shock and Awe"

The rapid success in this new war with Iraq lay in the unexpected. With the television cameras of the world following the coalition's every move during the buildup, it was impossible to take advantage of the element of surprise. Since it seemed most logical that the coalition would attack from just two directions, north and south, the enemy concentrated its forces at those obvious avenues of approach. Given the overwhelming strength of U.S. airpower, it was also assumed that prolonged air attacks would precede any ground attack, as had been the case in Kuwait (thirty-two days of air attacks) and Kosovo (seventy-eight days).

Counting on just such assumptions, Gen Franks and I MEF commander LtGen James T. Conway "shocked" the Iraqis—and the world—by launching simultaneous air and ground attacks, and "awed" them as well with the lightning strikes of its coordinated air and ground elements. This was not designed only to surprise the Iraqis. It had a two-fold purpose: 1) to prevent them from destroying their own oil fields—as they had done to the Kuwaiti fields a decade earlier—before the Marines and Brits could quickly capture the fields and keep the oil flowing for the benefit of the Iraqi people; and 2) to move so quickly that Iraqi troops would not have time to deploy any weapons of mass destruction, especially biological and chemical agents. (Gen Franks, in his 2004 book, *American Soldier*, relates how he had been warned personally by Jordan's King Abdullah II and Egyptian president Mubarak that Saddam Hussein had weapons of mass destruction and would not hesitate to use them. Thus it was Gen Franks's strategy to thrust into Iraq at all-out speed with fewer troops [130,000], as opposed to the recommendation of the Joint Chiefs of Staff of 500,000 troops and a conventional attack. SecDef Rumsfeld upheld Franks's strategy.)

Army units crossed the Kuwaiti-Iraqi border and barreled their way northward along the western bank of the Euphrates River to Baghdad. Elements of the 173d Airborne Brigade parachuted into northern Iraq to direct and assist the Kurdish militia there. Airborne Delta and Ranger special ops units secured SAM sites and airfields in western Iraq and in the north assisted indigenous Kurds, who were enemies of the Saddam regime. Meanwhile, SEAL and Marine special ops units were dropped in the east, to reconnoiter the avenues of advance, and around the southern seaports, to assist the Brits in clearing that area.

OPERATION IRAQI FREEDOM I
20 March—15 April 2003

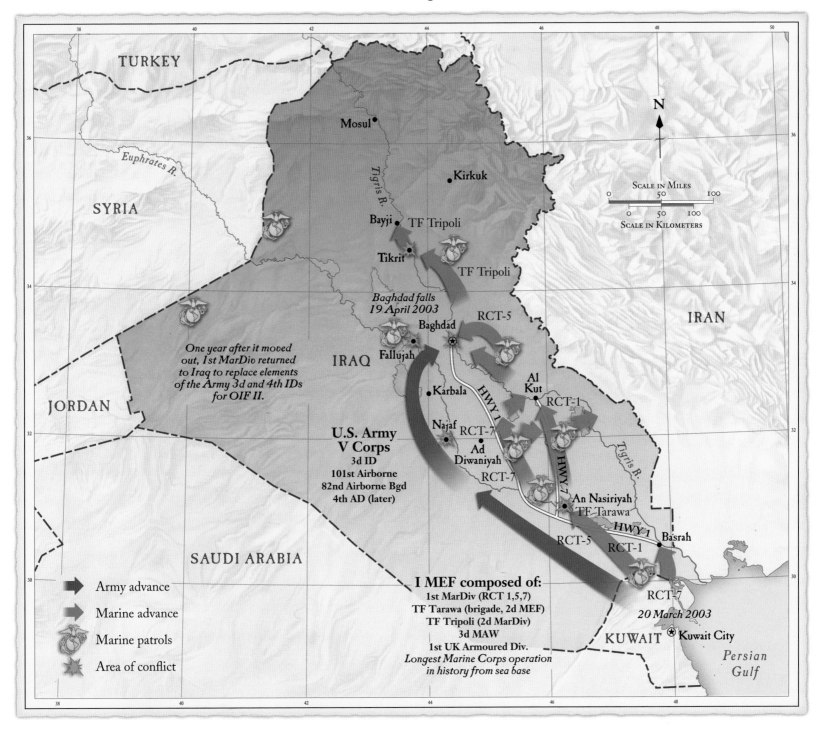

Simultaneously, I MEF's 1st MarDiv and 2d MEB seized the Rumaila oil field in southern Iraq and blitzed up the eastern banks of the Tigris River to Baghdad in their M1A1 main battle tanks, LAVs, and AAVs. Both Army and Marine forces attacked up two major paved two-lane highways, keeping their flanking protection and vanguard units well dispersed in the surrounding desert.

Foot-dragging in the UN and Turkey's decision not to cooperate had delayed the D-date past February, which would have afforded the optimal seasonal temperatures. Consequently, as U.S. forces advanced over the first two weeks, they were not only besieged by a two-day sandstorm, but the temperature began to rise into the upper eighties and nineties. These conditions made it difficult to operate in the cumbersome gas protective suits and required individuals to consume larger amounts of water. Assault elements had started in condition MOPP-2, which required that they wear a protective suit (and carry

Embedded Journalists, Combat Artists, and Military Analysts

For the War on Terrorism, an unusual approach to the handling of the press had been devised by the military, based on lessons learned from the Vietnam, Balkan, and Gulf wars. Some 150 journalists who were credentialed to go into battle were "embedded" with specific units. Prior to the Iraq War, those to be assigned to the Marines underwent a weeklong indoctrination course at the Basic School in Quantico, Virginia.

Press journalists, still photographers, military analysts, and on-camera reporters, with their camera crews and satellite dishes, accompanied their assigned units, giving running—if myopic—accounts of what they were able to see and experience. Unlike in any other war, the American public was able to watch the conduct and progress of the conflict from every aspect, twenty-four hours a day, seven days a week, on the major cable networks. For these journalists, being up front with the troops in a real shooting war was a once-in-a-lifetime experience, and gave them a healthy respect for the armed forces. During the period of major operations, three reporters died in combat, one in a vehicle accident and one by natural causes; four independent foreign journalists were captured for a short time and later released.

The Corps' own retired LtCol Oliver L. North served as an on-camera military analyst for the Fox News Network, accompanying RCT-5 and HMM-268 and 267 (heavy-helicopter squadrons) all the way to Baghdad. North, who gained national attention during the Reagan administration, is now a popular television host of the Fox News series *War Stories,* a syndicated columnist, and a prolific author. In *War Stories: Operation Iraqi Freedom* (Regnery), he describes his experiences in Iraq.

Also with 1st MarDiv, but in an independent capacity, were former Marine Lt F.J. "Bing" West and retired Marine MajGen Ray L. Smith, a decorated veteran of the Battle of Hue during the Tet Offensive in Vietnam in 1968. Their book, *The March Up: Taking Baghdad with the 1st Marine*

LEFT: Retired Marine LtCol Oliver L. North, back in combat as a military analyst for the Fox News Network, telephones a report to Fox News during the attack toward Baghdad, on 7 April 2003. This photograph was taken from a passing LVT by Marine Capt Sean Basco, a Forward Air Controller attached to 1st Battalion, 5th Marine Regimental Combat Team.

ABOVE: As in all recent wars, the Corps sent artists out of the History and Museums Division into combat. For OIF, Sgt Jack Carrillo was assigned from the Visual Imaging Section, Quantico. Here, he is shown sketching in a helicopter while flying over Al Kut, Iraq, in May 2003. A Reservist combat artist, SSgt Mike Fay was recalled and arrived shortly after Carrillo. Below and right are samples of Carrillo's and Fay's artwork, respectively.

155 ARTILLERY OUTBOUND SOUTHEAST OF BAGHDAD 5APR03

Division (Bantam)—the title a nod to Xenophon's account of the ten thousand Greek hoplites' similar "march up" to take Baghdad in 400 BC, in his classic, *Anabasis*—covers in vivid detail the entire I MEF operation.

On assignment as official historians were Col Nicholas E. Reynolds, USMCR, who in civilian life works for the government, and Maj Theodore R. McKeldin, USMCR, a civilian contractor. Combat art was covered by Sgt Jack Carrillo, of the Combat Visual Imaging Center at Quantico (under former Gulf War combat artist Capt Charles Grow), which also sent combat photographers. Reserve SSgt Michael Fay, who covered the Afghanistan war, was called back to active duty by the Marine Corps History and Museums Division and arrived with I MEF after the siege of Baghdad.

The Public Affairs Office at HQMC benefited from the direction of BGen Andrew B. Davis, USMCR, a former newspaper reporter and editor on leave from his media management position at Northwestern University.

—HAC

an extra one) but not gas masks, gloves, or boots. Still, wearing a helmet plus the suit with a flak jacket on top made the oppressive heat almost unbearable. When the Army and the Marines reached Baghdad, the temperature hovered near one hundred degrees Fahrenheit.

The Ground War Strategy

The strategy in Operation Iraqi Freedom was not to go slowly and engage Iraqi ground units, but to blitz north at night without lights, using night-vision equipment, straight to Baghdad in two giant columns along the two major paved highways, bypassing towns and cities wherever possible to avoid civilian casualties and collateral damage. On the left, the U.S. Army V Corps, consisting of the 3d ID and the 82d and 101st Airborne divisions, sped up the west bank of the Euphrates River, while elements of the 173d Brigade, along with Delta Forces, struck enemy targets in the north, in lieu of the Army 4th ID's planned attack from Turkey.

To the east, I MEF (commanded by LtGen James T. Conway), composed of 1st MarDiv (commanded by MajGen James N. Mattis, veteran of the Afghan war), elements of 2d MarDiv (commanded by BGen Richard F. Natonski) and II MEF, and the British 1st Armoured Division—covered by 3d MAW's (commanded by MajGen James F. Amos) 130 fixed-wing aircraft, 60 helicopter gunships, tanker transports, and CH-46 supply and MedEvac choppers—raced up Route 1, a double-lane, divided highway between the Euphrates and Tigris rivers.

The first objective was dispatched quickly: seizure of the Rumaila oil field and oil pumping station, near Basrah in the south. Plagued only by a blinding, two-day sandstorm, the three Marine Regimental Combat Teams (RCTs 1, 5, and 7) smashed their way up Route 1, then up the west side of the Tigris, then onto Route 7, a paved two-lane road. Both roads were used for landing strips by Marine KC-130 four-engine prop, cargo, and fuel resupply aircraft. Blasting through several bloody encounters and gaining 250 kilometers in the first four days, the RCTs destroyed everything

ABOVE: Victorious officers confer following the combat phase of OIF: from left to right are LtGen James T. Conway, CG, I MEF; Col John F. Dunford, CO, RCT-5; Col John C. Coleman, Chief of Staff, I MEF; and MajGen James N. Mattis, CG, 1st MarDiv.

After eighteen days of crushing advance—halted briefly by a sandstorm—the Army 3d ID captured the major airport a dozen miles west of downtown Baghdad, changing its name from Saddam International to Baghdad International Airport. Astonishingly, one of its armored columns executed a daring twenty-five-mile mechanized combat task force raid through a section of the city itself that startled both residents and irregular remnant defenders alike. It also made a mockery of the regime's claims that the Americans were more than a hundred miles away and would never be allowed to enter the city.

The Marines on the east had to bridge their way across a tributary, but also entered the city and seized several of the deposed dictator's bomb-wrecked palaces and the university. Marine Task Force Tarawa also assisted jubilant Iraqi citizens in pulling down an enormous bronze statue of Saddam that sat atop a tall pedestal in Firdos (Paradise) Square—an image caught by embedded TV camera crews and televised to the whole world. That image became the icon of the two-week war, much as the Iwo Jima flag-raising by Marines did in the Pacific war in World War II.

After Task Force Tripoli (from II MEF) was sent to capture Saddam's hometown of Tikrit, two hundred

ABOVE: A sniper team from Marine Reserve 2d Battalion, 23d Marines, 4th MarDiv (activated from San Bruno, California) moves quickly for a better firing position during the advance to Baghdad. Although impeded by their heavy gas suits (and carrying an extra one)—and the intense heat—they proved lethally effective with their sniper rifles and scopes.

in their path and bypassed five other enemy divisions, which proceeded to dissolve as their soldiers deserted. Then, instead of following the obvious—and expected—direct route into Baghdad and directly into two Republican Guard divisions, the three RCTs abruptly turned east onto Route 17, between the two rivers. They then fought their way across the Tigris and continued the attack on the paved highway on the east bank of the river, right into the east side of the Iraqi capital.

The feat was remarkable in military annals. Thirty thousand Marines in eight thousand vehicles—with some convoys stretching fifty miles long and at times averaging forty-five miles per hour—advanced from the line of departure at the Kuwaiti border some five hundred miles up to the enemy capital in just ten days, knocking out all resistance they met and taking relatively few casualties in the process.

kilometers north of Baghdad, they returned, and I MEF moved back to Kuwait, as the Army 4th ID replaced them for what turned out to be a lingering, terrorist-guerrilla war that ultimately resulted in more casualties than the initial assault phase.

The End of OIF I

President Bush declared an end to major combat operations in Iraq on 1 May 2003. Both the Marines and the Army took moderate casualties up to this point; a total of 150 had been killed in action (including 23 Marines), and more than 400 were wounded. However, those numbers grew in sporadic action during the postwar occupation. A year after President Bush declared victory, U.S. KIAs numbered 1,000 and WIAs more than 6,000. Nevertheless, the losses in the three-week, 375-mile assault to Baghdad were fewer than had been taken in the four-day, 45-mile assault into Kuwait City twelve years earlier.

Weaponry had improved markedly over the decade following the first Gulf War, giving the planners of the new war advantages in both strategy and tactics. The astonishing accuracy of aerial bombing in Operation Desert Storm was now perfected to pinpoint precision. The American armed forces were a marvel of technical efficiency, with improved bombs, such as JDAMs, GBUs (Guided Bomb Units) and MOABs (the 21,000-pound "Mother of All Bombs"), new Tomahawk cruise missiles, tried-and-true B-52 high-altitude bombers with improved ordnance, untried B-1B Lancer bombers, B-2 Spirit (radar invisible) bombers, E-8 Joint Stars, new and improved artillery, Predator unmanned aerial vehicles, and newer Patriot missile interceptor rockets. The use of night-vision equipment, in particular, made the Americans an unstoppable force.

ABOVE: The thirty-third commandant, Gen Michael W. Hagee (2003–present).

LEFT: Marines of 3d Battalion, 1st Marines, roar past a raging fire on their way to Baghdad on 8 April 2003. The almost three-hundred-mile blitz was interrupted by sporadic resistance from Iraqi forces—which the Marines quickly destroyed.

M249 Squad Automatic Weapon (SAW)

A 5.56 x 45mm NATO–caliber belt-fed light machine gun, the SAW (also called the MINIMI) is a squad-level weapon that fires the same ammunition as the M16A4 rifle. The SAW, shown here with a lightweight canvas belt holder, replaced the BAR, and is the weapon around which the Marine fire team is built. Note that every fifth tracer round is red-tipped, which allows the gunner to see where his fire is hitting.

ABOVE: During the first battle for Fallujah in April 2004 when I MEF had returned to Iraq for its second tour, the new interim Iraqi government halted the Marine advance and tried to negotiate with the insurgents to give up. Although the Marines halted their house-to-house fighting, they still had to contend with sporadic sniper and mortar fire. Here, a Marine sniper sights his M107 at the source of a rocket-propelled grenade (RPG) attack.

BELOW: A Barrett M107 .50-caliber (.50-BMG) sniper rifle with a 10-round magazine.

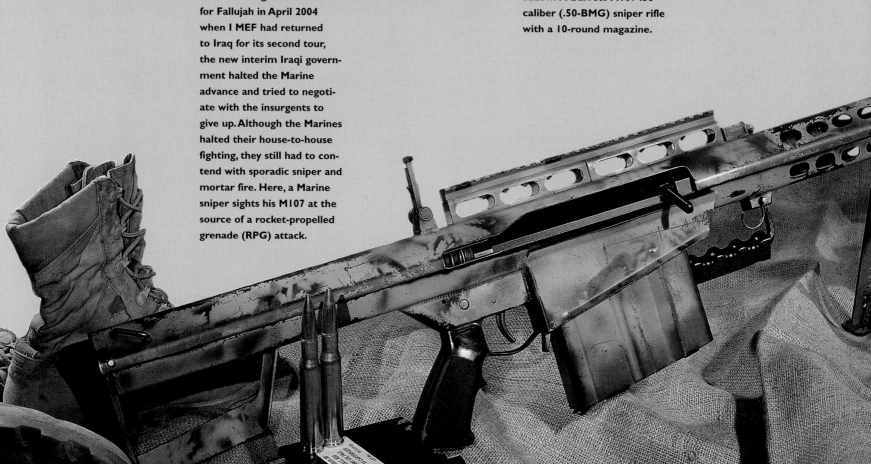

Designated Marksmen

While all Marines are expected to qualify with the rifle as "expert rifleman," "sharpshooter," or "marksman," the Corps continues to improve the combat capability of its basic infantry unit, the squad. To this end, the Thompson submachine gun was added to the squad in the 1920s and '30s, while an automatic BAR or M249 and a grenade launcher was added to each of the three four-man fire teams from 1943 to the present.

The latest innovation, and one that has greatly increased the combat effectiveness of the Marine rifle squad, is the designated marksman (DM). The best shot in each rifle squad will be provided with a rifle with a telescopic sight. The rifle would be the M14A2 with sight or the same M16A2 the other riflemen use, but with a sight added. The telescopic sight will enable the DM to seek out obscure targets, those hidden from the naked eye, that might oppose the squad at the midranges of two hundred to five hundred yards. This role is in contrast to that of the sniper teams armed with a more powerful and accurate rifle with telescopic sight, and who search for targets from hidden positions and at much longer ranges.

—BN

ABOVE: A new sniper rifle field tested in combat in Afghanistan in January 2002. Modified by the weapons section of Marine Corps Combat Development Command, Quantico, this M14 DMR (Designated Marksman Rifle) is used effectively here by Sgt Jason E. Capozzoli, of the 26th MEU(SOC) recon team.

BELOW: Providing a measure of extra security at the U.S. Embassy at Kabul, Afghanistan, LCpl Jeremy R. Riddle, designated marksman for Task Force Kabul, scopes a target with his DMR M14. The task force is part of the 4th MEB (Anti-Terrorism).

ABOVE: A Marine Harrier from VMA-542, piloted by LtCol Russell A. Sanborn, CO, refuels from a Marine KC-130T Hercules tanker over the largest lake in Iraq, Buhayrat al-Tharthar. The refueling enabled Sanborn's squadron to continue providing close air support over Fallujah during a renewal of the fighting there in September 2004.

RIGHT: Marines of Alpha Company, 1/5, use a Humvee for partial cover during close-in street fighting on the outskirts of Fallujah. The Humvee mounts a 40mm grenade launcher.

Once again the American public had reason to be proud of their Marine Corps, Army, Navy, and Air Force—and even the Coast Guard, which patrolled the Persian Gulf, sweeping for mines. All had performed their unique roles splendidly and professionally. But, not necessarily commented upon, all of the services notably acted together—*jointly*—in concert, as smoothly as a lubricated watch. The old snafus of the USS *Mayaguez*, the bungled attempt to rescue the Iranian hostages, the foul-ups of Haiti, Grenada, Panama, and Somalia—and even the glitches of the first Gulf War—had been worked out. The result was an astounding performance of expertly coordinated and highly efficient fighting by the best armed forces the world has ever witnessed.

Restraint was prevalent in every respect. Only military targets were hit—and those precisely. Major cities were bypassed, and collateral damage and civilian casualties were limited. The rapid pace of the twin-pronged attack threw the enemy off balance. The elimination of military objectives was swift and efficient, and allied casualties were relatively moderate. The number of enemy prisoners of war was extraordinarily high, as was the number of enemy casualties. Not only did the magnificently coordinated attack rid the world of a ruthless dictator and free the Iraqi people, but it also proved once again that the United States had no territorial intentions in the region.

KIMBER MODEL 1911-TYPE .45-ACP ICQB WITH INTEGRATED MILITARY PISTOL LIGHT

Dropping the 9mm M9 Beretta pistol after two decades, the Marine Expeditionary Unit, Special Operations Capable [MEU(SOC)] continued to rebuild and upgrade existing Model 1911A1 pistols, adding the SureFire tactical light, a special Safariland holster, and a GemTech lanyard. When Detachment One (DET-1) was formed from MEU(SOC) as the Corps' first element of the U.S. Special Operations Command (USSOCOM), known as MCSOCOM, it adopted a special version of the Kimber 1911 called the Interim Close Quarter Battle pistol (ICQB), shown here. MEU(SOC) will follow with the general adoption of a .45-caliber CQB pistol. The Kimber ICQB is the first 1911-type pistol to be marked "USMC."

RIGHT AND BELOW: In the holy Shia city of Najaf and in the nearby cemetery, Marines saw close hand-to-hand combat, often with knives, and faced intense fire from the AK-47s, mortars, and rocket-propelled grenades of Muqtada al-Sadr's Mahdi militia. At right, Marine SSgt Robert Willis, crouching at center, takes over from his wounded and evacuated platoon lieutenant and instructs his men to press the attack. Below, Sgt Yadir Reynoso helps treat wounded comrades. Several hours later, Reynoso himself was killed in action. During the three-week battle in the summer of 2004, nine Marines were killed and one hundred were wounded; Iraqi casualties were estimated to be in the hundreds.

Continuing Insurgency

Officially, combat ended after twenty-seven days; however, sporadic firefights with insurgents continued, and mopping-up operations were necessary in Baghdad and Tikrit, which had been Saddam's principal home and which had been taken with little opposition. After a period of stabilization and restoration of a semblance of law and order, the Marines were relieved by the Army 4th Mechanized Division and moved south into the Basrah area, before shipping out to their various home stations. Saddam's notorious sons, Uday and Qusay, were killed by U.S. soldiers, and more than fifty of the top Baathist leaders were captured. On 13 December 2003, soldiers of 3d ID tracked down the deposed dictator himself, and ignominiously extracted him, disheveled and unkempt, from the shallow "spider hole" bunker where he had hidden himself.

Once again, the U.S. Marines had risen to the call. They had spearheaded their sector in a rapid advance under fire that culminated in the destruction of all enemy forces in their way and the capture of all of their objectives. Thus a fifty-first battle streamer was added to the Marine Corps' long and glorious history. In the combat phase of OIF, five Navy Crosses were awarded to Marines, along with numerous Silver and Bronze Stars. As of this writing, no Medals of Honor have been awarded for the Iraq War.

The Beginning of OIF II

With Operation Iraqi Freedom complete, the initial Marine and Army units were replaced by fresh units. However, this put such a strain on U.S. military forces, already spread thinly around the globe, that replacements had to be drawn from other deployed units, and a continuous call-up of Reservists and National Guardsmen was issued. These measures, in turn, caused a decline in recruiting in all armed forces.

In April 2004, I MEF returned to Iraq (OIF II), and units of 1st MarDiv engaged in sporadic but bloody engagements in areas they had not seen before: Fallujah, Mosul, the Syrian border, Najaf, and other hot spots.

On 28 July, a new interim Iraqi government was installed, to serve until free elections could be held in January 2005 under its new constitution. The mission of U.S. occupying forces changed to that of providing overall security, of backing up Iraqi civil authorities, and of organizing and training a new Iraqi national constabulary and army. These efforts were thrown off balance by stepped-up insurgent activity throughout the country. As of this writing, Saddam Hussein remains in U.S. custody, under the direction of newly elected Iraqi prime minister Ibrahim Jaafari, awaiting trial by an Iraqi free-court system.

Unexpectedly, instead of concentrating on restoring peace and rebuilding infrastructure, U.S. forces have had to fend off attacks by rebel insurgents while training the fledgling Iraqi police force and army.

In 2007, al-Qaeda and Iranian terrorists continue to foster and reinforce Sunni/Shiite instability. Islamic terrorists have also upgraded Improvised Explosive Devices (IEDs) with deadlier, aimed propellants. As a result, U.S. casualties are increasing at a time when equipment is wearing out. Additionally, regular, Reserve, and National Guard troops must now serve multiple combat tours.

LESSONS AND INNOVATIONS

Through the 2001 war in Afghanistan, the uniqueness of Marine Corps missions and combat forces lay in the basics of moving from ship to shore by air, and in its indigenous aviation that provided close air support for front-line troops.

The Iraq War of 2003, however, called for and demonstrated some basic tactical innovations for both the Marines and the Army.

MK19 MOD-3 Automatic Grenade Launcher

Amounting to a 40mm machine gun, the MK19 MOD-3 fires high-explosive 40mm grenades from a belt. It can be mounted on a tripod for ground use or on a pedestal atop a vehicle and fires at a rate of 325 rounds per minute.

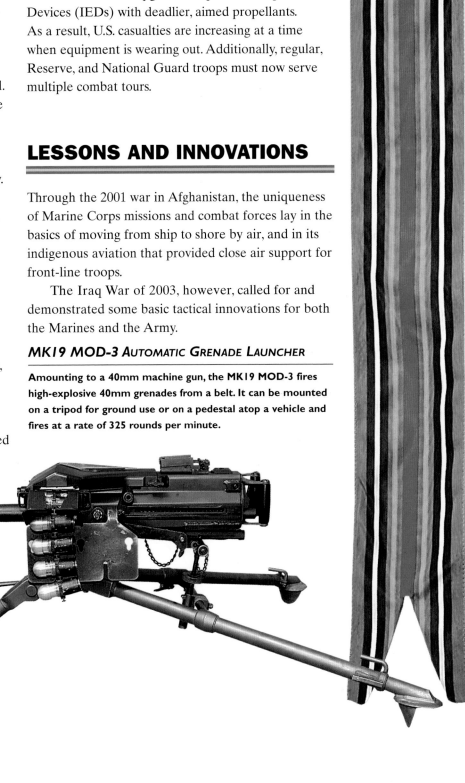

The Urban Warfare Test: The Battles for Fallujah

The spring-to-fall 2004 Marine siege of the insurgent-held city of Fallujah, thirty-five miles west of Baghdad, demonstrated the feasibility of the "three-block" urban warfare concept, involving civilian, political, and asymmetrical military operations first advocated by CMC Victor Krulak ten years earlier. As retired Col Gary W. Anderson pointed out in a *Marine Corps Gazette* analysis, in urban fighting by Marines in the so-called Sunni Triangle (Baghdad, Tikrit, Ramadi), the Quantico Warfighting School's study of urban warfare paid off.

Especially effective, according to Anderson, was the issuance of orders to all lower echelons via signals, runners, and squad radios in order to avoid bunching up; the maintenance of a constant 360-degree defense called back clearing to stem the enemy's attempts to encircle and strike; and the precise use of combined and focused fire from supporting arms, tanks, MC-130 gunships, and Cobra attack helicopters, to avoid civilian casualties. Increased long-range sniper fire proved particularly effective and precise, with no civilian casualties, as did the Marines' adaptability to changing situations in the heat of combat, responding quickly to the enemy's changing tactics as in a previous battle at Najaf—where the Shiites tried to use searchlights to negate Marine night-vision capability. In Fallujah, the Sunni insurgents aped Marine tactics in many instances, since they had no training or fixed battle doctrine of their own.

Marine emphasis on cultural intelligence was also effective all the way down to the rifleman, and was applied to humanitarian and nation-building efforts in cooperation with local tribal leaders and sheiks

in battle areas. Thus the Corps' humanitarian concern for noncombatants persuaded many Iraqis to help the Marines.

Tactical commanders had the unprecedented ability to look down from low level on enemy positions and around corners using the new remote-operated, Dragon and Silver Fox unmanned aerial vehicles (UAVs). Improved body armor saved lives, and improved breaching equipment took care of heretofore deadly obstacles. One of the only major unsolved problems was the enemy's use of innocent civilians and holy sites and schools as shields, and their exploitation of combat-related damage or casualties for propaganda purposes. Nevertheless, despite what the enemy tried,

the Marines dominated both the ground and the airspace over the battle sites. Command of I MEF had passed to LtGen John Sattler, 1st MarDiv was commanded by MajGen Richard Natonski, and the 5th Marines spearheaded the attack. Former Marine and ex-Assistant Secretary of Defense Bing West reported from Fallujah how "The Watchdogs" of VMU-1 on the perimeter operated the Pioneer and Predator unmanned aerial vehicles. In one case, they guided a Hellfire-missile-equipped Predator, launched from Baghdad but crewed from a base in California, to a target inside Fallujah using GPS coordinates to align these weapon platforms. Then, they contacted two Marine Harriers on station at nineteen thousand feet and guided them via the monitoring UAVs to eliminate the target.

On 8 November 2004, the final attack on Fallujah was ordered by the Iraqi interim prime minister. The 1st MarDiv, shepherding the untried 36th Iraqi Commando Battalion, jumped off in Operation Phantom Fury, later renamed Operation al-Fajr (Arabic for "dawn"), first securing an insurgent-held hospital on the western perimeter, then storming into the city from the northwest and driving house-by-house southward into a neighborhood they dubbed Queens. Meanwhile, elements of the 1st Army ID advanced on the left flank. It took a grueling weeklong battle to ferret out the remaining insurgents, most of whom had abandoned the city along with the civilian population. Ruthless Abu Musab al-Zarqawi, the Jordanian leader of the insurgents, did not stand and fight but fled with most of his militia, made up in part of Syrian, Jordanian, Iranian,

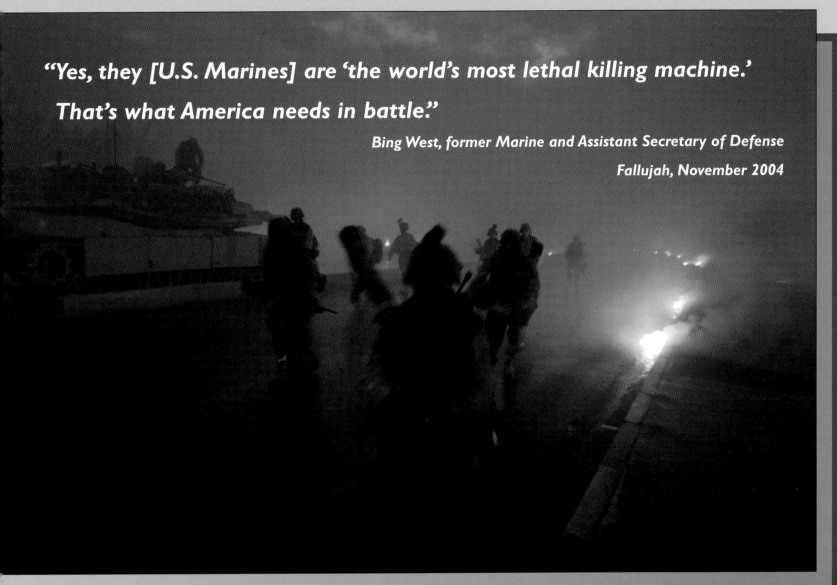

"Yes, they [U.S. Marines] are 'the world's most lethal killing machine.' That's what America needs in battle."

Bing West, former Marine and Assistant Secretary of Defense

Fallujah, November 2004

Moroccan, Saudi, and Afghan fighters, many of whom were allied with al-Qaeda, Hezbollah, or Islamic Jihad. Their aim, of course, was to upset the establishment of a secular, free government in Iraq. An estimated one thousand of them were killed, while the Marines and Army sustained some forty KIA and three hundred WIA (wounded in action).

West also commented on remarks by a British correspondent covering the insurgents' side, who observed, "The U.S. Marines are the world's most lethal killing machine." West, a Vietnam veteran and former Assistant Secretary of Defense, retorted, "If America needs a hard job done, the Marines will do it, and they won't lose their humanity in the process or any sleep over pulling the trigger. Yes, they are 'the world's most lethal killing machine.' That's what America needs in battle."

As the Marine Corps gains more experience in urban/asymmetrical warfighting, the introduction of newer effective weapons is inevitable. Promising is a mobile prototype of the active denial system (ADS), which is a nonlethal weapon (NLW) that uses millimeter-wavelength technology to incapacitate human targets by causing a burning sensation on the skin. The weapon's tiny radiated waves excite the fluid molecules just under the surface of the skin. The effect, while dramatic, causes no permanent damage. Such weapons will be highly effective in crowd control. They could also win urban battles without the destruction of buildings or the necessity of room-to-room fighting. The use of vehicle-size robots is also being explored.

–HAC

OPPOSITE: Designed to drive rebel insurgents out of Fallujah, Operation Phantom Fury, later renamed Operation al-Fajr (Arabic for "dawn"), was a joint effort involving both American and Iraqi forces. Here, exhausted Marines of Company I, 3d Battalion, 5th Marines, catch a breather inside a secured building during the fighting in early November 2004.

ABOVE: Marines of Bravo Company, 1st Battalion, 8th Marines, scurry for cover after a Marine artillery "short round" of white phosphorus that was intended to set a smoke screen in front of them lands in their midst. Fortunately, no one was burned or otherwise injured.

Above and Beyond: Humanitarian Aid

During the final capture of Baghdad in April 2003, lawlessness and looting were rampant. Some ten thousand priceless artifacts of the Mesopotamian-Sumerian civilization were stolen from Iraq's National Museum. Unjust criticism fell on the United States for failing to safeguard them.

CENTCOM assigned Marine Reserve Col Matthew Bogdanos to form a team to investigate the thefts and track down the missing antiquities. As a civilian, Bogdanos was a Manhattan assistant district attorney with a master's degree in classical studies. He had already been sent to Afghanistan in a similar capacity. Bogdanos assembled agents from multiple U.S. and international agencies, along with his Marines. Their mission was to find and return the missing artifacts to the Iraqi people, not to pursue criminal prosecutions.

In an atmosphere of utter chaos, with few records or catalogs of artifacts available, Bogdanos' strategy was to win the trust of Iraqi civilians through personal contact, and to rely on their informing on the looters. His strategy not only succeeded in the recovery of artifacts, it also created great goodwill among the liberated populace. And, in the yearlong effort, more than 5,500 stolen artifacts were recovered, including some of the finest pieces of the period, such as the Treasure of Nimrud, the Warka Vase, and the fabled Golden Harp of Ur.

Marines have always assisted civilians and the helpless in war zones. Their generosity, especially toward children, is almost legendary. Iraq and Afghanistan were no exceptions. While the daily news concentrated on isolated suicide bombings by irreconcilable former Baathists, the positive news of assistance by Marines in rebuilding Iraq's infrastructure, its schools, its roads, its hospitals, and in training Iraqi security forces, all the while working with the interim government to secure the first free elections ever in that country, went virtually unreported.

–HAC

ABOVE: The right man for the job, Marine Reserve Col Matthew Bogdanos. An assistant Manhattan district attorney, boxer, and classicist, Bogdanos went on active duty after his apartment near the World Trade Center was destroyed on 11 September 2001. He organized and led the task force to recover antiquities stolen from the Iraq National Museum.

RIGHT: Marine Cpl Troy Merrill of Col Bogdanos' task force holds a priceless artifact found and returned to the Iraq National Museum. It is a five-thousand-year-old Sumerian baked-clay tablet with cuneiform writing on it. Baghdad is situated in the heart of the Fertile Crescent, the area between the Tigris and Euphrates rivers where the ancient cities of Babylon and Nimrud blossomed.

Mobility and Jointness

The rapid advance of twin U.S. Army and Marine mechanized units into Iraq from Kuwait—bypassing nonstrategic cities on the way to the main target, Baghdad—astonished the world. The Army infantry and mechanized divisions raced to battle in their Bradley fighting vehicles and M1A1 Abrams tanks, while the Marine MEF dashed forward in their LAVs and AAVs (amphibious tractors that carried troops, supplies, and ammunition), led by M1A1 Main Battle Tanks. Both Army and Marine units were, of course, supported by their own artillery, mostly 155mm howitzers, which had to keep pace, displace, set up, align targets, and fire in front of the rapidly advancing forces.

Both the Marines and the Army had helicopters: the Army, troop-carrying Chinooks, smaller Huey Black Hawks, and Apache gunships, all comparable to Marine CH-53Es, CH-46s, and Cobra gunships. The Marines, however, also had AV-8B Harriers for close air support and interdiction and carrier-based F/A-18 Hornets for long-range and combat air patrol. The Air Force A-10 Warthogs provided an on-call form of close air support and tank-busting for the Army.

The Air Force provided all forces with AWACS (Airborne Warning and Control System) and enemy target location information from their specialized 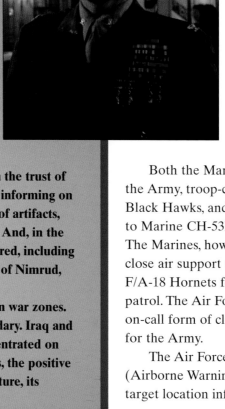 Joint Star aircraft. The Air Force, Army, and Marines all utilized unmanned aerial vehicles to observe the enemy and relay televised images of targets, and even to hit them with remote-guided missiles. Satellite imagery was also used by the overall command, and GPS transponders were ubiquitous, used by individuals and missile and bomb guidance systems alike.

After decades of working to achieve it, a coordinated jointness of Army, Marine, Air Force, and Navy operations was finally perfected. The usual friction between the Marines and the

Army, in particular, seemed to have vanished. In fact, in the eyes of the Marines, the Army's 3d ID and elements of the 82d and 101st Airbornes performed magnificently—as aggressively and efficiently as the Marines themselves. Both stormed up parallel routes to capture the capital with few casualties and little collateral damage.

The first apparent lesson of Gen Tommy Franks's new "lightning" style of mechanized raids (not exactly patterned after the German blitzkrieg or Gen Patton's WWII tactics) was that light, highly mobile units performed better in such limited warfare. This put to bed once and for all Army plans to develop a giant field-artillery piece and other heavy weaponry designed for conventional warfare.

The 70-ton M1A1 tank, while performing extraordinarily, was found to be too heavy and difficult to support and maintain at great distances. Future plans call for an air-transportable 30-ton tank. The prospect arose that even artillery should be lighter, in order to move more rapidly and be more easily transported. Night-vision capabilities proved their importance, as did the unmanned, remote-controlled surveillance aircraft.

Most Extraordinary Heroism

There is no more poignant example of personal bravery in battle than the action that earned Brad Kasal, First Sergeant of Weapons Company, 3rd Battalion, 1st Marines, the Navy Cross.

One tough, "Robo-Grunt" Marine, Kasal was assigned to support the engaging infantry. But, on 13 November 2004 in Fallujah, Iraq, when his men got into trouble in a fierce firefight inside a house controlled by insurgents, he fearlessly dashed in to extricate the wounded.

Literally bumping into an enemy, he fired a burst of ten M16 rounds into the heart and two more into the forehead of his opponent before finally killing him.

Kasal, under a hailstorm of enemy fire, rushed to aid a fallen Marine, sustaining seven bullet wounds himself and, falling on top of the wounded Marine to protect him from an exploding grenade, took forty-four additional shrapnel hits.

Losing blood rapidly, Kasal instead tended the other Marine's wounds then guarded them both for forty-five minutes until the firefight raging around them ceased and they were rescued.

The photograph of Kasal being helped by two Marines—with his smoking Beretta pistol still at the ready—epitomizes his extraordinary heroism and fighting spirit.

Full recovery from his wounds took many surgeries over two years. Besides his well-deserved award, Kasal was promoted to the highest enlisted rank, Sergeant Major.
                                   –HAC

LEFT: Maintaining his will to fight following an intense battle in Fallujah, 1st Sgt Brad Kasal is helped to medical treatment for the fifty-one bullet and shrapnel wounds he sustained in the hour-and-a-half firefight.

INSET: Sergeant Major Brad Kasal

ABOVE: Appointed on 25 April 2007 as 16th Sergeant Major of the Marine Corps—the senior enlisted Marine and advisor to the Commandant—Carlton W. Kent completed recruit training at Parris Island in 1976. During his 31-year career, SgtMaj Kent served in embassy security detachments, attended the Army Airborne and Parachute Riggers schools, and was senior drill instructor and battalion master at both Marine Recruit Depots. In 2001, he was assigned Sergeant Major of Marine Forces Europe in Stuttgart, Germany, then as Sergeant Major of the I Marine Expeditionary Force.

RIGHT, TOP: A 70-ton Marine M1A1 main battle tank lists deeply to starboard into the soft mud of a shallow canal on the outskirts of Baghdad.

RIGHT, CENTER: A tank retriever quickly arrives on the scene to pull the monster vehicle out and get it back on its intended mission.

CheyTac M200 Sniper Rifle

A new sniper rifle, field-tested during combat in Afghanistan in January 2002, was introduced in Iraq. The CheyTac (pronounced "SHYtak") Intervention System M200 is capable of soft-target interdiction at 2,500 yards. Firing a .408-caliber 419- or 305-grain round, the rifle's various sighting aids can be coupled with its tactical handheld ballistic computer to ensure long-range accuracy.

The National Museum of the Marine Corps

More than a decade of planning, fund-raising, and construction culminated with the opening on 10 November 2006—the 231st anniversary of the Corps—of the National Museum of the Marine Corps on 135 acres just outside the Main Gate at Marine Corps Base Quantico in Virginia. President George W. Bush cut the ribbon in the presence of senior Marine officers and thousands of former Marines and guests.

The unique skyline profile of the 210-foot slanted spire, suggesting the Iwo Jima flag raising, can be seen from Interstate 95. This magnificent, contemporary structure houses the ultimate repository of some 60,000 significant artifacts of Marine Corps history, 8,000 works of combat art, and other fascinating, historical items.

Designed in the round and banked by sloping berms, the new $80-million dollar, 200,000-square-foot museum is the center-piece of the future Marine Heritage Center. When fully completed, the complex will include a parade deck, memorial walking trails, chapel, IMAX theater, conference center, and hotel.

It is a military museum like no other in the world, highlighting the Corps' glorious history, great traditions, and some of its momentous battles. Aircraft from the inception of Marine aviation in 1912 to the present are suspended from the ceiling and both flags raised on Iwo Jima are on display.

Exhibits incorporate state-of-the-art graphics and technology, including surround sound, temperature changes, and other special effects that startle and amaze. Nothing is static; multimedia screens project images while narrations guide and elucidate. There is little blood and gore, but the simulated conditions of the battlefield will arouse sharp memories in veterans and inspire awe in civilians. Vintage tanks, landing craft, helicopters, aircraft, weapons, artillery pieces, machine guns, and small arms proliferate—most in battle configurations—are dramatically lit to stunning effect.

Museum Director Lin Ezell, who was previously program manager of the Smithsonian's Air & Space Museum annex at Dulles, oversees a staff of 48. She coordinates with Marine Corps Headquarters, the University of the Marine Corps, the Marine Corps Heritage Foundation, and the Center's designers and contractors. In addition to the exhibit areas, only two thirds of which are completed, there are collection storage, archival, and restoration areas as well as tutorial facilities.

The University of the Marine Corps on the Quantico base—which includes the Gen Alfred Gray Research Center, the historical division, and the photo and material archives—also operates the NMMC. University President, retired Marine Major General Donald R. Gardner, says, "In

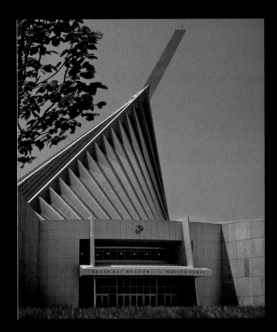

essence, this is a museum that will set the bar for all other military museums in the future. We are justly proud of it and of all the people who have made it possible."

Visit www.usmcmuseum.org.

ABOVE AND BELOW: A monument to honor and courage, the National Museum of the Marine Corps (above) highlights the Corps' illustrious history through its collection of artifacts and exhibits, such as the World War II gallery (below). Other areas of the museum educate visitors about the Vietnam and Korean wars, what it takes to be a Marine, and the global war on terror.

The Corps Attains Top Commands

Marine Gen Peter Pace was nominated in 2005 by President George W. Bush to the senior military position in the United States, the Chairman of the Joint Chiefs of Staff. Although he has no direct chain of command, Gen Pace represents the Commandant of the Marine Corps, the Chief of Naval Operations, the Chief of Staff of the Army, and the Chief of Staff of the Air Force to the Secretary of Defense.

A class of 1967 Naval Academy graduate, Gen Pace is a decorated Vietnam infantry combat veteran, has served in various commands and schools, has a master's degree in business administration from George Washington University, commanded the Marine operation in the first Somalia humanitarian relief mission, and headed the U.S. Southern Command. From there, he was designated Vice Chairman of the Joint Chiefs before his selection to the top post.

For the Marine Corps it has been a long haul since the National Security Act of 1947 that created the Defense Department (from the old War Department). The Marine Corps did not at first achieve equal status; indeed, until recently other military services considered it to be no more than a sub-function of the Navy.

After his tour as CMC, Marine Gen James Jones was named Supreme Allied Commander, Europe. For Marine officers to have achieved these two highest military posts speaks of a new awareness, in the post-9/11 War on Terrorism, of the Marines' unique training in land, sea, and air warfare and in expeditionary Navy-Marine task forces. The Corps' exemplary warfighting record in previous and present wars and conflicts also affirms their eminent qualification. The Defense Department policy of "Jointness" introduces each service superficially to one another, but when it comes to comprehensive strategy and tactics in combined arms, the Marine Corps' demonstrated ability and versatility has at last been properly recognized.

—HAC

ABOVE: Marine Gen Peter Pace, the first Marine to serve as chairman of the Joint Chiefs of Staff.

BELOW: Marines have always made friends with the populace, assisting in every humanitarian way. Typical are these Marines' sharing a treat with an Iraqi mother and her child.

A new generation of aircraft will join the new land vehicles with the upcoming addition of the tilt-rotor MV-22 Osprey (the larger capacity, longer range, V/STOL semi-helicopter) to not only the Marine Corps, which developed it, but to the Army, Air Force, and Navy as well. The adoption of the Osprey and the new Lockheed JSF (joint strike fighter) means that the Marine Corps, Navy, and Air Force will all use the most advanced aircraft in the world.

The all-volunteer American armed forces performed even better than they did in the first Persian Gulf War. That fact, and the resurgence of respect for the military, combined with newer, lighter, more efficient weaponry, augurs well for this country's continued posture as the dominant world power.

LOOKING TOWARD THE FUTURE

As would be expected, the Marine Corps performed brilliantly in operations Iraqi Freedom I and II. Its coordination of land, sea, and air components in a lightning thrust through almost four hundred miles of enemy territory—annihilating all opposition before it and capturing the enemy's capital—awed the world. As an elite assault force, the Corps demonstrated its unique efficiency, proficiency, mobility, versatility, and aggressive "warfighting" ethos.

As a consequence, Pentagon long-range planners began to see the superiority of agility over heavy mechanization, which had been the dominant legacy of World War II. The planners began thinking of lighter tanks, and newer, radical weapon designs emerged from the drawing boards—weapons that would be more effective in future urban conflicts, including improved body armor and armor plating and better protection for vehicles from buried explosive devices and lethal rocket-propelled grenades. More emphasis has also been given to unmanned aerial reconnaissance and interdiction.

Military minds are turning to previously unimagined scenarios, foreseeing a plethora of smaller, hard-to-track guerrilla-terrorist adversaries on the one hand, and the still larger threat of confrontation with China and possibly Iran and North Korea on the other. U.S. forces must be honed to defeat this host of unpredictable threats.

The long overdue realignment of U.S. forces worldwide, too, brought 2d ID units from South Korea and an armored division from Germany to Iraq, leaving in their wake further withdrawals back to the United States. Impressed by the Marine Corps' prescient use of prepositioned supplies and weaponry that allows for shorter response time to any conflict anywhere and which the Marines have demonstrated since the first Gulf War, the Army began such planning itself.

The Air Force will no doubt continue to concentrate on its strategic long-range bombing ability (as demonstrated so effectively by the missions mounted over Afghanistan and Iraq from bases in the U.S. Midwest), shorter-range fighter-bomber tactics, and mass air transportation of the Army. And the Army, while trying to lighten its cumbersome load, will likely continue to play the "follow-on" role of major occupying force, usually after the Marines have initially captured the objective. But it is the Navy-Marine "team" that has emerged even stronger by indisputably proving its effectiveness.

Unlike the epic land, sea, and air battles of the twentieth century, it is thought that the major conflicts of the twenty-first century will consist of quick-strike, short-term encounters. In any case, patrolling naval battle groups and Navy-Marine "expeditionary" task forces will continue to be the lightning rods for quick response anywhere on earth, and the unprecedented tripartite Marine land-sea-air muscle of the Navy-Marine team will continue to be at the forefront.

"First to Fight."

chapter nine

Twenty-First Century "Warfighting"

"Marines are a breed apart—born of epic battles and tempered in the ultimate crucible of combat. We will carry our rich legacy forward and continue to honorably serve our Nation. The Marine Corps is committed to providing the Nation its expeditionary 'Force of Choice' for tomorrow's challenges."

James T. Conway, General
34th Commandant of the Marine Corps

As of 2010 the two separate wars in Afghanistan (Operation Enduring Freedom/OEF) and Iraq (Operation Iraqi Freedom/OIF) continued; the former entering its ninth year, the latter potentially concluding its sixth.

On the humanitarian front, Marine units provided aid in response to natural disasters such as Hurricane Katrina, which struck New Orleans in 2005, and the 2004 tsunami in Indonesia, while also providing U.S. Embassy security throughout the world.

The brigade, composed of two regiments or a regimental combat team/Marine Air-Ground Task Force (RCT/MAGTF), remains the Marines' basic combat element. The reinforced battalion-sized expeditionary unit (MEU) is the principal force for worldwide crisis response due to its rapid adaptability, while the rifle company is the smallest tactical Marine formation capable of sustained independent operations on the battlefield. (In Vietnam, the basic combat element was the battalion; in Korea, the regiment).

For both OEF and OIF, Marine Reservists of infantry, armor, and artillery battalions from the 4th MarDiv, plus affiliated Civil Affairs personnel as well as combat historians and combat artists were activated.

The second battles of Fallujah and Ramadi against Muslim extremists and al-Qaeda in Iraq had been won decisively in 2004 and 2006 respectively by elements of I and II Marine Expeditionary Force (MEF) and U.S. Army units. Marine units then moved westward into the barren Al Anbar province bordering Syria and, with the increasing cooperation of Sunni Muslim residents and Iraqi military trainees, eventually gained control and subdued the area. Stability steadily improved as al-Qaeda fighters were eliminated from the area. When the "surge" strategy was applied, beginning in 2007, Iraq took a pronounced step toward political stability, allowing the Marines to step back their involvement.

Ostensibly the surge involved deployment of an estimated 30,000 additional troops, but, more significantly, it called for allied troops to move out from their compounds and into the regions and villages to

interact with and win the confidence of the populace, assisted by the growing Iraqi National Army and police. The Marines had done this successfully in the Vietnam War with their Combined Action Platoon (CAP) strategy of placing infantry squads in villages to live among the civilians and to provide protection from indigenous Viet Cong (VC), particularly during harvest times.

While a resolution in Iraq seemed imminent, success in Afghanistan was proving to be a tougher challenge. Marines from Task Force 58 had landed deep in Afghanistan on 24 October 2001 when, as the first U.S. ground force, they performed an incredible 400-mile heliborne forcible entry to capture Kandahar and set up a Forward Operating Base (FOB) with airfield. However, the situation nine years later was not promising.

U.S. strategy of counterterrorism against al-Qaeda and counterinsurgency against the Taliban in Afghanistan remained the same as it had been from the start of the conflict, and all coalition military had been put under NATO command to involve European nations. Yet Afghanistan's elected but weak government failed to effectively coalesce the disparate tribes, ethnic groups, and fragmented political parties within the country. This allowed the Taliban insurgents, now augmented by al-Qaeda, to reemerge as a threat. Afghanistan's rugged, barren mountainous terrain, too, presented far more tactical problems than the flat deserts of Iraq: less grazing fire, more mortar and howitzer high-trajectory requirements, limited vehicular support, less effective close-air support, communication transmission complications, and greater individual fatigue.

As conditions improved in Iraq, the Marines commenced a widespread drawdown in 2009, moving a substantial number of troops to Afghanistan to augment the 24th Marine Expeditionary Unit (MEU) already in southern Helmand province. As of November 2009 there were 68,000 total U.S. troops and 42,000 NATO allied troops in Afghanistan.

TACTICAL AND TECHNICAL CHANGES

Adaptability is a basic philosophy of the expeditionary Marine Corps. All wars present unique characteristics which Marines quickly assimilate, from jungle to desert to mountain. In both Iraq and Afghanistan, Marines followed a strategy of decentralizing opera-

tions, winning tribal confidence, and demonstrating that there is no better friend—nor worse enemy—than a U.S. Marine.

Former CMC Charles Krulak's innovative concept of a "Three-block War" proved itself in Iraq as Marines fought face-to-face on one street, performed humanitarian deeds on another, and confronted political issues on a third. In urban house-to-house fighting tactics, they developed a "Stack-3" and "Stack-4" maneuver in which the fire team—four members back-to-back—covers itself either by 240- or 360-degrees. Use of unmanned aerial vehicles (UAV) also increased small unit effectiveness and lethal potential. As of 2010 most I and II MEF and rotating III MEF units had served four combat tours each in Iraq and Afghanistan.

The non-traditional, asymmetrical warfare experienced in both theaters presented new threats, including suicide car bombings. The Russian-made 7.62mm Kalashnikov AK-47 automatic rifle was encountered thirty-five years prior in Vietnam, but the now ubiquitous shoulder-fired, long-tube Russian Rocket-Propelled Grenade (RPG) in the hands of terrorists and insurgents wreaked havoc, especially with vehicles. In response, the Humvee was up-armored and its roof gun turret shielded, yet still vulnerable.

Other unanticipated, more menacing, lethal devices encountered in Iraq were the roadside buried-mine and vehicle-borne Improvised Explosive Device (IED) and the Explosively Formed Penetrator (EFP). These necessitated the quick development of the Mine Resistant Ambush Protected (MRAP) vehicle, a 20-ton, 2.5-ton load or ten combat-armed Marine carrier with a V-shaped hull to deflect explosions outward.

For combat in Afghanistan, where IEDs are becoming more prevalent and where the MRAP is limited by terrain, a lighter, MRAP All Terrain Vehicle, or M-ATV, was developed as was a smaller one-man vehicle named a "Husky," with a V-shaped hull and blast resistant armor. When its magnetic panels detect a mine, the driver safely detonates it under the Husky.

The individual Marine is also being issued improved Flame Resistant Organizational Gear (FROG) with sweat-wicking undershirts and gloves, a lighter Modular Tactical Vest (MTV) with Enhanced Small Arms Protective Inserts (ESAPI) for chest, back, and sides that can stop a 7.62mm round. The vest also has built-in pouches for ammo magazines, bayonet, and an intersquad radio. An alternative to the MTV is the Scalable Plate Carrier (SPC), which provides great mobility and reduces heat stress. Quad Guards protect the arms and legs. The CamelBak insulated, anti-microbial water system holds more than three quarts. Footwear is now rugged, all-terrain (RAT) boots with a two-year life. On the new lighter weight Kevlar helmet is a rack for an improved, single eyepiece, monocular AN/PVS-14 Night Vision Device (MNVD). For daytime, dark and clear UV lenses, fog resistant, ventilated and particle filtered, anti-reflective, high impact goggles with fabric covers are now standard. Cold weather gear has also been upgraded and a new three-season sleeping bag replaces the old. The rugged battlefield computer is ubiquitous, affording two-way access and coordinations from higher to squad levels heretofore unimagined.

In weaponry, the current 5.56mm Modular Weapon System (MWS) consists of the short M4 Carbine and the M16A4 semi-automatic rifle, the latter of which has been upgraded with a 4-power rifle optic (RCO) sight attached to the rifle's new rail adapter system. Near its muzzle is a laser aiming and infrared illumination device with a high-powered LED flashlight. More durable and accurate than the standard M16, is the new SCAR (Special Operation Forces Combat Assault Rifle) that is currently issued to the Marine Special Operations Regiment (MSOR) under the Special Operations Command based at Camp Lejeune. The lighter, more durable 5.56mm

Infantry Automatic Rifle (IAR) is replacing the M249 Squad Automatic Weapon (SAW). Other replacement weapons include the M32 40mm Multi-Shot Grenade Launcher and a new Scout Sniper Capability rifle.

In the Aviation Combat Element (ACE), the innovative tiltrotor MV-22 Osprey vertical/short take-off and landing (V/STOL), utility/troop carrier was first deployed for combat in Al Anbar, Iraq, in 2007. They soon became a critical element of the Marines air support capabilities, participating in an estimated 3,000 combat sorties, as of July 2008.

In the Ground Combat Element (GCE), the Expeditionary Fighting Vehicle (EFV), which replaces the amphibious assault vehicle (AAV), is designed for irregular warfare, and the Joint Light Tactical Vehicle (JLTV), designed with better capacity to combat IEDs, will supplement, and potentially replace the ubiquitous Humvee (HMMWV). A new truck-mounted High Mobility Artillery Rocket System (HIMARS) will complement the lightweight, helo sling-transportable 155mm howitzer.

In the Afghan mountains, valleys, and undulating plains, Marines developed a tactic of "cordon and knock." When unable to flush the enemy out of rocks and ravines, Marines surround and close in on the

ABOVE: MajGen Walter E. Gaskin Sr. was appointed commanding general, 2d MarDiv and II MEF (FWD) and as CG of the Multi-National Force-West, in Iraq's Sunni Al Anbar province on 9 February 2007. Gaskin's basic plan was to drive the insurgents from the cities, thus implementing a strategy of clearing, holding, and building that would win over the populace. Marines gave direct assistance in repairing or building infrastructure, medical facilities, schools, solar-powered lights, generators, water and sewer systems, and even mosques. By the end of 2007, most provincial cities had their own mayors and city councils, and for the first time in many years, children attended schools and received basic medical treatment.

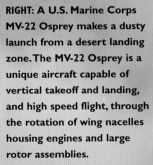

RIGHT: A U.S. Marine Corps MV-22 Osprey makes a dusty launch from a desert landing zone. The MV-22 Osprey is a unique aircraft capable of vertical takeoff and landing, and high speed flight, through the rotation of wing nacelles housing engines and large rotor assemblies.

ABOVE: On 18 May 2008, a Marine from the 24th Marine Expeditionary Unit (MEU) has a close call after Taliban fighters opened fire on his unit near Garmser in Helmand Province. The Marine was not injured. The 24th MEU had moved into the opium-growing region and Taliban stronghold in late April to clear a road. They ended up engaging with the Taliban almost daily for several weeks before the region quieted down in late June.

targets for a final, overwhelming knockout punch, often augmented by close-air napalm runs.

Marine Commandant James T. Conway points out that the Corps is educating troops about Afghan culture and using locals in operations in the region to avoid being misunderstood as conquerors or occupiers, as they engage in counterinsurgency (COIN) and search-and-destroy missions. Afghanistan is radically different from Iraq: tougher terrain is forcing Marines to adapt tactics and medevac capabilities; and tribal dialects and affiliations are more complex. Marines are working out of numbers of firebases, establishing security networks, giving medical aid and helping assure Afghans adequate water and land to stabilize the economic structure.

The war that began with U.S. air strikes in Afghanistan in October 2001 in response to the 9/11 attacks by al-Qaeda on the United States continues, while the one initiated by the United States in Iraq in 2003 is phasing down. At the same time, neighboring Iran is making nuclear threats, as is North Korea, while China is strutting its armed might as a challenge to the world's sole remaining superpower, the United States, its largest financial debtor. Russia is angling for a comeback as well, while NATO and numerous allies try to remain neutral. Adding to regional instability, Afghanistan's two eastern neighbors, Pakistan and India, remain at a nuclear standoff, while al-Qaeda and Osama bin Laden still use the former as a sanctuary.

PLANNING FOR 2025 AND BEYOND

The U.S. Defense Department asserts that the United States—and the world—is entering an era of persistent conflict and long wars, and, as do all other services, the Marine Corps constantly prepares for future eventualities.

In 1907 the U.S. began strategic studies of potential conflicts that could occur during the twentieth century. One, the "Orange Plan," pinpointed potential conflict with Japan and was instrumental in preparing the U.S. Navy and Marine Corps for the war in the Pacific (Pearl Harbor notwithstanding) in the 1940s. Similarly, the Marine Corps Warfighting Laboratory, under the Marine Corps Combat Development Command (MCCDC) at Quantico, studies various plausible scenarios the U.S. military could face in the twenty-first century. In 2007, CMC Conway created a Strategic Vision Group (SVG) of current and former Corps leaders to develop the "Marine Corps Vision & Strategy 2025."

THE CONTINUING MISSION

After 1st MarDiv's brilliant performance in the Korean War, in 1952 Congress enacted a bill that permanently defined the United States Marine Corps as a three infantry division/three air wing—with a fourth Reserve division/wing—"Force-in-Readiness" for the nation. It was to be equal to and supported by its sister force, the U.S. Navy, and its Commandant would sit equally as a member of the Joint Chiefs of Staff. In 2009 the Corps' end strength topped 202,000.

There will be no change in the qualifications, standards, or performance of future Marines, nor will there be in the overall structure, mission, or naval character of the Corps. Its Warfighting functions of Command and Control, Intelligence, Maneuver, Fires, Force Protection, and Logistics will be continually honed.

For foreseeable global challenges, two major scenarios emerge: one, major power struggles among several leading nations; and, two, irregular, asymmetrical, hot spots in restive regions.

Regarding the first scenario, the Marine Corps must maintain its superiority, hence, adoption of the Lockheed-Martin supersonic, stealth, Short Takeoff, Vertical Landing (STOVL) F-35B Lightning II Joint

Strike Fighter, which is expected to enter Marine Corps service in 2012. (The F-35A U.S. Air Force conventional takeoff and landing version and the F-35C U.S. Navy carrier variant will follow in subsequent years.) The new versatile aircraft will replace the F/A-18 Hornet, the AV-8B Harrier II, and the EA-6 Prowler in the Marine Corps air fleet. The MV-22 Osprey tiltrotor V/STOL utility/troop carrier will replace the 40-year-old CH-46 Sea Knight medium helicopters; it has a combat radius of 430 nautical miles (796 km), and can carry 24 combat-loaded Marines at 255 knots. Plans are also in place to update the heavy lift CH-53E helicopter with the Sikorsky-built CH-53K series; this upgrade, expected to enter service in 2015, will retain the CH-53E Super Stallion footprint but will double its range and capability, while maintaining its ability to perform close-in logistic support and extraction. Other new generation helicopters include the AH-1Z Viper, and the all-new UH-1Y Venom.

The primary mission of the Nation's Force-in-Readiness for both threats will remain expeditionary, requiring the Corps' basic force structure of MEF, MEB, and MEU in flexible Marine Air-Ground Task Forces (MAGTFs) to be able to respond quickly anywhere in the world. They will be lighter, faster, harder-hitting and more reliant on speed, maneuver, and

surprise. Sea-based in Expeditionary Strike Groups (ESGs), they are centered around a major Marine assault ship leading two Marine Expeditionary Brigade assault echelons spread on thirty-eight amphibious warfare ships, twelve of which are aviation-capable: amphibious assault ships (LHA/LHD), amphibious transport, dock (LPD) (Amphibious Transport Dock), and landing ship, dock (LSD). The newest LHA-6, USS *America*, which is expected to go into service in 2013, will have enhanced aviation capabilities to accommodate V/STOL tiltrotors, the fixed-wing STOVL, and other aircraft in use currently or planned for the near future.

The Navy-Marine team concept for Joint Forcible Entry Operations (JFEO) will be stronger than ever, with more seabasing and maritime prepositioning of ships and supplies necessary for operational maneuver from the sea (OMFTS) in littoral as opposed to blue water scenarios. From Guam, now a major Pacific Fleet command center, the Pacific Rim will be constantly monitored. This calls for both increasing Navy-manned Marine assault shipping and for Naval Surface Gunfire Support covering up to 200 nautical mile inland ranges with new shipboard electromagnetic rail artillery. A remote controlled 16-inch Scramjet, liquid oxygen-powered, Mach 15, Supersonic Combustion Ramjet

ABOVE: On the ground in Iraq, female Marines were assigned to MP guard duty and, in consideration of Muslim customs, dealt primarily with Muslim women. Female Marines also were assigned to Public and Civil Affairs positions, and to specialized computer, photographic, and technical duties. Although they did not have direct combat roles, many female Marines were exposed to enemy fire on the ground and in the air in Iraq. On 6 December 2006 U.S. Naval Academy graduate Maj Megan McClung became the fifth female Marine killed in action when she was killed by a roadside IED in Ramadi.

LEFT: On 19 February 2010— just a few days after the beginning of the anti-Taliban offensive known as Operation Moshtarak (from the Dari for "together")—a sergeant (standing) yells to the Marines in his squad to engage a target after taking fire from a mosque in the city of Marjah, Afghanistan.

will have a range of 460 miles, and surface- and submarine-launched Tomahawk cruise missiles will range farther with more accuracy. Such innovations might call for the reactivation of battleships for larger surface platforms.

UAS DOCTRINE: UNMANNED AIR SUPPORT

Unmanned Aerial Vehicles (UAVs) are extremely effective for battlefield reconnaissance, damage assessment, force protection, and convoy security. Cost-efficient, reliable, lightweight, and portable, these tiny drones can be hand-launched from ground positions, are programmed for GPS autonomous navigation, and can provide real-time high-resolution or infrared images. The Marine Corps uses the Dragon Eye and, increasingly, the Raven B at the company level, and is also introducing the Wasp III Micro Air Vehicle (MAV), which

weighs less than a pound and can operate for 45 minutes at up to 1,000 feet in altitude. Its RQ-7B Shadow and ScanEagle UAVs are used for higher, longer-range operations—the ScanEagle can operate for as long as 24 hours at a stretch and can reach altitudes of up to 16,000 feet. The larger Predator is armed with deadly Hellfire missiles and in the future will carry directed-energy high-power microwave systems that will fry enemy electronic systems. This will be followed up by high-powered destructive laser beams. By 2018, such drones will be equipped with various sensors, electro-optical infrared systems, and wide-angle Synthetic Aperture Radar (SAR), and will be accurately controlled from the ground—even continents

away. Further development centers on Micro Aerial Vehicles (MAV), tiny flying devices disguised as insects capable of photographing and even attacking the enemy—undetected. Such state-of-the-art advances could reduce the role of the Air Combat Element in the future.

Command & Control, Intelligence and counter-intelligence, communications, cybernetics, robotics, and other sophisticated support elements are constantly being upgraded to correspond to developing weaponry and tactics, particularly the threat of cyberterrorism. Computerized Battlefield Management is evolving along with satellite and Unmanned Aircraft Systems (UAS). In addition to lethal weaponry, non-lethal weapons are being developed to reduce civilian casualties.

As technology increasingly takes over manned combat functions, the future might hold more opportunities for women in virtual combat roles. The armed forces of the United States today are the best educated in its history; ninety-five percent of Marine enlisted ranks are high school graduates.

Nor is the individual Marine, his or her quality of life, family, and the stress of deployment and dwell time overlooked. Efforts are being made to reduce multiple combat deployments for active and reserve components. For those wounded in action or suffering the residual effects of battle, the newly formed Wounded Warrior Resource Center of the DoD is dedicated to treating Post–traumatic Stress Disorder (PTSD) and Traumatic Brain Injury (TBI) treatment, and extended care and rehabilitation.

CONFLICT CONTINUES

A 30,000-troop increase beginning in 2010 notwithstanding, whether the Afghan war will end in defeat like Vietnam, or in moderate success like Iraq is conjecture.

The Islamic Republic of Afghanistan is historically a nation composed of disparate, indigenous tribes; even today some thirty-five languages, including two official national languages, are spoken there. In 1919 Afghanistan won its independence from British rule, and in 1989 defeated an occupying Soviet army. The rise of the radical Sunni Muslim Taliban in the mid-1990s created yet another source of internal strife in Afghanistan. A fundamentalist sect known for its strict interpretation of Muslim sharia law and for its oppression of women, the Taliban initially seemed to

be a strict, albeit effective, force for maintaining law and order. Giving sanctuary to al-Qaeda terrorists, they continue to spread asymmetrical guerrilla warfare into nuclear neighbor Pakistan. The United States claimed victory over the Taliban in 2001, following the 9/11 attacks, however, the Taliban has risen again and remains a threat to the future of both the Afghan people and the world.

Not to be dismissed is the nuclear threat from Afghanistan's western neighbor, Iran; the United States is engaged in wars on both sides of that unstable Muslim nation. As the Israelis unilaterally destroyed an Iraqi nuclear WMD plant in 1981, they are again poised in self-defense to take out Iran's fledgling nuclear plants to prevent the latter's stated vow to erase Israel from the map.

Iran also presents the potential threat of cutting off the Persian Gulf by blocking the narrow Strait of Hormuz, an act that could necessitate U.S. Navy-Marine intervention.

Thus, the first decade of the twenty-first century is turning out much like that of the twentieth; a harbinger of another 100 years of conflict rather than peace.

Spearheaded by the Expeditionary U.S. Marine Corps, America's military might is still the planet's best keeper of the peace. As long as the Corps exists, it will remain an agile "Two-Fisted Fighter" capable of handling major contingencies as well as a multi-capable force to eradicate smaller irregular conflicts worldwide.

BELOW: Cpl. Jason Dunham, who died in April 2004 from injuries sustained after using his body to shield fellow Marines from a hand grenade in Husaybah, Iraq, became the first Marine to receive a Medal of Honor in the Iraq War. Sgt. Major Michael Templeton, \Dunham's former company first sergeant, carefully clutches Dunham's dress blue uniform as Maj. Trent A. Gibson, Dunham's former company commander, Sgt. Bill Hampton and Cpl. Kelley Miller, the two Marines whose lives were saved by Dunham, stand at the position of attention during the christening of the Navy destroyer bearing Dunham's name 1 August 2009 at the Bath Iron Works in Bath, Maine. Dunham's parents donated his dress blue uniform to be displayed on the ship's quarterdeck.

Epilogue

The United States Marine Corps, despite being the smallest of the four branches of the American armed forces, has nevertheless played a significant role throughout its more than 230-year history. That role has often been to serve as the projection or reaffirmation of American power, both in neighboring countries and in lands on the other side of the world.

Every country likes to have an elite force, and many have their own brand of Marines. The French have two small groups of marines, the navy's *Fusiliers Marins* and the army's *Troupes de Mer*. While many European countries (Great Britain, the Netherlands, and Italy) and certain Asian nations (South Korea, the Republic of China, Thailand, and Indonesia), as well as some Latin American states (Mexico, Venezuela, Brazil, Argentina, and Chile), also have marines, none of these groups possess the combined air-sea-land components and coordinated functions of the United States Marine Corps.

As the twenty-first century witnesses the birth of a new type of warfare against Islamist terrorists ("terrorism" is a tactical weapon, not an enemy, per se), it is becoming clearer than ever that with irregular adversaries, the United States will turn to Navy-Marine task forces for quick deployment anywhere on the planet to extinguish bushfire conflicts wherever they ignite, to stop terrorists, and to protect American lives and property. The Marine Corps Combat Development Command and the Marine Corps Warfighting Laboratory at Quantico continue to contemplate strategy, tactics, weaponry, and possible scenarios decades into the future in order to be prepared to win any future battles against enemies whose identities and abilities can only be conjectured at present. And the Corps will always remain the same in its primary aspect: it will continue to attract the best recruits, to be the best-trained of the U.S. military forces, and to be counted on as the most ready to take on any threat to the United States. That is, the Corps will continue to serve as America's on-call, "911 Force-in-Readiness."

Message from the thirty-fourth Commandant of the Marine Corps:

We are calling a new generation of Marines to serve. They will carry the battle-tested colors of our Corps just as you once carried them—with honor and with pride. We still make Marines, win battles, and create quality citizens! I ask for your continued commitment to ensure this tradition endures and our proud legacy prevails.

Semper Fidelis and Keep Attacking.

James T. Conway
General, U.S. Marine Corps
Commandant of the Marine Corps

Appendix A
United States Marine Corps Rank Insignia

General
(Gen)
Commandant of the Marine Corps
Pay Grade O10

Lieutenant General
(LtGen)
Pay Grade O9

Major General
(MajGen)
Pay Grade O8

Brigadier General
(BGen)
Pay Grade O7

Colonel
(Col)
Pay Grade O6

Lieutenant Colonel
(LtCol)
Pay Grade O5

Major
(Maj)
Pay Grade O4

Captain
(Capt)
Pay Grade O3

First Lieutenant
(1stLt)
Pay Grade O2

Second Lieutenant
(2dLt)
Pay Grade O1

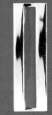

Chief Warrant Officer
(CWO-5)
Pay Grade W5

Chief Warrant Officer 4
(CWO-4)
Pay Grade W4

Chief Warrant Officer 3
(CWO-3)
Pay Grade W3

Chief Warrant Officer 2
(CWO-2)
Pay Grade W2

Warrant Officer 1
(WO-1)
Pay Grade W1

Sergeant Major
of the Marine Corps
(SgtMajMC)
Pay Grade E-9

Sergeant Major
(SgtMaj)
Pay Grade E-9

Master Gunnery Sergeant
(MGySgt)
Pay Grade E-9

Master Sergeant
(MSgt)
Pay Grade E-8

First Sergeant
(1stSgt)
Pay Grade E-8

Gunnery Sergeant
(GySgt)
Pay Grade E-7

Staff Sergeant
(SSgt)
Pay Grade E-6

Sergeant
(Sgt)
Pay Grade E-5

Corporal
(Cpl)
Pay Grade E-4

Lance Corporal
(LCpl)
Pay Grade E-3

Private First Class
(Pfc)
Pay Grade E-2

Medals and Decorations

Listed in order of precedence are Navy-Marine medals for valor in combat (Medal of Honor, Navy Cross, Silver Star, Bronze Star) and service and campaign awards. For those that are both heroic and meritorious (Navy Distinguished Service Medal, Legion of Merit, Distinguished Flying Cross, Navy & Marine Corps Medal, Bronze Star, Air Medal, Navy & Marine Corps Commendation Medal, Navy-Marine Corps Achievement Medal) a small gold "V" device is added to indicate a medal awarded for combat. The Purple Heart is awarded for each wound sustained in combat. Small silver and bronze stars denote multiple awards.

Medal of Honor
Established: 3 March 1863

Navy Cross
Effective: 6 April 1917

Defense Distinguished Service Medal
Established: 9 July 1970

Navy Distinguished Service Medal
Effective: 6 April 1917

Silver Star
Approved: 7 August 1942

Defense Superior Service Medal
Effective: 6 February 1976

Legion of Merit
Effective: 8 September 1939

Distinguished Flying Cross
Established: 2 July 1926

Navy & Marine Corps Medal
Effective: 6 December 1941

Bronze Star
Effective: 7 December 1941

Purple Heart
Effective: 5 April 1917

Defense Meritorious Service Medal
Effective: 3 November 1977

Meritorious Service Medal
Effective: 16 January 1969

Air Medal
Effective: 8 September 1939

Joint Service Commendation Medal
Effective: 1 January 1963

Navy & Marine Corps Commendation Medal
Effective: 7 December 1941

Joint Service Achievement Medal
Effective: 3 August 1983

Navy & Marine Corps Achievement Medal
Effective: 1 May 1961

Prisoner of War Medal
Effective: 5 April 1917

Marine Corps Good Conduct Medal
Established: 20 July 1896

Selected Marine Corps Reserve Medal
Effective: 1 July 1925

Marine Corps Expeditionary Medal
Authorized: 15 August 1936

China Service Medal
Effective:
7 July 1937–7 September 1939;
2 September 1945–1 April 1957

American Defense Service Medal
Effective: 8 September 1939–
7 December 1941

American Campaign Medal
Effective: 7 December 1941–
2 March 1946

European-African-Middle Eastern Campaign Medal
Effective: 7 December 1941–
2 March 1946

Asiatic-Pacific Campaign Medal
Effective: 7 December 1941–
2 March 1946

World War II Victory Medal
Effective: 7 December 1941–
31 December 1946

Navy Occupation Service Medal
Effective: 8 May 1945–various

Medal for Humane Action
Effective: 26 June 1948–
30 September 1949

National Defense Service Medal
Effective:
27 June 1950–27 July 1954;
1 January 1967–14 August 1974

Korean Service Medal
Effective: 27 June 1950–
27 July 1954

Antarctica Service Medal
Effective: 2 January 1946

Armed Forces Expeditionary Medal

Effective: 1 July 1958

Vietnam Service Medal

Effective: 4 July 1965– 28 March 1973

Southwest Asia Service Medal

Effective: 2 August 1990– 30 November 1995

Kosovo Campaign Medal

Effective: 24 March 1999

Afghanistan Campaign Medal

Effective: 24 October 2001

Iraq Campaign Medal

Effective: 19 March 2003

Global War on Terrorism Expeditionary Medal

Effective: 11 September 2001

Global War on Terrorism Service Medal

Effective: 11 September 2001

Korea Defense Service Medal

Effective: 28 July 1954

Armed Forces Service Medal

Effective: 1 June 1992

Humanitarian Service Medal

Effective: 1 April 1975

Outstanding Volunteer Service Medal

Effective: 31 December 1992

Armed Forces Reserve Medal

Effective: 1 August 1990

French Croix de Guerre Medal (World War I)

Authorized: 8 April 1915

Republic of Vietnam Gallantry Cross with Palm

Effective: 1 March 1961– 28 March 1974

Philippine Defense Medal

Effective: 8 December 1941– 15 June 1942

Philippine Liberation Medal

Effective: 17 October 1944– 3 September 1945

Philippine Independence Medal

Effective: 8 December 1941– 3 September 1945

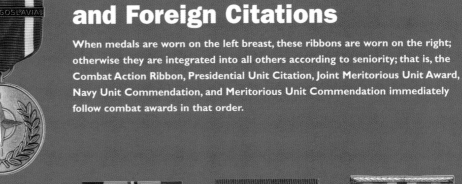

Unit Commendations and Foreign Citations

When medals are worn on the left breast, these ribbons are worn on the right; otherwise they are integrated into all others according to seniority; that is, the Combat Action Ribbon, Presidential Unit Citation, Joint Meritorious Unit Award, Navy Unit Commendation, and Meritorious Unit Commendation immediately follow combat awards in that order.

United Nations Service Medal (Korean Service)
Effective: 27 June 1950–27 July 1954

United Nations Medal
Authorized: 20 July 1959

NATO Medal (For Service in the Former Yugoslavia)
Effective: 1 July 1992

Combat Action Ribbon
Effective: 1 March 1961

Presidential Unit Citation
Effective: 16 October 1941

Joint Meritorious Unit Award
Authorized: 22 July 1982

NATO Kosovo Medal
Effective: 13 October 1998

Multinational Force & Observers Medal
Effective: 3 August 1981

Republic of Vietnam Campaign Medal
Effective: 1 March 1961–28 March 1973

Navy Unit Commendation
Effective: 6 December 1941

Meritorious Unit Commendation
Authorized: 17 July 1967

Navy "E" Ribbon
Effective: 1 July 1974

Sea Service Deployment Ribbon
Effective: 15 August 1974

Navy Arctic Service Ribbon
Effective: 1 January 1982

Navy and Marine Corps Overseas Service Ribbon
Effective: 15 August 1974

Marine Recruiting Ribbon
Effective: 1 January 1973

Marine Drill Instructor Ribbon
Effective: 6 October 1952

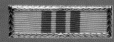

Marine Corps Security Guard Ribbon
Effective: 28 January 1949

Kuwait Liberation Medal (Saudi Arabia)
Effective: 17 January–28 February 1991

Kuwait Liberation Medal (Emirate of Kuwait)
Effective: 2 August 1990–31 August 1993

Republic of Korea War Service Medal
Effective: 25 June 1950–27 July 1955

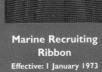

Philippine Presidential Unit Citation
Effective: 14 September 1946

Korean Presidential Unit Citation
Effective: 27 June 1950–27 July 1953

Vietnam Presidential Unit Citation
Effective: 1 March 1961–28 March 1974

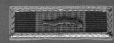

Republic of Vietnam Unit Citation Gallantry Cross
Effective: 1 March 1961–28 March 1974

Republic of Vietnam Unit Citation Civil Actions
Effective: 20 January 1968–28 March 1974

United States Marine Corps Battle Streamers

The official Battle Colors of the Marine Corps are permanently housed at Marine Barracks, Washington, D.C., and bear a colored streamer for each expedition, period of service, and campaign in which Marines have participated, as well as U.S. and foreign unit awards. Presently, there are fifty-four streamers, recent additions for the ongoing campaigns in Afghanistan and Iraq.

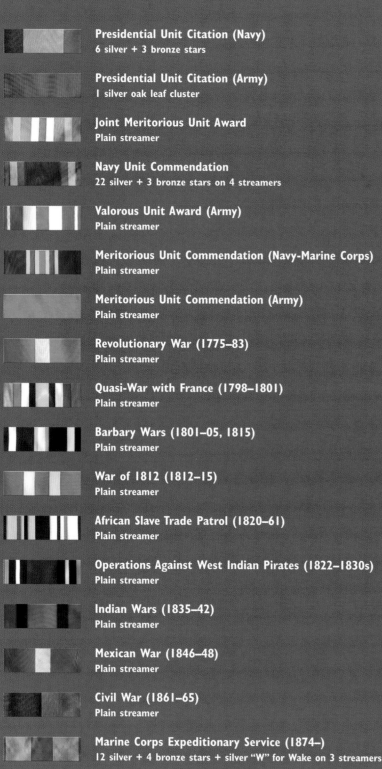

Presidential Unit Citation (Navy)
6 silver + 3 bronze stars

Presidential Unit Citation (Army)
1 silver oak leaf cluster

Joint Meritorious Unit Award
Plain streamer

Navy Unit Commendation
22 silver + 3 bronze stars on 4 streamers

Valorous Unit Award (Army)
Plain streamer

Meritorious Unit Commendation (Navy-Marine Corps)
Plain streamer

Meritorious Unit Commendation (Army)
Plain streamer

Revolutionary War (1775–83)
Plain streamer

Quasi-War with France (1798–1801)
Plain streamer

Barbary Wars (1801–05, 1815)
Plain streamer

War of 1812 (1812–15)
Plain streamer

African Slave Trade Patrol (1820–61)
Plain streamer

Operations Against West Indian Pirates (1822–1830s)
Plain streamer

Indian Wars (1835–42)
Plain streamer

Mexican War (1846–48)
Plain streamer

Civil War (1861–65)
Plain streamer

Marine Corps Expeditionary Service (1874–)
12 silver + 4 bronze stars + silver "W" for Wake on 3 streamers

Spanish Campaign (1898)
Plain streamer

Philippine Campaign (1899–1906)
Plain streamer

China Relief Expedition (1900–01)
Plain streamer

Cuban Pacification (1906–09)
Plain streamer

Nicaraguan Campaign (1912)
Plain streamer

Mexican Service (1914–17)
Plain streamer

Haitian Campaign (1915, 1919–20)
1 bronze star

Dominican Campaign (1916)
Plain streamer

World War I (1917–18)
1 silver + 1 bronze star + Maltese cross + Siberia and West Indies clasps

Army of Occupation of Germany
Plain streamer

Second Nicaraguan Campaign (1926–33)
Plain streamer

Yangtze Service (1926–27, 1930–32)
Plain streamer

China Service (1936–39 and 1945–57)
1 bronze star

American Defense Service (1939–41)
1 bronze star

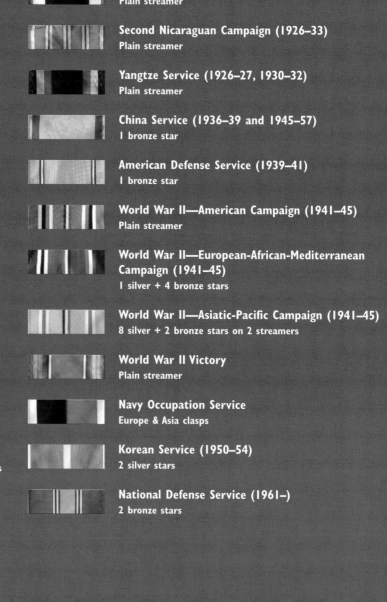

World War II—American Campaign (1941–45)
Plain streamer

World War II—European-African-Mediterranean Campaign (1941–45)
1 silver + 4 bronze stars

World War II—Asiatic-Pacific Campaign (1941–45)
8 silver + 2 bronze stars on 2 streamers

World War II Victory
Plain streamer

Navy Occupation Service
Europe & Asia clasps

Korean Service (1950–54)
2 silver stars

National Defense Service (1961–)
2 bronze stars

Armed Forces Expeditionary Service (1958–)
5 silver stars

Vietnam Service (1962–73)
3 silver + 2 bronze stars

Southwest Asia Service
3 bronze stars

Kosovo Campaign (1999–)
2 bronze stars

Global War on Terrorism—Expeditionary (2001–)
Plain Streamer

Global War on Terrorism—Service (2001–)
Plain Streamer

Afghanistan Campaign (2001–)
Plain streamer

Iraq Campaign (2003–)
Plain streamer

Philippine Defense
1 bronze star

Philippine Liberation
2 bronze stars

Philippine Independence
Plain streamer

French Croix de Guerre (World War I)
2 bronze palms + 1 gilt star

Philippine Presidential Unit Citation
2 bronze stars

Korean Presidential Unit Citation
2 bronze stars

Republic of Vietnam Armed Forces Meritorious Unit Citation of the Gallantry Cross
1 bronze palm

Republic of Vietnam Meritorious Unit Citation Civil Actions
1 bronze palm

Commandants of the Marine Corps

Name	Service	Final Rank as CMC
1. Samuel Nicholas	28 Nov 1775–Aug 1781	Major
2. William W. Burrows	12 Jul 1798–6 Mar 1804	Lieutenant Colonel
3. Franklin Wharton	6 Mar 1804–1 Sep 1818	Lieutenant Colonel
4. Anthony Gale	3 Mar 1819–16 Oct 1820	Lieutenant Colonel
5. Archibald Henderson	17 Oct 1820–6 Jan 1859	Colonel
6. John Harris	7 Jan 1859–12 May 1864	Colonel
7. Jacob Zeilin	10 Jun 1864–31 Oct 1876	Brigadier General
8. Charles McCawley	1 Nov 1876–29 Jan 1891	Colonel
9. Charles Heywood	30 Jan 1891–2 Oct 1903	Major General
10. George Elliott	3 Oct 1903–30 Nov 1910	Major General
11. William P. Biddle	3 Feb 1911–24 Feb 1914	Major General
12. George Barnett (GNA)	25 Feb 1914–30 Jun 1920	Major General
13. John A. Lejeune (GNA)	1 Jul 1920–4 Mar 1929	Major General
14. Wendell Neville (GNA) (MOH)	5 Mar 1929–8 Jul 1930	Major General
15. Ben H. Fuller (GNA)	9 Jul 1930–28 Feb 1934	Major General
16. John H. Russell Jr. (GNA)	1 Mar 1934–30 Nov 1936	Major General
17. Thomas Holcomb	1 Dec 1936–31 Dec 1943	Lieutenant General
18. Alexander A. Vandegrift (MOH)	1 Jan 1944–31 Dec 1947	General
19. Clifton B. Cates	1 Jan 1948–31 Dec 1951	General
20. Lemuel C. Shepherd Jr.	1 Jan 1952–31 Dec 1955	General
21. Randolph McCall Pate	1 Jan 1956–31 Dec 1959	General
22. David M. Shoup (MOH)	1 Jan 1960–31 Dec 1963	General
23. Wallace M. Greene Jr. (GNA)	1 Jan 1964–31 Dec 1967	General
24. Leonard F. Chapman Jr.	1 Jan 1968–31 Dec 1971	General
25. Robert E. Cushman Jr. (GNA)	1 Jan 1972–30 Jun 1975	General
26. Louis H. Wilson (MOH)	1 Jul 1975–30 Jun 1979	General
27. Robert H. Barrow	1 Jul 1979–30 Jun 1983	General
28. Paul X. Kelley	1 Jul 1983–30 Jun 1987	General
29. Alfred M. Gray Jr.	1 Jul 1987–30 Jun 1991	General
30. Carl E. Mundy Jr.	1 Jul 1991–30 Jun 1995	General
31. Charles C. Krulak (GNA)	1 Jul 1995–30 Jun 1999	General
32. James L. Jones	1 Jul 1999–13 Jan 2003	General
33. Michael W. Hagee (GNA)	14 Jan 2003–13 Nov 2006	General
34. James T. Conway	14 Nov 2006–present	General

(MOH) = Medal of Honor Recipient (GNA) = Naval Academy Graduate

Sergeants Major of the Marine Corps

Name	Service
1. Wilbur Bestwick	23 May 1957–31 Aug 1959
2. Francis D. Rauber	1 Sep 1959–28 Jun 1962
3. Thomas J. McHugh	29 Jun 1962–16 Jul 1965
4. Herbert J. Sweet	17 Jul 1965–31 Jul 1969
5. Joseph W. Dailey	1 Aug 1969–31 Jan 1973
6. Clinton A. Puckett	1 Feb 1973–31 May 1975
7. Henry H. Black	1 Jun 1975–31 Mar 1977
8. John R. Massaro	1 Apr 1977–15 Aug 1979
9. Leland D. Crawford	16 Aug 1979–Jun 27 1983
10. Robert E. Cleary	28 Jun 1983–26 Jun 1987
11. David W. Sommers	27 Jun 1987–27 Jun 1991
12. Harold G. Overstreet	28 Jun 1991–29 Jun 1995
13. Lewis G. Lee	30 Jun 1995–30 Jun 1999
14. Alford L. McMichael	29 Jun 1999–26 Jun 2003
15. John L. Estrada	26 Jun 2003–25 Apr 2007
16. Carlton W. Kent	25 Apr 2007–present

Appendix B

Military Staff System

Offices	Joint Staff (Commands)	General Staff (Division > Regiment)	Smaller-Unit Staff (Battalion)
Manpower & Personnel	J-1	G-1	S-1
Intelligence	J-2	G-2	S-2
Operations	J-3	G-3	S-3
Logistics	J-4	G-4	S-4
Strategic Plans	J-5		
Civil Affairs		G-5	S-5
C4 Systems	J-6		
Communications		G-6	S-6
Operational Plans	J-7		
Inspector/Evaluation		G-7	
Force Structure	J-8		

Basic U.S. Marine Corps Structure

Unit	Command	Components/Size
Operating Forces (replaces Fleet Marine Force)	CMC	3 MarDivs, 3 MAWs, 1 Reserve (nonactive) division and air wing
COMMARFOR/LANT (replaces FMF/Lant)	lieutenant general	2d MarDiv; 2d MAW
COMMARFOR/PAC (replaces FMF/Pac)	lieutenant general	1st and 3d MarDivs; 1st and 3d MAWs
MEF	lieutenant general	2+ infantry divisions, 1 aircraft wing (formerly "Amphibious"; changed to "Expeditionary" in 1988)
MarDiv	major general	3 infantry and 1 artillery regiments + (25,000 men)
MEB	brigadier general	2+ regiments
Regiment (called "Marines," e.g., 1st Marines)	colonel	3 infantry battalions, 4 artillery batteries
MEU	colonel	1+ infantry and artillery battalions; air
MEU(SOC)	colonel	1+ infantry and artillery battalions; air

Unit Sizes and Commands

A basic triangular structure carries downward (although a fourth element is sometimes added to afford a larger, rectangular, configuration). Although configured or augmented for specific assignments, i.e., with additional artillery, armored units, etc., the three-unit structure allows for two units to be "up," that is, on the attack, while one is held "back" in reserve or is used as a base of fire to protect the advancing units. This can be reversed for tactical or terrain reasons so that one unit attacks while the other two provide a covering base of fire. But theoretically all three sides can face the enemy, as in a 360° tactical area of responsibility (TAOR).

Unit	Command	Components	Size
theater	general	unlimited	unlimited
army	lieutenant general	3+ corps	250,000 (approx.) (refers to whole army)
corps	lieutenant general	3+ divisions	80,000 (approx.)
force	lieutenant/major general	2+ divisions (up to 24: AEF)	100,000 (approx.)
division	major general	3 infantry + 1 artillery regiments	25,000
brigade	brigadier general	2 regiments (now a MEB/MAG)	9,000
regiment	colonel	3 battalions	3,200
battalion	lieutenant colonel	3 companies	1,100
company	captain	3 platoons	250
platoon	2d lieutenant	3 squads	48
squad	sergeant	3 fire teams	13
fire team	corporal	3 Pfcs (privates)	4

Structure of Marine Aviation

The Marine Corps' aviation force, composed of fixed-wing and rotary-wing (helicopter) air components, is among the top ten largest in the world. Marine Air is designed to operate from aircraft carriers (CVs and LHAs), but is also capable of operating from land bases.

Marine Air fixed-wing aircraft include the F/A-18 Hornet fighter, the A-6 Intruder attack-bomber, the FB Prowler electronic-warfare fighter-bomber, and the AV-8B Harrier attack-fighter. Its rotary-wing aircraft include the CH-46 Sea Knight, the CH-53E Super Stallion, and the new MV-22 Osprey.

Unit	Command	Size
MAW	major general	3+ MAGs
MAG	colonel	4–6 squadrons
VMF, VMF/A, VMO, VMQ	lieutenant colonel	6–15 aircraft in 7–8 sections
Section	major, captain	2 aircraft
Flight	2d lieutenant, 1st lieutenant, captain	1 aircraft

Appendix C

United States Marine Corps Innovations in Warfare

To keep its cutting edge, the Marine Corps has over its 230 years constantly innovated to increase its effectiveness in weaponry and tactics; many of the Corps' innovations have been appropriated by other U.S. and foreign military services.

1880s Development of specialized weaponry, small arms; Gatlin gun

1895 Marines adopt the 6mm Browning-Colt automatic machine gun and the 6mm Remington-Lee 5-shot rifle (the Army did not adopt a machine gun until 1908)

1900 Advanced Base Force (ABF) concept is developed following the Spanish-American War to defend new overseas bases

1913–1914 Beach Defense concept is formulated (ignored by European powers in favor trench warfare)

1915 Marines develop first U.S. armored unit (the King armored car)

1915 The improved Lewis light machine gun is adopted by the Marines (the Army rejected it)

1920 War plan against Japan is formulated by Marine LtCol Pete Ellis

1921 Thompson submachine gun is adopted

1921 Thompson submachine gun as weapon for rifle squad leader

1920s Marine Corps makes rifle marksmanship a priority, an example followed by other services

1920s Invention of the portable gas can (copied by the Germans)

1920s–1930s Marines adopt khaki uniforms for hot weather, field herringbone twill utilities for Pacific War

1920s–1930s Marines win most National Rifle Marksmanship contests

1920–1945 Amphibious Doctrine and amphibious vehicles are developed

1920–1940 Close air support; dive bombing (copied by the Germans)

1930 Invention of the Cole cart

1930s Invention of light machine-gun ammo cart with motorcycle wheels

1930s Wrote Small Wars Manual

1930s Invention of the Van Orden sniper rifle M1903C with 8-power Unertl scope

1930s Marine Melvin Johnson, Jr., invents the Johnson rifle and machine gun

1938 Johnson invents a self-loading semiautomatic rifle used by parachute battalions

1941 Adoption of utility field/battle uniform

1941–1944 Marine amphibious landing forces train Army units for North Africa, Sicily, and Pacific campaigns

1940s Tactical Air Control Party (TACP) and ground aviation support/direction systems

1942 Adoption of Australian battle jacket

1943 Development of flame-thrower tanks

1943 Cloth camouflage helmet covers

1943 Fire Team concept is developed

1946 Development of vertical envelopment helicopter use

1947 Toys for Tots program initiated by Marine Col W. Hendricks and Disney Studios

1952 Development and adoption of body armor, thermal boots

1960 Marine Small Wars Manual influences President John F. Kennedy regarding Vietnam

1967 Marines inaugurate Combined Action Programs to assist civilians in Vietnam

1960s Former Marine Eugene Stoner develops the AR-15 and M16 rifles

1960s Col George Chinn invents the MK19 grenade machine gun

1960 Tactical Area of Responsibility (TAOR) concept is developed

1960s Marines develop Landing Platform Helicopter (LPH)

1960s Development of Short Air Takeoff System (SATS)

1960s First Marine Marathon run in Washington, D.C., for charity

1960s Adoption of British "wooly-pully" sweater

1970–1980 Marines adopt V/STOL Harrier aircraft

1975 LCAC (Landing Craft, Air Cushioned) is adopted

1978 First to adopt jungle-camouflage utilities/ combat uniforms

1970s Global Prepositioning Supply Points concept

1980s Opening of the Sniper School at Quantico

1980s Development of Amphibious Assault Ship (LHA); Marine troop/air assault ships

1980s Adoption of "tanker's jacket," followed by other services

1990s Night-vision technology and tactics

2000 The Crucible, the final test to finish boot camp and become a Marine, is inaugurated

2000 Initiation of Martial Arts program for all hands

2001 Adoption of new digital-pattern (MARPAT) camouflage utility/combat uniform

Glossary of Marine Lingo

aft Rearward

AWOL Absent without leave

birthday ball Annual celebration of the creation of the Marine Corps on 10 November 1775

boondocks, boonies Field training areas, remote locations, woods

boondockers Field boots

boot A recruit

boot camp A recruit training depot

brass Officers; metal buttons or buckles; spent shell casings

break out Take out, unpack, unload

brig A prison or jail, as on a ship

bulkhead A wall, as on a ship

"By your leave, sir" "May I have your permission?"

cammies Camouflaged utility uniform

cash sales Designated sales area for non-issued items

chocolate chips Gulf War desert-pattern cammies

chow Food

chow down Eat

commissary Base grocery store

corpsman Navy medic assigned duty with Marines

Crucible, the The final test for recruits at boot camp

Devil Dogs World War I appellation for Marines

dress blues Dress uniform

field day Period of time devoted to cleaning, usually in barracks

field scarf Khaki-colored cloth necktie

fore Forward part or direction, as on a ship

foul-up, fubar Make a mistake, Fouled Up Beyond All Repair

galley, chow hall, mess Mess hall kitchen; dining hall

gear, 782 gear Necessary possessions; weapons-related equipment

globe and anchor Marine Corps emblem (adopted 1868)

gunny Gunnery sergeant

gung ho "Let's go!"; extremely enthusiastic (adj.)

gyrenes World War II appellation for Marines

hash mark Sleeve service stripes for enlisted Marines

hatch Door, as on a ship

head Bathroom, as on a ship

jarhead Pejorative name for a Marine used by other services; comes from the look of a close haircut

ladder Stairs, as on a ship

leatherneck Appellation for a Marine (from the leather collar once part of the Marine uniform)

liberty Off duty (enlisted); leave (officers)

mess dress Very formal Marine uniform

office hours Commanding officer's nonjudicial punishment

"ooo-rah!" Affirmative verbal response meaning "yes," "will do," or "Way to go!"

overhead Ceiling, as on a ship

parade deck Area or field for marching, drilling, or parading

piece Rifle or gun

"piss-cutter" Fore-and-aft visorless cap

pogey bait Candy, sweets

pogey rope Shoulder braid for the French Croix de Guerre medal bestowed on the 5th and 6th Marines in World War I

police To clean up

port Left or left side, as on a ship

MCX Acronym for Marine Corps Exchange; a general store on a Marine base; also PX (Post Exchange); BX (Base Exchange)

rack, sack; sack out Bed; to go to bed or lie down

rear-echelon pogue Anyone not in a combat unit

rockers Curved chevrons under sergeant stripes

scuttlebutt Water fountain, on a ship; a rumor

secure Keep in place, put away, stop activity

seabag Canvas bag for clothing and personal items

Semper fi Shortened form of Marine slogan "Semper fidelis," meaning "always faithful"

ship over Reenlist

short-timer Marine nearing the end of his enlistment or tour

sick bay Dispensary or first-aid room, as on a ship

sick call Specified time for sickness or injury treatment

skivvies Underwear

slop chute Bar/restaurant club for enlisted ranks on base

smoking lamp, "lit" vs. "out" Permissible times for smoking, as on a ship

spit and polish A neat, sharp, appearance with all brass shined, as for a uniform

spit kit Small spitoon in a barracks or on a ship

spit shine Shining shoes with a bit of saliva

square away Get things or people in order, as on a ship

starboard Right or right side, as on a ship

topside Upstairs, above

Teufel Hunden World War I appellation for Marines meaning "devil dogs" (incorrect German)

utilities Work or field uniforms

watch Duty, guard duty, officer of the day, as on a ship

Selected Marine Corps Acronyms

AAAV Advanced Amphibious Assault Vehicle (formerly AAV, derived from LVT amphibious tractor "amtrac"; now called EFV)

AAV Assault Amphibious Vehicle

AC Amphibious Corps

ACE Aviation Combat Element

AMC Air Mobility Command

AN/PSN-11 precision lightweight global positioning system receiver

ANGLICO Air/Naval Gunfire Liaison Company

ARG Amphibious Ready Group

ASP Ammunition Supply Point

ATF Amphibious Task Force

ATGM Anti-Tank Guided Missile

BLT Battalion Landing Team

Bn Battalion

C2 Command and Control

C2PC Command and Control, Personal Computer

C3I Command, Control, Communications, Intelligence

C4I Command, Control, Communications, Computer and Intelligence

C4I2 Command, Control, Communications, Computer, Intelligence and Interoperability

CATF Commander Amphibious Task Force

CBIRF Chemical/Biological Incident Response Force

CDR; DCDR Commander; Deputy Commander

CDRUSEUCOM Commander, U.S. European Command

CE Command Element

CENTCOM Central Command

CFC Combined Forces Command

CG Commanding general

CIC Commander-in-Chief, the President of the United States

CI/HUMINT Counterintelligence/Human Intelligence

CJCS Chairman, Joint Chiefs of Staff

CLAWS Complementary Low Altitude Weapon system

CMC Commandant of the Marine Corps

CO Commanding officer

Co Company

COBRA Coastal Battlefield Reconnaissance and Analysis

COMMARFOREUR Commander, Marine Forces, Europe

COMMARFORLANT Commander, Marine Forces, Atlantic

COMMARFORPAC Commander, Marine Forces, Pacific

COMMARFORRES Commander, Marine Forces, Reserve

CP Command Post (any unit)

CQB Close Quarter Battle (Kimber 1911-type pistol)

CRRC Combat Rubber Recon Raft

DOA Days of Ammunition

DoD Department of Defense

DoN Department of the Navy

DSRP Defense Space Reconnaissance Program

EMW Expeditionary Warfare Maneuver

EOD Explosive Ordnance Disposal

EPW Enemy prisoner of war

FARP Forward Arming and Refueling Point

FAST Fleet Antiterrorism Security Team

FDNF Forward Deployed Naval Forces

FEX Field Exercise

FLC fighting load carrier

FLIR Forward Looking Radar

FMFPac/Lant Fleet Marine Forces Atlantic/Pacific (replaced by "Operational Forces")

FOB Forward Operating Base

FSCC Fire Support Coordination Center

FSSG Force Service Support Group

GCCS Global Command and Control System

GCCS-MC Global Command and Control System-Marine Corps

HERCULES Heavy Equipment Recovery Combat Utility Lift and Evacuation System

HET Human Exploitation Team

HIMARS High Mobility Artillery Rocket System

HMH Marine Heavy Helicopter Squadron (CH-53E Super Sea Stallion)

HMLA Marine Light Attack Helicopter Squadron (AH-1W Cobra)

HMM Marine Medium Helicopter Squadron (CH-46 Sea Knight)

HMMWV High Mobility Multipurpose Wheeled Vehicle (Humvee)

HMX Marine Executive Helicopter Squadron

HQMC Headquarters, Marine Corps

HVT High-Value Target

ICQB Interim Close Quarter Battle (Kimber 1911-type pistol)

ID, AD Army designations of infantry and armored divisions

IED Improvised Explosive Device

IFF Identification Friend or Foe

ISMT Indoor Simulated Marksmanship Trainer

JCS Joint Chiefs of Staff

JFCOM Joint Forces Command

JIC Joint Intelligence Center

JOA Joint Operations Arena

JSF Joint Strike Fighter

JTF Joint Task Force

JWFC Joint Warfighting Center

KIA Killed in Action

LAR Light Armored Reconnaissance unit

LAV Light Armored Vehicle

LCAC Landing Craft Air Cushion

LHA Amphibious Assault Ship (General Purpose)

LHD Amphibious Assault Ship (Multipurpose)

LIC Low Intensity Conflict

LPD Amphibious Transport Dock

LPH Landing Platform Helicopter (converted CVE); Amphibious Assault Ship

LSD Landing Ship Dock (Cargo Variant)

LVT Landing Vehicle, Tracked

LW155 Lightweight 155mm Howitzer

M1A1 Marine main battle tank

MAG Marine Aircraft Group

MAGTF Marine Air-Ground Task Force

MARCENT Marine Corps Central Command

MARCORSYSCOM Marine Corps Systems Commands

MarDiv Marine Division

MarForLant/Pac Marine Forces Atlantic/Pacific (no longer used)

MAW Marine Aircraft Wing

MBL Main Battle Line (has replaced MLR)

MBT Main Battle Tank

MCAS Marine Corps Air Station

MCB Marine Corps Base

MCCB(TW),(HW) Marine Corps combat boots; temperate and hot weather

MEB Marine Expeditionary Brigade

MEB(AE) Marine Expeditionary Brigade (Assault Element)

MEB(AT) Marine Expeditionary Brigade (Anti-Terrorism)

MEF Marine Expeditionary Force

MEU(SOC) Marine Expeditionary Unit (Special Operations Capable)

MIA Missing in Action

MLR Main Line of Resistance (between friendly and enemy forces)

MOLLE Modular Lightweight Load Carrying Equipment (replaced the ALICE pack)

MOOTW Military Operations Other Than War

MOPP Mission Oriented Protective Posture (gas, chemical suit/mask)

MPF Marine Prepositioning Force

MPS Maritime Prepositioning (Ships) Squadrons

MSR Main Supply Route

MTACCS Marine Tactical Command and Control Systems

NBC Nuclear, Biological, Chemical

NCO / Non-com Non-commissioned officer

NEO Non-combat Evacuation Operations

NGO Non-governmental organization

NLW Non-Lethal Weapons

NORAD North American Aerospace Defense Command (U.S. & Canada)

NORTHCOM Northern Command (Continental United States, Alaska, Canada, Puerto Rico, U.S. Virgin Islands)

OGA Other Government Agency

O-in-C Officer-in-Charge

OTH Over the Horizon

OTV interceptor outer tactical vest

PACCOM Pacific Command (Hawaii and U.S. Pacific territories)

PASGT personal armor system ground troops

PhibRon Amphibious Squadron (Marine attack ships in a task force)

Plt Platoon

PMF Para-military force

POW Prisoner of War

PSYOPS Psychological Operations

Rgt or (Mar) Regiment (also called "Marines," as in 1st Marines)

RLT Regimental Landing Team

ROE Rules of Engagement

RPG Rocket-Propelled Grenade

SACEUR Supreme Allied Command, Europe

SAR; CSAR Search and Rescue; Combat Search & Rescue

SATCOM Satellite Communications

SATS Short Airfield for Tactical Support

SAW Squad Automatic Weapon (M4 machine gun, Fire Team weapon)

SERE Survival, Evasion, Resistance, Escape

SMAW Shoulder-Launched Multipurpose Assault Weapon

SOA Sustained Operations Ashore

SoCOM; T-SOC Special Operations Command; Theater-Special Ops Commands

SOP Standing Operating Procedure

SOUTHCOM Southern Command (Central and South America)

SPMAGTF Special Purpose Marine Air-Ground Task Force

Sqd Squad

SRAW Short Range Antitank Weapon

STOM Ship-to-Objective Maneuver

STRATCOM Strategic Command (merger of SpaceCom and StratCom)

TACAIR Tactical Aviation

TAOR Tactical Area of Responsibility (360°)

TF Task Force (Navy)

T/O Table of Organization

TOW Tube-Launched Optically-Tracked Wire-Guided Missile

UAV Unmanned Aerial Vehicle, Reconnaissance

UCAV Unmanned Combat Aerial Vehicle, Weapons Delivery

UCP Unified Command Plan

V/STOL Vertical/Short Take-Off and Landing (AV-8B Harrier; JSF)

VMAQ Marine Tactical Electronic Warfare Squadron (FB Prowler)

VMF/A Marine heavier-than-air squadron, fighter/attack (F/A-18 Hornet)

VMFA(AW) Marine All-Weather Fighter/Attack Squadron (Hornet)

VMGR Marine Aerial Refuel and Transport Squadron (KC-130J Hercules)

VMM Marine Medium Tiltrotor Squadron (VM-22 Osprey)

VMO Marine heavier-than-air squadron, observation

WIHA Wounded by hostile action

WIA Wounded in Action

WMD Weapons of Mass Destruction

WWMCCS Worldwide Military Command and Control Systems

Further Reading

Alexander, Col Joseph H. and Don Horan. *The Battle History of the U.S. Marines: A Fellowship of Valor.* New York: Lou Reda Productions, 1997. A fascinating page turner that covers the major battles in the Corps' history.

Boot, Max. *The Savage Wars of Peace: Small Wars and the Rise of American Power.* New York: Basic Books, 2002. From the Barbary Wars of 1801–1805 to Somalia in 1992, small wars have been the Marines' frequent occupation. This book is exhaustively researched and well documented.

Brady, James. *The Marines of Autumn: A Novel of the Korean War.* New York: St. Martin's Press, 2000. A fascinating novel about the fighting withdrawal of the 1st Marine Division from the Chosin Reservoir in 1950.

_____. *The Scariest Place in the World: A Marine Returns to North Korea.* New York: St. Martin's Press, 2004. Brady returns to hilltop sites along the DMZ where he served as a second lieutenant during the Korean War.

Chenoweth, Col H. Avery, USMCR (Ret.). *Art of War: Eyewitness U.S. Combat Art from the Revolution through the Twentieth Century.* New York: Barnes & Noble/Friedman-Fairfax, 2002. Includes combat art from the Marine Corps collection, as well as examples from all the military services.

David Douglas Duncan. *War Without Heroes.* New York and Evanston, Ill.: Harper & Row, 1970. Magnificent and unforgettable combat photographs of the Vietnam War by the dean of combat photographers, a former Marine himself.

Fox, Col Wesley L., USMC (Ret.). *Marine Rifleman: Forty-Three Years in the Corps.* Dulles, VA: Brassey's, Inc., 2002. This book details Fox's career from private to colonel, with two wars and a Medal of Honor along on the way.

Gordon, Michael and LtGen Bernard E. Trainor, USMC (Ret.). *The Generals' War: The Inside Story of the Conflict in the Gulf.* New York: Back Bay Books, 1995. An insightful and eye-opening account of the developing strategy and execution of the liberation of Kuwait from Iraq Gordon was a *New York Times* correspondent during the war.

Hanson, Victor Davis, Ph.D. *Carnage and Culture: Landmark Battles in the Rise to Western Power.* New York: Random House, 2001. This eminent Classical scholar and historian traces the rise of modern weaponry and battle in the West from antiquity to the present.

Heinl, Col Robert Debs, USMC (Ret.). *Soldiers of the Sea: The United States Marine Corps, 1775–1962.* Annapolis: U.S. Naval Institute, 1963. This is a complete and highly personal history of the Corps, including the first post–World War II history of the Corps.

Hoffman, Col Jon T., USMCR. *Chesty: The Story of Lieutenant General Lewis B. Puller, USMC.* New York: Random House, 2001. The most complete biography of the famous, highly decorated (five Navy Crosses) Marine legend.

_____. *USMC: A Complete History.* Westport, Conn.: Hugh Lauter Levin Associates, Inc., 2002. An expansive volume of an almost day-to-day calendar of events in the history of the Marine Corps.

Krulak, LtGen Victor H., USMC (Ret.). *First to Fight: An Inside View of the U.S. Marine Corps.* Annapolis: Naval Institute Press, 1984. With ample historical examples, Krulak describes the prime qualities of the Corps: brotherhood, valor, institutional pride, loyalty, intellect, obedience, originality, and parsimony.

Millett, Col Allan R., USMCR (Ret.). *Semper Fidelis: The History of the United States Marine Corps.* New York: Simon & Schuster, 1980. A definitive work on the subject, this scholarly book stresses the organizational and administrative history of the Corps.

North, LtCol Oliver, USMC (Ret.) *War Stories: Operation Iraqi Freedom.* New York: Regnery Publishing, Inc. An eyewitness account from a famous combat veteran who was embedded with elements of I MEF during its lightning assault into Iraq and the capture of Baghdad.

Sherrod, Robert. *History of Marine Corps Aviation in World War II.* Washington: Combat Forces Press, 1952. A definitive account that includes statistics and squadron histories.

Simmons, BGen Edwin H. and J. Robert Moskin, eds. *The Marines.* Westport, Conn.: Hugh Lauter Levin Associates, Inc., 1998. Essays by noted Marines highlighting various historic events in Marine Corps history.

Simmons, BGen Edwin H., USMC (Ret.). *The United States Marines, 1775–1975.* New York: Viking Press, 1976. Concise and authentic history, by the former Director of the Marine Corps History and Museums.

Simmons, BGen Edwin H., USMC (Ret.). *United States Marines, A History,* 4th Edition. Annapolis, MD: Naval Institute Press, 2003. A concise history written by the former director of the Marine Corps History and Museums Division.

_____. *Dog Company Six.* Annapolis, MD: Naval Institute Press, 2000. A gripping novel about a Marine Reserve officer's experiences in Korea.

Spooner, Major Rick, USMC (Ret.). *The Spirit of Semper Fidelis. Reflections from the Bottom of an Old Canteen Cup.* Williamstown, NJ: Phillips Publications, 2005. Salty memories of the "Old Corps" during World War II.

Stavisky, Samuel E. *Marine Combat Correspondent: World War II in the Pacific.* New York: Ballantine Publishing Group, 1999. A vivid first-hand account of a professional newspaper-man who became a Marine combat correspondent, covering some of the fiercest battles in the Pacific.

Taplett, Col Robert D., USMC (Ret.) *Darkhorse Six: A Memoir of the Korean War, 1950–1951.* Williamstown, NJ: Phillips Publications, 2002. An account of the Korean War, from Camp Pendleton to the Pusan Perimeter, Inchon-Seoul, and the Chosin Reservoir, as experienced by the commander of the 3rd Battalion, 5th Marine Regiment.

Thomason, John W. *Fix Bayonets! And Other Stories.* Annapolis, MD: Naval Institute Press, 1994. Written and illustrated by World War I Marine Thomason—the "father of combat art." The book hit the bestseller list in the 1920s and brought even more fame to the Corps.

Also recommended are the Marine Corps Association's *Leatherneck* magazine and *Marine Corps Gazette* as well as official monographs from the Marine Corps University, Quantico.

Photography Credits

AC—Arms Communications
www.armscomm.com

ART—USMC Art Collection, Marine Corps Historical Center, Washington Navy Yard, Washington, D.C.

AU—Aurora Photos
www.auroraphotos.com

AV—www.av8rstuff.com

BB—Brown Brothers
www.brownbrothersua.com

BS—Bob Schwartz
www.ww2wings.com

CW—Charles Waterhouse
www.usmcartist.com

DDD—David Douglass Duncan, The Photography Collection, Harry Ransom Humanities Research Center, The University of Texas at Austin

DS—Don Stivers www.donstivers.com

DT—Don Troiani Collection
www.historicalartpirnts.com

FCM—Four Corners Media
www.fourcornersmedia.net

FNH—FNH USA, Inc. www.fnhusa.com

GH—George Hall/Check-6
www.planepix.com

GPJ—Gary Paul Johnston

HAC—H. Avery Chenoweth

JD—Jim Dietz www.jamesdietz.com

JPC—Jim Phillips Collection

JWT—J. Walter Thompson, Atlanta, GA

KUC—Kevin Ullrich Collection

LOC—Library of Congress
www.loc.gov

MCHC—Marine Corps Heritage Center, Quantico, VA

MCM—National Museum of the Marine, Marine Corps Historical Center, Washington Navy Yard, Washington, D.C.
www.usmcmuseum.org

MCU—Marine Corps University Research Center Archives, Quantico, VA

MK—Mort Künstler
www.mortkunstler.com

MOA—Medals of America
www.usmedals.com

MP—Michael Patterson
www.arlingtoncemetery.net

MS—Marc Stewart
www.aviationart.homestead.com

NA—National Archives
www.archives.gov

NHC—Naval Historical Center
www.history.navy.mil

NR—printed by permission of the Norman Rockwell Family Agency ©2005 the Norman Rockwell Family Entities

NRA—National Rifle Association
www.nra.org

RG—Roy Grinnell
www.roygrinnell.com

RH—Robert Hodierne, © 2004 reprinted with permission
www.vietnamphotography.com

RSC—Maj. Richard Spooner Collection

SI—Smithsonian Institution
www.si.org

SW—Steve Wiper
www.classicwarships.com

TBZ—The Battle Zone, Ltd.
www.thebattlezone.com

TL—Tom Lovell,
www.greenwichworkshop.com

USNI—US Naval Institute
www.usni.org

VIR—Visual Information Repository, Marine Corps University, Quantico, VA

WPN—World Picture News
www.worldpicturenews.com

FRONT MATTER

1: official USMC photo; 2: photo courtesy JWT; 3: emblem courtesy of the author; 5: photo ©AC; 6-7: streamers courtesy USMC; 9: photo courtesy USMC; 10: photo courtesy of the author; 11: photo courtesy Brooke Nihart; 12: photo courtesy James Brady/Tom Eckerle; 13: Official USMC photo.

INTRODUCTION

14-15: photo courtesy JWT; 16: official USMC photos; 17: emblems courtesy RSC; 18-19: official USMC photo; 20: Courtesy JWT, inset photo LOC; 21: artwork ©Donna Neary/ART, photo courtesy MCU; 22: photo ©Reuters/Corbis, patch courtesy TBZ; 23: background photo ©Peter Turnley/Corbis, medal MOA, streamer courtesy USMC; 24-25: official USMC photos; 26: ©Reuters/Corbis; 27: both photos ©Peter Turnley/Corbis, ribbons courtesy MOA; 28: photo ©Bettmann/Corbis, inset official USM; 29, clockwise from top: official USMC photos, photo ©Bettmann/Corbis, poster courtesy ART; 30: official USMC photos; 31: official USMC photo.

CHAPTER 1

32: streamer courtesy USMC, button courtesy; MCM 32-33: background photo ©Donna Neary/ART; 33: photo NA; 34: artwork courtesy ART, inset artwork ©HAC/ART; 35: artwork ©Donna Neary/ART; 36: artwork ©CW; 36-37: sword courtesy MCM; 38: map LOC; 39: map LOC, artwork ©CW, powder horn courtesy MCM; 40-41: muskets courtesy MCM; 41: artwork courtesy U. S. Naval Academy Museum; 42: grenade courtesy MCM; 42-43: artwork ©CW; 44: band artwork ©Donna Neary/ART, artwork ©John Magruder/ART, uniform courtesy MCM; 45: artwork ©Donald Dickson/ART.

CHAPTER 2

46: streamer courtesy USMC, emblem courtesy RSC; 46-47: background photo LOC; 47: poster LOC; 48: photos & sword NA; 49: artwork ©CW, drawing NA, streamer courtesy USMC; 50: artwork ©HAC/ART, chapeau courtesy MCM; 50-51: artwork ©MK; 51: weapon courtesy MCM, streamer courtesy USMC; 52: shako plate courtesy RSC, artwork ©CW; 53: artwork ©John Clymer/ART, battle rattle courtesy MCM, drummer artwork ©Donna Neary/ART, pistol courtesy MCM; 54: map LOC; 55: artwork ©John Magruder/ART, photo courtesy JWT, swords courtesy MCM; 56: band & marine private artwork ©Donna Neary/ART, drumsticks & drum courtesy MCM; 57: cap, sword & shako plate ©DT, artwork ©Donna Neary/ART, streamer courtesy USMC; 58: artwork ©HAC/ART, artwork ©CW; 58-59: rifle courtesy MCM; 59: artwork ©Charles Cureton/ART, streamer courtesy USMC; 60: streamer courtesy USMC, pistol & shako courtesy MCM, artwork ©Donna Neary/ART; 61: pistols courtesy MCM, artwork ©CW; 62: artwork ©Charles Cureton/ART; 62-63: artwork courtesy USMC Historical Center; 63: uniform courtesy MCM, map ©AC; 64: streamer courtesy USMC, artwork ©DT; 64-65: musket courtesy MCM; 65: artwork ©TL; 66: artwork ©Donald Dickson/ART, chapeau courtesy MCM; 67: artwork ©DS, photo ©BB; 68: patches courtesy RSC, officer's coat courtesy MCM; 69: artwork ©DT, photo NA, button courtesy MCM; 70: photo LOC, bugle courtesy MCM; 70-71: photo LOC; 71: sword courtesy MCM, photo LOC; 72: powder flask courtesy MCM, photo NA; 72-73: panoramic photo LOC; 73: weapons courtesy MCM; 74: photo LOC, uniform & shako courtesy MCM; 75: artwork ©DT; 76: officer's & enlisted kepis courtesy MCM, dress buckle courtesy RSC; 77: artwork ©CW, photo LOC, background map LOC; 78-79, from top: Spencer rifle and detail courtesy James Crane Collection, bullets courtesy KUC, Sharps rifle ©SI, rifled musket, navy rifle & bayonet courtesy MCM; 79: streamer courtesy USMC; 80: photo NA, drum courtesy MCM, marine band & drummer artwork ©Donna Neary/ART; 81: all shako plates courtesy RSC, photo NA; 82: artwork ©Donald Dickson/ART, emblem & epaulette courtesy RSC, official USMC photo; 83: photo LOC, shako & detail courtesy MCM 84: medal courtesy MCM; 84-85: rifle courtesy MCM, photo Detroit Photographic/LOC; 85: medal MOA, photo NA, canteen courtesy MCM; 86: photo Detroit Photographic/LOC, drum & overcoat courtesy USMC Museum, portrait official USMC photo; 87: photo Detroit Photographic/LOC, tunic courtesy MCM, artwork ©Donna Neary/ART; 88: portrait official USMC photo, photo courtesy NHC; 88-89: rifle courtesy MCM; 89: photo NA, streamer courtesy USMC; 90: medals courtesy RSC, official USMC photo; 90-91: sword courtesy MCM; 91: official USMC photos; 92: official USMC photo, medals and coat courtesy RSC; 93: official USMC photos; 94: photo courtesy MCU, marine band artwork ©Donna Neary/ART, shoulder knots & emblem courtesy RSC, helmet courtesy MCM; 95: top photo NA, uniform courtesy MCM, bottom official USMC photo; 96: official USMC photo, cartridge box courtesy MCM; 96-97: background official USMC photo, rifle and bayonet courtesy MCM; 97: inset photo NA, streamer courtesy USMC.

CHAPTER 3

98: streamer courtesy USMC, emblem courtesy RSC; 98-99: background photo NA; 99: poster NA; 100: top & bottom photos NA, field hat courtesy MCM, portrait official USMC photo; 101: photo LOC, enlisted cap & medal courtesy RSC; 102: pistols & case courtesy MCM, photo ©Chicago Historical Society, medal courtesy RSC, portrait official USMC photo; 102-103: machine gun courtesy MCM; 103: official USMC photos, streamer courtesy USMC; 104: photos courtesy NHC, enlisted cover courtesy MCM; 105: top photo courtesy private collection, background official USMC photo; 106: streamer courtesy USMC, background photo NA, inset photo courtesy Ted Twordowski Collection; 107: pistol courtesy MCM, clip and bullets courtesy KUC, background photo LOC; 108-109: photos LOC,

streamer courtesy USMC; 110: photos courtesy MCU; 111: posters LOC, background photo LOC; 112: top & bottom photos NA; 113: top photo NA, background official USMC photo; 114: streamer courtesy USMC, top official USMC photo, center photo NA; 114-115: panoramic photo LOC; 115: left poster courtesy ART, right poster LOC; 116: top poster LOC, bottom poster courtesy ART, medal courtesy RSC, portrait photo courtesy MCU; 117: top photo courtesy JPC, bottom photo NA, streamer courtesy USMC; 118: official USMC photos; 119: photo NA; 120: official USMC photo; 121: top & bottom official USMC photos, portrait photo courtesy MCU; 122: poster LOC; 122-123: panoramic photo courtesy JPC, rifle courtesy MCM, bullets courtesy KUC; 123: marksmanship badges MOA; 124: left poster courtesy ART, center & right posters LOC, tommy gun and bullets courtesy MCM; 125: official USMC photos; 126: patches courtesy MCM; 127: artwork ©Harding/ART, uniform courtesy MCM, photo NA; 128: poster LOC, official USMC photo, collar discs courtesy RSC; 129: artwork ©Samuel J. Woolf/ART, portrait official USMC photo; 130: map ©Exner Cartography; 131: top & bottom official USMC photos, poster LOC; 132: photo courtesy MCU, medal courtesy RSC; 133: streamer courtesy USMC, background official USMC photo, bayonet and sheath courtesy private collection, poster LOC 134: photo LOC; 134-135: panoramic photo LOC; 135: poster LOC; 136: streamer courtesy USMC, top official USMC photo; 136-137: background official USMC photo; 137: portrait official USMC photo, inset uniform photo ©AC, mini fourragère courtesy Robert Volpe/JPC; 138: official USMC photos; 139: official USMC photos, wings MOA; 140: portrait photo courtesy MCU, medal courtesy RSC; 140-141: artwork ©Jim Butcher/ART; 142: poster LOC; 143 artwork ©Tom Lovell/ART; 144: artwork ©F.C. Yohn/ART, map ©AC; 145: official USMC photos, streamer courtesy USMC; 146: top photo courtesy private collection, artwork ©John W. Thomason/ART; 146-147: panoramic photo courtesy MCU; 147: cap courtesy UMSC museum, center official USMC photo, streamer courtesy USMC; 148: official USMC photo; 148-149: rifle courtesy MCM; 149: photo courtesy JPC, medal

©Corbis, streamer courtesy USMC; 150: patches courtesy RSC, top & bottom official USMC photos; 151: artwork ©John Magruder/ART courtesy of the author, field hat courtesy MCM; 152: enlisted cap courtesy RSC; 152-153: photo NHC; 153: poster LOC, patches courtesy RSC; 154: streamer courtesy USMC, top official USMC photo, center photo courtesy JPC 154-155: panoramic photo courtesy MCU 155: official USMC photo, artwork ©HAC/ART; 156-157: artwork ©JD, photo courtesy JPC; 157: poster courtesy ART, photo courtesy JPC; 158: streamer courtesy USMC, photo NA; 159: all photos courtesy JPC; 160: top photo courtesy JPC, bottom photo courtesy Dave Ostrowski Collection; 161: hat plates courtesy RSC, photo courtesy JPC, fur cover courtesy MCM; 162: streamer courtesy USMC; 162-163: photo LOC; 163: photo NA; 164: top posters courtesy Richard Claar, bottom poster courtesy ART; 165: poster courtesy ART, background photo collection of the author, inset photo ©Corbis.

CHAPTER 4

166: streamer courtesy USMC, emblem courtesy RSC; 166-167: background photo Corbis; 167: poster courtesy MCHC;168: portrait official USMC photo, white cap courtesy MCM, inset photo NA; 168-169: photo NHC; 169: portrait official USMC photo; 170: bugle and skin fabric all courtesy MCM, photo NA; 171: photo NHC; 172: photo © Bettmann/Corbis; 173: official USMC photos, patches TBZ; 174: photo Corbis; 175: letter courtesy MCM, portrait official USMC photo, medal courtesy USMC; 176: streamer courtesy USMC, artwork ©John Shaw/Liberty Studios, photo NA, emblem & bars courtesy MCM; 177: portrait photo NA, artwork ©MS, patch courtesy RSC; 178: official USMC photos, medal courtesy MCM; 179: artwork collection of the author, ribbon & medal courtesy RPC; 180: photo Corbis, streamer courtesy USMC; 180-181: photo courtesy SW; 182: background photo Corbis, field message courtesy MCM, inset photo Corbis; 183: photo Corbis; 184: map ©Exner Cartography; 185: artwork ©RG, portrait official USMC photo, siren courtesy MCM; 186: photo LOC, rifle courtesy MCM, bullets courtesy KUC; 187: photo courtesy MCU, bayonet and bandolier courtesy KUC; 188: poster courtesy ART, official

USMC photos, medal courtesy USMC; 189: top photo Corbis, submachine gun courtesy MCM, background photo courtesy MCU; 190: top & center knives and sheath courtesy private collection, bottom knife courtesy KUC, photo courtesy MCU; 191: photos Corbis; 192-193: artwork ©JD; 193: portrait photo MCU; 194: artwork ©NR; 194-195: photo ©Bettmann/Corbis; 195: medal courtesy RSC, photo Digital Stock; 196: official USMC photo, medal courtesy USMC; 197: top photo courtesy MCU, center photo Corbis, uniform courtesy MCM; 198: streamer courtesy USMC, medal MOA; 198-199: photo courtesy NRA; 199: photo courtesy J. Doug Bailey Collection; 200: top two patches courtesy private collection, bottom patch MOA, inset photo NA; 200-201: photo courtesy MCU; 202: photo courtesy MCU; 203: top & bottom photos courtesy MCU, patch courtesy private collection, portrait official USMC photo; 204-205: artwork ©TL/ART; 206: photo courtesy MCU, uniform courtesy MCM; 207: sketch ©Kerr Eby/ART, bottom photos courtesy MCU; 208-209: all photos courtesy MCU; 210: photo Corbis, boots courtesy MCM, streamer courtesy USMC; 210-211: photo courtesy MCU; 211: inset photo courtesy Norm Hatch; 212: photo courtesy Norm Hatch; 213: portrait official USMC photo, medal courtesy USMC; 214: photos courtesy Norm Hatch; 215: top & bottom photos Corbis; 216: patches TBZ, photo courtesy MCU; 217: photo Corbis; 218: patches TBZ, photo courtesy MCU; 219: photos courtesy MCU, canteen courtesy RSC; 220: artwork ©Nicholas Trudgian, portrait official USMC photo, life vest courtesy MCM; 221: medal courtesy KUC, POW pass courtesy Robert Plouffe, bottom photo Corbis; 222: photo courtesy MCU; 223: photos courtesy MCU 224: photo collection of author; 225: photo courtesy MCU; 226: photo courtesy MCU, dog tags, snapshot, canteen & cup all courtesy John S. Rothe Collection; 227: photo courtesy MCU, portrait photo ©BS; 228: photo courtesy Jeremiah O'Leary Collection; 230: photos courtesy MCU; 231: ©Associated Press; 232: artwork ©Harry Jackson/ART, sketch ©Donald Dickson/ART, photo courtesy Harry Jackson; 233: sketch ©Kerr Eby/ART; 234: photo courtesy MCU; 234-235: panoramic photos LOC; 235: photo

courtesy MCU; 236: photos courtesy MCU; 236-237: photo courtesy MCU; 237: inset photo Digital Stock, portrait official USMC photo, helmet ©DT; 238: artwork ©C.C. Beall/ART; 238-239: photo Corbis; 240: top left official USMC photo, top right & bottom photos courtesy MCU; 241: background & inset photos courtesy MCU, portrait official USMC photo; 242: photos courtesy MCU, flag courtesy MCM; 243: top photo courtesy MCU, all portraits official USMC photos; 244: flag raising film footage courtesy VIR, top photo ©Associated Press, bottom photo courtesy MCU; 244-245: flag courtesy MCM; 245: photo Corbis; 246-247: photo ©Time Life Pictures/Getty Images; 247: top photo courtesy MCU, bottom photo Corbis; 248: portrait official USMC photo, poster courtesy ART; 248-249: photo NA; 249: web belt courtesy Joe Lanselatto Collection; 250: photo NA, poster courtesy ART; 251: background photo Corbis, inset artwork courtesy ART; 252: left photo NA, portraits official USMC photos; 253: portraits official USMC photos, streamer courtesy USMC, medal courtesy USMC; 254: streamer courtesy USMC, medal courtesy KUC, poster courtesy ART, helmet courtesy MCM; 254-255: photo NA; 256: photos courtesy MCU; 257: background photo Digital Stock, inset photo courtesy MCU, streamer courtesy USMC; 258: streamer courtesy USMC, photo courtesy MCU; 258-259: rifle courtesy MCM; 259: background photo courtesy MCU, bayonet & sheath courtesy private collection; 260: top & bottom photos NA, portrait official USMC photo; 261: all photos courtesy MCU; 262: medal courtesy KUC, patch MOA, photos courtesy MCU; 263: photos courtesy MCU, patch John Helvey; 264: portrait official USMC photo; 265: official USMC photos; 266: background & top photos courtesy MCU; 267: top photo Corbis, bottom photo courtesy MCU, streamer courtesy USMC; 268: official USMC photo; 269: official USMC photos, portrait courtesy RSC; 270: streamer courtesy USMC, photo courtesy MP; 271: portrait official USMC photo; 272: photo Corbis; 273: official USMC photo; 274: medal MOA; 275: ©NR, streamer courtesy USMC; 276: streamer courtesy USMC, patches MOA; 277: Photo ©Mark Wilson/Getty Images, patches MOA.

CHAPTER 5

278: streamer courtesy USMC, emblem courtesy RSC; 278-279: background photo ©Bettmann/Corbis; 279: poster LOC; 280-281: photos ©DDD; 282: top photo courtesy MCU, bottom photo collection of author; 282-283: rocket launcher courtesy MCM; 283: photo collection of author; 284-285: all photos ©DDD; 286: seal courtesy USMC; 288: portraits official USMC photos; 289: portraits official USMC photos; 290: photo collection of author; 290-291: photo courtesy MCU; 291: portrait official USMC photo; 292: photos collection of author; 293: photo ©DDD; 294: portrait photo courtesy MCU; 294-295: background photo collection of author; 295: grenades courtesy MCM, bottom inset photo Corbis; 296: photo collection of author; 297: top & bottom photos collection of author; 298: photo Corbis; 298-299: photo courtesy NHC; 298: inset portrait official USMC photo, medal courtesy USMC; 300: photo courtesy collection of author; 301: photo Corbis; 302: photo Corbis; 303: top portrait official USMC photo, right portrait photo courtesy MCU, medal courtesy USMC; 304: photos courtesy collection of author; 304-305: photo courtesy collection of author; 306: portrait official USMC photo, medal courtesy USMC; 307: top photo ©DDD, bottom photo courtesy collection of author; 308-309: photo courtesy collection of the author; 309: portrait official USMC photo, medal courtesy USMC; 310: portrait official USMC photo, medal courtesy USMC; 311: grenade courtesy private collection, photo courtesy collection of author; 312: helmet courtesy MCM, photo NA; 313: top & bottom photos courtesy MCU, inset photo courtesy Dennis M. Giangreco Collection; 314: helmets courtesy MCM, official USMC photo; 315: background & inset photos courtesy MCU, portrait official USMC photo; 316: map ©Exner Cartography; 317: photos courtesy MCU, winter hat courtesy MCM, streamer courtesy USMC; 318: top photo courtesy collection of author, bottom official USMC photo; 319: photos courtesy collection of author, portrait official USMC photo; 320: photo courtesy Dennis M. Giangreco, vest courtesy MCM; 321: photo courtesy collection of author; 322: portrait official USMC photo, medal courtesy USMC, inset photo courtesy James Brady; 322-323:

background photo Corbis; 323: medals MOA, photo Corbis; 324: photo Corbis, mess kit courtesy private collection; 325: photo courtesy collection of author.

CHAPTER 6

326: streamer courtesy USMC, emblem courtesy RSC; 326-327: background photo ©DDD; 327: poster courtesy ART; 328: portrait official USMC photo, poster courtesy ART; 329: ©Larry Burrows/Time Life Pictures/Getty Images, helmet courtesy MCM, portrait official USMC photo; 330: photo Corbis, medal MOA; 331: portrait official USMC photo, medal courtesy USMC; 332: photo courtesy MCU; 332-333: photo ©Camera Press Ltd; 333: inset photo courtesy collection of author, medal courtesy USMC; 334-335: photo Corbis, rifle courtesy MCM; 335: inset photo Getty; 336: photos ©HAC; 337: map ©Exner Cartography; 338: photo ©TRH Pictures; 338-339: machine gun courtesy MCM; 339: photo ©Larry Burrows/Time Life Pictures/Getty Images; 340: photo ©Larry Burrows/ Time Life Pictures/Getty Images; 341: top photo ©Larry Burrows/Time Life Pictures/Getty Images, bottom photo Time Life Pictures/Getty Images, streamer courtesy USMC; 342: portrait official USMC photo, medal courtesy USMC; 343: top photo ©HAC, bottom photo courtesy MCU; 344: photo ©HAC; 345: top photo ©Larry Burrows/Time Life Pictures/Getty Images, bottom photo courtesy MCU; 346: top photo ©LarryBurrows/Time Life Pictures/ Getty Images, bottom photo ©Larry Burrows Collection; 347: photo ©HAC, portrait official USMC photo, medal courtesy USMC; 348: photo ©HAC; 348-349: rifle courtesy MCM; 349: top photo ©RH, background photo ©Bettmann/UPI; 350: streamer courtesy USMC, photo ©DDD; 351: top photo ©DDD, bottom photo Bettmann/UPI, grenade launcher courtesy MCM; 352-353: ©Bettmann/UPI; 354: top & bottom photos ©DDD; 355: official USMC photos, medal courtesy USMC, camera courtesy MCM; 356: photo ©Larry Burrows/Getty Images, boots courtesy MCM; 357: photo Corbis, inset portrait official USMC photo, medal courtesy USMC; 358-359: photo ©DDD; 359: photo Corbis; 360: top photo Corbis, center photo ©DDD; 360-361: rifle courtesy MCU; 361: top photo Corbis,

Index

Page numbers in italics indicate illustrated material or information found in a caption.

A

Abbott, Sgt Todd, *418*
Abrams, Gen Creighton W., Jr. (USA), 367
Abrams tank, 402, *405*, 454, 455, *456*
Academy Award, 214
Accelerated Pacification Plan, 368
Aces, Marine flying, 252, *252–253*
Active denial system (ADS), 453
Adams, John, 34
Adaptability of Marine Corps, 462–464
Advanced Base Force (ABF), 104, 106, 172–173
  after Spanish-American war, 22, *105*
  exercise, on Culebra Island, 107
  in World War II, 172–173
Afghanistan
  air operations in, 427, *427*
  base at Kandahar, 427
  casualties in, 428
  continuing future conflict in, 467
  "detainees" taken in, 427–428
  devices in, 462
  Operation Enduring Freedom (OEF), 460–467
  sea-land-air integration in, 201
African-American Marines, *247*, 275, 288
Aguinaldo, Emilio, 90
Airacobra, 185
Air Boss, *404*
Aircraft, enemy
  Badger (Russia), *394*
  MiG (Russia), 318
  Mitsubishi G4M3 "Betty" bomber (Japan), *249*
  Naka-jima Ki-43 "Oscar" fighter (Japan), *249*
  YAK-3 (Russia), 284
Aircraft, fixed-wing
  A-4 Skyhawk, 341, *344*
  A-1 Skyraider, *292*, *345*
  AV-8B Harrier, *397*, 403, *404*, *421*, *426*, *432*, 448
  B-36 bomber, 288
  Boeing F4B-3, *156*
  B-29 Superfortress, 210, 218, 223, 225, 248, 269, 325
  C-130 transport, 340, *366*
  Curtiss P-40 Kittyhawk, *191*
  DeHavilland DH-4, 138, *138*, *139*, *141*, *148*
  EA-6B Prowler, *397*, *433*
  FA/8D Hornet, *16*
  F/A-18 Hornet, *395*, *426*, *433*
  F-117A Stealth bomber, 434
  F4F-3A Wildcats, *162*, 176, *177*, 185
  F3F-2 "Flying Barrel," *160*

F6F Hellcat, 284
F9F Panther, *315*
F-4 Phantom, 341
F86 Sabre, *314*
F80 Sabre jet, *313*
F-80 Shooting Star, 318
F-4S Phantom II, *390*
F4U Corsair, *220*, 226, *255*, *260*, *294*, *312*, *313*
N-9 seaplane, 138
Piper L-5 "Bird Dog," 265
P-38 Lightning, 185, 222
P-51 Mustang, 210, 284
R4Q/C-82 cargo plane, 310
SBD Dauntless dive-bomber, 185, *250*
Sopwith Camel, 138
Vought SB2U Vindicator, *182*
Vought Corsair O2U-1, 155, *156–157*
Aircraft, general
  helicopter development, *315*
  jet development, *315*
  and vertical-envelopment doctrine, 289, 318, 320
Aircraft, rotary-wing, 25
  AH-1G Cobra, 341
  AH-1W Cobra, *404*, *435*
  Bell 47G, 318, *318*
  Bell P-39 Airacobra, 185
  Bell UH1 Huey, 341
  CH-53E Super Stallion, 427, *428*
  CH-46 Sea Knight, 289, *329*, 341, *371*, *432*
  CH-53 Sea Stallion, *26*, 341, *354*, *374*, *418*, *420*
  "Flying Grasshopper," *356*
  HRP-1, 289
  HRS utility, 289
  RH-53D, Navy, 378
  Sikorsky HRS-1, *318*, *319*, 320
  UH-1 Huey, *374*
  UH-34 Sea Horse, *329*, *332*, *338*, *339*, 341, *341*, *348*
  and vertical-envelopment doctrine, 289, 318, 320
  VH-3D Sea King, 22, *22*
Aircraft, tilt-rotor, *395*, *424*
Aircraft carriers. See also individual ship names
  Marine squadrons on, 250
  Yorktown, commissioning of, *162*
Airfields
  expeditionary, *344*
  Short Airfield for Tactical Support, 329, *344*
Air Force, U.S.
  and atomic bomb, delivery of, 269
  and F-80 Shooting Star, 318
  and SS *Mayaguez* incident, 377
  25th Squadron, 51st Fighter Interceptor Wing, *314*
  Transportation Command (TRANSCOM), 25
Air-ground team concept, *152*

Air Naval Gunfire Liaison Company (ANGLICO), *372*
Air operations, in Persian Gulf, 402–403
Al Asad, Iraq, *16*
Aldrich, Capt Donald N., *253*
Al-Jazeera, 434
Allen, Ethan, 34
Alli, Joe, 229
Almond, MajGen Edward M. "Ned," 298
al-Qaeda, 426, 460, 461, 464, 467
al-Sadr, Muqtada, *449*, *450*
al-Zarqawi, Abu Musab, 452
American Asiatic Squadron, 89
American Expeditionary Force (AEF), 22
  in World War I, 124
American Soldier, 440
Amos, MajGen James F., 443
Amphibious Assault ships, 25
Amphibious doctrine, 23, 183
  codification of, pre-World War II, 161, 163
Amphibious operation(s), 155.
  See also individual campaigns
  integrated sea-air-land, in South Pacific, 201
  on Okinawa, 256–265
  in Revolutionary War, 37
Amphibious Ready Groups, 25
Amphibious Triad, *417*
Amphibious units
  Amphibious Squadron 7, 427
  Amphibious Squadron 8, 427
  3d Marine Amphibious Unit, 327, 328
  22d Marine Amphibious Unit, 382, *384*
  III Amphibious Corps, 222, 256, 264, 271
  III Marine Amphibious Force (MAF), 340, 372, 377
  5th Marine Amphibious Brigade, 328
  9th Marine Amphibious Brigade, 373
  24th Marine Amphibious Unit, 382
  34th Marine Amphibious Unit, 376
  V Amphibious Corps, 201, 226, 234, 271
  V Amphibious Corps Reserve, 216
Anacostia Naval Auxiliary Air Station, 22
Analysts, military, 442–443
Anderson, Col Gary W., 452
Anderson, Pvt James, Jr., *347*
Antiaircraft guns, *172*, *173*, *181*, *387*
Antiwar movement, 338
Appellations
  "Chosin Few," 311
  and Devil dogs, 142, *142*
  nicknames, 16–17
  origins of, 16–17
  "Ridge Runners," *319*
  from World War I, 142
Aristide, Jean-Bertrand, 418
Arlington National Cemetery, 275

Armed forces, U.S.
  consolidation, proposed, 286–289
  post-World War II, 280–281
Armed Forces Qualification Test, 371
Armistice, 137
Armor, body, *320*, 323
Armored car, *119*
Army, U.S.
  2d Army Division, 143
  2d Division, 22, *121*
  Eighth Army, in Korea, 284
  field army, Marine command of, 265
  Military Assistance Command, Vietnam (MACV), 341
  rivalry, with Marine Corps, 286–289
  1st Cavalry Division, 226
  321st Regimental Combat Team, 81st ID, 226
  77th Division, 222, 226
  165th Infantry, Reserve Army 27th Division, 218
  7th Infantry Division, 300
  24th Infantry Division, *280*
  25th Infantry Division, *280*
  VII Army Corps, 405
  XVIII Army Corps, 405
  XXIV Army Corps, 256
Arndt, GySgt Charles C., *189*
Arnold, Benedict, 34
Arnold, Hap, 286
Art, Marine Corps combat collection, 231. See also Artists, combat
Artillery. See also Howitzer; Missile; Rocket; Tank
  battery, in Dominican Republic, *118*
  bombardment, of Tripoli, 49
  broadside gun, *117*
  combined arms, 24
  deck gun, *105*
  fire support, on Tinian, 223
  at Fort Fisher, 77
  French GPF, in Cuba, *113*
  gun crew, *219*, *223*
  landing guns, 24, *24*
  "Long Toms," 256
Artists, combat, 229, 231, 442–443
  in Lebanon, *384*
  in Vietnam War, *335*
  in World War I, *129*
  in World War II, *204*, *207*
Assunpink Creek, 38, *39*
Atom bomb
  and Japanese surrender, 269–270
  Marine exposure to, 271, 324–325, *325*
  testing of, 324–325, *325*
Aviation, Marine, 23, 116, 119. See also Aviation units
  aboard Navy carriers, 250
  birth of, 115, 119
  close air support, in Korean War, 318
  developments in, 1980s, 395
  effectiveness of, in Okinawa, 265

  flying aces, *252*, *253*
  and Forward Air Controllers (FAC), 318, *319*
  glider program, 186
  insignia of, *254*
  recruiting posters for, *156*, *328*
  tactical, 260
  in World War I, 138–141
Aviation units. See also Units
  Aircraft Group 21, 168
  2d MAW, 26, 328
  3d MAW, 26, 400, 443
  3d MAW, MAG 16, *31*
  Forward Air Controllers (FAC), 318, *319*
  HMM 264, 410
  HMM 266, *432*
  HMR 161, *318*, *319*, 320
  HMX 1, 22, 289
  MAG 11, 326
  MAG 13, 216
  MAG 21, *223*
  MAG 22, 182, 216
  MAG 31, 216
  MAG 33, 264
  1st Marine Aeronautic Company, 138, *138*
  1st Marine Aviation Force, *140*
  1st Marine Aviation Squadron, *138*
  1st MAW, *313*, 341
  3rd MAW, *16*
  VMA 542, *448*
  VMAQ 2, *432*
  VMF 111, *162*
  VMF 114, 226
  VMF 122, *220*, 226
  VMF 124, *255*
  VMF 213, *255*
  VMF 214, *220*, *221*, *313*
  VMF 312, *312*
  VMF 323, 264
  VMFA 115, *394*
  VMFA 121, *397*
  VMFA 251, 427
  VMFA(AW) 242
  VMO 6, 265
  VMS 3, *250*
  VMU 1, 452
Awacha Pocket, 261
Awards. See also Medal of Honor
  Dewey Medal, 92
  foreign citations, 465
  George Medal, *195*
  Marine Corps Brevet Medal, *149*
  Navy/Marine, by precedence, 462–465
  ribbons, campaign, 466–467
  Sampson Medal, 90
  unit commendations, 465
Axtell, Maj George C., Jr., 252, *271*

B

Badger, *394*
Bagaduce Peninsula, *42*, *43*
Baghdad, 444, *445*, *456*

Bahamas, 45
Bailey, PFC David R., 440
Balkans, 419–421
"Banana" wars, 109, 113, 114
Band, Marine. See also Music
    drummer in, 53
    early history of, 20–21
    early photo of, 70
    and John Philip Sousa, 21
    uniforms of, 21, 44, 56, 94
Bangladesh, 410
Barbary Wars
    Presley O'Bannon in, 48–49, 48
    and Mameluke sword, 49
    Philadelphia incident in, 48
Barber, Capt William E., 306
Barnett, CMC George, 107, 124, 129
Barnum, Lt Harvey C., 340
Bartlett, Tom, 229
Basco, Capt Sean, 442
Basilone, GySgt John, 238
Bataan death march, 160, 180
Bataan (film), 427
Battalion Landing Team (BLT), 326, 340,
    383, 422, 424, 436
Battle streamers. See Streamers
Bauer, LtCol Harold W., 252
Bayler, LtCol Walter L.J., 174, 271
Bayonet, 133, 187, 190, 389
Beall, Col Lloyd J., 66
Beaufort, MCAS, 26
Belgium, 140
Belgium, Thielt, bombing of, 141
Bell, Sgt James, 103
Belleau Wood, 134, 145
    4th Brigade in, 131
    map of, 144
    Marine casualties at, 132, 134
    painting of, 143
Bell UH-1 Huey, 374
Benes, MajGen Tom, 394
Bennett, LtCol Drew, 407
Berkeley, Maj Randolph, 114
Berlin Wall, 328
Berndt, Col Martin, 420
Bestwick, SgtMaj Wilbur, 328
Betio. See Tarawa
Bey of Alexandria, 20
Biddle, Anthony Drexel, 190
Biddle, CMC William, 107, 119
Black, Cpl Harlon H., 243
Black, John, 229
Black Sheep squadron, 220, 221
Bladensburg, 52
Blair, Tony, 430
Blanc Mont, 102, 127, 142
Blaz, BGen Vincente, 224
Blitzkrieg, 166
Block Island, 36
Blunderbuss, 51
Bodenwiser, Lt Alec, 361
Bodnar, Sgt John, 271
Body armor, 320, 323
Bogdanos, Col Matthew, 454

Bolt, Maj John F., 253, 314
Bonin archipelago, 225
Bonnyman, 1stLt Alexander, Jr., 212,
    213
Books
    "Archie Smallwood" series, 151
    Fix Bayonets!, 146, 147
    Marine Combat Correspondent,
        229
    memoir, of BGen Vincente Blaz, 224
    Small Wars Manual, 159, 332
    This Is War, 285
Boomer, LtGen Walter, 402, 409
Boot camp, 26, 27, 30–31. See also
    Training
    the "Crucible," 419
    recruits, 27
Booth, Sgt George, 233
Bougainville, 183, 191, 200
Bouker, BGen John H., 329
Bourne Field, MCAS, 250
Boxer Rebellion, 98, 101
Boyington, Maj Gregory, 221, 252
Bradley, Gen Omar N. (USA), 286, 288,
    298
Bradley, PM2 John H., 243
Brady, 1stLt James, 323
Brainwashing, of POWs, 330
Breckinridge, Lt Henry B., 52
Breed's Hill, 34
Brenner, Sgt Bob, 228, 229
Brewer, BGen Margaret A., 28, 29
Brodie, Bernard, 299
Brooklyn, 89
Broome, Capt John, 76
Brown, John, 66, 67
Brown Bess musket. See Musket
Buchanan, James, 66
Buckner, LtGen Simon Bolivar, 256, 256,
    259, 264, 268, 268
Bugle, 170
Bull Run, first battle of, 68
Bundy, MajGen Omar, 125
Bunker Hill, 34
Burdwell, LCpl David, 361
Burgoyne, Gen John, 40
Burris, Sgt Daniel J., 426
Burrows, Larry, 338, 339, 346
Burrows, William Ward, 46
Bush, Cpl Richard Earl, 263
Bush, George H.W., 387, 396
Bush, George W., 426, 430
Bush, Lt William S., 50, 51
Bushido, code of, 219, 272–273
    vs. Marine esprit de corps, 272–273
Butler, BGen Smedley, 113, 114, 158,
    160
Butler Coliseum, 146
Buttersworth, Thomas, 41

C
Caco rebellion, 113, 148. See also Haiti
"Cactus Air Force," 193
Cadwalader, BGen John, 38, 39
Cameron, Cpl R., 320

Cameron, Lt F.H., 67
Camouflage, 25, 206, 237, 436–439
Campbell, 2dLt John F., 30
Campbell, Pfc Robert R., 242
Camp Lejeune, 26, 29, 275
Camp Neville, 154
Camp Pendleton, 26, 275
Capolino, John, 48
Capozzoli, Sgt Jason E., 447
Capra, Frank, 213
"Capstone" concept, 428–429
Carl, LtGen Marion, 185, 252
Carlson, Col Evans F., 158, 160, 210
Carmick, Capt Daniel, 48, 54
Carrillo, Sgt Jack, 442
Cartagena, Colombia, 34
Casey, Pvt, 103
Cates, CMC Clifton B., 132, 145, 219,
    223, 287, 288, 288
Catlin, Col Albertus W., 125
Central Command, U.S. (CENTCOM),
    396, 431
Ceremonies, 21
Chamberlain, Maj William C., 264
Champagne, Cpl David B., 322
Chapelle, Dickie, 346
Chaplains, Navy, 262, 398, 402
Chapultepec, citadel of, 62, 63, 64
Charlo, Pfc Louis C., 242
Château-Thierry, 130, 132, 134, 135
    77th Co, 6th Marines at, 133
Chemical-Biological Incident Response
    Forces (CBIRFs), 14
Chenoweth, Col H. Avery, 34, 58, 333,
    334, 467
Cherry Point, MCAS, 26, 275
Chiang Kai-shek, 158, 274
China
    and Korean War, entry into, 298,
        300–301
    legation guard duty in, 158
    post-World War II, concern with,
        274
    4th Regiment in, 161
Chosin Reservoir, 301–310
    arduous conditions at, 304, 305, 306,
        307, 308
    "attacking in another direction," 306
    and the "Chosin Few," 311
    Marine air support at, 304
    "no man left behind," 304, 307
"Chowder Society," 287
Chow time, 104, 154
Christie, Walter, 412
Chu Lai, 341, 345
Cincinnatus, 39
Cinematography, combat, 212–214.
    See also Photographers, combat
    on Iwo Jima, 244
Civil insurrections, 113, 115
Civil War
    and battle of Bull Run, 68
    Confederate Marines in, 66
    Fort Fisher, attack on, 76, 77
    weapons used during, 78

Clark, Ramsey, 366
Clinton, Bill, 411
Clymer, John, 231
Cobb, Capt Llonie, 433
Code of Conduct, 330–331
Codetalkers, Navajo, 191
Cold War
    beginning of, 270
    and combat air patrols, 394
    and Cuban Missile crisis, 328
Coleman, Col John C., 443
Collins, Lawton, 286
Collins, MajGen William, 341
Collins Plan, 286–289
Colombia, 34
Combat Development Command, 385,
    460
Combat Information Bureau (CIB),
    340
Combined Action Program (CAP), 337,
    337, 462
Combined arms, 24
Commandant of the Marine Corps, 23,
    223, 467
Communications
    difficulties of, with Wake Island,
        174–175
    and Joint Amphibious Signal
        Company (JASCO), 260
    modern innovations in, 423
    and tactical aviation, 260
Communism, 326
Conestogoe Wagon tavern, 34
Confederate Marines, 68, 69
Confederate stars and bars, 264
Continental Congress, second, 22, 34
Continental Marines, 32, 34, 35, 36–37
    first successful amphibious
        operation, 45
    uniforms of, 35, 37
Conway, Gen James T., 440, 443, 460,
    464, 467
Cook, Capt Donald Gilbert, 331
Coral Sea, battle of, 180
Core values, 30, 31
Cornwallis, MajGen Lord Charles, 38,
    40
Corpsmen, Navy, 248, 249, 262, 262,
    263, 266, 311
Corregidor Island, 180
Correspondents, combat, 228–229. See
    also Journalists; Photographers,
    combat
    in World War I, 132
Corsair. See Aircraft, fixed-wing
Cortez, Col Chris, 407
Counterinsurgency (COIN), 464
"Country Fairs," in Vietnam, 337
Craig, BGen Edward A., 291, 292, 296
Croatia, 424
Croix de Guerre, 136, 137, 143
Cuba, 24
    and Spanish-American War, 89–90
Cuban missile crisis, 328
Culebra Island, 105, 150

Cunningham, Cdr Winfield S., 175, 177
Cunningham, Maj Alfred A., 119, 138
Cureton, LtCol Charles, 57, 59, 62
Cushman, CMC Robert, 219, 223, 355,
    368, 376

D
Dakeshi Ridge, 261
Daly, GySgt Daniel, 98, 101, 116, 132,
    132
Da Nang
    Marines on patrol, 341
    and Tet Offensive, 358
Davies, Rodger, 376
Davis, BGen Andrew B., 443
Davis, Jefferson, 68
Davis, MajGen Raymond G., 308, 310,
    368
Davis, Richard Harding, 82
"Death Rattlers," 269
DeBlanc, Capt Jefferson Joseph, 196
Debusk, Sgt Jerry M., 317
Defense Battalions, creation of,
    172–173
DeHavilland, 138, 139, 141, 148
Delaware River, 38
Demo, Pfc Christopher, 214
Denig, BGen Robert L., 228
"Denig's Demons," 228–233, 228, 233
Department of Defense, 288
Desegregation, 275
Desert Storm. See Persian Gulf War
Designated marksman, 447. See also
    Sniping
Devereux, Maj James P., 175, 176–177,
    178
"Devil dogs," 17, 132, 142. See also
    Appellations
Dewey, Commo George (USN),
    89–90
Dickson, Col Donald L., 45, 66, 82, 231,
    232
    Sgt. Stoney Craig (comic book), 231
Diego Garcia, 378
Diet, Sgt Ernest J., 214
Dietz, Jim, 156–157, 193
Direct Air Support Center, tactical
    control, 260
Dive-bomber, 185, 250
Divisions
    1st Marine Division, 26, 128, 187,
        225, 229, 256, 258, 261, 275, 291,
        300, 301, 304–305, 320, 405,
        411, 452
    2d Marine Division, 26, 128, 214,
        218, 223, 256, 271, 275, 328, 398,
        405
    3d Marine Division, 222, 234, 341,
        346, 359, 371
    4th Marine Division, 215, 218, 219,
        223, 234
    5th Marine Division, 234, 271, 346
    6th Marine Division, 256, 257, 261,
        274
Dixon, Pfc Fermin, 214

Doctrine
  aerial dive-bombing, 155
  air-ground team concept, 152
  amphibious, development of, 161, 163
  Capstone concept, 428–429
  force-in-readiness, 312, 326, 460
  maritime prepositioning, 378, 399
  mechanized raids, 454
  From the Sea, 410
  "three block war" concept, 419, 452–453
  vertical-envelopment, 289, 318, 320
"Dodge City," 368
Dog tags, 226
Dominican Republic, 113, 118, 329
Domino effect, 326
Donahue, Maj Archie G., 252
Dong Ha, bridge at, 372, 373
Donohue, Vic, 231
"Doolittle Commission," 284
Doolittle Raid, 179, 180
Douglas, Paul, 287, 288
Douglas-Mansfield Bill, 23, 314
Douglass, SgtMaj Fredrick, 382
Doyen, BGen Charles A., 130
Draft, the, 375
Draper, Lt Herbert L., 91
Drum and Bugle Corps, 21, 95
Drums, 80, 86
Drysdale, LtCol Douglas, RM, 306
Duncan, David Douglas, 229, 280, 285, 292, 307, 351, 354, 366
Dunford, Col John F., 443
Dunham, Cpl Jason, 467
Dunn, Tom, 231
Dupont, RAdm S.F. (USN), 72
Dyer, Maj Jack, 384

E

"Easter Offensive," 372
Easy Company, on Mt. Suribachi, 240, 242
Eby, Kerr, 207, 233
Eddy, LtCol William A., 268
Edson, Capt Alvin, 64
Edson, MajGen Merritt Austin, 189, 210, 287, 288, 330
Edson's Raiders, 189
Egyptians, ancient, 34
Eisenhower, Dwight D., 286
Ellis, LtCol Earl Hancock "Pete," 155, 155, 412
Ellis Hall, 155
Elrod, Capt Henry Talmage, 174, 175
El Toro, MCAS, 275
Ely, Pfc Jack, 214
Embassy duty, 101
  in Beirut, 382
  London detachment, 270
  in Tehran, Iran, 378
Emblems. *See also* Insignia; Patch, unit
  bronze collar disks, 128
  of the Corps, 17
  dress ornaments, 94

eagle, globe, and anchor, 82
  Indian Head, 126
England, Gordon, 467
Eniwetok, 216
Enola Gay, 269
Ercole, SSgt John, 212, 214
Erskine, MajGen Graves, 239
Escobar, LCpl Richard, 455
Esprit de corps, 16
  vs. Japanese code of bushido, 272–273, 273
Estrada, SgtMaj John L., 456
Ethical standards, 31
Evans, Maj Francis T., 138
Exercises
  Advanced Base Force (ABF), 107
  CARAT, 416
  Phibex, with Croatia, 424
Expeditionary Maneuver Warfare (ENW), 14, 428–429
Expeditionary units. *See also* Units
  I MEF, 400, 405
  I MEF, recon team Piglet-2-1, 408
  3d MEB, 417
  4th MEB(AT), 430
  4th MEB, 400
  5th MEB, 400, 405
  7th MEB, 400
  9th MEB, 340, 342
  13th MEU(SOC), 422
  15th MEU, 416
  15th MEU(SOC), 427
  22d MEU, 403
  22d MEU, BLT 1/6, 429
  24th MEU, 410
  24th MEU(SOC), BLT 2/8, 422, 436
  26th MEU, 403, 420
  26th MEU, Bravo Battery, 1/2, 455
  26th MEU(SOC), 420, 427
  26th MEU(SOC), BLT 2/2, 424
  26th MEU(SOC), recon team, 447

F

Fairbairn, Capt William, 190
Falls, C.B., 131
Fallujah, 448, 449, 452–453, 452, 453, 459
  digital warfare in, 25
  sniping in, 446, 447
Farley, Cpl James, 338, 339
Farrister, William J., 356
Fay, SSgt Michael, 442
Feher, Pfc Michael, 329
Fenton, Capt F.I. "Ike," 266, 284
Fenton, Col Frank, 266
Fenton, Mike, 266
Fields, MajGen Jeff, 347
Field-stripping exercise, 121
Films. *See* Movies
Finley, Pvt, and dog Jack, 188
"Fire Brigade," 291, 294
Firepower Control Teams (FCTs), 372
Fire teams, 195
Fitzpatrick, 2dLt John, 36
Flagg, James Montgomery, 116

Flag-raising on Iwo Jima. *See* Iwo Jima
Flak jackets, 320, 323
Fleet Antiterrorism Security Teams (FASTs), 14, 386
Fleet Marine Force (FMF), 22, 152
  post–World War II, 275
Flintlock. *See also* Machine gun; Musket; Rifle
  blunderbuss, 51
  French Charleville, 44
  Mexican, 64
Flying boxcars, 310
"Flying Grasshopper," 356
"Flying Tigers," 251
Force-in-readiness, 214, 312, 326
Forces Françaises de l'Intérieur (FFI), 270
Ford, John, 213
Forrestal, James, 243, 286
Fort Fisher, 75, 76, 77
Fort McHenry, 52, 54
Fort Rivière, 113, 115
Fort Sumpter, 76
Foss, BGen Joseph F., 193, 252
Foss's Flying Circus, 192
Fourragère, 136, 137, 137
Fragging, in Vietnam, 375
Franklin, Benjamin, 40
Franks, Gen Tommy R. (USAF), 431
  and shock and awe strategy, 440
Frazier, Capt Kenneth D., 252
Fulford, Col Carlton W., 407
Funchilin Pass, 310

G

Gagnon, Cpl Rene A., 243
Gale, LtCol Anthony, 58
Galer, BGen Robert E., 315
Gamble, Lt John Marshall, 50
Garand, John, 199
Garland, 2dLt Addison, 50
Gaskin, MajGen Walter E., 463
Gas suits, 444
Gear, changes to and newly issued, 462–463
Geiger, MajGen Roy, 222, 241, 256, 256, 264, 271, 271, 286
Gemayel, Amin, 382
Gemayel, Bashir, 382
Genaust, Sgt William H., 212, 229, 242, 244
Geneva Convention, 178, 179
Geneva Peace Accords, 326
Geneviève de Brabant (song), 17
George III (king), 32
Geraghty, Col Timothy, 383
Gerlach, LtCol Larry, 383
Gettysburg battlefield, 80
Ghent, Treaty of, 54
Gibbons, Floyd, 132, 136
Gibson, Maj Trent, 467
Gilbert Islands, 196, 265
Gillespie, 1stLt Archibald, 62
Glenn, Maj John, 313
Glider program, 186

Gloucester Fox Hunting Club, 35
Gneckow, Capt Gerald, USN, 387
"Golden Fleece," 337
Gonzalez, Sgt Ernesto, Jr., 31
Good Neighbor Policy, 159
Gray, CMC Alfred M., 385, 388
Great Depression, 162
Great White Fleet, 105
Greene, Lt Israel, 66
Grenada, 384, 385
Grenade, 42, 283, 295, 311
  launcher, 351, 389, 423, 451
Grinnell, Roy, 185
Gromyko, Andrei, 280
Grumman Ironworks, 160
Guadalcanal, 185, 187, 194
  air defense of, 185
  "Edson's Raiders" on, 189
  Henderson Field, attacks on, 185, 185
  weapons used on, 187
Guam, in World War II, 222, 224. *See also* Mariana Islands
Guantanamo Bay, 24, 91, 93, 328
Gulf War. *See* Persian Gulf War
"Gung ho," 160
Guns. *See* Artillery
Gunther, LtCol Chris, 420

H

Hagee, CMC Michael W., 445, 460
Haguru-ri, 306
Hahn, LCpl Michael, 429
Haiti, 113, 148, 148, 156, 418
Hajek, Pvt, 103
Half Moon Ridge, 261
"Halls of Montezuma," 64–65
Hampton, Sgt Bill, 467
Hanke, Col Robert, 394
Hanneken, Cpl Herman, 148
Hansen, Sgt Henry O., 242
Hanson, 1stLt Robert M., 252
Harbord, MajGen James G., 127, 132, 135
Harding, Capt George Matthews, 127
Harpers Ferry, 66, 67
Harrier, 397, 403, 404, 421, 426, 432, 448
Harris, LtCol John, 65, 70
Hatch, SSgt Norman T., 204, 207, 210, 212, 212, 214, 243
Hatfield, Capt Gilbert D., 154
Hathcock, GySgt Carlos, 360
Havana Harbor, 86
Haversacks, 149
Hayes, Cpl Ira H., 243
Hayward, Capt Louis, 214
Hearst, William Randolph, 89
Heinl, Col Robert, 287
Helgoland, 365
Helicopter. *See* Aircraft, rotary-wing
Hellcat, 284
Henderson, CMC Archibald, 28, 58, 58, 59, 59, 65
Henderson, Maj Lofton R., 185

Henderson Field, 185, 201
Hendricks, Col William, 214
Henri, Capt Raymond, 231
Hessians, 38, 40
Heywood, CMC Charles, 82, 88
Higgins, Andrew J., 183
Hill 382, Iwo Jima, 248
Hill 400, Vietnam, 346
Hill 484, Vietnam, 346
Hill 861, Vietnam, 349
Hill 881, Vietnam, 349
Hindenberg Line, 143
Hiroshima, 269
Hispaniola, 46
History, of the Marine Corps, 457
Hittle, BGen James Donald, 287, 289
HMS *Cyane*, 54
HMS *Glasgow*, 36
HMS *Levant*, 54
HMS *Reindeer*, 53
HMS *Serapis*, 41
Hoar, Gen Joseph, 411
Ho Chi Minh, 366
Ho Chi Minh trail, 355, 371
Hochmuth, MajGen Bruno, 355
Hodge, MajGen John, 256
Hoffman, Clare, 287
Hogaboom, Gen Robert Edward, 287, 289
Holcomb, CMC Thomas, 134, 168, 179, 197, 228
Holcomb, 2dLt Franklin, 270
Hollywood. *See* Movies
Honor guard, Marine, 19
Hootches, 375–376
Hopkins, Esek, 37
Hornet, 16, 395, 426, 433
Horse Marines, 155, 158
Horseshoe Ridge, 261
Hospital ships, 365
Howitzer. *See also* Artillery
  battery, in Pusan, 290
  on Bougainville, 200
  fire-support base, 370
  gun crew, 393
  in Iraq, 455
  on Iwo Jima, 247
  self-propelled, 388
Hue, Vietnam
  casualties at, 364, 364
  combat action in, 359, 361, 363
Huey, 374
Hulbert, Henry Lewis, 102
Humanitarian efforts
  in Bangladesh, 410
  in Iraq, 454, 454, 458
  in natural disasters, 460
  in Vietnam, 337
Humvee, 448, 466
Hunt, Pvt, 103
Huntington, LtCol Robert, 90, 93
Hussein, Saddam, 396, 400, 430, 434, 444, 451
  sons of, 434
Hygiene, 308, 324

I

Identity card, World War I, *145*

IJN *Akagi*, 182, 185

IJN *Hiryu*, 182

IJN *Kaga*, 182

IJN *Kikusui*, 256

IJN *Soryu*, 182

IJN *Yamato*, 256, 264

Inchon, 294, 298, *298*

Indian head patch, *126, 128*

Indian Wars, 59

Indoctrination, 27, 30

Infantry units. *See also* Units

    1st Marines, D Co, *103*

    1st Marines, 7th Batt, *440*

    1st Marines, *106*, 226, 294, 405

    1st Marines, 2d Batt, *318*

    1st Marines, 3d Batt, *445*

    2d Marines, *103*, 201, 208, 210, 218

    2d Marines, C Co, *112*

    2d Marines, 2d Batt, F Co, *16*

    2d Marines, 3d Batt, 326, *429*

    4th Marines, 101, *114*, 158, 160, *161*, 274

    4th Marines, 2d Batt, 373, *374*

    4th Marines, 3d Batt, *337*

    4th Marines, 3d Batt, L Co, *351*

    5th Marines, 120, 124, *125*, 130, 143, *154*, 294, 296

    5th Marines, 52A Co, *155*

    5th Marines, Antitank Company, *321*

    5th Marines, Antitank Platoon, *297*

    5th Marines, 2d Batt, *280*, 361

    5th Marines, 3d Batt, 30, 294, *452*

    5th Marines, 3d Platoon, A Co, *298*

    5th Marines, 1st Batt, *398*, 405

    5th Marines, 1st Batt, B Co, *284*

    6th Marines, 130, 143

    6th Marines, 2d Batt, *134*, 440

    7th Marines, 148, 265, 294, 303

    7th Marines, Combat Assault Batt, *416*

    7th Marines, 1st Batt, 405

    7th Marines, 2d Batt, 405

    7th Marines, 3d Batt, *316*, 405

    7th Marines, 3d Batt, I Co, *371*

    8th Marines, BLT 1, *383*

    8th Marines, 2d Batt, *384*

    8th Marines, 1st Batt, *384*, 453

    8th Marines, 1st Batt, B Co, *458*

    8th Marines, 148, *208*, 264

    9th Marines, 148, 367, 405

    9th Marines, 1st Batt, *375*

    9th Marines, 2d Batt, G Co, *365*

    9th Marines, 3d Batt, 405

    9th Marines, 3d Batt, M Co, *351*

    13th Marines, *146*

    14th Marines, 215

    22d Marines, 216, 222, 261, *261*

    23d Marines, 215, *444*

    24th Marines, 215

    25th Marines, 215

    26th Marines, 355, 371

    28th Marines, *248*

    29th Marines, 222, 258, 261

Ingres, Jean-Auguste-Dominique, *50*

Insignia. *See also* Emblems; Patch, unit

    cap devices, 68, 81, 161

    chevrons, 150, 153

    collar, 1stLt, 176

    corpsman, Navy, 262

    defense battalion, 173

    fourragère, 136, 137, 143

    marksmanship badges, 123

    rank, all, 461

    wings, Navy/Marine Corps, 254

Intelligence, 217, 356–357

Interrogation, 219

Iran, future conflict with, 467

Iraq War

    air operations in, 432, 433, 434, 435, 448

    artillery support in, 455

    Baghdad, operations in, 444, 445, 456

    casualties in, 445

    devices in, 462

    digital warfare in, 23

    embedded journalists in, 442, *442–443*

    Fallujah, battle of, 25, 446, 447, 452, *452–453*, 453, 455, 459

    ground war strategy in, 443–445

    humanitarian aid in, 454, *454*, 458

    insurgency in, 449, 450, 451

    joint operations in, 449

    looting of Iraq National Museum, 454

    map of U.S. advance, 441

    maritime prepositioning in, 431

    Najaf, battle of, 449, 450, 452

    "shock and awe" in, 434, 440–441, 443

    sniper team in, 444, 446, *446*, 447, *447*

    "surge," 460–461

    tactical innovations resulting from, 451, 454–455

    "Three-block War," 462

    urban warfare in, 450, 452, 452–453, 453, 459

    weapon systems used in, 445

    women Marines in, 29

Ishihara, Capt (IJN), 264

Island hopping, 215

Isom, Pfc Paul E., 257

Israel, 382

Iwo Jima

    African-Americans at, 247

    casualties at, 248

    flag raising on, 237, 239, 240–245

    Green Beach, 422

    Japanese airfield at, 248–289

    Mount Suribachi, 234

    terrain of, 234, 238–239, 246

Iwo Jima Memorial, 275

J

Jackson, Donald, 288

Jackson, MajGen Andrew, 54

Jackson, Pfc Harry, *232*

Jacques Farm, 186

Japan

    atrocities committed by, 178–179

    and Bushido warrior code, *219*, 272–273

    in China, 160

    on Guam, *224*

    occupation of, 274–275

    scheduled invasion of, 256, 269

    surrender of, 270, 271, *271*

"Jar head," 17

Jet-assisted takeoff (JATO), *367*

Jingoism, 89

Johnson, Louis, 280, 288

Johnson, LtCol Chandler, *240*

Johnson, Lyndon, 332, *333*, *371*

Johnson, Capt Melvin, 199

Johnson, Pfc Ronald F., *317*

Johnston, LtGen Robert, 411

Johnson rifle. *See* Rifle

Joint Chiefs of Staff, 23, 288

    Marine chairman of, *458*

Joint Direct Attack Munitions (JDAM), 434

Joint Forcible Entry Operations (JFEO), 465

Jointness, 454, *458*

Jones, CMC James L., 27, 424, 428, *429*

Jones, John Paul, 40, *41*, 42–43

Jones, Sgt Joseph Michael, *349*

Journalists. *See also* Correspondents, combat

    embedded, 442–443

    in Vietnam, 336, 338, 340, *346*

Judo, 30

K

Kamikazes, 250, 256, 271

Kandahar Air Field, *432*

Karch, BGen Frederick, 340

Kasal, 1stSgt Brad, 455, *455*

Kelley, CMC Paul X., *384*

Kelly, Pvt John Joseph, *137*

Kennedy, John F., 328, 332

Kepi, *17*, 76

Kerr, Col James, 287

Kerr, Sgt F.C., *304–305*, 307

Kessler, 1stLt Woodrow M., *176*

Key, Francis Scott, 54

Keys, MajGen William M., *409*

Khe Sanh, 355–357, *356*, *357*, 368

    abandonment of, 368

    aerial photo of, *369*

    Marine sniping at, *360*

Kickboxing, 30

Kimberly, Capt L.A., *83*

Kleitt, Pfc V., *247*

Knight, Pfc Curtis W., *159*

Knives. *See also* Weapons, bladed

    innovations in, *190*

    Ka-bar, *190*

Knowles, 1stLt Brian, 408

Korean Military Advisory Group (KMAG), 278

Korean War, 23

    allied counteroffensive in, 314

    cargedores, *292*

    casualties of, 323

    China's entry into, 298, 300–301

    close air support in, 318

    map of, *316*

    Reservists in, 311–312

    South, invasion of, 278, 280

    tanks, condition of, 284

    and the 38th Parallel, 311

    UN line, collapse of, 300–301

    unpreparedness for, 278, 280–281

    women Marines in, 28

Kosovo Liberation Army (KLA), 421

Koto-ri, 310

Krulak, CMC Charles C., 29, 418–419, *419*, 462

Krulak, LtGen Victor H., 213, 287, 289, *337*

Krusa-Dossin, BGen Mary Ann, 28, *29*

Kunishi Ridge, 265

Kuwait, 396, 405, *408*

Kwajalein, 215–216, 217, *413*

L

Laidman, Hugh, 231

Lake Champlain, 34

Land, Maj E.J., *360*

Landing craft, 183, 412–417

    advanced amphibious assault vehicle (AAAV), *417*

    air-cushioned (LCAC), 393, *416*, *419*

    amphibious assault vehicle (AAV), *414*, 422

    amphibious tractors, 202, *202*, 204

    armored barge, *150*

    development of, *183*, 412–413

    Higgins boats, 183, 217

    at Inchon, *298*

    at Iwo Jima, *234*, 235, *236*

    LVTs, 217

    at Tarawa, *204*, 217

    tracked, 162

Landing Force Air Support *Control Units (LFASCU)*, 260

Landing Platform Helicopters (LPH), 328

Lanzalotto, Joseph C., 245

Larder, John, *238*

Lasswell, Fred, 233

Latour, Maj A., *54*

Laub, Pvt, *103*

Leadership, 428–429

Leahy, Maj Mike, *371*

Leahy, Pfc Gordon W., *297*

"Leatherneck," 17

Leatherneck magazine, 28, 229, 231, 233

Lebanese-Christian militia, 382

Lebanon, 326, *380*, 382

    barracks bombing in, 382, *383*, 384

Lee, BGen Harry, *113*

Lee, Pvt John W., *247*

Lee, Robert E., 68

Lejeune, CMC John, 107, *114*, *121*, *127*, *131*, 143, 147, 148, *160*

Lejeune, Eunice, 28

Leopold, WO John F., *214*

Lepanto, battle of, 34

Lerner, Alfred, 457

LeRoy, Catherine, *346*

Lewis, Al, 228

Lewis, LtCmdr Fred L., Jr. (USN), *320*

Lewis, Pvt Harry, 85

Lewis gun, *119*, *120*, *121*

Leyendecker, Joseph C., *111*

Leyte Gulf, 250

    kamikaze attacks at, 250, 256

    Marine fighter squadrons after, 250

Life belt, inflatable, *206*

Life vest, *221*

Lincoln, Abraham, 66, 68, 80

Lindberg, Cpl Charles W., *242*

Litzenberg, Col Homer, 303

Liversedge, BGen Harry, 248

Logistics

    air, in Vietnam, 364

    and Maritime Prepositioning Force, 399, *399*

    in Persian Gulf War, 419

    prepositioning concept, 378

Long, Paul, 228

Lopez, 1stLt Baldomero, 298, *299*

Louisiana purchase, 62

Lovell, BGen Solomon, 43

Lovell, Tom, *143*, 231

Lowe, MajGen Frank E., *321*

Lowery, Sgt Lou, 229, 244

Lucas, Jim, *334*

Ludwig, Verle, 151

Luftwaffe, 23

LVT *Alligator*, 163

Lytle, Capt Robert, *139*

M

M1014 combat shotgun, *423*

M9A1 2.36-inch rocket launcher, *282–283*

MacArthur, Gen Douglas (USA), 101, 180, *184*, 225, 271, 278, 281, 294, *294*, 295, 298

Machine gun. *See also* Flintlock; Musket; Rifle

    .30-caliber, *226*

    .50-caliber, *216*, 226

    M2 Browning, *393*

    M3 submachine gun, *189*

    M60, 329, *336–337*

    M240, *429*

    M1917A, *195*

    M1895 Colt, 24, *102*

    MP5, *423*

    M249 (SAW), *401*, 444–445

    M1921 Thompson, *124*

    NATO-caliber "Minigun," *396*

    Potato Digger, *102*

MacIntyre, Col Neil, *314*

Mackin, Elton E., 122

Mae West, life vest, *221*

Magazines, Marine Corps, 233
Magruder, Col John, 44, 151
Makin Island, 188, 206
Manassas, 68
Maneuver from the sea, 14
Manila Bay, 89
"Manpack" receiving station, 25
Mansfield, Mike, 288
Manzo, Cpl Francisco, 25
Mao Tse-tung, 274
Maquis resistance fighters, 270
Marble Mountain, 345
Mare Island, 50
Mariana Islands, 218–223. See also
    Guam; Saipan; Tinian
    amphibious landing on Saipan, 218
    casualties on, 223
    clearing entrenched enemy fighters,
        219
    consequence of attack, 222
    tank action on Guam, 222
Marine Air-Ground Task Forces
        (MAGTFs), 14, 460, 465
    warfighting role of, 25
Marine Barracks, 21, 46, 48, 467
Marine Combat Correspondent, 229
Marine Combat Correspondents
        Association (MCCA), 228,
        228–233, 230, 231
Marine Corps, U.S.
    creation of, 45
    and Executive Order 969, 105
    expeditionary role of, 25–27
    flexible response role of, 328
    force-in-readiness plan, 312, 326
    future preparedness, 464
    mission, evolution of, 22–23, 25–27,
        464–466
    status, clarification of, 312
    strength, personnel, 26
    transitions in, post-Korea, 328–329
    and unification plan, 286–289
Marine Corps Gazette, 233
Marine Corps Heritage Center, 457
Marine Corps Reserve Officers
        Association, 287
Marine Corps University, 388
Marine Corps War Memorial, 275
Marine divisions (MarDivs), 14. See also
    Divisions
Marine Expeditionary Brigades (MEBs),
    14, 25, 465. See also
    Expeditionary units
Marine Expeditionary Forces (MEFs),
    14, 25, 460, 465. See also
    Expeditionary units
Marine Expeditionary Units (MEUs),
    14, 465. See also Expeditionary
    units
    and maritime prepositioning, 399
Marine Expeditionary Units with
        Special Operations Capabilities
        (MEU/SOC), 25. See also
        Expeditionary units
Marine Guard Detachment, 104

Marine honor guard, 19
Marine One, 22, 22
Marines, foreign, 460
Marines' hymn, 17, 18–19, 21
    lyrics, 18
Maritime Prepositioning Force, 399
    in Iraq War, 431
Marksmanship, 110, 447. See also
        Sniping
    designated, 447
    poem concerning, 110
    qualification badges, 123
    in World War I, 132
Marne River, 134
MARPAT digital camouflage, 25, 439
Marsden, Capt M.M., 123
Marshall, George C., 286
Martial arts program (MCMAP), 30
Matanikau River, 189
Matjasic, Capt Raymond A., 214, 230
Matkanikau river, 189
Mattis, MajGen James N., 407, 424, 427,
    434, 443
Maxwell, MSgt Heber D., 213
Mayaguez, 377
McCawley, CMC Charles G., 86
McClung, Maj Megan, 465
McCutcheon, BGen Keith B., 260, 319,
    341
McDonald, Cpl Jack, 103
McInally, Sgt Andrew, 418
McKeldin, Maj Theodore R., 443
McKonkey's Ferry, 38
McNamara, Robert, 336, 347
Meal, ready-to-eat (MRE), 393
Medal of Honor, 102
    awarded at Iwo Jima, 248
    China relief expedition, 101
    Haitian campaign, 116
    Korean War, 299, 303, 309, 310,
        322
    Nicaragua campaign, 156
    Vietnam War, 331, 333, 340, 347,
        355, 357, 370
    World War I, 132, 139, 140
    World War II, 175, 188, 189, 196,
        203, 213, 253, 263
Medals. See Awards
Medical
    corpsmen, Navy, 262
    wounded, evacuation of, 265
Medical Civic Action Patrols (Med
        CAP), 337
Medinet Habu, 34
Megee, LtGen Vernon, 260
Mercer, BGen Hugh, 38, 39
Merrill, Cpl Troy, 454
Messenger dogs, 188
Meuse-Argonne
    capture of Blanc Mont, 142
    Last Night of the War, 144
Mexican War, 62–65
Mexico City, 64, 65
Meyers, LtGen John, 98, 100
Michels, Pfc James R., 242

Midway, battle of, 180, 181, 182, 182
Mielke, Art, 228
MiG, 318
Military occupational specialties, 28
Miller, Capt Samuel, 52
Miller, Cpl Kelley, 467
Miller, LtCol Harvey L., 159
Millet, Alan, 287
Milosevic, Slobodan, 420
Minefields, clearing, 405
Mine Resistant Ambush Protected
        vehicle (MRAP), 462, 466
Minutemen militia, 34
Miranda, LCpl Albert, 361
Missile. See also Artillery; Rocket; Tank
    surface-to-air (SAM), 403
    surface-to-surface (SCUD), 400
    TOW guided missile system
        (M220E4), 392
Mitscher, Adm Marc (USN), 222
Mobility, 454–455
Monroe Doctrine, Roosevelt Corollary,
    113
Montagnards, 371
Monteverdi, Sgt Al, 228, 229
Moon, Pvt, 103
Moorer, Cdr Thomas, 250
Moran, Sherwood F., 219
Mortar, 324. See also Artillery
    heavy German, 131
    platoon, 81mm, on Okinawa, 267
Mottoes, 16–17. See also Appellations
Movies
    combat footage, 212–214
    on exploits of Peter J. Ortiz, 269
    from World War II, 164, 165
Mulcahy, MajGen Francis, 256
Mullan, Capt Robert, 34, 35
Mullen, 1stLt Paul A., 220
Mundy, CMC Carl E., Jr., 410
Murphy, John Alphonsus, 101
Murray, MajGen Raymond L., 303, 303
Museum of the Marine Corps, 457
Music. See also Band, Marine
    Continental drummer, 35
    the Marine band, 20, 20, 21
    Marines' hymn, 17, 18, 21
Musket, 74, 75, 78. See also Flintlock;
        Machine gun; Rifle
    Charleville, 40–41
    M1861 rifled, 79
    Tower (Brown Bess), 40–41
Mustang, 210, 284
Mutter, LtGen Carol A., 28, 29, 29
Myatt, MajGen James M., 398, 409
Myers, Gen Richard (USAF), 431

N
Nagasaki, 270
Naha, Japan. See Okinawa
Najaf, 449, 450, 452
Napalm, 227
Nassau Hall, 39
National Guard Association, 287
National Rifle Association, 287

National Security Act of 1947, 23, 287
Natonski, BGen Richard F., 443, 452
Navajo codetalkers, 191
Naval Academy, 163, 385
Naval Committee, 34
Naval Reserve Officer Training Corps
        (NROTC), 30, 163
Navy, United States. See also individual
        ship names
    carriers, Marine squadrons on, 250
    Continental, creation of, 36
    medical support, to Marines, 262
Navy Reorganization Act of 1947, 288
Navy Task Force 58, 222
Neary, Col Donna, 21, 44, 53, 56, 60,
    80, 87, 94
Neville, CMC Wendell, 114, 127, 132
Newcomb, Cpl Obie, 207, 209, 212,
    214, 230
New Jersey, college of, 39
New Orleans, battle of, 54, 54, 57
New Providence, 36, 45
Nicaragua, 108, 154
Nicholas, Capt Samuel, 34, 35, 36, 37
Nicknames, 16–17. See also
        Appellations
Nightingale, Cpl Earl, 168
Nihart, LtCol Brooke, 178, 318
Nimitz, Adm Chester W. (USN), 184,
    215, 225, 250, 271
Nixon, Richard M., 371
Norge, R. Ray, 199
North, LtCol Oliver L., 442
North Atlantic Treaty Organization
        (NATO)
    and the Balkans, 412
    and Korea, 281
Northern Troops and Landing Force
        (NTLF), 218
North Island, NAS, 114

O
O'Bannon, Lt Presley, 48, 48–49, 54,
    190
Obs, GySgt William, 139
Ocotal, battle of, 154
Offenbach, Jacques, 17
Office of Strategic Services (OSS), 270
Officer Candidate School (OCS), 31
Officers
    commissioning sources for, 30–31,
        163
    general, number authorized, 27
    and tombstone promotions, 288
O'Grady, Capt Scott (USAF), 420
O'Halloran, Maj James S., 182
Okinawa, 266, 267
    American objectives at, 256, 258
    amphibious capabilities, under-
        utilization of, 259, 265
    Awacha Pocket, 261
    casualties at, 265
    death of LtGen Buckner at, 264,
        268, 268
    Japanese strategy at, 256

Marine/Navy aviation, role of, 269
Naha, 258, 261, 261, 265
    Shuri Castle, 257, 258, 264
Oland, SSgt Roy, 214
Old Glory, 48
Old Ironsides, 51, 54
O'Leary, SSgt Jeremiah, 228, 229
O'Malley, Sgt Robert, 333
Operating forces, 14, 26
Operation al-Fajr, 452
Operational Maneuver from the Sea
        (OMFTS), 14
Operation Beaucharger, 348
Operation Cadillac Ranch, 429
Operation Coronet, 269
Operation Desert Shield and Desert
        Storm. See Persian Gulf War
Operation Dewey Canyon, 368, 371
Operation Double Eagle, 345, 347
Operation Eagle Claw, 378
Operation Enduring Freedom. See
        Afghanistan
Operation Fortress Entry, 359
Operation Harvest Moon, 345
Operation Iraqi Freedom. See Iraq War
Operation Just Cause, 388–389
Operation Mameluke Thrust, 371
Operation Olympic, 269
Operation Pegasus, 364
Operation Shufly, 340
Operation Starlight, 341
Operation Task Force Hotel, 368
Operation Union II, 347
Operation Uphold/Support Democracy,
    418
Operation Urgent Fury, 384
Orange plan, 172, 412, 464
Orden, George Van, 191
Ormsby, Pvt, 103
Orsoba, Pvt, 103
Ortiz, Maj Peter J., 270
Orton, Cpl James, 214
Osprey, controversy over, 424
Ottoman Empire, 34, 398
Owens, Sgt Forest, 214

P
Pace, Gen Peter, 458
Pacification, in Vietnam, 337, 368
Packwood, TSgt Norval, 233
Pakenham, Sir Edward, 54
Pakistan, 201
Palacio Nacional, 64
Panama, 109, 112, 388–389
Panmunjom, 321, 323
Papake, Cpl C., 319
Parachute Marines, 199
Paris Peace Accords, 373
Park, Capt Matthew, 40
Parkinson, Capt Chip, 407
Parris Island, 119, 120, 419
Patch, unit, 126. See also Emblems;
        Insignia
    3d MAW ACE(F), 397
    Amphibious corps, 200, 203

Fleet Marine Force Pacific, *216*, *218*
Flying Tigers, *251*
history of, *126*
HMLA-775, *433*
HMT-301, *432*
Indian Head, 126, *126*
Marine divisions, World War II, *274*, *275*
Marine fighter squadrons, *395*, *397*
VMA(AW)-242, *395*
VMA(AW)-533, *404*
VMAQ-2, *432*
VMAT-203, *397*
VMF-211, *177*
VMF-214, *433*
VMFA 115, *395*
VMFA-333, *404*
VMFT-401, *395*
VMGR-252, *428*
Pate, CMC Randolph, *328*
Pay issues, *31*, *36*
Payne, 2dLt Frederick R., *253*
Pearl Harbor
   antiaircraft fire, *170*
   Arizona memorial, *169*
   Arizona under attack, *169*
   Japanese attack on, 168–169
   Marine casualties of, *169*
   Marine barracks at, *171*
Peleliu, 225–226, *226*, *227*, *255*
   casualties on, *226*
   Marine advance on, *225*, *226*, *227*
Pendleton, BGen Joe, *114*, 148
Pendleton, Col John A., *112*
Penobscot Bay, battle of, *43*
Peralte, Charlemagne, *148*
Perkins, Cpl William T., *355*
Per Marem, Per Terram, *16*
Perry, Commo Matthew C. (USN), *271*
Pershing, Gen John J. (USA), 23, 120, 124, 128, *133*, 147
Persian Gulf War
   aerial phase of, *402*–403, *403*, 404
   Al Khafji, battle of, *403*
   battle plan for, *402*
   buildup phase of, *400*, *400*, 401
   camp conditions during, *402*, *402*
   casualties in, *409*
   the ground war in, *405*, *405*–409, *406*
   Iraqi capabilities preceding, *400*
   map, Marine operations in, *408*
   Marine Observation Post 4, *406*
   oil-well fire, *406*
   origins of war, *396*
   Recon team, Piglet 2-1, *409*
   Republican Guard in, *396*
   Saudi restrictions in, *398*
   task forces in, *405*
   training exercises during, *401*
   Umm Hajul, battle of, *403*
Persians, ancient, *34*
Personnel, demographics, 30–31
Phantom, *315*, *341*

Philippine Insurrection, 96, 97, 106
Philippines, 90, 92, *107*
Philippine Sea, battle of, *222*
Photographers, combat, *229*, *280*, *285*.
      See also Cinematography, combat
   in Korean War, *280*, *285*, *304*
   in Vietnam War, *334*, *346*
   in World War I, *136*
   in World War II, *208*, *240–245*
Photography
   Camera, Bell & Howell, *355*
Piaseki, Frank, *289*
Pinup girl, *203*
Pirates, 48–49
Pistol. *See also* Revolver
   Beretta semiautomatic, 9mm, *389*
   Kimber ICQB, *449*
   M1836, *60*
   M1842, *61*
   M1843, *61*
   M1911 Colt, *107*
Platoon Leaders Class (PLC), 30–31, *163*
Pless, Capt Stephen W., *357*
Plouffe, RM Robert (USN), *221*
Port-au-Prince, *156*
Porter, RAdm David D. (USN), 46, 50
Portteus, Pvt Kenneth N., *219*
Posters. *See* Recruiting poster
Potato Digger, *102*
Powell, Dick, *164*
Powell, Gen Colin (USA), *396*
Powers, LtCol Joel, *432*
Predator UVA, *452*
Pregnancy, *29*
Presidential Unit Citation, *265*
"President's Own," *20*
Princeton, battle of, 37, *38*, *39*, 40
Prisoners of war
   brainwashing of, *330*
   code of conduct, 330–331
   detainees, from Afghanistan, 427–428
   interrogation of, methods, *219*
   Marines as, from Wake Island, 178, *179*
   post-Pearl Harbor, *171*
   "safe conduct" pass, *221*
Privateer, French, *48*
Prowler, *397*, *433*
Public Affairs, 442–443
Public Relations, department of, *228*
Puerta Plata harbor, *48*
Puerto Rico, *105*
Puller, 2dLt Lewis B., III, *381*
Puller, MajGen Lewis B., Jr., 226, *295*, *301*, *305*, *381*
Punji sticks, *340*
Pusan Perimeter, *290*, *291*, *294*
Putnam, Maj Paul S., 176, *176*
Pyle, Ernie, *231*

Q
Quam, *224*
Quantico, 16, 120, *121*, *146*, 155
   Butler Coliseum, *146*

Ellis Hall, naming of, *155*
   and Marine Corps University, *388*
Quasi-war, with France, *46*
Quetzalcoatl, *64*
Quick, Sgt John, *90*

R
Rabaul, *220*
Raferty, J.J., *319*
Rainbow Plan, *172*
Ralls, Col Johann, *38*
Ranger, *40*
Rauenhorst, Maj Robert, *433*
Raymond, Maj Alex, 231, *251*
Reagan, Ronald, 378
Recruiting
   depots, 119, *121*
   post-Vietnam War, *381*
   publicity bureau, creation of, *119*
   in Vietnam era, *375*
   in World War I, 120, *124*
Recruiting posters
   as art form, *124*
   aviation, *156*
   early 19th century, *47*
   early 20th century, *111*, *115*, *116*
   Korean War, *279*
   modern era, *425*
   Teufel Hunden, *142*
   Vietnam era, *327*
   for women Marines, *29*
   World War I, *99*, *122*, *124*, *128*, *131*, *133*, *135*, *142*, *153*
   World War II, *167*, *191*, *250*
Refueling operations, in-flight, *428*, *448*
Regimental Combat Teams (RCTs), Marine, 443–444
Reid, 2dLt George C., *72*
Reisenberg, Sidney H., *111*
Republican Guards, *396*, *444*
Reservists, Marine, *311*, *314*
Retirement, *31*
Revere, LtCol Paul, *43*
Reverse-slope defense, *261*
"Revolt of the admirals," *288*
Revolutionary War, *41*
   Bagaduce Peninsula, assault on, *43*
   battle deaths in, *45*
   and Continental Marines, birth of, 32, 34
   and Continental Marines, end of, *45*
   first Marine casualties of, *36*
   first naval battle of, *36*
   map, Princeton, *39*
   map, Trenton and Princeton, *38*
Revolver, 73, *102*. *See also* Pistol
Reynolds, Col Nicholas E., *443*
Reynolds, Maj John, *71*
Reynoso, Sgt Yadir, *450*
Rhoades, Fred, *233*
Ribbons. *See* Awards
Rickover, Adm Hyman (USN), *89*
Riddle, LCpl Jeremy R., *447*
"Ridge Runners," *319*
Ridgway, Gen Matthew, *314*

Rieck, Pvt Roy F.W., *170*
Rifle. *See also* Flintlock; Machine gun; Musket
   CheyTac M200 sniper rifle, *456*
   DMR M14, *447*
   field-stripping exercise, *121*
   M14, 329, *342–343*
   M16, 348–349, *423*
   M16A2 Colt, *386–389*
   M1918 Browning automatic, *148–149*
   M1 carbine, *258–259*, 302
   M1 Garand, *133*, *186–187*
   M1816 Hall, *58–59*, 65
   M1941 Johnson, *198–199*, 199
   M1898 Krag-Jorgensen, *88*
   106mm recoilless, *368*
   M1862 Spencer, *78*
   M1861 Whitney Plymouth Navy, *79*
   Sharps carbine, *79*
   sniper, *360*, *446–447*, *456*
   Springfield, 73, 84, *123*, 131, *133*, *194*
   Winchester-Lee, 24, 96
Ripley, Col John L., *372*, *372*, *373*, 385
Risler, Sgt Jack, *271*
Robb, Capt Charles S., *371*
Robertson, MajGen Donn, *355*
Robinson, GySgt Robert G., *139*
Robinson, LCpl Christopher, *461–462*
Roche, John S., *226*
Rocket. *See also* Artillery; Missile; Tank
   antitank, *284*
   launcher, *282*
Rockey, MajGen Keller E., *237*
Rockwell, Norman, *194*, *272*, *273*
Roebling, Donald, *412*
Rogue nations, rise of, *396*
Roi-Namur, 215–216
Roosevelt, Franklin D., 32, *107*, 179
Roosevelt, Theodore, 105, 119
Rosenthal, Joe, *237*, *242*, *243*, *244*
Ross, Pfc H., Jr., *247*
Royal Air Force, 138
Rumaila oil fields, 443–444
Rumsfeld, Donald, *427*
Russell, CMC John H., 148, 161
Russian revolution, 148

S
Sabre, *313*, *314*
"Safe conduct" pass, *221*
Saint-Mihiel, 130, 142
Saint-Nazaire, *125*
Saipan, *218*, *219*. *See also* Mariana Islands
Salamis, battle of, *34*
Sally, *48*
Saltonstall, Dudley, *43*
Sanborn, LtCol Russell A., *448*
Sandino, Augusto César, *154*, 155
Sands of Iwo Jima, *165*, 212
Sandwich, French privateer, *48*
San Pascual, battle of, 63–64
Santa Rita River, *106*

Santo Domingo, *148*
Sarajevo, *420*
Sattler, LtGen John, *452*
Saudi Arabia, *396*, 398
Sawada, Kyoicha, *363*
Scharff, Hans Joachim, *219*
Schenk, Maj Fred, *397*
Schilt, 1stLt Christian, *157*, 158
Schlosberg, Lt Herb, *213*
Schmidt, MajGen Harry, 215, 234, *240*
Schools. *See also* Boot camp; Training
   basic, *16*
   consolidation of, 155
   Navy-Marine Corps Amphibious Training Command, *260*
   scout snipers', *123*
   sniper, *360*
Schrier, 1stLt Harold G., *240*, 242
Schwarzkopf, Gen Norman (USA), 405
Scott, Cpl Ernest J., *247*
Scout Snipers' School, *123*
"Scrambled eggs," *380*
Sea-air-land operational mode, *201*
Sea duty, *386*, *386*, 387
Sea Horse, *329*, *332*, *338*, *339*, 341, *341*, 348
Sea King, *22*
Sea Knight, *289*, *329*, 341, *371*, *432*
Seaplane, *138*
Sea Stallion, 26, 341, *354*, *374*, *418*, 420
Second Continental Congress, 32, 34
Segal, 1stLt Harold E., *253*
Seminole indian wars, 58, *59*
"*Semper Fidelis*," *31*
Senate Naval Affairs Committee, *287*
Sergeants Major of the Marine Corps, *467*
Sewall, Samuel, *46*
Sexual harassment, *29*
Sgt. Stoney Craig (comic book), *231*
Shah Isa Air Base, *397*
Shapley, LtGen Alan, *168*
Shaw, John D., *176*
Shepard, CMC Lemuel, *219*, *223*, 289, *323*, 330
Shepard, Cpl P., *247*
Shipman, 1stSgt Joe, *228*
"Shock and awe," *440–441*, 443
"Shores of Tripoli," 48–49
Short Airfield for Tactical Support, *329*
Shotgun, combat, *423*
Shoup, David M., *202*, *203*, *210*, 328, *329*
Shuey, Gen Clifford H., *190*
Shuri Castle. *See* Okinawa
Shuri Line, *261*. *See also* Okinawa
   tanks' role, in breaching, *259*
Sikorsky, Igor, *289*
Silent Drill Team, *21*
Simmons, BGen Edwin H., *142*, *164*
Sino-Japanese War, 160
Sitter, Capt Carl L., *309*
"Situation well in hand," *82*

Skyhawk, 341, *344*

Skyraider, *292*, 345

Slot, the, 196

Small Wars Manual, 159, 332

Smallwood, Archie, 151

Smathers, George, 288

Smith, Lt Bernard L., 119

Smith, LtCol Charles B., 291

Smith, Lt John, *199*

Smith, MajGen Holland M. "Howlin' Mad," *166*, 201, 218, *241*, 286, 287

Smith, MajGen Oliver P., *291*, 295, 300

Smith, MajGen Ralph, 218, 286

Smith, MajGen Ray L., 442

"Smith versus Smith" incident, 286

Snedeker, Col Ed, 265

Sniping. See also Marksmanship
   CheyTac M200 Sniper rifle, 456
   in Operation Iraqi Freedom, 444, 446
   training for, *123*
   in Vietnam, 360
   in World War I, 122
   in World War II, 186

Snyder, Sgt Rolland L., 297

Soissons, 143

Somalia, 403, 411

Sopwith Camel, 138

Soule, Capt Karl, 213

Sousa, John Philip, 17, 21, *21*, 82, *94*

Sousley, Pfc Franklin R., *243*

South Vietnamese Army (ARVN), *332*

Soviet Union. See also Cold War
   and Cuban Missile crisis, 328
   and domino effect, 326
   and Manchukuo, invasion of, 274
   and Russian revolution, 148

Spaatz, Carl, 286

Spanish-American War, 89–90, 92

Special Operation Capabilities (SOC), 14

Spooner, Maj Richard T., 268, *269*

Spruance, VAdm Raymond (USN), 201

Stackpole, LtGen Henry C., 410, *411*

Stars and bars, 264

Star-Spangled Banner, 54

Stavisky, SSgt Sam, *228*, 229

Stealth bomber, 434

Steele, SSgt Norm, *214*

Stennis, John, 381

Stewart, Marc, *177*

Stiletto, *190*

Stingray patrols, 352, 368

Stoner, Cpl Eugene, 348

Strank, Sgt Michael, *243*

Strategic lift, 25

Stratemeyer, Gen George E., 280

Streamers, 22, 466–467
   African Slave Trade Patrol, *60*
   American Defense Service, *166*
   Army of Occupation of Germany, *145*
   Barbary Wars, *49*
   China Relief Expedition, *98*

Civil War, *79*

Cuban Pacification, *103*

French Croix de Guerre, 136

Global War on Terrorism-Expeditionary, 451

Global War on Terrorism-Service, 427

Haitian Campaign, *117*, 149

Indian Wars, 59

Joint Unit Meritorious Unit Award, *448*

Korean Presidential Unit Citation, *317*

Korean Service, 278

Kosovo Campaign, *418*

Marine Corps Expeditionary Service, *106*, 176, *378*

Meritorious Unit Commendation, *258*

Mexican Service, *114*

Mexican War, 64

National Defense Service, *424*

Navy Unit Citation, *253*

Nicaraguan Campaign, *109*

Operations Against West Indian Pirates, *57*

Persian Gulf War, 22

Philippine Independence, *267*

Philippine Insurrection Campaign, *97*

Philippine Liberation, 254

Presidential Unit Citation, *133*, 350

Quasi-War with France, 46

Republic of Vietnam Armed Forces Meritorious Unit Citation of the Gallantry Cross, *364*

Republic of Vietnam Armed Forces Meritorious Units Citation of the Gallantry, *364*

Republic of Vietnam Meritorious Unit Citation Civil Action, *337*

Revolutionary War, 32

Second Nicaraguan Campaign, *154*

Southwest Asia Service, *23*, 400

Spanish Campaign, 89

Valorous Unit Award, *257*

Vietnam Service, *326*

War of 1812, *51*

World War I, *147*

World War II-American Campaign, *198*

World War II Asiatic-Pacific Campaign, *210*

World War II- European-African-Mediterranean Campaign, *270*

World War II Victory, *273*

Yangtze Service, *158*

Struble, VAdm Arthur D. (USN), 295

Stuart, Jeb, 68

Submachine gun. See Machine gun

Submarine warfare, 120

Sugar Loaf Hill, 261

Sundblom, Haddon, 280

Sunni Triangle, 452

Superfortress, *210*, 218, 223, 225, 248, 269, 325

Super Stallion, 427, *428*

Supporting Arms Liaison Teams (SALTs), 372

Suribachi, Mount, *234*, *235*, *237*, *240*

Swagger stick, *151*

Sweden, 365

Swett, 1stLt James E., *253*

Swords. See also Bayonet; Weapons, bladed
   Civil War, *71*
   dress, Revolutionary War, *37*
   Mameluke, *54–55*, 91
   officer's, 20, *57*
   presentation, to Presley O'Bannon, 48, *54*

Sykes, Sgt Eric, *190*

T

Tactical Airfield Fuel Dispensing System (TAFDS), 344

Tactical Air Navigation System (TACAN), 344

Tactical changes in warfare, 462, 463–464

Talbot, Lt Ralph, *139*, 140

Taliano, Sgt Charles A., *379*

Taliban, 426, 427, 462, 467

Tanks, *257*. See also Artillery; Howitzer; Missile; Rocket
   Abrams M1A1, *402*, *405*, 407, 454, 455, *456*
   bulldozer, *226*
   evacuation of wounded by, *265*
   flamethrowing, *261*
   M3 light, *187*
   M24 light, 284
   M26 Pershing, 284
   M4 Sherman, *222*, *223*, *237*, 256
   M26 Sherman, *290*, 297
   in Persian Gulf War, *405–407*
   PT-76 amphibious (Russian), *361*
   Shuri Line, used against, *259*
   threat, Korean War, 283
   T-72 (Iraqi), *406*
   T-34 (Russian), *282*, 284

Tanner, Cpl F., *247*

Taplett, LtCol Robert, 294, 308

Tarawa
   Betio, *208*, *209*, *211*
   casualties at, 202
   cinematography on, *212–213*
   commanders conference, *210*
   landing at, 202, *203*, *204–205*, *206*, *207*
   lessons learned at, 217
   sketches of action on, *207*, *232*, *233*

Task force
   Carib, *418*
   Contingency Marine Air-Ground Task Force (CMAGTF 2-91), 410
   Marine, organization, 14
   Naval Task Force 58, 426
   Navy, carrier-based, 216
   Ripper (Persian Gulf War), *407–408*

Tarawa (Operation Iraqi Freedom), *435*, 444

Tripoli (Operation Iraqi Freedom), *444–445*

Task force, joint
   Joint Guardian, 420
   Provide Comfort, 410
   Provide Relief, *411*
   Sea Angel, 410

Task Force Delta, 345, 347

Technical changes in warfare, 462–464

Templeton, SgtMaj Michael, *467*

Terpning, Howard, 231

Terror, war on, 426–427, 430

Tet Offensive, *362–363*
   intelligence failures preceding, 356–357
   misreporting of, 364, *366–367*
   strategic failure of, 359

Teufel Hunden. See Devil dogs

The Singing Marine (film), 164

Thomas, MajGen Gerald C., *189*, 287, 288, 314

Thomas, Sgt Ernest I., 242

Thomas, 1stLt Franklin C., Jr., 252

Thomas Clark House, 39

Thomason, Col John W., Jr., 146, *146*, 146–147, 231

Thomason, Sgt Clyde, *188*

Thousand-yard stare, *354*

38th parallel, 278

"Three Block War" concept, 419, *452–453*

Tibbets, Col Paul, Jr., 269

Tientsin, 98, 101

Tilton, Capt McLane, 72, 78

Tingley, Pvt, *103*

Tinian, 223

Tojo, Hideki, 222

"Tombstone" promotions, 288

Tompkins, MajGen Rathvon, 355

Tonkin Gulf Resolution, 332, 336

TOW guided missile system, 392

Towle, Col Katherine A., 28, *28*

Tractor, amphibious, *203*. See also Vehicle

Tradition
   esprit de corps, 16
   mottoes, 16–17

Training. See also Schools
   boot camp, 27, 30–31
   desert-warfare, *401*
   martial arts, 30

Transportation Command (TRANSCOM), 25

Transport Quartermasters, 386

Trench warfare, 120, *351*

Trenton, battle of, *37*, *38*, *39*, 40

Tripoli, battle of, 48, *48–49*, 49

Troiani, Don, 75

Trowbridge, 2dLt Eugene A., *253*

Trudgian, Nicolas, `

Truman, Harry S., 270, 280, 286, 287, 312

Tulagi, 185

Tun Tavern, 34, *34*

Turkey, 434

Turner, RAdm Kelly (USN), 201

Tuttle, Cpl Jerome D., 297

Tuttle, 2dLt Albert T., 244

Twelve-Mile Swamp, 58

Twiggs, Maj Levi, 64

Twining, Gen Merrill B., 287, *289*

U

U-boat patrols, 250

"Unification" plan, 286–289

Uniform, clothing, 20. See also Insignia
   boondockers, *210*, 234
   boots, in Vietnam, 356
   camouflage, history of, 436–439
   camouflage, MARPAT digital, *25*, 439
   camouflage utilities, 206
   Continental Marines, 35, *35*
   dress buckle, Civil War, *76*
   evening dress, *21*
   full-dress, *56*
   Marine band, 20, *21*, 44
   "Marine Green," *61*, *131*
   Mexican War period, 62
   Return to Green, 61
   sergeant major, c.1835, *59*
   undress tunic, *87*

Uniform, equipment
   armor, body, *320*
   belt, Sam Browne, *127*
   gas suits, 444
   782 gear, *149*, 154
   haversacks, *149*
   inflatable life belt, *206*
   mess gear, *324*
   Mission Oriented Protective Posture-2 (MOPP-2), *405*, 441–442
   powder horn, *39*, *72*
   water canteen, *85*
   web, M1910, *127*
   web, M1913, *131*
   web belt, World War II, *249*

Uniform, general
   c. 1800, *44*
   c. 1834, *50*
   c. 1875, *82*
   c. 1840s, *66*
   changes, post-World War I, *151*
   of Continental Marines, 35, 37
   details, traditions of, 20, *20*, *21*

Uniform, headgear
   aviator helmet, *254*, *312*
   campaign hat, *97*, *128*, *151*
   chapeau bras, *50*, *66*
   cover, officer's, *380*
   dress helmet, spiked, *94*, *104*
   enlisted cap, c. 1927, *152*
   fatigue cap, *57*
   helmet, camouflage, *237*
   kepis, *76*
   Kevlar helmet, *410*
   "Mongolian piss-cutter," *161*
   overseas cap, *147*

"scrambled eggs," 380

shako, 60, 74, 83

United Nations (UN)
  and Korean War, 280, 323
  and war on Iraq, 430

Units. See also Aviation units; Divisions; Expeditionary units; Infantry units
  1st Armored Car Squadron, 119, 148
  1st Marine Battalion, 92, 93
  1st Marine Brigade, 114, 156
  1st Marine Defense Battalion, 174, 178–179
  1st Marine Parachute Battalion, 185
  1st Marine Provisional Brigade, 280
  1st Provisional Brigade, 219, 222
  1st Tank Battalion, 261, 265, 405, 431
  2d Raider Battalion, 188
  3d Defense Battalion, Battery E, 3-inch Antiaircraft Group, 182
  3d Defense Battalion, Battery F, 172
  3d Parachute Battalion, L Company, 199
  4th Marine Brigade, 124, 130, 131, 132, 143, 146, 219, 275
  4th Tank Battalion, 4th MARDIV (Reserve), 407
  5th Marine Brigade, 146
  6th Machine Gun Battalion, 77th Company, 133
  6th Defense Battalion, 182
  7th Fleet, Special Landing Force, 359
  9th Defense Battalion, 173
  Air Tactical Control Unit, Marine Corps (MCATCU), 344
  Anti-Terrorism Brigade, 427
  photo section, 2d MARDIV, 214
  Reserve Public Affairs Unit 1-1, 233

Units, allied
  1st Armoured Division, 400, 402
  7th Armoured Brigade, 434
  36th Iraqi Commando Battalion, 452
  40 Royal Commando Regiment, 434
  41 Royal Marine Commando, 306, 310

Units, enemy
  Communist Chinese Forces (CCF), 302
  Iraqi Republican Guard, 400, 405
  NKPA 9th Division, 312
  NVA divisions, composition of, 356
  NVA 304th Division, 356, 368
  NVA 325th Division, 356

Unmanned aerial vehicle (UAV), 25, 452, 454, 466–467

Unmanned Air Support (UAS), 466–467

Urban warfare, 302, 452–453

Ushijima, Gen Mitsuru (IJN), 256

USS Alfred, 36

USS Alliance, 41

USS Arizona, 169

USS Bairoko, 312

USS Bennington, 250, 265

USS Block Island, 265

USS Blue Ridge, 374

USS Bonhomme Richard, 41, 42–43, 416

USS Bonhomme Richard vs. HMS Serapis, 41

USS Brooklyn, 89

USS Bunker Hill, 250, 265

USS Cabot, 36

USS California, 108

USS Carl Vinson, 427

USS Chickamauga, 68

USS Comstock, 427

USS Constitution, 46, 48, 51

USS Constitution vs. HMS Guerrière, 51

USS Dubuque, 427

USS Enterprise, 81, 171, 427

USS Essex, 250, 255

USS Franklin, 250, 251

USS George Washington, 386

USS Gunston Hall, 420

USS Hancock, 252

USS Harry S. Truman, 433

USS Indianapolis, 269

USS Iowa, 387

USS Kearsarge, 418, 420

USS Kitty Hawk, 427

USS Lexington, 180

USS Maine, 84, 86, 88, 89

USS Massachusetts, 104

USS Mayaguez, 377

USS Midway, 292

USS Missouri, 270, 271

USS Nassau, 26, 397, 404

USS Nevada, 153

USS New Mexico, 387

USS Okinawa, 340, 348

USS Panay, 158

USS Peleliu, 424, 426

USS Philadelphia, 48

USS Ponce, 420

USS Princeton, 348

USS Repose, 365

USS Sanctuary, 365

USS Saratoga, 178

USS Shreveport, 427

USS Tallahassee, 68

USS Theodore Roosevelt, 427

USS Tripoli, 359

USS Wasp vs. HMS Reindeer, 53

USS Whidbey Island, 427

USS Yorktown, 162, 180, 180

V

Valle, MajGen Pedro del, 258, 264

Vandegrift, CMC Alexander A., 28, 109, 113, 189, 197, 287, 288

Van Fleet, LtGen James, 314, 320

Vehicle. See also Landing craft; Tanks
  aerial, unmanned, 25, 452, 454
  armored car, 119
  Humvee, 448
  light attack, 401

mechanical "mule," 365

staff, in Persian Gulf War, 407

tractor, amphibious, 203

Veracruz, 109

Verdun, 142

Vernon, Edward, 32

Vertical-envelopment doctrine, 25, 289, 318, 320

Vessels, naval. See also individual ship names
  Marine detachments on, 386

Veterans of Foreign Wars, 287

Vietnam Veterans Memorial, 376

Vietnam War
  combat, nature of, 338, 340
  DMZ in, 347, 355
  map, of Marine operations, 335
  Marine landing, 342–343
  Marine presence in, 340–341
  and Mayaguez incident, 377
  micromanagement of, 336
  political complexity of, 332
  sniping in, 360, 360
  stingray patrols in, 352
  withdrawal from, 371–372
  women Marines in, 28

Vinson, Carl, 288

Vladivostok, 148

Voodoo, 148

W

Waffenstillstandstag, 137

Wahhabism, 396

Wainwright, LtGen Jonathan, 180

Wake Island, 174, 177, 178
  aerial view, 178
  battle of, 174–179, 177, 178
  Capt Elrod's letter home, 175
  communication difficulties with, 175
  final action, sketch of, 179
  surrender of, 273
  survivors of, 271, 274

Walker, James, 63

Walker, MajGen Walton, 284

Wall, the, 376

Wallace, Brevet Capt William, 72

Wallace, Col Clarence R., 264

Waller, Col L.W.T., 114

Waller, LtCol Ben, 98

Walsh, 1stLt Kenneth Ambrose, 253, 253

Walt, LtGen Lewis, 337, 341, 355

Wana Draw, 261

Warfighting Center, 385, 460

War of 1812, 49–57, 54

Washington, Gen George, 34

Washington, Lawrence, 32

Washington Conference for the Limitation of Naval Armaments, 155

Waterhouse, Col Charles, 36, 49, 58, 77

Watson, Col Samuel, 64

Wayne, Gen Anthony (USA), 61

Wayne, John, 165

Weapons. See also specific types
  changes to after 2000, 463
  updating, in 1980s, 382–393, 389

Weapons, bladed. See also Swords
  bayonet, 133, 190, 389
  Ka-bar, 190
  knives, innovations in, 190
  small arms, c. 1775-1855, 40, 40
  stiletto, 190

Weber, Lt Otto, 270

Weiland, PFC George R., 226

Weldon, Felix de, 275

Welsh, Capt John, 43

West, Lt F.J. "Bing," 442, 452, 453

Westmoreland, Gen William C. (USA), 356, 361

Wexler, Elmer, 231

Wharton, LtCol Franklin, 58

White House, 22, 52

Wike, HM Vernon R., (USN), 349

Wildcat, 162, 176, 177, 185

Williams, Capt John, 58

Williams, Capt Lloyd, 132

Willis, SSgt Robert, 450

Wilson, CMC Louis, Jr., 219, 223, 375, 379, 381

Winkle, SSgt Archie Van, 303

Wise, Col Frederic M., 122

With the Marines at Tarawa (film), 212

Wolf, Pvt, 103

Wolmi-do, 294

Women Marines, 28–29
  recruiting of, Post-Vietnam, 381
  Women's reserve (MCWR), 28
  in World War II, 275

Women's Armed Services Integration Act, 28

Woolf, Samuel Johnson, 129

World War I. See also individual battles
  American Expeditionary Force in, 120, 124
  Belleau Wood, 131, 132, 134, 136, 143, 144, 145
  Château-Thierry, 130, 132, 133, 134, 135
  Croix de Guerre awarded in, 142
  expansion during, 120
  map, of western front, 130
  maps, of Belleau Wood, 144
  Marine aviation in, 138, 141
  Marine casualties in, 146
  Marne River, 134
  Meuse River, 144
  Saint-Mihiel, 130, 142
  sniping in, 122
  uniform, changes to, 128

World War II. See also individual battles
  defense battalions, creation of, 172–173
  demobilization, 274–275
  Guam, 224
  island hopping, 201, 215
  Iwo Jima, 146, 234–250
  Japan, projected invasion of, 271

Japanese surrender, 270, 271, 274

lessons learned, 217

Leyte Gulf, 250, 256

map, of battles, 184

Marine actions, recap of, 275

origins of, 166

Pearl Harbor, 168–169, 170, 171

Peleliu, 225–226, 226

Tinian, 223

Wake Island, 174–179, 178

Worley, LCpl Kenneth L., 370

Wright brothers, 115

Y

Yalu River, 298, 300–301

Yamamoto, Adm Isoroku (IJN), 176, 222

Yohn, F.C., 144

Yom Kippur War, 376

Z

Zacharias, RAdm Ellis (USN), 287

Zeilin, CMC Jacob, 65, 76, 81–82, 82

Zilmer, LtCol Rick, 407